THE BAB AND THE BABI COMMUNITY OF IRAN

THE BAB AND THE BABI COMMUNITY OF IRAN

EDITED BY

FEREYDUN VAHMAN

ONEWORLD
ACADEMIC

Oneworld Academic
An imprint of Oneworld Publications

Published by Oneworld Academic, 2020

A CIP record for this title is available from the British Library

ISBN 978-1-78607-956-5
eISBN 978-1-78607-957-2

Typeset by Tetragon, London
Printed and bound in Great Britain by Clays Ltd, Elcograf S.p.A.

Oneworld Publications
10 Bloomsbury Street,
London, WC1B 3SR
England

Contents

Biographies

Abbas Amanat is William Graham Sumner Professor of History at Yale University. He is also the director of the Yale Program in Iranian Studies. His latest publications are: *Iran: A Modern History* (Yale University Press, 2017); *The Persianate World: Rethinking a Shared Space* (with Assef Ashraf, Brill, 2018); and, in Persian, *Az Tehran ta 'Akka, Babiyan va Baha'iyan dar Asnad-e Douran-e Qajar* (with Fereydun Vahman, Ashkar Press, 2016).

His other publications are: *Resurrection and Renewal: The Making of the Babi Movement in Iran, 1844–1850* (Cornell University Press, 1989); *Pivot of the Universe: Nasir al-Din Shah Qajar and the Iranian Monarchy, 1831–1896* (University of California Press, 1997); and *Apocalyptic Islam and Iranian Shi'ism* (I.B. Tauris, 2005). See further: https://history.yale.edu/people/abbas-amanat.

Armin Eschraghi is Lecturer in Islamic Studies at Goethe University Frankfurt (Germany) and the Sankt Georgen Divinity School. He is the author of a monograph on Shaykhism and the Bab's early writings (*Frühe Shaykhi- und Babi-Theologie. Die Darlegung der Beweise für Muhammads besonderes Prophetentum.* Einleitung, Edition und Erläuterungen. Brill: Leiden 2004) and of a translation and extensive commentary on Baha'u'llah's epistle to the influential Muslim cleric Aqa Najafi Isfahani (*Baha'u'llah. Brief an den Sohn des Wolfes, Aus dem Persischen und Arabischen übersetzt und herausgegeben*, Suhrkamp/Insel: Berlin 2010). He has also authored several research articles on the writings and early history of the Babi and Baha'i faiths and their relationship to Islam in general and Shi'ism in particular.

Omid Ghaemmaghami is Associate Professor of Arabic and Near Eastern Studies and Director of the Middle East and North Africa studies program at the State University of New York in Binghamton. He holds a PhD in Middle Eastern and Islamic Studies from the University of Toronto, an MA in Islamic and Near Eastern Studies from Washington University in

St. Louis, and certificates from the Dalalah Institute in Damascus and the American University in Cairo. He has taught and lectured on Arabic and Islamic Studies at universities and academic institutions in the United States, Canada, Europe, and Egypt, and is the author of the forthcoming book *Encounters with the Hidden Imam in Early and Pre-Modern Twelver Shīʿī Islam* (https://brill.com/view/title/34465?lang=en).

Stephen N. Lambden received his PhD in Religious Studies from the University of Newcastle upon Tyne in 2002 where he submitted a thesis about Islamo-biblica (Isra'iliyyat, Israelitica) and the emergence of the Babi-Baha'i Interpretation of the Bible. He specializes in Abrahamic religious texts and Semitic languages (Hebrew, Arabic, etc.) and has lectured in Babi-Baha'i Studies at the University of Newcastle upon Tyne and elsewhere. His work exhibits a special interest in the Bible and the Qur'an and their relationship to Babi and Baha'i Arabic and Persian primary scriptural texts and doctrinal teachings. Among his many publications are contributions to the *Encyclopædia Iranica*, *Encyclopedia of Language and Linguistics*, Studies in the Babi and Baha'i Religions (Kalimat Press series), and several other journals and books. He also contributed the "Islam" chapter for the *Blackwell Companion to the Bible and Culture* (Oxford, 2006). He is currently a Research Scholar at the University of California, Merced. Many of his papers and research notes are found on his personal website: http://hurqalya.ucmerced.edu.

Todd Lawson (PhD, McGill University 1987) is Emeritus Professor of Islamic Thought at the University of Toronto where he joined the Department of Middle East and Islamic Studies in 1988. There, he taught undergraduate and graduate students the Qur'an, Islamic theology, philosophy, and mystical thought. More recently, he taught courses and supervised graduate work on the dynamics between the literary and religious dimensions of Islamic discourses and texts. He has published widely on Qur'an commentary (*tafsir*), Shiʿi mystical and messianic thought, and the writings of the Bab in the context of the general religio-mystical milieu of his time. His two most recent books are *The Quran, Epic and Apocalypse* (Oneworld, 2017) a study of the Qur'an as literature, and *Tafsir as Mystical Experience: Intimacy and Ecstasy in Quran Commentary* (Brill, 2019) on the first major exegetical composition by the Bab (the *Tafsīr sūrat al-baqara*). His study of the Bab's annunciatory Qur'an commentary on the Surah of Joseph (Qur'an 12),

Gnostic Apocalypse, was published by Routledge in 2012. Also, in 2012, he edited, with Omid Ghaemmaghami, a collection of scholarly studies on the writings of the Bab entitled *A Most Noble Pattern* (George Ronald, Oxford). He also guest edited a special Baha'i issue of the *Journal of Religious History* (vol. 36, no. 4, December 2012), gathering articles by numerous academics on a variety of topics to do with the rise and development of the Baha'i faith. He lives in Montreal with his wife Barbara.

Moojan Momen is an independent scholar who was born in Iran but raised and educated in England, attending the University of Cambridge. He has a special interest in the study of the Baha'i faith and Shi'i Islam, both from the viewpoint of their history and their doctrines. In recent years, his interests have extended to the study of the phenomenon of religion. His principal publications in these fields include *An Introduction to Shi'i Islam* (Yale University Press, 1985); *The Bábí and Bahá'í Religions 1844–1944: Some Contemporary Western Accounts* (George Ronald, Oxford, 1982); *The Phenomenon of Religion* (Oneworld, Oxford, 1999, republished as *Understanding Religion*, 2008); and *The Baha'i Communities of Iran, 1851–1921: Volume 1: The North of Iran* (George Ronald, Oxford, 2015). He has contributed articles to encyclopedias such as the *Encyclopædia Iranica* and the *Oxford Encyclopedia of the Modern Islamic World* as well as papers to academic journals such as the *International Journal of Middle East Studies, Past and Present, Iran, Iranian Studies, Journal of Genocide Research*, and *Religion*. He is a Fellow of the Royal Asiatic Society.

Sholeh A. Quinn is Associate Professor of History at the University of California, Merced. She received her PhD from the University of Chicago in 1993. Her research focuses on the history of early modern Iran. She is the author of *Historical Writing during the Reign of Shah 'Abbas: Ideology, Imitation, and Legitimacy in Safavid Chronicles* (2000), *Shah 'Abbas: the King Who Refashioned Iran* (2015), and co-editor of *History and Historiography of Post-Mongol Central Asia and the Middle East: Studies in Honor of John E. Woods* (2006). She is currently completing a book on Persian historical writing across the Ottoman, Safavid, and Mughal empires.

Nader Saiedi is Professor of Baha'i studies at UCLA. He was born in Tehran, Iran. He holds a Master's degree in Economics from Pahlavi University in Shiraz and a PhD in Sociology from the University of Wisconsin. For over twenty-five years he was Professor of Sociology at Carleton College in Northfield, Minnesota. In 2013, he became the Taslimi Foundation Adjunct Professor of Baha'i History and Religion in Iran at UCLA. His main interests include Babi and Baha'i studies, social theory, Iranian studies, and peace studies. Among his published books are *The Birth of Social Theory* (1993), *Logos and Civilization* (2000), and *Gate of the Heart* (2008).

Fereydun Vahman is Professor Emeritus at Copenhagen University and former Iranian Studies Fellow at Yale University with more than forty years of teaching and research in old Iranian religions and languages. He is the author of quite a number of books and articles in several languages. His publications include: *The Iranian 'Divina Commedia' Ardāy Virāz Nāmak* (Curzon Press, 1983, repr. Routledge, 2017); *West Iranian Dialect Materials* (with Garnik Asatrian, 4 vols, Copenhagen, 1987–2002); *Acta Iranica* 28 (ed. with W. Sundermann and J. Duehesne-Guillemin, Brill, 1988); *The Religious Texts in Iranian Languages* (ed. with Claus Pedersen, Royal Danish Academy, 2007); *175 Years of Persecution: A History of the Babis & Baha'is of Iran* (Oneworld, 2019). In Danish: *Dansk-Persisk Ordbog* (Special-pædagogisk forlag, 1986, 12th print 2012); *Persisk-Dansk Ordbog* (Gyldendal, 1998). In Persian: *Diyanat-e Zartushti* (Bonyad-e Farhang-e Iran, 1348 Sh./1969); Salman-e Savaji's *Jamshid va Khorshid* (B.T.N.K, 1348 Sh./1969); *Farhang-e mardom-e Kerman* (Bonyad-e Farhang-e Iran, 1353 Sh./1974); *Baha'iyan va Iran* (Horizonte Publications, 1986); *Kasravi va ketab-e Baha'igari-ye ou* (Frankfurt, 2007); *Yeksad-o shast sal mobarezeh ba 'a'in-e Baha'i* (Baran, 2011); *Az Tehran ta 'Akka, Babiyan va Baha'iyan dar Asnad-e qajar* (with Abbas Amanat, Ashkar Press, 2016); *Bab va Jame'e-ye Babi-ye Iran. Yadnameh-ye devistomin salgard-e mild- Bab 1819–1920* (ed., Baran, 2020). He is the editor of the series devoted to Religion and Society in Iran; so far eight books have been appeared in the series, which is published by Baran in Sweden. Professor Vahman is also co-founder and President of the Danish-Iranian Society.

Siyamak Zabihi-Moghaddam is an independent scholar who holds a PhD in Middle Eastern History from the University of Haifa. His articles have appeared in the *Journal of Women's History*, *Journal of Religious History*, *Contemporary Review of the Middle East*, and *Iranian Studies*. In addition, he has edited a volume of Persian primary sources on the 1903 massacre of Baha'is (Bahá'í-Verlag, 2016).

Acknowledgments

This volume is the English version of the Persian book of the same title, which was published on the bicentenary of the birth of the Persian prophet Sayyid 'Ali-Muhammad Shirazi, the Bab (1819–50). I owe the publication of this book first and foremost to the colleagues and scholars who enriched this volume with their contributions. I am also indebted to Stephen Lambden and Sholeh Quinn for their constant support and encouragement during the preparation of this work. My thanks also go to Adib Masumian for translating the first chapter of this book from Persian into English. Finally, I would like to extend my thanks to Novin Doostdar of Oneworld Publications and to Jonathan Bentley-Smith for supervising the final editing of this edition.

FEREYDUN VAHMAN
University of Copenhagen, Denmark

A Note on Transliteration

The editor has respected the preferred transliteration style of each contributor to this volume.

Iran in the nineteenth century

Preface

FEREYDUN VAHMAN

This volume was first published in Persian on the occasion of the bicentenary of the birth of Sayyid 'Ali-Muhammad Shirazi on 20 October 1819. Known to history, by both supporters and opponents, as the Bab, an Arabic word meaning "door" or "gate," he began his brief ministry on the evening of 22 May 1844, and it ended with his public execution by firing squad in Tabriz on 9 July 1850. At the young age of twenty-five, the Bab had declared himself a messenger of God, announcing the beginning of a new age and a new religious order. During the course of the Bab's short mission, he attracted thousands of followers. While some characterized this movement as a seditious uprising, others attributed its popularity to his compelling spiritual charisma and radically new approach to the major religious themes of the time, which he conveyed through thousands of pages of original writings in both Persian and Arabic. His life coincided with an intense period of messianic expectation in Shiʿi Islam, anticipating the promised return of the Hidden Twelfth Imam after a prolonged period of occultation. Historians of the Qajar era describe the brief but tumultuous ministry of the Bab as a revolutionary and heroic period, in which a significant proportion of Iranians were seeking religious renewal and social transformation.

It is remarkable that the name and message of the Bab spread with such astonishing speed throughout nineteenth-century Iran. This was a time when even basic travel and rudimentary communication, such as post and telegraph, were virtually nonexistent for the masses. Factors such as the prevailing economic crisis, the corruption and cruelty of the Qajar government, and people's despondence over the corruption and hypocrisy among the Shiʿi clergy are among the reasons attributed by scholars to the widespread attraction to the Bab's religion during this period. They argue that, under such circumstances, many of those seeking change and hope turned to him, especially since his messianic claim fulfilled their religious expectation of the coming of the promised one. Beyond the tyranny and corruption of nineteenth-century Iran, this belief in his spiritual station is crucial to understanding the large-scale following of the Bab. The decline of the Iranian state was certainly not a new phenomenon. Furthermore, the Bab did not present a specific policy for resolving the nation's profound problems. Even as a matter of religious belief, his messianic claims were inconsistent with the expectations of the Shi'i faithful, who expected the promised one to arrive with a sword of revenge to kill infidels and oppressors. On the contrary, the Bab rejected violence, and prohibited his followers from spreading his religion through means other than reasoning and persuasion. He even considered the mere causing of grief as a sin. The vast difference between his message of religious renewal and the messianic expectations propagated by orthodox religious schools and clerical circles is all the more remarkable because many of the Bab's early followers were religious scholars and Islamic jurists.

It would seem that the speed with which the Bab's message spread should primarily be attributed to what has been described in various sources as his unique personality, genius, and charisma. Above all, his ability to inspire people was the result of his certainty that he was responding to a divine calling and an inexorable mission that was destined to be victorious, that his penetrative word came from a heavenly source, and that no power on earth could stop the progress of his divine religion. The view that his widespread and sudden influence was derived primarily from these factors, rather than frustration with material conditions, might seem "irrational" if belief in notions of destiny and divine power are considered irrelevant to historical analysis. But this understanding of ultimate triumph in the face of violent persecution and overwhelming odds was the defining characteristic of the Bab's teachings. It is what moved the masses who followed him, even if the price was their death through genocidal pogroms at the hands of both the government and clergy.

On the first evening of the proclamation of his divine mission, the Bab wrote the first chapter of the highly innovative *Qayyum al-asma* in the presence of his first follower, Mulla Husayn Bushru'i. In that treatise, he summoned rulers, kings, religious leaders, and people of both the East and West to respond to his message. He introduced himself unequivocally as a recipient of divine inspiration and the promised one of all ages. His message, however, was contrary to the traditional Shi'i understanding of the appearance of the promised Mahdi. The orthodox belief was that he must come to confirm Islam and renew the Muhammadan ethos, yet the Bab announced a new religious dispensation. He understood the coming of each historic messenger as the resurrection day for their respective time, the dawn of a new age. He presented the Babi religion as a "New Creation", or *khalq-e badi'*, which God has decreed for all the peoples of the world on this most recent Resurrection Day—a new order with new teachings and laws suitable for an unprecedented period of history.

In shaping this drama, the element of expectation (*intizár*) shared by almost all religious persuasions played an important role. It is a Shi'i belief that when the first Imam, 'Ali, was prevented from succeeding the Prophet Muhammad, a great catastrophe took place in the Islamic world which would one day be vindicated. The death of the eleventh Imam and the disappearance of his son, the twelfth Imam, in 260 AH (874 AD)—both victims of this usurpation—caused the Shi'i faithful to seek solace and hope in the belief that the Hidden Imam would one day reappear from a period of occultation. This return would vindicate the collective suffering and expectation of the Shi'i, and usher in an era of justice that would end all oppression. This eschatological tradition is attributed to the Prophet Muhammad from a narrative probably recorded in the early days of the expectation period. This *hadith* states that: "Even if only one day remains for the life of the world, God will prolong that day until a man from my descent will arise and fill the world with justice and fairness, as it is now full of oppression and injustice." During this period, the number of Shi'i traditions concerning the advent of the promised one started to increase and mingled with pre-Islamic Zoroastrian beliefs about the appearance of *Saoshyant*, the messianic figure of the Zoroastrians, which had remained in the shared memory of the Iranians for many centuries before the appearance of Islam. The belief is that with his coming, the dead will be resurrected and falsehood will disappear from the world. This is also similar to the Jewish expectation, described in the book of Daniel (two centuries before the birth of Christ), about the coming of Mashiah [משיח] (Messiah), as well as the Christian belief in the return (Parousia) or "second coming" of Christ descending from the sky. The clear reference in the Qur'an to the Day of Resurrection, the raising of the dead from the grave, the explanations of heaven and hell, and so on lent weight to the truth of these traditions.

The incredible and far-fetched conditions associated with the advent of the promised one rendered the actual occurrence of such an event physically impossible. Nonetheless, it was central to the teachings of Shi'i clerics, though it was subject to a paradox. On the one hand, such beliefs enflamed the enthusiasm of the believers for the coming of the promised Qa'im or Mahdi, while on the other hand they suppressed and suffocated any movement that might be deemed insurrectionary in fulfilment of that same promise. The disparaging of Babi and Baha'i beliefs as blasphemous and heretical is perhaps explained by orthodoxy and fanaticism, but it may also be attributable to the fact that with the fulfilment of the twelfth Imam's return, the Shiʿi clergy lose the primary justification for their religious authority, which is exercised in the absence of the promised Mahdi. The behavior of the Islamic Republic of Iran is an obvious example of this theocratic contradiction, branding the Baha'is as heretics deserving death. Yet many of the early Babis were deeply learned religious scholars, among the very same 'ulama that repressed this threatening theology. People from all walks of life who flocked to the Babi religion understood their acceptance of the Bab's claims as the ultimate realization of their belief in Shiʿi Islam. They also considered the sacrifice of their lives for the Babi cause as analogous to the martyrs of Islam, especially the Shiʿi who were killed in Karbala (10 Moharram 61 AH/10 October 680 AD.)

It is remarkable that, even today, Shiʿi intellectuals who are concerned with the decline of Islam and its apparent anachronism in modern times are not prepared to pay the least attention to this significant Iranian religious movement, although its message of religious renewal responds exactly to these concerns. It may well be argued that the revelations of the Bab and Baha'u'llah were the greatest revolutionary and religious movements in the modern history of Iran. They reflect the vitality and capacity of contemporary Iran to produce significant religious and social change, as well as sublime beliefs that can attract millions of people around the world, as demonstrated by the vast expansion of the Baha'i faith.

Two centuries from the birth of the Bab in 1819, we present this collection—the result of scholarly research by a group of Iranian and non-Iranian academics—as a gift to thoughtful people everywhere who seek knowledge of this extraordinary history.

FEREYDUN VAHMAN

Copenhagen

1

The Bab

A Sun in a Night Not Followed by Dawn

FEREYDUN VAHMAN[1]

On 9 July 1850, before a densely packed and clamoring crowd that had gathered on the rooftops of the barracks of Tabriz, Sayyid 'Ali-Muhammad Shirazi,[2] known as the Bab—a youth of thirty-one who had claimed to be the Qa'im and had brought a new religion—was executed by firing squad. The hostility of the Bab's enemies was such that, rather than return his body to his family, they threw it into a moat on the outskirts of the city so that wild animals might feed on it. This may well have been the first death by firing squad that was carried out in Persian history. This prophet of Shiraz was put to death at a time when his nascent faith had thrown people throughout Persia into a state of excitement. The execution of the Bab set in motion a series of events that would be just as astonishing, bloody, and ruthless as his own death had been.

1 Translated by Adib Masumian.

2 Sayyid is an honorific title denoting people accepted as descendants of Muhammad especially through Husayn, the prophet's younger grandson.

In stark contrast to the frenzied upheavals which the manner of his life and the nature of his claims incited among the people of Persia, and the profound grief and horror that seized his family and his followers as a result of his death, the birth of the Bab in a calm and peaceful spot in Shiraz—the upper chamber of the home of Mirza Sayyid 'Ali, his mother's uncle—brought abundant joy to his family. The first child of the Bab's parents had died just a few days after birth. In accordance with the prevailing custom, when his mother began to go into labor, she was taken to the home of Mirza Sayyid 'Ali, so that this newborn might live[3]—and it was this same newborn who would later bring to humanity such novel concepts that they inaugurated a new chapter not only in the annals of Persian history, but also in the history of the world's religions.

Sayyid 'Ali-Muhammad was born on 20 October 1819 to a family of reputable merchants of Shiraz. His father, Sayyid Muhammad-Reza, had a shop in the bazaar of Shiraz. The genealogy of the Bab indicates that six generations of his paternal ancestors were all *Sayyids* of Shiraz, some of whom also ranked among the celebrated clerics of that city.[4]

The mother of the Bab, Fatimih Bagum, came from a family of renowned merchants of Shiraz. Both her paternal ancestors and her brothers, the maternal uncles of the Bab, were all *Sayyids*. Hers was a respected family that enjoyed wealth and means. Among her brothers, most of whom would later become Babis and even Baha'is, were Haji Mirza Sayyid Muhammad (known as Khal-i Akbar in Baha'i literature), Haji Sayyid 'Ali (Khal-i A'zam), and Haji Mirza Hasan-'Ali (Khal-i Asghar). To this list of the Bab's maternal relatives must also be added Mirza Sayyid 'Ali, the paternal uncle of the Bab's mother, in whose home he was born, and

---

3 Fayzi, Muhammad-'Ali, *Hazrat-i Nuqta-yi Ula* (Bahá'í-Verlag: Langenhain, 1992), 80–81; henceforth, "Fayzi, *Nuqta-yi Ula*."

4 For more information on the genealogy and family of the Bab, see Fayzi, *Khandan-i Afnan-i, Sidrih-yi Rahman* (Tehran, 1971)—henceforth, "Fayzi, *Khandan-i Afnan*"—and Fayzi, *Nuqta-yi Ula*, 64–70. Refer also to Amanat, Abbas, *Resurrection and Renewal: The Making of the Babi Movement in Iran 1844–1850* (Cornell University Press: Ithaca and London, 1989), 110; henceforth, "Amanat, *RR*." Among the most eminent of the Bab's paternal ancestors was the son of his father's paternal uncle, Hujjatu'l-Islam Haji Mirza Muhammad-Hasan Shirazi, better known as Mirza-yi Shirazi (1815–96). Following the death of Shaykh Murteza Ansari, Mirza-yi Shirazi became the *marja'-i taqlid* (highest-ranking authority of Twelver Shi'ih world communities). He is famous for his religious edict prohibiting the use of tobacco, which was issued in support of the popular uprising against the Tobacco Concession, the so-called "Regie protest" (1891–92).

whose daughter, Khadijih Bagum, he would later marry. All these men were engaged in commercial enterprise, both in Persia and beyond, and they each operated their own businesses from the various cities of the country.[5]

The family of the Bab had a residence in Murgh-Mahalleh, one of the better districts of Shiraz where the reputable merchants of the city lived. The traditional makeup of communities in Persian cities was based on a very close relationship between the local bazaars and mosques, and this relationship took on a particularly religious form in the district of Murgh-Mahalleh. Abbas Amanat makes reference to the conflicts between the Haydari and Niʿmati groups, which in those days had become rampant between the districts of Shiraz.[6] In order to assert their own dominance, and also that of their supporters, the majority of the ruffians in every district would brawl with their opposing groups. The reputable merchants and families typically kept their distance from such conflicts, unprepared as they were to risk sacrificing their fame and wealth by openly associating with either side. Instead, these merchants and families worked to support one another; they formed guilds both as a show of solidarity and also as a means of ensuring their commercial success.

At a young age, the Bab lost his father, who died when he was forty-nine.[7] Following the death of her husband, and in accordance with the instructions he had left in his will, the Bab's mother went with her young child to live in the home of her brother, Haji Sayyid ʿAli (Khal-i Aʿzam).

---

5 See Chapter 3 in this volume, "The Shaping of the Babi Community," for more information on the Bab's maternal uncles.

6 Amanat, *RR*, 111.

7 The Bab must have been deeply affected by his father's death. Years later, he lamented in one of his letters how his father never had the opportunity to recognize his station once he had revealed himself. Therefore, he implored God in this letter to have the angels inform his father of his revelation so that he would be reckoned with the believers. The relevant passage from that letter is as follows: "O Lord our God! Verily, my father hath died, having never beheld me invested with the Greatest Word. Impart my Cause unto him, O my Lord, as he dwelleth with the angels of the heavenly Throne. Make him steadfast in the greatest word by your grace, and inscribe his name with such are deemed praiseworthy in the estimation of the Remembrance (qustas al-zikr) in the vicinity of the Bab."

(Provisional rendering of *Qayyumu'l-Asma*, Suriyih-i Jihad, verse 39 by the present translator with assistance from Ruwa Pokorny.) The original Arabic text of this passage has been published in Afnan, Abu'l-Qasim, *'Ahd-i Aʿla: Zindigani-yi Hazrat-i Bab* (Oneworld Publications: Oxford, 2000), 30; henceforth, Afnan, *'Ahd-i Aʿla*.

From then on, Sayyid 'Ali-Muhammad, the Bab, remained in the care of his maternal uncle.[8]

There are stories which attest to the inquisitiveness of the Bab's mind in his childhood, as well as the exceeding rigor with which he carried out the religious obligations of Islam. We have exact historical dates for most of the significant events in the Bab's life; these have been recorded, with remarkable precision, in his works such as the Persian Bayan, the Arabic Bayan, the Sahifih-yi Bayn al-Haramayn (written in response to Mirza Muhit Kirmani), the Qayyum al-asma, and others.

The Bab was five years old when, one day, his uncle enrolled him in a religious school headed by one of his friends. Shaykh 'Abid. Mulla Fathullah, who was a schoolmate of the Bab's and served as the class monitor, gives the following account:

> When the Bab was brought to the school, we beheld a child with narrow limbs and a feeble body; he was dressed in a green tunic and a skullcap made of cashmere, walking hand in hand with his uncle. Arriving behind them was a male servant, bearing a plate on which were placed some sweets and a copy of the Qur'an, which he presented to the instructor.[9]

Owing to his burgeoning mental development, his abundant talent, and superior mind—and because he was enrolled in a religious school that could not meet his intellectual needs—there was an air of dissatisfaction that attended the period of the Bab's childhood education. His uncle had previously told the schoolmaster how unusual his nephew was:

8 Haji Sayyid 'Ali not only raised the Bab as he would have his own son, but he was also the first person to believe in the Bab after the Letters of the Living. Haji Sayyid 'Ali went to visit the Bab while he was imprisoned in the fortress of Chihriq, and during his journey back to Shiraz, he was arrested in Tehran and martyred along with six other Babis. Fazil Mazandarani, Asadu'llah, *Tarikh-i Zuhur al-Haqq*, vol. 3 (Bahá'í-Verlag, Germany 2008), 176; henceforth, "Mazandarani, *Zuhur al-Haqq*." The significant role which Haji Saiyyid 'Ali played in the early years of the Babi religion is discussed in the following pages.

9 Afnan, *'Ahd-i A'la*, 30 n. 9 and 31. Mulla Fathullah succeeded his father as the chief custodian of the Vakil Mosque in Shiraz. Sometime thereafter, he embraced the cause of the Bab and was killed in the Battle of Fort Tabarsi.

> He does not act or behave like other children; he prefers to seclude himself and immerse himself in thought. He shows no interest in playing or engaging in recreational activities as other children do. There are times when he makes truly astonishing statements.[10]

Shaykh 'Abid, the instructor of the school, who would later embrace the cause of the Bab,[11] gives the following account:

> As was customary on the first day of class, I asked the Bab to recite the opening verse of the Qur'an: "Bismi'llah al-rahman al-Rahim."[12] This he did without any hesitation or error. I then asked him to memorize this verse: "Huwa al-Fattah al-'Alim."[13] The Bab said nothing, and when I asked him why he had remained silent, he responded, "I do not know the meaning of 'Huwa' ['He is']."[14]
>
> There were several occasions when the Bab arrived late to school. One day, I sent one of the students to find him. When this student returned, he said, "He is performing his obligatory prayers in a corner of his home."
>
> On yet another occasion when the Bab had arrived late, I asked him, "Where were you?" he responded meekly, "I was at the home of my Ancestor."[15]

Other anecdotes have been recorded which recount the Bab's vigilant observance of Islamic prayer and worship—even in his childhood—and describe how he would be sunk in thought in the middle of a lively class. One such anecdote involves a certain day when all the students in the class were repeating a phrase at the instruction of their teacher—except for the Bab, who did not say a word and refused to cooperate. When one of the other students asked him why he had remained silent, he replied with a

---

10 Ibid.

11 Fayzi, *Nuqta-yi Ula*, 81.

12 "In the Name of God, the Compassionate, the Merciful." (Translator's note.)

13 Qur'an 34:26. (Translator's note): "He is the Opener [of the gates of sustenance], the All-Knowing."

14 From the account of Mulla Fathullah as recorded in Mirza Habibullah (Afnan). *Tarikh-i Amri-yi Shiraz* (Handwritten ms., INBA, no. 1027d); henceforth, "Mirza Habibullah, *Tarikh*." See also Amanat, *RR*, 115.

15 Gulpaygani, Mirza Abu'l-Fazl, *Kashful-Ghita' 'an Hiyalil-A'da'*. (Tashkent, n.d.), 83–84; henceforth, "*Kashful-Ghita'*." Also quoted in Fayzi, *Nuqta-yi Ula*, 79; Afnan, *'Ahd-i A'la*, 35; and other sources.

couplet from Hafiz: "Hearest thou not the whistle's call, this snare should now thy prison be."[16]

We do not know for certain whether the Bab ever expressed his disapproval of the traditional and outmoded style of instruction he was receiving, which occasionally involved corporal punishment and other forms of violence towards children, to his mother and uncle. Nabil Zarandi has related the following account from Shaykh 'Abid:

> I felt impelled to take [the Bab] back to his uncle and to deliver into his hands the Trust he had committed to my care. I determined to tell him how unworthy I felt to teach so remarkable a child. I found his uncle alone in his office. "I have brought him back to you," I said, "and commit him to your vigilant protection... It is incumbent upon you to surround him with your most loving care. Keep him in your house, for He, verily, stands in no need of teachers such as I." Haji Mirza Sayyid 'Ali sternly rebuked the Bab. "Have you forgotten my instructions?" he said. "Have I not already admonished you to follow the example of your fellow-pupils, to observe silence, and to listen attentively to every word spoken by your teacher?"[17]

With this remonstrance from his uncle, the Bab returned to school—but the immensity of his spirit, the unusual measure of his insight, could not be restrained by the narrow confines of that place. At last, with the permission of his uncle, the Bab quit the school of Shaykh 'Abid at the age of ten and began to work at his uncle's mercantile business.[18]

Mirza Sayyid 'Ali did not give up hope that the Bab might resume his formal education. The Bab was fifteen (c. 1834) when Mirza Sayyid 'Ali took him to one of the well-known Shaykhi 'ulama, Mulla 'Abdul-Khaliq Yazdi, to learn the fundamentals of Arabic grammar and the principles of Islamic jurisprudence. Mulla 'Abdul-Khaliq Yazdi recounts the following in a conversation with Mulla 'Abd al-Rahim-i-Qazvini:

---

16 Mirza Habibullah, *Tarikh*, 7–8. Other stories of this nature can be found in Babi and Baha'i histories. This translation of the couplet from Hafiz taken from Amanat, *RR*, 115.

17 Nabil Zarandi, Shaykh Muhammad. *The Dawn Breakers: Nabil's Narrative of the Early Days of the Baha'i Revelation*, trans. and ed. Shoghi Effendi (Wilmette, Illinois: 1932), 75–76; henceforth, "*Nabil*."

18 Afnan, *'Ahd-i A'la*, 37 n. 20 cites a passage from the Bab's *Kitab al-Fihrist* which corroborates this historical detail.

> I was a leader of prayer in Shiraz and held teaching lectures there. Once the uncle of this reverent man [i.e., the Bab] brought him to me saying that "this is a soul who is adorned with piety and austerity, but lacks learning, and I beg you to pay him some attention." After I had admitted him, I left him in the custody of my younger son. A few days later, my son came back to me complaining that "the person you have left me has not accomplished any of the elementaries. He first must learn basic grammatical structure *Amthila*,[19] and teaching *Amthila* is not suitable to my position." After that they sent him to Bushihr for the purpose of trade. Now I see such magnificent writings and unequalled verses as to make me astonished."[20]

According to Amanat, there is nothing strange about the Bab's distaste for the traditional style of instruction that prevailed in his day, or his aversion to the rigidity that characterized the religious schools of that era. To that effect, Amanat quotes the observations of an English merchant who was in Shiraz in 1850:

> The usual studies in Persian colleges are the Persian and Arabic languages, the Koran and commentaries upon it, theology, law, moral philosophy, and logic. Of natural philosophy, geography, and general history, nothing is taught or known... The dry study of Arabic language is in general held more in estimation and repute than any other pursuit.[21]

He then adds:

> The grammar of Arabic is complicated and difficult... Volumes have been written on philological trifles and subtleties, which are calculated to perplex and confuse, rather than to assist and enlighten the student.[22]

19 A bilingual Persian-Arabic elementary text on Arabic accidence (the inflections of words; morphology, syntax, grammar...) by 'Ali ibn Muhammad al-Jurjani (d. Shiraz, 816/1413), also entitled Sayyid-i Sharif (the Noble Sayyid) and Mir (Notable, Commander). It was part of the madrasa curriculum and was first published from the early nineteenth century in India, Persia and elsewhere; Calcutta (1805), Lucknow (1843) and Bombay (1845), then slightly later in Tehran (1852, etc). See Amanat, *RR*, 116 n. 37.

20 Mazandarani, *Zuhur al-Haqq*, 138 n. 1.

21 Amanat, *RR*, 117, quoting Benning, R. B. M. *Journal of Two Years' Trade in Persia*. 2 vols. (London, 1875), vol. I, 282.

22 Ibid.

The Bab's lack of formal education, as well as the presence of grammatical irregularities in his writings, were used constantly by his enemies as a pretext to discredit him. These people would cite the occasionally unconventional style which the Bab employed in his Persian and Arabic writings as evidence of his poor grasp of both languages, which they used as a basis for rejecting his claim of having introduced a new religion. Yet, for the Bab's followers, his limited education, his lofty revolutionizing ideals, and his firm, flowing style of Arabic and Persian writing all served as testament to the truth of his claim and the divinity of his knowledge. In his Sahifih-yi 'Adliyyih, the Bab responds to those who objected to his language:

> The fact that on some occasions words were altered or words uttered contrary to the rules of the people of doubt is because people would be able to make certain that the claimant of this position [himself] received these verses and this knowledge not by the way of learning, but because his heart is illuminated with the divine knowledge. [Therefore] he justifies these innovative alterations and what is contrary to rules, with the divine rules, as the same matter frequently occurred in the Book of God [the Qur'an].[23]

It is truly remarkable that the Bab was so straightforward about his lack of formal education, openly asserting that whatever he said or wrote were the products of divine inspiration. In his Tafsir-i Ha', addressed to a group of the 'ulama, the Bab writes:

> I swear on my own soul that I did not read a word of the conventional sciences, and in the past there were no books of sciences with me whose words I have memorized, and there is no reason for this divine gift but God's generosity and his benevolence. Today if someone asks me of various scholarly matters cited in books, I swear to God that I do not know the answer, and I do not even know the grammar and syntax, and I am proud of it, since God in the Day of Resurrection will prove to all that I was assisted by his generosity.[24]

23 Amanat, *RR*, 117. *Sahifih-yi 'Adliyyih*, Iranian National Baha'i Archive, no. 82, 155 (henceforth, INBA).

24 Amanat, *RR*, 117. Tafsir-i Ha', INBA, vol. 67, 1–84 (56–57).

In contrast to his dislike for sciences that begin with words and end with words, the Bab, in his writings, praises the advances made by Westerners—whom he calls "the people of Christ"—in the applied sciences. In his Persian Bayan, he states explicitly that there are scholars of every discipline in other countries outside the domain of Shi'i Islam.[25] In that work, he gives the example of the telescope, with which the Europeans have been able to study the position of our moon and other celestial bodies.[26]

The Bab's advocacy of the study of new sciences—as well as his support more generally for the other hallmarks of Western civilization, such as the establishment of a postal service, the printing of books, and so on—in a religious work rooted in spiritual beliefs demonstrates his aversion to pure religious legalism and his alignment with a kind of secularism that rejects the commending of absolutely everything to the Will of God in favor of a more practical approach that encourages the pursuit of knowledge, the making of discoveries, and the creation of new inventions, and even characterizes these as religious principles in and of themselves.[27]

THE BAB DISCONTINUES HIS FORMAL EDUCATION AND BEGINS HIS MERCANTILE WORK

During the time of the Bab, it was customary for the children of merchants in Persia to apprentice at their fathers' shops and become acquainted with commerce. It is according to this tradition that the Bab, upon discontinuing his formal education, began to work at the shop of his uncle, Haji Mirza Sayyid 'Ali (Khal-i A'zam). Though little is known about the Bab's life in Shiraz, we can infer from the historical context that his spiritual tendencies, including his engagement as a child in prolonged acts of worship—documented years later in attestations dating to when he lived in Bushihr—made up a significant part of his life at that time.

Five years later, the Bab set off for Bushihr, where—with an inheritance that had been bequeathed to him by his late father—he formed a commercial partnership with his uncle, Haji Mirza Muhammad (Khal-i Akbar).

25 The Bab, Persian Bayan 6:13; henceforth, "Bayan."
26 Ibid.
27 See Amanat, *RR*, 118.

The Bab's commercial enterprise in Bushihr lasted five years (1835–40); he worked with his uncle for the first two years, but carried on with his own independent business for the remainder of that time.

The commercial network of the family was based in the south of Persia, extending from Bushihr, which was a thriving port city, to other such cities along the Persian Gulf, such as Bandar 'Abbas, and ports along the Gulf of Oman and Bombay, Calcutta, and even Zanzibar and Java. In another direction, this network also extended to England, chiefly by way of India, with three centers of operations—in Shiraz, Yazd, and Bushihr.[28]

On the basis of family documents, such as ledgers that describe the business transactions of the Afnans, Abu'l-Qasim Afnan provides a clear account of the Bab's commercial enterprise. The Bab's imports from India included sugar, tea, tin, indigo, and spices, as well as various kinds of calico used to make curtains, women's clothing, and tablecloths. To this list of goods can also be added different types of cashmere and brocade, along with English wool and cotton textiles imported from India. The Bab exported rugs, dried rose petals, rosewater, foodstuffs, and dried fruits, such as shelled almonds and raisins, and at times he also traded gold coins. According to these historical documents, the Bab also had dealings in such cities as Yazd, Isfahan, Kashan, and Qazvin.[29]

There were certain goods which the Bab did not trade. In none of the extant records is there any indication that he ever bought or sold weapons, liquor, or opium. He refrained even from dealing in such malodorous merchandise as asafoetida, for which there was a market in India, and also sheepskin, etc.[30]

It must be recognized that commerce in those days was far from easy. There was always the danger that commercial goods brought into Persia by way of Bushihr with a caravan of mules would be stolen by highwaymen. Similarly, maritime commerce was faced with the constant threat of pirates, frightening storms, and the possibility that ships might sink.

Babi and Baha'i histories regard the Bab's expansion of his commercial network into regions beyond the ones mentioned previously as an indication

28 See Amanat, *RR*, 121. For more information on Persian commerce in the Qajar era, see Chapter 3 in this volume, "The Shaping of the Babi Community," which includes Western sources on this subject.

29 Afnan, *'Ahd-i A'la*, 39–41. Afnan also describes how goods were transported by sailboat, or via mules that were made to cross the mountaintops between Bushihr and Shiraz.

30 Afnan, *'Ahd-i A'la*, 41.

of his ability to successfully carry on an enterprise. According to these histories, one factor that contributed to the Bab's commercial success was his maintenance of good relations with other merchants in southern and central Persia. The *Nuqtat al-Kaf* states:

> The most prominent among the class of merchants were astonished by the Bab's superior ability in matters of commerce, and found it very strange that so young a person could so effectively regulate the most vital of such affairs.[31]

That same text testifies to the Bab's renown among the people of Bushihr for his "good nature, his equanimity, his dignified bearing, his piety, his virtue, his work ethic, his generosity, his contentment, and his insight."[32]

The Bab resided in Bushihr at a time when that city was undergoing political and social upheaval. To protect their Indian colony and to expand their influence throughout the regions of the Persian Gulf, and strengthen their commercial ties with India, the British Government established a residency in Bushihr toward the beginning of the nineteenth century. In May 1837, as Muhammad Shah was taking military measures to reassert Persian control over the city of Hirat, the British Government responded at once by sending a fleet of warships to the shores of Bushihr and occupying the island of Kharg. This development led the people of Bushihr to show great anger toward the British. As tensions between the two nations were rising, in March 1839, at the instigation of the leader of the Akhbari sect in that region, Shaykh Husayn Al-i Usfur—and with the support of the governor of the province of Fars, Asadu'llah Mirza—the residents of Bushihr launched an insurrection that attempted to prevent the British rear admiral and his troops from landing in the Bushihr Residency. Left with no other choice, the British evacuated Bushihr and retreated to the island of Kharg. Naturally, these incidents disrupted trade in Bushihr for a relatively long time. In an effort to restore normalcy, the merchants of the city attempted to mediate between the two nations, but to no avail. Eventually, the British Residency was re-established in Bushihr three years later. Beyond these developments, a period of global economic stagnation

31 Kashani, Haji Mirza Jani, *Tarikh-i Nuqtat al-Kaf*, a history of the dispensation of the Bab and a chronicle of the first eight years of his ministry (ed. E. G. Browne; Leiden, the Netherlands: Brill), 109, 191; henceforth, "*Nuqtat al-Kaf*."

32 Ibid.

that lasted from 1838 to 1843 also yielded undesirable consequences for Persian commerce.[33]

These circumstances notwithstanding, the Bab continued to carry on his enterprise in Bushihr, and with every passing day he became increasingly well-known for his piety, devoutness, truthfulness, and trustworthiness. The latter two virtues served as firm foundations for commerce in Persia, reflecting themselves clearly in the dealings of those large families in which the mercantile profession was passed down from generation to generation. Merchants in those days enjoyed a close relationship with the mosques and the 'ulama, and a great many of those who came from merchant families belonged to the clerical class. At this juncture, the commercial culture of Persia was intertwined not only with the values of truthfulness and trustworthiness, but also an atmosphere of religiosity. The Prophet of Islam was himself a merchant who bore the title of "the Trusted One" [Amin], so it was only natural that a descendant of his should have considered trustworthiness a religious obligation. The *Farsnamah-yi Nasiri* states that the maternal uncles of the Bab "for generations...were engaged in trade and...known for their honesty."[34] With regard to the Bab specifically, Amanat writes:

> On one occasion, Haji Mirza Abu'l-Hasan Yazdi, a merchant in Bushihr on his way to the pilgrimage of Hajj, entrusted the Bab with some merchandise to be sold during his absence. The price of the merchandise fell and it was sold at a price cheaper than was expected. However, on his return to Bushihr, Sayyid 'Ali-Muhammad (contrary to the general practice of the time, which only obliged him to pay back the value of the sold merchandise), included 175 tumans extra, the difference between the original value and the price fetched, insisting that failing to pay the original price was contrary to the code of trustworthiness.[35]

33 For a detailed account of the events of this period, as well as information and research on the incidents in Bushihr and the Persian Gulf which then took place, see Amanat, *RR*, 122 n. 70.

34 *Fars-Nama*, vol. 2, 131. This translation taken from Amanat, *RR*, 127.

35 Mu'in al-Saltana Tabrizi, Haji Muhammad, *Tarikh-i Amri [Baha'i]*, INBA, 78; henceforth, "Mu'in." This excerpt taken from Amanat, *RR*, 128. *Nabil-i Zarandi*, 79, and other Baha'i histories have quoted the same account, with minor differences, from Sayyid Javad Karbala'i. Among the other innovations which the Bab brought to the realm of commerce was his breaking the custom of *dabbih* [bargaining for reduction after a transaction has already been settled], to which reference is made in most histories pertaining to the life of the Bab; see *Nabil*, 79; Amanat, *RR*, 128; Afnan, *Ahd-i A'la*, 41–42; and Fayzi, *Nuqta-yi Ula*, 90–91.

The *Nuqtat al-Kaf* recounts a similar anecdote, but in this case attributes the loss which the Bab incurred to the characteristically meticulous attention he paid to prayer and other acts of worship:

> So devoted was he to his religious observances that it is said he was once entrusted with some indigo that someone came to buy. This customer had come at a time when the Bab had intended to recite a certain religious text, and to this customer he said, "Wait one hour; then I shall be available." At first, the man agreed to wait—but when the hour had passed and the Bab had become ready to receive his customer, he found that he had gone. In addition, the price of indigo had fallen in that time. The Bab sold it at a lower price, sustaining a loss of 70 tumans in the process—a sum he ultimately paid with his own funds to the person who had entrusted this merchandise to him as compensation.[36]

Amanat writes:

> This moralistic attitude [of the Bab] was not devoid of pragmatism, however. The Bab's later instructions [in the Bayan] do not resonate the bookishness of madrasa jurists, nor do they lend themselves, at least as far as trade was concerned, to a puritanical enthusiasm.[37]

He continues in that vein:

> Contrary to the restricted regulations set up by the shari'a, but in compliance with common practice, [the Bab] allows a lawful interest on the borrowed money "as it is now practiced among the merchants," or allows agreement on the extension or delay of the repayment of exchange bills. He regards the mutual satisfaction of both parties as the essential condition for the lawfulness of any contract, whether they are "under age, adults, slaves, or free men."[38] On the subject of foreigners, he emphasizes that only those Christian merchants who follow useful trades and professions are permitted

36 *Nuqtat al-Kaf*, 109.
37 Amanat, *RR*, 129.
38 Bayan 5:18.

> to dwell in the countries of believers.[39] On another occasion, he refers to changes in the monetary system and acknowledges that depreciation of currency, both gold and silver, brings losses to the *tujjar* [merchants]. He hopes that in the future these fluctuations will settle.[40] He strictly forbids trade of opium, intoxicating drugs, and liquors for believers, but allows their use for medical purposes under certain conditions.[41]

Emphasizing the extent to which the Bab was known for his generosity, and also for the many consecutive hours he would spend absorbed in prayer and other acts of worship, the *Nuqtat al-Kaf* states:

> [The people would say] he would spend all his capital; on one occasion, he gave 70 tumans to an indigent...those same people wrote to the Bab's uncle to complain of his actions.[42]

From this account, one can perhaps deduce why the Bab separated himself from commercial partnership with his uncles. Mu'in al-Saltana ascribes this move on the Bab's part to "the existing necessities of the time."[43]

Amanat writes:

> For young Sayyid 'Ali-Muhammad engagement in trade served not only as a means of earning his livelihood, but more significantly as a way to emphasize moral standards he felt were declining, standards that were for him idealized in the words and deeds of the Prophet and Imams.[44]

In a letter to one of his followers, who was himself a merchant, the Bab states that God ordained the mercantile profession for Muhammad and 'Ali-Muhammad [the Bab]. In this letter, the Bab implores God to bestow his blessings upon them that are fair in their dealings and love those who are inferior to them even as they love themselves. He states,

39 Ibid., 7:16.
40 Ibid., 5:19.
41 Ibid., 9:24.
42 *Nuqtat al-Kaf*, 109.
43 Mu'in, 78. This translation taken from Amanat, *RR*, 129.
44 Amanat, *RR*, 129.

moreover, that those who engage in commerce "for the sake of God," and observe justice and fairness, will be safeguarded by God from every deceiving one.[45]

Business that was done for the sake of God, upon which the Bab placed great emphasis, harks back to the Islamic concept of "partnership with God," which in reality refers to the belief that God is present in commercial affairs. This constant awareness of the presence of God is intended to serve as the highest motive and greatest duty to observe justice and fairness, particularly toward the indigent and inferior. Included also in the Bab's letter is his allusion to having a profession similar to that of the Prophet Muhammad. The significance of this allusion is appreciated by the author of the *Nuqtat al-Kaf*, himself a merchant, who considers the similarities between the lives of the Prophet Muhammad and the Bab in every respect—even their being orphans in childhood—as evidences of divine wisdom, inasmuch as the Bab's engagement in trade

> was designed to accomplish the proof to the people, so they would not be able to claim that he lacked the capacity of dealing with people. Thus the same mysterious considerations behind the engagement of his venerated ancestor [the Prophet] in trade, could also be applied to him. So, in every sense he could be a sign of that original light even in his orphanhood.[46]

EPIPHANY, PIETY, AND INTUITION

Every work that has discussed the Bab's life, irrespective of whether or not its author was a Baha'i, has, as we have seen, invariably highlighted the unbending vigilance with which the Bab spent hour after hour engaged in prayer, worship, and other acts of piety. Another point on which all these works agree are some of the Bab's epiphanies, and also his ability to endure the rigors of an abstinent lifestyle. The uncle and guardian of the Bab, Haji Sayyid 'Ali, once said the following in a conversation with Shaykh 'Abid, who taught at the school which the Bab attended:

---

45 This letter, originally written in Arabic, appears in Mu'in, 28. Refer also to Amanat, *RR*, 129–30.

46 *Nuqtat al-Kaf*, 110. This translation taken from Amanat, *RR*, 130.

> From this nephew of mine, one sees such things as have never before been witnessed from any other child. Every day I hear from him a new word; at every moment I behold him in an unusual state. For instance, he will recount some of his strange and astonishing dreams, and it is most peculiar that a child of eight or nine should have such dreams.[47]

Some of these dreams are recorded in books that discuss the Bab's life. The following account comes from Haji Sayyid 'Ali, his uncle:

> On a certain day, [the Bab] was sleeping beside me in the Murgh bathhouse when he awoke suddenly, saying, "The roof covering the Mirza Hadi bathhouse has collapsed; one woman and three children have died." An uproar ensued in no time at all, with everyone asserting his own number of the fatalities, but eventually it became clear that the situation was exactly as the Bab had reported it.
>
> On another occasion some time ago, he told me, "I had a dream in which I beheld a pair of scales, suspended in the air between earth and heaven. The Imam Ja'far Sadiq sat in one of the scales, which was touching the ground. An invisible hand took hold of me and placed me in the empty scale. At that moment, the scale in which I was sitting lowered to the ground, and the scale bearing the seated Imam rose to the sky."[48]

These dreams persisted even after the Bab proclaimed his cause:

> In 1846 he dreamed that at the hour of the spring equinox (the Persian new year), some books were sent down to him. When he opened one of them he noticed that its pages were covered with the dust of [the Imam] Husayn's tomb. He looked more closely and saw a tablet in an excellent *shikastih* style bearing an astral seal at the bottom with the epigram "I entrusted my cause to God," signed "Mahdi."[49]

---

47 Ayati, 'Abdul-Husayn, *al-Kawakib al-Durriya fi Ma'athiri'l-Baha'iyyih* (Cairo, 1922), 33; henceforth, "*Kawakib al-Durriya.*"

48 Afnan, *Ahd-i A'la*, 31, and other historical sources on the life of the Bab.

49 Commentary on verse 35 of Suriy-i Nur (Qur'an, Surah 24), INBA, no. 98, 55–65 (57–59). (This translation taken from Amanat, *RR*, 131.) In that commentary, and on the basis of this dream, the Bab asserts the truth of his claim through the use of the Abjad notation and the numerical value of each letter of the Arabic alphabet.

As the Bab reached the age of maturity and beyond, these remarkable states, apparent in him since childhood, were gradually accompanied by an attitude of humility and innocence. To that effect, Haji Sayyid Javad Karbala'i notes:

> Whilst journeying to India, I passed through Bushihr. As I was already acquainted with Haji Mirza Sayyid 'Ali, I was enabled to meet the Bab on several occasions. Every time I met him, I found him in such a state of humility and lowliness as words fail me to describe. His downcast eyes, his extreme courtesy, and the serene expression of his face made an indelible impression upon my soul. I often heard those who were closely associated with him testify to the purity of his character, to the charm of his manners, to his self-effacement, to his high integrity, and to his extreme devotion to God.[50]

The Bab's five years in Bushihr were devoted not only to commercial pursuits, but also to the development of his lofty spiritual qualities—qualities he had evinced in his childhood, but which had not yet satisfied his perfection-seeking spirit. Every day, from the earliest hours of dawn until sunrise—and also from midday till late in the afternoon—the Bab dedicated himself to rapturous prayer and supplication, entirely absorbed in spiritual realms. He would spend several hours each Friday in continuous worship on the roof of his house, engaged in such fervent communion that even the burning rays of the sweltering summer sun of Bushihr could not deter him from his acts of devotion.[51]

This manner of worship was used, without due consideration of the Bab's other traits, as a pretext by Sipihr, the Qajar court historian, and other polemicists after him to ridicule the Bab.[52] In reality, such displays of piety and rigor are earnest attempts to discover the light of one's own internal splendor, and achieve an awareness of one's inner realities. In virtually every religious movement and school of thought, there is a precedent whereby saints and other such sages have embarked on these spiritual quests. It seems the Bab's spellbound states of devotion gave rise to widespread rumors

---

50 *Nabil*, 79.

51 Paraphrase of *Nabil*, 77–78.

52 Refer, for instance, to: Sipihr, Mirza Taqi Khan (Lisan al-Mulk), *Nasikh al-Tawarikh* (ed. Jamshid Kiyanfar), vol. 2 (Intisharat-i Asatir: Tehran, 1998), 827; henceforth, *Nasikh al-Tawarikh*.

that he was under the tutelage of a mystical guide. Babi and Baha'i sources reject these rumors, and instead regard the veracity of the Bab's claims, his spiritual ascendancy, his heavenly disposition, and the speed and force with which he composed his verses, as miraculous. The *Nuqtat al-Kaf* states:

> The widely-reported notion that the Bab would subject himself to the kind of bodily deprivation common to ascetics, or that he studied under some spiritual mentor, is sheer slander and patently false. Much to the contrary, that self-sufficient Point seemed to have no need for any one in any respect; it was only with regard to his Beloved that he was as one poor and needy.[53]

During the Bab's time in Bushihr, he would compose beautifully flowing verses—including prayers written for various individuals—without appending his own name to these writings:

> Though his formal education was limited to that brief span he spent at the school of Shaykh 'Abid, astonishing phrases and fitting words would flow nonetheless from his pen.[54]

THE BAB'S JOURNEY TO THE SACRED SHRINE CITIES OF 'IRAQ

After residing in Bushihr for five years, the Bab decided to travel to Najaf and Karbala. When he informed his family of this decision, they were very concerned. His mother, saddened by the distance that already existed between her and her son—and his uncle, Haji Sayyid Muhammad (Khal-i Akbar), who had a commercial center of operations in Bushihr but lived in Shiraz at the time—tried to dissuade the Bab from undertaking this journey, but their efforts were in vain.[55] The Bab even declined his uncle's suggestion to await his return to Bushihr before traveling. In a letter to him, the Bab wrote: "The time for my journey has come, and I have no choice but to travel."[56] After setting his commercial affairs in order and handing over the keys of

53 *Nuqtat al-Kaf*, 109–110.
54 *Kawakib al-Durriya*, 34.
55 For more information on these dissuasive efforts, see Afnan, *'Ahd-i A'la*, 43.
56 Ibid.

his shop to the custodian of the caravanserai, the Bab departed for Karbala in 1257 AH (1840–41). This journey opened a new chapter for the Bab; bidding farewell to the world of commerce, he was now entering the next stage of his life—a stage filled with turmoil and with no clear conclusion.

Not much is known about the Bab's time in Karbala apart from accounts that attest to the captivating quality of his speech and the charm of his virtuous character. A. L. M. Nicolas, a diplomat with the French Consular Service in Persia during the Qajar era and author of a book on the Babi religion, once met with one of the first Babis, Mulla Sadiq Khurasani, entitled "Muqaddas." On that occasion, Khurasani related to Nicolas an account of his first encounter with the Bab in Karbala, which Nicolas summarizes as follows:[57]

> On a certain day, I entered the Shrine of the Imam Husayn, intending to make pilgrimage there, when I beheld a youth in a kind of spiritual trance. He was immersed in a silent state of sanctification, and tears were streaming down his face. Without willing it, I began to go towards him—but as I did not wish to disturb him, I instead seated myself in a corner to wait until he had concluded his pilgrimage. The more attention I paid to him, the more fascinated I grew with his expressions of modesty and shame. I witnessed from him such things as I cannot possibly describe. When he had finished his pilgrimage, he went to the courtyard of the shrine. I did not succeed in conversing with him that day, but I resolved to make pilgrimage to the shrine again at the same time the following day, that perhaps I might be able to speak with him and restore my former serenity.
>
> When that next day came, my hope that I would see him in that same state and be stirred to my core once again was far greater than

57 Nicolas, who worked at the French Consular Service in Persia at the outset of the Bab's dispensation, began to study the new movement with interest. Towards the beginning of the twentieth century, his translation of the Arabic Bayan into French, along with some of his other writings on Babi history, were published in Paris (Nicolas, A. L. M., *Seyyèd Ali Muhammad dit le Bâb*, Paris, 1925, 191–92; henceforth, "Nicolas.")

Mulla Sadiq Khurasani, entitled "Muqaddas," was a follower of the Shaykhi school of thought and one of the first people to embrace the Bab's Cause. In Shiraz, Khurasani was subjected to aspersion and harassment. He and his son, known by his title of Ibn-i Asdaq, rendered great services to both the Babi and Baha'i religions. For a biographical account of Khurasani written by Ibn-i Asdaq, see Rafati, Vahid, *Payk-i Rastan* ('Asr-i Jadid: Darmstadt, Germany), 2005, 371–95.

> it had been the previous day. After conducting the rites of pilgrimage, I headed in his direction and said to him, "If you will allow it, I wish to have a word with you." He shook his head to decline my request, and went on his way. When the two of us had gained some distance from the Imam's tomb, that youth came towards me and apologized, stating that, "The vicinity of the tomb is a holy place; it is a place for prayer and contemplation, and I was oblivious of myself." So courteous was his demeanor, so cheerful his face as he spoke these words that I could not help but be totally captivated by him.[58]

With regard to the Bab's journey to Karbala and his pilgrimage to the Shrine of the Imam Husayn, the author of the *Nuqtat al-Kaf* writes:

> For close to a year, he made regular visits to that sacred spot. Such strange and astonishing things would be seen from him as he entered the sanctuaries of his immaculate ancestors and made pilgrimage to their tombs as would astound a great many of his onlookers. There is no truth to the well-known notion that he would participate in the classes of the late Sayyid [Kazim Rashti] as a mere pupil, though he did attend those classes in Karbala for nearly three months and also make appearances at the late *Sayyid*'s religious sermons from time to time. On all these occasions, the late *Sayyid*—may God exalt his station—would benefit immensely from the inner light of that lofty One, but the people in his midst were entirely unaware of the mystery of his Cause.[59]

As part of the efforts of Haji Rasul Bazargan, a Shaykhi merchant of Qazvin, to convince the members of his family of the truth of the Bab's claims, he states:

> Should the possessor of the divine voice be that same *Sayyid* I saw in Karbala, verily I say that whatever he claims is the truth.[60]

58 Afnan, *'Ahd-i A'la*, 45–46, and other sources.
59 *Nuqtat al-Kaf*, 110.
60 Haji Rasul Bazargan was the father of Haji Shaykh Muhammad (Nabil), one of the famous Babis of Qazvin. This original text of this passage has been published in Mazandarani, *Zuhur al-Haqq*, 299.

At the invitation of Mulla Sadiq Khurasani, the Bab attended a gathering at the residence of Sayyid Kazim Rashti, then the leader of the Shaykhis and himself present at the gathering, where a traditional eulogy for the martyrs of Karbala was being given. As the Bab entered, Mulla Husayn Bushru'i—who in Shiraz would later become the first person to believe in the Bab—was narrating a tragic account of the martyrdom of the Imam Husayn. Khurasani writes that, upon the Bab's entrance, Sayyid Kazim arose from his seat out of reverence, and that the others in attendance followed suit. The Bab seated himself by the front door in spite of Sayyid Kazim's insistence that he take a more prominent seat. Then, at the instruction of Sayyid Kazim, Mulla Husayn began to recite from the poetry of Shaykh Ahmad Ahsa'i. The Bab was so deeply moved as he listened to those poems that he began to weep, and he wept so bitterly that all those present at that gathering began to weep with him.[61]

The Bab lived in the sacred shrine cities of 'Iraq, known as the 'Atabat,[62] for nearly one year—eight months in Karbala, and three months in other cities of religious significance. According to nearly every Babi and Baha'i source, the Bab would occasionally attend the classes of Sayyid Kazim. These sources consider the writings of the Bab to be tokens of his divine knowledge. Muslim historians, however—beginning in the Qajar era and extending into subsequent periods—have mostly rejected this claim by alleging that the Bab attended Sayyid Kazim's classes on a regular basis, notwithstanding that these historians have failed to cite any evidence in support of their assertion.[63]

61 Nicolas, 192, and other Babi and Baha'i sources. Amanat considers it likely that this was a literary gathering known as the Divanu'r-Rashti, "a literary circle set up by Rashti for ritual mourning for the Imams as well as poetical, literary, and theological exchange, which met in his library. A spirit of patronage was augmented by Rashti's desire to broaden his sphere of intellectual and political influence...[this gathering] provided for substantial support not only from Persian religious students, but also from a large and heterogenous body of merchants, 'ulama, and literary and poetical figures [from Karbala]" (*RR*, 139). Amanat goes on to note that this gathering "survived a century after the death of its founder, up to 1941, when Rashti's grandson, Sayyid Qasim Rashti, died in Karbala. The library, which at one time housed more than ten thousand books, after suffering chronic waves of looting and arson was finally dispersed" (ibid., 139 n. 156).

62 Atabat: thresholds, more fully, *'atabāt-e 'alīyāt* "the lofty or sacred thresholds," the Shi'ih shrine cities of Iraq—*Najaf, Karbala, Kazemayn,* and *Samarra*—containing the tombs of six of the imams as well as secondary sites of pilgrimage.

63 For a detailed discussion of this subject, see Muhammad-Husayni, Nusratu'llah, *Hazrat-i Bab* (2nd ed.; Australia, 2016), 164–67; henceforth, "Muhammad-Husayni."

THE BAB'S RETURN TO SHIRAZ AND MARRIAGE

The Bab's time in Karbala ended not of his own volition, but that of his mother, who after six years of separation could not tolerate being so far from her only son any longer. Accordingly, the Bab's uncle, Haji Sayyid 'Ali, traveled to Karbala to persuade his nephew to return to Shiraz. At first, the Bab refused this plea. Ultimately, however, through the intercession of Sayyid Kazim Rashti—arranged at the request of Haji Sayyid 'Ali—the Bab acceded to his uncle's request, returning to Shiraz in 1842. Not long thereafter, the Bab's mother—in a move that may have been intended to prevent any future journeys her son might have wished to undertake—prepared the means for his marriage. The Bab's wife, Khadijih Sultan Bagum, was the daughter of Aqa Mirza Sayyid 'Ali, the paternal uncle of the Bab's mother. At the time of his marriage, the Bab was twenty-three years old.[64]

The various histories generally agree that, in spite of the turmoil that had spread not only in Shiraz, but also throughout the province of Fars,[65] the Bab lived in Shiraz for the two years leading up to the declaration of his cause in a state of peace and contentment. During these days, the Bab would devote some time to prayer and communion each morning before the sun had risen. He would spend several hours of the day at his uncle's business, and upon returning, he would stand in prayer and worship one hour after sunset. Years later, in the prison of Maku (1847), the Bab would fondly recall this period of his life, referring to them as "happy days."[66] According to an account from his wife, Khadijih Bagum, after having his dinner, the Bab would spend hours writing in what appeared to be a ledger, but what was actually a notebook reserved for his compositions on spiritual and religious subjects.[67] In response to his wife, who had expressed her surprise upon finding that the contents of this notebook bore no semblance whatsoever to commercial matters, the Bab said, "This is the people's account book."[68]

64 Afnan, *Ahd-i A'la*, 48. Family documents identify the date of the Bab's marriage as Friday, 18 Rajab 1258 AH (25 August 1842) and indicate that it was registered at the residence of his uncle, Haji Sayyid 'Ali (Khal-i A'zam). From this union was born a son named Ahmad, who died in Shiraz as a child. For more about Khadijih Bagum, see Balyuzi, Hasan, *Khadijih Bagum, the Wife of the Báb* (George Ronald, Oxford, 1981).

65 See Amanat, *RR*, 147.

66 Bayan 6:2.

67 Mirza Habibullah, *Tarikh*, 20–21. This translation taken from Amanat, *RR*, 147.

68 Fayzi, *Khandan-i Afnan*, 163. Amanat considers this remark by the Bab to be a reference to Qur'an 2:202, which states that God will calculate the deeds of his servants

On one occasion, he wrote for a cousin, Muhammad-Taqi Vakilu'l-Haqq, a piece which, according to that cousin's own testimony, "resembled the prayers of the Sahifih al-Sajjadiyyah [attributed to the Imam 'Ali]."[69]

We have little information about the Bab's writings from this period, but these brief allusions—along with his pure and virtuous lifestyle, for which he had become known in Shiraz—all speak to the spiritual ecstasy and the mystical inspiration he experienced, which prepared him to receive the divine message that lay in store for him. So great, in fact, was his spiritual excitement that some members of his family had begun to notice it and even grew concerned for him. The fervor unleashed by the advent of a new revelation from God had quickened the pulse of the world, and the flood of fate had swept up the Bab and his kin in its current. Is it possible to imagine that the Bab had spent those long hours in prayer and worship, and had endured such rigorous austerity, to attain that momentous event to which he had unwittingly been heading? Witnessing her husband's remarkable state, Khadijih Bagum had said to her family that the Bab was "preoccupied most of the time with prayers and worship," which clearly demonstrated that he was "a superior person."[70]

The historical documents at our disposal indicate that, in 1844, the Bab gradually became more conscious of his reality, accompanied as this growing awareness was by instances of spiritual inspiration. A few years later, in a letter the Bab sent to his family while imprisoned in the fortress of Maku, he states explicitly that, nineteen days before the passing of Sayyid Kazim Rashti—coinciding with the beginning of the year 1260 AH (1844)—"the concealed mystery" had been revealed to him.[71] In his Risalih-yi Baynu'l-Haramayn, he refers even more clearly to the revelation he had received:

> In truth, the first day that the spirit descended in the heart of this servant was the fifteenth of the month of Rabi'u'l-Avval [4 April 1844].[72]

---

on the Day of Resurrection: "It is they who have a portion from what they have earned, and God is swift in reckoning." See Amanat, *RR*, 147 n. 199.

69 Fayzi, *Khandan-i Afnan*, 111.

70 Mu'in, 77–79. Refer also to Amanat, *RR*, 149.

71 Passage from a letter of the Bab to his family, written while he was imprisoned in the fortress of Maku; INBA, no. 58, 66–160. A portion of this letter has also been published in Mazandarani, *Zuhur al-Haqq*, 177–78.

72 The Bab, *Kitab al-Haramayn*; this passage quoted in Nicolas, 206. This work was written in June 1845, later than the Sahifih-yi Bayn al-Haramayn. See also Amanat, *RR*, 168 and 168 n. 98.

In his commentary on the Surih-yi Baqarih of the Qur'an, written in February 1844—approximately three months before he declared his cause—the Bab recounts a dream which involves the death of Sayyid Kazim Rashti:

> Verily I saw, on that night in a dream, the Holy Land[73] fallen in pieces and lifted in the air till it stopped in front of my house. Then afterward, news came of my teacher's death, the great, kind scholar, may God have mercy upon him.[74]

Amanat evaluates the significance of the Bab's dream in this way:

> This symbolic dream not only alludes to the new claims of the Bab by the announcement of Rashti's death, but also hints at the termination of the 'Atabat era, which in the Bab's view is concurrent with the commencement of the new dispensation.[75]

Eventually, a few months before the Bab's declaration, he disclosed to his mother and uncle, Haji Sayyid 'Ali, that he had been chosen to champion a great cause: the promulgation of the commandments of God amid the people. In this vein, Amanat notes that:

> To substantiate his sincerity to his uncle, Sayyid 'Ali, and his mother, the Bab relied on his own religious devotion and personal integrity, stressing that he only reflected what had been revealed to him [by God].[76]

Sometime thereafter, in a writing known as the Kitab al-Fihrist, the Bab would explicitly state that he began to receive revelation approximately two months before he declared his cause.[77]

---

73 A reference to the 'Atabat.

74 INBA, no. 98, 4, 23–27. (This translation taken from Amanat, *RR*, 168. Translator's note.)

75 Amanat, *RR*, 168.

76 Amanat, *RR*, 149 citing Mu'in, 79.

77 Ishraq-Khavari, 'Abdu'l-Hamid. *Muhadirat*, vol. 2 (Bahá'í-Verlag, Germany, 1987), 669. See also Chapter 2 in this volume, "The Worldview of the Bab."

THE DECLARATION OF THE BAB'S CAUSE: THE BIRTH OF A NEW RELIGION

The Bab refers to the exact date and time of the inception of his dispensation, which he identifies as the fulfillment of the Qur'anic promise of "the resurrection of Islam," in one of the sacred texts of the Babi religion, the Persian Bayan: two hours and eleven minutes after sunset on the night of 22 May 1844. For such a resurrection to take place, the people must first rise from their graves—or, to put it in Babi terms, they who are fast asleep must be roused from the slumber of heedlessness—and a new dispensation of a single religious truth must be inaugurated.

Among the similarities between the lives of Christ and the Bab is that, just as the three Magi had gone from the East to Palestine in search of the promised one of Judaism, it was now a group of Persian seminarians—students of the Shaykhi school—who had traveled from Karbala to Persia to find the promised one of Islam.[78] These students had embarked on this journey at the instruction of their teacher and leader, Sayyid Kazim Rashti who, prior to his death in early 1844, had not appointed a successor for himself, but rather urged his pupils to set aside their theological studies and discussions, and instead seek out the promised one. This last exhortation from a teacher to his students was no mere coincidence. Not only had Sayyid Kazim and his own teacher, Shaykh Ahmad, founder of the Shaykhi school, believed that the advent of a new religious dispensation was imminent, but yet another

78 The founder of Shaykhism, a new school of thought in Shi'ism, was Shaykh Ahmad Ahsa'i, who was born in the Arabian city of Ahsa' in 1752. He lived for a time in Bahrain, the sacred shrine cities of 'Iraq, and Persia, and found followers in all these regions. Shaykhism adds new teachings to those five principles which are well-known in Shi'ism as "the pillars of Islam." Chief among these new teachings is the rejection of the idea that a physical resurrection will occur on the Day of Judgment in favor of belief in a spiritual resurrection, or the resurrection of a subtle body known as "Hurqalya." Following the death of Shaykh Ahmad in 1825, and per his instructions in his will and testament, Sayyid Kazim Rashti assumed leadership of the Shaykhi school and established its center in Karbala. When Rashti died and the Bab declared his cause, a large number of Shaykhis became followers of the Babi religion, but the Shaykhi school does still exist. Today one of its main centers is the Iranian city of Kirman, and a number of Sayyid Kazim's descendants [the Ibrahimi family] have, in the past century, served as the school's leaders. For more information on Shaykhi history and thought, see the *Encyclopædia Iranica*: (www.iranicaonline.org/articles/search/keywords:shaykhism), which also contains articles on the relationship between Shaykhism and the Babi religion. Refer also to: Denis MacEoin, *From Shaykhism to Babism: A Study in Charismatic Renewal in Shi'i Islam*, accessible online at: https://bahai-library.com/author/Denis+MacEoin. A brief discussion of Shaykhi beliefs is also included in Chapter 5 of this volume, by Todd Lawson.

group of mystics and even poets had also arrived at the same conclusion based on their understanding of Islamic texts and traditions.[79] Perhaps most astonishing is the fact that, in that same century, religious movements were also emerging within the Christian community, who, using prophecies in the Torah and the Gospel as their basis, considered the coming of Christ from the heavens—an event Christians throughout the world had been eagerly awaiting for centuries—to be close at hand.[80]

Following the death of Sayyid Kazim Rashti, a few of his most eminent students claimed that they were his rightful successors, and they each found support from the other Shaykhi seminarians. Another of his distinguished students, Mulla Husayn Bushru'i, obedient to the last instructions of his late teacher, assembled a group of like-minded seminarians to accompany him on his quest to find the promised one. To prepare themselves spiritually for this perilous journey, the members of that cohort secluded themselves for forty days in the Kufa Mosque where, in accordance with Islamic tradition, they engaged in fasting, prayer, and communion with God that lasted throughout the night.

Mulla Husayn Bushru'i, who would go on to play a historic role in the Babi movement, was no ordinary seminarian. His spirit, with its insatiable appetite for learning, could never find repose. He was a man of great determination, in constant search of a new challenge. So vast was his knowledge of his creed that others deemed him worthy to succeed Sayyid Kazim Rashti. The death of Sayyid Kazim in Karbala occurred at a time when Mulla Husayn had gone to Isfahan, at the instruction of his late teacher, to respond decisively to the objections and animosities that had been leveled against the Shaykhis by the Hujjatu'l-Islam, Sayyid Muhammad Baqir Shafti, and the other 'ulama of that city. The account of this debate, which took place in Isfahan, became the talk of the town. Mulla Husayn, an unpretentious seminarian of little means, was facing a man regarded as one of the greatest 'ulama in all Persia—an obscenely wealthy man whose power was said to have rivaled that of the Shah. While in Isfahan, Mulla Husayn made a living through manual labor, and with the wage he earned from that work, he spent the remainder of the week in fasts and other acts of austerity. It was in this state of self-denial that Mulla Husayn debated with Shafti and other 'ulama. In the end, Mulla Husayn utterly confuted Shafti—and after fulfilling similar duties in Khurasan, he returned to Karbala. From that point forward, the

79 See Amanat, *RR*, chapter 2, "Prophets and Prophecies," 70–105.
80 Ibid.

inhabitants of Isfahan would remark that, "A penniless seminarian came and reduced our Hujjatu'l-Islam to silence."[81]

When he had concluded his period of seclusion, Mulla Husayn—along with his brother and cousin, who were both students of Sayyid Kazim Rashti—entered Bushihr through Basrih by ship (apparently in mid-May 1844), and after a brief sojourn there, he set off for Shiraz. Mulla Husayn and his kin were gradually joined by the rest of his companions (nine of them, according to Nabil's account) once they had completed their own periods of seclusion. It is unclear what compelled Mulla Husayn to travel from Karbala to Shiraz. One account mentions a certain Mulla Hasan Gawhar, who had made a claim as successor to Sayyid Kazim and whom Mulla Husayn and his companions considered unworthy of that position. According to this account, they consequently set out with the intention of traveling to Kirman, where they would meet with Haji Muhammad Karim Khan Kirmani—who had advanced his own pretension to successorship—to assess the validity of his claim, passing through Shiraz along the way.[82] Nabil's account, however, states that Mulla Husayn felt a hidden power, magnetic in its force, drawing him northward towards Shiraz.[83]

We are likewise faced with conflicting accounts of the circumstances attending the meeting between Mulla Husayn Bushru'i and the Bab. Nabil Zarandi writes:

> a few hours before sunset [on the evening of 22 May 1844], whilst walking outside the [Kazirun] gate of the city [Shiraz], [Mulla Husayn's] eyes fell suddenly upon a youth of radiant countenance, who wore a green turban and who, advancing towards him, greeted him with a smile of loving welcome. He embraced Mulla Husayn with tender affection as though he had been his intimate and lifelong friend. Mulla Husayn thought him at first to be a disciple of Sayyid Kazim who, on being informed of his approach to Shiraz, had come out to welcome him.

Nabil, quoting Mulla Husayn, writes:

> The youth [the Bab] who met me outside the gate of Shiraz

81 For more biographical information on Mulla Husayn Bushru'i, see Amanat, *RR*, 153–62; Afnan, *Ahd-i A'la*, 55–60; Mazandarani, *Zuhur al-Haqq*, 94–116; and Ruhu'llah Mihrabkhani, *Mulla Husayn: Disciple at Dawn* (Kalimat Press, 1987).
82 Mazandarani, *Zuhur al-Haqq*, 96; Afnan, *'Ahd-i A'la*, 60.
83 *Nabil*, 52.

> overwhelmed me with expressions of affection and loving-kindness. He extended to me a warm invitation to visit his home, and there refresh myself after the fatigues of my journey. I prayed to be excused, pleading that my two companions had already arranged for my stay in that city, and were now awaiting my return. "Commit them to the care of God," was his reply; "He will surely protect and watch over them."[84]

The impression one receives from Nabil's account is that Mulla Husayn was so deeply moved by the Bab's kind demeanor, courteous conduct, and dignified bearing that he could not help but accept the Bab's invitation.

Amanat considers it likely that the Bab might have learned of Mulla Husayn's journey through his uncle or one of his relatives in Bushihr, and that he was in fact awaiting Mulla Husayn's arrival. Such a scenario would, according to Amanat, reinforce the possibility of a prior acquaintance between the Bab and Mulla Husayn during their days in Karbala.[85] The *Tarikh-i Jadid* relates an account from Haji Mirza Jani Kashani, quoting Mulla Husayn, in which the latter, in light of this prior acquaintance, heads straight for the home of the Bab upon entering Shiraz. After knocking at the door, Mulla Husayn hears the voice of the Bab from inside the house, asking, "Mulla Husayn, is that you?" With Mulla Husayn's response in the affirmative, the Bab opens the door and, with a smile on his face, says to Mulla Husayn, "I have been disinclined to go to the bazaar all day, and I see now that your coming here was the reason for this feeling." Recalling that remarkable interaction, Mulla Husayn states, "It did not occur to me at that moment how Sayyid 'Ali-Muhammad, without having seen me, had recognized who was knocking at his door."[86]

Setting aside the questions of what prompted Mulla Husayn to travel to

---

84 *Nabil*, 52. Nabil is quoting here from the account of Mulla Ja'far Qazvini, who states that he himself heard Mulla Husayn recount this anecdote several times. Qazvini also relates the same account in his own history (included as an addendum to *Tarikh-i-Samandar*; see 472.) For more information on other sources that have discussed this meeting between the Bab and Mulla Husayn, see Amanat, *RR*, 166–67 and 167 n. 96.

85 In the preceding pages, we have made reference to the presence of the Bab at the home of Sayyid Kazim Rashti while Mulla Husayn was delivering a religious sermon. The *Tarikh-i Jadid*, citing Mulla Husayn, states that Mulla Husayn had the honor of accompanying the Bab on his pilgrimages to the tomb of the Imam Husayn on numerous occasions. See Mirza 'Ali Hamadani, *Tarikh-i Jadid: The New history* (ed. E. G. Browne; Philo Press, Amsterdam, 1893), 34; henceforth, "Hamadani."

86 Hamadani, 34. Other accounts of the circumstances attending this encounter are discussed in various historical sources.

Shiraz and how he and the Bab met in that city for the first time, it must be noted that the Bab's numinous states; the allusions he made to his family concerning the profound spiritual transformations he was experiencing; and his dreams, to which he would refer in his later writings, all speak to the imminence of the hour of a revelation that could no longer remain hidden behind the veil of concealment. It was inevitable that this roaring torrent, with its irrepressible power and overwhelming magnitude, should have precipitated from the Bab's burning breast, that seat of copious inspiration, sweeping across the expanse of Persia with a force that—as is borne out by the pages of history—gained it immense renown in that land. It was not known to them that Mulla Husayn and his companions had become important characters in this design of destiny. Had they not taken that step into this fateful path, perhaps their lot would have fallen to some other group of people, though subsequent events would show that Mulla Husayn was the most obvious candidate to assume the role that he did.

There is more consistency among the various accounts of the ensuing conversations between the Bab and Mulla Husayn. After having tea, the Bab, who firmly believed in his own messengership, asked his guest confidently but delicately, "Do the Shaykhis not believe that the earth will never be left without God's proof? Now that five months have passed since the death of your teacher and leader, who is the 'possessor of the cause' that shall serve as Sayyid Kazim's successor?" Mulla Husayn replied, "Our teacher did not appoint anyone to that position; rather, he urged his students to spread out far and wide in search of the promised one." The Bab then asked, "What signs did your teacher say would indicate the promised one?" Mulla Husayn then proceeded to enumerate those signs of the promised one mentioned by Sayyid Kazim and described in the Shaykhi creed. As part of this explanation, Mulla Husayn placed special emphasis on the knowledge possessed by the promised one, stating, "Sayyid Kazim would always liken his own knowledge, when compared with the knowledge of the promised one, to a drop before the ocean." The Bab then inquired, "Do you see those signs in me?" Mulla Husayn, who had perhaps been jarred by this question, replied, "I do not see those signs in you." The Bab then remained silent. In the course of this conversation, Mulla Husayn's eyes fell upon a treatise on a shelf of that room—a commentary on the Surih-yi Baqarih. With but one glance over its contents, Mulla Husayn, without willing it, began to recite passages from that commentary. Eventually, he asked the Bab for the name of its author. The Bab replied, "This work was composed by a youthful beginner who has made a great claim." Mulla Husayn then asked, "Where does this youth reside?" The Bab replied, "You are seeing him now."[87] Mulla Husayn was exceedingly perturbed by this response. His brief acquaintance with the Bab from their days in Karbala notwithstanding, and despite the fact that he knew him to be a pure and devout youth, Mulla Husayn could not accept, under any circumstances, that the Bab had advanced so frighteningly momentous a claim.

The Bab then declared that the time had come to write a commentary on the Surah of Joseph.[88] Mulla Husayn had previously requested such a commentary from Sayyid Kazim Rashti, who told him that he was incapable of such a feat, stating that a person whose station far outranked his own would compose it.[89] The Bab then began to pen this commentary, known as the Qayyum al-asma, softly reciting its verses in a beautiful tone as he wrote.

The Qayyum al-asma must be unequivocally regarded as one of the most significant and eloquent writings which the Bab composed in the early days of his dispensation. The rapidity with which he wrote—the music of his intonation, the elegantly rhyming flow of his sentences—had utterly astounded Mulla Husayn. Not even for a moment did the Bab lift his pen from his paper. The light which illuminated their surroundings, coupled with the radiantly sinless face of the Bab—from whose pen the sentences seemed to stream forth like a flood—may well have reminded Mulla Husayn, on that fateful night, of this verse from the Qur'an, which the Prophet Muhammad had adduced to establish the truth of the revelation he had brought:

> Does it not suffice them [the objectors] that we have sent down unto thee the Book that is recited unto them? Surely in that is a mercy and a reminder for a people who believe.[90]

Considering what took place that night, one can easily appreciate the spiritual transformation Mulla Husayn underwent. The sensational conversation he had with the Bab—the power he had witnessed from that commentary on the Qur'an, the dignified demeanor and unusual charm he had seen—all had the potential to assure this searching Shaykhi that he was close to

87 *Nabil*, 61–65.
88 *Nabil* 57; Afnan, *Ahd-i A'la*, 63.
89 Afnan, *Ahd-i A'la*, 63 and other sources.
90 Qur'an 29:51. In a letter addressed to Mulla Ibrahim Shirazi, the Bab explicitly states that he finished writing the remainder of the Qayyum al-asma in forty days. See INBA, vol. 36, 170–80, cited in Amanat, *RR*, 172 n. 119.

the object of his quest. Yet, the one who had laid claim to this station was a youth—a former merchant with no religious education. Mulla Husayn's confusion and consternation did not escape the Bab's attention. When Mulla Husayn requested permission to leave and return to his companions, the Bab said, "If you leave in such a state, whoever sees you will assuredly say: 'This poor youth has lost his mind.'"[91] Mulla Sayyid Jalil Urumi, who was also in Shiraz at that time, notes that Mulla Husayn could not sleep at night as a result of his "inner struggle and mental occupation" after his meetings with the Bab.[92] Ultimately, however, his conversations with the Bab gave him the assurance he needed, culminating in his acceptance of the Bab on the night of 22 May 1844.[93]

Most Babi and Baha'i sources state that Mulla Husayn's dialogue with the Bab occurred during a single night, but there is other evidence at our disposal which indicates that it may have taken place over the course of up to three days. Aqa Sayyid Mu'min Khurasani, a friend of Mulla Husayn's, writes:

> One day in the presence of the Babu'l-Bab ["the gate of the Gate," a title which the Bab later gave Mulla Husayn] in Khurasan [probably Mashhad], we were passing a madrasa [a religious school]. He looked at the school and said: "Not one warm-hearted man [*ahl-i dil*] has ever come out of a madrasa. Down with these schools which are houses of ignorance." I said, "By the grace of God, eminent individuals like yourself have come out of these schools; why are you condemning them?" He replied, "Do not say that, Sayyid Mu'min; all that I ever learned in these wretched places was to make me argue with and oppose the Proof of God for forty days. I realized the meaning of the saying 'knowledge is the greatest veil' through the fruits of this ruined place. I wish I had no education."[94]

According to another account that dates to the upheaval at Fort Tabarsi (1848–49), Mulla Husayn once said:

---

91 *Nabil*, 61.

92 Qazvini, Mulla Ja'far, historical narratives appended to *Tarikh-i Samandar va Mulhaqat* (ed. 'A. 'Ala'i, Tehran, 1975, 472). This translation taken from Amanat, *RR*, 170.

93 As mentioned, the Bab refers to this date explicitly in his Bayan (2:7).

94 Mu'in, 62–63; this translation taken from Amanat, *RR*, 169. In Persian, the number forty signifies an unusually large quantity of something, and its usage here suggests that Mulla Husayn regarded his conversations with the Bab over the course of multiple days as lengthy and even excessive.

> I wish my steps had never reached the madrasa, so I would never have bothered the Proof of God for three days and nights.[95]

Mulla Husayn's acceptance of the Bab must be recognized as having largely stemmed from the teachings of the first two leaders of the Shaykhi school, Shaykh Ahmad Ahsa'i and Sayyid Kazim Rashti, who would occasionally pepper their praise of the Imams of Shiʿi Islam with exaggerations. In so doing, they would propound new interpretations of foundational Shiʿi beliefs regarding the Day of Resurrection, the Prophet Muhammad's nocturnal journey to heaven, and the advent of the promised one that differed from the conventional understanding of those concepts. The Shaykhi leaders regarded the existence of a "gate" to the Twelfth Imam—an intermediary role which, according to Shiʿi belief, was established with the occultation of the Twelfth Imam and the accession of four "gates" to that position, and was discontinued with their death—as a requirement stipulated by their religious law, and they also considered themselves "gates" to a certain degree.[96] The object of the quest on which Mulla Husayn and the other Shaykhi pupils who embraced the Bab had embarked was to find the promised "Gate"; having attained their goal, they set out at once to spread the news of their crucial discovery throughout the whole of Persia. It is difficult to imagine that, over the course of his conversations with the Bab, Mulla Husayn would have wished to receive an explanation of Babi teachings. For Mulla Husayn, the Bab represented the Proof of God on earth—given his descent from both the Prophet of Islam and its Imams—and from then on, whatever the Bab claimed or wrote took on the status of divine proof for his followers.

Amanat writes:

> [However,] Sayyid 'Ali-Muhammad did not consider himself merely Rashti's successor or even the Perfect Shiʿi, but assumed a position much closer to a prophetic status. It is with this consideration that titles like *Bab*, *Dhikr* (lit. "remembrance"), and *Nuqtih* ("point") were adopted, with a sense of deputyship delegated to him not merely

95 Account given by Waraqatu'l-Firdaws, Mulla Husayn's sister, relating it from Aqa Mulla Muhammad Hasan Bushru'i, one of the survivors (*Baqiyyat al-Sayf*, or "Remnants of the Sword") of the upheaval at Fort Tabarsi. Cited in: Fu'adi Bushru'i, Hasan, *Tarikhi-Diyanat-i Baha'i dar Khurasan* ('Asr-i Jadid: Darmstadt, 2007), 66. This translation and citation taken from Amanat, *RR*, 169 and 169 n. 103, respectively.

96 The title of Sayyid Kazim Rashti was *Babu'l-Muqaddam* ("the Primary Gate").

> from the Twelfth Imam but from a divine authority... As became more apparent to the Shaykhi converts over the next few years, Sayyid 'Ali-Muhammad's goal in assuming the gateship (*babiyyih*) was different from the aims of past Shaykhi leaders.[97]

The Bab had asked Mulla Husayn not to disclose his identity so that his companions could discover and recognize him on their own. Gradually, the Bab's station and claims were accepted by sixteen other people. Along with Tahirih (Qurratu'l-'Ayn), who had embraced the cause of the Bab after reading his writings while residing in Karbala, and also the Bab himself—nineteen people in all—this group constituted the first *vahid* ["unit"][98] of believers who formed the Babi movement, a group known as the Letters of the Living.[99] The Bab refers to this matter explicitly in his Bayan:

> Consider likewise the Source of the revelation of the Bayan. For forty days none except first the letter *sin* [Mulla Husayn] believed in the *ba* [the Bab] and then gradually the other letters of *bismillah* [*Bismillah al-rahman al-rahim*, "In the Name of God, the Merciful, the Compassionate"] adorned the cloak of recognition, till the first *vahid* was completed.[100]

---

97 Amanat, *RR*, 171.

98 In the Abjad notation, the term *vahid* is equivalent to the number 19, and it is a term which the Bab uses in his arrangement of chapters in the Bayan. The significance of the number 19 in the Babi and Baha'i religions, beyond signifying the concept of *vahdat* ["unity," or more literally "oneness"], is that it also serves as a reminder of the number of letters that compose the Qur'anic verse *Bismillah al-rahman al-rahim* ["In the Name of God, the Merciful, the Compassionate"] since, in Islamic tradition, the name of God is to be invoked before beginning any undertaking. The Bab refers to the Letters of the Living, the first *vahid* of people to believe in him, as the letters that compose the *bismillah* (Bayan 8:15). Similarly, in the Abjad notation, the word *hayy* ["living"] has a value of 18, which represents the number of people who first believed in the Bab.

99 According to *Nabil*, 80, the Letters of the Living include: Mulla Husayn Bushru'i, Mulla Hasan (the brother of Mulla Husayn), Mulla Muhammad Baqir (the nephew of Mulla Husayn), Mulla 'Ali Bastami, Mulla Khudabakhsh (Mulla 'Ali) Quchani, Mulla Hasan Bajistani, Mulla Husayn Yazdi, Mulla Muhammad (Rawdih-Khan) Yazdi, Sa'id Hindi, Mulla Muhammad Khu'i, Mulla Jalil Urumi, Mulla Ahmad Abdal Maraghi'i, Mulla Baqir Tabrizi, Mulla Yusuf Ardabili, Mirza Hadi Qazvini, Mirza Muhammad-'Ali Qazvini, Tahirih (Qurratu'l-'Ayn), and Mulla Muhammad-'Ali Barfurushi (Quddus). For a discussion of the chronological order in which each of these individuals accepted the Bab, see Amanat, *RR*, 176. Most of the Letters of the Living were killed in the first years of the Babi movement. The nineteen flower-filled terraces leading up to the Shrine of the Bab in Haifa symbolize the nineteen Letters of the Living.

100 Bayan 8:15. (All but the first sentence of this translation taken from Amanat, *RR*, 175. Translator's note.)

AFTER THE DECLARATION OF THE BAB'S CAUSE

Once the initial core of the Babis (or the Letters of the Living) was formed, the first and most important duty facing that small band of followers—and also the Bab himself—was to spread his message throughout Persia and the 'Atabat. The Bab sent each of the Letters of the Living, along with a few others who had embraced his cause after them, to various places to spread the news of his advent. Mulla Husayn, for instance, was given some letters and tablets, and then dispatched to various cities—including Isfahan, Yazd, and Tehran—where he was to share the Bab's message with anyone who was ready to hear it.[101] The Bab sent Mulla 'Ali Bastami to Karbala to teach the cause, and likewise assigned a different city to each of the others among his earliest followers. Afterwards, the Bab told them that Quddus (the last Letter of the Living to believe in the Bab) would be accompanying him on a pilgrimage to Mecca, where he would announce his cause, and thence depart for Karbala. It was decided that all the Babis were to eventually regroup in Karbala, where the emergence of the Hidden Imam from his occultation—as had been foretold in Islamic traditions—was to take place.

MULLA 'ALI BASTAMI

Mulla 'Ali Bastami became the first person after Mulla Husayn Bushru'i to embrace the Bab's cause when, according to his own testimony, he read just one verse from the Bab, who subsequently gave Bastami the title of "the second to believe." Bastami, who hailed from a village close to Bastam (now Shahrud) in eastern Khurasan, spent his days as a young seminarian in Mashhad—and because his teacher there had Shaykhi tendencies, he gained a familiarity with that school of thought. After some correspondence with Sayyid Kazim Rashti, Bastami set off for Karbala and became one of Rashti's students. With the death of Rashti, and also the emergence of contending groups among his students, Bastami joined Mulla Husayn and his other peers in their forty-day vigil, and from there accompanied them to Shiraz.

In obedience to the Bab's orders, towards the end of the summer of 1844,

101 For more on these duties given to Mulla Husayn, see Chapter 3 in this volume.

Bastami entered Najaf by way of Bushihr and Basrih. In Najaf, he went to see Shaykh Muhammad-Hasan Najafi, the pre-eminent Shiʿi *mujtahid* of that city. From the moment Bastami began to speak, this *mujtahid* had discerned his intent; he dismissed Bastami from his presence and expelled him from Najaf.

Bastami then went to Karbala, and although the Bab had forbidden him from divulging his name, Bastami was nonetheless able to attract a considerable number of Shaykhi seminarians to the new religion. As a basis for his arguments, Bastami cited the prophecies of Shaykh Ahmad Ahsa'i and Sayyid Kazim Rashti regarding the imminence of a new dispensation, and also presented these seminarians with the writings of the promised one, including sections of the Qayyum al-asma. In an atmosphere already charged with traditional conflict between Shiʿis and Sunnis, Bastami's efforts to teach this new cause turned not only the Shiʿi 'ulama, but also the would-be successors to Sayyid Kazim against him. The reports of the English consul in Baghdad attest to the tense and turbulent climate of Karbala in the context of Bastami's activities there.[102] Ultimately, through measures taken by the Shiʿi 'ulama of Karbala, Bastami was arrested and sent to Baghdad. The governor of 'Iraq, Najib Pasha, who always kept abreast of the sectarian tensions between Shiʿis and Sunnis with some concern—and who one year earlier had resorted to military force to quell an upheaval born of this tension, resulting in a mass killing—did not forfeit the opportunity that had now presented itself. He convened a council consisting of prominent Sunni and Shiʿi 'ulama to put Bastami on trial (16 January 1845), and placed his fate in their hands. We do not have exact details from the deliberations of that council, but the verdict appears to have been that the Sunni 'ulama, after perusing the Qayyum al-asma, concluded that the anonymous author of that work claimed to have received divine revelation, and deemed that this author and the bearer of his book, Bastami, were infidels, and sentenced them both to death. The Shiʿi 'ulama were more forbearing, and considered imprisonment or exile to be fitting punishments for Bastami. Here, too, the strife between Sunnis and Shiʿis, Turks and Persians—a constant source of unrest in the religious cities of 'Iraq—had manifested itself. Najib Pasha left the question of Bastami's fate to the discretion of the judges of Istanbul, and sometime later, a pronouncement was made

102 F.O. 248/114. Refer also to Amanat, *RR*, 216 n. 39.

that Bastami was to be transferred to Istanbul as a prisoner (25 January 1845). Documents from the Ottoman government show that Bastami was sentenced to hard labor in the imperial dockyard of Istanbul, and that he passed away about one year later, toward the end of 1846. Bastami was the first Babi to give his life because of faith in that cause.[103] As we will see, Bastami's assignment to proclaim the message of the Bab in the 'Atabat—as well as the events that followed—played a pivotal role in shaping the course of events which the Babi religion would take in its earliest days.

THE BAB'S EVENTFUL JOURNEY TO MECCA

On 10 September 1844, the Bab; his Ethiopian servant, Mubarak; and Quddus departed Shiraz and arrived at Bushihr on 19 September 1844.[104] A few days later, they boarded a ship that was leaving Bushihr for Jiddah. The Bab's purpose in undertaking this journey was to fulfill Shi'i prophecies, and perhaps the expectations of his followers, concerning the advent of the Mahdi. According to these traditions, the Mahdi was to announce his advent during the pilgrimage season while in the presence of other pilgrims; from there, he would go to Karbala to emerge from occultation with his companions, who would then devote their attention to a conquest of the world. The fulfillment of this prophecy held great importance for the Bab and his followers, insofar as it would vindicate his claim. The Bab refers to the significance of this matter in one of his sermons:

> Thus, in that month [Dhu'l-Hijjah], whatever is promised by your God to every young and old will happen. Soon he will appear in the Holy Land with the word that will "split asunder" whatever is in the

---

103 For a biographical account of Mulla 'Ali Bastami and his trial, see Mazandarani, *Zuhur al-Haqq*, 9–78; Amanat, *RR*, 175–80, 211–38; MacEoin, Denis, "The Fate of Mullā 'Alī Bastāmī", *Baha'i Studies Bulletin*, 2:1 (1983), 77; Momen, Moojan, *The Bábí and Bahá'í Religions, 1844–1944: Some Contemporary Western Accounts* (Oxford: George Ronald, 1981), henceforth "Momen 1981"; idem., "The Trial of Mulla 'Ali Bastami: A Combined Sunni-Shi'i Fatwa against the Bab," *Iran: Journal of the British Institute of Persian Studies* 20 (1982), 113–43; *Nabil*, 66–99, 87–92.

104 Afnan, *Ahd-i A'la*, 76.

> heavens and earth.[105] Behold his word; the righteous Qa'im who is the just Qa'im will arise in Mecca according to what has been uttered: "When the Qa'im appears, give him your support together with all those who will come to his assistance from distant corners." When [his opponents] "have corrupted the earth," then he will commence the new Cause in the hinterland of Kufa.[106]

It must be noted here that, in this brief span, the fame of a *Sayyid* born to a noble family from Shiraz had spread not only throughout Fars and Bushihr, but also throughout other parts of Persia and even 'Iraq. To protect his fledgling community, the Bab had bidden the Letters of the Living and his other followers not to reveal his identity. This order was followed to some extent. In his memoirs, Mirza Muhammad-Taqi Afnan writes:

> In the year 60 [1260 AH], it had become well known in Shiraz that a dear *Sayyid* had claimed to represent the Hidden Imam, but the blessed name of this *Sayyid* was never mentioned.[107]

With the increase in the number of his followers, and given how intensely they longed to teach his religion, it seems it was not possible for the Bab's name to have remained a secret:

> When a number of the Letters of the Living, as well as some of the veteran believers from among the Bab's companions, returned to Karbala, they began to teach the Cause, and a group of Arabs and Persians in Karbala, Baghdad, Kazimayn, and other cities embraced it. At the time when the Bab himself had set off for his pilgrimage, he foreshadowed the imminence of his public declaration at Mecca, his going to Karbala, and his fulfillment of religious prophecies. Furthermore, he instructed his followers to gather at Karbala.[108]

---

105 The word that "split asunder" probably refers to Qur'an 19:90, which in Shi'i prophecies is interpreted as the sign of Revelation. "When the Qa'im appears" is presumably a reference to a hadith related from Ja'far Sadiq (Majlisi, *Biharu'l-Anwar* 8/31, trans. 573). This translation and explanation taken from Amanat, *RR*, 238–39 and 239 n. 196, respectively.

106 The original Arabic text of this passage has been published in Mazandarani, *Zuhur al-Haqq*, 187.

107 Fayzi, *Khandan-i Afnan*, 110–11.

108 Mazandarani, *Zuhur al-Haqq*, 187.

This matter naturally raised the concern of religious and governmental authorities since, in their view, it had the potential to incite tension and provoke riots—particularly in Shiraz, which for years, and for various reasons, had experienced rebellion and disorder. Later, once he had returned from Mecca, the Bab alluded to his own apprehensions to that effect at a point in one of his letters where he communes with God:

> I had warned those who know me not to reveal my name. But I set out for pilgrimage to your House when I became terrified of the accomplices of the devil who were the corrupt people.[109]

In a similar letter, the Bab laments the carelessness of some of his followers:

> When I left this city [Shiraz] for the destination of the Holy Sanctuary, if after my departure no one had divulged my name, no one would have been tormented. But my believers are responsible toward God. Now there happened what ought to have happened.[110]

It seems that the Bab, being privy to the circumstances of the region, had deemed it likely even before his journey to Mecca that conflict and strife would break out between his supporters and opponents in Shiraz. To prevent this outcome, the Bab expedited his journey to Mecca, and may well have left Shiraz in haste. A letter he sent from Bushihr to his wife, Khadijih Bagum, speaks of this, and also points to the sorrow he felt as a result of being so far from his wife:

> My sweetheart, may God protect you. God is my witness that since the time of our separation, such griefs encircled me as are beyond description. But since destiny is so all-powerful, it is due to a fitting purpose that this [separation] occurred in this way. May God, in

109 Arabic letter to Mulla 'Abdul-Khaliq Yazdi written after the Bab's return from Mecca. INBA, no. 91, 94–102 (96). This translation and citation taken from Amanat, *RR*, 239 and 239 n. 199, respectively.

110 Nicolas, 61–69. This translation and citation taken from Amanat, *RR*, 239 and 239 n. 200, respectively. Amanat believes that this letter was written to Shaykh 'Ali Qaini, the son of Mulla 'Abdul-Khaliq, who may have asked the Bab why he decided not to travel to Karbala.

> the name of the Five Holy Souls,[111] provide the means of my return as may be best. It is two days since I entered Bushihr. The weather is intensely hot, but God will protect [me]. At any rate, it appears that in this very month the ship will sail. Gracious God shall protect us. It was not possible for me to meet with my esteemed mother at the time of my departure; do give her my regards, and ask that she pray for me.[112]

The voyage from Bushihr to Jiddah was challenging for the Bab. Beyond the tempestuous sea, the exceedingly hot weather, the scarcity of potable water, and the close quarters which all the travelers were forced to share, the Bab was deeply saddened by the coarse and quarrelsome behavior that the other pilgrims were exhibiting on so spiritual a journey.[113] On this voyage, Shaykh Abu-Hashim—the nephew of Shaykh Abu Turab, the Imam Jum'ah of Shiraz—induced a number of the pilgrims onboard from Shiraz and Bushihr to turn against the Bab and "not forego any opportunity to insult him or accuse him of overstepping his bounds."[114] After witnessing the Bab's meekness, and considering the possibility that the Shaykh's mischief might create serious difficulties on his overcrowded vessel, the captain of the ship warned Shaykh Abu-Hashim a number of times to refrain from his malicious behavior. The Shaykh, however, persisted in his provocations, and the captain had no choice but to order that he be thrown off the ship. Ultimately, the Bab interceded on the Shaykh's behalf and dissuaded the captain from pursuing that course of action.[115] However, Shaykh Abu-Hashim resumed his antagonistic activities, and upon returning from Mecca to Shiraz, began working to turn other 'ulama against the Bab.[116] In spite of these unfavorable circumstances, the Bab's time on the ship was spent revealing sermons, prayers, and commentaries on Surahs

111 A reference to the Prophet Muhammad, the Imam 'Ali, Fatimih, Hasan, and Husayn.

112 Fayzi, *Khandan-i Afnan*, 166–67. (All but the first and last sentence of this translation taken from Amanat, *RR*, 240–41. Translator's note.)

113 "On the way to Mecca, one matter that was most disgraceful towards God, and indeed diminishing to their [original] intention, was the pilgrims' quarrels with each other, since such behavior was prohibited, and remains so." Bayan 16:4; this translation taken from Amanat, *RR*, 242.

114 Afnan, *Ahd-i A'la*, 75. This opposition, directed toward the Bab just four months after he had declared his cause, demonstrates the fame which his name and claim had gained in so short a time.

115 Ibid.

116 Mirza Habibullah, *Tarikh*, 38–39. Refer also to Amanat, *RR*, 242.

of the Qur'an, all of which Quddus would write down as the Bab spoke. These writings, which had been kept in a saddlebag, were eventually stolen by an Arab thief.[117]

As to the nature of the Bab's proclamation at Mecca to the effect that he was the Qa'im, which was the very purpose of his journey to that city, an account has survived from Haji Abu'l-Hasan Shirazi, who would go on to accept the Bab and Baha'u'llah after him. According to Amanat, Abu'l-Hasan, who bore witness to all that had happened on the Bab's voyage from Bushihr to Mecca and Medina, writes that:

> at the end of Hajj rites, when the floor and the roof of Masjid al-Haram were entirely filled with pilgrims, the Bab stood against the wall, holding the ring knob of the Ka'bih door, and three times in "the most eloquent and exquisite voice" announced, "I am the Qa'im whom you were expecting." Abu'l-Hasan continues: "It was extraordinary, that in spite of the noise, immediately the crowd became so silent... All the pilgrims heard the Bab's call, [Abu'l-Hasan] maintains, and interpreted it for one another. They discussed it, and reported the new proclamation in letters to the people in their homelands."[118]

Abu'l-Hasan Shirazi believes that these developments occurred in the course of the Bab's debate with Mirza Muhit Kirmani, an eminent student of Sayyid Kazim's to whom reference was made earlier, and with whom the Bab had been acquainted from the days when he lived in Karbala. Following the death of Sayyid Kazim, Muhit made pretensions to leadership of the Shaykhi school and never accepted the claim which the Bab had advanced. Abu'l-Hasan Shirazi writes that, upon hearing the nature of the Bab's claim,

---

117 The Bab and his companions arrived at Jiddah on the first night of Zul-Hijjah 1260 AH, or 15 December 1844 (Afnan, *Ahd-i A'la*, 76). In his *Khutba al-Jiddah* [Literary Sermon at Jeddah], the Bab recorded the exact dates on which he entered and departed various seaports and other cities as part of his pilgrimage journey. In that sermon, he refers to the theft of his writings, which he identifies as having taken place at the third stop between Mecca and Medina. Based on the text of that sermon, Afnan has attempted to determine precisely where in the desert between Mecca and Medina these writings were stolen (*Ahd-i A'la*, 79). See also Lambden, Stephen N., "The Khuṭba al-Jidda (The Literary Sermon at Jeddah) of the Bāb" in: Lawson and Ghaemmaghani ed. *A Most Noble Pattern*, 146–59.

118 This quotation taken from Amanat, *RR*, 243–44. (Translator's note.)

Muhit was seized with terror, and from then on made efforts to keep his distance from the Bab.[119]

The Bab's own account of his proclamation at Mecca, however, speaks of his disappointment with the pilgrims' lack of interest in his claims:

> One thousand two hundred and seventy years from the [Prophet's] Designation have passed and each year innumerable people have circumambulated the House. In the final year, the founder of the House [the Bab] himself went for Hajj and saw that by God's grace, people from all creeds had come to Hajj. No one recognized him, but he recognized all. And the only one who recognized him was the one who accompanied him in his pilgrimage, and he is the one whose [name] is equal to eight *vahid* [Quddus],[120] and God is proud of him.[121]

Toward the end of his pilgrimage, the Bab decided against his original plan to go to Karbala and regroup with the other Babis who had gathered there, and chose to depart for Shiraz instead. He attributed this decision to *bada'*, which in Islamic jurisprudence denotes a change in the Will of God or an alteration in the fulfillment of an irrevocable promise. For those new Babi converts who had gathered at Karbala to announce the Qa'im's emergence from occultation and wage war against the infidels, the Bab's decision not to go to Karbala was an unexpected and disheartening development. There were, in reality, a number of factors that led to the Bab's decision. Examples include the arrest and imprisonment of his herald in 'Iraq, Mulla 'Ali Bastami, as well as the difficulties that had confronted Tahirih and resulted in her confinement to the home of the *mufti* of Baghdad, Abu al-Thana', Shihab al-Din al-Alusi (d.1270 /1854).[122] But perhaps the most important factor was that the Bab came to categorically reject the association of *jihad* with literal war and bloodshed committed in the name of religion.[123]

---

119 Mirza Habibullah, *Tarikh*, 40–41; Mu'in, 73; Afnan, *Ahd-i A'la*, 76–77; and other Baha'i histories on the Bab.

120 "In his writing, the Bab often computes from the year of *Ba'tha*, the beginning of the Islamic revelation, instead of the year of *Hijra*, which is the beginning of the Islamic calendar. *Quddus* has the numerical value of 152, which is equal to 8 x 19" (Amanat, *RR*, 244 n. 232).

121 Bayan 4:18; this translation taken from Amanat, *RR*, 244.

122 For more on Tahirih see Amanat, *RR*, chapter 7.

123 See also Chapter 2 in this volume. The Bab did not actually annul the law of *jihad*; rather, he conditioned it only upon his permission, which he never gave.

In a prayer he composed sometime after these events, the Bab explained his reasoning for not going to Karbala. The gist of the prayer is as follows:

> O Lord! you know of that command in which I ordered the divines [the early believers] to enter the Holy Land in order [to be prepared] for the Day of Return, when your hidden covenant was to be revealed and they were all obedient. And you know what I heard in the Mother of the Cities [i.e. Mecca] of the opposition of the ʻulama and the denial your servant encountered from those who were destined away from the Truth. Therefore, I gave up my goal, and did not travel to that land, hoping that the sedition (*fitna*) would settle and those who were obedient to you would not be humiliated, and no one would find a chance to inflict the slightest harm upon someone else. My Lord, you know what I envisaged in this decision, and you are the omniscient. My Lord, this is your decision and this is your command. If I failed in other duties, I have not failed in [implementing] your words. Therefore, you arbitrate between me and them with your justice, and forgive those who are repentant and obedient to your tradition...you know that at the time of my return [from Hajj] I intended what you commanded me, and you directed me toward what I understood from your Book. I did not desire the kingdom of this world or the next. This was not my initiative but it was your will, you Lord, the only one.[124]

The events mentioned above, and in particular the Bab's decision not to go to Karbala, disenchanted some Babis who had high hopes of a swift victory, and armed his enemies—including Mirza Muhammad Karim Khan Kirmani—with ammunition in their polemics against the Bab and the Babi religion to gleefully deem these developments as signaling the end of the movement.

Although the Bab's announcement of his messengership at Mecca did not yield the results he had expected, he did succeed in conversing with a number of Shiʻi, Sunni, and Shaykhi pilgrims, all of whom he unequivocally summoned to embrace his religion. Among the writings the Bab composed in this period is the Sahifih-yi Bayn al-Haramayn, which was written in

124 INBA, no. 8, 97–98, "tablet for Mulla ʻAbdul-Khaliq Yazdi," probably written toward the end of 1845. This translation and citation taken from Amanat, *RR*, 252 and 252 n. 277, respectively.

response to seven questions posed by Mirza Muhit Kirmani, a leading figure of the Shaykhi school.[125]

THE BAB'S RETURN FROM PILGRIMAGE AND THE EVENTS OF SHIRAZ

In late spring 1261 AH [1845], the Bab returned from his pilgrimage journey. From Bushihr he wrote letters to Muhammad Shah and Haji Mirza Aqasi, the prime minister, to solicit their assistance with freeing Mulla 'Ali Bastami from Ottoman captivity. Afterwards, the Bab sent Quddus to Shiraz with instructions to openly announce his cause. Prior to the Bab's own subsequent arrival at Shiraz, Mulla 'Ali-Akbar Ardistani ascended the minaret of the Masjid-i Naw and began to sound the call to prayer, to which he added a sentence testifying to the Bab's station.[126] Quddus likewise went to that same mosque, ascended the minaret, and began to recite from the Qayyum al-asma. There he unreservedly proclaimed the name of Sayyid 'Ali-Muhammad, which until that time had been kept secret. Mulla Sadiq Khurasani (Muqaddas) then took to the mosques, streets, and bazaars of Shiraz, where he declared, without the slightest inhibition, that "the Gate to the Hidden Imam" had appeared. Such outspoken propagation—along with rumors of the Bab's presence at the recent pilgrimage, which had been spread throughout the city by returning Shirazi pilgrims—triggered the excitement of the people and the agitation of the 'ulama of Shiraz. The governor of the city—Mirza Husayn Khan, the Ajudan-Bashi [chief adjutant]—arrested those audacious Babis and assembled a council whose charge was to better understand their beliefs, and these proceedings were to be held in the presence of 'ulama. Before that council, Quddus, Muqaddas, and Ardistani courageously adduced proofs to establish the legitimacy of the Bab's claim. By order of the governor, Muqaddas was brutally lashed, and the beards of all three men were set on fire. On the following day, once their faces had been blackened and their noses threaded with a horse's halter, the executioner pulled the cord that bound the three Babis and paraded them

125 For more on this writing, see Behmardi, Vahid, "Sahifih-yi Bayn al-Haramayn," *Safini-yi 'Irfan*, vol. 1 ('Asr-i Jadid: Darmstadt, Germany, 1999), 18–38. Only the first of Kirmani's questions pertains to the Bab's religion; the remainder deal with other Islamic matters and bear no relevance to that subject.

126 "I testify that 'Ali before Muhammad ['Ali-Muhammad], the Bab, is the Remnant of God."

throughout the city and markets before a crowd of clamoring spectators. As was then the custom, the tradesmen and other people gave money to the executioner as a means of encouraging him to inflict still greater harm on his captives. At sunset, the three Babis were taken to the gate of Shiraz and expelled from the city, but they returned there under the cover of night. So tragically inhumane was the punishment that had been meted out to them that it was covered in detail by *The Times*.[127]

Probably in June–July 1845, the Bab departed Bushihr for Shiraz, and was stopped en route by officials intent on arresting him. Upon entering Shiraz, these officials took the Bab to a small citadel near the governor's residence, where he was kept under supervision. In a trial that had drawn a great deal of attention—convened as it was before a judge, 'ulama, and grandees of the city—the Bab was subjected to insult and scorn on account of the candor and insistence with which he stated his claims. With a gesture from the judge, one of those present struck the Bab's face so forcefully that his turban fell from his head. Following some deliberation on how the Bab should be punished, eventually the Imam Jum'ah of Shiraz, Shaykh Abu Turab, consented—with the guarantee of his friend, Haji Sayyid 'Ali, the Bab's uncle—to the Bab's release from the citadel, on the condition that he not violate the terms of the house arrest to which he was now being sentenced. Sometime thereafter, at the request of the 'ulama of the city, the governor ordered that the Bab be brought to the Vakil Mosque to renounce his claims. As news of this impending event spread, a large number of people gathered there. Amid the commotion of the people, the Bab ascended the pulpit and disavowed his claim to be the representative of the Hidden Imam. He then professed his belief in the oneness of God, the messengership of the Prophet Muhammad, and the exalted stations of the other Imams of Islam. The Bab said nothing about his being the Qa'im, and no one asked him about it. The gathering drew to a close, and the Bab returned to his uncle's residence as the 'ulama raucously heaped verbal abuse upon him. The words which the Bab had spoken allayed the hostility of his opponents and instilled confidence and steadfastness in his followers.[128]

127 *The Times*, 19 November 1845, published in the *Literary Gazette* [15 November 1845]. This reference taken from: Balyuzi, H. M., *The Bab* (Oxford: George Ronald, 1973), 76–77.

128 For a more extensive treatment of this period, see *Nabil*, 145–56; Fayzi, *Nuqta-yi Ula*, 160–67; and other historical sources.

At this time, Mulla Husayn entered Shiraz and informed the Bab that a number of the people to whom he had written letters had embraced his cause. Gradually, more of the Bab's followers went to Shiraz, and they held secret gatherings at the home of the Bab's uncle. The conversion of celebrated 'ulama to the religion of the Bab—such as Sayyid Yahya Darabi (Vahid) and Mulla Muhammad-'Ali, a Hujjatu'l-Islam of Zanjan (Hujjat-i Zanjani), both of whom enjoyed great influence in their respective homelands—brought joy to the Bab in this time of crisis.

The coming and going of the Babis in and out of Shiraz once again threw the city into upheaval. At the instigation of the 'ulama, the governor of Shiraz ordered a certain 'Abdul-Hamid, the city's superintendent of police, to go with his horsemen to the home of the Bab's uncle and arrest him, the Bab himself, and whoever else he found there. Apart from the Bab and his uncle, the superintendent did not find anyone else; he arrested both of them and headed for the seat of the governor. An outbreak of cholera had caused panic in Shiraz, prompting many of its residents to leave. The governor of Shiraz, along with others in positions of power, had also left the city and taken refuge in villages and foothills. The superintendent took the Bab to his own home, where he was to remain until the governor's return—but eventually, as a result of the affinity he came to feel for him, the superintendent gave the Bab the freedom to go wherever he wished. Subsequently, the Bab encouraged his followers to travel to various parts of Persia to promulgate the new religion. After bidding farewell to his wife, his mother, and his uncle, the Bab and two of his followers—Aqa Sayyid Kazim Zanjani and Muhammad-Husayn Ardistani—set off for Isfahan.[129]

The Bab's decision to go to Isfahan was occasioned by the fact that the governor of that city—Manuchihr Khan, the Mu'tamidu'd-Dawlih—had responded positively to a letter that the Bab had written him. The presence of a relatively strong Babi community in that city, which had taken shape through the efforts of Mulla Husayn Bushru'i, also factored into the Bab's decision to travel there.[130] From the outskirts of Isfahan, the Bab sent a letter through Sayyid Kazim Zanjani to Manuchihr Khan, requesting that he

129 For a more detailed account of the events that took place in Shiraz at this time, see *Nabil*, 170–98; Afnan, *'Ahd-i A'la*, 115–56; Faizi, *Nuqta-yi Ula*, 91–146; and Muhammad-Husayni, 97–254.

130 For more information on the Babi community of Isfahan at this time, see Chapter 3 in this volume.

designate a place for him to stay. Manuchihr Khan asked Sayyid Muhammad Khatun-Abadi, the powerful Imam Jum'ah of Isfahan, to host the Bab at his own home. The Imam Jum'ah sent his brother, Mir Sayyid Muhammad, along with a number of other people to the city gate to receive the Bab. The Imam Jum'ah himself remained in front of his home, where he welcomed the Bab with praise and reverence.[131]

THE BAB IN ISFAHAN

The Bab's time in Isfahan can perhaps be accounted as the only period following his proclamation when he enjoyed relative peace and respect. His sojourn at the home of the Imam Jum'ah afforded him the opportunity to become acquainted with the religious climate of the city. At a gathering where a number of 'ulama were present, the Imam Jum'ah requested that the Bab write a commentary on the Qur'anic Surah of Va'l-'Asr. Without taking any time to contemplate this request, the Bab began penning that commentary, astounding those in attendance with the rapidity and eloquence of his writing to such a degree that they, along with the Imam Jum'ah himself, rose to their feet and kissed the hem of his cloak out of respect.[132] On another occasion, Manuchihr Khan paid a visit to the Bab and requested—at a gathering attended by several of the 'ulama—that he write a commentary on the "special prophethood" of the Prophet Muhammad. With that same speed and precision, the Bab penned a treatise on this theme spanning some fifty pages—a theme that is still the subject of much discussion by Muslims and Christians today.[133]

The support which Manuchihr Khan was lending the Bab, as well as the Bab's residence at the home of the Imam Jum'ah, became a matter of some concern to the mullas of Isfahan, who accused the Bab of being an infidel and a corruptive influence sowing the seeds of confusion in the minds of men. In light of this hostility from the mullas, the Imam Jum'ah excused himself from hosting the Bab any further. Following this, Manuchihr Khan gave the Bab a place to stay within the governor's seat. Then, in an effort to have their concerns dispelled and their questions answered, Manuchihr Khan invited the 'ulama to participate in a gathering. Some declined the

131 Fayzi, *Nuqta-yi Ula*, 192.
132 Afnan, *Ahd-i A'la*, 209.
133 *Nabil*, 202.

invitation, but others accepted. This gathering, featuring an exchange of questions and answers, ended without bearing any fruit, and the antagonism of the clerics continued as before. From the tops of their pulpits, the ʻulama vied with one another in their denunciations of the Bab and his heretical beliefs, adding to the climate of unrest that already existed. No less than seventy of those ʻulama issued *fatwas* calling for the Bab's death, and they registered complaints with Muhammad Shah and Haji Mirza Aqasi. What may well have saved the Bab's life was the diplomatic *fatwa* issued by the Imam Jumʻah, which he appended to the *fatwas* of the other ʻulama, and in which he characterized the Bab as insane and testified that he did not witness any unorthodox behavior from the Bab when he was a guest at his home.

Manuchihr Khan began to think of ways to extricate the Bab from the tumult of the ʻulama. He spread a rumor throughout the city that the Shah and the prime minister had summoned the Bab to Tehran. He then ordered a trusted army general to first escort the Bab out of Isfahan with a detachment of soldiers, so the people could see with their own eyes that he was leaving the city, and then secretly bring him back into Isfahan after nightfall.[134] From then on, the Bab remained hidden in a house adjacent to the seat of the governor, which served as his private residence, only one of the Bab's followers being aware of his location.

As a youth, Manuchihr Khan was one of the Georgian eunuchs who served at the harem of Fath-ʻAli Shah; he converted to Islam, and rose in the ranks as a result of his worth and intellect until he became governor of Isfahan. Muhammad Shah was so fond and trusting of Manuchihr Khan that Haji Mirza Aqasi—who had succeeded in dismissing and oppressing each and every one of the political operatives appointed by the Qa'im-Maqam, the previous prime minister—could not remove Manuchihr Khan from the governorship of Isfahan. Manuchihr Khan saw in the Bab a progressive and revolutionary prophet—one whose novel perspective on matters of religion struck him as far more sensible than the narrow confines of Shiʻi jurisprudence and Islamic religious law. The Bab and his movement had the potential to challenge the steadily increasing power of the ʻulama, who regarded themselves as the rightful leaders of Persia, and the government as the usurpers of that right. On the other hand, it is possible that the exceedingly shrewd Manuchihr Khan had envisioned a future in

134 *Nabil*, 109–11.

which this young prophet, whose message had been promulgated across the whole of Persia and whose popularity was growing with every passing day, would lend him his support, enabling him to prevail over his political rival and enemy, Haji Mirza Aqasi, and become the next prime minister.[135] It was perhaps to achieve this end that, during the Bab's stay at the governor's residence, Manuchihr Khan met with him privately, offered him his valuable ring, and sought his permission to use his power and wealth to remove Haji Mirza Aqasi from office. He said, moreover, that he would arrange for the Bab to be married to one of the Shah's sisters, and strive to spread his religion throughout the world. The Bab expressed his gratitude to Manuchihr Khan for his support, but refused to accept his offer, stating that that which God had ordained to befall him and his religion would inevitably come to pass.[136]

The Bab's stay at the governor's residence did not last more than three months, as Manuchihr Khan died in March 1847. Manuchihr Khan's nephew, Gurgin Khan, who was in pursuit of power and wished to seize his uncle's riches, wrote a letter to Haji Mirza Aqasi to apprise him of the events that had taken place in Isfahan and inform him that the Bab was staying at the governor's residence. In relaying this information, which he believed to be a meritorious service, Gurgin Khan was hopeful that he would be installed as governor of Isfahan. Haji Mirza Aqasi, who had also given consideration to the complaints of the mullas and the events that had transpired in Shiraz, ordered at once that the Bab be escorted to Tehran by a detachment of horsemen.[137] Before embarking on this journey, the Bab's turban was turned into a nightcap in an effort to conceal his identity.

The events that took place in Shiraz and Isfahan demonstrate the powerlessness of the government officials when compared with the immense influence of the mullas. Even after leveraging the Imam Jum'ah's impartial attitude toward the Bab, Manuchihr Khan, the powerful governor of Isfahan, could not provide the Bab with an environment in the city where it was safe for him to spread his enlightening and revolutionary ideas. The conclusion of the Bab's time in Isfahan marked the end of his relative freedom, and launched him into a tumultuous period, ultimately ending in his martyrdom.

---

135 Amanat, *RR*, 257.

136 *Nabil*, 212–13.

137 For more information on the events that took place in Isfahan, see *Nabil*, 199–216; Afnan, *Ahd-i A'la*, 208–41 and Muhammad-Husayni, 297–320.

FROM ISFAHAN TO AZARBAIJAN

The soldiers' behavior towards the Bab as they traveled from Isfahan to Kashan was exceedingly harsh. In a letter the Bab wrote to Muhammad Shah from the prison of Maku, he described the villainous and deceitful conduct of Gurgin Khan, who had initiated this journey in haste and completed it over the course of just seven nights, accompanied by only five guards and lacking the proper means for travel.[138] The Bab and his escorts arrived at Kashan on the night before Naw-Ruz (20 March 1847). One of the Babis of that city, Haji Mirza Jani Kashani, was able to persuade the commander of the soldiers to allow the Bab to be his guest for three days.[139] Mirza Jani Kashani and his brother, Muhammad Isma'il Kashani, surnamed "Dhabih," were both former disciples of Shaykh Ahmad Ahsa'i, and they arranged for a group of Shaykhis and Babis to meet with the Bab while he was sojourning at Kashan. These two brothers told the Bab that they were willing to prepare the means for his escape and devote the rest of their lives to serving him.[140] But the Bab—perhaps cherishing some small hope of a meeting with Muhammad Shah, and unwilling to become a fugitive—declined their offer.[141]

After passing through Qum, this small caravan reached the village of Kinargird, situated one day's journey from Tehran. There they received a message from Haji Mirza Aqasi, who was ordering that their prisoner, the Bab, be taken to the nearby village of Kulayn—which Aqasi himself owned—and that they should then await further instructions from him.[142] A few days later, a group of Babis traveling from Isfahan and Tehran arrived and attained the Bab's presence. While in Kulayn, the Bab sent a letter to Muhammad Shah in which he described the cruelty of Husayn Khan, the governor of Fars; recounted the kindnesses of Manuchihr Khan; and asked Muhammad Shah to meet with him. In response, Muhammad Shah wrote the Bab a letter in the style usually employed by the royal court in their

138 Afnan, *Ahd-i A'la*, 223, where the relevant passage from the Bab's letter is quoted.
139 A few years later, Mirza Jani wrote a book on Babi history entitled *Nuqtat al-Kaf*. Following an unsuccessful attempt by a few Babis to assassinate Nasir al-Din Shah, Mirza Jani was arrested and killed in Tehran.
140 Hamadani, 216.
141 For a more detailed account of the Kashani brothers and their family, see Chapter 3 in this volume.
142 Fayzi, *Nuqta-yi Ula*, 210, where an account from Mu'in al-Saltana on how a residence for the Bab was found at the village of Kinargird is also quoted.

correspondence. This letter begins: "Renowned and virtuous Sir..."[143] and goes on to say that his own favor encompassed all of Persia, remarking, "this applies especially to you, who come from an illustrious family of *Sayyids* and scholars." Regarding the Bab's request to meet with him, Muhammad Shah wrote that he had plans to travel, and instructed the Bab thus:

> Go to Maku; wait there and rest for a few days. God willing, my retinue and I will return to the capital; then will I summon you, and the proper arrangements be made to grant your request.[144]

The prospect of a meeting between the Shah and a charismatically pious person such as the Bab was unacceptable to Haji Mirza Aqasi. Privy as he was to the temperament of Muhammad Shah, Aqasi feared that the Shah would likely develop a devoted affinity for the Bab—an affinity he believed would pose a threat to his own political designs. In addition, Aqasi, who ostensibly had Sufi tendencies, regarded the Bab and his movement as yet another challenge that only compounded the meddling of the ambitious mullas in affairs of state. For this reason—and with consideration to other problems confronting the country, including an uprising led by a certain Salar in Khurasan[145]—Aqasi preferred to mitigate the Babi crisis for the time being by sequestering the Bab at Maku pending further developments.

At the command of Muhammad-Baig, and accompanied by a group of horsemen, the Bab departed Kulayn for Tabriz in April 1847, and was warmly received by the Babis and other people he encountered along the entire way. A number of Babis from Qazvin and Zanjan had hastened to a vineyard near Qazvin to see the Bab, and ask that he permit them to help him flee from his escort. On this occasion, too, the Bab declined their offer.[146]

From that vineyard, the Bab wrote a letter to Muhammad Shah requesting that he reconsider his decision, stating that it would be wrong for the Shah

143 The full incipit of the letter is as follows: "Renowned and virtuous Sir—the epitome of courtesy, descendant of the Pure Ones, leader of the loved ones: Haji Mirza 'Ali-Muhammad Shirazi, upon him be the blessings of God."

144 The full text of this letter has been published in Fayzi, *Nuqta-yi Ula*, 214.

145 Muhammad Hasan Khan Salar was one of the leaders and distinguished men of the Qajar era who, in 1846, launched a revolt in Khurasan with the hope that he would accede to the throne by occupying the capital. After five years of guerrilla warfare with the government, Salar was eventually defeated and killed during the reign of Nasir al-Din Shah.

146 For more information on the Babis of Qazvin, see Mazandarani, *Zuhur al-Haqq*, 292–309, and also Chapter 3 in this volume.

to treat him this way regardless of whether he considered him a believer or an infidel. To prove his innocence in this letter, the Bab asked the Shah to read his writings. In conclusion, the Bab wrote:

> Shouldst thou find me deserving of death, then by the sanctified Essence of God, know that I long for it more than the babe yearneth for its mother's breast.[147]

At this stage in the development of his movement, the Bab's confinement to a remote and unfamiliar place—inhabited by Turkish-speaking Sunnis—was designed to seclude him and keep him far away from his followers. This was not a matter he could accept easily. Disappointed at not having received an answer from Muhammad Shah, the Bab arranged for a letter to be sent from Miyanih—174 kilometers from Tabriz—to Bahman Mirza, the Shah's brother and the governor-general of Azarbaijan, requesting that he permit him to remain in Tabriz and not be consigned to Maku.[148] Bahman Mirza had high political ambitions, intent as he was to succeed his sick brother as king. Additionally, Bahman Mirza did not have a good relationship with Haji Mirza Aqasi. Thus, any inclination to the Bab's wishes could have been interpreted by his watchful opponents in Tabriz and Tehran as a sign of opposition to the Shah and proven very costly from a political perspective.[149] These circumstances notwithstanding, during the Bab's forty-day sojourn in Tabriz, Bahman Mirza attempted to arrange a debate between the Bab and a number of the 'ulama of the city—but these 'ulama, who were aware of what had transpired in the Bab's meetings with the 'ulama of Isfahan, refused to grant him any interviews.[150]

---

147 For the full text of this letter, see Fayzi, *Nuqta-yi Ula*, 220–21.

148 Mu'in 136. Refer also to Amanat, *RR*, 373 n. 6 and Fayzi, *Nuqta-yi Ula*, 225–29. The bearer of this letter was Muhammad-Baig Chaparchi, the commander of the soldiers who were escorting the Bab. A man trusted by Haji Mirza Aqasi, Muhammad-Baig was a Sufi and follower of the Ahl-i Haqq creed, but with time he grew so impressed by the Bab that he eventually became a Babi.

149 "An educated prince and a patron of literature and scholarship, Bahman Mirza was a member of the anti-Aqasi coalition that toward the end of Muhammad Shah's reign unsuccessfully tried to remove the premier" (Amanat, *RR* 373 n. 7). For more information, see E. B. Eastwick, *Journal of a Diplomate's Three Years' Residence in Persia*, 2 vols. (London, 1864).

150 For more information on the Bab's stay in Tabriz, see Mu'in 137–49. Amanat writes that Javad Khan Atash Bigi, who had met the Bab at the small citadel in Tabriz where he was being held, commented that "the 'ulama were fearful of the Bab because 'he made redundant their parasitic tutelage'" (*RR*, 374 n. 8).

At the beginning of July 1847, the Bab was conducted by an escort from Tabriz to the fortress of Maku, where he was imprisoned. This fortress had been built near the border shared by Persia, Russia, and the Ottoman Empire at the foot of a massive boulder, and in those days a vast and uninhabited plain was stretched out before it. A letter the Bab wrote from Maku to Muhammad Shah speaks to the sadness and loneliness he felt as a result of his desolate banishment. In this letter, the Bab complains of the tyranny of the governor of Fars, informs the Shah of the suffering dealt him over the past four years by government officials and army soldiers, and courageously calls on him to embrace his religion:

> Wert thou to be told in what place I dwell, the first person to have mercy on me would be thyself. In the heart of a mountain is a fortress...the inmates of which are confined to two guards and four dogs. Picture, then, my plight... I swear by God! Shouldst thou know the things which in the space of these four years have befallen me at the hands of thy people and thine army, thou wouldst hold thy breath from fear of God, unless thou wouldst rise to obey the Cause of him Who is the Testimony of God and make amends for thy shortcomings and failure.[151]

Contrary to the expectations of Haji Mirza Aqasi, the Bab's imprisonment at Maku became an abundantly fruitful period for him. At first, and at the instruction of Aqasi, 'Ali Khan Maku'i—warden of the fortress—prevented the Bab's followers from visiting him. With time, however, Maku'i grew so captivated by the Bab's innocence and prophet-like behavior that he lifted these constraints, to the extent that even he at times would not withhold his aid from the Babis. Soon, Babis from the various cities of Azarbaijan—and even from Khurasan—were setting off for the fortress to see the Bab. During the Maku period, the Bab continued to write letters to his followers and family, and also compose other addresses. It was during this period that the Bab wrote his most important work, the Persian Bayan. Another work he composed was the Dala'il-i Sab'ih (the Seven Proofs), written to prove his claim in response to one of the students of Sayyid Kazim Rashti. And it was also at this time that the Bab, for the first time, announced explicitly and

151 The Bab, *Selections from the Writings of the Bab*, 13.

unequivocally the full extent of his claim to be the Qa'im. In his Risalih-yi Qa'imiyyih, addressed to Mulla 'Ali Turshizi, surnamed 'Azim—one of his most eminent followers in Azarbaijan[152]—the Bab, invoking his unshakable belief in his own messengership, not only portrays the advent of his religion as the fulfillment of all the prophecies concerning the coming of the Qa'im, but also, in that work, proclaims the inauguration of a new period of religious truth and announces the abrogation of the religious law of Islam.[153] In that treatise, the Bab states:

> I am that divine fire which God kindles on the Day of Qiyamat. By which all will be resurrected and revived, then either they shun away from it or enter the Paradise through it. Say! those who enter the gate (*bab*) with reverence, by the Lord of the Heavens and the Earth, the Lord of both worlds, God will add to the number of their fire [*naruhum*: *nar* numerically equals 251] the number of the bab [i.e., the value of 5] and thus will place upon them the light [*nur*: 256]; then they will know that he is the Qa'im in whose Day they all expected and to all he was promised.[154]

The Bab emphasizes that, in abrogating the religious law that came before his own, he did not utter even a single word that ran counter to "the Primal Book" [the Qur'an], taking God as his witness that whatever he has annulled or established has been done at the behest of God.[155]

Amanat writes:

> The clear assumption of Mahdihood and declaration of Qiyamat were the Bab's most straightforward statements so far. Although even in his first utterances in *Qayyum al-asma'* he had implicitly claimed the status of Qa'imiyyih...but contrary to the conventional notion of the Mahdi rendered by the Shi'i orthodoxy, such a declaration did not strive for the consolidation of the Islamic shari'a and the

152 This epistle pertained to the Bab's trial and was sent to Turshizi in Tabriz. See Muhammad-Husayni, 420.

153 In Babi and Baha'i literature, the abrogation of Islam refers to "a passing beyond Islam, or the *irtifa'* (exaltation) of Islam." See Chapter 2 in this volume.

154 For the original text of this passage, see Mazandarani, *Zuhur al-Haqq* 132–33. This translation is taken from Amanat, *RR*, 375–76.

155 Ibid., 133.

> reaffirmation of the Muhammadan order. Quite on the contrary, the "new creation" on the Day of Resurrection required the replacement of the past dispensation with a new order.[156]

In his Risalih-yi Qa'imiyyih, the Bab expounds the signs and conceptions of the Qa'im and his advent not according to Islamic and in particular Shi'i traditions—which state that he will come with a large, fully-equipped army intent on spilling blood—but rather according to the school of Illuminationism, inherent to the primordial underpinnings of ancient Persian culture that still remain alive and well in the Iranian collective consciousness today. The basis of Illuminationist philosophy is the manifestation of the "divine glory,"[157] which was to take place concurrently with the advent of Saoshyant, the promised one of Zoroastrianism, in the end times. The "divine glory" here is a reference to the divine fire (or divine light) previously discussed. It is a life-giving fire, a ray that enkindles and bestows worthiness, a light that confers life and coherence, with which "Ahura Mazda (Lord of Wisdom) calls into being countless creations—creations that are good, beautiful, astonishing, brimming with life, and resplendent."[158] It is that very fire and light which, if a person were to step into it, that person would, according to the Bab, be admitted into heaven.[159]

In spite of his circumstances, the Bab never neglected to write to his family—and in light of the conflicting reports about him that likely reached them, the Bab did what he could to assuage his family's concerns.[160]

156 Amanat, *RR*, 376.

157 This "divine glory" [*farr-i izadi*] is the same as the Avestan word "khvarnah," or "khwarrah" in the Pahlavi language.

158 Avesta, *Yasht* 10.

159 This subject demands an extensive discussion that lies beyond the scope of this chapter. In the writings of the Bab and Baha'u'llah, one can find much evidence of the influence of the Illuminationist thought of ancient Persia. See Ekbal, Kamran, "Angiziyih-yi Huriyyih ya Da'ina, va Din, va Radd-i Pay-i Fikr-i Mazdayasna dar Lawh-i Mallahu'l-Quds," *Safini-yi 'Irfan*, vol. 1, 24–110; and Vahman, Fereydun. "Baha'u'llah: Farr-i Izadi," *Payam-i Baha'i*, October–November 2017, 39–51.

160 "In his correspondence with his wife, Khadijih Bagum, the Bab nevertheless extended his usual reassurances and his affection. In a letter presumably from Tabriz, he consoles his 'dearest soul' for the unfortunate turn of events that caused their separation. He also sends her a piece of velvet and a bottle of perfume (INBA, vol. 59, 166–69). In another letter from Maku, he informs his family that he has sent a booklet containing 'prayers for the people of the house' and asks for five scarves and ten handkerchiefs (INBA, vol. 58, 160–62). He also orders for his personal use a volume of his own prayers to be written on *tirma* paper with golden illumination and in best calligraphy (INBA, vol. 91, 179)." (Amanat, *RR*, 375 n. 13).

The Bab's presence at Maku drew the attention of the inhabitants of cities and villages in that region, who sought to benefit from visits to this *Sayyid* who had claimed to represent the Hidden Imam. In a report written toward the end of 1847 and addressed to the Russian ministry of foreign affairs, Prince Dolgorukov, the Russian minister in Persia, stated that at his request—and as a result of fears that the presence of the Bab in the border region of Maku might lead to unrest—the Persian government had relocated the Bab from the fortress of Maku to a different place. In reality, however, the Bab was still at Maku when Dolgorukov sent this report; indeed, his transfer to Chihriq did not take place until a few months later.[161] This delay suggests that, after receiving Dolgorukov's report, the Persian authorities could not easily decide where the Bab should be imprisoned next.

On 10 April 1848, after nine months of incarceration at Maku, the Bab was transferred from Maku to Chihriq, located in a border region inhabited by Kurds, a distance of four kilometers from the city of Salmas. The inhabitants of that small region were Sunni Kurds—consisting of Naqshbandis, Yazidis, and Ahl-i Haqqs—as well as a small number of Nestorian Christians. The chief of that area and warden of the fortress of Chihriq was Yahya Khan Shikkaki, a Kurd from the Shikkak tribe.

During the Bab's first few months of imprisonment at Chihriq, Yahya Khan, wishing to satisfy Haji Mirza Aqasi, spared no opportunity to treat his prisoner harshly. The Bab entitled Chihriq "Jabal-i Shadid," or "the Grievous Mountain."[162] Only a few people were permitted to visit the Bab; others had to get up on the rooftops of nearby houses and see him from a distance. The severities only increased with the resignation of Haji Mirza Aqasi toward the end of 1848. Those who had permission to meet with the Bab were thoroughly searched, and when it came to the question of his writings, they were subjected to unusually intense scrutiny. In his first few

161 Momen 1981, 72 and Amanat, *RR*, 378 n. 23. The following is a passage from a letter by Mulla Ahmad Abdal Maraghe-i to one of the Bab's maternal uncles: "The reason the Bab was transferred from Maku is that the Russian minister heard that the Bab was at Maku, and this made the minister fearful of possible sedition. He told Haji Mirza Aqasi to relocate the Bab to another one of his provinces, as the Bab was currently near the border and close to Russian land, and expressed his fear of sedition" (Afnan, *Ahd-i A'la*, 314–15). This letter is undated, but it is highly likely that it belongs to that same period in which the Bab was transferred from Maku to Chihriq.

162 This in contradistinction to Maku, which the Bab entitled "Jabal-i Basit," or "the Open Mountain." In the Abjad notation, "Shadid" ["Grievous"] is numerically equivalent to "Chihriq."

months at Chihriq, the Bab wrote two letters—one to Muhammad Shah, the other to Haji Mirza Aqasi—known as "the Sermons of Wrath." In these two sermons, written in an explicitly condemnatory tone, the Bab demands justice for the cruelty meted out to him by Muhammad Shah and Haji Mirza Aqasi. He challenges the Shah thus:

> If you are not afraid of the triumph of the truth and the abolition of the falsehood, why then are you not summoning the 'ulama of the land and not calling me forth to put them in their place...? If, however, you intend to shed my blood, then why do you hesitate...? For me this is blessing and mercy from my God and for you and those who act like you this is toil and suffering from him.[163]

In his sermon to Haji Mirza Aqasi, the Bab similarly holds him responsible for his captivity, and deems him as an opponent of all that is true and right.[164]

These letters demonstrate the Bab's despair at the limbo into which he had been placed as a result of the government's inability to decide what to do about him and the message he was propounding. The Bab had reached the conclusion that the government and the 'ulama had now joined forces and risen against him. He had neither made any political claims, nor did he care for wealth or rank. The Bab's belief in the truth of his message—his firm conviction that he had been chosen for a great cause, which he was obligated to spread to all humanity—made it difficult for him to tolerate his confinement to the four walls of a prison. At the same time, the Bab was aware that his claim to be the Qa'im would not only shake the foundation of the Shi'ah clergy to its core, but also assail the mental conceptions of religion which the people of Persia had built for themselves with myriad conflicting ideas all at once. It was not possible for the Bab to meet a challenge of such great proportions from his cell in the remote prison of Chihriq. In the face of the government and the clerical establishment, who both wished to silence him, the only means at the Bab's disposal were his writings and his letters to Muhammad Shah and Haji Mirza Aqasi, whom he still hoped would come to their senses. But the Bab was dealing with a sick and indecisive Shah, as well as a crafty and deceitful prime minister who devoted all his efforts to

163 This translation taken from Amanat, *RR*, 382.

164 For a summary of this letter in Persian, see Muhammad-Husayni, 854–55. Muhammad-Husayni's book, *Hazrat-i Bab*, contains multiple chapters on the writings of the Bab during his ministry.

making arrangements with his political opponents that were designed to keep him in a place of power.

The Bab's imprisonment in Azarbaijan resulted in the spread of his religion throughout such cities as Maku, Khoy, Maraghah, Salmas, Urumiyya, and Tabriz, as well as large villages like Saysan. This success was made possible by the efforts of a small but active group who had hastened to meet the Bab, and then disseminated his message with a fresh vitality. Similarly, it was in this period that a number of distinguished Babis were able to meet with the Bab, including Mulla 'Ali Turshizi ('Azim), who from the earliest days of the Bab's incarceration at Maku was among those who were close to him and would handle his affairs. There was also Asadu'llah Khu'i, surnamed Dayyan (meaning "judge"), who had familial ties to the court and spoke Syriac, Hebrew, Turkish, and Arabic. Mulla Husayn Bushru'i, the first person to believe in the Bab, journeyed from Khurasan to see him. Mulla 'Abdul-Baqir Tabrizi was another Letter of the Living who visited the Bab at Maku. Mulla Adi-Guzal (known as Sayyah) of Maraghah was entrusted with the duty of delivering the Bab's letters, and he traveled constantly between Maku and the other regions of Persia. Haji Sayyid 'Ali, the uncle of the Bab who had embraced his cause, was likewise able to visit his nephew in this period. Mulla 'Abdul-Karim (Ahmad) Qazvini, a transcriber of the Bab's writings, served as his conduit to the Babis of Tehran, and delivered, at the Bab's instruction, copies of his Dala'il-i Sab'ih to various Qajar grandees and princes.[165]

THE TRIAL OF TABRIZ

Some three months after the Bab had been imprisoned in Chihriq, Reza Khan Afshar, one of the guards of the fortress, received orders from Haji Mirza Aqasi to conduct the Bab to Tabriz—a decision actuated by the written complaints of the 'ulama of Tabriz and Azarbaijan,[166] who were protesting the people's acceptance of the Bab. Owing to the Babi upheavals that had

165 For biographical accounts of the well-known Babis of Azarbaijan, see *Zuhur al-Haqq*, 35–72, and Amanat, *RR*, 383–84. A comprehensive treatment of the Chihriq period, which includes letters from some of the Bab's companions to his uncles in Shiraz and Yazd that discuss important matters pertaining to the history of that time, can be found in Afnan, *Ahd-i A'la*, 308–76.

166 'Abdu'l-Baha, *A Traveller's Narrative Written to Illustrate the Episode of the Bab* (Wilmette, Illinois: US Baha'i Publishing Trust, 1980), 14.

recently broken out in Mazandaran and Khuy, Reza Khan Afshar, who would go on to embrace the Bab's cause, decided to deliver the Bab to Tabriz by way of Urumiyya. The governor of Urumiyya, Malik Qasim Mirza, was the uncle of Nasir al-Din Shah and an enlightened, educated man. He received the Bab warmly and accorded him a fitting residence. During the Bab's ten-day sojourn in Urumiyya, the governor made arrangements for him to meet with the 'ulama of that city, and on a few occasions the Bab went to see some of those 'ulama on his own.

Due to its geographical location, as well as its minority populations of Jews and Nestorian Christians, Urumiyya had a distinct religious climate that differed from that of the other cities of Persia, in that the 'ulama held less sway there. A number of people there had also converted to the Babi religion. Yet in spite of all this, the Bab's stay in the city came to be accounted as an important historical event. Belief in the innocence of the Bab and his lofty spiritual station was such that, on a certain day after he had exited a public bath, the people of the city rushed inside to buy cupfuls of his bathwater from the bath-keeper, believing it to be laden with blessings and curative properties.[167] It was in Urumiyya that Aqa Bala Bayg, a painter at the court of Malik Qasim Mirza, drew a black-and-white, pen-and-ink portrait of the Bab on paper at the governor's behest.[168]

Before entering Tabriz, the Bab had summoned 'Azim and told him that he intended to candidly assert his claim to be the Qa'im at a convocation where the 'ulama and the crown prince himself would be present. 'Azim, who was one of the Bab's closest companions and most obedient followers—and had theretofore believed Sayyid 'Ali-Muhammad Shirazi only to be "the Gate to the Imam"—was both astonished and perturbed by this remark, and he departed the Bab's presence. The next day, 'Azim approached the Bab and told him that he had spent the entire night in agitation and ardent communion with God, until at last he came to recognize the veracity of the Bab's claims. After composing the Risalih-yi Qa'imiyyih for 'Azim, the Bab then instructed him to share that treatise openly with those whom he felt would be receptive to it.[169] 'Azim prepared several transcripts of the

---

167 Fayzi, *Nuqta-yi Ula*, 285 and 285 n. 1.

168 While the Bab was imprisoned at Chihriq, Shaykh 'Ali Turshizi ('Azim) met with Malik Qasim Mirza apparently to "seek his mediation for the release of the Bab and a place of refuge [in Urumiyya] under his protection but the prince being an ally of the late Manuchihr Khan—was hostile to Aqasi and on bad terms with the Shah, declined this request." Amanat, *RR*, 385.

169 *Nabil*, 313; Fayzi, *Nuqta-yi Ula*, 286.

treatise, which he sent to the eminent Babis of the time. In addition, he sent these transcripts, along with some letters of his own, to the Babis of Tehran, Kashan, Isfahan, Yazd, and Bushihr, and asked them all to strive to spread that message far and wide.[170] This treatise had a profoundly significant effect on how these Babis understood the truth of the Bab's message.

News of the Bab's arrival at Tabriz aroused such great excitement and expectation among the people that the governor of the city decided to give the Bab a place to stay on the outskirts until such time as the furor had subsided. One of the ʻulama of the time gives the following account in a letter he wrote:

> The ordinary people of Tabriz, too...began to entertain illusions about [the Bab]. They were waiting for his arrival and for the gathering of the ʻulama so that if in that gathering he triumphed or if the verdict of that gathering turned out to be in his favor, then the learned and the lay, the stranger and the native, and even the government troops would pay their allegiance to him without hesitation and consider obedience to whatever he commands an obligation.[171]

The ʻulama could not reach a consensus on how the convocation should be conducted, prolonging this state of suspense by another week as a result.

At this time Tabriz was considered a city of great religious significance by virtue of the fact that, after Isfahan, it was home to the largest population of ʻulama, whether Shaykhi or Usuli. With the banishment of the Bab to Azarbaijan, that province became the center of Babi traffic and activity, and the clerics were naturally alarmed by the spread of this religion throughout the cities and villages of the region.

Eventually, in July 1848, the Bab entered Tabriz, a city still ablaze with the fire of anticipation. In those days, Nasir al-Din Mirza, an adolescent of seventeen, was the crown prince of Persia and governor-general of Azarbaijan. His uncle, Amir Aslan Khan Quvanlu, and his steward, Fadl-ʻAli Khan ʻAli-Abadi, served as his advisors on matters of governance. All three of them, along with a few other high-ranking members of the government, were present at the trial of the Bab.

---

170 Mazandarani, *Zuhur al-Haqq*, 131-33.

171 From a letter of Mulla Muhammad-Taqi Mamaqani, cited in Mudarrisi-Chahardahi, *Shaykhigari va Babigari* (Tehran, 1972), 311. This translation taken from Amanat, *RR*, 386.

Amanat writes:

> Staging an inquisitorial gathering was the best Aqasi could conceive in order to exploit the complaints of the clergy [regarding the spread of the Babi religion] for his own advantage. In staging the trial of Tabriz, Aqasi hoped to achieve two objectives. By exposing the Bab to the hostile Shaykhis, who had already called for his execution, the premier was sending a signal to the Babis and warning them of the fatal consequences of any militant action. He was also using the occasion to remind the troublesome 'ulama of Tabriz of their ultimate dependency on his good will.[172]

In light of the Bab's previous meetings with the 'ulama of Isfahan, each and every one of the Usuli 'ulama cited some reason to be excused from attending that convocation. Only the Shaykhi 'ulama accepted Aqasi's invitation—but the government did not invite the Shaykhu'l-Islam of Tabriz, a Shaykhi, or his nephew, Abu'l-Qasim, who both wished to see the Bab executed.[173]

The mullas, observing with disbelief the ever-growing number of converts to the Bab's religion, hoped that this convocation might humiliate the Bab and tarnish his holy and cherished image. When the Bab arrived at the gathering, not one of the attendees—all seated next to each other in a tight-knit circle—offered the Bab a place to sit. After a brief pause, Nasir al-Din Mirza, whose sensibilities had likely been offended by the portentous disrespect that had been shown the Bab, offered him a seat even more prominent than his own. In the words of a chronicler at the Qajar court, the crown prince, agitated by the discourteous behavior of those in attendance, "accorded the Bab his attention and favor."[174] The 'ulama, of course, were opposed to this unexpected gesture of goodwill.[175]

The Nizamu'l-'Ulama, the tutor of the crown prince who had been appointed to interrogate the Bab on behalf of all those present, began by asking him about the exact nature of his claims and the authenticity of the writings that were being distributed in his name. Amanat writes that in response, "the Bab admitted the sole authorship of his works then in public

172 Amanat, *RR*, 387.

173 Ibid.

174 Amanat, *RR*, 388, citing Hidayat, Reza-Quli Khan, *Rowzat al-Safa'-i Nasiri* (Tehran, 1960), vol. 10, 423; henceforth, *Rowzat al-Safa'*.

175 Amanat, *RR*, 388. Some historians of the Babi and Baha'i religions believe that the Bab went to the front of the convocation and seated himself there.

circulation,"[176] and goes on to say that the Bab replied to the question about the nature of his claim in this way:

> He declared that his position of "specific gateship" resembled that of [the Imam] 'Ali in relation to Muhammad. He recited the famous hadith "I am the city of knowledge and 'Ali is its gate," then stated: "It is incumbent on you to obey Me, by virtue of [the verse] 'Enter the gate with reverence!' But I did not utter these words. He uttered them who uttered them." Asked "Who then is the speaker?" he replied: "He who shone forth on Mount Sinai." He then read the famous verse: "[If to say] 'I am the Truth' be seemly in a Tree, why should it not be seemly on the part of some favored man?" and continued, "There is no selfness in between. These are God's words. I am but the Tree [the Burning Bush] on Sinai. At that time [the divine word] was created in it, now it has been created in Me."[177]

It is clear from these remarks that the Bab regarded himself as the light that shone upon Moses on Mount Sinai. The Nizamu'l-'Ulama, who had not expected the Bab to make such a stupendous claim, said sarcastically, "If this is indeed the case, then grant me the honor of being the watchman of all our shoes by the door!" With that, a marked change took over the atmosphere of that convocation, and the Nizamu'l-'Ulama proceeded to provoke all his seminarian pupils to prevail over the Bab. He and the other clerics began to inundate the indignant Bab with all sorts of questions, ranging from Arabic grammar to the exegesis of Islamic traditions, the circumstances attending the revelation of Qur'anic verses, subtle points on the subject of divinity, philosophy, matters of religious jurisprudence (including certain laws pertaining to sexual intimacy and homosexuals), Hippocratic medicine, and the effects of mixing the four humors proposed by the ancient Greeks. Even if the Bab had responded to all these questions, in the eyes of his audience, none of his replies would have constituted an adequate proof of his claim.[178]

The Bab's straightforward admission of his unfamiliarity with the aforementioned disciplines further emboldened the clerics. With that same haughty demeanor, the Nizamu'l-'Ulama told the Bab that, if he truly did possess wondrous abilities, he should perform a miracle and restore the

176 Ibid., 389.
177 Ibid.
178 Amanat, *RR*, 385–91.

health of the ailing Muhammad Shah. Immediately thereafter, Nasir al-Din Mirza, supposedly wanting to make things easier on the Bab, asked him to dispense with that request, and instead return the Nizamu'l-'Ulama to his youth. The Bab, for his part, gave a simple response to these whimsical demands: "It is not within my power."[179] Rather than satisfying their requests, the Bab, wishing to establish the truth of his claim on his own terms, began to reveal Arabic verses in the manner of the Qur'an—a feat he always considered the single greatest miracle he could perform. When the Bab had recited just one verse, Mulla Muhammad Mamaqani interrupted him to criticize his solecisms. In response, the Bab said, "I am unlettered, and have not studied the learning current amongst men. I speak forth the things that flow from my tongue." The Bab then proceeded to remind the 'ulama of some of the grammatical irregularities in the Qur'an. Following this, he was asked, "If you have not studied these sciences, where then have you learned the things you are now saying?" to which the Bab replied, "Through divine revelation." The Bab's repeated emphasis on his lack of familiarity with the prevalent disciplines of his day added fuel to the fire of this debate between a prophet and the old guard of Islamic law. The Bab deemed this an opportune moment to declare openly, for the first time and amid accusations of heresy and deception from the 'ulama, that he was, in fact, the Hidden Imam—the promised Qa'im whose return the people had eagerly anticipated for thousands of years.[180] In voicing so prodigious a claim, the clerics had now been pushed to the peak of their outrage. Mulla Muhammad Mamaqani rebuked the Bab harshly and used unseemly language toward him. Filled with bewildered fury, the Nizamu'l-'Ulama and others in attendance imperiously demanded, as proof of the Bab's claim, that he manifest the rod of Moses, the ring of Solomon, and the leaders of men, the *jinn*, and their forty thousand followers, who all must accompany the advent of the Qa'im according to Shi'i traditions. The Bab attempted a few times to shift the focus of the discussion back to the claim he had just advanced, but the attendees did not give him a chance to speak. Faced with a deluge of taunts, curses, and abusive mockery from the 'ulama, the Bab thought it best to spend the rest of the trial in silent protest.

179 The Bab's response that it was not within his power to accomplish these feats is similar to the words of Jesus as recorded in the New Testament: "Why do you call me good?...No one is good except God alone" (Mark 10:18), and also Qur'an 41:6, in which God bids Muhammad to say that he is a man like any other, with the exception that he receives divine revelation.

180 Fayzi, *Nuqta-yi Ula*, 290, and other Babi and Baha'i histories.

Astonishingly serene as the Bab's behavior was, it had no discernible effect on the resentful hearts of the 'ulama or the caprices of the crown prince. The Bab did not see himself as some sort of sorcerer who could manifest the white hand of Moses at will; rather, he believed himself to be a prophet who needed only his revelation of verses and his claim to Mahdihood as proofs of his station. The claim of the Bab stands without parallel in the annals of Shi'i history, insofar as it not only signaled a clear breaking of the Babi religion with Islam, but it also more palpably marked the inception of a religious fervor that would soon arouse an almost unprecedented degree of irrepressible excitement throughout the whole of Persia. Amid the clamoring of the 'ulama, the trial ultimately ended without a verdict.[181]

The unyielding insistence of the clerics that the Bab be executed on charges of *bid'at*[182] forced the crown prince to choose between two dangerous decisions. If he acquiesced to the powerful clerics of Tabriz by condemning the Bab to death, the Babis would likely rise up and throw the country into turmoil. On the other hand, if he chose not to abide by the will of the clerics, the crown prince would be accused of heresy himself and barred from accession to the throne. In an effort to solve his dilemma, the crown prince's advisors, including the Nizamu'l-'Ulama, persuaded him to send his personal physicians—one of whom was a certain Dr. William Cormick—to examine the Bab and assess his mental health. Their predictable diagnosis—one of insanity—was, according to Cormick himself, an expedient measure designed both to extricate the crown prince from his predicament and also to save the Bab's life. Years later, Cormick wrote: "Our report to the shah at that time was of a nature to spare [the Bab's] life."[183] To placate those clerics who were intent on the Bab's death, the government spread rumors that the Bab had recanted during his trial. They even composed a

181 For accounts of the trial of the Bab at Tabriz, see MacEoin, Denis, "The Trial of the Bāb: Shi'ite orthodoxy confronts its mirror image," in: Carole Hillenbrand (ed.) *Studies in Honour of Clifford Edmund Bosworth* (Brill, 2000), 272–317; Amanat, Abbas, "The Prophet and the Priests," in *The Pivot of the Universe: Nasir al-Din Shah Qajar and the Iranian Monarchy, 1831–1896* (University of California Press, 1997), 84–88; *Nabil*, 309–23 and Afnan, *Ahd-i A'la*, 322–33, which cite numerous reports on the matter from various sources.

182 *bid'at*: "Lit. innovation. A belief or practice for which there is no precedent in the time of the Prophet or the Imams. The prohibited innovation [is] generally considered as unacceptable but distinguished from heresy." Amanat, *RR*, 418. (Translator's note.)

183 Browne, E. G., *Materials for the Study of the Babi Religion* (Cambridge, 1918), 261; henceforth, "Browne, *Materials*."

written recantation, which did not resemble the Bab's style of writing and bore no signature.[184]

Despite these developments, Mirza 'Ali-Asghar, the Shaykhu'l-Islam of Tabriz and adjudicator on matters of religious law—who was not present at the Bab's trial but was determined to see him executed—issued a *fatwa* himself condemning the Bab to death. This *fatwa*—which was also signed by the nephew of the Shaykhu'l-Islam, the *mujtahid* Shaykh Abu'l-Qasim—stated that the Bab's claim amounted to apostasy, which warranted his death, and that this sentence would be carried out in the event that his insanity could not be proven.[185] Since, however, the Shaykhu'l-Islam was aware that the government was disinclined to execute the Bab, he insisted that the prophet of Shiraz at least be subjected to corporal punishment, with the hope that the whip might compel him to recant his claim. The decision to carry out this punishment was not unanimous. According to Reza-Quli Khan Hidayat, even the *farrashes*[186] at the court of the crown prince "because of their great sympathy [towards the Bab] refrained from administering the punishment."[187] Consequently, the Shaykhu'l-Islam issued his own edict for a punishment to be meted out to the Bab. Of the twenty lashes intended for the Bab's feet, a number of those blows were dealt to his face, which became so badly wounded and swollen as a result that it required a second visit by Dr. Cormick in the Bab's prison cell.[188] Nasir al-Din Mirza wrote an extensive report to Muhammad Shah in which he falsely stated that the Bab "had apologized, recanted, and repented of and asked pardon for his errors, giving a sealed undertaking that henceforth he would not commit such faults," adding that he was now "awaiting the decision of his Most Sacred Royal and Imperial Majesty, may the souls of the worlds be his sacrifice!"[189]

---

184 This letter is so obviously inauthentic that few polemics written in the past several decades have even mentioned it. It was formerly claimed that this letter was housed at the library of the Iranian parliament, but shortly after the Islamic revolution of 1979, it was reported in the newspapers that the letter had been stolen!

185 For a facsimile of this *fatwa* and a translation of it into English, see Browne, *Materials*, 259.

186 "Servants in charge of punitive duties" (Amanat, *RR*, 391). (Translator's note.)

187 *Rawzat al-Safa'*, vol. 10, 428. This translation taken from Amanat, *RR*, 391. The *Nuqtat al-Kaf* states: "The crown prince said to his *farrashes*, 'The *siyyid* must be bastinadoed.' In response, the *farrashes* said, 'Give us the order to throw ourselves off the roof, and we will comply—but this we will not do'" (138).

188 Browne, *Materials*, 261.

189 The translations of these passages taken from Amanat, *RR*, 392. For the full text of the report, see Afnan, *Ahd-i A'la*, 324–25.

Amanat writes:

> The trial of Tabriz symbolized the ongoing encounter between two opposing interpretations of religion. Whatever the outcome, here was a messianic claimant who sought to restore the long-overshadowed authority of the Imam by challenging the legitimacy of the *mujtahids* who claimed the Imam's collective deputyship in their own right. The confrontation between the "prophet" and the "priests" brought to the surface the deep tension ingrained within the body of Shiʿism. The gulf of difference between the two world views could not have been bridged by a theological disputation. The irreconcilability of the two positions was clear at the outset and neither side seems to have had any illusions.[190]

THE RETURN TO CHIHRIQ PRISON

About two months after his trial in Tabriz, the Bab was remanded to the fortress of Chihriq. Despite the scornful behavior of the ʻulama toward him, as well as the corporal punishment he had suffered, the Bab left the convocation of the crown prince with his head held high. Though it astounded the ʻulama, the Bab's unequivocal claim to be the Qa'im—a claim that entailed the advent of the Day of Resurrection—was embraced by the majority of his followers, and thousands of those devoted lovers would go on to give up their lives to establish the truth of that claim. The treatment that was shown the Bab only added to his popularity among the masses, who saw him as an oppressed *Sayyid* trapped in the clutches of a tyrannical government and cruel *mujtahids*.

Following his arrival at Chihriq, the Bab wrote Haji Mirza Aqasi an indignant letter, which he entrusted to one of his followers to take to Tehran and deliver to Mulla Muhammad-ʻAli Zanjani (Hujjat), who was then to give it to the prime minister.[191] Additionally, he wrote a letter to the ʻulama of Tabriz, calling on them to cast off from their eyes the veils of ignorance and prejudice, and apprehend the truth of his cause. In this letter, the Bab reminded the ʻulama that his movement had, from its earliest days, enjoyed a state

190 Amanat, *RR*, 393.

191 This letter was written in Arabic; an excerpt has been published in Fayzi, *Nuqta-yi Ula*, 304–6.

of constant growth, and that no power or circumstance could ever hinder its progress. He told the ʿulama that every objection they raised against his religion was equally applicable to Islam, and stated that their rejection of this new religion was tantamount to a rejection of Islam.[192]

The summer of 1848 witnessed two historical events in the nascent Babi community: the Conference of Badasht, and the march of Mulla Husayn and a group of Babis toward Mazandaran (22 July 1848). Similar to the Bab's claim in Tabriz that he was the Qa'im, "both these events were symbolic of a new dynamism within the movement" that "consciously aimed at two objectives":[193] the first, establishing the independence of the Babi movement by breaking completely with Islam and cementing its status as a new religion, which was the main subject of discussion by the Babi leaders at Badasht; the second, forming a resistance that would likely attempt to save the Bab by rescuing him from the fortress of Chihriq—an objective pursued by Mulla Husayn and his companions. It is difficult to ascertain whether the concurrence of these two events was purely coincidental, or whether the Babi leaders deliberately planned them to occur simultaneously with the convocation of the crown prince. Whatever the case, each of these events may be regarded as a turning point in the history—and ultimately, the fate—of the Babi movement.[194]

With the Bab's return to Chihriq, in spite of the severities that attended the first few months, a number of Babis were gradually able to visit him, and his correspondence with Babi leaders and the members of his family continued once again.[195]

At the time when the Bab was transferred to the fortress of Chihriq, the sickly Muhammad Shah finally succumbed to his illness. Subsequently, Nasir al-Din Mirza went to the capital, where a coronation was held and he was crowned the new king of Persia. Concomitant with this development was the installment of Mirza Taqi Khan as prime minister, and he quickly

192 For the full text of this letter, see Afnan, *Ahd-i Aʿla*, 332–37.

193 These quotations taken from Amanat, *RR*, 393.

194 Ibid., 393–94. For a discussion of the Conference of Badasht, see Amanat, *RR*, chapter 7.

195 The Bab's letters to his family, whether sent from Maku or Chihriq, demonstrate his concern that his wife and other family members might become confused or worried by hearing conflicting reports of his situation. Even as he contended with his own difficult circumstances, when he did not have the opportunity to compose letters himself, the Bab would ask his amanuensis (Sayyid Husayn) and others to write to his uncles to assure them of his safety. For the text of some of these letters, see Afnan, *Ahd-i Aʿla*, 327–41.

gained power as he earned such titles as Atabak-i A'zam ("the chief tutor") and Amir Kabir ("the great commander"). It was in those very days that Mulla Husayn and the other Babis who had gathered in Khurasan made their entrance into Mazandaran. After reaching Barfurush, this band of Babis was drawn into unwanted conflict with a belligerent local *mujtahid*, the Sa'idu'l-'Ulama, and his followers. Having no other recourse, the Babis took refuge in the fort of Shaykh Tabarsi in Mazandaran. The choice of this fort was entirely accidental, and the Babis began to repair it and supplement it with towers and ramparts to defend themselves.[196]

THE EXECUTION OF THE BAB IN TABRIZ

The trial of the Bab in Tabriz, as well as the abusive treatment he was shown there, encouraged the mullas in various cities and villages to openly oppose the Babis. The draconian politics of Amir Kabir, which did not allow the slightest trace of disorder in his domain, compelled him to engage the military to combat the Babis. The harrowing reports of the incidents that ensued brought great distress to the Bab, who would spend hours in tearful prayer and supplication. He wept, for instance, as he stood listening to the traditional eulogy for the martyrs of Karbala, considering every one of the martyrs of his own religion, striving in the path of truth and justice, each to be another Imam Husayn. In Tehran, and at the bidding of Amir Kabir, seven Babi leaders—including the Bab's own beloved uncle, Mirza Sayyid 'Ali (Khal-i A'zam)—were publicly executed, though it seems the companions of the Bab kept this matter hidden from him.[197] When the Battle of Fort Tabarsi had ended, and the Bab learned that the Sa'idu'l-'Ulama had hacked the body of Quddus to pieces, he mourned for nineteen days, refusing any food or visitors during that time. Reports of skirmishes between the Babis and government forces in Nayriz and Zanjan only added to the Bab's sorrow. Amir Kabir, who held the Babis responsible for all this unrest in the country, decided to eradicate the movement altogether. The victories of the government forces over the Babis prepared the ground for the execution of the Bab—a measure Amir Kabir imagined would quell this turmoil once

196 For more information on the Battle of Fort Tabarsi, including the skirmishes between the government forces and the Babis that lasted some eight months, see Chapters 3 and 6 in this volume.
197 *Nuqtat al-Kaf*, 222.

and for all—and to that end he issued an order to the governor-general of Azarbaijan, Sulayman Khan Shahsavan, instructing him to arrange for a detachment of thirty horsemen from Sa'in Qal'ih to conduct the Bab from Chihriq to Tabriz. Mu'in al-Saltana writes that, throughout the Bab's stay in Salmas, "He predicted the imminence of his martyrdom,"[198] and also that some of the Babis of the city had hidden their swords under the prayer mats in the local mosque with the intention of rescuing the Bab after clashing with the troops who were escorting him.[199] When the Bab learned of this plot through 'Azim, he summoned him to his presence and said to him most prudently, "I have committed my affairs to God, and do not approve of a plan such as this." With great difficulty, 'Azim eventually dissuaded those Babis from pursuing their misguided designs any further.[200] A group of Babis, however, did follow the Bab's escort the entire way, but maintained enough distance to avoid being noticed and arrested by them.[201] Eventually, on 19 June 1850, the Bab, whose turban and cloak had now been replaced with a nightcap and a long-sleeved jacket as a sign of disrespect for him,[202] arrived at Tabriz, where he—along with his amanuensis, Sayyid Husayn Yazdi, and also Mirza Muhammad-'Ali Zunuzi, who never left the Bab's side for so much as a single moment—were imprisoned in the citadel of 'Ali-Shah.[203]

Amir Kabir's decision to execute the Bab was beset with challenges from the outset. In the capital, Nasir al-Din Shah and Mirza Aqa Khan Nuri (the I'timadu'd-Dawlih), aide to the prime minister, each disagreed with the execution for their own reasons. Nasir al-Din Shah believed that the Babi movement would gradually dwindle away on its own, and thus saw no need to execute the Bab.[204] It may also be the case that he feared the Babis would rise up to avenge the killing of the Bab. Mirza Aqa Khan Nuri argued that the insurrections of the Babis had nothing to do with this *Sayyid*, who had been relegated to a distant prison and prevented from exercising his influence in any respect.[205] There may well have been a connection between the opposition of Mirza Aqa Khan Nuri to the Bab's execution and his lofty ambition to become the next prime minister, hoping as he did that he might

198 Mu'in, 289. This translation taken from Amanat, *RR*, 396.
199 Ibid. Refer also to Amanat, *RR*, 396.
200 Ibid.; Afnan, *Ahd-i A'la*, 391.
201 Afnan, *Ahd-i A'la*, 391.
202 *Kawakib al-Durriya*, 236.
203 Afnan, *Ahd-i A'la*, 391.
204 *Nasikh al-Tavarikh*, vol. 3, 302.
205 *Nabil*, 502–4.

one day be able to count on the support of the Babis against his political rivals.[206] Amir Kabir was in dire need of a *fatwa* from the ʻulama to justify the measures he was taking to execute the Bab. Yet his politics had deeply offended the ʻulama, whose power he had sought to limit, and not one of them was prepared to issue the edict he needed. The prospect of retaliation from the Babis was another factor that deterred the ʻulama from involving themselves with the Bab's execution. Even among the members of government, Prince Hamzih Mirza, the governor of Tabriz, was for political reasons reluctant to have any hand in the Bab's execution, insofar as he did not think it his place to shed the blood of an innocent *Sayyid*.[207] Thus, Amir Kabir commended the task to his own brother, Mirza Hasan Khan, secretary of the army of Azarbaijan. The government's efforts to reconvene a tribunal of clerics, who this time might sentence the Bab to death, were fruitless. Taking the previous trial as a precedent, not one of the ʻulama—whether Shaykhi or Usuli—was willing to participate in such a gathering.

Amir Kabir, however, was in a hurry to execute the Bab. In Zanjan, not far from Tabriz, the Babis were still fighting government forces.[208] Amir Kabir was hopeful that the Bab's execution would demoralize the Babis and put an end to the upheaval in Zanjan. Consequently, he sent Sulayman Khan Afshar, who had fought the Babis at Fort Tabarsi—along with his own brother, Mirza Hasan Khan—to Azarbaijan, where, "with threats and enticement,"[209] they eventually induced three *mujtahids* to issue a *fatwa* calling for the Bab's death. Preliminary measures for the Bab's execution were taken over the course of three weeks. During this time, a number of religious figures—including a certain "Haji Aqa Kashshi," a descendant of Shahabu'd-Din Suhravardi and a celebrated mystic of his time, as well as Mulla Faraju'llah Aʻma and a few others—met with the Bab.[210]

The day before his execution, the Bab and two of his followers, Aqa Mirza Muhammad-ʻAli Zunuzi and Sayyid Husayn Yazdi, were taken through a bustling mass of people first to the residence of Mulla Muhammad Baqir,

---

206 Amanat, *RR*, 396.

207 By order of Prince Hamzih Mirza, the Bab and his amanuensis, Sayyid Husayn Yazdi, were secretly brought one night from the prison where they were being held to the residence of the prince, who received the Bab with respect, conversed with him about his claim, and asked him to adduce proofs, which added to the prince's respect for him. See *Kawakib al-Durriya*, 234–39.

208 See Chapter 6 in this volume.

209 Muʻin, 303–4.

210 Afnan, *Ahd-i Aʻla*, 391–92, quoting Muʻin.

the Imam Jum'ah of Tabriz, and then to the home of Mulla Mortiza Harandi (the 'Alamu'l-Huda). Both of these men refused to meet with the Bab, and signed his death warrants without exchanging any questions or answers with him.[211] From there, the Bab was conducted to the residence of the renowned Shaykhi *mujtahid*, Mulla Muhammad Mamaqani, who wished to have a discussion with him. An account of this dialogue is recorded in the memoirs of Mamaqani's son, Mulla Muhammad-Taqi Mamaqani, who states that he witnessed it, and that even beyond that occasion he had heard anecdotes of this meeting from his father.[212] He writes:

> On a certain morning, [the Bab] and two of his followers—one of them Aqa Muhammad-'Ali Tabrizi [*recte* Zunuzi], the other Sayyid Husayn Khurasani [*recte* Yazdi]—was conducted through a densely-packed crowd in the city first to the home of the late Haji Mirza Baqir, the son of the late Mirza Ahmad, a *mujtahid* of Tabriz, where [the Bab] made no mention of his beliefs.
>
> From there, he was taken to the residence of my illustrious father, the Hujjatu'l-Islam [Mamaqani], and I myself was present at the meeting that ensued. [The Bab] sat opposite my late father, who imparted his sage advice and tender counsel to the Bab, and extended the utmost kindness and sympathy to him—but these drops of rain had no effect on the hard stone. Despairing at the apparent futility of his actions, my late father then asked:
>
> "As to the claims you had previously advanced at the convocation of the crown prince—that you have brought a new Cause, opened the gate of revelation, produced verses like those of the Qur'an, and so on—do you still hold these to be true?"
>
> "Yes," the Bab replied.
>
> "Renounce these claims," my father responded, "for it is unseemly

211 *Nabil*, 215–16 and other histories of the Babi and Baha'i religions disagree on the number and names of these *mujtahids* (with the exception of Mulla Muhammad Mamaqani), as well as the order in which they issued their *fatwas*.

212 *Namus-i Nasiri, Guft o Shunud-i Sayyid 'Ali Muhammad-i Bab ba Rawhaniyun-i Tabriz* (ed. Hasan Mursalvand; Tarikh-i Iran, 1995), 9 ff. The original manuscript of *Namus-i Nasiri*—in the handwriting of Mulla Muhammad-Taqi Mamaqani, son of Mulla Muhammad Mamaqani—is housed at the library of Ayatullah Mar'ashi in Mashhad. Muhammad-Taqi Mamaqani wrote this book in 1306 AH [1888–89 CE] in honor of Nasir al-Din Shah, to whom he presented it as a gift in Tabriz as the shah was undertaking his third trip to Europe.

of you to so vainly misguide yourself and others down the path to perdition."

"I will do no such thing," said the Bab.

My father then offered a few counsels to Aqa Muhammad-'Ali [Zunuzi], which proved entirely ineffective.

At that moment, the agents of the government wished to remove the Bab and his companions, but he turned to my father and said: "Will you now issue the edict for my death?"

"There is no need for my edict," my father replied. "These remarks of yours are themselves proof of your apostasy, and constitute the warrant for your death."

"What I seek," said the Bab, "is your own opinion on the matter."

My father responded, "Now that you insist, yes—so long as you persist in maintaining these vain pretensions and corrupt convictions, which redound to your apostasy, the pronouncement of your death is, according to the lucid laws of our religion, a necessity. Yet, as I am willing to accept the recantations of those who are apostates by nature, I shall free you from your fatal plight should you choose to retract your claims."

"Absolutely not," declared the Bab. "The matter is precisely as I have said it; there is nothing for me to recant."[213]

The *fatwas* of Mulla Muhammad Mamaqani and the Imam Jum'ah focused on the corrupt nature of the Bab's beliefs and his apostasy, but also affirmed that he was of sound mind and capable of logical reasoning, when just two years prior these same *mujtahids* had exempted the Bab from capital punishment by virtue of his "insanity." The *fatwa* of Mulla Muhammad Mamaqani states:

> [The Bab] is of totally sound intellect, and is convinced of the truth of his mission; indeed, he has prepared the means for his accession to the throne, cherishing the hope that he might rule as king.[214]

In his last day on this earth, the Bab instructed his amanuensis, Sayyid Husayn Yazdi, to disavow his faith so that he might live to tell others those details of the Bab's life that he had gleaned from the time he was in his

213 Ibid., 58–59. This account appears in a footnote in Fayzi, *Nuqta-yi Ula*, 334–36, as a passage from *Shaykhigari va Babigari*, 208 ff.

214 Mu'in, 304–5, quoted in Fayzi, *Nuqta-yi Ula*, 334.

company. To Sayyid Husayn Yazdi was also entrusted the task of delivering the Bab's letters into the hands of their addressees. The Bab's other cellmate, Muhammad-'Ali Zunuzi—known in Baha'i literature by his title, "Anis" [intimate companion]—was the son of Mirza 'Abdul-Vahhab, descended from the 'ulama of Zunuz. It seems that, from the Bab's first journey to Tabriz, Anis was so completely captivated by him, and grew so wholly devoted to him, that he openly declared his belief in him. When the Bab had left Chihriq and entered Tabriz for the last time, Anis betook himself there and joined the Bab in his cell, insisting right away that he also be executed. The family of Anis attempted to persuade him to recant his faith and free himself in so doing, but their efforts were in vain. On the day when Anis and the Bab were taken to be executed, even the wife and young daughter of Anis were sent to see him, with the hope that a word from them might induce him to abandon the path to martyrdom, but he refused their pleas. So great was the faith which Anis had placed in the Bab that on the night before the execution, when the Bab told his cellmates that he would rather be slain by one of them than by the bullets of the enemy—a remark that moved all those present to weep bitterly—Anis arose and said, "If this is your wish, then I am prepared to fulfill it." This immense sacrifice gladdened the Bab, who assured Anis that he would be martyred with him on the following day. Sayyid Husayn Yazdi writes that the Bab's face that night "was aglow with joy,"[215] exuding tranquility and contentment.

On the morning of the execution, the *farrash-bashi* and the soldiers conducted the Bab, barefooted and bereft of his green turban, cloak, and sash—all symbols of his lineage from the Prophet Muhammad—throughout the city and market to demonstrate the power of the government. When the Bab entered the barracks square, a number of the inhabitants of Tabriz led by Mulla Muhammad-Taqi Tabrizi received permission to see the Bab, and they implored him, for the last time, to recant his claim and save himself, but their appeal was to no avail.[216]

At around noon on 9 July 1850, when a multitude of the people of Tabriz had gathered at the barracks and on the surrounding rooftops, the *farrash-bashi* went to the room where the Bab and his companions were and brought him out to the square. The soldiers charged with the execution were from

215 *Nabil*, 507.
216 Za'im al-Dawla, Mirza Muhammad Mahdi. *Miftah al-Bab al-Abwab aw Tarikh al-Babiyya* (Cairo, 1903), 338, quoting the recollections of his father, an eyewitness to these events. This reference taken from Amanat, *RR*, 402 n. 115.

the Bahaduran regiment, headed by Sam Khan Urus, and divided into three files in the square.[217] This regiment, mostly composed of captives from the second Russo-Persian War, was likely chosen because Muslim soldiers might have been unwilling to execute an innocent *Sayyid*. The arrangements that had been made to carry out this execution indicate the great concern of the government. A number of armed soldiers stood on the rooftops of the barracks to keep an eye on the crowd that had gathered. It seems that, in the event that the spectators started a riot, the choice of a confined space like the Tabriz barracks square would have allowed these soldiers to easily neutralize any disturbance. The large number of soldiers served to counteract potential panic which the execution might have provoked, guard against any attempts by the public to rush onto the scene and free the Bab, and divide the responsibility for killing the prophet of Shiraz—and a *Sayyid*, at that—among an anonymous mass of people, rather than restrict it to any one identifiable person.[218] Historical sources agree that Sam Khan approached the Bab to express his reluctance to proceed with the execution, and then asked to be excused from carrying it out. In response, the Bab instructed Sam Khan to fulfill the duty that had been given him and to commit this affair to God.[219]

The Bab and Anis were suspended from two ropes, each held in place by a nail hammered into the wall. Anis, at his own request, was positioned in such a way that his body shielded that of the Bab, and his head rested against the breast of his beloved. Three rows of soldiers each fired in turn at the Bab and Anis. A few minutes later, the thick cloud of smoke that had ascended from the discharged muskets cleared, and there suddenly came from the crowd a cry of astonishment. Anis, totally unscathed, was standing by the wall, and the Bab had disappeared. "The Bab has gone from our sight!" the people shouted.[220] The bullets had torn the ropes into pieces and freed the two condemned. With haste and agitation, the *farrash-bashi* and a few soldiers searched for the Bab, and eventually found him in that

217 Sam Khan, or Samsam Khan, was a Russian army officer who in the time of Fath-'Ali Shah had been captured by the Persians during the second Russo-Persian War. In Persia, he converted to Islam and adopted the title of "Khan." He commanded a group of Russian and Assyrian soldiers, who were themselves all captives of that same war and made up the Bahaduran regiment, which participated in most of the military campaigns undertaken in the time of Muhammad Shah. See Fayzi, *Nuqta-yi Ula*, 337–38.

218 Amanat, *RR*, 402.

219 Fayzi, *Nuqta-yi Ula*, 338.

220 *Nabil*, 513.

same room where he had previously been conversing with his amanuensis, Sayyid Husayn Yazdi. One of the soldiers, Quch-ʻAli Sultan, dealt heavy blows to the Bab's face and head, dragged him out of the room, and took him back to the execution site.[221] Sam Khan was not willing to carry out this task a second time; he gathered his soldiers, and they all exited the square. Immediately thereafter, the duty was passed on to the regiment of Aqa Jan Baig Khamsih-i. The Bab and Anis were suspended just as before, and the order to fire was given. The thundering roar of the bullets and thick smoke from the gunpowder filled the arena. This time, the bullets hit their target, so shattering the bodies of the Bab and Anis that they had melded into one—but the face of the Bab had sustained only a slight wound.[222] Their bodies were later thrown beside a moat outside the city so that wild animals might feed on them.

Sipihr, the Muvarrikhu'd-Dawlih and court chronicler of the Qajar period, regards the Bab's survival of the first attempt as the will of God, who had wished to demonstrate the falsity of the Bab's claim:

> if [the Bab] exposed his bosom and cried out: "O, ye the soldiers and the people, didst thou not see My miracle that of a thousand bullets not even one hit Me but instead untied My bonds," then no one would have fired a shot at Him anymore and surely the men and women in the barracks would have assembled around Him and a riot would have broken out. [But] it was God's will that the truth should be distinguished from falsehood and doubt and uncertainty be removed from among the people.[223]

Sipihr, a man accustomed to the lying and deception that had permeated his environment, could never have understood the immensity of the Bab's spirit or apprehended the measure of his sincerity. Had the Bab done what Sipihr imagined, it would have made him a charlatan like countless others throughout history. Yet the Bab, who stated time and again, in his works and at the convocation of the crown prince, that his only miracle was his revelation of verses—the same Bab whose writings surged with his longing to be martyred—proved, through his appearance at the square where he

221 For accounts of the Bab's martyrdom, see *Nabil*, 500–23; Fayzi, *Nuqta-yi Ula*, 312–60; Afnan, *Ahd-i Aʻla*, 390–416; and Muhammad-Husayni, 573–609.

222 Fayzi, *Nuqta-yi Ula*, 344.

223 *Nasikh al-Tawarikh*, vol. 3, 1075–76. This translation taken from Amanat, *RR*, 403.

was executed, that he was a legitimate prophet who, Christlike, gave up his life for a message he had been chosen to deliver.

Through the efforts of the Babis, the bodies of the Bab and Anis were recovered from the moat where they had been cast, and concealed for fifty years as they were transferred to various parts of Persia for safekeeping. At the instruction of 'Abdu'l-Baha, what remained of their bodies was eventually taken to Haifa—then in Palestine—and on 21 March 1909, they were interred in a shrine on Mount Carmel that had been built solely to house their remains.[224]

Toward the end of his life, the Bab witnessed the defeat of the Babis in the upheavals of Fort Tabarsi, Nayriz, and Zanjan. He had neither called on the Babis to launch these upheavals, nor had any doubts as to how disastrously they would end. From the earliest days of his ministry, he strove to erase from the minds of his new followers the conception of the bloodthirsty and vindictive Qa'im mentioned in Shi'i hadiths, and replace it instead with an image of a peace-seeking prophet who had made it abundantly clear, orally and in writing, that he did not wish to see even the saddening of any soul.[225]

This revolutionary prophet, a standard-bearer who had withstood such great suffering, was deeply invested in reforming the foundations of religious belief and putting an end to the injurious influence of the mullas on society. By passing beyond Islam and announcing an independent religious law, the Bab inaugurated a new era—an era in which hidebound dogmatism had now been substituted with a widening of horizons and a freshness of thought. Up until the very last days of his life, the Bab expected that the government would enter into a dialogue with him. But the iron-fisted Amir Kabir, ever striving to establish order in the land, neither saw any need for this dialogue, nor deemed it in his best interest to make himself the target of accusations of heresy from the mullas and his other opponents

224 For additional information, see *Kawakib al-Durriya*, 248–51; Fayzi, *Nuqta-yi Ula*, 352–67; Afnan, *Ahd-i A'la*, 406–61; and Muhammad-Husayni, 582–98.

225 "[God] hath cherished and will ever cherish the desire that all men may attain His gardens of Paradise with utmost love, that no one should sadden another, not even for a moment, and that all should dwell within His cradle of protection and security" (The Bab, Bayan 6:16; this translation taken from *Selections from the Writings of the Bab*, 86).

by finding any sort of common ground with the Babis. Perhaps his intent was to first deal with the Babi question, and then place constraints on the uninhibited power of the *mujtahids*—but he had failed to appreciate the profoundly influential degree to which those clerics had embedded themselves into the sleep-stricken society of nineteenth-century Persia. His enemies—consisting of 'ulama, noblemen, and courtiers—began to conspire against him much more quickly than he had anticipated. The shah removed Amir Kabir from the office of prime minister and then, in January 1852—a year and a half after the Bab's execution—gave the order that he be put to death.

In reality, the juxtaposition of Amir Kabir with the Babis represented two different interpretations of modernity that had come face to face: one, the dictatorial implementations of secularist reforms, the pursuit of an inflexibly resolute prime minister; the other, a far-reaching, full-scale revival in the form of a new religion that revolutionized moral foundations and naturally entailed radical changes to the present culture and society. Each embodied a sentiment that rebelled against the firmly rooted religious and political institutions of its day. The Bab, from the very beginning, sought a kind of reconciliation and dialogue with the government, on the condition that the legitimacy of his religion be recognized and his community allowed to exist peacefully in Persia. But Amir Kabir, influenced by the Ottoman Tanzimat reforms, was vehemently opposed to any seriously fundamental re-evaluation of religious law, especially if it bordered on heresy and threatened the security of the country. It was inevitable that these two forces would eventually clash.

During a turbulent period in which the Babi community had lost its guiding light, a few of its members made an attempt on the life of Nasir al-Din Shah (15 August 1852) as retribution for the Bab's execution. The assassination was unsuccessful, but it had bloody consequences for the Babi community nevertheless. As part of the widespread, savage killing of the Babis that ensued, the final remnants of Babi leadership—including Tahirih; Mirza Jani Kashani, chronicler and author of the *Nuqtat al-Kaf*; Mulla 'Ali Turshizi, known as 'Azim; Sayyid Husayn Yazdi, the amanuensis of the Bab; and Sulayman Khan Tabrizi were all arrested and put to death in the most horrendous of ways. The only one in the leadership to survive was Mirza Husayn-'Ali Nuri, who would later come to be known as Baha'u'llah. After enduring four months of imprisonment, Baha'u'llah was exiled from Persia to Baghdad. With his teachings, and in the years that followed, Baha'u'llah was able to establish, in the form of the Baha'i religion, the community that the Bab had always intended to build.

These developments brought the government and the Usuli *mujtahids* closer together. Such alliances had existed in the Persian political sphere from the inception of the Qajar regime, in particular during the reign of Fath-'Ali Shah. Gradually, however, the indifference of Haji Mirza Aqasi toward the 'ulama and the severe measures of Amir Kabir served to diminish the role of the clerics. The persecution of the Babi community, and the subsequent execution of Amir Kabir, restored that lost power to the 'ulama. One can imagine the influential position which the leaders of the Shi'i community occupied in Persian politics from that point on, whether in terms of their close collaboration with the government or, at times, their opposition to it—a position that would culminate in the formation of an Islamic republic governed by a guardianship of religious jurists.

BIBLIOGRAPHY

English sources

Amanat, Abbas. *Resurrection and Renewal, the Making of the Babi Movement in Iran 1844–1850*. Cornell University Press. Ithaca and London, 1989.

Balyuzi, H. M. *The Báb*. Richard Clay. England, 1966.

Browne, E. G. *Materials for the Study of the Babi Religion*. Cambridge University Press. Cambridge, 1918.

Hamadani, Mirza 'Ali (Husain). *Tarikh-e Jadid. The New History*, edited by E. G. Browne. Philo Press. Amsterdam, 1975. (First published by Cambridge University Press, London, 1893.)

Lambden, Stephen N. "An Episode in the Childhood of the Báb." In *In Iran*, edited by Peter Smith, 3:1–31. Studies in Bâbî and Bahâ'î History. Los Angeles: Kalimát Press, 1986.

Mehrabkhani, Rouhollah. *Mulla Husayn, Disciple at Dawn*. Kalimát Press, 1987.

Momen, Moojan. "The Trial of Mullá 'Alí Bastámí: A Combined Sunní-Shí'í Fatwá against the Báb." *Iran: Journal of the British Institute of Persian Studies*, 20. 1982.

______. ed. *The Bábí and Bahá'í Religions, 1844–1944: Some Contemporary Western Accounts*. George Ronald. Oxford, 1981.

Zarandi, Mulla Muhammad. *The Dawn Breakers: Nabil's Narrative of the Early Days of the Baha'i Revelation*. Trans. and ed. by Shoghi Effendi. Wilmette Ill., 1932.

Nicolas, A. M. B. *Seyyèd Ali Muhammad dit le Bab*. Paris, 1905.

Persian and Arabic sources

INBA = Iran National Baha'i Archive.

Afnan, Abu'l-Qasim. *'Ahd-i A'la, zindigani-yi Hazrat-i Bab*. Oneworld Publications. Oxford, 2000.

______. Mirza Habibullah. *Tarikh-i Amri-yi Shiraz*. INBA nr. 1027.

'Ayati, 'Abd al-Husayn. *Kawakib al-Durriya fi m'athir al-Baha'iyya*, 2 Vols. Cairo, 1923–24.

Fasa'i, Hajji Mirza Hasan. *Farsnamah-yi Nasiri*. 2 vols (in one). Tehran, 1313/1894–1895.

Fayzi, Muhammad 'Ali. *Khandan-i Afnan-i, Sidra-yi Rahman*. Tehran, 1971.

______. *Hazrat-i Nuqta-yi Ula*. 3rd print, Bahá'í-Verlag. Germany, 1994.

Fu'adi Bushru'i, Hasan. *Tarikh-i Diyanat-i Baha'i dar Khorasan*. Asr-i Jadid publishers. Darmstadt, Germany, 2007.

Gheybi, Fazil. *Rag-i Taak, Goftari dar bari-yi naqshi din dar tarikh-i 'ijtema'i-yi Iran*. Available at: www.gheybi.com/resources/U1+U2%20Und%20 Ihnhalt%20+U3+U4.pdf.

Gulpaygani, Mirza Abul-Fazl and Gulpaygani, Sayyid Mahdi. *Kashf al-Ghita' 'an Hiyal al-'A'da*. Tashkand n.d. (1919?).

Hidayat, Riza Quli Khan. *Rowzat al-Safa-yi Nasiri*. 3rd edition, VIII–X. Tehran, 1338–1339/1959–1960.

Kashani, Haji Mirza Jani. *Tarikh-i Nuqtat al-Kaf*, ed. E. G. Browne. Brill. Leiden, 1910.

Mu'in al-Saltana Tabrizi, Haji Muhammad. *Tarikh-i Amr [-i Baha'i]*. INBA, A. 78.

Qazvini, Mulla Ja'far. Historical account published in *Tarikh-i Samandar va Mulhaqat*, ed. 'Abdul'ali 'Ala'i. Tehran 131 BE/1975.

Ra'fati, Vahid. *Peyk-i Rastan*. Bahá'í-Verlag. Germany, 2005.

Sipihr, Mirza Muhammad Taqi (Lisan al-Mulk). *Nasikh al-Tawarikh (Tarikh-i Qajariyah)*, ed. J. Kiyanfar. Tehran, 1998.

Za'im al-Dawla, Mirza Muhammad Mahdi. *Miftah-i Bab al-Abwab aw Tarikh al-Babiya*. Cairo, 1342/1903.

2

The Worldview of the Báb

The Reconstruction of Religion and Society

NADER SAIEDI

Abstract: Writings of the Báb, the founder of the Babi religion, brought about a new spiritual paradigm in which the ideas of religion, human identity, and social order are reinterpreted and reconstructed. He introduced a this-worldly dialectical, historical, and dialogical consciousness in the realm of religious discourse, affirmed the dignity of all beings as spiritual realities, rejected the culture of traditionalism, advocated the imperative of independent thinking for each human being, and called for fundamental transformations of the social order. His project of the spiritualization of life may be seen as a mediating link between the violent millenarian expectations prevalent among the Shiʿis of his time, and the peaceful approach to modernity in the writings of Baha'u'llah.

The Babi movement founded in 1844 by Sayyid 'Ali-Muhammad, the Báb, was a spiritual movement which offered a new interpretation of religion and mysticism, suggesting that religion is inseparable from a project of social reconstruction. Therefore, as noted by some impartial historians, it aimed to modernize Iran and bring fundamental social transformations to the backward Qajar society of the time.[1] By claiming that the age of Islam was over and that he had brought a new religion, the Báb challenged both the culture of traditionalism and the established order of Iranian society, calling for foundational changes in its cultural, religious, social, and political structures. While the form of his writings was influenced by the Islamic idioms and symbols of his time, the content of his writings questioned traditional ideas and reinterpreted traditional symbols.

Some authors have equated the Babi movement with the Protestant reform movement begun by Martin Luther in the sixteenth century. Although there are similarities between the functions of these two movements, the extent of the questioning of tradition called for in the writings of the Báb is far greater. Luther never claimed that he had brought a new religion. What led to the success of Luther's movement was that, despite the opposition of the Roman Catholic Church, many rulers of the time supported his cause and accepted his reforms. What we find in the case of the Báb is exactly the opposite. Even a patriot and liberal like Amir Kabir, who was interested in implementing various reforms in Iran, instead of confronting the conservative clerics and supporting the Báb, joined the religious leaders in their opposition and brutal suppression of the Babi movement. Ironically, therefore, the greatest reformer of mid-nineteenth-century Iran was also the most vehement suppressor of this advocate of reform and modernity.

In order to understand the depth of the novelty and creativity of the writings of the Báb, in the following sections we discuss his worldview and the social and political ideas emphasized in his writings.

---

1 Abbas Amanat, a historian of the Qajar period, writes: "This revolutionary step set the Babis on the road to a complete break from Islam... The mind that conceived this break, and set about to achieve it, though primarily religious, shared the modernity of a secular mind as it traced the stagnation of the community not in the irreversible fate of its members but in their failure to see the incompatibility of their past religious values with the realities of a new era" (*RR*, 406–7).

RECONSTRUCTION OF THE IDEA OF RELIGION: DIALECTICAL LOGIC AND HISTORICAL CONSCIOUSNESS

Iranian intellectuals of the twentieth century became familiar with dialectical logic and historical consciousness through the writings of Hegel and Marx. However, it is noteworthy that in the middle of nineteenth-century Iran both dialectical logic and historical consciousness were discussed in the writings of the Iranian prophet, the Báb. The writings of the Báb, who was executed in 1850, and the early works of Karl Marx were written at the same time; and both of them, in different ways, address a dialectical and historical consciousness. In regard to the question of religion, Marx simply rejected religion in general, whereas the Báb rejected traditionalism and called for a dialectical reconstruction of religion.

Much has been said about dialectics and its meaning. Yet, the essence of dialectical logic is contained in the German word *Aufhebung* which is the core concept in all the writings of Hegel. The word *Aufhebung* indicates two opposite meanings. On the one hand, *Aufhebung* means cancellation, elimination, negation, and destruction. In traditional religious discourse this sense is expressed by the word abrogation (*naskh*). On the other hand, *Aufhebung* means preservation, elevation, and exaltation. It is the unity of these two opposite meanings of *Aufhebung* that defines Hegel's dialectical philosophy. In other words, in the movement of history, each new and higher stage of history is the realization of the previous stage in a higher form. The more developed stage is the *Aufhebung* of the previous stage because it cancels and elevates the previous stage. Thus, *Aufhebung* is a synthesis that contains within itself both the thesis and the anti-thesis: it both preserves and negates the previous stage. *Aufhebung* is the unity of negation and affirmation.[2]

One of the most significant and central ideas of the Báb is precisely this dialectical and historical concept.[3] According to the Báb, each new stage of the development of humanity is an *irtifa'* of the previous stage. Consequently, each new religion is an *irtifa'* of the previous religion. The word *irtifa'*, which means both cancellation and elevation, is used by the Báb as his

2 See for example: Hegel, Georg W. F., *The Philosophy of History*.

3 It may be argued that the thesis of evolution and historical consciousness is the most important idea of the nineteenth century social theory in the West. However, at the same time, usually the opposite point of view was dominant in religious cultures since the followers of various religions defined their own religion and religious laws as unchanging and eternally binding.

key conceptual term to convey the unity of two opposite meanings. On the one hand a new religion is the negation and abrogation of the previous religion. On the other hand, the new religion is the same previous religion which appears in a higher more elevated form. Therefore, the truth of all religions is one, but this same truth appears in higher forms in subsequent revelations. For example, according to the Báb the Qur'an is the same as the Gospel. Although the Qur'an abrogates the laws of the Gospel, that same spiritual truth appears in the Qur'an in a higher form corresponding to the development of history. The word *irtifa'* as used by the Báb is exactly the word *Aufhebung* as it was used by Hegel.[4] The Báb believes that religion and culture are ever advancing, and there is no end to this renewal and development. Religion is a dynamic and changing reality because the human being is a historical being and society is a dynamic reality. The logic of religions is the logic of *irtifa'*. Thus, each religion corresponds to its own historical moment and is subject to abrogation/elevation by the next religion in accordance with the dynamics of the historical development of humanity.

Before discussing other aspects of this dialectical and historical logic, it is necessary to take note of a major difference between the approach of the Báb on the one hand, and that of Hegel and Marx on the other. While Hegel and Marx applied the concept of dialectics and historicity to the realm of society and history, neither of them believed in the relevance of dialectical logic to the realm of religion or divine revelation. Marx did not believe in divine revelation and rejected religion in general. However, Hegel whose philosophical approach was of a spiritual and religious nature, believed that with the emergence of Christianity religious dialectic had reached its endpoint, and that Jesus had pronounced the final and ultimate word on religious truth. In other words, Hegel believed that Christianity is the final revelation of religious truth. According to Hegel, the words of Jesus are the synthesis of two previous stages of religious consciousness. In the first stage, nature and the natural world were deified, whereas in the second stage, human beings worshipped a God who transcended the realm of nature. Hegel maintained that the Christian thesis of the Holy Trinity is a dialectical synthesis of the previous two stages. Through it, religious dialectic reaches its ultimate end and perfection.[5] We can see that even Hegel conceived of the word of God as something absolute and, therefore, exempt from the historical and dialectical logic. In other words, human and social phenomena

4 See for example: The Báb, The Persian Bayan, 3:3, 3:16, 6:6, 8:3, 8:16, and 9:5.
5 See for example: Hegel, Georg W. F., *Lectures on the Philosophy of Religion*.

are subject to historical dynamics, but the realm of religion, which is the divine word and revelation, has already reached its absolute truth and is immune to the exigencies of historical development.

The Báb, on the contrary, not only sees all aspects of culture and society as subject to historical transformation, he also applies the logic of historicity to the realm of religion and to the word of God, which was previously thought of as being absolute and above history. This new conception leads to two apparently opposing conclusions—yet it is precisely the unity of these two opposites that defines his worldview. On the one hand, all religions are one religion, all prophets are the same reality, and all scriptures are one identical word of God. On the other hand, religion is a progressive and dynamic reality, and the word of God is a living and dynamic entity. This identical living word of God appears in new and more elevated forms parallel to the development of the changing needs of society. Each revelation of God is preserved and elevated in a new expression of the same word. The Báb gives the example of a living human being who is the same person at different ages, but when he is twelve years of age he appears in a higher and more developed form compared to when he was only two years of age. According to the Báb, each Book of God yearns to reach its maturation and elevation in the form of the next Book of God. And yet, the religious traditionalists who claim to love their scripture prevent their sacred text from realizing its progress, and they reject the new scripture. That is why the Báb finds the previous expressions of the word of God to be in profound sadness.[6]

Therefore, through the reconstruction of religion in the writings of the Báb, religion becomes a dynamic reality which must be renewed in each new stage of the historical development of humanity. Yet, all these religions are one and the same reality. Consequently, religions must be reconciled together, since no prophet of God is superior to any other. The word of God and the prophets are the same; it is the human reality that has changed. Therefore, only differences in the outward appearance of religions, corresponding to their historically specific conditions, have changed. The truth of all religions is one and the same. Followers of different religions must remember this essential unity of all religions and overcome the

6 The Báb writes: "Today the Furqán [Qur'an] bestoweth salutations unto those letters who have uplifted it, and caused it to enter in the Bayán... Thus, today, nothing is more afflicted with anguish than the Furqán. All recite it, yet they fail to receive its blessing, and attain naught but its torment, even as those who were reciting the Book of Alif in the day of the Revelation of the Furqán" (Persian Bayan 3:3).

fundamentalist tendency to become obsessed with the legalistic aspects of their traditions, forgetting the common and essential truth of all religions.

RECONSTRUCTION OF THE IDEA OF THE HUMAN BEING AND HUMAN IDENTITY

The historical and dialectical approach to religion in the writings of the Báb provides the foundation for a new understanding of both humans and society. Before directly addressing the reconstruction of the concept of the human being in his thought, it is useful to give an example of how the new conception of religion requires a new definition of humans.

The Babi movement begins with the "Declaration" of the Báb, his initial announcement of his mission and the conversion of his first disciple. In his book, the Persian Bayan, the Báb gives the precise date, hour and minute of this Declaration, which took place at two hours and eleven minutes after the sunset on 5 Jumadi I 1260 A. H. (22 May 1844).[7] According to the Báb, this moment is the moment of the birth of the Babi religion and the inception of the Day of Resurrection. However, this discussion in the Persian Bayan expresses a revolutionary transformation of the idea of religion, as well as the concept of human beings. Traditionally, it has been believed that the inception of any religion is defined by the moment that the prophet receives his first revelation from God and becomes conscious of his prophetic station. However, the writings of the Báb make it clear that he had received divine revelations previous to the date of his Declaration.[8] Thus, the birth of the Babi religion is not equated with the first revelation/conversation between God and his chosen prophet. Rather, the Babi religion is born at the moment that God, through the mediation of his prophet, the Báb, engages in a dialogue with a human being. His Declaration was a conversation between the Báb and an ordinary human being, Mulla Husayn, during which the Báb announced his claim to him, and Mulla Husayn accepted the Bab's claim and became his first believer.

The Declaration of the Báb, therefore, represents a profound reinterpretation of the meaning of religion and its recipients. Traditionally, religion is

7 Persian Bayan 2:7.

8 For example, in his work, Kitab al-Fihrist, the Báb speaks of receiving divine revelation in the middle of the month Rabi' I, namely 50 days before his Declaration. (Kitab al-Fihrist, 2)

perceived as a monological entity, a product of the absolute will and knowledge of God that is above history. Therefore, religion becomes an arbitrary imposition of the divine will on humanity. In this approach, religion is an absolute and trans-historical reality. Consequently, each religion is perceived by its followers to be the last religion, and its laws are conceived to be binding laws for eternity. That is why, perceived in this way, religion turns into a grave obstacle against human progress and development. However, the Báb's concept of religion defines religion as a dialogue between God and humanity, a product of an interaction between divine knowledge/will and a specific stage of human development, need, and conditions. Religion is not an absolute divine command. It is instead the reflection of the divine will in the mirror of human historical receptivity. Consequently, religion becomes historical and dynamic. The source of religion is absolute, but religion is the relative manifestation of this absolute in the mirror of human reality. All religions, therefore, become historically specific, and no religion is a final revelation.

Such reconstruction of religion as the product of the dialogue between God and humanity presupposes a new definition of human beings. Humanity now participates in the construction of religion and engages in a dialogue with God. So now, divine revelation appears and changes in accordance with the content of this conversation. In other words, humans become partners with God and play a necessary role in the construction of religion. Thus, humans appear as the image of God, a sacred and spiritual being. It is for this reason that in this worldview humans no longer could be degraded, humiliated, or objectified.

Another expression of this same concept is the centrality of the Covenant in the writings of the Báb. The idea of a covenant is present in all religions. However, in the worldview of the Báb this concept is also reinterpreted.

A pact or agreement presupposes the existence of two units of will and consciousness who enter into a binding contract with freedom and choice. In the worldview of the Báb, religion is fundamentally a covenant with God, and this means that human beings appear as a spirit, a consciousness, before God to become a partner in the divine Covenant. Therefore, the very concept of covenant leads to a new definition of humans. Human beings are now defined by reason, consciousness, freedom, choice, and spiritual powers. She or he is now a being who is endowed with rights and must actively participate in determining her or his own destiny.[9]

9 For example, see the Báb, *Tafsiri Ha'*, 116.

Reinterpretation of the Covenant means a new social and political definition of human beings.

In order to better understand this point, a reference to one of the works of the Báb, his Interpretation of the Letter Ha', may be helpful. This work which is a commentary and explanation of the alphabetical letter H, is written in reply to a questioner who in his letter to the Báb asked of the nature of Truth as well as the true station of the Báb. His letter to the Báb begins with the words "He is the Mighty" (*Huva'l 'Aziz*). In response, the Báb mentions that by pursuing a spiritual and mystical method all humans can discover the truth for themselves. All reality is interconnected, and therefore, the answer is potentially present in the very question itself. In order to both answer the question of the questioner and to convey this emphasis on the nobility and power of human beings, the Báb devotes his entire reply to a discussion of the very first alphabetical letter that is mentioned in the letter of the questioner, namely the letter *Ha'* or H.[10] Here we are not concerned with the details of the answer of the Báb. But it is important to note that the young prophet believes in the nobility of human beings to the extent that when asked a question, he invites his questioner to engage in independent thinking, attain self-consciousness, and achieve mystical insight. In the worldview of the Báb, all things are organically connected with each other, and therefore the truth of everything is present within everything else. By understanding one's own truth, humans can understand the truth of all reality. Realization of true self-consciousness is identical with achieving knowledge of all reality.

To understand this new approach to human beings in the worldview of the Báb, we need to discuss his concept of identity. This is a central principle throughout the writings of the Báb. In the past, human identity was usually defined in terms of the characteristics that separate us from each other. Likewise, in the postmodern approach, human identity is defined in terms of one's gender, ethnicity, language, class, age, nationality, culture and the like. Such conceptions define humans in contrast with each other and affirm identity in terms of a diversity which is devoid of unity. The writings of the Báb propose an entirely different philosophy. For the Báb, humans are spiritual beings, and this means that a human being consists of two aspects. One aspect is what distinguishes us from each other, whereas the other aspect affirms our common unity. In the language of the Báb, the

10 Ibid., 109.

two aspects of human being are called essence and existence, or servitude and divinity. According to him, we are like a mirror. This mirror has a specific glass which distinguishes it from other glasses. Yet the real truth of all mirrors lies in the fact that an identical image is reflected in them. God is like a sun, and humans are all different mirrors who are reflecting the divine names and attributes. The glass is our essence, our created and finite character, our servitude as a specific created being. Yet our true identity, the Báb maintains, is the image of God, our existence, the divine attributes that are reflected in our heart.[11] The Báb, therefore, intends to create a new culture in the world. In this culture people see themselves and others as the reflections of divine attributes, a divinity that is common to all human beings. The consequence of this approach to identity is that all humans are endowed with the same truth, all become sacred and beautiful, and all are endowed with rights. This dual aspect of human identity implies that we are one with other humans. Yet, we remain independent and unique beings. We achieve happiness and fulfillment when we are conscious of the spiritual unity of all human beings, see ourselves as organically linked to each other, and at the same time celebrate our individuality, uniqueness, and diversity.

RATIONALISM AND HUMANISM

As we noted before, the Báb sees humans as noble beings who are endowed with the inherent capacity to think for themselves and, therefore, are obligated to engage in the independent investigation of truth. In order to convey this fact, the Báb metaphorically mentions that: if in this day an ant were to decide to discover the most complex and hidden truth of the Qur'an through an analysis of the very blackness of its own eye, it will assuredly succeed, for this is the day that divine revelation is vibrating in all beings.[12] Needless to say, the message of the Babi movement was the very opposite of the message of the Usuli school of Shi'i Islam, which had become victorious over its rival, the Akhbari school, by the beginning of nineteenth century. The

11 Persian Bayan 4:1.

12 The Báb writes: "Know thou, verily, that God revealed the Qur'án, even as He hath created all things. Therefore, in this day, should a tiny ant desire to unravel all its verses, and its abstruse meanings, and its stations, through the black of its own eye, it shall be capable of achieving that, inasmuch as the mystery of Lordship and the effulgence of the eternal vibrate within the very atoms of all created things" (Commentary on the Surih of Kawthar, 12).

Usuli school taught that for an individual to understand the application of Islamic law to the details of his own life, one must emulate and obey a high Shiʿi cleric, rather than rely on one's own independent thought and judgment. The consequence of this doctrine, as demonstrated by recent history, was the negation of the equality of human beings, negation of democracy, dependence of the masses on the clerical authority, brainwashing of the people, and an offensive assault on the humanity of the Other. However, at this same time, namely prior to the middle of the nineteenth century, the prophet of Shiraz emphasized the universal imperative of independent thinking as the prerequisite of the realm of religion, ethics, and mysticism. In what follows we examine some of the expressions of this rationalism in the writings of the Báb.

Equality of the Believers and Canceling of the Authority of the Clerics

The writings of the Báb eliminated the clerical institution and prohibited them from mounting the pulpit. In his Persian Bayan the Báb writes that the use of the pulpit is prohibited. Instead, all are commanded to sit on chairs, seats and the like, so that no one would be removed from the station of dignity. For the places of public sermon, the Báb says that a seat may be mounted on a throne so that all can hear the recitation of the divine words. He continues to say that the purpose of this law is this; that in the Day of the Revelation of the promised one, people would be honored by direct learning from that supreme source of knowledge. Then the Báb contrasts this ideal of direct learning from the prophet and his words, to the prevalent habits of the people of his time who, as the Báb says, desire to recognize the prophet through their reliance on the judgment of clerics whose source of knowledge is, in turn, their claim to have understood the words of some other people, who in the past have recognized the previous prophet! That is why, the Báb says, that they fail to recognize their Beloved.[13]

In the above pronouncement, the Báb is eliminating the basis of clerical authority. He prohibits ascending the pulpit, which is a symbol of the superiority of the clerics and a signal for their emulation by the people. He finds such ascent, as well as the seating of the people beneath the cleric, an

13 Persian Bayan 7:11.

insult to the dignity of all human beings. Equally important is the emphasis the Báb places on the idea that all people should investigate the words of the prophets for themselves and refuse to depend on the judgment of the clerics, whose source of knowledge is their indirect understanding of the words of other people who interpret the words of the prophet. According to the Báb all prophets are one and the same. The previous prophet now has appeared as the Báb, and people instead of learning directly from him and his words, ignore him and rely on the judgment and understanding of the clerics. This is the main reason that the people fail to recognize the truth. Understanding truth, therefore, is antithetical to the entire idea of clerical authority.

The writings of the Báb also prohibit congregational prayer which requires following the clerical leader of the prayer. According to the Báb, worship of God does not require human mediation, and all must engage in prayer with the purity of their own heart. Even when the Báb makes an exception in the case of the prayer for the dead, he emphasizes that no one should stand ahead of others. All must stand in equal rows to honor the deceased.[14]

Centrality of the Word and the Rejection of Miracles

One of the central teachings of the Báb is that miracles, as the breaking of the laws of nature, have no relevance to the mission of the prophet—which is the spiritual and moral education of humanity. Therefore, miracles cannot function as legitimate evidence of truth. The rejection of the obsessive Shiʿi preoccupation with miracles was intended by the Báb to remove a great obstacle against the progress of society towards rationalism and an emerging empirical foundation, and was intended to purify the realm of religion from superstition and a magical orientation. The greatest evidence of the presence of God, the Báb believes, is the beautiful order of the world and the laws of nature, not their interruption. Instead, the supreme miracle of God belongs to the realm of spirit, namely the divine words. The evidence of the truth of a prophet is the revelation of the creative word of God which unveils the requirements of the age, brings about a new culture and value system, and helps humanity to actualize its spiritual potentialities.[15]

14 Ibid., 9:9.
15 See for example: Persian Bayan 2:1, 2:14, 2:16, 6:8.

Reconstruction of Heaven, Hell, and the Day of Resurrection

One of the most significant expressions of the Báb's rationalistic teachings is the fact that he reinterprets all those traditional religious concepts that are opposed to reason, justice, and the nobility of human beings. Through his novel reinterpretations, those same concepts turn into evidence for rationalism, human dignity, and historical consciousness. One of the most important of these concepts is the prevalent idea about the Day of Resurrection, heaven, and hell. The common understanding of these issues is based upon a literal reading of the Qur'anic verses. This view finds society and history as static, opposes the requirements of reason, and negates the justice of God. This God loves to inflict eternal torture on humans who have committed some sins. Likewise, heaven is perceived primarily in terms of materialism and sexuality. It appears to be the fantastic projection of the basest physical dreams and desires of men.

The first point is that according to the Báb, heaven and hell are not confined to human beings. Instead, all things have their own heavens and hells. For all things, heaven, the Báb maintains, is the state of the realization of its own potential. Likewise, hell is the deprivation of a thing from realizing its perfection. The Persian Bayan believes that not only humans but also all beings in nature are manifestations of divine attributes. Consequently, all things are beautiful and sacred, and nature is also endowed with moral rights. All things yearn to attain the state of their own perfection, which is their paradise. Humans are obligated to help everything, including the realm of nature, to achieve its paradise. Thus, protection of the environment is a fundamental spiritual duty of all human beings. Two examples of this message follow:

> Rather, He hath commanded, in regard to each thing, that whoever possesseth power over anything must elevate it to its uttermost perfection that it wouldst not be deprived of its own paradise.[16]
>
> It is forbidden that one bring any object into being in a state of imperfection, when one hath the power to manifest it in full perfection. For example, should one build an edifice, and fail to elevate it to the utmost state of perfection possible for it, there would be no moment in the life of that edifice when angels would not beseech

16 Persian Bayan 4:11.

> God to torment him; nay, rather, all the atoms of that edifice would do the same. For each thing, within its own station, yearneth to attain unto the utmost height of excellence in its own level.[17]

In regard to human beings, paradise is the state of the realization of one's spiritual potentialities. Since humans are historical beings and since there is no end to their spiritual advancement, therefore, heaven and hell are also dynamic and historical phenomena. The Day of Resurrection is not the end of history. Instead, it is the day of the revelation of a new prophet of God who begins a new stage of development of human history. Living in accordance with new spiritual values implies resurrection from the graveyard of ignorance and stagnation. Those traditionalists who oppose the advancement of culture and history are depriving themselves and others from realizing their spiritual potentialities. This deprivation is hell itself. The Báb writes:

> That which is intended by the Day of Resurrection is the Day of the appearance of the Tree of Divine Reality... For example, from the inception of the mission of Jesus—may peace be upon Him—till the day of His ascension was the Resurrection of Moses... And from the inception of the Revelation of the Apostle of God—may the blessings of God be upon Him—till the day of His ascension was the Resurrection of Jesus—peace be upon Him—wherein the Tree of Divine Reality appeared in the person of Muhammad... And from the moment when the Tree of the Bayán appeared until it disappeareth is the Resurrection of the Apostle of God, as is divinely foretold in the Qur'án.[18]

Therefore, the new human-centered interpretation of the Day of Resurrection becomes an affirmation of the ceaseless advancement of human history, and a basis for the emphasis on human rights and the protection of the environment.

Reconstruction of the Concept of the Occultation and Return of the Imam

Another reflection of the creativity of the Báb is his new interpretation of the concepts of the Twelfth Imam, his occultation, and his return. Although

17 Ibid., 6:3.
18 Ibid., 2:7.

the prevalent and literal understanding of these ideas contradict both reason and ethical values, the Báb reinterprets the same ideas in ways that affirm rationality and the nobility of human beings.

Needless to say, the Báb considers himself to be the Return of the Twelfth Imam. However, as it is explicated in his later writings, by Twelfth Imam he means the common spiritual truth he shares with all other sacred figure of Islam. Yet, in one of his mystical works, Commentary on the Occultation Prayer, he provides an alternative interpretation for the occultation of the Twelfth Imam. This work of the Báb is a commentary on a prayer attributed to the Sixth Imam, called the Prayer of Occultation. This prayer consists of three sentences and the Shiʿa believers are encouraged to recite this prayer in order to hasten the return of the Twelfth Imam. The Báb interprets this prayer in a mystical and philosophical way. According to him, the Twelfth Imam, his occultation, and his return do not refer to any particular historical event, rather they are symbolic expressions of the dynamics of human self-alienation and self-consciousness.[19]

According to the Báb, God has created the primordial truth of human beings in the utmost state of perfection and nobility. This idea, namely the original spiritual perfection and powers of all human beings, is symbolically represented as the birth and the childhood of the Twelfth Imam. However, despite its potential nobility and glory, human beings in the course of their ordinary pursuits become preoccupied with selfish and materialistic concerns, forgetting their own spiritual identity and truth. This state of self-forgetfulness and self-alienation is symbolized by the idea of the occultation of the Twelfth Imam. The age of occultation is the age of tyranny and injustice because the essence of tyranny is none other than the negation of spiritual values and the reduction of self to the level of beasts. That is why the emancipation from tyranny and the realization of the age of freedom require the reawakening of human spiritual consciousness in such a way that one's potential spiritual powers become operative at the level of one's concrete life. This return to one's spiritual identity is symbolically presented as the return of the Twelfth Imam. For such overcoming of tyranny, it is necessary to engage in prayer, since the spirit of prayer is the dynamic of discovering the infinite within one's own finite reality.[20]

19 Saiedi, Nader, *The Phenomenology of Occultation and Prayer in the Bab's Sahifih-yi Ja'fariyyih*, 196–216.

20 The Báb, Commentary on the Occultation Prayer, 70.

EQUAL RIGHTS, SOCIAL JUSTICE, AND ETHICS

As Foucault has noted, in the past the social and cultural order was based upon the logic of resemblance.[21] In this logic, the relation between humans and God becomes the binding model of all social relations. For example, the relationship between slave owner and slave, between males and females, believers and infidels, religious leaders and their followers, and kings and their subjects were all reproductions of the relationship of God to human beings. Consequently, in traditional logic the notion of God was reduced to an instrument for the legitimization of all kinds of oppressive social inequalities. Needless to say, the worldview of religious clerics usually further strengthened this logic. The revolutionary worldview of the Báb, however, defines all beings as mirrors of divine attributes. The implication of this principle is that since the truth of all humans is the reflections of divine attributes, therefore, they are all equal, sacred, and endowed with rights. In other words, the Báb destroys the traditional logic of resemblance and replaces it with a new logic of equality and social justice.

Comparing the social rank of farmers with kings, in his work the Kitab al-Asma' (the Book of Divine Names), the Báb argues that *farmer/cultivator* is one of the supreme names of God. God is a farmer because he plants the seeds of his divine words in the hearts of human beings. Humans must purify the soil of their souls so that these seeds will yield fruit. He continues that since farmers, who are apparently the lowest rank in society, are a reflection of divine names, and since kings are also a reflection of divine names, therefore, people should treat farmers exactly in the same way that they treat their kings. Both are one reality and both are living by God's bidding. We can see that here the very notion of God turns into a powerful justification for social equality.[22]

Another expression of the same logic is the spiritual approach to language in the writings of the Báb. Mythological, authentic language is a system in which the name of anything unveils the truth of that thing. Of course, no real language can perform this function. However, the writings of the Báb indicate that in this age the truth of things should become manifest in their

21 Foucault, Michel, *The Order of Things*, 17–75.

22 The Báb writes: "Say! God verily cultivateth on earth as He pleaseth, at His bidding. Will ye not behold? Think ye that ye are the sowers? Say! Glorified be God! We are, verily, the Cultivators. Say! Gaze ye then upon all even as ye behold the most exalted of the renowned amongst you. Verily that which is shared by both the rulers and those who farm the lands is one thing: they all abide by the bidding of God." Kitab al-Asma', 383.

names. The solution of the Báb to this problem is that in thinking of anything, we should examine the alphabetical letters that constitute its name. We should then take each letter of that name as an abbreviation of one of the names of God. In this way we can see everything as the embodiment of various divine attributes. Everything becomes sacred and beautiful, because it is a reflection of divinity. Since the truth of everything is the reflection of divine names and attributes, we can remember the truth of things by just naming them. The Báb intends to create a culture in which people get habituated to seeing everything as wonderful and majestic. People should treat all beings with love and respect. The Persian Bayan gives the example of the word *sang* (a pebble or rock, consisting of the Persian letters, SNG) which is apparently devoid of any value. According to the Báb, one should see in the letter "S" the divine name *subbuh* (All-Glorious), and in the letter "N" the name *nur* (Light), and in the letter "K" (the Arabic equivalent of the Persian "G") the name of God *karim* (All-Bountiful). And so, all objects become beautiful and sublime:

> inasmuch as God hath commanded the people of the Bayán to elevate all things to their uttermost limit of perfection, He hath granted them permission to call everything, through the letters of their names, by the names of God, lauded and magnified is He, that none may see in anything aught save the Countenance of the Revelation of the Will, in Whom naught is seen but God. For example, the lowest rank in the mineral kingdom is that of the stone (sang, consisting of three Arabic letters s, n, and g). Then in its letter Sín (s) naught would be seen but the All-Glorious (subbúh), in its letter Nún (n), Light (núr), and in the letter Káf (k, g) the All-Bountiful (karím).[23]

Station of Women, Rejection of Patriarchy

Emphasis on the noble station of women and the necessity of treating them with respect and dignity is one of the teachings of the Báb. In one of his early writings the Báb defines the moral norm for treating women as "the utmost path of love," and affirms that hurting women even to the extent of a twinkling of an eye is a transgression from the command of God.[24] In the Persian Bayan, the Báb emphasizes that one should bring happiness

23 Persian Bayan 5:9.
24 The Báb, Sahifih-yi 'Adliyyih, 38.

and delight to the hearts of the people. However, he defines bringing joy to the hearts of women as twice as moral and of twice the spiritual significance.[25] However, perhaps the most important expression of the views of the Báb regarding women is the way he treated the revolutionary activities of his female disciple, Tahirih Qurratu'l-'Ayn. Both before and after the Conference at Badasht, Tahirih actively undermined traditional cultural structures, including the structures of patriarchy. Despite frequent criticism and resistance even by many followers of the Báb, the prophet continued to support her activities, and affirmed an extraordinarily high spiritual station for her. It was in the summer of 1848, in the village of Badasht at a conference of Babi leaders, that she undertook the historic mission of announcing the true claim of the Báb and the independence of the Babi religion from Islam. She declared the end of the traditional order by appearing without a veil in front of the Babi male participants at the conference, announcing that a new day and a new order had dawned in the world. Writing in the same year, the Báb in prison in Chihriq affirms the station of Tahirih in extraordinary ways, equating her station with that of all other seventeen male Letters of the Living combined.[26] These eighteen Letters of the Living are the first believers, the disciples of the Báb who occupy the highest spiritual station after the prophet himself. This new Babi culture which rejects the patriarchal culture turns into the principle of the equality of the rights of men and women in the subsequent Baha'i religion.

The Ethical Maxim: For the Sake of God

The writings of the Báb offer a universal ethical maxim. He says that human deeds should be done "for the sake of God and for the sake of his creatures." This ethical rule which has strong affinity with the moral maxim of Kant ("act on the basis of good will"), emphasizes that not only should actions be accompanied with purity of motive, but that acting for the sake of God is inseparable from acting for the sake of all the creatures of God. Human action should be motivated by the desire to serve the human race as well as all beings, rather than being a means for attainment of one's selfish desires.[27]

25 Persian Bayan 7:18.
26 The Báb, Commentary on Basmalah II.
27 Persian Bayan 7:2.

In one of his works, Fi al-Suluk ila Allah (On the Virtuous Journey Towards God), the prophet of Shiraz, in discussing this ethical principle, affirms two central points. First, he argues that acting for the sake of God is in fact an imitation of God's pattern of creative action. God's creative action is not caused by any particular need or selfish desire, rather it is an expression of his pure love and grace. Likewise, humans should follow the divine method and refrain from reducing their deeds to a mere instrument for the realization of their selfish desires. Second, the Báb states that the divine providence of God is universal, and it makes no distinction between believers and non-believers. Even when humans deny God, he continues to provide his bounties to them. According to the Báb, all should follow this same universal ethical model and treat believers and non-believers in the same way.[28]

Culture of Affirmation

One of the main aims of the Báb is the creation of a culture of affirmation in which all see themselves as responsible for the needs and welfare of all others. In his Persian Bayan, he writes that if one receives a letter, or is asked a question, one has to answer it in the most responsive way. He then says that one must go further, and insists that if someone is in need of something, even if he does not ask for help, one should respond to the call of his condition. All must feel obligated to answer the objective needs of all others. He writes:

> it is enjoined in this Revelation that should anyone receive a letter from any other, it is his duty to write him back... Likewise, should one's condition silently call upon others, it is the duty of men of discernment to answer his call. In like manner should one's place of

28 The Báb writes: "Be thou for God and for His creatures even as God hath been for God Himself and for His creatures. Just as God hath verily created thee out of nothing, in like manner must thou adore Him in utter devotion, for the sake of His Countenance, without desire for reward or fear of punishment. Act likewise in all conditions and with regard to all matters and phenomena. Shouldst thou unlock this gate to thy heart, thou wouldst assuredly be adorned with the virtues of the All-Merciful. Then, were all the people to wrong thee, thou wouldst forgive them and, indeed, do good unto them, even as God, glorified be He, provideth, through His grace, for those who have ungratefully repudiated Him. Thus, apply the same maxim with regard to all phenomena and matters." (Fi al-Suluk ila Allah)

> residence call for answer, or any other manifestation discernible to men of vision, it is binding upon them to reply, that at no time, no one may witness that which would cause him grief.[29]

This end, namely "that at no time, no one may witness that which would cause him grief," is one of the most important ethical and social principles of the Báb. It states that not only one should not cause sorrow and grief for others, but rather, one should bring joy and delight to the hearts of others. As the Báb says, "in the Bayán there is no act of obedience that ensureth greater nearness to God than bringing joy to the hearts of the faithful, even as naught yieldeth more remoteness than causing them grief."[30]

One of the various expressions of this culture of affirmation in the writings of the Báb is an emphasis on eradication of poverty, prohibition of begging and the duty to engage in work and employment. In his Arabic Bayan, the Báb emphasizes the social responsibility of the rich and the government to help the poor, while at the same time he prohibits begging. The Báb prohibits begging because he believes that begging degrades humans and deprives them of their nobility and dignity. Work is required from everyone. However, if one is unable to work due to some physical or mental reason, it is the duty of society to help him.[31]

Development and Modernization: Perfection and Refinement

Another manifestation of the nobility of human beings in the writings of the Báb is his frequent emphasis on the necessity of a spiritual reconstruction in the realm of the economy and industry. In works like The Persian Bayan, and The Book of Divine Names, the Báb commands that one has to perform his economic and industrial work in the utmost state of perfection. The Báb affirms that when one engages in productive labor in the highest state of perfection possible at one's level, one is acting as the image of God. The sacred and spiritual character of humans, therefore, must manifest itself at the most "materialistic" level of social life, namely in the realm of economics and work. This spiritualization of economic activities turns the

29 Persian Bayan 6:19.
30 Ibid., 7:18.
31 Arabic Bayan 8:17.

realm of economy into a moral domain. The imperative of seeking perfection in one's labor is the logical result of the Bab's concept of heaven and hell. (See p. 90.)

In the writings of the Báb, the idea of seeking excellence in work is inseparable from the imperative of refinement and beautification in all things. It is necessary to beautify the world for, as he says, no ordinance is more emphasized in the Bayan than the binding principle of refinement.[32] This beautification extends to all levels of human life beginning with physical cleanliness to the beautification of cities as well as the creation of art. Such beautification is a spiritual project which turns the material world to a mirror of the spiritual realm. The Báb wants to see that his followers reach the utmost state of excellence in the realm of industry, as well. For that reason, he praises Europeans for attaining a high degree of perfection in their production techniques. The Babis are asked to develop excellence and beautification in industrial work to the extent that among the faithful of the Bayan nothing may be seen except that it has attained perfection in its own station. Thus, according to the Báb, just as today the letters of the Gospel are distinguished among other communities in the art of ornament, the dwellers in the Bayan should become likewise.[33] That is why, while the Báb prays for the spiritual development of Europeans, he encourages Iranians to move toward excellence in their economic and industrial activities.[34]

In order to realize this industrial development as well as social justice, the Báb emphasizes the direct responsibility of the state and political rulers. For example, he states that kings must create a postal service and other means of communication throughout their realms. Yet he emphasizes that this service should become available to all people and not turn into a privilege for the rich and powerful.[35] Likewise, in one of his writings he discusses in detail the responsibility of kings to fight poverty, develop society, advance and perfect industry and the arts, encourage and sponsor scientific and industrial innovation, and to love people as they love their own dear ones. He says that the purpose of these duties is that nothing which may cause sadness to anyone would be observed in their kingdom. In that same work, the Báb says that the most beloved and the nearest of the rulers before God is the one who is the kindest and most compassionate to the people. At the end

32 Persian Bayan 6:3.
33 Ibid., 3:17.
34 Kitab al-Asma', 627.
35 Ibid., 4:16.

of his discussion, the Báb addresses the rulers and asks them to fear God and not desire for anyone that which they do not desire for themselves. He asks them to be watchful, that in their dominion there should not be found anyone who goes to sleep with an afflicted heart because of the rulers.[36]

CONCLUSION

In the short period of his mission (1844–50), the Báb confronted an avalanche of opposition and persecution, and yet he succeeded in producing, with amazing creativity and novelty, a myriad of works in relation to religion, mysticism, and social order. The worldview of the Báb offered a dialectical logic in the realm of religion and history, emphasized a historical consciousness, and promoted a rational, human-centered, and justice-oriented culture. It was the Báb who outlined the first holistic project of social reform in modern Iran. In this sense, he joins the example of the other Iranian prophet, Zoroaster. The fact that the most important work of the Báb, the Persian Bayan, is written in Persian demonstrates the fact that, while respectful of Islam, it (like the subsequent Baha'i religion) emphasizes Iranian spiritual ideas and in many ways celebrates Iranian traditions. For example, unlike many early Islamic high clerics who tried hard to define Naw-Ruz as a form of idolatry and fire worship, the Persian Bayan not only constructs the Babi calendar on the basis of a solar year, but identifies Naw-Ruz as the first day of the Babi New Year, considering it to be the most sacred day on the calendar.[37]

Likewise, every prophet of God is defined as 'the sun of truth," while fire, like the burning bush, is glorified as the symbol of the highest spiritual reality. The writings of the Báb, as in Zoroastrianism, define nature and its elements as sacred, even commanding the Babis to recite once a week facing the sun a short verse of exaltation, which is always identified as the supreme symbol of divine revelation to all beings.[38] Nor should it be forgotten that the emphasis of the prophet of Shiraz on human freedom is thoroughly compatible with the Iranian spiritual worldview. In the worldview of the Báb, the idea of the reform of Iran turns into a basis for the reform of the entire world, linking the love of Iran to the love of the whole of reality.

36 The Báb, Fi al-Sultah (Tablet on Sovereignty).
37 Persian Bayan 5:3.
38 See Saiedi, Nader, *Gate of the Heart*, 210–16.

BIBLIOGRAPHY

Amanat, Abbas. *Resurrection and Renewal, The Making of the Babi Movement in Iran, 1844–1850*. (London: Cornell University Press, 1989).

Báb (The). Commentary on Basmalah II. Archives of the Bahá'í World Centre.

Báb (The). Commentary on the Letter Ha', INBA 99:86–154.

Báb (The). Commentary on the Occultation Prayer. INBA 57:60–154.

Báb (The). Commentary on the Surih of Kawthar.

Báb (The). Fi al-Sultah (Tablet on Sovereignty), Archives of the Bahá'í World Centre.

Báb (The). Kitab al-Asma'. INBA 29.

Báb (The). Kitab al-Fihrist.

Báb (The). Fi al-Suluk ila Allah (On the Virtuous Journey Towards God). Archives of the Bahá'í World Centre.

Báb (The). Persian Bayan.

Foucault, Michel. *The Order of Things: An Archaeology of the Human Sciences*. (New York: Pantheon Books, 1970)

Hegel, Georg W. F. *Lectures on the Philosophy of Religion*. 3 Vols. (Berkeley: University of California Press, 1984–85).

Hegel, Georg W. F. *The Philosophy of History*. (New York: Willey, 1900).

Saiedi, Nader, 'The Phenomenology of Occultation and Prayer in the Báb's Sahíifiyi Ja'faríyyih' in *A Most Noble Pattern: Collected Essays on the Writings of the Báb*. Lawson, T. and Ghaemmaghami, O. (eds.) (Oxford: George Ronald, 2012), 196–216.

Saiedi, Nader. *Gate of the Heart: Understanding the Writings of the Báb*. (Waterloo: Wilfrid Laurier University, 2008).

3

The Shaping of the Babi Community

Merchants, Artisans, and Others

ABBAS AMANAT

Abstract: The early Babi community included a range of believers, often from underprivileged social groups, who sought in the Bab's movement new social bonds and a fresh social message in line with their religious quest and their secular discontents. Two groups in particular: the young students of the Shaykhi school, who were critical of the mainstream Shiʿi establishment, and a younger generation of merchants who were exposed to serious vacillations in the economic market, were in the forefront of movement. Other groups including lower- and middle-rank government administrators, petty landowners, villagers, and members of guilds also joined the nascent community from all over the country. As such the Babi movement was the first nationwide protest, and later revolutionary, movement in modern Iran. This chapter explores interactions between the religious and the secular as well as the appeal of the messianic thought within the social and economic context of the period.

In 1262/1846, Hajji 'Abd al-Karim Baghbanbashi, a Qazvini merchant of some substance, read to a gathering of Shaykhis a letter from his son, Mohammad Mahdi, in Isfahan. In this letter, to which he had attached a booklet containing extracts from the writings of the Bab, Mohammad Mahdi informed his father of the loss of merchandise during a journey to Bombay: "Five thousand tumans worth of silk that belonged to us, to my uncle, and to others, was totally sunk in the sea. Divers and rescue workers tried to salvage it, but with no success. However, God granted us an inexhaustible treasure of which not a particle will be lost if we consume till the Final Day. Here I send it to you to benefit and let others benefit without fearing of its exhaustion."[1] Mulla Ja'far Qazvini, who was present, relates that after reading the letter the weeping 'Abd al-Karim complained, "How on earth can this booklet provide money for the expenses of my family?"[2] Mohammad Mahdi's letter sums up the moral attitude of many Babi converts of the younger generation who, sometimes contrary to the wishes of their fathers, found in the new movement a message of salvation and moral renewal. For Mohammad Mahdi material loss in business became unimportant compared to his spiritual gains when he visited the Bab in Isfahan. Yet the new venture in which he had invested his faith and his means proved to be no less hazardous than the perils of the sea. Four years later he fought and died in the fortress of Tabarsi, together with other Babi mullas, merchants, artisans, and peasants who, like himself, looked upon the merchant of Shiraz and his mulla lieutenants as sacred models of moral perfection.[3]

THE CHANGING ECONOMY

In the early years of the movement, parallel to the conversion of the Shaykhi 'ulama, some progress was also made in converting members of the merchant class (*tojjar*). The conversion of the tojjar, predominantly from the lower ranks but also including some prominent merchants, and following them the conversions of members of the guilds (*asnaf*)—shopkeepers,

1 Qazvini, Mulla Ja'far, historical account published in *Tarikh-e Samandar va Molhaqqat*, ed. 'A. 'Ala'i, Tehran 131 Badi'/1975, 473–74. (Hereafter cited as *Qazvini.*)

2 Ibid., 474.

3 Ibid., 494; *Tarikh-e Samandar va Molhaqqat*, ed. 'A. 'Ala'i, Tehran 131 Badi'/1975, 158–59. (Hereafter cited as *Samandar.*)

wholesalers, and artisans—created the second largest group of believers after the ʻulama in the early Babi community. The Bab's emissaries also gained ground among other urban and rural groups: civil servants and local functionaries, court renegades and ex-officials on the fringe of the state establishment, Sufis and wandering dervishes in the cities, small landowners, semi-nomadic chiefs, and peasants in villages and small agricultural towns. The nationwide network that was thus created in a short span of time, often on the pattern of the existing Shaykhi network, witnessed to the effectiveness of the Babi message to remold groups with heterogeneous origins and persuasions into a dynamic community with a common loyalty and sense of purpose. At no other juncture in modern Persian history, at least since the suppression of the Noqtavis in the early seventeenth century, had a religious movement of protest achieved such a degree of popularity and social mobilization. After the failure of the Babi attempt, it took another half-century before a mass mobilization of any significance could unite people under the joint aegis of the ʻulama, the merchants, and the lay intellectuals.

In the conversion of merchants and the affiliated guilds at least two factors may be traced. First, the intercommunal bonds between this group and the ʻulama. The mutual links between the madrasa and the bazaar, a familiar feature of Persian urban life, were reasserted in a new context. Unlike their non-Babi counterparts, the Babi merchants did not look to the Babi ʻulama merely for protection and guidance, but rather tended to see themselves as equal partners in a joint undertaking. Second, for converts with similar professional backgrounds and similar ascetic and mystical preoccupations, Sayyed ʻAli Mohammad Shirazi presented a role model to whom they could look for moral inspiration, and with whose message they could identify themselves.

A number of questions arise concerning the motives of the merchants and guilds, and the nature of their involvement. To what extent did economic activities or occupational connections contribute to the shaping of the new affiliation? Bearing in mind the economic climate of the time, it is vital to see in the new movement a reflection of the growing aspirations, or the dissatisfaction, of the business community. To what extent did awareness of economic stagnation serve as an impetus for the renewal of messianic interests? Equally important are the aspirations of the converts and the way conversion affected the material well-being and social status of the new believers. Addressing these questions tests the validity of those interpretations that stress the role of the merchants and artisans, often merely as a mechanical response to the prevailing economic condition, almost to the exclusion of all other elements. To assume that the professional identity of these groups, and consequently the fluctuations in their economic fortune, were the only mobilizing forces behind their participation in the movement would be an oversimplification. Yet there is enough evidence to suggest that the parallel between the rise of the movement and changes in the economic conditions of the time was no coincidence.

The majority of tojjar converts had been brought up in families that were traditionally engaged in commerce. Either by means of inheritance or collaboration with senior members of the family, the new generation enjoyed the respect and social standing that usually accompanied a reasonable amount of capital in the form of the family business. Toward the end of the 1830s and in the early 1840s, when most of these younger tojjars, including the Bab himself, became active, the economy was in the throes of major change, particularly in sections of urban industry and trade.

In the early nineteenth century, a rapid increase in the volume of foreign trade, followed by a degree of internal security under the Qajars, brought about a commercial revival. The opening of new trade routes and a rise in the consumption of the home markets made it possible for the merchants to re-emerge as an influential group. Thanks to their professional bonds, internal and international contacts with colleagues at home and abroad, financial credit and relative immunity from government intervention, they seem to have prospered throughout the first third of the century.[4] By the mid-1830s, however, although commerce was still expanding, Persian merchants found themselves surrounded with unexpected difficulties, chiefly due to an increasing European presence. During this period the full impact of Western commercial domination, in terms of industrial superiority as well as political presence, made itself felt for the first time. Communities of local traders, craftsmen, and those engaged in small-scale urban industries began

4 Limited research has been carried out so far on the position of merchants in early Qajar Iran. Two examples are: G. Hambly, "An Introduction to the Economic Organisation of Early Qajar Iran," in *Iran* 2 (1964), 69–81, and A. K. S. Lambton, "The Case of Hajji 'Abd al-Karim: A Study on The Role of the Merchants in Mid-nineteenth Century Persia," in *Iran and Islam, in Memory of the Late Vladimir Minorsky*, ed. C. E. Bosworth (Edinburgh, 1971), 331–60. See also W. M. Floor, "The Merchants (*tojjar*) in Qajar Iran," *Zeitschrift der Deutschen morgenländischen Gesellschaft*, 129 (1976), 101–35, and *Cities and Trade: Consul Abbott on the Economy and Society of Iran, 1847–1866*, ed. Abbas Amanat (Oxford, 1983), xxxv–xi, and cited sources.

to suffer the effect of foreign competition. The rapid rise in the volume of European imports made Iran not only less self-sufficient, but susceptible to fluctuation in international trade.[5]

Trade in the south, which up to then had flourished through ports of the Persian Gulf, had begun to stagnate by the end of the 1830s, mainly because of the competition of the northwestern route. The decline of the southern trade, owing also to the insecurity prevailing in the region, piracy in the Gulf, remoteness from the markets of central and northern Iran, and the incompatibility of the prices of imports, jeopardized the business of many southern tojjar, forcing them to seek other exporting alternatives.[6] By the 1840s the southern trade began to suffer a serious setback. The import of cotton fabrics in particular, which in the early 1830s amounted to about two-thirds of the volume of Persian Gulf trade, was reduced to one-seventh of the total by the late 1840s.[7]

The competition of the trade centers of the north was not the only reason for this decline. Southern merchants were also faced with trade restrictions and high tariffs imposed by the British in India, particularly with regard to the import of opium, tobacco, and wool. Reporting on the plight of Persian merchants, the British consul in Tehran, Keith Edward Abbott, emphasizes: "If some of the few exportable productions which Persia possesses continue to be prohibited as returns for what she takes from India, there is no doubt that increased difficulties will attend the future prosecution of the trade; indeed they are already beginning to be experienced without any other cause being assignable than the gradual exhaustion of the country under the partial state of commercial restriction abroad, and the continual drain upon her of the precious metals."[8]

---

5 A. K. S. Lambton, "Persian Trade under the Early Qajars," in *Islam and the Trade of Asia*, ed. D. S. Richards (Oxford, 1970), 215–44. See also G. G. Gilbar, "The Persian Economy in the mid-19th Century," *Die Welt des Islams*, 19 (1979), no. 1–4, 196–211.

6 On the trade of southern Iran in this period see Lambton's "Persian Trade," 235, 239; J. B. Kelly, *Britain and the Persian Gulf* (1795–1880) (Oxford, 1968), 260–89, 343–53; *Lorimer Gazetteer* 1/2, 1956–59, 1976–81; Issawi, *Economic History*, 85–91; and R. T. Olson, "Persian Gulf Trade and the Agricultural Economy of Southern Iran in the Nineteenth Century," in *Modern Iran: The Dialectics of Continuity and Change*, ed. M. E. Bonine and N. R. Keddie (Albany, 1981), 173–90.

7 *Cities and Trade*, 86–89 (on Bushehr and Shiraz), 79–85 (on Yazd, Kirman, and Bandar 'Abbas), and the relative appendixes provide an account of the southern trade in the late 1840s. For a comparison with the 1860s see L. Pelly, "Remarks on the Tribes, Trade and Resources around the Shoreline of the Persian Gulf," in *Transactions of the Bombay Geographical Society*, 17 (1864).

8 "Report on Commerce," *Cities and Trade*, 89.

The volume of the Basra–Baghdad trade with cities in western and central Iran underwent similar crises. In addition to the frequent Ottoman attempts to redirect commercial vessels to the Ottoman port of Basra rather than Persian Mohammara, the insecurity on the western frontiers and the additional custom duty levied by the Baghdad government on exports to Iran[9] made it difficult for Persian merchants to operate successfully on this route.[10] Writing in 1843, Edward Burgess states that the Baghdad route is more competitive than any other trade route to Persia, yet due to a variety of obstacles such as the "disturbed state of the Arab tribes," which made the river navigation "dangerous and uncertain" and disturbed frontiers between Iraq and Iran, it is very doubtful whether this trade can survive.[11] The long, drawn-out dispute between the Persian and Ottoman governments frequently disrupted the normal flow of trade. The Ottoman authorities lost no opportunity to exert a "forcible interruption in the commerce of Mohammara,"[12] which served as a better alternative to Basra for long-distance merchants.

One example of these difficulties is revealed in the correspondence of Manuchehr Khan Mo'tamad al-Daula, the governor of Isfahan, Lurestan, and Khuzestan. In March 1845 he reports to Tehran that as a result of the recent Ottoman attack on Mohammara, some 200,000 tumans' worth of merchandise belonging to Persian merchants established in Iraq and Kermanshah was damaged and lost.[13] Shortly afterwards, Manuchehr Khan strongly objects to the measure taken by the Ottoman fleet in preventing the entry of commercial vessels to the port of Mohammara and forcibly redirecting them to Basra.[14]

In Baghdad itself, the discriminatory treatment of the Persian tojjar by Ottoman authorities put an extra burden on those who were already suffering from the insecurity on both sides of the border. The negligence of the Persian representative in Baghdad, plus the shortcomings of the central government to raise the matter with the Ottomans, made the Persian tojjar even more susceptible. Rawlinson, the British consul in Baghdad, reports:

9 F.O. 195/237, no. 22, 15 May 1844, Rawlinson to Canning.

10 An account of the trade of Baghdad and Mohammara in the late 1840s appears in Abbott's "Report on Commerce," *Cities and Trade*, 89–93.

11 Letters from Persia, 53.

12 F.O. 60/114, no. 611, 28 May 1845, Sheil to Canning, enclosed in Sheil to Aberdeen, 3 June 1845.

13 Manuchehr Khan Mo'tamad al-Daula, in reply to the inquiry of Comte de Meden (the Russian envoy) about the events in Mohammara. French translation enclosed in F.O. 60/ n 3, no. 25, 18 March 1845, Sheil to Aberdeen.

14 F.O. 60/ n 4, no. 61, supp. 3 June 1845, Manuchehr Khan to his agent in Tehran, translation.

"A strong feeling of dissatisfaction has long prevailed among the numerous and wealthy Persian community of Baghdad at the conduct of their national representative at this court. They allege, apparently with reason, that he is devoid of the local weight or influence necessary for the due vindication of the interest committed to his charge."[15]

The trade of northern and northwestern Iran, however, enjoyed greater prosperity. Thanks to the flourishing Russian trade through the ports of the Caspian, especially Barforush, Persian merchants as far as Kashan and Isfahan could export their products to the Caucasus and beyond. But the conclusion of the Treaty of Torkamanchay (1828) gave great commercial advantages to Iran's northern neighbor. As an outcome of Russian infiltration into Persian markets, by the late 1830s an increase had occurred in the volume of Russian imports.[16] More significantly, the reopening of the Tabriz–Trebizond route in the mid-1830s made the volume of the European imports grow even higher.[17] Irregularities in the price of imported goods,[18] and the arrival of European entrepreneurs as well as colonies of Greeks and Armenians in Tabriz acting as agents and factors to the European manufacturers, however, threatened Persian traders, who feared a complete takeover by their privileged foreign rivals. A series of Persian bankruptcies in the early 1840s and futile protests by the Persian merchants were the results of this unfair competition.[19]

Other economic problems contributed to the crisis as well. The constant drain of precious metals and the resultant scarcity of money, the rapid fall in

---

15 F.O. 195/237, no. 25, 29 May 1844 and 248/114, no. 28, 12 June 1844, Rawlinson to Sheil.

16 In the period under consideration, some details appear in: Lambton, "Persian Trade," 226–28, 240–41; M. L. Entner, *Russo-Persian Commercial Relations, 1828–1914*, University of Florida Monographs, no. 28 (1965), chapters 1 and 2, 1–38; F.O. Confidential Papers no. 136 (Persia): "Report by Consul Abbott of his journey to the coast of the Caspian Sea, 1847, 1848," in *Cities and Trade*, 11–14 (on Barforush), 19–21, 39–40 (on Astarabad); and various other reports by Abbott including F.O. 60/117 on trade of Tehran and Tabriz. Also, Issawi, *Economic History*, 142–46, and MacKenzie, *Safarnamih*, 80–102, 185–95.

17 C. Issawi, "The Tabriz-Trabzon Trade, 1830–1900: Rise and Decline of a Route," *International Journal of Middle East Studies* (1970), 18–27. Also, *Economic History*, 92–103.

18 Lambton, "Persian Trade," 241.

19 F.O. 60/107, "Translation of the Petition from the merchants of Tabriz to the Prime Minister of Persia presented at Tehran in November 1844," enclosed in no. 16, 25 November 1844, Sheil to Aberdeen. Also F.O. 60/107, no. 13, 1 July 1844, Bonham to Sheil; and F.O. 60/117, no. 3, 31 March 1845, Abbott to Aberdeen. For the discussion on this subject see W. M. Floor, "Bankruptcy in Qajar Iran," *Zeitschrift der Deutschen Morgenländischen Gesellschaft*, 127 (1977), 61–76.

the value of the tuman contrasted by a rise in prices and a ravaging inflation, the gradual accumulation of a vast deficit in Iran's balance of payments, a decrease in the international demand for certain Persian export products, the exaction of new limitations on Persian exports by neighboring countries, and the implementation of the Anglo-Persian commercial treaty of 1841, which provided extra commercial advantages for British subjects and their proteges, all had deleterious effects on Iran's fragile domestic economy. The amount of pressure exerted upon the economy, particularly in the sector of local manufacturers and local merchants involved in the distribution and export of their products, is most visible in the vulnerable textile industry. In the early 1830s, owing to the increased consumption of European goods, production of all sorts of Persian cloths declined in the domestic weaving centers. A considerable number of cotton-weaving workshops in Isfahan, Kashan, and other industrial cities, which had prospered in the earlier part of the century, were completely wiped out. A Russian regulation prohibiting the entry of silk piece goods into the Caucasus also contributed to the decline of silk weaving and other workshops dependent on their exports.[20]

By the mid-1840s, local manufacturers and distributors felt the full effect of this decline. The merchants of Kashan and Isfahan, who like their colleagues in Shiraz, Yazd, or Tabriz had been alarmed by the prospect of bankruptcy and loss of business, could do little more than express their discontent in the form of petitions and delegations to the state authorities, who were either unsympathetic or incapable of any effective measures. Abbott's March 1845 dispatch is one of many accounts documenting the unsuccessful attempts of Persian merchants and manufacturers to resist foreign competition. Reporting on Mohammad Shah's apparent lack of interest in a previous petition forwarded by the manufacturers of Kashan "praying for protection to their commerce which...[was] suffering in consequence of the introduction of European merchandise," the British consul continues:

> Deputations from the traders and manufacturers both of Kashan and Isfahan have however just arrived and though it is said their principal object is to complain of some Regulations of the Russian Government by which the entry into the Caucasian Provinces of silk piece goods having gold embroidery or figuring, the manufacture of the above

20 On the Russian commercial and customs policy in the Caucasus and the effects of the frequent closing of the border between the 1820s and 1880s see Entner, *Russo-Persian Commercial Relations*, 21–25.

> named towns, is prohibited, I understand they have also the intention of making observations on the injury which European trade has occasioned them. They say that in Fath 'Aly Shah's reign there were in Isfahan alone 2,000 looms in use in the manufacture of the above mentioned goods, but that in consequence of the increased consumption of European manufactures and the change in the fashions at Court, only a very few now remain of that number, and that these as well as the manufacturers of Kashan are threatened with ruin by the refusal of the Russian Government to admit the goods within its frontier. They represented this before to His Majesty when at Isfahan and they were promised that the matter should be made the subject of a communication to the Russian Minister but the restriction still continues.

Abbott also expresses concern at the grievances of the Tabriz delegate over the issue of Greek competition: "He can find no one to listen to him. The Prime Minister's aversion to business of any kind is too well known to leave him anything to hope for from that quarter, and the other Ministers will do nothing without a sufficient bribe. I should fear the present deputations had little chance of succeeding in the avowed object of their journey."[21]

From the 1830s onwards, most of the European observers noticed the sharp decline in the textile industry. Eugene Flandin, passing through Kashan in 1841, maintains: "If a few industries have still survived, the majority of them are unfortunately inactive only waiting to vanish altogether."[22] He states that the devastating effects of European competition were not solely the outcome of the incompatible prices or the low cost of British products, but also the deliberate trade policy of the British Government.[23] Changes in fashion, particularly among the women of the royal household, and Mohammad Shah's austere lifestyle and avoidance of silk and embroidered clothes in the style of his grandfather Fath 'Ali Shah, also affected the production of luxurious piece cloths.[24] With the production of cotton fabrics

21 F.O. 60/117, no. 3, 31 March 1845, Abbott to Aberdeen, Tehran. The Persian government however raised the matter with the Russian authorities, though not with much immediate success (F.O. 60/116, no. 127, 14 November 1845, Sheil to Aberdeen, Tehran, including translation of Hajee Meerza Aghasi's letter to Comte Meden).

22 E. Flandin and P. Coste, *Voyage en Perse de M.M. Eugene Flandin, peintre, et Pascal Coste, architecte, 1840–41*, 2 vols. (Paris, 1851) I, 267–68.

23 Ibid.

24 See Comte de Sercey, *Une Ambassade extraordinaire: La Perse en 1839–40* (Paris, 1928), 226–27.

hampered by foreign competition, the religious prohibition in Shiʿite fiqh on the use of pure silk dresses prevented manufacturers from turning to silk weaving as an alternative product for the home market.[25]

Ruination of domestic manufacturers, decline in the export of textile products, and diversion of trade from south to northwest were particularly felt in central and southern Iran, though merchants in the north did not remain untouched. Commercial communities in Kashan, Isfahan, Shiraz, and Yazd, as well as those in Tabriz and Qazvin, came under heavy pressure to adapt themselves to the prevailing conditions. The troubled years of the 1840s thus witnessed a transition in the Persian economy, with lasting effects. Many import merchants with larger capital and resilience managed to stay in business either by acting as wholesale agents and factories of European manufacturers or by gradually diverting to new exporting fields, most noticeably cash crops: tobacco, cotton, silk (before the 1860s), and opium. Export merchants, domestic distributors, and middle- and lower-rank manufacturers faced a harder choice. Tied to domestic products for which there was little demand, they could not easily be absorbed into the tight imports market. Some went bankrupt or withdrew from trade; others were reduced to mere petty traders and shopkeepers.

THE BABI MERCHANTS

Perhaps more than its immediate impact on the material well-being of the merchants, the message of this rapid, inexorable process of change was one of far-reaching decline. Without the logic of the modern mind, which makes a distinction between the sacred and the profane, for the Persian merchant of the period this growing awareness of material decline could only emerge within a religious frame of reference. The boundaries between material and spiritual were not, and perhaps could not have been, clearly drawn, and their correlation was subtle and complex. For a merchant of some sophistication who was acquainted with something beyond the parochial world of jurists and theologians, such an awareness was likely to bring about a crisis of values far broader than mere economic concerns. The sense of moral complacency

25 It was sometime later, during the first years of the reign of Nasir al-Din Shah, that Mirza Taqi Khan Amir Kabir encouraged the manufacturers of Kashan to overcome the religious restriction by introducing new mixed silk-cotton fabrics known as qadak and qatni. Sheil, *Glimpses of Life and Manners in Persia* (Note H., 378).

and religious superiority so apparent in members of the clerical class could more easily crumble for a merchant when the bare realities of his professional life forced him to recognize his material inferiority. For the older generation the set practices of religious devotion, professional fortitude, and godliness, for which they were known and of which they were proud, could still guarantee a reward, if not in this world at least in the hereafter. For the younger generation, however, facing the harsh realities of a changing world led to moral predicaments of a different nature.

Exposure to the world of scholastic learning had already transformed some younger individuals of unusual vigor into crossbreeds of mullas and merchants. Those who were inclined to Shaykhism and similar tendencies found it ever more gratifying to engage themselves, in conjunction with their business, in theological and mystical endeavors for which the esoteric discourses of Shaykhis and Sufis were the departure points. The outlook of these merchants, like that of the Bab himself, was no doubt profoundly pietistic, but it was not bound by the rationale of devotion for salvation. Nor was it petrified in the arid wilderness of principles of Osul or entangled in the tedious web of applied fiqh (foru‘). Shi‘ites, as their world view and frame of mind might have been, were able to carve for themselves an intellectual niche in the labyrinth of religious learning where they could erect an edifice of religiosity and messianic faith. These merchants on the fringe of the learned domain questioned the time-honored norms of the conventional mind and vigorously searched for new definition for the fundamentals of the faith. For them, as for their Babi clerical counterparts, acts of devotion or mystical experiences could only be meaningful if they carried a tangible message of comprehensive redemption. Such eschatological preoccupations, the reverse of the jurists' depersonalization of the Shi‘ite faith, became impregnated with expectations for a messianic figure who in character and aspiration would personify their moral ideals. Concern with resurrection was thus an attempt to bring about a new moral order that can translate the otherworldly promises to worldly realities.

Such aspirations are evident, albeit under a guise of unworldliness, in the careers of young Babi merchants. In Isfahan, Kashan, Tabriz, Yazd, and Shiraz, the same concurrence between material concern and messianic expectations can be observed. Sayyed Mohammad ‘Ali and Sayyed Mohammad Hadi Nahri Tabataba'i, two brothers from a well-established Shaykhi family of Isfahan who were known for their religiosity and social status, provide good examples. Their attention was first drawn to the new claimant, the Bab, when they were in the 'Atabat in 1260/1844. The Nahris' association with the Shaykhi community of the 'Atabat started with their father, Sayyed Mahdi, who emigrated from India to Najaf and later became a devoted adherent of Shaykh Ahmad Ahsa'i.[26] He gained a reputation as a religious benefactor by founding a number of charitable endowments, such as a caravanserai and public bath in Najaf, and constructing a channel to supply drinking water.[27] He invested the family fortune in land and property and acquired a number of shops in the area. Upon the Wahhabi invasion of southern Iraq, he returned to Isfahan, where he married a relative of Sayyed Mohammad Baqer Shafti.[28]

His son Sayyed Mohammad 'Ali, brought up in a devoted Shaykhi environment, joined the ranks of the 'ulama. He finished his primary studies in Isfahan, and later joined Sayyed Kazem Rashti's circle in Karbala'. His brother, Sayyed Hadi, though a Shaykhi, developed close relations with Shafti and later married his niece, Khorshid Baygom.[29] Later, Hadi also moved to Karbala', where he and his wife both attended Rashti's lectures.[30]

Like their father, the Nahri brothers represented an intermediary link between the 'ulama and the tojjar. Parallel to their enthusiasm for religious studies, Mohammad 'Ali and Hadi, as members of the Persian mercantile community of Iraq, were also conducting trade from their office in Baghdad.[31] Their brother in Isfahan, Sayyed Ibrahim, who was also involved in trade, probably acted in partnership with them.[32] The fortune they accumulated during the next few decades came not only from trade, but mainly from

26 Sayyed Mahdi's father, Hajji Sayyed Mohammad Tabataba'i of Zavareh, emigrated to India at the end of the eighteenth century and married into a wealthy Shi'ite family ('Abd al-Hamid Eshraq Khavari Nurayn-e Nayyerayn [Tehran, 123 Badi'/1967], 11–12, and Mazandarani [Fazel], Asadullah, *Ketab-e Zohur al-Haqq* vol. III. [Tehran, n.d. (1323 Sh/1944?)], 96 (hereafter cited as *Mazandarani*)). See A. Rafi'i Mehrabadi *Atashkadeh-ye Ardestan* (Tehran 1336 Sh/1957) for an account of the Tabataba'i Sayyeds of Zavareh (I, 166–206).

27 His surname, Nahri, is derived from the word *nahr* (channel, stream) because of his useful endowment.

28 Eshraq, *Nurayn*, 13–14. Both Sayyed Mahdi's wife and Shafti's wife were Shaykhi.

29 Later known as Shams al-Zuha. She was a devoted Babi and a companion of Qurrat al-'Ayn, who accompanied her on her journey from Baghdad to Qazvin. Both 'Abd al-Baha', *Tadhkirat al-Wafa'*, 268–90, and Eshraq, *Nurayn*, 41–52, give her biography.

30 Sayyed Ibrahim remained in Isfahan, presumably to look after the family business (*ZH*, 98).

31 Ayati Tafti, 'Abd al-Hosayn. *al-Kawakib al-Durriya fi Ma'athir al-Baha'iya*. 2 vols. Caurim 1342/1923–24. (Hereafter cited as *Kawakib*.) 410.

32 Ibid., 413.

their investments in land, agriculture, and property.[33] The pattern of collaboration between Sayyed Ibrahim and some of the religious figures in Isfahan suggests that the Nahris acted for a time as agents and bankers to such mojtaheds as Mohammad Hosayn Imam Jom'a and Shafti, who were always on excellent terms with them.[34]

Conversion to the new movement, however, brought about some dramatic changes in the life of the family. The two brothers had met Sayyed 'Ali Mohammad Shirazi during his pilgrimage in 1258/1842, and like many others, were impressed.[35] By the time the Bab announced his mission in Shiraz, Hadi and Mohammad 'Ali, who had probably heard of the new claims through Bastami, were among the first to give their allegiance. When they arrived in Shiraz, the Bab had already left for Hejaz.[36] On their return to Isfahan, they met Mulla Hosayn, whom they knew from the 'Atabat and to whom they declared their faith.[37] Later, in 1261/1845, they made another journey to Shiraz to pay a visit to the Bab.[38] Afterward, Mohammad 'Ali returned to Karbala'. Hadi, however, remained in Isfahan. As Shaykhi dignitaries, the Nahris were able to encourage others to give their support to the movement. Yet their brother, Sayyed Ibrahim, showed no great enthusiasm at this time.[39]

The family's economic condition was also affected by the new movement. After their conversion, the Baghdad trade was gradually liquidated, probably as a result of the economic stagnation in southern Iran and in particular the Baghdad trade. At the same time, the Nahris were gradually pulling out of business, devoting their time, money, and effort to the progress of the movement.

33 Ibid., 413 and Eshraq Khavari, 28.

34 *Kawakeb*, 413, and Nabil Zarandi, Shaykh Mohammad, *The Dawn Breakers: Nabil's Narrative of the Early Days of the Baha'i Revelation*, trans. and ed. Shoghi Effendi (Willmette, Ill, 1932), 208 (hereafter cited as *Nabil*).

35 Eshraq, *Nurayn*, 15–16, 31.

36 Ibid., 16, 31–32, 42–43 (citing from an autobiographical risala by Sayyed Mohammad 'Ali). Also, *Mazandarani*, 97, and *Kawakeb*, 410.

37 Eshraq, *Nurayn*, 31–32; cf. *Nabil*, 100.

38 Eshraq, *Nurayn*, 16, 32; cf. *Mazandarani*, 97.

39 *Kawakib*, 411. In a letter that is partly cited in Eshraq, *Nurayn*, 28–30, Qorrat al-'Ayn, writing in 1262/1846 to Sayyed Mohammad 'Ali, advised him to return from the 'Atabat to Isfahan and try to convince his elder brother of the truth of the Zohur. This attention to Sayyed Ibrahim is perhaps owing to his relations with the prominent 'ulama in the city. Later in 1263/1847 when the Bab was residing in Isfahan, the three brothers arranged for a feast in his honor at which Sayyed Mohammad Imam Jom'a, his brother Sayyed Hosayn, Mohammad Taqi Harati, Mohammad Reza Paqal'a'i, and others were present (ibid., 18–20, 28; cf. *Nabil*, 208–9).

The Nahris' preoccupation with messianic prophecies is evident in a number of inquiries that they made to Rashti prior to 1260.[40] In their correspondence with the Bab, they later asked about certain remarks in the first part of *Qayyum al-Asma'* regarding "the signs and the evidences" of the "pure religion."[41] Further, their inquiries on the esoteric meaning of prayers, intercession, and the angels of the grave witness their search for a more realistic interpretation of religious beliefs and practices. They also asked the Bab's view about those who prior to the Advent of the Qa'im preached his impending Zohur, a clear effort to link the Bab with Ahsa'i and Rashti. Quoting a Tradition attributed to 'Ali, they asked the meaning of bada' (change in God's intention, an issue of pivotal importance to Shaykhi theology)[42] in order to explain perhaps the incompatibility of the new revelation with the promises of the Shi'ite tradition. In reply, the Bab cited a verse from the Qur'an: "God blots out and he establishes whatever He will; and with Him is the Essence of the Book."[43] To justify bada' in the case of his earlier cancellation of the 'Atabat declaration, the Bab in effect goes against the deterministic bent of the Shi'ite prophecies. Such adjustment to the realities of the world, its perils and possibilities, must have been particularly appealing to his mercantile audience accustomed to change.[44] The Nahris further inquired about the meaning of the word *hojja* (proof) in the visitation prayer of the Seventh Imam, and the esoteric meaning of related Qur'anic verses. Acknowledging the seven evolutionary stages of divine emanation, the Bab emphasizes that God reiterated bada' in all seven Imams in the same way that He renewed His bada' in the case of the new hojja, the Bab. But in his case, he points out in his usual invocatory style, it is reason that determines human salvation: "My Lord! You know that I do not like any one to face your countenance except with the proof of reason. This is the status of man and by this the people of *Bayan* are distinguished from perplexed people."[45]

In the course of the next few years, the Nahris were instrumental in the

40 al-Qatil al-Karbana'i. "Risala." Published in Fazel Mazandarani, *Zohur al-Haqq*, III, appendix 2, 502–32, 516.

41 Letter in reply to the questions of Mulla Mahmud, Sayyed Mohammad Ali Nahri, and other believers, Iran National Baha'i Archive. Library and private photosat publications. (Hereafter cited as INBA), no. 91, XXXIII, 154–61 (156).

42 Ibid., 157.

43 Qur'an, XIII 39.

44 INBA, no. 91, 158.

45 Ibid. Also the Bab's letter in reply to questions asked by Mirza Mohammad Hadi and Sayyed Mohammad 'Ali Nahri, INBA, no. 91, XXXI, 152–53.

conversion of a number of believers from among merchants. Their pietistic approach to the Bab's message is best reflected in their opposition to Qorrat al-'Ayn's unveiling in the Badasht gathering. Yet it appears that Shams al-Zuha', Hadi's wife, held more liberated views. Her association with Qorrat al-'Ayn, and possibly her unveiling, may have aroused her husband's misgivings about the Babi heroine. Immediately after Badasht, Hadi was killed during a night attack in Niyala. Mohammad 'Ali returned to Isfahan. After the events of Tabarsi and the execution of the Bab, he remained largely inactive, though he remained firmly committed to his Babi and later Baha'i beliefs.[46]

Hajji Mohammad Reza Jawahiri, a young merchant in his twenties, was also converted when the news of the appearance of the Bab first spread to Isfahan. Like many other mystical experiences of early Babis, Mohammad Reza's recognition was preceded by a dream in which he had visited the Imam of the Age at the time of his pilgrimage to the shrine of Hosayn. This dream, as he himself related, inspired him to pursue the Imam in the world of reality. Like the Nahris, he also conducted trade through the Baghdad route, and enjoyed inherited wealth. After his conversion, his new commitments not only cost him financial loss and finally bankruptcy, but the hostility and antagonism of his relatives. He was arrested for a brief period in 1266/1850 and jailed in Tehran prison before an Armenian merchant paid for his freedom. Two years later he was arrested and executed in Tehran together with a few other Babi merchants.[47]

There were Babi converts in other commercial centers. One of the most celebrated was Hajji Mirza Jani (sometimes called Parpa), a young merchant from Kashan who is mostly known for his authorship of the important historical account, *Nuqtat al-Kaf*.[48] He was first attracted to

46 Two of Sayyed Ibrahim's sons, Sayyed Hasan and Sayyed Hosayn Tabataba'i, faithful followers of Baha'u'llah, continued with the family trade in Isfahan, where they ranked among the well-known merchants in the 1860s and 1870s. They continued their collaboration with the imam jom'a, which brought substantial benefits for both parties. However, the excessive debts of the imam jom'a to his creditors and partners finally persuaded him to join the powerful mojtahed of the city, Mohammad Baqer Najafi Esfahani (Aqa Najafi), in issuing a condemnation of the Tabataba'is' heretical beliefs and demanding their death. The fatwa was finally confirmed by the governor, Zell al-Soltan, and the two brothers met their death in 1296/1879 (Eshraq, *Nurayn*, 52 ff); Wills, *Land of the Lion and Sun*, 153–56.

47 *Mazandarani*, 101–3; cf. Browne, Edward, (ed.), *Nuqtatu'l Kaf* [*Nuqtat al-Kaf*] *Compiled by Hajji Mirza Jani of Kashan* (London and Leiden, 1910), xv, 111–12 (hereafter cited as *Nuqtat al-Kaf*).

48 For further details on the account and its authenticity, see bibliography.

the Bab when, in 1844, he met Mulla Hosayn in Kashan. Mirza Jani's earlier enthusiasm originated in the admiration he felt for the eminent Shaykhi leaders, rather than in a systematic study of the Shaykhi doctrine. "Although because I had not studied the principals of the sciences [of religion]," he writes, "I was not formally affiliated to this highly elevated order [Shaykhism], yet in my inner self I adored the excellencies the two illustrious babs [Ahsa'i and Rashti], and therefore was attached to their sympathizers."[49] His preoccupation with Zohur is not inseparable from his sectarian sympathies: "I visited the holy shrines of Karbala' and Najaf shortly after the death of Hajji Sayyed Kazem [Rashti], and learned from his disciples that during the last two or three years of his life he had spoken in the lecture room and pulpit of little else but the approaching advent of the promised Proof, the signs of his appearance and their signification, and the attributes by which he would be distinguished, declaring that he would be a youth of the clan of Hashim, untaught in the learning of men."[50]

At the time of the Shaykhis' retreat in Kufa,[51] Mirza Jani must have been present in the 'Atabat.[52] Considering his commercial links with Baghdad, it is not unlikely that he was in contact with the Shaykhi community there, and therefore was aware of the developments within the circle. Mirza Jani's younger brother, Hajji Mirza Mohammad Isma'il Kashani, known as Zabih, also acknowledged Ahsa'i and Rashti.[53] In his *Masnavi*,[54] Zabih stresses the spiritual insight that enabled the Shaykhi leaders to unveil the truth of the forthcoming Zohur. The author's anticlerical feelings are evident:

49 *Nuqtat al-Kaf*, 102.

50 Browne, Edward G. (ed. and trans.), *The New History (tarikh-e-jadid) of Mirza Ali-Muhammed the Bāb* by Hosayn Hamadani (Cambridge University Press, 1893, rep. 1975) (hereafter cited as *New History*), 30.

51 See Amanat, Abbas, *Resurrection and Renewal: The Making of the Babi Movement in Iran 1844–1850* (hereafter *RR*), chapter 4.

52 *New History* 30–33, 39 and Browne's introduction, xiv–li.

53 This title, apparently bestowed on him by the Bab, alludes to the tale of Ibrahim's offer for the sacrifice of his son Isma'il in Qur'anic stories. He also sometimes refers to himself by his other pen names Fani and 'Aref. Later, the title of Anis was conferred upon him by Baha'u'llah in the tablet of Ra'is. (Mirza Abul-Fazl Golpayegani, *Risala Eskandariya*, in reply to A. Toumansky [Cairo, 1318/1900], also partly cited in Zapiski of the Oriental Section of the Russian Imperial Archaeological Society (1893–94), 33–45, and translated by E. G. Browne in *New History*, xxxiv–xlii [xii]. Reference to Anis appears in Baha'u'llah Majmu'a-yi Alwahi Mubaraka [Cairo 1338/1920], "Lauh-i R'ais" [Arabic], 90.)

54 For details of the *Masnavi* see bibliography.

> The ʻulama of the time are the false lights. They are obstacles to the appearance of the sun, for this reason, the sun of universe ordered: "Unveil the curtain from his face."
>
> The emergence of the Shaykh [Shaykh Ahmad] and Kazem [Sayyed Kazem] disclosed all the hidden veils.
>
> They lifted the false curtain from the face of the truth, therefore the ʻulama became their enemies, and prevented people from understanding.[55]

Nuqtat al-Kaf and the *Masnavi* of Zabih show certain similarities that in turn suggest their authors' common intellectual background. *Masnavi*'s clear mystical influence is evident not only in the style of the poetry and the extensive usage of Sufi vocabulary but in its treatment of the Bab's (and later Baha'u'llah's) spiritual status. The same influence is evident in the introduction of *Nuqtat al-Kaf*, which gives a Shiʻite-Sufi justification of the Bab's revelation.[56]

The origins of this mystical interest must be traced back to Shaykhism. Yet a Sufi connection, particularly through the study of classical texts and possible contact with dervishes, cannot be ruled out. Mirza Jani sometimes refers to dervishes who accompanied him on his journeys in Iran and Iraq, both for the purpose of trade and later for visiting the Babis in other cities.[57] Indeed, the pantheistic tone and narrative style of both *Nuqtat al-Kaf* and *Masnavi*, as well as Mirza Jani's interpretation of the signs of Zohur, betrays mystic influence.[58] This influence must have been reaffirmed by the writings of the Bab and later by the pantheistic ideas current in Babi circles.[59] In the early phases of the Baha'i thought, Zabih too must have shared the mystical bent of its founder.[60] It is difficult to imagine that such a tendency could have been developed without a previous knowledge of Sufi terminology

55 *Masnavi*, 68 a.

56 *Nuqtat al-Kaf*, 1–98 (particularly 86–98).

57 Fo'adi Boshru'i, Hasan. *Tarikh-e Diyanat-e Baha'i dar Khorasan*, eds. Minou Fo'adi and Fereydun Vahman, ʻAsre Jadid, Darmstadt, 2007. (Hereafter cited as Fo'adi) 54.

58 For Sufi messianism see *RR*, chapter 2.

59 N. K., 252–63, gives a good example of the prevailing Babi views after the execution of the Bab. The authenticity of the section in N. K. is questioned by H. M. Balyuzi (*Edward Granville Browne and the Baha'i Faith* [London, 1970], 42–48), yet it could still be regarded as a sample of the current tendencies.

60 In his *Masnavi*, Zabih refers to his visits to Baha'u'llah on several occasions. He met him first in Baghdad in 1265/1849–50 (39b), and in 1270–1271/1853–1854 (41a–b). In 1285/1868, he met Baha'u'llah in the port of Gallipoli and accompanied him to his new exile at ʻAkka (Acre) (46b–54a). He gives a vivid picture of Baha'u'llah and the evolution of his ideas.

and content, however. Zabih's *Masnavi* seems largely inspired by the *Masnavi* of Jalal al-Din Rumi; it is divided into seven books (compared with five of Rumi's) and in many parts has clear signs of the allegorical stories and parables of the above work. The style of *Nuqtat al-Kaf*, however, is in some parts reminiscent of such Sufi biographical works as Farid al-Din 'Attar's *Tadhkirat al-Awliya'*.

This mystical tendency laid the foundation for the reshaping of eschatological expectations. The sense of awe and respect for Shaykhi leaders gradually turned into a sense of anticipation for the promised one. For Zabih as for his brothers, the Advent of the Imam was primarily defined in terms of the Shi'ite expectation, but it also benefited from the concept of the Perfect Man. In a passage of the *Masnavi* that is reminiscent of the Shaykhi visitation dreams, Zabih describes a vision of the Lord of the Age. After a long and laborious vigilance, Zabih became aware of the material existence of the Imam, whom he is able to visit later in reality in the character of the Bab:

> Twenty years ago, in the state of *khalsa*,[61] I saw that perfect countenance.
>
> From then onwards, in order to come to his presence, I sought for Sahib al-Zaman [the Lord of the Age]
>
> Because I was aware that the lord of the universe is alive, therefore I sought for his visit... Whether it was a vision or a dream, I cannot say what state I was in, I only know that I saw him, twenty years prior to his Advent.[62]

In 1263/1847, when the Bab was passing through Kashan on his way from Isfahan to Tehran, Zabih expresses his own eagerness for visiting the Bab in the form of another anticipatory dream:

> Before "the lord of the people" sets out for Kashan, every day and night, I prayed to God for the honor of his sight.
>
> One night, I had a serene dream, that his excellency, who resembles the sun, shone in Kashan.
>
> Next morning, I said to my brother, that soon the sublime sun will rise.
>
> He said, there is no news of him in the whole world. I briefly

61 *Khalsa* is a state between sleep and wakefulness in which the soul witnesses the occurrence of certain matters in advance. Tahanawi, *Kashaf*, 597.

62 *Masnavi*, 2b–3a.

> replied: "He will come today." It so happened that his excellency arrived the same day, shining like the sun.[63]

It was the Bab's visit to Kashan that brought to the surface the devotion of the Kashani brothers.[64] They arranged several meetings between the Bab and some sympathizers among the Shaykhi 'ulama and tojjar. The Kashani Babis also offered their assistance to the Bab to be rescued from the government escort that was taking him to the capital. Zabih, in conformity with the other believers, declared that they were ready to provide the necessary means for his escape: "and we will attend and accompany you wherever it be; for we will thankfully and gladly give up our lives, our wealth, our wives, and our children for your sake."[65] The Bab's response to this offer was his usual unwillingness to take any violent action lest such action would ruin his dim chances of coming to terms with the government: "We need the help and support of none but God, and His will only do we regard."[66]

The Bab's reluctance did not turn the Kashani brothers away. Over the next few years, their growing adherence to the movement lessened their popularity in Kashan and harmed their good name as honest and forthright merchants:

> About 'Aref [Zabih] and Hajji [Mirza Jani] people believed that "these youths are the most pious people of the time.
>
> Both brothers are generous and openhanded, not even for one moment did they ignore the name of God...
>
> Both are crusaders [mojtahed] for the truth, they never search in the world for anything but the truth."
>
> Then the ignorant ones said, "It is a pity that these two, in spite of all their invocations and prayers, abandoned their faith and became infidels.
>
> They became Babi and shunned the truth.
>
> They deserted their forefathers' religion, and became alienated with their own souls."[67]

63 Ibid., 2b.

64 In addition to other well-known sources, such as *Nabil*, 217–22 and N. H., 213–16, the account of the Bab's abode in Kashan is also described in *Masnavi*, 3a–4b, and Nateq Esfahani, *Tarikh-e Amri-ye Kashan*, 14.

65 *New History*, 216. A similar account appears in *Masnavi*, 2b.

66 Ibid.

67 *Masnavi*, 152a.

Despite mounting criticism and open hostility, especially after 1265/1849, both brothers remained "the slaves of [the Bab's] threshold."[68] Zabih refers to his brother as "a lost-hearted Hajji, who was ready to sacrifice his life"[69]—an aspiration that soon turned into reality. After the unsuccessful attempt on the life of Nasir al-Din Shah in 1268/1852, together with many other Babis, he was arrested in the shrine of Shah 'Abd al-'Azim near Tehran, where he probably compiled his historical account. Soon, however, the sanctuary was invaded, and he was taken by government agents to the Anbar dungeon, to be killed shortly after by Aqa Mahdi Malik al-Tojjar and other merchants of Tehran—a highly uncharacteristic brutality to be committed toward a fellow merchant.[70] Zabih remembers his brother's death in the following words:

> That lover of the truth, the adorer of the *Rabb-e A'la'* [the Bab]
> He dedicated his possession and his life in the path of his Lord...
> He was finally taken to the dungeon of oppression, and then they strangled him with a piece of rope.
> No man the like of that devoted man ever came to this world.
> His death burnt the heart of sorrowful Zabih.
> A mystic like him the world never witnessed, he finally was martyred in the path of truth.
> His name would remain in the book of lovers, his soul would ascend to Heaven.[71]

The Shaykhi merchants of Isfahan and Kashan were not the only converts in the tojjar ranks. In Qazvin the Farhadis were among the first who supported the new cause, as early as 1261/1845.[72] Prior to 1260, two brothers of Azarbaijani origin, Hajji Allah-Verdi Farhadi and Hajji Asadullah Farhadi, who had been engaged in the internal trade between

68 Ibid., 2b.
69 Ibid.
70 An account of the execution of Hajji Mirza Jani appears, in among other sources, *Vaqayi'-i Ittifaqiya* no. 82 (10 Zu al-Qa'da 1268/26 Sept. 1852); also cited in *Shohada-ye Amr* III, 271.
71 *Masnavi*, 29a. On the Kashani brothers: Golpayegani, *Kashf al-Ghita'*, 42–45, and *Nuqtat al-Kaf*, 113, 120–24, 259, 175–76 and 198. Besides references in *Masnavi*, both *Samandar* (222–23) and *New History* provide further information on Zabih.
72 Information on the Farhadis in *Samandar*, *Mazandarani*, and *Kawakib* are based on the recollections of Aqa Mohammad Jawad Farhadi. *Qazvini* and *Nabil* provide further details. Accounts on Qorrat al-'Ayn also have references to the Farhadis.

the Caspian ports and Yazd, had established themselves in Qazvin.[73] The fortune they accumulated in the silk trade brought them affluence and was one reason for their social distinction. Their religious affiliation, on the other hand, made them chief defenders of non-orthodox cause.[74] Whether it was due to their previous acquaintance with Ahsa'i or their association with 'Abd al-Wahhab Qazvini,[75] the Farhadis became devoted Shaykhis and on Ahsa'i's last visit to Qazvin, around 1235/1819, played host to him.[76] In the tense struggle for religious control of Qazvin, the Farhadis were in 'Abd al-Wahhab's camp, and thus in opposition to Mulla Mohammad Taqi Baraghani.

What other elements beside personal affection for Shaykhi leaders attracted merchants like the Farhadis to Shaykhism? Above all, the Shaykhis were critical of the vigorous participation of prominent mojtaheds in economic life. By the 1840s, the economic power of high-ranking Usuli 'ulama, either by direct investment or by other means such as expropriation of endowments or exorbitant commissions from commercial contracts, had reached such a point that merchants, especially those who lacked reliable ties to mojtaheds or could not afford their high fees for protection and legal backing, sought an alternative clerical body in Shaykhism. On a few occasions, for instance, Mulla Mohammad Taqi Baraghani's controversial verdicts on transactions and contracts annoyed merchants of Qazvin, who protested against his shady practices.[77]

Moreover, it is possible that Shaykhism was more lenient toward certain forms of interest taking; a practice that was later legalized by the Bab. But primarily, it was on moral and intellectual grounds that Shaykhi mullas were deemed superior. The conduct of some Usuli mojtaheds, on the other hand, was deplored not only because of their assumed corruption and profligacy but because they were viewed as narrow-minded and intellectually sterile. They were frequently criticized for their rigidity and lack of interest in matters beyond trivial details of fiqh.

73 *Mazandarani*, 372, and *Samandar*, 91.
74 *Nabil*, 165. Allah-Verdi was known in Qazvin for his holy dreams.
75 For 'Abd al-Wahhab see *RR*, chapter 7. Also Tonkaboni, Mirza Mohammad ibn Solayman, *Qisas al-Ulama'*, Tehran 1304/1886, 2nd ed, Tehran, n.d., 22–24, 35 (hereafter cited as *Qisas*); Tehrani, Agha Bozorg (Mohammad Muhsin), *Tabaqat A'lam al-Shi'a* (in 3 parts) Najaf 1373–88/1954–68), II/2, 809–12 (hereafter cited as *Tabaqat*). Tehrani points out that Tonkaboni's doubts on 'Abd al-Wahhab's qualifications for ijtihad are baseless.
76 *Kawakib*, 95.
77 *Qisas*, 24, 32–33.

The polarization of the Qazvin community into two camps inevitably drew the Farhadis further into a confrontation. In the elder generation, opposition to the Usuli jurists was expressed in terms of moral and financial support for the Shaykhi leaders; in the younger generation it turned into a more militant approach. It is not a coincidence that animosity between the two sides intensified at a time when the decline in the southern trade, particularly the fall in demand in the Indian market for Persian silk and ensuing restrictions, made the tojjar more dependent on their agricultural and urban holdings in Qazvin, a source of revenue that possibly caused friction with Mohammad Taqi Baraghani.

After the death of Allah-Verdi Farhadi in 1844, his four sons, who had married the four daughters of their uncle, Haji Asadullah, continued the family business in collaboration with him.[78] The news of the proclamation of the Bab came through Hajji Mirza Mahmud, a merchant from Shiraz. He visited Qazvin after his pilgrimage of Hajj, during which he traveled with the Bab in the same boat.[79] Enthusiasm for learning the identity of the Lord of the Age encouraged Hajji Asadullah to dispatch Mulla Jawad Valiyani to Shiraz.[80] Afterward, when 'Abd al-Jalil Orumi, a Letter of the Living, came to Qazvin, the Farhadis became fully converted to the Bab.[81] In the course of the next few years, they were in the center of Babi activities and played host to many Babi missionaries. In moments of need, they also gave them financial help.[82]

The second of the four brothers, Aqa Mohammad Hadi Farhadi, gradually emerged as one of the leaders of the Qazvin Babis.[83] This was in part due to the changing religious climate in Qazvin. Mulla 'Abd al-Wahhab, who was then in his seventies, remained undecided over the Bab's claims. Despite his sons' attempts to convince him, he never publicly endorsed the Bab.[84] The task of the protection and security of the Babis thus inevitably transferred to persons who had the courage and the means of defying the opposing 'ulama. In the face of mounting hostility in 1263–64/1847–48, the Farhadis used all they had at their disposal, including their money and

78 *Samandar*, 91–92, 229–31.

79 *Mazandarani*, 372, citing Aqa Mohammad Jawad's notes.

80 Ibid., citing the same source. For Valiyani see *RR*, chapter 6.

81 Ibid., citing the same source.

82 *Samandar*, 353.

83 The eldest of the four, Mohammad Rafi', who was a resident of Yazd, was not a Babi. The other two were Mohammad Mahdi and Mohammad Jawad.

84 *Qazvini*, 494–95.

their connections with the artisans and the lutis, to defend themselves and their fellow Babis. Shortly after the return of Qorrat al-'Ayn and her companions to Qazvin, the departure under duress of Mulla 'Abd al-Wahhab for the 'Atabat left the stage clear for Mohammad Taqi to attack the Babis from the pulpit, denouncing them as infidels and religiously unclean.[85] Violent clashes and physical attacks on the Babis followed the verbal onslaught.[86] When 'Abd al-Jalil Orumi, who was preaching in Qazvin under the protection of the Farhadis, was attacked by the mob and dragged to the madrasa of Mulla Mohammad Taqi to be bastinadoed in his presence, Mohammad Hadi, his brother Mohammad Jawad, and their supporters climbed over the walls of the madrasa and rescued him.[87] Earlier, in 1263/1847, when the Bab was passing through Miyana on his way from Tehran to Azarbaijan, Aqa Mohammad Hadi and a group of his followers offered to rescue him. But as on other occasions, the offer was turned down.[88]

In the next two years, as the Bab in his isolation in the fortress of Maku and Chehriq was more and more cut off from his adherents, the Babis turned more toward a militant and uncompromising struggle. Aqa Mohammad Hadi, preparing for the jihad, set up a workshop in the basement of his house to produce swords, and distributed them among the followers.[89] When Vabid Darabi, who appears to have been experienced in warfare, arrived in Qazvin that year, Aqa Mohammad Hadi even arranged for training sessions in his house.[90]

The assassination of Mulla Mohammad Taqi in the middle of 1263/1847 brought the conflict to its peak. As we have seen, Mohammad Hadi may have assisted the assassin. Consequently, the Farhadis came under strong suspicion and were accused of being the chief instigators and accomplices in the crime. Riots broke out in the city and the house of the Farhadis was twice sacked by the mob. Hajji Asadullah and one of his nephews, Mohammad Mahdi, were arrested and detained in the government house, together with

85 Mulla 'Abd al-Wahhab died in Moharram 1264/Dec.-Jan. 1847–48 in the Atabat (*MAV*, 1736).

86 *Samandar*, 351–52, and *Qisas*, 56–57.

87 *Samandar*, 352; cf. *Mazandarani*, 347–48, citing Mohammad Jawad Farhadi.

88 K. D. I., 95–96, and *Mazandarani*, 374. According to *Nabil* (235) and *Samandar* (97–99), an earlier meeting took place in Siyah Dihan (a village southwest of Qazvin) between the Bab and some of the *Qazvini* and Zanjani followers. Mulla Ja'far Qazvini and others met the Bab at other stages in the villages around Qazvin (*Qazvini*, 479–80).

89 *Mazandarani*, 374, citing Mohammad Jawad.

90 Ibid.

seventy other Babis.[91] Later, at the insistence of Mohammad Baraghani, husband of Qorrat al-'Ayn, who now succeeded his father, Hajji Asadullah and other Babis were sent to Tehran where he soon died in prison.[92]

Mohammad Hadi avoided certain arrest and persecution by escaping to Tehran in disguise, but daringly returned to Qazvin in the disguise of a Yazdi caravaneer to rescue his younger brother from government detention.[93] The rescue of Qorrat al-'Ayn was more difficult. She was under strict surveillance in her father's house, guarded by trusted women of the household and a group of lutis at the gate.[94] Mohammad Hadi, in collaboration with Baha'u'llah, drew up a plan for her rescue. Aqa Mohammad Hadi's wife, Khatun Jan, disguised as a laundress, smuggled a message to Qorrat al-'Ayn. Aqa Hasan Najjar, a carpenter, and Vali and Qoli, both lutis, helped Mohammad Hadi to free Qorrat al-'Ayn by night, and the party rode all the way from Qazvin to Tehran without the Baraghanis being able to stop them.[95]

The escape of Qorrat al-'Ayn was a blow to Mulla Mohammad and the rest of the Baraghanis. For the third time *tollab* (seminary students) and lutis sacked the house of the Farhadis. Fearing for their lives, Khatun Jan and her three sisters, all admirers of Qorrat al-'Ayn, took refuge in the ruined tomb of Emamzada Ahmad outside the city for four months.[96] Mohammad Hadi accompanied Qorrat al-'Ayn on her journey to Badasht, but no further trace of him is found. He was probably killed in the Niyala incident.[97]

The other Babis of Qazvin were also persecuted. Their houses and properties were confiscated as a surety for payment of larger ransoms and they were either imprisoned or forced into exile.[98] But in spite of the harrowing experiences of 1848, the spirit of dissent persisted, and even intensified. In a narrative written some years later, Hajji Mohammad Naser Qazvini, a domestic trader and one of Tabarsi's "Remnants of the Sword," after describing the Babis' sufferings in Tabarsi, concludes with a militant note undiminished by the emerging Baha'i moderation: "The opponents [of the Babis] who are still around would soon come out of their garb of Pharaonism and instead wear the cloak of poverty and misery so that this

91 *Samandar*, 92, and *Mazandarani*, 375.
92 *Samandar*, 230.
93 *Mazandarani*, 375.
94 *Samandar*, 362, and *Mazandarani*, 376.
95 *Samandar*, 363–66.
96 *Mazandarani*, 378–79, and *Samandar*, 369.
97 *Samandar*, 93, and *Mazandarani*, 337.
98 *Qazvini*, 486–88, and *Samandar*, 21.

pure land would be purged of these abominables and the tree of morality which is planted would bear fruit."[99] In the years ahead, his diehard Babi activism frequently exposed him to persecution and arrest on charges of conspiracy against the state.[100] Shaykh Kazem Samandar, Naser's partner in business, states that "because of successive persecutions his commercial affairs were completely disturbed."[101] In 1300/1882–83 he was again arrested in Rasht and died in jail.[102]

Shaykh Mohammad Qazvini (later known as Nabil Akbar), father of Kazem Samandar, another domestic merchant and a colleague, may not have matched Naser in radicalism but shared his aspirations. His father, Aqa Rasul, a devout Shaykhi residing in Karbala', was among those who met the Bab in 1258/1842.[103] Shaykh Mohammad, like the Nahri brothers, studied under Rashti and named his son Kazem after him. Returning to small-scale trade after his conversion,[104] his house was a center of Babi gatherings. In the aftermath of Mulla Mohammad Taqi's assassination, though he escaped persecution in his home town, he was later arrested in Tabriz, where he had temporarily sojourned, and was severely bastinadoed by order of Mulla Ahmad Mojtahed. Subsequently, he was bailed out by merchants sympathetic to his plight and, fearing the same fate in Qazvin, was helped to set up an office in the Tabriz bazaar.[105] About the same time, when he visited the Bab, presumably in Chehriq, Sayyed 'Ali Mohammad bemoaned the injury and indignity inflicted upon his follower and fellow merchant. "It was not you who was punished, it was me," he said.[106]

In Khorasan, some members of the local merchant community also joined the movement. Hajji 'Abd al-Majid Nishaburi perhaps is the most remarkable example. He was a dealer in turquoise and high-quality shawls,[107] and his father enjoyed prestige as the owner of the best-known turquoise mine in Nishapur.[108] Though nothing is known about any past connections,

99 Narrative of Hajji Mohammad Nasir Qazvini, appendix to *Tarikh-e Samandar*, 517–18. Only a portion of this account is now extant.
100 Ibid., 518–20, and *Samandar*, 215.
101 *Samandar*, 215.
102 Ibid., 216.
103 Ibid., 17–18.
104 Shaykh Mohammad, like most other merchants of Qazvin, was chiefly engaged in the distribution of raw silk (ibid., 24).
105 Ibid., 24–30.
106 Ibid., 30.
107 Fo'adi, 55, and *Mazandarani*, 162.
108 *Nabil*, 125.

his name appears among the first converted through Mulla Hosayn, when he was passing through Nishapur in 1846.[109] Not fully convinced of the validity of the Bab's claims, he embarked on a personal quest. After visiting the Bab,[110] he returned to Mashhad, where he continued his trade in luxury goods.

On the eve of the Tabarsi episode, 'Abd al-Majid accompanied Mulla Hosayn on his march to Mazandaran, and not only paid most of the expenses with valuable shawls and Nishapur turquoise, but also participated actively in the fighting of Tabarsi, although he was in his mid-fifties.[111] After the fall of Tabarsi, he was captured and brought to the city of Barforush together with Qoddus and the others. The prince commander, Mahdi Qoli Mirza, realized that 'Abd al-Majid, being a prosperous man, was too valuable to be slaughtered by the crowd, and saved his life.[112] Subsequently he escaped from the Tehran jail, after paying a ransom of a hundred tumans.[113] Returning to Mashhad, Hajji 'Abd al-Majid remained a devout Babi and later Baha'i. Some twenty-eight years after Tabarsi, in 1294/1877, he met his death, in his mid-eighties. Aqa Mohammad Baqer Najafi Esfahani (better known as Aqa Najafi),[114] the notorious enemy of the Babi-Baha'is, who had temporarily moved from Isfahan to Mashhad, put his seal of approval on the fatwa concerning his blasphemy, and after much controversy, the unrepentant 'Abd al-Majid was executed.[115]

Aqa 'Ali Reza Tajer Shirazi, a less conspicuous but more typical example of the Babi merchants of Khorasan, stood as an intermediary link between bazaar and madrasa. A merchant from Shiraz who had long settled in

109 Fo'adi, 55.

110 *Mazandarani*, 162.

111 Most of the Tabarsi accounts, including Tarikh-e Mimiya, narrative of Mirza Lotf 'Ali, and Nabil, refer to his role as the treasurer of Tabarsi.

112 Zavarehi, *Tarikh-e Mimiya*, 109.

113 *Samandar*, 175, and Malek Khosravi, *Tarikh-e Shohada-ye Amr* II, 75.

114 Shaykh Mohammad Baqer Esfahani (son of Shaykh Mohammad Taqi), better known as Aqa Najafi, was the inheritor of his father's clerical fame and the founder of the Najafis' financial power (*Tabaqat* 1/1, 198–99, 247–48 and Il/1, 215–17). The wealth and the influence of the Najafis and their dispute with the governor of Isfahan Zell al-Soltan over legal and economic domination in the city made them outstanding in the clerical history of the nineteenth century. Their anti-Babi-Baha'i stand, which is apparent in Tabataba'i affairs (see above), caused them to receive opprobrious treatment in Baha'i sources.

115 Fo'adi (56–65) contains a full account of the events that finally led to the execution of Hajji 'Abd al-Majid. Hajji 'Abd al-Majid's son Mirza Buzurg, later titled Badi', was for some time in doubt about his father's Babi-Baha'i faith. Later, he was converted and while on a mission to the court of Nasir al-Din Shah to deliver Baha'u'llah's tablet of the shah of Iran, he died under torture and became one of the hero martyrs of Baha'i history. This was six years before the execution of Hajji 'Abd al-Majid.

Mashhad, he was at one stage a talaba in the madrasa of Mirza Ja'far, where he swore an oath of fraternity with his classmate Mulla Mohammad 'Ali Barforushi (Qoddus).[116] His recognition of the Bab was apparently due to this earlier friendship.[117] It also appears that he and Qoddus belonged to a group of which Mulla Hosayn was also a member.[118] At the time of his departure from Mashhad Qoddus reportedly withdrew his oath since he believed that it would be impossible for Aqa 'Ali Reza to fulfill the strict terms of the pledge.[119] Nonetheless, his erstwhile membership in the Khorasan circle made 'Ali Reza respond to Mulla Hosayn's call for jihad and subsequently offer financial aid to the Khorasani followers. During the turmoil of 1848 in Mashhad, 'Ali Reza, while preparing himself to join the Babi marchers on their way to Mazandaran, was arrested by Sam Khan, the Mashhad chief of police, who flogged him on the pretext of blasphemy and extorted a large sum from him.[120] Later in his life, perhaps because of financial troubles, he abandoned his trade and became a local grain merchant.[121]

Hajji 'Abd al-Jawad Yazdi, a relative of Mulla 'Abd al-Khaleq Yazdi and presumably one of his close adherents,[122] joined the Babiya in its early days, perhaps through Yazdi's influence.[123] Established in Mashhad as a reliable broker, he was basically a commission-agent for the merchants in the city. His son-in-law, himself a Babi, acted as the representative of the uncles of the Bab in Yazd.[124] Their connection with the Bab's uncles in Shiraz and Bushehr sheds light on the channels through which merchants like 'Abd al-Jawad and Aqa 'Ali Reza Shirazi may have first heard of the Bab. The trade

116 Ibid., 74.

117 Ibid. This was a common practice among tollab. It served not only practical purposes such as sharing meals and rooms, but often indicated a common orientation or primary training. After completion of studies, sometimes these links served as basis for alliance between the mojtaheds; for example, the oath between Mulla Mohammad Baqer Shafti and Hajji Ibrahim Karbasi (QU 140).

118 *Mazandarani*, 174. Fazel Mazandarani seems to draw his information from a certain 'Abd al- Mu'min, who is perhaps identified Aqa Sayyed Mu'min, cited in Mu'in, 62–63.

119 Fo'adi, 74.

120 Ibid. Samsam Khan Urus, the commander-in-chief of the regiment of Bahaduran, was the beglarbagi of Mashhad (RS X, 329, 416–20). He was the first official in Mashhad to become aware of Mulla Hosayn's activities in the city, and to report to the governor Hamza Mirza (RS X, 422). See also Lady Sheil, *Life and Manners*, 141.

121 'Allaf, possibly a vendor of fodder (Fo'adi, 74).

122 Fo'adi, 104–5. Among the relatives of Mulla 'Abd al-Khaleq there were other Babis-Aqa Mohammad Hasan Muzahheb (book illuminator), his nephew, and Mirza Mohammad Hosayn E'tezad al-Atibba', his son-in-law, who was a physician.

123 Ibid.

124 Ibid.

organized by merchants on the Shiraz-Mashhad route, with representatives in Tabas, Yazd, and Bushehr, provided a Shaykhi network often linked to Shaykhi 'ulama throughout the country.

In Shiraz and Bushehr, the conversion of the merchants, even from Shaykhi persuasion, seems to have been hindered by the harassment the Bab underwent after 1845. Though a number of merchants, often connected to the Bab's uncles, were attracted in the early stages, only a handful joined the Babi ranks. One example was Mirza Ahmad Shirazi Ishik Aqasi, a descendant of a merchant family and later the author of a general history that contains some new details on the Bab and the beginning of the movement. Mirza Ahmad's curiosity is apparent throughout the pages of his narrative. As the claims and objectives of the movement unfolded, however, he became disillusioned with the Bab, and critical of his disciples. He apparently was not alone in this change of attitude. Babi sources refer to the presence of other sympathetic merchants in the early debates of Mulla Hosayn and Moqaddas in Shiraz.[125] But only the names of a few who remained loyal to the Bab are known: Mirza Abul-Hasan Shirazi, who met the Bab in the hajj, Aqa Mohammad Karim Shirazi, and Hajji Mirza Mohammad.

For the Afnans, the maternal side of the Bab's family, the claims of the young Sayyed 'Ali Mohammad posed an agonizing dilemma. His eldest and the youngest uncles, Hajji Sayyed Mohammad and Hajji Sayyed Hasan 'Ali, a resident of Yazd, categorically refused to recognize his claims and chastised him for his heretical utterances.[126] Hajji Mirza Sayyed 'Ali, closest of the Bab's three maternal uncles, however, was a devout follower from the start. In contrast to most other members of his family, who showed apprehension and embarrassment on the publication of the new claims, he missed no opportunity to support his nephew. In 1216/1845, after the Bab's return from Hajj, in an important letter from Bushehr to his brother in Shiraz, Sayyed 'Ali declared his full conviction.[127] A few months later, during the first round of the anti-Babi persecution, when the Bab was taken into custody by the governor of Fars, Hosayn Khan Ajudanbashi, Sayyed 'Ali

125 *New History*, 36, and *Nabil*, 65.

126 See *RR*, chapter 3 on the Afnans.

127 The letter is partly cited in Fayzi, *Khandan-e Afnan*, 25–31. The author believes that these letters were written by the elder brother, Hajji Mirza Sayyed Mohammad, but the contents of the letter, the fact that the other brothers showed no sympathy toward the new claim, and the presence of Hajji Sayyed 'Ali in Bushehr at the time prove that the writer is none but Sayyed 'Ali.

guaranteed bail and acted as his nephew's sponsor.[128] Even after the Bab's departure from Shiraz he did not lose contact with him. In 1265/1849 he visited the Bab for the last time, in the fortress of Chehriq. A few months later he was arrested in Tehran, together with a number of other Babis, by order of Mirza Taqi Khan Amir Kabir. Admitting his commitment to the Bab and refusing to retract, he and six other Babis, known as the Seven Martyrs, were found guilty of conspiracy and corruption of belief, and put to death in the Sabzih Maydan market. "Eminent merchants of Shiraz and Tehran," including Malik al-Tojjar himself, interceded to save his life, offering ransom, but "he refused to heed their counsel and faced the persecution to which he was subjected."[129]

THE BABI ARTISANS

The main contribution of the Babi tojjar in the movement was perhaps their role as intermediaries in attracting members of various guilds (*asnaf*), small manufacturers and artisans, to the Babi ranks. Although no mass conversion ever took place (except in the case of Zanjan, later, which culminated in the uprising of 1849–50), many individuals were drawn to the new faith through local contacts and association with the Babi tojjar and 'ulama.[130]

The trade routes of central and western Iran give one indication of the way Babism spread among local merchants and their associated groups. Hajji Mirza Jani's pilgrimage to Iraq in 1843–44 doubled as a journey connected to his trade. Zabih was also present in Baghdad on a few occasions between 1849 and 1854, presumably for the same purpose.[131] Sometime prior to 1264/1848 we find Hajji Mirza Jani in Barforush "for the purpose of trade."[132]

A group of young local merchants and manufacturers who assembled around Hajji Mirza Jani and Zabih in Kashan typifies Babi communities

128 *Nabil*, 151; cf. Mirza Habibullah, *Tarikh*, 45–46, and *Nuqtat al-Kaf*, 113.

129 *Nabil*, 442–64 (447). The full incident is recorded in various sources, including *Nuqtat al-Kaf*, 215–22. Also see Momen, *Religions*, 100–105.

130 Gobineau, with regard to the mutual relation between the artisans and merchants, points out: "It is clear that these organized cooperations are backed on the one hand by the merchants for whom they work and on the other by the mullas who, their prestige requiring that they be surrounded by the masses, are glad to take up the interests of apprentices, craftsmen (artisans), and even master craftsmen" (Trois ans en Asie, translation cited in Issawi, *Economic History of Iran*, 37).

131 *Masnavi*, 39b, 41a.

132 *Nuqtat al-Kaf*, 175–76.

around the country. In addition to the younger brothers, Mirza Ahmad and Aqa Mohammad 'Ali,[133] Mirza Mahdi Kamranibaf,[134] Hajji Sayyed Mahmud,[135] Mirza Aqa Tajer Kashani,[136] and Hajji Mirza Mohammad Reza Makhmalbaf Kashani[137] were all manufacturers and local merchants who were in professional contact with them. Mohammad Reza Makhmalbaf, for example, owned a number of velvet-weaving workshops, and operated a trade with India, Istanbul, and Baghdad,[138] the same pattern of trade as Mirza Jani and Zabih, who both seem to have been engaged in the export of silk products to Baghdad and the Caucasus.

In Isfahan, the conversion of members of various professions was due chiefly to the efforts of the Babi mullas, but Nahris were also instrumental. Among the Babis of Isfahan, Ja'far Gandom Pakkun (sifter of wheat), Ahmad Saffar (tin-plater), Hosayn Mesgar (coppersmith),[139] and 'Ali Mohammad Sarraj (leather worker)[140] all bore the title of *mulla*. In other cases, such as Kazem Banna (mason) in Kerman,[141] Mahdi Kurehpaz (kiln worker), Mohammad Musa Namadmal (felt-maker) and Ja'far Mozahheb (book gilder), all in Nayriz,[142] the same title is used for the Babi artisans. One may assume that while engaged in various professions, the title Mulla was added to their names as an acknowledgment of their literacy or possibly religious training, a fact that may indicate the success of the Babi recruitment among literate guild members.

A special place in the early success of the movement in Isfahan is attributed to Ja'far Gandum Pakkun. Nabil Zarandi believes that he was the first

---

133 *Kashf al-Ghita'* (45) and *Kawakib* (I, 90–92) believe that there was a fourth brother but this is not confirmed by Natiq (*Tarikh-e Amri-ye Kashan*, 4), which seems to be more reliable. On Mirza Ahmad and his fate see Browne, Edward G., ed. and trans. *A Traveller's Narrative Written to Illustrate the Episode of the Bab*. 2 vols. Cambridge 1891, 332, 371 (hereafter cited as *Traveller's Narrative*); *New History* 391 (n.) Balyuzi, *E. G. Browne and the Baha'i Faith*, 64, and Ahmad Ruhi Kermani (?), *Hasht Behesht*, 282.

134 *Tarikh-e Amri-ye Kashan*, 4–5, and *Nabil*, 221. Mirza Mahdj was executed in Tehran in 1268/1852 (*Vaqayi'-i Ittifaqiyyih*, no. 82, and Recollections of Aqa Hosayn Ashchi cited in *Tarikh-e Shohada-ye Amr* 111, 310–12).

135 *Tarikh-e Amri-ye Kashan*, 3.

136 *Samandar*, 227.

137 Mo'in al-Saltana Tabrizi, Hajji Mohammad. *Tarikh-e Amr* [-e Baha'i]. INBA Library MS A. (Hereafter cited as *Mo'in*.) 75.

138 Ibid.

139 Nabil, list of the participants in Tabarsi, 421 n. 5 and 6.

140 *Mazandarani*, 105.

141 Ibid., 398.

142 SAMB, 402 n. citing an anonymous Babi account.

person to become a Babi in Isfahan,[143] due to "a close association with Mulla Hosayn."[144] He later fully recognized the Bab at the latter's arrival in Isfahan in 1262/1846.[145] Emphasis on the early acceptance of Gandum Pakkun is perhaps attributable to his low status. Indeed, the Babi sources regard the conversion and wholehearted devotion of Gandum Pakkun, which ended in his death in the fortress of Tabarsi,[146] as an example of the attention paid by the poor and underprivileged to the new message. The Bab himself points up the significance of this conversion by portraying Mulla Ja'far as a humble man who grasped the reality of his cause: "Look at the Land of Sad [Isfahan] which in appearance is the greatest of lands where in each corner of its schools numerous students are found under the name of knowledge and ijtihad, yet, at the time of refining Gandum Pakkun will put on the garb of primacy. This is the secret of the word of the People of the House regarding the time of Manifestation when they say: 'The lowest of the people shall become the most exalted and the most exalted shall become the lowest.'"[147]

Further spread of the Babi word among craftsmen, local traders, and other humble people was often the result of personal and intercommunal contacts. Aqa 'Ali Akbar Najjar (carpenter) and Aqa Mohammad Hanasab (henna miller), for instance, first learned of the new Bab and his claims through Mulla Hosayn. Aqa Sayyed 'Abd al-Rahim, who was one of Mohammad Baqer Shafti's bailiffs in the village of Siyafshad, in turn heard of the movement through 'Ali Akbar Najjar.[148] On a trip to Isfahan, while in the city to complain about a recent robbery in the village, he accidentally met his close friend 'Ali Akbar and noticed in his possession a tablet written in red ink, probably a copy of *Qayyum al-Asma'*. 'Ali Akbar Najjar revealed that he had received the tablet from a "learned man" who had recently arrived from Shiraz, and directed his friend to the quarter of Darb-e Kushk, where during his first visit to Mulla Hosayn, 'Abd al-Rahim professed his conversion. His belief was strengthened after he had paid a visit to the Bab

143 *Nabil*, 99.
144 Ibid.
145 Both *Kawakib* I, 71 and Mo'in, 98, refer to a dream that led Mulla Ja'far to recognize the Bab in Isfahan.
146 *Nuqtat al-Kaf*, 202, and *Nabil*, 99.
147 Bayan VIII/14 296. Neither *Nabil* Zarandi's quotation of the above remark (99) nor Nicolas's French translation (A. L. M. Nicolas, *Le Beyan persan* [Paris, 1914) IV, 113) is accurate.
148 INBA Lib. MS. no. 1028 D, Miscellaneous notes, 32–33.

in Isfahan in 1263/1847 and received a tablet from him in which he was addressed with a grand title.[149]

By 1848–50 the number of artisans, craftsmen, and skilled workers who had joined the Babi ranks formed a sizable part of the movement's urban population. There is no comprehensive record of the number, the identity, and the occupation of the Babis to enable us to make any accurate assessment, but even judging by the names of those who participated in Babi resistances in Tabarsi, Nayriz, and Zanjan, it is evident that a sizable body of guild members with a variety of occupations were present. Among the 360 participants in Tabarsi, for instance, there were forty-one Isfahanis, of whom the occupation of thirty-two were specified. Besides eight mullas and seminarians there were twenty-four members of various guilds and professions: eleven masons; five workers in the hand-weaving industry (one handloom weaver, two knotters, two cloth-stampers); four other skilled workers (a coppersmith, a tin-plater, a leather worker, and a sifter of wheat); and four shopkeepers and traders (two apothecaries, a butcher, and a cloth dealer). Of forty-one Isfahanis, forty were killed in Tabarsi and one "Remnant of the Sword" was later executed in Tehran.[150]

If, due to its wide geographical distribution, the occupational pattern of the participants of Tabarsi can be taken as representative of the Babi community throughout the country around 1264/1848, it is evident that the participation of the guilds in the movement is second only to that of the 'ulama. As a whole, of 222 participants whose occupations are known, 60 percent were middle- and lower-rank mullas, 26 percent were from guilds, about 8 percent were small landowners, and the remaining 6 percent were merchants, lower- and middle-rank government officials, and other professionals. Of thirty-eight participants whose occupations are unknown, we can assume that a large proportion were either artisans or else peasants who, because of their humble occupations (or because of the inadequacy of the sources), remained unspecified.

The urban nature of the Zanjan uprising is evidenced by the large number of "the poor, the traders of the bazaar, the sadat, and the students."[151] Among them were three ironsmiths (Hajji Kazem, Mashhadi 'Abbas, and Ostad Mehr 'Ali, who together improvised two makeshift cannons for the Babi defense), two hatters (Ostad Sa'il, the chronicler of the Zanjan events, and

149 Ibid., and *Mazandarani*, 101.

150 See geographical distribution and occupations of the participants of Tabarsi overleaf.

151 Mirza Hosayn Zanjani *Tarikh*, INBA Lib. MS. no. 3037, folio 10.

Geographical distribution and occupations of the participants of Tabarsi

	Mullas	Guilds	Small landowners	Merchants	Government officials	Other	Unknown	TOTAL	%
Khorasan	55	10	–	1	2	–	43	111	30
Mazandaran	27	7	14	–	1	1	36	86	23
Isfahan	8	24	–	1	–	–	8	41	11
Sangsar & Shahmirzad	10	6	1	–	–	–	15	33	9
Qazvin	5	2	–	2	–	–	7	15	4
Fars	5	–	–	–	–	1	5	11	3
Ardestan	1	1	2	–	–	–	7	11	3
Azarbaijan	6	1	–	1	–	–	2	10	2.7
Zanjan	1	–	–	1	–	–	8	10	2.7
Yazd & Kerman	1	4	–	–	–	–	4	9	2.5
Tehran	2	–	–	–	1	1	1	5	1.3
Other places	13	3	–	–	–	–	2	18	5
Total	134	58	17	6	4	3	138	360	100
% of 222 known occupations	60	26	7.6	1.6	1.8	1.3			

Note: This table is based on information supplied by four major sources—narrative of Mirza Lotf'Ali Shirazi; *Tarikh-e Mimiya*; *Nabil*; and narrative of Aqa Mir Abu-Taleb Shahmirzadi. The totals do not add up to 100%, because percentages have been rounded up and down to avoid giving the impression that they are precise figures rather than estimates.

Ostad Khalil), an apothecary, a shoemaker, a carpenter, a dyer, a clothier, a tobacconist, a gardener, and a maker of gunpowder. Also, among the Babi defenders in Zanjan were two gunners, a courier, a wandering dervish, a reformed thief, and a few lutis.[152]

152 The above list, only a sample of the participants in Zanjan, was compiled from several narratives: Mirza Hosayn *Tarikh*; Aqa 'Abd al-Ahad Zanjani "Personal Reminiscences," trans. by E. G. Browne, *JRAS*, 29 (1897) and 761–827; and narrative of Hashim Fathi Moqaddam Khalkhali, INBA Lib. MS no. 3037.

In the urban resistances of 1267/1851 in Isfahan and 1268/1852 in Tehran, members of the guilds, under the direction of the ʻulama and the merchants, again played an effective role. Sadiq Tabrizi, a confectioner, and Mulla Fathullah Qomi, an engraver, who was the son of a bookbinder, were two of the three main participants who made an attempt on the life of Nasir al-Din Shah and later were executed together with many other Babi merchants, small landowners, and lower-rank state officials who were assembled from all over the country in Tehran.[153]

In addition, some of the new converts to Islam (*jadid al-Islam*), Jews of Torbat-e Haydariya, for instance, who were involved in local trade, became curious about the Bab. The Jewish converts of Torbat, originally from Yazd, had suffered persecution and forced conversion in 1839–40 in Khorasan and were often adhering to a crypto-Judaic faith.[154] In 1850, at the time of Mulla Ahmad Azghandi's arrest and banishment, six of these Jews, who were on friendly terms with him, sympathized with the Babis, though their full conversion took place a few years later.[155] The motives behind this interest, shared by Jews of Hamadan during Qorrat al-ʻAyn's visit, are to be found in the manner in which a deprived minority expressed itself in the face of persecution, forced conversions, and strict control. Increasingly in later decades of the century, the members of the Jewish community sought messianic salvation in the promises of the Bab and later Baha'u'llah. They were seeking consolation in a movement which could restore to them, not security, prosperity, or their lost faith, but a sense of ecumenical solidarity, courage in the face of hostile forces, and hope for ultimate relief.

The merchants and artisans who were attracted to the Bab constituted only a tiny minority of that class but their conversion was symptomatic of a dual crisis, both economic and moral. Not surprisingly, the Babi movement spread rapidly along major trade routes of Iran and received support in almost all commercial centers. The opening of the Persian market to foreign trade had already changed the traditional commercial network. Conversion

153 For quantitative analysis of the background, occupations, and distribution of the early Babis see M. Momen, "The Social Basis of the Babi upheavals in Iran (1848–53): A Preliminary Analysis," *International Journal of Middle East Studies*, 15 (May 1983), 157–83.

154 Fo'adi, 83–85; cf. Lavi, *Tarikh-e Yahud-e Iran* III, 634. See also Wolff, J., *Narratives of the Mission to Bukhara*, London 1847, 163, 199–200; W. J. Fischel, "The Jews of Persia 1795–1940" in *Jewish Social Studies* 12 (1950), 119–60 (124 and sources in footnote 18); RS X, 248.

155 Fo'adi, 76, 185–86.

to the Babi faith demonstrated the potentials of a new generation of merchants to embrace an ideology responsive to their widening intellectual horizons. Their pietistic ethos and mystic preoccupations served as an impetus to bring out the merchants' aspiration upon a messianic stage on which the chief actor was one of their own. For many of these merchants, already exposed to the esoteric discourses, the only conceivable vision for moral and material reconstruction was that of a messianic renewal. Rather than encouraging the merchants to take action against material disadvantages and reversals, the changes in the economic climate only made them keener in their moral crusade. Attraction to esoteric and millennial ideals came with a sense of criticism of the moral decline, if not resentment and contempt for material life. This did not mean, however, that they were turning away from the respected norms of the merchant class. Rather, their conversion to a movement with a radical puritanistic message, at least as they saw it, was to reaffirm their loyalty to the values characteristic of their class. During the first phase of the movement, the presence of the merchants in the Babi ranks hardly managed to divert the course of the movement toward further moderation. On the contrary, the Babi merchants willingly pursued the apocalyptic millennium of the Babi mullas at the expense of their own. Only later, after 1852, did the exclusion of the militant activism from the Babi agenda allow the remnant of the Babi merchants to seek in the Baha'i faith moral values congruent to their own mercantile worldview.

CONVERTS FROM THE GOVERNMENT RANKS

The efforts of the Babi activists among the non-clerical population were not limited to the merchants and their associated groups. Civil servants (*ahl-e divan*) of the lower ranks and individuals on the fringe of the Qajar government, both in the capital and in the provinces, also responded to the Bab's message. In Tehran, the early Babi nucleus included young sons of court functionaries, provincial ministers, and army chiefs, as well as low-ranking officials in the central administration. In the provinces, especially in Khorasan and Azarbaijan, there were Babis belonging to the local bureaucratic families. In general, the converts did not represent any one faction within the Qajar administration, nor did their adherence to the Bab stem from overt political ambitions. In a few cases, conversion even resulted in voluntary relinquishment of a governmental post; in even fewer cases, it was a consequence of involuntary exclusion from the state establishment. Previous Shaykhi adherence was often a factor in conversions, though there were other religious affiliations as well.

Among the early followers in Tehran who were in some way associated with the government, Mirza Hosayn 'Ali Nuri (d. 1309/1892), known as Baha' and later Baha'u'llah, was probably the first who responded favorably to the new claims.[156] During Mulla Hosayn's stay in Tehran, Nabil tells us, Mulla Mohammad Mo'allim Nuri, a private tutor to the children of the Nuri household, handed Mirza Hosayn 'Ali a written message from the Babi missionary to which he responded with enthusiasm.[157] However, it is after 1847 that he becomes openly active in the Tehran Babi circle.[158] Other members of Mirza Hosayn 'Ali's large family, including Mirza Yahya (later known as Sobh-e Azal), Mirza Musa and four other brothers, an uncle, and a nephew, also joined the movement.[159]

Mirza Hosayn 'Ali (Baha'u'llah) was born in Tehran to a family of Mazandarani landowners, in 1233/1817.[160] His father and grandfather, judging by the size of their households and their estate, were established rural notables in the district of Miyanrud in the Nur region.[161] His father, Mirza 'Abbas Nuri (also known as Mirza Bozurg), a distinguished master calligrapher of the early Qajar era,[162] had moved to the capital sometime in the early 1880s. Owing to the Qajars' patronage of artists as well as their

156 The extensive primary sources on the life and thoughts of Baha'u'llah, including his own works, deserve a separate treatment. Worth mentioning among the existing studies are: H. M. Balyuzi, *Bahá'u'lláh: The King of Glory* (Oxford, 1980); three entries under BAHA'ALLAH in *Encyclopædia Iranica* (EIr) by E. G. Browne, in EIr by A. Bausani, and in EIr by J. Cole; Momen, *Religions*, 177–306. M. A. Malik Khusravi Eqlim-e Nur (Tehran 118 Badi'/1962) contains new material on Baha'u'llah's family background and early life. Beside Babi-Baha'i primary accounts, including Nabil, which covers Baha'aullah's life in some detail, three other accounts are of special importance: Sayyed Mahdi Dahaji, Browne Or. MSS no. F.57(9); Mirza Jawad Qavini, Browne Or. MSS no. F.26, trans. E. G. Browne in MSBR, 3–112; and 'Izziya Khanum *Tanbih al-Na'imin* Browne Or. MSS no. F.60(8) and F.61(9).

157 *Nabil*, 104–8. Mulla Hosayn distributed copies of the Bab's *Qayyum al-Asma'* among other notables in the capital (Mo'in, 71).

158 *Traveller's Narrative*, 58–62; M. J. Qazvini, "Epitome" (Browne, E. G., *Materials for the Study of Babi Religion*, Cambridge 1918, 3–4); *Kawakib* I, 257–70; and *Nuqtat al-Kaf*, 200, 239–40.

159 *Nabil*, 109–19; *Traveller's Narrative*, 373–74; *Samandar*, 16r.

160 Shaykh Mohammad Nabil Zarandi, "Chronological Poem," Browne, *JRAS* (1899) B. II, 985.

161 *Eqlim Nur*, 2–16, 86–97.

162 See in Elr: 'ABBAS (P. P. Soucek) for his calligraphical works and administrative career.

special predilection for employing Mazandarani officials (and because of his co-citizenship with Mirza Asadullah Nuri, father of Mirza Aqa Khan Nuri), Mirza 'Abbas joined the central army office as a junior secretary and accountant.[163] He was gradually promoted to private secretary, then minister (i.e., the chief administrator: *vazir*) to the chief of the imperial guard, Imam Verdi Mirza, Fath 'Ali Shah's twelfth son and the head of the Qajar tribe (*Ilkhani*).[164] He also received royal approbation for his excellent calligraphic work.

In the events immediately after the death of Fath 'Ali Shah, in spite of Imam Verdi's collaboration with one of the pretenders to the throne, Mirza 'Abbas seems to have escaped the consequences of his affiliation with the prince, though only temporarily. Because of his past amicable relations with Mirza Abul-Qasim Qa'im Maqam Farahani, he was even promoted to the post of vazir of Borujerd and Lurestan.[165] Less than a year later, however, in a widespread purge of the old administration under the newly appointed premier, Aqasi, Mirza 'Abbas lost not only his office and his tenure but a great portion of his fortune.[166] His brief, ill-fated marriage to Ziya' al-Saltana, the celebrated daughter of Fath 'Ali Shah, contributed to his downfall.[167] Whatever purpose this marriage was initially intended to serve, its outcome was ominous for Mirza 'Abbas and his family. Between 1835 and 1839, mainly under the pretext of resisting the reimbursement of Ziya' al-Saltana's huge marriage portion (*mahr*), apparently after being forced to divorce the princess, Mirza 'Abbas was disgraced, put under house arrest, and bastinadoed by the prime minister's agents and collaborators.[168] The family's houses were confiscated and Mirza 'Abbas's wives and thirteen children were separated. In 1839, Mirza 'Abbas died in isolation and despair.[169]

His father's unhappy fate and sudden ruination appears to have generated in Baha'u'llah a distaste for temporal power. His own later experiences further confirmed his denunciation of "worldly ambitions," even when in

163 Bamdad, *Rijal* VI, 126–29.
164 *Eqlim Nur*, 113–14; Bamdad, *Rijal* VI, 127.
165 For his relations with Qa'im Maqam see the latter's *Munsha'at* ed. J. Qaim Maqami (Tehran, 1337/1958) 37, 116, 117, 126, and 181.
166 Bamdad, *Rijal* VI, 128; *Eqlim Nur*, 11–26; *Nabil*, 109.
167 *Eqlim Nur*, 205–8, 122.
168 Ibid., 121–22; cf. Baha'u'llah *Lawh Mubarak Khatab bi Shaykh Mohammad Taqi* (Tehran, n.d.), 199, trans. Shoghi Effendi, *Epistle to the Son of the Wolf* (Wilmette, Ill., 1941).
169 *Eqlim Nur*, 122–23; Bamdad, *Rijal* IV, 128.

the late 1840s and early 1850s he stood a chance to secure a government post. In spite of a brief rapprochement with Aqasi[170] and later with Aqa Khan Nuri, the ministers' suspicion and lack of interest kept him away from administrative positions. The affairs concerning the ownership of the village of Quch Hesar, a private property in the southern outskirts of Tehran belonging to Mirza 'Abbas to which Aqasi laid a claim, renewed animosity between Baha'u'llah and the chief minister.[171] During the premiership of Mirza Taqi Khan Amir Kabir (1848–51), Baha'u'llah's disclosed Babi leanings met with the premier's disapproval, and in the summer of 1851 he went briefly into voluntary exile in the 'Atabat.[172] On his return to Tehran, a few months later after the downfall of Amir Kabir, Baha'u'llah's hopes of reaching an understanding with the new premier Mirza Aqa Khan Nuri (a distant relative) were shattered when, in the wake of the 1852 Babi assassination attempt against Nasir al-Din, he was imprisoned on suspicion of involvement in the plot. Though Mirza Aqa Khan was effective in saving him from execution, his ensuing exile to Baghdad severed his remaining links with the Tehran political establishment.[173]

The events of 1848–52 and Baha'u'llah's unsuccessful efforts to maintain a middle ground between his fellow Babi co-religionists and the state no doubt confirmed his original ambivalence toward political power. In 1868, when he was imprisoned in 'Akka, on the tablet of Ra'is addressed to the Ottoman grand vazir, Baha'u'llah related a childhood memory when a scene of puppetry unfolded to him the elusive nature of temporal power. At the end of the show, the puppeteer told the astonished boy that all the displayed pomp and circumstance of Sultan Salim's court, including the sultan, his chiefs, and his ministers, were inside a chest. "From that day," Baha'u'llah recalls, "all the [material] instruments of this world in the eye of this slave [himself] resembled that performance, and had no significance whatsoever [for me], even as much as a grain of mustard. The people of insight can see with the eye of certainty beyond the pomp of possessors of material power its decline. Like those puppets, soon the superficial instruments [of power], the apparent treasures, the worldly ornaments, the military ranks, the luxurious clothes, and their arrogant possessors will proceed toward the grave

170 *Nabil*, 120.

171 Ibid., 120–21; cf. Eqlim Nur, 182–85.

172 *Nabil*, 32, 587, 593–94.

173 For Baha'u'llah's involvement in the events of 1852 and its aftermath see *Nabil*, 595–602, and Momen, *Religions*, 128–46.

chest. In the eyes of the people of insight, all those conflicts, struggles, and arrogance resemble children's toys."[174]

This attitude permeates the writings of Baha'u'llah, demonstrating a mystical trait not unrelated to his earlier exposure to Sufism of his own time. His acquaintance with Sufi dignitaries in Mohammad Shah's court and his attraction to wandering dervishes may suggest a vigorous interest in Sufism. In his youth, reportedly, "he was keen to speak about saints and mystics... In any feast or gathering, if someone criticized the sayings of the mystics or brought forward a problem about the words of the saints, he would reply to the criticism or resolve the problem without any hesitation."[175] Some of his later works composed in the Sufi tradition, as well as his later retirement in the refuge of Khalidi-Naqshbandi convents in Kurdistan (1854–56), reveal a mystical outlook pivotal to his later messianic claims and his socio-moral reforms.[176] Yet, it seems that his earlier preoccupation with mysticism did not prevent him from regarding the claims of his contemporary Sufis with skepticism.[177] Baha'u'llah's mystical bent was in harmony with the growing popularity of Shi'ite-Sufi orders, particularly Ne'matullahis, among the notables of Mohammad Shah's time. But for Baha'u'llah, as for some Sufis who joined the movement, mysticism provided a channel through which the notions of human perfection and moral renewal could be contemplated, and tenets of orthodox Islam could be re-evaluated, and at times rejected.

An essential feature of Sufi thought: the doctrine of the Perfect Man, the need for a living spiritual guide together with the methods of purification and self-denial were synonymous with Shaykhism. In spite of Ahsa'i's denunciation of Sufism, many of its features were adopted into his theosophy. The point of confluence between the apparently diverse streams of Shaykhism and Sufism was the yearning for moral perfection. Baha'u'llah's vision of such perfection, however, was as different from that of Babi mullas and merchants as his social background and his causes of grievance. Yet the

174 "Lawh'i Ra'is" in *Majmu'a Alwahi Mubaraka* (Cairo, 1920), 107–11.

175 *Kawakib* I, 264.

176 Among his works with evident mystical leanings are Haft Wadi, Chahar Wadi va Jawahir al-Athar (Tehran, 129 Badi' 1972) trans. 'Ali Qoli *Nabil* al-Daula as *The Seven Valleys and the Four Valleys* (Wilmette, Ill., 1945, rev. ed. 1952) and *"Kalamat Maknuna" Majmu'a-yi Alwah-i Mubaraka* (Cairo, 1338/1920) trans. Shoghi Effendi as *The Hidden Words* (Wilmette, Ill.,1939). See also J. Cole "Bahá'u'lláh and the Naqshbandi Sufis in Iraq, 1854–1856," in *From Iran East and West* ed. J. Cole and M. Momen (Los Angeles, 1984), 1–28, and A. Taherzadeh, *The Revelation of Bahá'u'lláh*, 2 vols. (Oxford, 1974–76) I, 45–149.

177 Abul-Fazl Golpayegani *"Risala Iskandariya" Si risala* (Cairo, 1318/1910).

appeal of the nascent Babism was broad enough to allow a convergence of views; a consensus upon which converts from all walks of life could share a common goal. Baha'u'llah's later re-diversion of the course of militant Babism after 1852 (and more noticeably after 1864) toward moderation was in sharp contrast to the policies of the radical wing of the movement, headed, at least nominally, by his own brother, Mirza Yahya Nuri Sobh-e Azal. The politically pacifist current founded by Baha'u'llah, which eventually evolved into the Baha'i religion, was no doubt affected by his frustration with the disastrous outcome of the Babi experience. Unlike many of his co-religionists, who were preoccupied with the Shi'ite vision of a utopian political order under the aegis of the Imam of the Age, Baha'u'llah focused his efforts on disentangling moral ideals from political claims; a Sufi legacy that he stretched to new frontiers in order to resolve an eternal problem of Islamic faith. By forging a new source of loyalty on a largely moral basis, Baha'u'llah envisaged a suprareligious ecumene free from the political claims of the Islamic community (*umma*). The later Baha'i–Azali division, which plunged the Babi community into a bitter sectarian conflict, was above all a division over policy and outlook, though the dispute over succession, legitimacy, and leadership played its role as well. Unlike the Azali faction, still largely reminiscent of the early years, Baha'u'llah urged a compromise with the state, perhaps as early as Badasht days of 1848. In later years, in bitter disillusion with their political defeat, the majority of the Babis turned to him for a leadership free of political ambitions but not devoid of a socio-moral program.

Baha'u'llah was not typical of the Babi converts with administrative or courtly backgrounds. Most other believers of this category showed a greater degree of militancy and zeal, which though directed primarily against the religious establishment were not free from anti-state sentiments. One of the most active, and probably the closest to court circles, was Mirza Reza Qoli Turkaman, son of the Turkman chief Mohammad Khan Mir Akhur, head of the royal stable under Mohammad Shah (Mohammad Khan, later known as Sepahsalar A'zam, the prime minister under Nasir al-Din Shah, was his brother-in-law.)[178] Like Baha'u'llah, Reza Qoli Khan became acquainted with the Babis through Mulla Hosayn's contacts in Tehran, Mulla Mohammad Mo'allem Nuri and the Kani brothers. A man of wealth and influence, Reza Qoli did not hesitate to publicize his Babi beliefs, nor to spend large sums,

178 For his account see Bamdad, *Rijal* III, 228–32.

four to five thousand tumans, to promote the Babi cause.[179] His house in Tehran was the gathering place for some Babis, a refuge for the others. In 1263/1847, in the village of Khanluq on the outskirts of Tehran an offer to rescue the Bab from government detention was turned down. A year later, an unsheathed sword on his shoulder, he was in Barforush defending Qoddus against growing physical threats from his opponents.[180] He then joined Mulla Hosayn in Mashhad, during the earliest Babi clashes in that city. After Badasht, he returned to Tehran, where he joined the Qajar contingency forces and left for Tabarsi, presumably in the hope of mediating between the Babis and the prince governor, Mahdi Qoli Mirza. When negotiations failed, he defected to the Babi side and fought against government troops before surrendering himself at the end of the fighting. Eventually, by the order of Mahdi Qoli Mirza, he was torn to pieces.[181]

In close contact with Reza Qoli Khan and Baha'u'llah was another convert from Nur: Mirza Solayman Qoli, son of Shatirbashi, chief of the royal footmen. His recitation skills earned him the title *Khatib al-Rahman* (the Orator of the Merciful). His missionary activities took him throughout Iran before being captured and executed, at the insistence of his brother,[182] in the massacre of 1268/1852 in Tehran.

Another well-known member of the Tehran Babi group to perish in the 1852 massacre was Solayman Khan Tabrizi, the son of Yahya Khan, an army chief and previously commander of the royal stewards of the crown prince 'Abbas Mirza.[183] An adherent to Shaykhism, presumably from the Shaykhi quarter of Amir Khiz in Tabriz, Solayman Khan spent some time in Karbala', where he frequented Rashti's lectures.[184] In a second journey to the 'Atabat, through his acquaintance with Mulla Mahdi Khu'i and other Azarbaijani activists, he joined the Babis. In Tehran, in collaboration with Baha'u'llah, he tried in vain to reverse the death sentence imposed on the Bab.[185] In the same year, Solayman Khan's brother Farrukh Khan, who was sent to Zanjan to crush the Babi uprising, was killed by followers of Mulla

179 *Nuqtat al-Kaf*, 195.
180 Ibid., 195.
181 Zavareh-e Mimiyeh; cf. *Nuqtat al-Kaf*, 196.
182 Malik Khosravi Shohada-ye Amr III, 264–65, citing 'Abd al-Baha'.
183 For Yahya Khan's services to the Qajars during the Russo-Persian wars see RS IX, 670–71. During the Salar revolt of 1847–49 he was given the charge of transferring the captive Salar to Tehran (RS X, 381–84).
184 *Mazandarani*, 23.
185 Ibid., 24.

Mohammad 'Ali Hojjat Zanjani.[186] Mirza Taqi Khan Amir Kabir, knowing of Solayman Khan's Babi leanings, tolerated him. He was ordered by the prime minister to change his white Arabian dress and wear a civilian hat instead of a turban, presumably to underline his disapproval of Solayman's involvement with the radical mullas.[187] After 1266/1850, the house of Solayman Khan became the center of the Babi clandestine activities led by Shaykh 'Ali 'Azim.[188] Following the unsuccessful attempt on Nasir al-Din and the ensuing Babi killing of 1852, Solayman Khan was captured and put to death. His cruel and painful death earned him a special place in the chronicles of the Babi martyrs.[189]

Other members of Tehran group with bureaucratic backgrounds included Mirza Hasan Tafrishi Mustaufi (accountant), Mirza Mohammad, the deputy chief of the Chapar Khana (the postal service), Mirza Masih Nuri, a nephew of Mirza Aqa Khan Nuri, and three low-rank scribes who were executed in 1852 in Tehran.[190] It is not unlikely that at some stage before 1852 the Tehran Babis had attracted other sympathizers among state officials.

At the provincial level, governmental functionaries with local tribal or urban bases were attracted to the Babis. A remarkable example was Reza Qoli Khan, son of Solayman Khan Afshar Sa'in Qal'a and son-in-law of Sayyed Kazem Rashti.[191] He was an Afshar chief with the rank of *sartip* (brigadier) in the Azarbaijan army. In spite of his father's zealous adherence to Mohammad Karim Khan Kermani, Reza Qoli showed sympathy and respect to the Bab during his mission of transferring him from Maku to Chehriq in 1264/1848.[192] His Babi leanings added fuel to what appears to have been an old dispute with his father. The breach between the two widened following the key role played by Solayman Khan in crushing the Babi resistance in Tabarsi, and shortly after, in the execution of the Bab.[193] Some years later, Solayman Khan's complaints to the provincial government

186 Mirza Hosayn Zanjani, *Tarikh* folio 19 a-b; cf. Sepehr, Mirza Mohammad Taqi [Lisan al-Mulk], *Nasikh al-Tawarikh Qajariya*, ed. J. Kiyanfar, Tehran 1998, 111–295 (hereafter cited as *Sepehr*).

187 *Mazandarani*, 24.

188 Vaqayi' Ittifaqiya, no. 82; cf. Malik Khusravi, *Shohada-ye Amr*, 227.

189 The account of Solayman Khan's brutal execution is recorded by many sources including Vaqayi' *Ettefaqi-ye*, no. 82; *Sepehr* IV, 42; *Mazandarani* 26 (n.). For European accounts see *Traveller's Narrative*, 330–31, and Momen, *Religions*, 128–46.

190 *Mazandarani*, 216–17.

191 For Solayman Khan see *RR*, chapter 5.

192 Mo'in, 169–72. See *RR*, chapter 9.

193 For his involvement in Tabarsi see *Sepehr*, 111, 244.

concerning his son's heretical beliefs—accusing him of even cutting off the ear of a muezzin at the height of his anti-Islamic rage—ended in Reza Qoli's detention and probably loss of his family estate in Sa'in Qal'a. Residing in Tehran during the later Nasiri period, he was reportedly poisoned by his own son for reasons of religious enmity.[194] Other Babi converts of Azarbaijan included Mirza Lotf 'Ali Salmasi (possibly from Ahl-e Haqq), a steward in Mohammad Shah's court. Following his conversion by Vahid he was instructed to deliver Bab's addresses to the monarch and his minister. As a result, he was dismissed from service and took residence in Salmas, where he played host to the Bab in 1266/1850.[195]

A small group of low-ranking local officials among the early converts in Khorasan also deserves some attention. During his first mission to Khorasan, when passing through Sabzevar, Mulla Hosayn paid a brief visit to a number of local *mostaufis* (government accountants), who had perhaps had Shaykhi sympathy. Later, two brothers, Mirza 'Ali Reza Mostaufi and Mirza Mohammad Reza (later Mo'taman al-Saltana), and some of their relatives became supporters of the Bab.[196] Their affiliation to the movement largely remained secret, but they donated funds to the Mazandaran march,[197] and in the following years provided comfort for the Babis at times of persecution and trouble.[198] Toward the 1290s/1870s, both brothers were promoted: Mirza 'Ali Reza became a revenue accountant "in the royal presence,"[199] and Mo'taman al-Saltana, the chief accountant of Khorasan.[200] Nasir al-Din Shah, highly suspicious of Mo'taman al-Saltana's Babi sentiments, ordered his transfer to the city of Kashan, where he was in virtual exile. Later, the shah summoned him to the capital, where he reportedly was forced to marry the shah's sister, then to drink "poisonous coffee" (1310/1892–93).[201]

Mirza Mohammad Taqi Jovayni, another early Babi convert, was a humble scribe and accountant from the village of Jovayn. He encountered Mulla Hosayn on one of his visits to Sabzevar. Jovayni's active participation

194 Mo'in, 173–76.
195 *Mazandarani*, 66.
196 Fo'adi, 30, 67.
197 Ibid., 67.
198 Ibid., 67–71. *Tarikh-e Amri-ye Khorasan* uses many local sources, including oral accounts from the members of the Mostaufi and Mustashar Daftar families (30, 73).
199 Mohammad Hasan Khan E'temad al-Saltana Mir' at al-Buldan-e Nasiri (Tehran 1296/1878) III, supp. 12.
200 E'temad al-Saltana *al-Ma'athir wa'l-Athar* supp. 29, 55; *Tarikh-e Muntazam-e Nasiri* III, supp. 23.
201 Fo'adi, 70–72. See also Sheil, *Glimpses of Life and Manners*, 92.

began during the Tabarsi upheaval, when he held the responsibility for receipts and expenditure of the common funds[202] and on a few occasions acted as the representative of the Babi party in negotiations with the local chiefs and state officials.[203] His most dramatic act, which could be seen as a final declaration of war against the government, was the slaying of Khosrau Khan Qadikala'i, a tribal brigand in the service of the local government, as a reprisal for his deceitful behavior toward the confused Babi column. In the final surrender of the Babi fighters, Mirza Mohammad Taqi was captured and put to death. His head was spiked on a spear and carried around the city of Barforush.[204]

THE BABI COMMUNITY: AN ASSESSMENT

The activities of the Babi disciples influenced a spectrum of individuals with diverse affiliations and stretching over a broad geographical span throughout Iran and Iraq. In this nationwide appeal, the largest and the most prominent body of believers were from the religious class, often from lower and middle echelons and always with non-orthodox leanings. Merchants and the members of the guilds made up the second largest group. Together with urban mullas and state officials, the merchants formed the intellectual elite of the Babis, with the seminarians, the guilds, and the peasantry as its rank and file. The counterparts of the Babi 'ulama in the countryside, the village mullas, also had some success in converting their small constituencies. A few landowners of higher status and economic caliber and chiefs of settled nomadic clans also joined, especially in Mazandaran and Fars. Notwithstanding the Sufis' apathy toward Babism, a few Ne'matullahis, theosophists (*hekami*), and wandering dervishes were also in the Babi ranks. The state officials, not a large group, gained some prominence, for they were able for a time to provide limited protection for their co-religionists.

The Babis' geographical distribution can be divided into six regions. Khorasan probably contained the largest number of Babi believers, some from the provincial capital Mashhad and smaller cities such as Sabzevar,

202 *Sepehr* III, 236. *Nabil* (417) refers to his "literary accomplishment."
203 *Tarikh-e Mimiya*, 22 (negotiations with the governor of Mazandaran Khanlar Mirza), 34–35 (with 'Abbas Qoli Khan Larijani).
204 *Nabil*, 417.

Nishabur, and Qa'in but mostly from rural regions of central-southern Khorasan. Mazandaran contained the second-largest number, with some concentration in Barforush, and with exceptionally large numbers in rural regions of Nur, 'Allabad, Bahnamir, Sangsar, and Shahmirzad and smaller numbers in Sari, 'Arab-Khayl, Savad-Kuh, Amol, and the surrounding villages. The third region included communities in central and western provinces roughly corresponding to provinces of Isfahan, 'Iraq 'Ajam, and beyond. A sizable group existed in Isfahan, a large community in Ardestan, and a noticeable group in Kashan and the surrounding villages: Naraq, slightly later in Qamsar, Jausheqan, Vadeqan, and Natanz. The larger bodies of converts in Tehran, Qazvin, and Zanjan (by 1850 probably the largest single Babi community in Iran) were mostly of urban origin, with some rural connections. While the first two included some notables, the latter was predominantly constituted of lower classes. Other Babis were scattered in small groups in Kerend, Sahna (both of Ahl-e Haqq), Hamadan, Kermanshah, Qum, and Ishtihard. The fourth region was Iraq, with concentration among the Shaykhis of Karbala' and a few others in Kazemayn and Baghdad. The fifth region, Fars and Yazd, consisted of both urban and rural Babis. In Shiraz they were mostly artisans and lower-rank merchants. Nayriz, a base for Sayyed Yahya Darabi (Vahid) and the scene of later conflict during 1849–52, housed a semi-rural community under the joint leadership of the landed notables and religious leaders. Other communities in Estahbanat, including Hendijan and Mehrijerd, another in Sarvestan, and individuals in villages and towns throughout southeastern districts, were mostly converted through Vahid. The Babis of Yazd and the environs, including mullas, merchants, a physician, and members of guilds as well as peasants and small landowners, were also among his followers. Azarbaijan, the sixth region, witnessed noticeable examples of mass conversion in the rural areas as well as individual conversions in the cities. Smaller Babi groups were also scattered in Kerman, Astarabad, possibly Lurestan, Kurdistan, and even the Shi'ite kingdom of Lucknow in India.

The entire population of the Babis in the late 1840s can hardly have exceeded the rough estimate of a hundred thousand indicated by various observers.[205] The Babi minority constituted some 1.6 percent of Iran's total population of a maximum six million in the same period. Quantitatively, the ratio does not present a breakthrough. But of the total population,

205 See P. Smith, "A Note on Babi and Baha'i Numbers in Iran," *Iranian Studies* 17 (Spring–Summer 1984), 295–301, and cited sources.

about three million were nomads, and of the remaining half perhaps only 2 percent, or six hundred thousand, were urban. The rest were villagers. As far as can be ascertained, there were no nomadic Babis. Moreover, the ratio of the urban to rural Babis was probably no less than one to three. Thus, the Babis perhaps constituted over 4 percent of the urban population and some 3 percent of the village population.

By the token of its message, Babism was bound to remain a minority movement even during its short history as a dynamic social force. But its broad diffusion and intensive proselytism made its bold message audible throughout the country out of proportion to its size. Regional nuances no doubt influenced both the pattern of Babi conversion and the reception of its message. One definitely influential factor was the pre-existence of numerous heterodox communities, both open and semi-secret, on the highly diverse map of religious adherence. Above all these were Shaykhi nuclei and communities of various size. If not converts defecting from mainstream religion, the Shaykhi adherents were often individuals or groups with heterodox history who resisted assimilation by choosing Shaykhism as a replacement for the older affiliation. Of all the alternatives to majority Shiʿism in the mid-nineteenth century Shaykhism probably had the largest adherence, widest distribution, and greatest visibility, superseding both Sufi orders and the declining Akhbaris. Such extensive grassroots support was the most effective factor in the success of the Babi recruitment.

The Babis were able to recruit from other nonconformist minorities, however. Though often overlooked, the conversions from the Ahl-e Haqq and associated "extremists" to the Babi movement were perhaps second only to the Shaykhis. Both as individuals and occasionally as a community, they showed greater receptivity, since their messianic expectations and their outlook, especially on the doctrine of prophethood, could be accommodated by the Babi Zohur. By the nineteenth century, Ahl-e Haqq had become largely a peasant religion with a syncretic belief system that had survived openly only in Kurdish, Persianized Kurdish, and Azari communities of western and northwestern Iran. But in all probability the geographical distribution of the Ahl-e Haqq included many scattered localities in central, northern, and even eastern Iran. The same is true with Isma'ili village communities in central and southern Khorasan. Their receptivity to Shaykhism and then Babism came at a time when the Isma'ili revival, first through the Ne'matullahi and then under Shah Khalilullah and Aqa Khan had already kindled the messianic hopes of the 'Ataullahi tribe in Southern Khorasan and Kerman.

Mass conversion among the followers of Mulla Mohammad 'Ali Zanjani (Hojjat), himself a militant Akhbari, is another indication of Babi appeal to nonconformist minorities. The socio-religious background of Zanjan Babis still remains a mystery, but certain peculiarities in their mass behavior betray the likelihood of religious extremism far distinct from the learned Akhbarism of the *madrasa* tradition. While to contribute the rapid expansion of Babism solely to the pre-existence of heterodoxies would be a gross simplification, it must be stressed that even in the mid-nineteenth century, Persian society was far less monolithic, less religiously homogeneous, than often acknowledged. The network of heterodoxies—whether those that re-emerged in the post-Safavid era in the Sufi guise or those that survived in their original form—was still not conquered by the Twelver Shi'ism of the Usuli 'ulama. More often than not, the plethora of invisible heterodoxies found a common ground in a single current that could shield them against the pressure of the majority religion. The upsurge of Babism was thus a point of confluence for diverse trends that shared as much common messianic aspiration as repulsion of the religious establishment and hatred for the oppressive temporal power. The potential of the movement was immense, even unique, as it was able to fuse the popular messianism of the countryside with the socially complex and intellectually elaborate nonconformism of the cities of eastern Iran.

The catalysts of this process were sectarian conflicts, material decline, and naked oppression. In such circumstances, the special appeal of the Babi movement was to individuals and groups on the fringes of society who were troubled, more in heart than in mind, by the increasingly visible manifestations of disorder and decay. In its formative stages, the movement was fluid enough to project grievances of groups as diverse as mullas and women. What cemented these groups into one and gave them a focus and a symbol of sanctity was the Bab, and under him a circle of semi-prophetic figures to whom the Babis could attach new bonds of loyalty beyond their professional and regional affiliations. The symbolic presence of the Bab, and the message he advocated in conjunction with the evolving aspiration of his followers, at least for a time, maintained the momentum and guaranteed the solidarity of the movement.

SELECTED BIBLIOGRAPHY

al-Qatil al-Karbala'i. *Risala*. Published in Fazel Mazandarani *Zohur al-Haqq*, III, appendix 2, 502–32.

Amanat, Abbas. *Resurrection and Renewal, The Making of the Babi Movement in Iran, 1844–1850*. Cornell University Press, 1989.

Ayati Tafti, 'Abd al-Hosayn. *al-Kawakib al-Durriya fi Ma'athir al-Baha'iya*. 2 vols. Caurim 1342/1923–24.

Bab, Sayyed 'Ali Mohammad Shirazi. *Qayum al-Asma'* (Commentary on Surat Yusuf). Browne Or. MSS. No, F. 11 (9).

Beyza'i Zuka'i, Ne'matullah. *Tazkereh-ye Sho'ara-ye Qarn-e Awwal-e Baha'i*. 3 vols. Tehran, 121–122 Badi'/1965–70.

Browne, Edward G. (ed. and trans.) *The New History (tarikh-e-jadid) of Mirza Ali-Muhammed the Bāb* by Hosayn Hamadani. Cambridge University Press, 1893, rep. 1975.

___ (ed.) *Nuqtatu'l Kaf* [*Nuqtat al-Kaf*] *Compiled by Hajji Mirza Jani of Kashan*. London and Leiden, 1910.

___ (ed. and trans.) *A Traveller's Narrative Written to Illustrate the Episode of the Bab*. 2 vols. Cambridge, 1891.

Fayzi, Mohammad 'Ali. *Hazrat-e Nuqta-ye Ula*. Tehran, 132 Badi'/1973. repr. Bahá'í-Verlag, Germany, 1994.

___. *Khandan-e Afnan, Sedra-ye Rahman*. Tehran, 127 Badi'/1971.

Fo'adi Boshru'i, Hasan. *Tarikh-e Diyanat-e Baha'i dar Khorasan*. Eds. Minou Fo'adi and Fereydun Vahman. 'Asre Jadid, Darmstadt, 2007.

Gobineau, Comt Joseph A. de. *Religions et philosophies dans l'Asie Centrale*. Paris, 1865 (2, ed, 1890).

Golpayegani, Mirza Abul-Fazl and Golpayegani, Sayyed Mohammad. *Kashf al-Gheta'*. Tashlend, n.d.

Hedayat, Reza Qoli Khan. *Rouzat al-Safa'i Nasiri*. 3rd ed., VIII–X. Tehran, 1338–39 Sh./1959–60.

INBA Iran National Baha'i Archive. Library and private photosat publications.

Levi, Habib. *Tarikh-e Yahud-e Iran*. 3 vols. Tehran, 1339/1960.

Malik Khosravi, Mohammad 'Ali. *Eqlim-e Nur*. Tehran, 118 Badi'/1962.

Malik Khosravi, Mohammad 'Ali. *Tarikh-e Shohada-ye Amr*. 3 vols. Tehran, 130 Badi'/1972.

Mazandarani [Fazel], Asadullah, *Ketab-e Zohur al-Haqq* vol. III. Tehran, n.d. [1323 Sh. /1944?].

Momen, M. *The Bábí and Bahá'í Religions, 1844–1944: Some Contemporary Western Accounts.* Oxford, 1981.

Mu'in al-Saltana Tabrizi, Hajji Mohammad. *Tarikh-e Amr* [*-e Baha'i*]. INBA Library MS A.

Nabil Zarandi, Sheykh Mohammad. *The Dawn Breakers: Nabil's Narrative of the Early Days of the Baha'i Revelation.* Trans and ed. Shoghi Effendi. Willmette, Ill., 1932.

Nateq-e Esfahani, Mohammad. *Tarikh-e Amri-ye Kashan.* INBA Library, MS. No.2016D.

Nicolas, A. L. M. *Seyyèd Ali Mohammad dit le Bab.* Paris, 1905.

Qatil → al-Qatil.

Qazvini, Mulla Ja'far. Historical account published in *Tarikh-e Samandar va Molhaqqat.* Ed. 'A. 'Ala'i. Tehran, 131 Badi'/1975.

Samandar *Tarikh-e Samandar va Molhaqqat.* Ed. 'A. 'Ala'i. Tehran, 131 Badi'/1975.

Sheil, M. *Glimpses of Life and Manners in Persia.* London, 1856.

Sepehr, Mirza Mohammad Taqi [Lisan al-Mulk], *Nasikh al-Tawarikh Qajariya.* Ed. J. Kiyanfar. Tehran, 1998.

Tehrani, Agha Bozorg (Mohammad Mohsen). *Tabaqat A'lam al-Shi'a* (in 3 parts). Najaf, 1373–88 Sh./1954–68.

Tonkaboni, Mirza Mohammad ibn Solayman. *Qisas al-'Ulama'.* Tehran, 1304/1886. 2nd ed. Tehran, n.d.

4

From a Primal Point to an Archetypal Book

Literary Trajectories through Select Writings of the Bab (1819–50)

STEPHEN N. LAMBDEN

Abstract: This chapter is about the voluminous Persian and Arabic writings of the nineteenth-century Qajar-era religious revolutionary known as the Bab. These several hundred scriptural texts are mostly in manuscript, mostly unpublished, and mostly untranslated. Here, a trajectory is set forth giving some historical, contextual, and direct scriptural information about key elements within the Bab's massive literary output in excess of 1,500 items considered divine revelations. Certain of the major writings of the Bab from the earliest period until his several, latter years' imprisonment in Azarbaijan (northwestern Persia, 1847–50) are placed in context. This is at times on the basis of the five or more modes (e.g. Revealed Verses; Devotional Inspirations, Commentaries; Learned Surahs; Persian Revelations and Literary Orations)—into which the Bab himself divided his writings.

> ...until a Herald from heaven (*munad min al-sama'*) cries out...then hasten quickly along [to join him]. By God! It is as if I perceive him (the messianic al-Qa'im, "Ariser") [in Mecca] between the pillar [corner of the Ka'ba] (*al-rukn*) and the locale ("station" of Abraham, *al-maqam*). He will spread out his arms in initiating a new religious Cause (*amr jadid*), offering a new Book (*kitab jadid*), and instituting a new sovereign rule from heaven (*sultan jadid min al-sama'*). His eternal banner (*rayat abada*^{an}) will not be layed down until the time of his death.[1]

The religious, Arabic and Persian scriptural writings of the mid-nineteenth-century Persian Shiʿi merchant and messianic claimant known as the Bab (Ar. Gate), are numerous, often theologically weighty compositions. Within them their author, Sayyid 'Ali Muhammad Shirazi (d. Tabriz, 9 July 1850) claims to have fulfilled many such early Islamic messianic traditions as that cited above. Largely authored between 1844 and 1850 CE (= 1260–67 AH), his writings often presuppose a knowledge of the Qur'an and of twelver, Imami Shiʿi traditions as well as diverse other Islamic and related sources. There is much within them, however, that extends, reinterprets, or abrogates Islamic norms in revolutionary and challenging ways. The new religion they articulate was early referred to by the Bab himself as the *al-din al-khalis* ("the pure religion").[2] Its sacred writ claimed to embrace, recreate, transcend and transfigure its Abrahamic religious roots and background. As the generative alphabetic locus, the Bab claimed to be the first alphabetical locus, the Primal Point (*nuqtat al-awwaliyya*) from which traced or scribed a sacred scripture that came to be viewed by many as expressive of an Archetypal Book (*umm al-kitab*) of guidance for all humanity.

---

1 This Islamic prophetic tradition derives from the fifth Imam, Muhammad al-Baqir (d. c.126/743) and is cited by al-Nu'mani in his *Kitab al-Ghayba*, 1403/1983:171 f. as well, for example, as by Majlisi, in the *Bihar*, vol. 52: 235, 293. The Bab himself cites (with full isnad, "chain of transmission") and interprets an Imami Shiʿi version of this hadith in his T. Kawthar (f. 28), P. Dala'il (29) and elsewhere.

2 QA 1:5; 12:16, etc.

THE WRITINGS OF THE BAB, SOME PRELIMINARY OBSERVATIONS

For the Bab himself, his writings initiated a new eschatological age of inner (*ta'wil, 'irfan*), deep-level (*batini*) revelation from God (*wahy*), intended to herald a new era of inclusive, yet post-Islamic, religious evolution. Sometimes addressed to all humankind, a good many of these mid-nineteenth-century (early Qajar era, 1794–1925) writings were disturbing to the uninitiated who imagined their sacred books to be the last word from the creator on high.[3] These writings were—and remain—religiously challenging to many of their Muslim and other readers. Yet, for Babi-Baha'i believers, they prelude and prepare for the arrival of an era within which renewed religiosity and a new order of justice (*al-'adl*) and peace (*al-sulh*) predominate. For past followers of the Bab, as well as for contemporary Baha'is, the writings of the Bab are viewed as revealed sacred scripture.

Religious texts deriving from the Bab are extant in scores of Middle East and globally diffused Arabic and/or Persian manuscripts. They have been little analyzed and studied by modern academics and remain inadequately known, largely unpublished (in facsimile or critical editions) and untranslated.[4] No comprehensive survey or even listing of all the major and minor writings of the Bab can be set down here. Only a few brief summary notes as trajectories through certain of these writings will be possible. Issues surrounding manuscript location and availability, dating, authenticity, and historical *sitz im leben* (setting in life) will be kept to a minimum. The fascinating history of the Azali Babi, Baha'i, western "orientalist," and modern academic approaches to the religion and writings of the Bab, will likewise very largely be bypassed.[5]

The new, revealed book(s)-centered religion of the Bab came into

---

3 Aside from universal addresses in the QA and elsewhere, an example of a scriptural (c. 1848) Tablet of the Bab which at times seems to be addressed to the people of the world, can be found (in facsimile) in Afnan, 2000:473.

4 Critical editions of the writings of the Bab are virtually non-existent. The few semi-critical Azali Babi publications (P. Bayan, K-Panj Sha'n, Haykal al-Din, etc.) dating from early the post-WWII decades, remain useful, though their nature and history are beyond the scope of this summary paper.

5 On the writings of the Bab, see though, for example, MacEoin, 1992 (Sources), Mohammad Hosseini, 1995, Afnan, 2000, Saiedi, 2008, Lawson and Lambden, personal websites (see Bib. at the end of this chapter, p. 217).

being from 5 Jumadi al-Awwal 1260/22–23 May 1844, when he communicated Arabic verses (*wahy*) before his first disciple, the Shaykhi initiate and Letter of the Living (*hurūfat al-hayy*), Mulla Husayn Bushrū'i (c. 1813–49).[6] The Bab was more precise since this took place on that day, two hours and eleven minutes after sunset. For him, the rule of God commenced then and creation was renewed.[7] The Bab held that at that time, the Abrahamic, latter-day eschaton, the Day of Resurrection and Judgment (*yawm al-qiyama*), had inwardly and to some degree outwardly commenced.[8] This was 1,000 years or so after the alleged death of the young, ultimately messianic son of the eleventh Imam, Hasan al-Askari (d. Samarra, c. 260/873–74) known as Muhammad al-Mahdi.[9] Indeed, the Bab gradually claimed to be the spiritual "return" (*raj'a*) of this ethereal figure as well as the second coming of Jesus, the Prophet Muhammad (d. 632), Imam 'Ali (d. 40/661), and Imam Husayn (d. 61/680), with new revealed books, treatises, and other writings.[10] While the Bab frequently underlined his humanity or being a (mere) servant (*'abd*) of God, he also came to make very elevated claims. His human persona was often related to these elevated claims in the light of a tradition from Imam Ja'far Sadiq which has it that devotional "servitude" (*'ubudiyya*) is a state (*jawhara*), the true nature [essence] (*kunh*) of which is Lordship [Divinity] (*al-rububiyya*).[11]

For the remaining post-1844 six years of his life, the Bab wrote, dictated or revealed verses in the form of letters, scriptural Tablets (*lawh*, pl. *alwah*), literary "orations," "discourses" (*khutba*, pl. *khutub*), devotional writings (*munajat*), supplications (*du'a*), treatises (*risala* pl. *rasa'il*), scriptural divisions (*sūrah*, pl. *suwar*), scrolls or documents (*ṣahifa*, pl. *ṣuhuf*),

6 In many of his writings, the Bab refers to a 1270 (lunar) year period from the call of the Prophet in c. 610/2 CE until his own call to prophethood in 1260.

7 It may be that the two (hours) can indicate commencement through the diacritical point of the letter "B" (*abjad* 2) and the 11 (minutes) indicate the H and W (5+6 = 11) of *Huwa* = "He is [God"]. A new theophany began at a theologically meaningful, predestined time.

8 P. Bayan, II:7, 30; cf. VI:13.

9 As a child, this son of Hasan al-'Askari was believed to have entered into occultation (*ghaybat*) in a celestial world beyond. He has long been expected to emerge in the fullness of time as the messianic Qa'im ("Ariser," with the sword or the religious cause, etc.) or final twelfth Imam, named above.

10 See al-Ahsa'i, Sh-Ziyara, III:37.

11 The Arabic text of this hadith can be found in the Sufi influenced 100th section on al-'Ubudiyya ("devotional servitude") in the Misbah al-Shari'a (282) ascribed to Imam Ja'far al-Sadiq.

commentaries (*tafsir* pl. *tafasir* cf. *sharh*, also commentary), and books (*kitab*, pl. *kutub*). This as well as many *haykal*s, pentadic (five pointed) or star-shaped ('humanoid') and circular talismans (*dhari'a*) as well as other less esoteric forms of communication.[12]

The scripture-centered religion of the Bab was gradually, though speedily, communicated in both Arabic and Persian. If Abrahamic, Islamic and other world faiths can be viewed as "religions of the [single] Book (*kitab*)," the religion initiated by the Bab fast became a veritable "religion of the library" (*maktab*). Devotees believed this massive corpus to be expressive of a supra-cosmic codex, an *umm al-kitab* (Archetypal-Mother Book) evident within a multiplicity of diverse books and treatises. These writings were texts either written down by the Bab himself, in his stylish *naskh* (calligraphic script), or dictated to nearby scribes or amanuenses.[13] Several important writings of the Bab or portions of specific works have multiple Arabic and/or Persianized titles, sometimes as utilized by the Bab himself or invented by others. As will be seen, his early Tafsir Sūrat Yūsuf (Commentary on the Surah of Joseph mid. 1844) has at least three other titles.

The Bab variously and repeatedly mentioned the rapidity of his power of revelation and estimated the magnitude of his writings. As a proof of his elevated religious status, he states in his R. Dhahabiyya that he could reveal a well-established *Ṣahifa* (Treatise) in six hours.[14] In his 1846 T. Sūrat al-kawthar (see p. 182), he underlined his ability to reveal a thousand verses in six hours.[15] In the P. Dala'il he states that he is capable of revealing the equivalent of the whole Q. (revealed over twenty-three lunar years, c. 610–632 CE) in just five days and nights.[16] Within the Persian Bayan, he estimated that he could rapidly reveal 1,000 or more verses (bayt) in just five hours.[17] Therein, at this time (c. 1848), he also

---

12 On types of talismans see P. Bayan, V.10 (165); VII.10 (252–53) and later in this chapter. The most detailed treatment of the talismanry of the Bab is found in the works of MacEoin, especially his 1985 article.

13 A few of such scribes (*katib*), including the seventh "Letter of the Living," Sayyid Husayn Yazdi (d. Tehran, 1268/1852) and Mulla 'Abd al-Karim (Ahmad) Qazvini (d. Tehran, 1268/1852), became well-known. For some useful details and references, see MacEoin, Sources, App. 2 and 3, 204–5.

14 INBMC 86:79.

15 T. Kawthar, fol. 5a.

16 P. Dala'il, 26.

17 P. Bayan, II.1.17.

estimated that the totality of his verses amounted to 500,000.[18] Later still, in his K. Asma' (c. 1849), he again stated that in just two days and nights he could produce the equivalent of the approximately 6,236 verses of the Qur'an.[19] Similarly, in a late Chahriq-period Arabic and Persian letter to the 'ulama' of Tabriz, the Bab underlines his messianic claims when he states that in four days and nights he could reveal what had previously taken twenty-four years.[20]

The major and minor writings of the Bab apparently exceed 1,500.[21] They are obviously much greater in volume and length than both the Bible and the Qur'an. These writings vary greatly in length. Some are just a few lines or verses such as his brief personal or expository letters and messages. There exist short works such as the approximately 100-Arabic-word Khasa'il-i sab'a (The Seven Directives). Additionally, there are very large compositions extending for several hundred and even a thousand and more pages. There exist very lengthy treatises and books, set forth over a period of weeks or months; examples being the Kitab-i panj sha'n (about 350 pages) and the Kitab al-asma', "Book of Names" (perhaps 2–3,000 pages).

To date, the writings of the Bab have not all been collected together, authenticated, or analyzed in detail. Some exist in numerous manuscript versions, others in a few very rare or even single manuscripts. Many autograph manuscripts seem to be lacking or lost. Manuscripts of the writings of the Bab are scattered throughout Iran, the Middle East and elsewhere. A proportion, however, through travelers, diplomats, missionaries, and collectors, ended up in western university libraries, museums, and private collections. Aside from Iran itself and the Baha'i World Centre in Haifa (Israel), important collections are located in Europe (London, Cambridge, Paris, Leiden), Russia (St. Petersburg), the USA (New York, Princeton), and elsewhere.[22]

18 P. Bayan, VI. 11, 218.

19 K. Asma' XVI.18; SWB:139.

20 Afnan, 2000:335.

21 In a 2002 letter of the Research Department of the Baha'i Universal House of Justice (Haifa, Israel) we read, "With regard to the Writings of the Báb, the Archival collection holds approximately 135 original Tablets, and 55 photocopies [of writings]" (cited in Lights of Irfan vol. 10, 2009, 350). Since that time, it has become clear that the corpus of the Bab's writings in Persian and Arabic, extant and lost, amounts to around 2,000 items (personal communication from Steven Phelps, February 2020).

22 Cf. MacEoin, *Sources*, index.

BAYAN/MUBIN ("CRYSTAL CLEAR") YET "ABSTRUSE, BEWILDERINGLY ABSTRUSE (SA'B MUSTASA'B)": EXEGETICAL CLARITY AND ESOTERIC DEPTH IN THE WRITINGS OF THE BAB[23]

On one level, the purpose of the Bab was to clarify (*bayan*), through new levels of interpretation, various key religious, philosophical and social issues, and concerns. The exegetical clarifications of the Bab, however, seem to be something of a syzygy, a "unity of opposites." At times they are refreshingly clear and straightforward, and at times stunningly erudite and complex. His "gnosis" was directed toward all humanity as well as written in response to questions posed by, and issues sought after by stunningly erudite masters of Shi'i-Shaykhi philosophy and discourse (*kalam*). Deep literary complexities are wedded to numerous statements of succinct clarity and straightforward simplicity. Many of the demythologizations of Qur'anic and Islamic doctrine by the Bab reduce Islamic scriptural complexity to something approaching common sense or rationalistic thought. In P. Bayan II. 8, for example, on the literal and eschatological senses of "death" (*al-mawt*), the Bab interprets the often complex senses of *barzakh* (interworldly partition, ithmus, interworld... Q. 23:100, etc.) within Qur'anic-Islamic teaching, Shaykhi cosmology and popular religiosity, in a straightforward, allegorical way: "The term *barzakh* indicates [the time period] between two [successive] Manifestations [of God] (*bayn al-zuhurayn*)."[24]

In the P. Dala'il, to offer another example, the Bab makes clear that "heaven" or "paradise" (*jannat*) indicates being possessed of the deep "knowledge of God" (*irfan-i haqq*), while being consigned to "hell"

---

23 I draw here on an Islamic prophetic or Imam transmitted tradition. It is a tradition which indicates that the prophetic hadith/khabar or amr ("tradition," "discourse" or "Cause") of Shi'i Islam is something deeply esoteric or complex, sa'b mustasa'b ("abstruse, bewilderingly abstruse"). This widely cited tradition can be found, for example, in al-Kulayni. Kafi 1:401–2 and Majlisi, Bihar[2] 2:183 ff. 52:318; cf. 66:232–33. It is many times cited and interpreted by the Bab. We find it in, for example, the S. Bayn al-haramayn f.103b and K. Panj Sha'n X.1, 338 (in an alchemical context). cf. also Lawson, 2018:102. Note also that I use here the English translation of sa'b mustasa'b by Shoghi Effendi within his rendering of the Kitab-i iqan of Baha'u'llah (89/trans. 82).

24 P. Bayan II, 34. One might note here that the Bab generally avoids the complexities implied by such terms as the Ishraqi-Shaykhi Arabic seven-letter loanword (in somewhat garbled transliteration) *hurqalya* [sic.] and related expressions having to do with celestial interworlds and resurrection bodies.

is indicative of being veiled from Reality (*ihtijab az haqq*).[25] The P. Bayan explains the "Day of Resurrection" (*qiyamat*) for the religion of the Bayan (followers of the Bab) as the coming manifestation of *man yuzhiru-hu Allah* (Him whom God shall make manifest).[26] We find the following basic theological axiom in the P. Dala'il: "Know that the gnosis of God (*ma'rifat Allah*) in this world can never be disclosed, save through the gnosis of the Manifestation of Reality [God] (*ma'rifat-i maẓhar-i haqiqat*).[27]

There are, then, many clear and straightforward statements of the Bab about piety, refinement, cleanliness, justice, ethics, and numerous other religious matters. There are also clear legalistic directives. Legal, ritualistic statements and directives are often straightforward, though they are occasionally very challenging. In this connection, it is frequently the case within the Bab's writings that outward circumstances and inner ethics revolve around the future well-being of the person of the coming messiah of the religion of the Bab, "Him whom God shall make manifest" (*man yuzhiru-hu Allah*). Many pre-eminently clear statements and directives of the Bab are preparations for the future era of *man yuzhiru-hu Allah*. The Bab declared, "I Myself am, verily, but a ring upon the hand of Him Whom God shall make manifest."[28] In Arabic Bayan IV. 11 he states that no one should overstep the regulations of the Bayan (*hudud al-Bayan*) such that they become saddened. Avoidance of passing on this sadness is said to be the greatest eschatological directive (*a'zam hadd*). It is so, lest the coming elevated messianic "He Whom We shall make manifest" (*man nuzhiru-hu*) be saddened.[29]

THE SHAHADA (TESTIMONY OF FAITH) AND ITS ALPHABETICAL MYSTERIES

Bayan, then, means clarity and the writings of the Bab are sometimes exactly this. They yet contain much that is deep, esoteric and challenging. A few examples must suffice to illustrate this point. We first turn to the

25 P. Dala'il, 44.
26 P. Bayan II.7, 31.
27 P. Dala'il, 65.
28 SWB, 119, trans. 168.
29 Cf. Ar, Bayan IV, 11 as partly cited in Bausani, 2000:387.

question of alphabetical and numerological teachings of the Bab. Rooted in *abjad*-based number–letter relationships, these configurations form hermeneutical keys to many dimensions of his thought from the Qayyūm al-asma' until the Kitab-i panj sha'n (1844–50), and including the two Bayans and P. Dala'il.[30] In this connection, the Bab gave theological and numerological centrality to the opening half of the simple and straightforward Islamic *shahada* (testimony of faith), for him the perennial quintessence of religion and its causative genesis.[31] In part, this is classically expressed as follows:

لا اله الا الله

The Kalimat al-Tawhid or "Word of the Divine Unity."

ل ا ا ل ه ا ل ا ا ل ل ه

The twelve detached letters of the above La ilaha illa Allah, "There is no God except God."

For the Bab, the twelve Imams—from 'Ali the first Imam to Muhammad al-Mahdi the twelfth—are on one level symbolically represented by the twelve letters of the important Arabic theological phrase known as the *kalimat al-tawhid.* This is the Islamic affirmation of the Divine Unity made up from twelve Arabic letters (as above). This important Qur'an-based formula (see Q. 37:35; 47:19, etc.) contains twelve letters in four words, all constructed from three different letters (أ + ل + ه = **A** + **L**+ **H**). It is a short testimony, *la ilaha illa Allah,* meaning "There is no other deity [God] but God."

Interpretations of this twelve-letter *shahada* are centrally important in many of the writings of the Bab. At times its two halves encapsulate twin, syzygy-type categories of theological negation ("There is no God") and theological affirmation ("save God").[32] The five "letters of negation" are, "There is no god/Deity" which are followed by the seven Arabic "letters of affirmation", spelling, *illa Allah,* "but God." Thus, in total, 5 + 7 letters = 12 letters, representative of the twelver Shi'i Imams who were considered

30 In his P. Dala'il, the Bab states, that the commencement of every theophany (*ẓuhūr*) of the religion of God has always been the *kalimat al-tawhid,* "There is no God but God," 65.

31 K.Panj II, 8, 285 ff., 305 ff., etc.

32 P. Dala'il, 68–69.

the successors of the Prophet Muhammad from the time of his death in 632 CE until the passing of the eleventh Imam in 260/873–74, and his youthful future messianic son a few years later. For the Bab, these holy figures were believed to be ever-present or active in the invisible spiritual worlds as loci of divine guidance and inspiration. The meanings of the *shahada* are simultaneously clear and complex. They encompass the doctrine of the Divine Unity (*tawhid*), its affirmation and its negation, as well as imamological and number-letter mysteries having messianic, theophanological and other implications. Within his writings, the Bab gives very frequent attention to these matters.

ESOTERICA, THE ABSTRUSE, SCIENCES OF THE UNSEEN (ʿULŪM AL-GHAYB)

If the above seems esoteric, there are writings of the Bab or many passages within them which are even more esoteric. They draw on centuries of insights into the *ʿulūm al-ghayb*, the Islamic occult sciences of the unseen, believed to have originally been communicated by Muhammad, Imam ʿAli and others. Like Shaykh Ahmad al-Ahsa'i, the polymathic generator of al-Shaykhiyya (Shaykhism), the Bab claimed to be especially adept in these areas, including *jafr* (number letter configurations and prognostication), alchemy, and talismanry. The knowledge of *jafr* specialized to him as the Qa'im (the messianic "Ariser"), enabled him to compute the lengths of religions' dispensations of the past and of the future.[33]

The Bab also expounded deep aspects of Jabirean rooted alchemy in various writings, including the Xth and other sections of his K. Panj S.[34] This latter alchemical "work of God" (*sanaʿ Allah*) is reckoned something subtle and beloved, the "most perfect ornament" (*taraz al-akmal*) of an exalted gnosis (*ʿilm*). The Bab declares that only a meagre portion of the lower aspects of alchemy were commonly known. This, since true alchemy involving the extraction of "gold," is something "abstruse (*saʿb*), bewilderingly abstruse" (*mustasaʿb*). This especially since "sulphur" (*al-kibrit*) is incinerated the moment that "fire" touches it! Outwardly and metaphysically, this is a miraculous though vaporous issue.[35] Having said this, it should be noted

33 KPS: IX.4, 315 ff.; XII.1, 405 f.
34 On this see, for example, Syed Nomanul Haq, 1993.
35 KPS. X. 1, 338.

that the Bab was not primarily an alchemist, although he did answer questions about the alchemical elixir (*al-iksir*) and the so-called "philosopher's stone" (*al-hajar*) in an esoteric though personal inward ascent fashion. Like Shaykh Ahmad, he discoursed a number of times about the alchemical operation (*al-san'a*, "the work, task"), often maintaining that the secret of the elixir exists in everything. He related the alchemical process to the capturing of the celestial theophanic "Fire" which must be made to "blaze forth" so as to remove any impediment from the inmost heart (*al-fu'ad*). The inner alchemical retort (*al-qar'*) must then be placed upon the "brim of the alembic" (*hadd al-inbiq*) such that the mystic wayfarer might "partake of the fruit of the Tree which emerges from Mount Sinai." This, it seems, can pour forth transformatively.[36]

On numerous occasions, the Bab held that his revelations expressed an esoteric or doubly esoteric, especially deep-level (*batini*) exegesis of the Qur'an, Islamic traditions and other sources. In addition to their esoteric depth, the writings of the Bab often comment on particularly complex Islamic materials. They presuppose a knowledge of unusual dimensions of imamocentric Islamic learning and philosophy. This and the nature of his grammar and syntax (see p. 164), are among the factors which make certain of his writings difficult to translate and understand. They often expound highly complex aspects of Shiʿi-Shaykhi and other streams of thought.[37]

Examples of complex, esoteric works of direct or indirect influence on the Bab include portions of the composite K. Shams al-ma'arif al-kubra (The Sun of Sublime Gnosis) and other writings of the Sunni theologian Ahmad ibn 'Ali al-Būni (d. Cairo 622/1225), some of whose writings were commented upon by al-Ahsa'i (see p. 162). Therein talismanry, the Mightiest Name of God (*al-ism al-a'zam*), and related ideas are prominent. Aspects of the theology of the Divine Name *al-Qayyum* (Deity Self-Subsisting, *abjad* 156) in relationship to the Islamo-biblical patriarch Joseph (Yusuf, *abjad* 156) and to the Divine Name *al-Wahid* ('the Unique'; *abjad* 19) are variously set forth.[38]

36 The Bab, Q. Elixir.

37 In his P. Dala'il (45–46) the Bab notes both the originality as well as the treasured depth and hidden beyondness of his talismanic related disclosures summed up as the Kitab-i hayakil-i vahid (Book of the Temples of Unicity) perhaps a section within his K. Panj Sha'n.

38 This esoteric theologian and mystical writer wrote something like forty books in Arabic. He has somewhat unfairly been dismissed as a mere occultist magician.

Another key channel of esoteric influence upon the Bab is the Imam 'Ali attributed compilation, Mashariq anwar al-yaqin (The Dawning Places of the Lights of Certitude) of Radi al-Din Rajab ibn Muhammad al-Bursi (d. Tus, c. 814/1411). At one point, for example, we read in this deeply esoteric often letter-number inspired compilation:

> Secondly, it [the *basmala* of Q. 1] is meaningful on account of the number of its letters (*hurūf*) which are nineteen. And the number of the name w-a-h-d, *wahid* (Unique) is also nineteen. For such [letters], conjoined are indicative of oneness (*al-wahdat*), the divine Unity (*tawhid*) and the Divine Unicity (*al-wahdaniyya*). And the Unique (*al-wahid*) is an attribute of the One (*ahad*).[39]

These and other influences upon the Bab were often filtered or channeled through the many works and treatises of the Shiʿi-Shaykhi sages, Shaykh Ahmad al-Ahsa'i (d. Mutayrif near Medina, 1241/1826) and Sayyid Kazim al-Husayni al-Rashti (d. Karbala, 1259/1843).[40] Though these two learned and prolific Shiʿi thinkers were sometimes very critical of Ibn al-'Arabi and Mulla Sadra, the direct and indirect influence of such major Islamic philosopher-theologians is clear in their own writings as well as in those of the Bab. The al-Ziyara al-jami'a al-kabira, attributed to the tenth Imam 'Ali al-Hadi (d. c. 214/868), upon which Shaykh Ahmad wrote a lengthy (around 1,500 pages) commentary, was especially influential.[41] The Bab

---

Within certain of his books al-Būni associates the Name of God *al-Qayyūm* (Self-Subsisting) with that of Joseph (both abjad 156) and with the al-ism al-a'ẓam (the Mightiest Name of God) (see Shams, 185, 481, cf. on Wahid (the Unique), 187). Al-Būni also spelled out and commented upon versions of the Imam 'Ali generated Shiʿi graphical form of the Mightiest Name of God (ibid., 89, 93–94; cf. 242 ff., 373, 419) and constructed numerous talismans often similar to those written by the Bab (ibid., 89, 236, 242 ff., 318, 329, 370, 424). Additionally, he wrote about *jafr* (number-letter divination) on which subject the Bab claimed to be an initiate (Shams, 342 f.; K. Panj, 315). For the Bab, Joseph is the prototype of the messianic Imam Husayn (see QA 5). This is indicated in that the words *Qayyūm* ([Deity] "Self-Subsisting") and the prophetological name Yusuf (= Joseph) both have an identical *abjad* (numerical) value of 156.

39 Cited Bursi, Mashariq, 158.

40 Written from Maku (1847 or 48) for a Shaykhi enquirer, the Bab in his P. Dala'il, refers to these two as *mazharayn-i muqaddimayn*, "dual previous divine manifestations" of Reality (70). The Bab also wrote a very effusive Ziyarat-Nama for al-Ahsa'i (see p. 178).

41 Note that the chronological periods between Moses, David and Jesus given by the Bab in his P. Dala'il (18), reflect that given in the Sharh al-ziyara of al-Ahsa'i.

directly cites it within his writings,[42] along with other treatises of the fountainhead of al-Shaykhiyya (Shaykhism).[43] The Bab associated and studied with Rashti in Karbala for a considerable period (a year or so) in the early 1840s.[44] He makes explicit, direct, and indirect reference to Shaykhi sources, including the K. al-Fawa'id and/or Sharh al-fawa'id of al-Ahsa'i and the Lawa'mi al-Husayniyya (Husaynid Brilliances) and Sharh al-Khutba al-tutunjiyya (Commentary on the "Sermon of the Gulf") of al-Rashti.[45]

In the light of the numerous passages relating to number-letter (*abjad*) theological paradigms and configurations within the writings of the Bab, it should be noted that he was, as a messianic figure, expected to be a master of *jafr* (sometimes "numerological divination or prognostication"). Responding to a question about this subject, Shaykh Ahmad al-Ahsa'i had it that this would be the exclusive inheritance of the messianic Qa'im. Imam 'Ali had inherited an aspect of *jafr* as the *'ilm al-hurūf* (science of letters) from Muhammad via Gabriel when (mystically speaking) he was upon Mt. Paran (*jabal faran*).[46] The Bab claimed knowledge of the secrets of this *jafr* in the sense of numerical, chronological, talismanic, or gematria related insights.[47]

Dimensions of *jafr* referred to by the Imams as *jafr al-jami'* ("Comprehensive Jafr") could also indicate modes of lettrist (number–letter) prognostication.[48] This *jafr* is mentioned by many esoteric-minded twelver savants and by Baha'u'llah in his L. Hurūfat al-muqatta'a ("Tablet of the Isolated Letters," see Bib.). *Jafr*-related doctrines pertaining to such numbers as 19 and 361 (= *abjad kull shay'*, "All things") are so common within the writings of the Bab that he was quite frequently moved to call his followers in such late writings as the K. Panj, as his "pleroma" (*kull shay'*). He addressed them with the words "O Kull Shay'" (O Everything/ "All-Thingers"). On one occasion he told them that they were, in this respect, originated from a single proto-cosmic entity or (loosely) "Soul" (*nafs wahida*).[49]

42 See, e.g., Sharh al-Ziyara in P. Bayan 4.11.
43 See P. Dala'il, 52, 59, 61.
44 See P. Bayan 5.15.
45 See, for example, the Bab, Kh-Jidda; Sh-Kh-Tutunjiyya; P. Dala'il, 59.
46 JK. 1/ii: 87–88.
47 Refer K. Panj: IX. 3, 305 f.; IX. 4, 315 f.; XII.3, 428 ff.
48 See [pseudo-Imam] 'Ali, 1987.
49 KPS, XII. 3, 423.

THE STYLE, GRAMMAR, AND SYNTAX OF THE BAB

> Few of these books [of the Bab] are easy reading...they defy the most industrious and indefatigable reader. (Browne, 1909: 305)[50]

The Arabic and Persian of the Bab are sometimes grammatically and syntactically loose or creative in the sense of disdainful of inhibitive linguistic rules. They are not always in conformity with either Qur'anic or classical Arabic or standard modern Persian. This, it seems, before the creative weight of the "stream of consciousness" inspirations of the Bab, which he considered new forms of *wahy*, "divine revelation," comparable to that of the verses of the Arabic Qur'an and reminiscent of the *shatihiyyat* (ecstatic utterances) of certain Sufi mystics. The Arabic and Persian of the Bab sometimes coalesce or are intermixed. In P. Bayan II. 14, the Bab associates the sacred word of this largely Persian text with the Arabic of the Qur'an, Arabic being "the most eloquent of all languages" (*afṣah az kull-i ilsan*).[51] His Arabic can be syntactically Persianized and his Persian Arabized. In response to such matters, the Bab, in c. 1845–46, wrote a *Risala fi'l-nahw wa'l-sarf* (Treatise on Grammar and Morphology/Syntax) in which he defended the seemingly ungrammatical, innovative, and revealed nature of his writings.[52]

The Bab saw both Arabic and Persian as befitting vehicles for the communication of sacred revelations. Though not a neologism of the Bab, in his P. Bayan (especially II. 16, 57 f., nine times here) and elsewhere (e.g., P. Dala'il, five twice, nine twice, etc.), he quite frequently used the compounded Arabic then Persian superlative adjective (*a'ẓam-tar* = "extra greater than great").[53] This in order to highlight the supreme greatness of his verses and other aspects of his new religion. Like the architects of Shaykhism who at times utilized a lengthy multiplicity of complex adjectival expressions, the Bab at one point in his P. Bayan refers to the messianic theophany of *man yuzhiru-hu Allah*, as like the "Sun of Reality in its Radiance" (*shams*

50 On the criticism of the Bab's grammar, see further Wilson, PTR 1915: 636–38.

51 P. Bayan II.14, 52.

52 See the Bab, INBA 4011C:167–71; INBMC 67:121–25; McCants, 2012. Also, P. Dala'il, 28. In the paragraphs to follow, only a few examples of seldom if ever used verbal and nominal forms derived from various Arabic roots will be given. The matter of solecisms and grammatical errors cannot be dealt with in detail here.

53 See, for example, P. Bayan I. 2, 7; II.1 18; II. 16, 57 f. five nine times; III.2, 76 twice; III. 8, 84; III.13, 93; IV.2, 111; IV.3, 112f., three times; V.6, 161f. twice; V.13, 171; V.16, 178; VII.11, 253, etc.) and P. Dala'il, five twice, nine twice, etc.).

al-haqiqat bi-diya'iha). The latter divine figure is, furthermore, an elevated being characterized by the following complex, rhyming Arabo-Persian expressions: "Divine Reality (*haqiqat-i ilahiyyat*), Lordly Being (*kaynuniyyat-i rabbaniyyat*), Camphorated Essence (*kafuriyyat-i jawhariyyat*) and Aphophatic Isolatedness (*sadhijiyyat-i mujarradiyyat*)."[54]

The writings of the Bab contain a fair number of neologisms, new items of vocabulary or words not found in classical Arabic or in standard Persian dictionaries. These new formations are not simply errors, but often serve to capture and invoke deep, theologically weighty, inner (*batini*) and rhyming dimensions of religious truth. Generally unused or non-existent derivatives of the Arabic root b-h-w (forms I, III and VI are used), for example, from whence the verbal noun baha' (= splendor, glory, beauty, etc.) derives, are quite common in such later writings of the Bab as his K. Asma' and K. Panj. Such unused formations include Xth verbal and other adjectival forms which theoretically express the basic sense (of form I = "to be beautiful, glorious, radiant," etc.) with a further possibly seeking or practical connotation. A few examples of this can be found in the following scattered though not unrelated sentences within the K. Panj:

...سبحان الله

فما ابهی بهائه حیث کل ذا بهاءٍ یستبهی ببهائه

> Glorified be God!... There is no Supreme Glory (*abha*) beyond His Baha' (Glory) since every possessor of baha' (glory) is rendered glorious (*yastbaha* [sic.] = Xth form) through His Baha' (Glory)... O my God! His Baha' (Glory) is beyond that of every possessor of baha' (Glory)... *Man yuzhiru-hu Allah* (Him whom God shall make manifest) is His Baha' (Glory)... Nothing is supremely Glorious (*abha*) [save] the supreme Glory of His Baha' (Glory) (*wa ma abha abha baha'-ihi*)...Every possessor of baha' is prostrate before Thy Baha' (Glory)... All manner of inner glorification ('baha'iness') is even as Thy Glorification thereof (Xthform twice; *istabha' istabha'ika*).[55]

54 P. Bayan III.11 on the new *basmala*, 89.

55 K. Panj. 17, 34, 57, 84, 114, 116. See also the Bab, KPS, 51 (bahiyy wa istibha) 52 (ibtiha' ibtiha' mustabahiyy), 80 (wa ibtiha' mustabahiyy bahiyy), 143 (tustabaha [iyy] tustabahiyyūn), 168 (mustabha used in Persian in K. Panj, V.5). cf. 76 (buhyan al-buhya'), 79, 83 (dhalik al-bahiyy al-mutabahiyy al-mutabah), 108 (mutabahiyy bahiyy), 123–24, 128, 131, 135 (reference is made here to Baha'i mirrors), 142, 144, 147, 153, etc.

Elsewhere in the same book, the Bab uses other Xth verbal and nominal forms of Arabic roots, whether commonplace or unused. Towards the beginning of K. Panj XI. 3, he has it that the genesis of religion is ma'rifa ("gnosis"). Having said this, he poses a series of rhetorical questions using Xth and other related, rare or unused forms of Arabic roots. Successively present (in the same paragraph) are Xth forms of [1] 'a-r-f ("to know," Xth form = "to recognize"), [2] '-b-d, "to serve" Xth form = "to subjugate"). [3] sh-h-d, "to witness," Xth form = "to call upon." [4] n-t-q, "to articulate," Xth form = "to interrogate," [5] h-k-y, "to relate," Xth form = unused neologism and [6] sh-'-a', "to beam, radiate," the Xth form is an unused neologism:

... تستشعشع المشتشعشعات بشعشاع

Here, the context is that the Bab poses the rhetorical question as to how somebody can irradiate (*tastsha'sha'a*) radiant beams (*al-mustasha'sha'at*) with their own radiance (*bi-sha'sha'a*).[56] His use of such rhythmic word patterns incorporating neologisms, is typical of his uninhibited creative style. Translation of such passages is inevitably speculative and inadequate.

Something of a clarificatory theology behind the multiple, seven or more forms of Arabic roots utilized by the Bab can be found in P. Bayan VIII. 2 on the seven degrees of inheritance and its related theological foundations. Reference is made to seven levels expressive of the *maratib-i tawhid* ("modes of the Divine unity") associated with part of the aforementioned *shahada* (testimony of faith) or *harf-i ithbat*, the "locus of affirmation" (= *illa Allah*, "but God" which has 3 + 4 = 7 letters). For the Bab, this has to do with seven ways of describing or naming God, all deriving from the triliteral (threefold) Arabic root w-h-d which basically indicates singularity, oneness or uniqueness; most famously, coming to signify the divine unity (*tawhid*) in the Qur'an and elsewhere. As given by the Bab, these seven forms of the Name of God based on w-h-d are as follows—the superlative form taking precedence as it does in many new *basmala* type (In the Name of God the X, the Y) literary commencements and other invocations of the Bab:

56 See K. Panj, XI.3, 380. The Bab uses several Xth form related derivatives from the root sh-'-a' in various of his writings aside from K. Panj XI.3. Cf. the Musha'sha'iyya, indicating a fifteenth to nineteenth century CE., Shi'i ghuluww ("extremist") messianic faction looking to Muhammad ibn Falah (fifteenth century CE).

1. Awhad ("Supremely Singular")
2. Wahhad ("Causing Unity/Unicity")
3. Wahid ("the One/the Unique")
4. Wahid ("One Single/the Matchless")
5. Mutawahhid ("The Solitary/Single")
6. Muwahhid ("The Affirmer of the Divine Unity")
7. Muwahhad ("The One United/Unified")[57]

In certain of his late writings, the Bab goes beyond this sevenfold theological paradigm. As indicated, he quite frequently applies other rarer or non-existent forms of Arabic roots, thereby supplying unique items of vocabulary. Such often rhapsodic theological intimations are perhaps meant to be heard and internalized as well as pondered in a state of awe.

Not infrequently, the poetical rhyme within the writings of the Bab relies on the repetition of standard though sometimes esoteric religious vocabulary. Such innovative rhythmical texts can have an almost hypnotic depth of rhythmic, *dhikr*-like intensity. An example of such rhyme involving the use of words ending in the long "a" with (the glottal stop) *hamza*, is eight times repeated in the opening phrases of the Khutba al-jaliliyya ("The Discourse of the Divine Majesty"), which precedes some versions of the T. 'Asr. This may be summed up with the following emboldened transliterated phrases: a divine self-revelation (*tajalli*) is expressed through the use of following rhyming words, (1) divine Splendor (**al-diya'**), (2) his glorious self-revelation nigh the theophanic Cloud (**al-ama'**), (3), through the Divine Glory (**bi'l-baha'**), (4) relative to a lauditive doxophany (**al-thana'**) associated with the divine Resplendence (**al-sana'**) before this theophanic Cloud (**li'l-'ama'**). Consequently, even heaven (**al-sama'**) withdrew beneath the shadows of the divine sublimity (**zalala al-kubriya'**).[58]

Another similar, sevenfold example of this *alif* + *hamza* as a word end-rhyme can be found in a letter or brief scriptural Tablet of the Bab to an unidentified though very elevated follower. In this brief communication we

57 P. Bayan, 273–78. In some mss. of the P. Bayan [2] and [3] (above) are reversed. These personal translations and transliterations are sometimes very loose. This section of the P. Bayan also mentions invoking God 100 times by each of these sevenfold Names. Here also I am partially indebted to Browne's observations in his summary of the P. Bayan VIII. 2 (in Momen, ed. 1987: 394–95) and Trav. Narr II: 'Note R', 312 ff. where he offers the following comparable Latinized forms: "[1] Unissimus, [2] Unator, [3] Unicus, [4] Unus, [5] Unatus, [6] Unficiens and [7] Unificatus. See also p. 210 on K. Panj.
58 INBMC 40: 1.

find the following successive rhyming phrases: (1) nur **al-baha'** (Light of Glory), (2) dhikr **al-insha'** (*dhikr* of regeneration), (3) sirr **al-qida'** (mystery of the decree), (4) mushir **al-imda'** (the governor of realization), (5) kafur **al-thana'** (the camphor of laudation), (6) tur **al-sina'** (Mount Sinai), and (7) ẓuhur rukn **al-hamra'** (the theophany of the crimson pillar). Shortly after this, a similar rhyme is maintained with words ending in ab, **kitab** (book), **wahhab** (the generous), etc.[59]

The Bab commented upon poetry and was himself highly poetical. Select poetry by the one-time Ibadi then Kaysani follower of al-Mukhtar and finally a prolific Shi'i poet, Sayyid al-Himyari (d. c. 178/789), was early on commented on by the Bab.[60] The poetry of the female Sufi mystic Rabiya al-Adawiyya of Baṣra (d. c. 185/801) seems to have been influential, perhaps as mediated through 'Attar's *Tazkirat al-awliya'* ("Memorials regarding those Intimate with God," sect, VI).[61] Coming from Shiraz, one of the focal centers of Sufism, Persian poetry, 'Irfani philosophy and esoteric "gnosis," it is not at all surprising that the Bab was so creative and poetical. Among many other poetical illuminati, Shiraz was the homeland of Ruzbihan Baqli Shirazi (d. 606 /1209), Abu Muhammad Sa'di (d. c. 690/1291), and Muhammad Hafiẓ-i Shirazi (d. 792/1390). Rhyme and poetical phrases, benedictions and elevated rhyming laudations inform many of the writings of the Bab.

PERSONAL LETTERS, "SCRIPTURAL TABLETS" (LAWH, PL. ALWAH)

In the following paragraphs, I shall introduce something of the writings of the Bab other than those dealt with in summary form later in this chapter, under the heading of the "Five Modes of Revelation," into which the Bab divided his writings.

---

59 See the letter or Tablet of the Bab to an unidentified individual in the Browne coll. Ms. F23 (9) [143–49], 144.

60 On Sayyid al-Himyari and his poetry see, for example, Ibn Shahrashub, Manaqib (Himyari is often cited here); Majlisi, Bihar, 10: 232–33, 53: 131–32 and the article on him in EI² by Wadad Kadi. Among the lost works of the Bab is a commentary on a poem (or poems) of al-Himyari (see Kh-Jidda, trans. IX. 6–7).

61 In P. Bayan VII:19 (271–72, on Salat) the Bab clearly (directly or indirectly) draws on this poetry of Rabiya. He defines true *'ibadat* (worship) in a distinctly Rabi'an fashion when he directs that God should be worshipped intensely, outside a fear of hell-fire (*nar*) or the hope of Paradise (*jannat*) (see Lambden, 2002).

Letters or Scriptural Tablets

The Bab wrote many personal letters to family members, relatives and his own Babi followers. In addition, for example, he wrote to contemporary notables, clerics (Sunni, Shiʿi and Shaykhi), governors and rulers or monarchs.[62] Like the hundreds of questions put, for example, to such leading clerics as his near contemporary, Shaykh Ahmad al-Ahsa'i, a considerable number of the writings of the Bab were written in reply to questions about religious matters. It was in reply to questions about theological and other issues that the Bab wrote numerous treatises (*risala*, pl. *rasa'il*), epistles or booklets (*ṣahifa*, pl. *ṣuhuf*) and prayers (*munajat*). Messianic and eschatological prophecies and their possible contemporary fulfillment scenarios were always a matter of great interest and constant inquiry. Almost every major book about the Bab and his writings contains texts of his letters or scriptural tablets (*lawh* pl. *alwah*) and treatises.[63]

Like Muhammad, the Bab also wrote to certain of the Middle Eastern rulers of his day. In light of messianic and apocalyptic expectations, he had a global, if not cosmic outreach.[64] He called for the universal and world-wide spread of his new religion. From very early on, he addressed (and continued to address, at least five) major epistles to Muhammad Shah Qajar (r. 1834–48) and his main minister 'Abbas Iravani (of Yerevan), Hajji Mirza Aqasi (d. 1265/1848).[65] From Muscat (now in the Sultanate of Oman) in early 1845, he also wrote to the 31st Ottoman Sultan, Abdülmecid I (= 'Abd al-Majid, d.

62 For the facsimile of a brief mid-1844 Persian letter of the Bab to his wife Khadijah Khanum (d. Shiraz, 1299/1882) written from Bushire just prior to the onset of his 1844–45 pilgrimage journey, see Balyuzi, 1973: opposite the title page. This letter begins with a slightly truncated *basmala* then an address to *jan-i shirin-i man*, "my sweet soul" (see further, Balyuzi, 1973: 57; see also the facsimile letter in Balyuzi, 1981 opposite 27). Numerous letters to the Afnan (lit. "twigs" of the Sacred Tree) or family of the Bab can be found, for example, in the several books about the Afnan family (which cannot be listed here though reference should be made to Rabbani, 2008).

63 E.g. see Afnan, 2000. See, for example, the thirty-eight early letters of the Bab mentioned in his Kitab al-Fihrist and those cited in INBA 6007C and the first three vols. of Mazandarani, KZH (cf. MacEoin, Sources, 50–53).

64 The Bab made many addresses within his mid-1844 QA to inhabitants of celestial levels of being including the ahl al-'ama' (denizens of the theophanic cloud) and the ahl al-'arsh (angelic beings surrounding the celestial Throne).

65 Aside from the address to Muhammad Shah and Aqasi in QA1, the Sūrạt al-Mulk, at least five letters to Muhammad Shah are extant (Afnan, 2000: 460; Quinn, 2012: 160 f.). Note also the c. 1848 Khutba Qahriyya, the Khutba[s] of Wrath for Hajji Mirza Aqasi (see Amanat, Resurrection, 381; MacEoin, Sources, 92–93).

1861). In this latter brief epistle, there is an address to all the people of the world (*ahl al-ard*), including the inhabitants of Constantinople (Istanbul) and beyond (*al-rum*). As with his communications with Muhammad Shah (cf. QA1), he requested that this Sultan make a universal proclamation of his new religion as expressed in his inspired writings.[66] From Muscat, the Bab boldly wrote to the then Ottoman Sunni Sharif al-Hijaz (Sherif of Mecca) Muhammad ibn 'Abd al-Mu'in ibn 'Awn (d. 1274/1858). Aside from the two Shaykhi recipients of the early 1845 Ṣahifa bayn al-haramayn (Epistle between the two Shrines), the Bab during his pilgrimage, also wrote to other such leading Shaykhis as Mulla Hasan Gawhar [Jawhar] (d. 1849), namely Shaykh Hasan ibn 'Ali al-Tabrizi of the village of Qaraja Daghi near Tabriz.[67]

The Bab wrote many further letters to other Shi'i and some Sunni 'ulama' of his day, as well as to groups of the 'ulama' collectively (cf. QA. II), such as those resident in Isfahan and Tabriz.[68] Among the most important early writings (c. early 1845) addressed to the 'ulama', is his five to ten page Kitab al-'ulama' (Book for the clerics).[69] Therein, the Bab presents himself as a servant (*'abd*) and one unlettered (*al-ummi*), a Persian (non-'Arab, *al-a'jami*) who has received an undoubtedly revealed book. This book (perhaps the QA) constitutes a "proof" (*hujjat*) from the occulted Remnant of God (*baqiyyat Allah*) who is a channel of divine revelation. It contains addresses to both Muslims and the people of the Book (*ahl al-kitab*, primarily Jews and Christians) and affirms that the "Spirit," Jesus and/or the Holy Spirit (*al-ruh*) assists him [the Bab] under all circumstances.[70]

The letters of the Bab to kings, rulers, clerics, major disciples and devotees, etc., are of very great doctrinal importance in the evolution of his new religion. So too are his letters or epistles and treatises written to his followers or major disciples such as the eighteen "Letters of the Living One" (*hurūf al-hayy*; *hayy* = abjad 18), including Mulla Husayn Bushrū'i and Fatima Baraghani (entitled Tahira, "The Pure One" and Qurrat al-'Ayn, "Solace of the Eyes," d. 1852 CE).[71] Some such communications were very

66 This though the Ottoman sultan was castigated as a "follower of Satan" for his treatment of the emissary of the Bab, his disciple Mulla 'Ali Bastami (partially cited Afnan, 2000: 90, cf. Momen, 1982).

67 Partially cited in Afnan, 2000: 89.

68 Mazandarani, KZH II: 110 f.; Afnan, 2000: 107–111.

69 Kitab al-'ulama' in INBMC 67: 212–13; INBMC 91: 89–90 and Afnan, 'Ahd, 109.

70 K.'Ulama' in Afnan, 2000: 108. The great Muhyi al-Din Ibn al-'Arabi similarly claimed that Jesus was always intimately associated with him.

71 The eighteen (the *abjad* numerical value of *hayy* = 10+8 = 18) "Letters of the Living"

brief, while others were lengthy and complex, like several of the weighty letters written in reply to questions of Sayyid Yahya Darabi, Vahid.[72]

An example of a doctrinally important letter of the Bab is that addressed in late 1846 (or early 1847) to the prominent Khurasani Shaykhi then Babi, Mulla Shaykh Ali Turshizi, entitled 'Azim (d. Tehran 1852). Therein the Bab selects this then prominent follower to make more generally and publicly known his claim to Qa'imiyya, to being the Shi'i Islamic messiah. He is described by the Bab as one chosen to be as an angel or messenger (*mala-k*[an]) with the duty of crying out at the behest of the Qa'im, to the effect that he is indeed made manifest.[73] Written from Maku (dated c. 1848), another important letter of the Bab on similar messianic lines, was addressed to the widely respected, 'Alid Sunni, Abu al-Thana', Shihab al-Din al-Alusi (d. 1270 /1854), a one-time mufti of Baghdad.[74] Within it the Bab claims (subordinate) divinity and to be the awaited Sunni-Shi'i Mahdi (Rightly-Guided One), "I manifested myself on the Day of Resurrection... I am the Mahdi."[75]

Certain manuscripts of writings of the Bab contain examples of his prayers and letters written in reply to questions and other matters. An example is the Browne Coll. manuscript F21 (9) which contains thirty-two Arabic letters of the Bab, including one to the crypto-Babi, the Georgian Christian born Chongur Enakolopashvili, a eunuch renamed Manūchihr Khan Gurji (d. 1847), the Mu'tamid al-Dawla, a one-time governor of Isfahan. Another text in this manuscript was written for Fatima Baraghani, Tahira, Qurrat al-'Ayn (d. 1852).[76] Many other manuscripts and a few printed texts also contain important letters of the Bab.[77]

---

are variously identified. They are, for example, listed in Dawn-Breakers (see preliminary facsimile of letters to all eighteen and others and, 80–81; Balyuzi, 1973: 26–27 and many other sources. They largely have a Shi'i - Shaykhi background and received many scriptural communications and directives from the Bab (for examples see DB:65–70, 80–84; SWB:148, 159–index).

72 See EGB Coll. F21, item 5, 35–44.

73 Printed in facsimile in [Anon] Qismati az alwah, and reproduced in MacEoin Sources (end pages); cited N-Kaf, 209; Mazandarani, KZH III: 164–46; 2nd ed. III: 132–33, 166–69; cf. DB: 313, 303.

74 Alusi is best known for his tafsir work, the Ruh al-ma'ani fi tafsir al-qur'an al-'azim... (The Spirit of the Meaning in Commentary upon the Mighty Qur'an). At the time of the trial of Mulla 'Ali Bastami (d. Istanbul, 1846) for alleged heresy, he was among those clerics who condemned him.

75 Za'im al-Dawla, Miftah, 212–15.

76 Nicholson, 1932: 62.

77 Aside from numerous ms. compilations see especially Hasani, al-Babiyyūn; Anon, Qismati az alwah; Taherzadeh, SWB (1976+78); Afnan, 2000.

THE GENESIS OF THE NEW SHARIʿA (LAWS), THE KHASAʾIL-I SABʿA (MID. 1845)

The laws, rituals and shariʿa-related directives of the Bab are scattered throughout many of his writings and were never systematized or finalized into one sacred book. They have their genesis in the Khasa'il-i sabʿa, or (Ar.) al-Shaʿa'ir al-sabʿa (The Seven [Religio-Legal] Directives').[78] Dating immediately after his return to Bushire in 1845, this work is the first major though very brief (100 Arabic words) preliminary implementation of the religio-legal hallmarks of the new religion of the Bab.[79] It called for the practice of seven new signs of Babi piety. These directives were an intimation of the fullness of the coming, largely 1847–50, eschatological shariʿa (religious law) of the Bab. Aside from (sometimes identical) religious stipulations within select surahs of the Qayyūm al-asma'[80] and a few other pre-1845 writings, the Khasa'il constitutes one of the earliest legal-ritualistic writings of the Bab. Its seven tokens, hallmarks or directives for the conduct of the true believer from mid. 1845 are as follows:[81]

خصائل سبعه

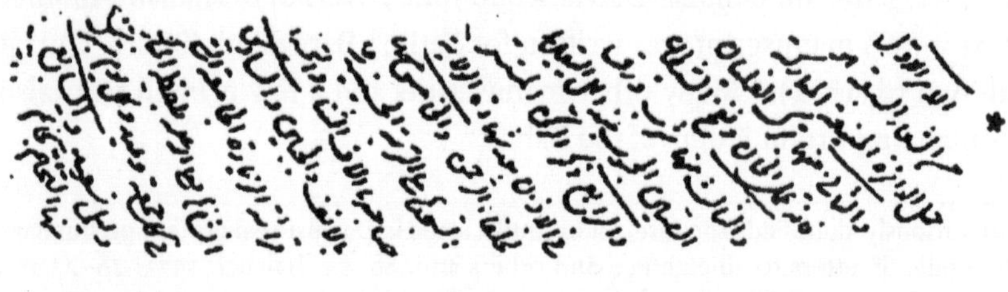

78 The text of the [Risala-yi] Khasa'il-i sabʿa (= KS) or al-Shaʿa'ir al-sabʿa, is cited in a letter of Mulla ʿAbd al-Karim Qazvini (d. 1268/1851–52) to the greatest uncle of the Bab, the Khal-i Aʿzam Hajji Mirza Sayyid ʿAli. It can be consulted in facsimile in Afnan, 2000: 99. A typed and summarized form of it also exists on page 100. The very brief Khasa'il was first communicated to the greatest uncle of the Bab, the Khal-i Aʿzam, Hajji Mirza Sayyid ʿAli in 1845 by Muhammad ʿAli entitled Quddus (the Most Holy) who had accompanied the Bab on pilgrimage.

79 Afnan, 2000: 83.

80 See especially QA 49, sūrat al-nida' and QA 50–51 sūrat al-ahkam I and II as well as the two Sūrat al-ahkam III and IVc at QA 104–5.

81 The slightly expanded image of the Khasa'il here is reproduced from Afnan, 2000: 99.

1. the carrying of an inscribed circular talisman,
2. the abandonment of smoking the "hubble-bubble" or "water-pipe" (*qalyan*),
3. the drinking of white Chinese tea in the company of the "people of certitude" (*ahl al-yaqin*),[82]
4. mention of the [Bab as] the Secreted Pillar [the Bab] (*al-rukn al-mustasirr*) in the Shiʿi *adhan* ("Call to prayer") after the twelver form of the *shahada* ("the testimony of faith"),
5. devotional praise and prostration through the clay turbat al-Husayniyya ("token shrine" of Imam Husayn),
6. the recitation of the Ziyarat al-jamiʿa (the "Comprehensive Visitation Prayer," originating with Imam ʿAli through ʿAli al-Hadi or as renewed by the Bab himself) at certain devotional and other gatherings, and
7. the wearing of an engraved white carnelian signet-ring indicative of Babi allegiance.[83]

These seven directives were a challenge to many of the adherents of the emergent religion of the Bab, especially the publicly proclaimed addition to the Shiʿi *adhan* (call to prayer).[84] The claim of Babiyya (Gate-hood) of the Bab was only cryptically or allusively set forth at this time. Thus, for example, in the seventh directive of the Khasa'il, the Bab recommends the wearing of a "white carnelian signet-ring" (*al-ʿaqiq al-abyad*) with the number 273 engraved on it after the words, "There is no God, but God," "Muhammad is the Messenger of God (*rasul Allah*)" and "ʿAli is the wali-Allah" ("The legatee of God"). The final 273 here is the abjad numerical value of the phrase "ʿAli Muhammad (= 202) is the Gate of God" (Bab Allah = 5+66 = 71), which numerically (202+71) adds up to 273.

82 In Khasa'il 3b it is stated that refined Babi tea-drinking should take place in the company of the *ahl al-yaqin* (people of certitude), a Sufi phrase found, for example, in the writings of Muhammad ibn ʿAli, al-Hakim al-Tirmidhi (d. c. 320/932) among many other Sufi writers. The phrases *ʿayn al-yaqin*, *haqq al-yaqin* and their like are quite common in the writings of the Bab. See, for example, SB Haramayn and Kh-Qahriyya, Afnan, 2000: 360.

83 It might be noted here that Mulla ʿAbd al-Karim Qazvini (d. 1268/1851–52), later a secretary of the Bab known as al-Katib, had a key role in attempts to alter the Shiʿi adhan ('call to prayer') formula. For more on the Bab and the early jihad cancellation see Lambden 2005:21 ff.

84 For a full translation, summary detailed commentary on the Khasa'il see Lambden website and 2011/2020 (forthcoming).

THE ALL-COMPREHENSIVE BAYAN (EXPOSITION) OF THE BAB

> The Bayan is in truth Our conclusive proof for all created things, and all the peoples of the world are powerless before the revelation of its verses. It enshrineth the sum total of all the Scriptures, whether of the past, or of the future.[85]

For the Bab, then, the Q. rooted term Bayan (Q. 55:4b; 75:17–19) indicates both the pre-Babi (Abrahamic) as well as the eschatological (Qajar era/nineteenth century) exposition, disclosure and clarification of religious truth. The Bab taught that all of the revelatory categories or modes of revealed writing are registered in his Bayan ("Exposition"). This all-embracing term or title echoes the title of the Qur'an (or "Recitation") or Furqan (the "Criterion," Q. 25:1 f.). That the totality of the sacred writings of the Bab constitute the Bayan ("Exposition"), is thousands of times presupposed and often explicitly stated by the Bab. In his P. Bayan he stated that all of his sacred writings (*athar-i nuqta*) constitute the Bayan.[86] In the prolegomenon of his Arabic Bayan he explains that whatsoever was set down in the Bayan is expressive of his religion (*dini*). As an inimitable expression of his verses (*ayat*). His Bayan (Exposition) is his Proof (*hujjat*) unto and for everything (*kull shay'*) within all the worlds (*al-'alamin*). It enshrines all of revealed verses, be they of the past, or of the future.[87]

According to the directives within the P. Bayan and other writings, such revelations as the Bayan should be well-written, calligraphed or printed, sometimes with colored or precious inks. The Bab taught that beautiful new styles of calligraphy should be used in setting down his revelations.[88]

THE FIVE MODES OF REVELATION

The Bab divided his writings into five (cf. the *abjad* value of Bab and the Arabic letter "h" = five) or more *sha'n* (pl. *shu'un*), revelatory modes,

85 The Bab Ar. Bayan cited SWB:113; trans. 159.

86 P. Bayan III.17, 102. The Bab called his followers (Per.) ahl-i Bayan, the people or community of the Bayan (P. Dala'il, 68).

87 Ar. Bayan 1:11, 21–22.

88 P. Bayan IX. 2, 313. On the Persian and Arabic Bayans, see p. 204 in this chapter.

categories, grades, or styles of revelation.[89] Though without clear-cut, simplistic definitions, these revelatory modes are largely derived from Qur'anic terminology, though they also reflect select Islamic and pre-Islamic sacred literary genres.[90] These categories sometimes overlap. At times they seem virtually synonymous. Within the writings of the Bab we find alternative, slightly variant or reordered versions of the five categories.[91] In simplified terms they are (the Bab often gives them in plural form): [1] Ayat (verses), [2] Munajat (devotions), [3] Tafasir (commentaries), [4] Suwar (sing. sūrah) or scriptural divisions, and [5] Kalimat-i Farsiyya (Persian texts). In more detail, with some notes in clarification and examples, they are:

[1] **AYAT** (SING. **AYA**): REVEALED, QUR'AN-LIKE ARABIC TEXTS

The production of such verses by the Bab are said to have constituted (like that of the Prophet Muhammad) his true, inimitable miracle.[92]

In an unpublished, unstudied letter of the Bab, modes (pl. *shu'un*) of *tafsir* are especially associated with the Prophet Muhammad (*al-nabi*), the *munajat* mode with the *wali* (sanctified Imam, cf. 'Ali), that of *al-'Ilm*, "knowledge" (presumably surahs or the suwar al-'Ilmiyya, no. 4, p. 190) with the *abwab* (gates; perhaps here Shaykh Ahmad and Sayyid Kazim, cf. QA. 24:80). It is then stated by the Bab that "We" (God through himself) had generated these "modes" (*shu'un*) and ultimately specialized them to the manifestations of the "Living One" (*al-hayy*), perhaps himself and his eighteen "Letters of the Living" (*hurūfat al-hayy*). The *ayat* (verses), as the first of the modes, are directly associated with God through the instrumentality of the Bab as his elevated *Dhikr* (Remembrance).[93]

For the Bab, revealed *ayat* (verses) are foremost. His revelations reflect Qur'anic verses. As we shall see, he produced many thousands of these

---

89 See P. Bayan II.9, 14–15; III.17; IV.9–10; VI.1; IX.2; P. Dala'il, 26 ff.; K. Panj, 274–75, 366–67, etc.; Mohammad Hosseini, 1995:724–25).

90 The Qur'an rooted scriptural terminology of the Bab has Hebrew, Syriac/Aramaic origins. It is basically Abrahamic (pre-Islamic, Islamo-biblical) rooted scriptural terminology.

91 In his c. 1868–70 Sūrat al-haykal (Surah of the Temple) Baha'u'llah similarly refers to his verses as being "in nine styles" (*shu'un*) of revelation (AQA 4:273). It is not clear exactly what is meant by these "nine styles," though the use of nine is obviously related to the abjad numerical value of the word Baha' (2+5+1+1 = 9) as may be contrasted with the five grades into which the Bab (*abjad* = 5) divided his writings.

92 P. Bayan III.16, 101; P. Dala'il, 10, etc.

93 Untitled Tablet of the Bab in Browne Coll. ms. F 23 (9), 143, cf. Browne 1892a.

verses. In the third of his "seven proofs" he specifically states that the confirmation of divine power (*ithbat-i qudrat*) is possible through the production of *ayat* (verses).[94] They occupy the primary level of sacred writ (*bi-haqiqat-i avvaliyya*). The four other modes of revelation exist to some degree on lower levels.[95] The Bab held that the revelation of the verses of the Q. was the pre-eminent proof of the prophetic mission of Muhammad. So too his own. His "seven proofs" are closely related to the miracle of the verses of the Islamic holy book. Before this God-generated "miracle" of the revelation of *ayat* (verses), the performance of outward miracles (*mu'jizat*) is deemed unimportant. The revelation of the Bayan (Exposition) by the Bab was, he held, the inimitable (*i'jaz*) miracle of a 25-year-old *nafs-i ummi* ("an unlettered person").[96]

In the Q., a verse (*aya*) may extend for a mere two isolated letters (such as *ha'-mim* and *ya-sin*) or a word or two, to a quite lengthy sentence or paragraph (e.g., Q. 2:282). In his P. Bayan, the Bab defines a revealed verse (*bayt*, synonymous with *aya*) as extending for thirty letters (*harf*) or forty with vowels (*i'rab*).[97] This though many of his writings contain lengthy, complex verses, extended sentences and pericopes of many more than thirty to forty letters.

[2] MUNAJAT (PL.): DEVOTIONAL INSPIRATIONS, REVELATIONAL SUPPLICATIONS OR PRAYERFUL, INVOCATORY DISCOURSE

At one point in his T. Kawthar, the Bab speaks of his writing a Ṣahifa fi'l-munajat (Treatise of Devotional Revelations) in just six hours. This would be expressive of the "greatest level of nobility (*sharaf al-akbar*) in the station of [revealed] verses" (*fi maqam al-ayat*). Such would be an outer (*zahir*) as well as an inner (*batin*) insight into a matter "abstruse, bewilderingly abstruse" (*sa'b mustasa'b*).[98] In the later P. Dala'il also, the Bab accords *munajat* with (and from) God, an especially noble (*sharaf*) status. The *munajat* mode of communion with God as revelation from Him, is here said to be akin to the *kalam Allah* (theology, Word/Speech of God) Himself (cf. no. 1, p. 175, *ayat* of God). There is the Word communicated from God and the *munajat*

94 P. Dala'il, 9.
95 P. Bayan III. 17, 102.
96 cf. Q. 7:157; Dala'il, 10 f., 25.
97 P. Bayan VI.1, 187. See further on the revelation of verses P. Bayan, VI, 7; VI, 8; VI, 15; VII.13.
98 T. Kawthar, f. 103b.

with God. For the Bab, the latter has an exalted, God-empowered interior dimension (*ruh al-munajat*).[99]

Furthermore, in his P. Bayan and elsewhere, the Bab mentions his great facility in revealing many verses of *munajat* (devotional texts).[100] For him, *munajat* as revealed devotions have a very elevated status. Such a conviction is no doubt expressive of the depth of his own devotionalistic piety. Some of his opponents were critical of this God-fearing devotion, imagining it a sign of depravity. For the Bab himself, however, it was the opposite, a certain sign of divine communication.

DEVOTIONAL WRITINGS OF THE BAB

Like Imami Shiʿi Islam, the religion of the Bab is very rich in devotional literature. Devotional invocations, benedictions, and prayers are everywhere apparent within the universe of Shiʿi Islam as well as within the writings of the Bab. Loosely falling within the munajat mode of scriptural communication, are writings of the Bab such as prayers (*salat*), devotions (*munajat*), supplications (*du'a*), repetitive benedictions, and the practice of ecstatic remembrance (*dhikr*). They are also dialogue-type prayers of the Bab in reply to specific questions. The writings of the Bab are full of prayers and devotional invocations, supplications, litanies, and *dhikr*-type chants. A specific directive within P. Bayan is to repeat the pious Arabic chant "O God" (*ya Allah*, "O God!") no less than 4,000 times.[101]

Such calls to invocational devotion are so numerous in the writings of the Bab, that it would prove impossible for any single person, no matter how devout, to carry them all out. Rhythmic invocations, *dhikr*-like chants, and prayers constitute a major proportion of his writings though he does say in his P. Bayan that a single act of sincere inner *dhikr* (remembrance)

99 P. Dala'il, 26–27. In his P. Dala'il (26), the Bab holds a very elevated view of *munajat* in the light of the opening passage (no.1 = entitled in Persian 'Ta'rif-i Bayan, "The Determination of the Exposition") within the Misbah al-shari'a (Niche of Islamic Law) (9) ascribed to Imam Ja'far al-Sadiq (see Misbah, 9 and 14 ff.). One translation of a recension of this Arabic work into Persian with a commentary was made by 'Abd al-Razzaq Gilani in the seventeenth century (c. 1087/1676). Its influence on the Bab would seem to have been immense. Miraculously, the Bab states that he could reveal 1,000 munajat devotional verses in just six hours (P. Dala'il, ibid.).

100 P. Bayan, II.1, 13.

101 P. Bayan VIII.19, 209. See further MacEoin, 1994:12 f.

with delicate spiritual intimacy (*ruh va rayhan*), is preferable to a thousand repetitions.[102] Especially important in this respect is P. Bayan V.11 because it includes details about *salat* (prayer) for the times of both birth (*mawlud*) and death (*mawt*). Additionally, there are many prayers of the Bab for specific times of day, for holy days, festivals, and special occasions.[103] The Islamic daily obligatory prayer (*salat*) appears to have been replaced with nineteen prayerful devotional prostrations (*rak'at*) carried out between noon and sunset.[104]

Moreover, there are many sometimes lengthy *Ziyarat-nama* (Visitation Tablets) texts of the Bab, commemorative writings of varying length written in honor of certain twelver Imams and other new age worthies such as the *hurūfat al-hayy* ("Letters of the Living One"), including Mulla Husayn (Letter no.1) and Muhammad 'Ali, Quddus ("The Most Holy," Letter No. 18).[105] Such texts are often meant to be recited at the shrine or resting place of whomsoever they honor and commemorate. The Bab composed a very effusive Ziyarat-nama for Shaykh Ahmad al-Ahsa'i.[106] Towards its beginning we read:

> May the quintessences of the eras (*jawhariyyat al-midad*) in the world of Sarmad, Perpetual Eternality, circle around thee [Shaykh Ahmad], O Light of Glory-Beauty (*nur al-baha'*), the Dhikr-Remembrance of Regeneration (*dhikr al-insha'*) and the Mystery of Accomplishment (*sirr al-qida'*). And upon [thee be] the Secreted Mystery of Realization (*mustasirr al-imda'*), the Camphor of the Sinaitic Mount (*kafur tur al-sina'*), the theophany of the Crimson Pillar (*zuhur rukn al-hamra'*) and the mid-most Locus of mine inmost heart (*buhbuhat fu'adi*) which is most beloved (*ahabb*) of God, My Lord.[107]

Among the distinctly devotional writings of the Bab, for example, is the fourteen-section Du'a-yi Ṣahifa (see p. 199), the similarly organized Ṣahifa a'mal al-sana ("Treatise on the Religious Practices of the Year"), and the

102 P. Bayan IX.4, 318.
103 The Islamic five daily Islamic prayer times are: [1] morning (al-subh), [2] noon (al-zuhr), [3] afternoon (*al-'asr*), [4] midday (*al-maghrib*), and [5] night (*al-isha'*).
104 Ar. Bayan VII.19.
105 See esp. the Bab in TBA. ms. 6007C.
106 The resting place of al-Ahsa'i was in the (desecrated since 1925, if not earlier) Jannat al-Baqi' ("Paradise of tree stumps") cemetery near Medina (in Saudi Arabia).
107 Browne, ms. CUL, 85–87.

seven-section Ṣahifa bayn al-haramayn (Epistle between the two Shrines). Of uncertain early date are his own versions of two major recreated Shi'i Ziyara (Visitation) texts, the al-Ziyarat al-jami'a al-saghira (Lesser Comprehensive Visitation Supplication), and the al-Ziyarat al-jami'a al-kabira (Greater Comprehensive Visitation Supplication).[108] Such later writings as the K. Panj and the K. Asma' also contain numerous devotional and invocatory aspects.

A considerable proportion of the writings of the Bab are commentaries upon and re-creations of Shi'i Islamic invocations and devotional texts. The Tasbih al-Fatima (The Glorification of Fatima), for example, is a fairly brief conflation of 100 invocations, consisting of thirty-four times *Allah Akbar* ("God is greatest" = the *takbir*), thirty-three times *al-hamdu li'llah* (the *tahmid*), and thirty-three times *subhan Allah* (Glorified be God) (the *tasbih*).[109] On this, the Bab wrote a detailed, twenty-page commentary in which Fatima and two of her children, the Imams Hasan and Husayn, are greatly glorified.[110] The Bab commented at least once on the Shi'i morning prayer ascribed to Imam 'Ali, the Du'a al-Ṣabah or such phrases within it as "O Thou the testimony of whose Essence (*dhat*) is by virtue of Thine Essence (*dalla 'ala dhatihi bi-dhatihi*)."[111] The Shi'i Ramadan dawn prayer, the Du'a Sahar (Dawn Prayer), or Du'a al-baha'(Prayer of Glory) for the fasting period, attributed to the fifth Imam Muhammad al-Baqir (d. c. 126/743), along with the closely related Du'a yawm al-mubahalah (Supplication for the day of Mutual Execration) transmitted by the eighth Imam 'Ali al-Rida' (d. 201/818), were massively influential within the writings of the Bab.[112] In both versions this supplication opens:

108 There are scores of Shi'i Islamic Ziyara texts for all of the fourteen immaculate ones, including the twelver Imams, from the Prophet and his daughter Fatima, from 'Ali ibn Abi Talib (d. 40/661) to Imam Muhammad al-Mahdi (d. 260/874), the twelfth Imam. There are even Shi'i Ziyara texts honoring pre-Islamic Abrahamic figures.

109 See Majlisi, Bihar 85:334.

110 T. Fatimah, 180 ff.

111 INBMC 14:400–9; 40:55–62.

112 For Shi'i Muslims, this day was that upon which 'Ali was appointed wali (legatee), which is set a few days earlier (on the 22nd or the 18th day of this month). "The Day of Mutual Execration" (*yawm al-mubahila*) denotes the day on which Muhammad all but engaged in mutual execration (*mubahala*) with select Christians of Najran. It was on this Day that he is believed to have gathered the proto-Shi'i (subsequently named) "people of the cloak" (*ahl al-kisa'*, cf. Qur'an 33:32), namely (apart from [1] Muhammad himself), [2] 'Ali, [3] Fatima, [4] Hasan, and [5] Husayn.

> O my God! I beseech Thee by Thy Baha' (Splendor) at its most splendid (*abha*) for all Thy Splendor (*baha'*) is truly resplendent (*bahiyy*). I, verily, O my God! beseech Thee by the fullness of Thy Splendor (*baha'*).[113]

This rhythmic devotion was frequently cited and rewritten/revealed by the Bab. In his P. Dala'il, he related the Du'a al-Ṣabah to Muhammad, Ali and Imam Husayn, especially since its divine attribute, *nur* (Light) is reckoned to be especially indicative of this Sayyid al-Shahada' (prince of Martyrs).[114] Often the various nineteen or more successive attributes within this prayer, *baha'* (splendor), *jalal* (glory), *jamal* (beauty), *'azimat* (grandeur), *nur* (light), etc., initiate devotional paragraphs and benedictions in the later writings of the Bab. Many of his uses of the words *baha'* and *abha* and *baha'-Allah* are rooted therein.[115] Within the K-Asma' and K. Panj Sha'n this is strikingly evident. The Bab named the nineteen new months of his innovative Babi or Badi' (new) calendar after the successive divine attributes occurring in certain of, or at the commencement of, these devotional texts.[116]

Among the numerous other Shi'i devotional texts of influence upon the Bab, are the Du'a al-Ṣabah attributed to Imam 'Ali[117] and the Du'a al-Simat ("The Prayer of the Signs").[118] The latter around five-page Arabic supplication was evidently well-known to the Bab. It commences with a solemn beseeching of God through a prayer beginning with a key, answer-invoking reference to the *al-ism al-a'zam*, the Most Powerful Name of God:

113 al-Qummi, Mafatih, 238.

114 P. Dala'il, 58

115 Early in his mission, the Bab creatively refashioned the almost identical opening lines of the Du'a yawm al-mubahala (INBA 6006C: [90–95] 92 f.) as he did very frequently toward its end. See especially his weighty K. asma' (Book of Names) (INBMC 29:4 f., 26, 31 f., etc.) and K. Panj S. (Book of the Five Grades) (I/I:3 f.; VII/1:316; VII/2:224, etc.).

116 P. Bayan V. 3, 153 f.

117 A Commentary of the Bab on this morning prayer, the Du'a al-Ṣabah (Morning Prayer) of Imam 'Ali dates from the Maku period (the Bab refers to being *fi wast al-jibal*, the "in the center of the mountain," 145). It was written for Sayyid Abu'l Hasan ibn Sayyid 'Ali Zunūzi (see Browne ms. F 21(9), 143–55).

118 An early recension of the Du'a al-simat can be found, for example, in the Misbah mutahajjid al-kabir (p. 417) of al Tusi (d. 460) and the Mafatih al-jinan (The Keys of the Paradises) of al-Qummi (d. 1359/1941). It is traditionally recited in Shi'i devotional circles around the time of sunset, especially during the last hour of a Friday, the Islamic sacred day of the week. Fatimah, the daughter of the Prophet Muhammad, is said to have recited it at sunset or thereabouts.

"I, verily, O my God! beseech Thee by Thy Mighty, Greatest, Mightiest Most Powerful, Most Glorious, Most Noble Name."[119] Sayyid Kazim Rashti wrote an important commentary on the Du'a al-Simat and there are numerous Babi-Baha'i related intertextualities incorporating terminology derived therefrom (e.g., faran = [Mount] Paran).[120]

The Bab also, we may further note, cited at length from a Friday prayer or Du'a supplication allegedly shown in Mecca by the occulted twelfth Imam, to a certain Abu'l-Hasan al-Darrab al-Isfahani. It is found within the devotional works and compilations of Ibn Tawus and al-Tusi. Within it there is reference to the expected Qa'im and Khalifa (successor) and to his messianic role and victory. In his P. Dala'il, the Bab specifically related this prayer to his mission and presence in Maku.[121]

[3] **TAFASIR** (SING. **TAFSIR**): COMMENTARIES

This indicates exegetical (interpretive) and/or rewritten, often deep level revelatory, sometimes letter-rooted and generated Qur'an commentaries.[122] This mode of commentary renews and transfigures the Islamic sacred text. The importance of the Q. to the Bab can hardly be overestimated. The Q. is all but omnipresent his writings. He constantly cited it, creatively refashioned it, and expounded it in an often *batini* or deeply allegorical fashion. In his P. Bayan he refers to himself as the one who originally uttered the Q., as the "Revealer of the Qur'an (*manzil-i qur'an*)."[123] From the outset, many of the writings of the Bab were distinctly neo-Qur'anic in form; having isolated letters, being divided into surahs and written in rhyming prose (*saj'*). The Bab often associated his revelations with the *ta'wil* (inner

119 Imami Shi'i sources have it that the Du'a al-simat was transmitted from the persons of both the fifth Imam Muhammad al-Baqir (d.126/743) and his son the sixth Imam Ja'far al-Sadiq (d. c. 148/765). An at times biblically influenced or islamo-biblical in devotional style (see especially Deut. 33:2), it is said to have been recited by Joshua son Nun (d. c. 10 century BCE!) as well as by Fatima and various twelver Imams. Its transmission history is complicated, allegedly spanning thousands of years.

120 See T. Kawthar.

121 P. Dala'il, 66–68.

122 The Bab sometimes uses the at times synonymous term *sharh* (commentary). The Tafsir works of the Bab are first, Q. related commentaries, second, commentaries on Islamic traditions, and third, commentaries upon other sacred and related texts such as Shaykhi writings. Here, Tafsir for the most part indicates Q. commentary of the Bab. For further details on the Tafsir works of the Bab see esp. Lawson, 1986+ bib. and Lawson personal website.

123 P. Bayan II.2, 21; II.12, 49.

sense) or *batin* (interior dimension) of the Q. For the Bab, the Qur'an has intertextual depths down to the minutest level, expressive of the *kull shay'* (everything) of its deep level of mystery, its pleroma, fullness or wholeness. For him the Q. has a depth of interpretation incorporating meaning within "everything" down to its individual letters, their morphology and at times their voweling (cf. Qur'an 65:12b; 36:12b, and 7:145). Something of this is expressed in the T. Kawthar (Commentary on the Surah of the Abundance, Q. 107) where we read:

> God revealed the Qur'an according to the likeness of the creation of all things (*bi-mithl khalq kulli shay'*)... For every single letter of the Qur'an, as accords with its being totally encompassed by the knowledge of God, to the level of its existent particles (*min dhawat al-ashya'*), there is a *tafsir* (interpretation). For every *tafsir* (interpretation) there is a *ta'wil* (deeper interpretive sense). For every *ta'wil* there is a *batin* level ("especially deep inner sense"). For every batin there are also further deep inner senses (*batin*), dimensions to the extent that God wills.[124]

The use of non-literal *ta'wil* in his first major work, the Tafsir Sūrat Yūsuf (= QA; mid. 1844), suggests that he saw this Qayyūm al-asma' (Self-Subsisting reality of the Divine Names) as a work which unlocks the deeper messianic and other senses of the entire Q. "O people of the earth," the Bab writes toward the end of this early, neo-Tafsir, "This Book (= the QA) is the tafsir of everything (*li-kulli shay'*)."[125] In his early Kitab al-ruh and Kitab al-'ulama', the Bab again associates the *batin* (interiority) of the Q. with revelations sent down through himself ("Our servant 'Ali"), as a "proof" (*hujjat*) from the eschatological *Baqiyyat-Allah* (occulted Remnant of God).[126]

Several closely Qur'an-related items written by the Bab were stolen in early 1845 during his pilgrimage months.[127] Three or four years later, during the time of his imprisonment in Maku (1848), the Bab dictated to his amanuensis perhaps five (possibly complete) Qur'an commentaries

124 T-Kawthar, fol. 8b.
125 QA 111:448. See also QA 104:414; 41:151; 38:142; 44:164; 61:242. Only a few aspects of the Tafsir works of the Bab have been the subject of academic analysis (see Lawson, 1986 + bib. of articles and books listed on the Lawson personal website).
126 Ar. text, Afnan, 2000:107.
127 See the Bab, Kh-Jidda, VIII:1 ff. and Lambden trans. 2012 esp. 154–58.

(also now lost).[128] Without registering full details, a few major, all-Arabic *tafsir* (Q. centered) works of the Bab will now be listed, loosely, according to their Qur'anic surah numbers:[129]

- Tafsir [hurūf al-] Basmala (*Bismillah al-rahman al-rahim*, Q.1:1, etc.). Includes a fourfold commentary on the nineteen letters of the *basmala* (In the Name of God, the Merciful, the Compassionate) and more besides. Early, pre mid-1845.
- Tafsir al-Ha' (Exegesis of the [Arabic] letter "H") in one or two, probably both early versions (I & II) though with alternative titles. This letter "h" is found at the commencement of the *huwa* ("He is [God]") and the *huwiyya* (Divine Self-Identity or Ipseity) as well as being the final letter of Allah (God) and *wajh* (Face, Countenance, see Q. 55:27 and Q. 97:1). Its *abjad* numerical value is five, like the word Bab (Gate).

TAFSIR SŪRAT AL-HAMD (PRAISE) OR AL-FATIHA ("THE OPENING," Q. 1)

In this commentary, the Bab dwells upon the three-letter opening word *bism* ("In the Name" Q. 1:1b) of the nineteen letter *basmala* (first letter "b"). Typical of his exegesis, he makes mention of the *nuqta*, the diacritical subdot or "Point" (•) at the base of the first letter "B" of the *basmala*. The Bab further comments upon the elided or hidden letter *alif* ("A") [hidden] in the *bism* ("In the Name") as an expression of the Unseen (*al-ghayb*).[130] He adds that the [first] letter "B" (*al-ba'*) [of the *bism*] is an allusion unto [His] Lordship (*rububiyya*) above everything. Its second letter "**s**" (*al-s̱in*) alludes to His immanence or repose (*s̱akinah*) which is agreeable relative to His existing in servitude (*al-'ubudiyya*) through the concomitant "Glory of His Lordship" (*jalal al-rububiyya*). The "m" (*al-m̱im*) is an allusion to

128 DB:31; Sources:88.

129 See also MacEoin, Sources, index, tafsir. An example of a Qur'an related work of the Bab without the Tafsir title is the explanation of Q. 85:22 usually referred to as the Su'al 'an al-lawh al-mahfuz (Question regarding the "Preserved Tablet", see TBA. ms. 6006C:79–80).

130 The word bism is actually bi-i[a]sm) in the Arabic of the bi/asm. The elided or "hidden" letter "A" is the first letter of the Arabic word for name, <u>a/i</u>+s+m, "In the Name..." cf. Q. 96:1).

the Glory of God (*majd Allah*) which was Self-revealed (*tajalli*) unto Him and through Him for God made this "Glory" (*majd*) expressive of His own Logos-Self (*nafs*) in that "Sanctified Temple" (*haykal al-muqaddas*) and the "Luminous Countenance" (*tal'at al-munawwar*).

The Bab continues to explain that the Greatest Name (*al-ism al-a'zam*) [of God] is he who is hidden between the "B" and the "s" in the world of the Unseen (*'alam al-ghayb*), a hidden letter "A" who is found between the two diacritical dots or points (*al-nuqtatayn*) of the two letter "b"s in the word *bab*, "gate." This is allusive of the Bab himself as the locus [the letter A] of the servant (*harf al-'abd*) and the manifestation of the Point (*al-nuqta*) between the two alphabetical shapes (the letter "A" stands between two letter "B"s in the word **Bab**).[131]

- **Tafsir Sūrat al-Baqara** ("The Cow," Q. 2) dating to early 1260/ 1844 and perhaps into 1845. The Bab had a very high estimate of this, his very early, pre-declaration tafsir work. Addressing Sayyid Yahya Darabi in his May 1846 T. Kawthar, he specifically refers to its sublimity when he writes:

> [Shaykh] Aḥmad [al-Aḥsā'ī] did not speak out aforetime about this matter, neither subsequently did the Sayyid [Kāẓim Rashtī]. They could not match what I expounded in the commentary (sharḥ = tafsīr) on the Sūrat al-Baqara [composed] for such as are weak ones among the possessors of insight. Indeed, they [the Shaykhī leaders] could not equal this insurmountable commentary (al-sharḥ al-manī') by producing any such Book of wondrous designation (al-ism al-badī')... (T. Kawthar, EGB ms. CUL F.10 (9), f.16a; INBMC 53:206).

- Tafsir Ayat al-Kursi ("The Throne verse," Q. 2:255) – now lost, early 1845 (pilgrimage period).[132]
- Tafsir Sūrat Yūsuf (Q. 12 Joseph), the Qayyūm al-asma' (= QA). mid 1844 or slightly later).
- Tafsir Ayat al-Nūr (Light Q. 24:35), ("The light Verse") [I].

131 T. Hamd, 69:134. Toward the end of this Tafsir, the Bab sets out some detailed instructions for the construction of a talismanic device, a subject detailed throughout his lifetime (INBMC 69:147 ff.; MacEoin, 1989).

132 The T. Ayat al-Kursi has 200 surahs, each with twelve verses. It was written just before 11 Safar/15 February 1845 during the pilgrimage period. This was stolen by a Bedouin and is now lost.

- Tafsir Ayat al-Nūr (Light Q. 24:35), and a few others verses in Q. 24 [II].
- Tafsir Q. 37:1a, "By those [angels] arrayed in rows." On the opening letter waw ("w") of this verse, ***w**a'l-Saffat saffa* = وَالصَّافَّاتِ صَفًّا.
- On Q. 50:16 and Q. 112:4 for Hasan Waqa'i'-yi-Nigar ("The Chronicler").
- Tafsir Laylat al-Qadr (Q. 97 "The Night of Destiny").
- Tafsir Sūrat al-'Asr (Q. 103 The Era [Afternoon]).
- Tafsir Sūrat al-Kawthar (Q. 107, "The [Eschatological] Abundance"). إِنَّا أَعْطَيْنَاكَ الْكَوْثَرَ (108:1)

"We indeed proffered thee al-Kawthar (The Abundance)."

- **Tafsir Sūrat al-Tawhid** (Q. 112, "The Divine Unity").[133]

Aside to some degree from the 1259–60/1843–44 T. Baqara, most of the Tafsir works of the Bab are not comparable to classical Islamic tafsir compositions.[134] In form and content, they are more often rewritten or re-revealed, neo-Qur'anic, tafsir works. Sometimes exhibiting Sufi type, or rewritten (targum-like) *tafsir* characteristics in a revelation (*wahy*) mode, the Bab's often eisegetical (inwardly self-interpretive) works challenge the inimitability (*i'jaz*) of the Q. Innovative post-Qur'anic dimensions and eschatologically suggestive levels of meaning are subtly or boldly in evidence in many of the Tafsir works of the Bab. They often include fourfold, individual letter-generated (sometimes acrostic, alphabet focused) modes of interpretation. An example of this letter-based exegesis of the Bab can be found in one of his interpretations of the letter kaf ("k") of al-**K**awthar ("Abundance"):[135]

- [1] Now the letter **K [of Kawthar]** is indicative of the Primordial **Word** (***k**alimat al-ula*) before which the Greatest Abyss (*'amq al-abkar*) was held back, for it cried out with laudation in praise of its Creator in the Seventh Citadel (*qasaba al-sab'a*) nigh the snow-white thicket of the Divine Realm (*ajmat al-bayda al-lahut*).

133 There are, of course many other Q. related writings of the Bab. The list here is highly selective.
134 See Lawson, 2019.
135 Here the Bab cites or reflects the Du'a al-simat (Prayer of the Signs) and operates on the classical Islamic cosmological hierarchy of the four worlds (lahūt; jabarūt; malakūt; nasūt).

- [2] Then the letter **K** [further] indicates the **Word** (*kalimat*) which divulged His glory upon Mount Sinai (*jabal al-sina'*). He cried out from the Crimson Tree (*shajarat al-hamra'*) at the right-hand side of the Mount (*al-tur*) in the Blessed Spot within the Omnipotent realm (*ard al-jabarut*).
- [3] Then the letter **K** [also] indicates the **Word** (*kalimat*) which divulged His glory above the Ark of the Testimony (*tabut al-shahada*) emanating fiery weapons (*ghumud al-nar*) upon Mount Horeb (*jabal al-hurib*) in the land of the Kingdom (*ard al-malakut*).
- [4] Then [this letter **K** furthermore] indicates the **Word** (*kalimat*) divulged upon Mount Paran (*jabal al-faran*) through the hosts of the sanctified myriads (*bi-ribwat al-muqqadisin*) beyond the ken of the cherubim (*ihsas al-karubiyyin*) within the clouds of Light (*ghama'im al-nur*) above thc waystation (*al-waqif*) in the sphere of this mundane world (*ard al-nasut*).[136]

Though details cannot be set down here, some good examples of the early allegorical exegesis of the Bab are found in his T. Sūrat al-Qadr (Q. 97:1 ff.), the event of the laylat al-qadr ("the Night of destiny"). Its opening words, "We sent it [= hu] down on the night of power!" are centered on the undefined letter "h" ("it," traditionally the Qur'an itself). The suffix in *anzalna-**hu*** with its *abjad* numerical value of five, is understood on prophetological and imamological lines. It suggests Fatima, 'Ali and Imam Husayn, the fifth (*abjad* h = 5) of the "people of the cloak" (*ahl al-kisa'*). The "angels (*mala'ikat*) and the Spirit (*al-ruh*)" in Q. 97:2 are the Imams (= "angels") and the messianic Qa'im (= "the Spirit").[137]

HADITH COMMENTARY

In addition to commentaries on Qur'anic surahs and texts, the Bab also cited and commented upon scores of traditions, commonly designated hadith or *khabar* (pl. *akhbar*). Thousands of hadith ("traditions") exist in hundreds of Shi'i Islamic compilations some of which attained a more or less canonical status. These texts deriving from the Prophet Muhammad, various of twelver Imams, and others were written down over several

136 T. Kawthar EGB ms. f. 15b–16b; INBAMC 53:207.
137 T. Laylat al-Qadr, INBMC 69:17 ff.

centuries (seventh to ninth century CE and beyond). They formed the basis of many aspects of Islamic theology, philosophy, and practice. Inquiries about aspects of such traditions led to a massive Islamic literature. The Bab was often asked about them and quite frequently cited the massive Bihar al-anwar (Oceans of Lights) of Muhammad Baqir Majlisi (d. 1111/1699).[138]

Many hadith-generated ideas were integrated into the wide-ranging vocabulary and thought of the Bab. Full comprehension of his writings is virtually impossible without some knowledge and appreciation of these sacred hadith texts. Hadith citations are, for example, especially numerous in the T. Kawthar and the P. Dala'il-i sab'a where many traditions are seen as prefiguring messianic and other aspects of the person and religion of the Bab. There exists a quite lengthy and complex letter of the Bab to the erudite Sayyid Yahya Darabi (d. Nayriz 1266/1850), Vahid awwal, ("The primary Vahid"). Within it as within the P. Dala'il (p. 37), the following suggestive eschatological tradition is cited as attributed to Muhammad and various of the twelver Imams (see P. Dala'il, 37). It is a tradition found in multiple versions in both Sunni and Shi'i sources and contains an apt prediction about the genesis of the religion of the Bab. It concludes with a beatitude upon eschatological religionists considered gharib (persons "strange"):

فَطُوبَى لِلْغُرَبَاءِ

> The Messenger of God [or Imam 'Ali] said, "Islam began strange (*gharib*[an]) and will return strange (*gharib*[an]) just as it had begun. So Blessed be such as are strange! (*fa-tuba li'l-ghuraba'*)."[139]

138 This very influential thematized collection of Shi'i traditions was quite frequently cited by the Bab.

139 Cited by the Bab, EGB ms. F21 (9), [9–26], 20. The Bab cites the full text of a version of this tradition concerning the "strange" (*gharib*) return. It stands among hundreds of such early Islamic traditions believed to predict or say something profound about the person and religion of the Bab. The word *gharib* in this tradition could also, for example, be translated, "obscure," "hidden," "unusual," "extraordinary." A version of this tradition of Muhammad is found in the *Kitab al-ayman* of the Sunni collection *al-Sahih* (the Reliable) of al-Muslim (as relayed from the companion Abu Hurayrah – translated above), the early Sunni, Musnad of Ahmad ibn Hanbal and the al-Sahih of al-Tirmidhi. Shi'i sources for this tradition include the Kitab al-ghayba of al-Nu'mani (d. 360/970; K. al-Ghayba, 220 f.). Therein several versions are cited as transmitted from Imam 'Ali as well as the fifth and sixth Imams (twice from sixth Imam). It can also be found in the Kamal [Ikmal] al-din of al-Saduq (d.381/991) and (citing al-Numayni) in the Bihar al-anwar (2nd ed. vol. 52:366–67, nos. 147 and 8) of Majlisi.

There are hardly any Islamic traditions more frequently drawn upon or cited by the Bab relative to his cosmology, theophanology, and self-understanding than the following three examples deriving from the Prophet Muhammad and Imam ʻAli:

> There is no single thing on the earth or in heaven save [it came to be] through seven [*khisal* = factors, dimensions of reality], namely [1] *Mashiyya* ("the [Divine] Will"); [2] *Irada* ("the [Divine] Intention"); [3] *Qadar* ("the [Divine] Foreordainment"); [4] *Qida'* ("the Divine Accomplishment"); [5] *Idhn* ("the Divine] Authorization"), [6] *Ajal* ("the [Divinely] alotted Time") and [7] *Kitab* ("the [Cosmic] Book").[140]

> Manifold and mysterious is my relationship with God! I am He himself (*ana huwa*) and He is I myself (*huwa ana*). Except that I am that I am (*ana ana*) and He is that He is (*huwa huwa*).[141]

> All that is in the Qur'an is in the [Sūrat] al-Fatiha ('The Opening', Q.1) and all that is in the [Sūrat] al-Fatiha is in the *Bismillah al-Rahman al-Rahim* ("In the Name of God, the Merciful, the Compassionate", Q. 1:1) and all that is in the *Bismillah al-Rahman al-Rahim* is in the [first letter] ba' ("B") of *Bism* ("In the Name..."). And I [Imam ʻAli] am the Point (•) [subcritical dot] (*al-nuqtah*) at the base of the [letter] B (*al-ba'*).[142]

The claim of being a member of humanity or a (mere) servant (*ʻabd*) of God is found in many of the writings of the Bab. His human persona is sometimes, however, as previously noted, related to his most elevated claims based on hadith texts. This in the light of a tradition from Imam Jaʻfar Sadiq which has it that devotional "servitude" (*ʻubudiyya*) is a state (*jawhara*) the true nature [essence] (*kunh*) of which is Lordship [Divinity] (*al-rububiyya*). [143]

---

140 al-Kulayni, al-Kafi, 1:149.

141 This hadith is important in the opening section of the R. Jaʻfarriyya of the Bab (INBMC 60:57 f.; 67, 73).

142 Trans. Lambden as cited in al-Jili [Gilani], al-Kahf wa'l-raqim. cf. Bursi, Mashariq, 23.

143 The Arabic text of this hadith can be found in the Sufi influenced 100th section the Misbah al-Shariʻa (282) ascribed to Imam Jaʻfar al-Sadiq (see p. 201 in this chapter).

Many questions posed to the Bab inquire about the implications of Islamic hadith or traditions and their meaning or levels of their alleged eschatological fulfillment. Though such commentaries seem not to be directly counted as one of the five modes of his revelation, their importance is paramount. What follows is a list, with occasional notes, of traditions commented upon by the Bab, though it should be borne in mind that many of his other writings contain sections or paragraphs devoted to such Islamic traditions.

COMMENTARIES ON HADITH TEXTS BY THE BAB

The commentaries of the Bab may divided into several (somewhat simplified) categories including, (1) Traditions with theological, theophanological, and Imamological implications about God, the will of God, the prophets, messengers and manifestations of God, his creation and his creatures, (2) Explanations of traditions pertaining to ethical, spiritual, devotional and related subjects, (3) Traditions reflecting or interpreting pre-Islamic sacred writings, and (4) Traditions pertaining to messianism, apocalyptic, and eschatology. The following are a few examples of traditions ascribed to the Prophet of the Imams upon which the Bab specifically commented:

- **Hadith al-Jariyya** ("The Tradition about Ever-Flowing [Post-Mortem] Charity").
- **Hadith al-haqiqa** (On the Ultimate Reality), records a dialogue between the first Imam 'Ali and Kumayl ibn Ziyad al-Nakha'i (d. c. 85/704).
- **Hadith al-'ama'** (On the Tradition of the theophanic Cloud).
- **Nahnu wajh Allah...** ("We are the Countenance of God"), a statement sometimes ascribed to Imam 'Ali.[144]
- "The [true] believer is alive in both of the [two] worlds (*al-darayn*)."
- **Hadith 'allamni akhi rasūl Allah** ("He taught me my brother, the Messenger of God").
- **Kull yawm 'Ashura** (Every day is the 10th [of Muharram, when Imam Husayn was martyred in 61/680]).
- **Man 'arafa nafsahu fa-qad 'arafa rabbahu** (Whoso knoweth himself

144 Cf. P. Dala'il, 57–58.

assuredly knoweth his Lord). An Islamic form of a delphic maxim ascribed to Muhammad or Imam 'Ali.

- **Sharh Khutba Tutunjiyya** [Tatanjiyya] (Commentary on an extract from the Sermon of the Gulf). Ascribed to Imam 'Ali this text was partially commented upon by Sayyid Kazim Rashti (Sh-Ttnj, see bib.) and the Bab.

The Bab, it may be noted in concluding this section, did not reckon all Shiʿi (or Sunni) hadith as authentic. Shiʿi messianic and eschatological proof texts are very numerous and at times highly contradictory. Citing such texts in his P. Dala'il, the Bab directs his questioner to the massive Bihar al-anwar of Majlisi, though he boldly has it that the authenticity of certain traditions can be suspect (*tahqiq-i in ahadith ithbat nist*).[145] Going further in a complex commentary upon the prophetic import of certain isolated letters of the Q., thc Bab cites, then disagrees with Majlisi, holding that he had even failed to grasp the true *zahir* (outer) import of the Qur'anic isolated letters which he had applied to his own time.[146]

[4] SUWAR AL-ʿILMIYYA (SING. SŪRAH)

Often Indictive of Arabic Q. type sūrahs, ("divisions," "chapters") this division is also referred to as (Per.) **'ulūm-i hikmiyya**, modes of knowledge, divine wisdom, philosophy, or gnosis. The precise meaning is unclear. It would seem to indicate that the Arabic surahs of the Bab are expressions of religio-philosophical wisdom.

The Bab often divided his Arabic works into surahs. While the Q., for example, has 114 surahs, the QA. has 111, the (lost) T. Ayat al-Kursi (the Throne Verse. Q. 2:255) 200, and the partially lost distinctly neo-Qur'anic, 1845 K. Ruh (Book of the Spirit), 700.[147] Of great interest in this connection are the titles given by the Bab in his K. Fihrist to the 111 surahs of the QA. Thus, for example, QA. 1 is the Sūrat al-mulk ("The Surah of the Dominion"); QA.5 the Sūrat Yūsuf ("The Surah of Joseph"); QA. 10 the

145 P. Dala'il:51. The massive (2nd ed. 110 vols.). Bihar of Majlisi is a large and influential thematized collection of Shiʿi traditions. It and a few points of commentary therein, was quite frequently cited by the Bab.

146 Bihar 2 52:107; INBMC 98:35 ff.

147 Cf. P Dala'il, 28. In P. Bayan III.16 the Bab differentiates his T. Sūrat al-baqara from his two other pre-1848 Q. commentaries expressive of verses (*ayat*; like the Qayyūm al-asma'), by placing it with the category of shu'un-i 'ilmiyya which might be loosely translated "(revelatory) modes expressive of knowledge" (101).

Sūrat al-'ama' ("The Surah of the Theophanic Cloud"); QA. 29, the Sūrat al-huriyya ("The Surah of the Maiden"); and QA. 110, the Sūrat al-Sabiqin ("The Surah of the Forerunners"). These titles provide important gateways to doctrinal dimensions of the earliest thought of the Bab.[148]

SŪRAT AL-RIDWAN

Some works of the Bab, such as the probably early (c. 1844–46) Sūrat al-Ridwan (The Surah of the Divine Good-Pleasure/Felicity/ Paradise), are separate, self-contained though closely Q. related writings. Such is the case with the S. al-Ridwan, a five- or six-page rhythmic, Qur'anic related disclosure of the meanings of Ridwan as a heavenly or eschatological realm of paradise. It is expository of a few Qur'anic verses making use of the term Ridwan, including the following text:

> With the Lord are gardens and running streams of water for those that keep from evil and follow the straight path, where they will live unchanged, with the purest of companions [spouses] (*ajwaj muttaharat*) and the Ridwan of/from God (*ridwan min Allah*) (Q. 3:15, cf. 48:29).[149]

Toward its commencement, the Bab describes the Sūrat al-Ridwan as follows:

> This Book was assuredly sent down on the part of thy Lord at the genesis of Riḍwan (*bad' al-ridwan*) just as thou were promised. Such indeed is the *Sirat* (Path) of Thy Lord throughout the heavens and the earth for He does recite unto thee the verses of the scriptural Tablet (*ayat al-lawh*). This to the end that thou assuredly attain the Encounter with God (*liqa'Allah*) and be numbered among such as are assured in faith.[150]

---

148 See Lambden H* website.

149 The masculine noun Ridwan is found thirteen times in seven Surahs of the Qur'an (Q. 3:15 [13],162 [156], 174 [168]; 5:2, 16 [18]; 9:21, 73 109 [110]; 47:28 [30]; 48:29; 57: 20 and 27; 59:8).

150 S. Ridwan, cited Afnan, 198.

A constant, around thirty times repeated refrain in the S. Ridwan is, "So Blessed be the Name of thy Lord! No God is there except Him," which is often followed by the exclamatory verse, "Never indeed have eyes ever envisioned their like!" (cf. Q. 55:15 ff). Within this piece, an important role is given to the figure of the houri or heavenly maiden. Her or their divine beauty is said to have had a stunning effect throughout all the regions of the earth and beyond. When the houris or "maidens" were perceived, whole regions (*al-abdan*) were entranced by the twinkling of their eyes. The Divine Countenance (*al-wajh*) was evident in the very hair (*sha'rat*) of their heads.[151]

[5] KALIMAT-I FARSIYYA

Persian verses, revelations, or written communications. The Bab supplemented his revelations in Semitic Arabic with other (less in quantity) Indo-Iranian or Indo-European, Persian sacred writings.

Centered on the theology of the sacred Kitab (Book), P. Bayan II.15 has occasion to comment on Persian modes of revelation (*shu'un-i farsiyya*) in the context of other such modes as have been previously mentioned. In Arabized Persian the Bab writes, "Persian modes of revelation (*shu'un-i farsiyya*) are, in their essence, like unto [Arabic] verses (*ayat*) since they all flow forth from the [same, God revealing] Ocean of Reality (*bahr-i haqiqat*). If someone should gaze with the eye of the inmost heart (*bi-'ayn-i fu'ad*) upon such [revealed] Persian words (*kalimat-i farsi*), they would observe that they, in their inmost essence (*bi-'ayni-ha*), are [as naught but] eloquently perspicuous [Arabic] verses (*fasahat-i ayat*)."[152] Persian revelations of the Bab (no. 5 above) are essentially as Arabic sacred verses like those of the Qur'an (no. 1, p. 175) or his Bayan in the widest sense implied by this term. Aside from Persian letters, most of the early scriptural communications of the Bab are in Arabic.

This was the case until he wrote his c. 1262/1846 treatise on religious fundamentals, the Ṣahifa-yi 'Adliyya (Treatise expressing Justice) which is very largely in Persian. Like many of the Bab's writings, this work opens by setting forth an apophatic theology of the unknowability of God. His "sanctified Essence" (*dhat-i muqaddas*) cannot be depicted or approached, being beyond the most lofty dimensions of gnosis (*ma'rifat*). In line with a well-known hadith much cited by the Bab, it is declared

151 S. Ridwan, cited in Afnan, 198.
152 P. Bayan II.15, 54.

"the perfection of *tawhid* (the Divine Unity) is the [apophatic] negation of the [Divine] Attributes and the [Divine] Names (*nahy sifat va asma'*) from His sanctified [Unknowable] Essence (*dhat-i muqaddas*)." Certain important and potentially controversial Islamic doctrines, such as the bodily *mi'raj* (the "night ascent" from Jerusalem) are straightforwardly affirmed. The Prophet went up with "his clothes and his two sandals" (*bi-libas va na'layn*).[153] A greater guardedness and orthodoxy on the part of the Bab seems to have been necessary, perhaps because Persian texts were more accessible to the possibly hostile Persian masses. This Ṣahifa paved the way for his other major Persian works, the Persian Bayan (c. 1848), Persian Seven Proofs (c. 1848–49), and other Persian writings (e.g., a fifth of the KPS) in which there is little dissimulation. Arabic verses of the Bab had primacy in his first revelations, as they were compared and contrasted with the Arabic Qur'an. As the religion evolved and attained some stability, this was supplemented with Persian revelations. The late letter of the Bab to the 'ulama' of Tabriz, for example, is in both Arabic and Persian.[154]

KHUTBAS, LITERARY ORATIONS[155]

> Praise be to God Who hath cleft the firmaments asunder (cf. Q. 21:30), split up the atmosphere, suspended the margins of the heavens (Q. 69:17), caused the solar luminary (ḍiya') to shine forth, quickened the dead and made the living to die. I render Him such praise as rises resplendent, a praise at once radiant, then brilliant, a praise which, on being communicated, ascends unto heaven and which, in its directness, traverses the celestial sphere. He created the heavens without pillars and set them upright without supports (cf. Q. 13:2; 31:10). Then He adorned them with radiant stars [constellations] (*al-kawakib al-mudi'at*) and caused many a dusky cloud (*saha'ib mukfahirrat*) to be restrained in the celestial sphere. He created the oceans and the mountains upon dashing, surging, concomitant,

153 S.'Adliyya, 34.
154 Afnan, 2000:232–337.
155 Khutbas (loosely, sermons, homilies, etc.) in the writings of the Bab are not so much oral discourses as literary phenomina. Hence the translation "oration" which can bypass the usually oral, Christian related sermonic meaning.

> flowing waves. He tore their floodgates asunder such that their waves formed a vast billowing sea.

These are the opening cosmological words ascribed to Imam 'Ali within the khutba al-tutunjiyya [tatanjiyya] ("Sermon of the Gulf").[156] It gives an idea of what a Shi'i Islamic theological khutba (allegedly delivered between Kufa and Medina) can be like. This text, which extends for several more highly imamologically centered paragraphs, was influential upon and much cited and interpreted by the Bab.[157]

Though not always counted one of the five modes of revelation, khutbas, loosely and inadequately "sermons" but more accurately (something like) "literary orations" or discourses of the Bab, are numerous and of tremendous centrality and importance. This literary genre is reckoned by the Bab himself to be a centrally important category of his writings.[158] His K. Panj includes the following order of the five modes of revelation, (1) *ayat*, (2) *munajat*, (3) *khutba*, (4) *tafsir*, and (5) *farsi* (see p. 210). In this work it even precedes *tafsir* and is placed (as number 3) where we often find *suwar 'ilmiyya* (religio-philosophical or theological divisions). For him the term *khutba* ("literary discourse") is at times synonymous with all manner of his revealed writings (as within his S. Radawiyya). Within the writings of the Bab, *khutba* can have overarching literary senses. The Bab certainly reckoned khutbas a major mode of his revelations. At times it is associated with the discourses or the very elevated communications of Imam 'Ali, Shaykhi treatises, and other forms of religious knowledge. He wrote or revealed khutbas throughout the whole of his six-year ministry.

As the latter-day messianic 'Ali of the new age of fulfillment, the Bab (like the first Imam, 'Ali, d. 40/661) throughout his mission (1844–46), wrote scores of khutbas. He emulated, for example, parts of the compilation of sayings, over 230 khutbas and other materials ascribed to Imam 'Ali in the Nahj al-balagha (The Path of Eloquence) of Sharif al-Radi (d. 406/1015). This compilation was highly valued by the Bab, who occasionally referred to or specifically cited it.[159] Like the first sermon of the

156 Cited al-Bursi, Mashariq, 166 f.

157 See further Lambden website "The Khutbat al-Tutunjiyya [Tatanjiyya] 'Sermon of the Gulf" ascribed to 'Ali ibn Abi Talib (d. 40/661), its Translation and Studies in its Shaykhi and Babi-Baha'i Interpretations."

158 P. Dala'il, 27.

159 See KPS. VIII. 4, 274–75.

Nahj al-balagha (The Path of Eloquence) and the deeply imamocentric Khutba al-tutunjiyya [tatanjiyya], the khutbas of the Bab often deal with deep theological issues. Among the khutbas ascribed to Imam 'Ali that were especially influential on the Bab were the khutba al-Yatimiyya[160] and the khutba for the day of Ghadir Khumm ("The Creek/Pond at Khumm," between Mecca and Medina).[161]

When travelling on his almost ten- (Gregorian) month extended pilgrimage journey (1844–45), the Bab often wrote or dictated khutbas. Certain of their titles are listed in his Kitab al-fihrist. Later examples of important literary khutbas of the Bab include the Khutba qahriyya ("Sermon of Wrath") addressed (among others) to 'Abbas Iravani (of Yerevan), Hajji Mirza Aqasi (d. 1848).[162] A fifth of the roughly 460-page Kitab-i Panj Sha'n consists of twelve (probably ideally nineteen) literary khutbas occupying almost seventy Persian pages.

THE KHUTBA AL-JIDDA (LITERARY ORATION NIGH JEDDAH)

The roughly twelve-page Arabic Khutba al-Jidda was written between Jeddah and Muscat (now in the Sultanate of Oman) in 1845, during the course of the Bab's return pilgrimage journey to Bushire then Shiraz. Its opening lines clearly reflect the opening words of the al-Khutba al-tutunjiyya [tatanjiyya] (loosely, "Sermon of the Gulf") ascribed to Imam 'Ali:[163]

> Praised be to God! Who raised up the Celestial Throne (*al-'arsh*) upon the watery expanse (*al-ma'*) and the atmosphere (*al-hawa'*) above the surface (*wajh*) of the watery expanse (*al-ma'*). And He separated between these two through the word "Benefits" (*ala'* –first

160 See T. Baqara, R. Dhahabiyya, INBMC 86:94

161 See P. Dala'il, 47. This prophetic hadith is very widely cited in Sunni and Shi'i literature.

162 This khutba can be found in INBMC 64:127–150. Aqasi at one point in this khutba is referred to as a *maẓhar al-iblis* ("manifestation of Satan") and counted an infidel (ibid., 133, 135).

163 Both the Bab and Baha'-Allah saw themselves as the eschatological theophany of the Divine Sinaitic speaker with Moses (mukallim al-tūr), whose future advent was predicted by 'Ali in the Sermon of the Gulf (Bursi, Mashariq, 168; Lambden 1986).

> letter = "A"). Then he divided the firmaments from the sphere of the theophanic Cloud (*'alam al-'ama'*). Betwixt these twain a division (*hifz^{an}*) suggestive of the (shape of the initial form of the Arabic) letter "H" (al-ha' = ھ). And from this atmosphere (*al-hawa'*) there emerged the Sinaitic Tree (*shajarat al-sina'*), its subtle graciousness overshadowing the ocean of laudation (*bahr al-thana'*) nigh the watchtower of the Light of radiant Glory (*li-matla' nur al-baha'*) above the crimson Thrones (*sara'ir al-hamra'*).[164]

This Kh-Jidda is infused with eschatological excitement and theological-chronological precision. As the text makes clear, the Bab was not just performing a pilgrimage to Mecca in 1844–45, but strongly believed that he was acting in accordance with a predestined divine plan. This work contains much striking theological, cosmological and biographical information.

THE KHUTBA ON 'ILM AL-HURUF (ON THE "SCIENCE OF THE LETTERS")

The Khutba on 'ilm al-hurūf (On the science of Letters), among the 'ulūm al-ghayb ("esoteric sciences"), also contains much of interest about letter/number exegesis. It was an esoteric knowledge which the Bab, like Imam 'Ali with his K. Jafr (Book of Occult Prognostication) and his fellow 1844–45 pilgrim, Sayyid Ja'far al-Kashfi (d. Burujird, 1267/1851), was especially expert. In this fairly brief text the Bab says that the dawn time (*al-subh*) of a new era has broken through the Light of Glory (*nur al-jalal*) and poses the rhetorical question promising that he would divulge the universe of "the science of the letters" (*'alam 'ilm al-hurūf*) and the mystery of their eschatological culmination (*akhirati-ha*).[165]

Finally, in this connection, the Bab in his Persian Ṣahifa-yi 'Adliyya, again accords khutbas a very exalted position. He refers to khutbas as a category of the "sanctified levels" of revelation appropriate to the exalted twelver Imams since they are characterized by "the most elevated discourse" (*bi-a'la kalimat*) of the "people of pristine Arabic fluency and

164 Kh-Jidda, Mulla Husayn ms., 61; INBMC 91:61.

165 Kh-'Ilm al-hurūf, INBA 6004C:209–13; INBMC 91:30–36; INBMC 67:228–33.

clarity" (*ahl-i fasaha va bayan*). This, he maintains, flows from "the Divine Pen of supernal Eloquence" (*qalam-i ashal*) registering everything (*az kull-i shay'*).[166]

SELECT TREATISES (RISALA, PL. RASA'IL), EPISTLES (ṢAHIFA, PL. ṢUHUF) AND OTHER SCRIPTURAL COMMUNICATIONS

Aside from letters or epistles of the Bab addressed to individuals or groups, there exist a large number of Risalas and Ṣahifas (loosely, "Epistles," "Treatises") as well as other kinds of scriptural communication. Some are independent treatises in Persian or Arabic. A proportion were designated or came to be known as *risala* (here = R.).[167] Among the important works so designated are the R. Dhahabiyya, for the Dhahabi Sufis of Shiraz,[168] and the R. fi'l-jasad al-nabi (or Sharh kayfiyyat al-mi'raj), on the earthly-celestial translocation of the "body" (*jasad*) of the Prophet Muhamad during his *isra'* (night journey) and *mi'raj* (night ascent).

The very brief R. fi'l-nahw wa'l-sarf ("Treatise on Grammar and Syntax," c. late 1844–early 1845) was written in defense of the, sometimes ungrammatical, revelatory style of the Bab. Within it, he states that personified grammar and syntax/morphology have "wept in the land of the tablets" and that he forgave them as they exhibited humble powerlessness in approaching him.[169] Here the Bab defends (as has been indicated) the often loose, free-flowing, creative nature of his grammar and syntax against Muslim criticism. Though he frequently violated standard grammatical rules, he held that he was not in error but essentially neo- or supra-grammatical. He believed that his revelations set a new scriptural and literary standard.[170]

166 S-'Adliyya, 7.

167 Note that the following very brief work is sometimes entitled (Per.) Risala-yi Khasa'il-i sab'ah (see p. 172 in this chapter).

168 Cf. Afnan, 2000:449.

169 Trans. McCants, 2012:64.

170 For details see McCants, 2012, especially the excellent translation on pages 64–66 and the informative notes. See also the few pages I devote to this subject.

THE RISALA FI'L-NUBUWWA AL-KHASSA (A TREATISE ON THE SPECIFIC PROPHETHOOD OF MUHAMMAD)[171]

This approximately fifty-page Risala is an especially important response to an inquiry of Manuchihr Khan (d.1262/1847), the governor of Isfahan or Mu'tamad al-Dawla (Chancellor of the Empire). He was a Georgian eunuch who had outwardly embraced Islam or become a crypto-Muslim.[172] He asked the Bab to write this treatise in proof of the veracity of the person and mission of the Prophet Muhammad on specific religio-historical lines. Within it the Hebrew Bible and New Testament are not cited or directly interpreted. The phrase *nubuwwa al-khassa* ("specific Prophethood") is found in the prophetologically related writings of Ibn al-'Arabi and his devotees. In this complex treatise there are, for example, acrostic type explanations of the names of Adam and Muhammad as well as *'ilm al-hurūf* (number-letter) informed speculations about the chronology of the latter's mission. The Bab identifies the *mashiyya* ("Divine will") as the bearer of the *nubuwwa khassa* in the being or body of the Prophet Muhammad.[173]

EPISTLES, TREATISES, BOOKLETS (ṢAHIFA, PL. ṢUHUF)

Ignoring alternative titles, something like a dozen major works of the Bab are commonly designated Ṣahifa (=S.). They especially include works of the first few years such as the following titles.

S. Bayn al-Haramayn (Epistle between the two shrines) was written in seven sections between Mecca and Medina in early 1845. It is primarily addressed to the three Shaykhi inquirers, Mirza Muhammad Husayn,

171 A semi-critical text of this work has recently been made by Eschraqi, Ph.D 2004 + 2012. On the concept of the *nubuwwa khassa* ("specific prophethood") as opposed to the *nubuwwa 'amma* "general prophethood" reference should be made to such writings of Ibn 'Arabi as his al-Futuhat al-Makiyya and Fusus al-hikam and those of his many commentators and disciples (see further, Lambden Ph.D).

172 A somewhat tyrannical though excellent administrator, this faithful servant of Muhammad Shah had responded favorably to a letter from the Bab requesting asylum (the Bab, Epistle to Muhammad Shah, cited SWB:15/trans. 13–14; Zarandi, DB:144 f.; Balyuzi, 1973:109 f.).

173 INBMC 14:321 333b.

Muhit-i Kirmani, and Sayyid 'Ali Kirmani, who were on pilgrimage at the same time as the Bab (1844–45). In this treatise, the Bab refers to himself as the *Dhikr Allah* (messianic "Remembrance of God"), the *fata al-'arabi* (Arabian youth), as well as the *kalimat al-'ama'ayn* ("doubly beclouded Word"), and the *khatt al-qa'im* ("upright script" = the letter "A") between the worlds. He is one subject, at all times, to inspiration from the Spirit (*al-ruh*).[174] Apart from discussions of such subjects as the paths of the stars and the science of talismans, the Ṣahifa bayn al-Haramayn contains a fair amount of material illustrative of the Bab's interest in novel aspects of *'ilm al-fiqh* ("jurisprudence") and devotional piety.

S. Hujjatiyya (The Treatise of the Proof).[175] This is a work of twenty-five to thirty pages in fourteen sections of devotional prayers or meditations between the Bab, the Hidden Imam, and God. They are closely associated with key Shi'i Islamic sacred days or events.[176] Every one of its fourteen sections uses the word Du'a prior to the mention of the date or occasion for each division. Apparently written for a certain Muhammad ibn Hasan,[177] it concludes with words to the effect that the [Hidden] Imam has given divinely sanctioned permission for the Shi'ah [rooted] believers (*li-shi'at*) to recite this al-Ṣahifa al-maknūna (Hidden Treatise) in every circumstance that they desire.[178]

Like many other of the writings of the Bab, this work commences with expressions of tahmid ("In praise of God"), theological meditations with and in glorification of God, Muhammad and his family (al), the Imams as channels of wilaya, intimate guidance, providence and leadership. Subsequently, a second section is linked with devotions for 'Id al-Ghadir Khumm (18 Dhu'l-Hijja) and 5 Jumada I when the Bab, as the

174 S. Haramayn, EGB ms. F7 (9): fol. 6 f.
175 At the commencement of this text the Bab himself refers to it as the al-Ṣahifa al-Hujjatiyya. It has at least two other titles: Ṣahifa Maknun [Makhzuna] (The Hidden [Treasured] Epistle) or (Per.) Du'a-yi Ṣahifa (Devotion-centered Treatise). All of its above-mentioned titles seem appropriate in the light of the manuscripts I have consulted.
176 See MacEoin Sources, 59 for a very useful list of these sacred days. Some manuscripts (see fn. 22) alter somewhat the order of certain of the 14 sections, e.g. [2] 'Id al-Ghadir Khumm (18 Dhu'l-Hijja), celebration of the appointment of Imam 'Ali in 632 CE and of the 5 Jumada I (declaration of the Bab), [3] 'Ashura', 10 Muharram (martyrdom of Imam Husayn) and [4] 'Id al-Fitr (1 Shawwal), in celebration of the end of the fasting month of Ramadan, etc. [5] 'Id al-Adha (10 Dhu'l-Hijja) the Feast or Festival of the Sacrifice, etc.
177 Saiedi, Gate, 31.
178 Afnan ms. 499.

new Imam 'Ali, declared his mission (cf. though sect. 11).[179] This second section refers to the time when "worlds found their consummation" relative to this world, on the eschatological Day when the very purpose of creation (*ghayat al-ibda'*) returned unto the "Apex of His Cause (*muntaha amrihi*)". Muhammad, it is underlined, was created for the purpose of the *Hujjat*, the messianic Proof.[180] The last two sections are both Qur'an-related; section 13 celebrates the 23rd of Ramadan when, according to the Bab, the Q. was first revealed to Muhammad. The final section 14 is related to the act of the completion of the reading or recitation of the Q. Throughout much of this work, the Bab holds to a thinly veiled "messianic secret."

Ṣahifa a'mal al-sana (Treatise on the Annual Devotional Practises). Dating to mid-1845, this "Book of the *Dhikr* (Remembrance)" is described by the Bab as a *kitab mubin* ("Perspicuous Book").[181] It is a very rare, approximately forty-page, fourteen-section (with subsections) work. Much of this text revolves around sacred doctrine, prayers and related observances for important dates throughout the Islamic year. It commences with the Qur'anic *basmala* and the disconnected letters A-L-M (cf. Q. 2:1), referring also to aspects of the Muharram month of fasting (*shahr al-siyam*). Its opening section is, according to the Bab, related to the Q., which was believed to have been revealed to humankind through Muhammad on the 23rd of the month of Ramadan (cf. above). Its best of directives (*ahkam*) is said to be "the mention/*Dhikr* of Justice" (*dhikr al-'adl*). The devotee should perform the most gracious of deeds by reciting (among other Qur'anic surahs) the *ahsan al-qisas* ("Best of Narratives" = Q. 12, "The Surah of Joseph") during the hours of the night.[182] Toward its conclusion, there is positive mention of al-bada' of God (cf. Q.13:39) in relation to the operations of the divine al-mashiyya (the Will of God). In the new age, God can legitimately reconstruct the future or (loosely) "change his mind."[183]

179 I translate here from a photocopy of an unidentified (probably Haifa located) manuscript given to me in the early 2000s by Muhammad Afnan (d. Canada, 2017).
180 Unpublished ms. 441.
181 So 6007C:413.
182 S. A'mal, ms. 416.
183 S. A'mal ms. 450, P. Dala'il, 51.

Ṣahifa Ja'fariyya.[184] This sixty or so page work is in part a commentary on the following supplication:

> O Zurayra. If you desire to interface with that time [of occultation] then recite this supplication, "O my God! Initiate me regarding Thyself, for if Thou do not inform me about Thyself, then I cannot claim to know Thy Prophet (*nabi*). O my God! Initiate me regarding Thy Messenger [= Muhammad] (*al-rasul*) for if Thou do not inform me regarding Thy Messenger, then I cannot become aware of thy [messianic] *Hujjat* (Proof). O my God! Acquaint me with Thy *Hujjat* (Proof), less I slip away from my religion."[185]

This variously titled, fourteen-section Arabic work, was composed in Shiraz around 10 Muharram 1262/8 January 1846. It has been well-summed up by Mohammad-Hosseini under the heading Tafsir al-ha' (other titles are noted) and partially introduced and commented upon by Saiedi as the Ṣahifa-yi Ja'fariyya.[186] Also known as the Ṣahifa Sharh Du'a zaman al-ghayba, it is (in part), a treatise in commentary on a brief prayer for personal experience of the hidden Imam (see p. 199), attributed to the sixth Imam, Ja'far al-Sadiq (d. c.148/765).[187] The Du'a text cited by the Bab (with detailed *isnad*) is that recorded in the al-Kafi of al-Kulayni.

Especially rich in deep theological discourse and hadith citation, this work can hardly be briefly or easily summarized though a few brief summary sentences on the certain of its fourteen sections follow: [1] On the phrase *huwa huwa* ("He is that He is") and other biographical and devotional matters.[188] [2] On *wasiyya ilahiyya* ("Divine successorship"), with reference to

---

184 See INBMC 60:57–154. INBMC 98:48–108 and Saiedi, Gate, 32.

185 Hadith from Ja'far al-Sadiq through Zurara recorded in the al-Kafi of al-Kulayni 1:336–37; also cited Majlisi, Bihar 52:146–47. This supplication can also be found in many other sources, including the K. al-Ghayba of al-Numayni. The text cited by the Bab from al-Kafi vol. 1:336–37 is quoted in S. Ja'fariyya, section 4 in INBMC 60:69 f. Further commentary on this tradition is found in sections 11–13 of the in S. Ja'fariyya (see Saeidi, 2012 and cf. the Saeidi trans. in 2012:201).

186 See Mohammad-Hosseini 1995:774–81, Saiedi in Lawson ed. 2012:196–216.

187 See Saiedi, 196 f. Loosely translated this title means, "Treatise in Commentary on the Supplication for [an engagement with the era of the advent of the messianic] Occultation [twelfth Imam/Qa'im]."

188 This *huwa* ("He is") phrase is most famously found in a tradition ascribed to the Prophet Muhammad, quite frequently cited by the Bab and Baha'-Allah.

Shaykhi issues and to certain speculations of Sayyid Ja'far Kashfi.[189] [3] A theological prolegomenon (*muqaddama*) dealing with foundational dimensions of the gnosis of reality (*usul al-ma'rifat*) as well as issues pertaining to the apophatic theology of the unknowability of the Divine Essence. There is also a negative evaluation of the level of the gnosis (*al-ma'rifa*) of the followers of Mulla Sadra (*al-sadra'iyyin*). [4] On the text of the supplication relating to the time of the *ghayba* (occultation) of the Imam, as cited from al-Kafi of al-Kulayni (with full isnad) (see trans. and fn., p. 201)... [8] On the gnosis of the most sublime verses of God (*ayat Allah al-kubra*). This section commences with the citation of Q. 38:67 (cf. Q. 78:2 al-naba al-'azim), referring to a "Mighty Announcement" (*nabw'u 'azim*) in the light of the advent of the Baqiyyat Allah (Remnant of God). Key theological statements are found here such as "The Divine Will (*mashiyya*) of the Essence of God (*dhat*)" being "the very Will of God Himself (*mashiyyat Allah*)" for this in the year that the Mashiyya (Divine Will) [= the Bab] is among the people.[190] [9] On the gnosis of the Mighty Benefits or Favors of God (*ma'rifat ala' Allah*). The Quranic word benefits (*ala'* see esp. Q. 53) which commences with the letter "A," is interpreted in this light and in terms of the Shi'i "family of God" (*al Allah*), the Imams as progeny of the Prophet Muhammad.

The Ṣahifa al-Radawiyya (c. mid Muharram 1262/Jan 1846). This eighth 'Imam Rida' (d. 203/818)-related treatise is again divided into fourteen sections which are all designated *khutbas* (literary orations), though they are further listed as four *kitabs* (Books) and ten *ṣahifas* (Treatises).[191] Its first item is the Risala or Khutba al-dhikriyya (The Treatise/Oration of the Remembrance),[192] which is essentially a listing of select earlier writings spanning a two-year period, dating from 1 Muharram 1260/22 January 1844 to 15 Muharram 1262/14 January 1846.[193] Some of the

189 The Bab makes specific reference to Kashfi's Sana-Barq ("The Brilliance of Lightning"). This poet, theologian, and mystic was the father of the Shi'i cleric then major disciple of the Bab, Sayyid Yahya Darabi, Vahid.

190 S. Ja'fariyya, VIII:97–98.

191 MacEoin, Sources, 50–51, 207; Saiedi, 32. This after the various names or titles of the Prophet Muhammad, his daughter Fatimah as well as the twelve Imams, in total, the fourteen "immaculate ones".

192 Confusingly, MacEoin refers to this work as the Risala Dhahabiyya ("The Golden Treatise") (Saeidi, Gate 51, etc.). On the Kh-Dhikriyya, see Afnan, 2000:47; Vahid Brown, 2005.

193 The Bab does not seem to have written later, post-1846 indexes of his writings though in many later writings he does make reference to earlier texts.

fourteen works listed in his Kh-Dhikriyya have obvious identities with works much better known by other titles. The early Qayyum al-asma', for example, is referred to as the third book, the Kitab al-Husayniyya (The Husaynid Book). This latter, alternative title is not suprising given the typological relationship between the new Joseph and the third Imam Husayn.

Ṣahifa-yi 'Adliyya (The Treatise expressing Justice). Another important Ṣahifa is the Persian Ṣahifa-yi'Adliyya (The Treatise expressing Justice) written in Muharram 1262/ January 1846. It is probably so titled because the establishment of *'adl* (justice) is one of the central purposes of the messianic Qa'im. The foundations of twelver Shi'i doctrine are examined in a fairly orthodox manner and in a state of partial dissimulation (see also under the fifth mode of revelation, p. 210).

Ṣahifa [Risala] furū' al-'Adliyya (The Treatise regarding the Branches of Justice). This rare, probably authentic work perhaps dating from early to mid-1846. It deals with and comments upon some of the major aspects of Islamic law and religious life. Its seven *fiqh* or jurisprudence-related sections are on (1) the *ziyarat jami'a al-saghira* (the "Lesser comprehensive visitation supplication"), (2) *Salat* (Obligatory prayer), (3) Regulations surrounding the obligatory prayer (*ahkam al-salat*), (4) Almsgiving (*zakat*), (5) On the fifth level taxation (*khums*), (6) on *jihad* (holy war), and (7) on the resolution of debts (*dayn*).

A few major writings of the final years in Adhirbayjan (NW Persia) (1847–50 CE). The Bab was imprisoned in Maku in Adhirbayjan (NW Persia) for around eight months (August 1847–April 1848). This period witnessed a more open proclamation of his teachings. During this time, the Bab continued to write Q. commentaries, in addition to the three mentioned in the P. Bayan.[194] After these months in Maku, the Bab was transferred to the fortress at Chahriq near the Turkish border.[195] This second imprisonment lasted for another two years and two months (1264–66/April/May 1848–July 50). It ended when Bab was executed (aged thirty-one) at Tabriz on 8 Sha'ban 1266/9 July 1850.

194 See P. Bayan III.16, 101.
195 Chahriq (or Chihriq) is between Khoy and Urumia and about twelve miles SW of Salmas. See Cole EIr. article in bib.

The Persian and Arabic Bayans and the new shari'a (law). Perhaps the best-known works of the Bab are his two closely related Bayans, the over 300-page Persian Bayan (Bayan-i farsi) and the terse, seventy-five-page Arabic Bayan (*al-bayan al-'arabi*). They are doctrinal-legal and ethico-religious "expositions" dating to the final few years of the Adhirbayjan (NW Iran) period of imprisonment. Both works exist in nine *wahids* (literary unities), each with nineteen sections (literary babs, pl. *abwab*) though the P. Bayan lacks the final ten sections (babs).[196] The contents of the Bayans are not easy to sum up.[197] There are numerous key interrelated themes with many subsidiary doctrines. The theology of the pleroma of the *kull shay'* ("everything"), as it is (*abjad*) 19x19 or 361, is an especially central numerological motif. The Bayans of the Bab provide something of a multifaceted summary of his developed religious thought, including his new laws and regulations.

The new shari'a (religious law). The genesis of the first religio-legal aspects of the laws of the Bab has been sketched previously in connection with the Khasa'il-i sab'a (The Seven Religio-Legal Directives). It will be appropriate here to mention something of the later ethical, spiritual, and legalistic directives of the Bab expressed in the Bayans and elsewhere. Many such legalistic guidelines are mild, undemanding, and easily implemented. Special importance was given, for example, to truthfulness, honesty, cleanliness, refinement, good-character, devotional piety, and non-violence. There exist many levels of spiritual ethics as well as admonitions to Islamic type and extra-Islamic piety. The observance of the Jewish, Christian, and Islamic "golden Rule" was a major teaching of the Bab.[198] Refinement (*lutf*) of character, taste, and disposition is central. Central to Qur'anic, Sufi, Imami Shi'i, and other ethical imperatives was the necessity of expressing the fear of God (*taqwa' Allah*) and the love of God (*hubb Allah*). These two qualities are central to the religious pathways enjoined by the Bab. Divine love (*al-hubb*) revolving around faith and certitude in the Bab and the coming

196 Though differently divided, the Kitab-i iqan (c. 1861–62) of Baha'-Allah is viewed by Baha'is as the "spiritual" completion of the (Persian) Bayan. For Azali Babis, the Mutammim-i Bayan (Completion of the Bayan) of Mirza Yahya Nuri (d. Famagusta, 1912) is viewed similarly. See further Browne in Momen ed. 1987:316–406; MacEoin, Sources, 83–84; esp. 84 fn. 25 and Lambden-Quinn, EIr. 2010 [2018].

197 Perhaps the best brief, lucid summary of the P. Bayan is that of the polymathic Italian Baha'i writer A. Bausani in his *Religion in Iran* (2000:385–89).

198 For details, see Lambden 2002.

messianic *Man yuzhiru-hu Allah* as manifestations of God (*mazahir-i ilahi*), was often celebrated and enjoined. In QA. 91, the Bab addresses the *ahl al-hubb* (community of love), possibly members of the Dhahabiyya Sufi order of Shiraz or other Shirazi Sufis known to the Bab.[199] The Bab invited such a community of love (*ahl al-hubb*) to listen to his call from the light of his inmost heart (*nuri al-fu'ad*). This, spiritually speaking, nigh the celestial *masjid al-aqsa* (furthermost Mosque cf. Q. 17:1) and the elevated Throne of God (*'arsh Allah*)".[200]

Some legalistic directives of the Bab are demanding, harsh, sometimes disturbing, and definitely revolutionary. Some may never have been intended to be carried out, though the Bab did expect his followers to obey or implement his new law and legalistic religious directives. The call to combat and jihad (loosely "holy war"), for example, was there from the beginning as evidenced by seven or more adjacent surahs of the QA., having titles relating to a coming eschatological combat and warfare (see surahs 95–102).[201] Around the time of his pilgrimage, the Bab called for a jihad-oriented gathering in Kufa or Karbala (in Ottoman Iraq). Such a congregation is something which must take place according to hundreds of Shi'i Islamic traditions. Yet global "holy war" was not to be in the light of the Bab's invoking the theology surrounding *al-bada'*, a "re-determination" or neo-genesis, a change in the divine decree of God (cf. Q.13:39).[202]

It was during the post-pilgrimage month in Bushire (c. June 1845–c. 1 Rajab 1261/5 July 1845), that the Bab wrote that God made the knowledge of *al-bada'* (re-determination) something very elevated, relative to the celestial throne of baha' (*'arsh al-baha'*).[203] In a supplication, he stated that

199 Here, as elsewhere, there are signs of the Bab's association with Sufis and a mystically oriented love ethic (T. Basmala, 361; cf. T.'Asr, f. 96 ff.).

200 QA. 91:364.

201 Though many of the laws and regulations of the Bab were never strictly implemented, the Bab did call upon his followers to observe them all.

202 An important section on bada' can be found in the al-Kafi of Kulayni, vol.1:146–49. See also the articles in EI–EI³ and EIr. with many further references; most recently, Amir-Moezzi, "Bada'," in EI³ (2015–14). Amanat's *Resurrection and Renewal* (1989) has an excellent section about this period and issues surrounding the Bab and the question of *al-bada'* (see ch. 5 esp. 243 ff.). It is in his "Tablet of the Bab to Mulla 'Abd al-Khaliq Yazdi" where (in a supplication) the Bab asserts that he had no desire for the mulk al-dunya (rulership of this world) nor for that of the hereafter (*al-akhira*) (see INBMC 91:[94–102] 98).

203 The Bab, Q. Bada' of God', INBMC 67:172–73.

he desired neither the *malik al-dunya* (rulership of this world) nor that of the hereafter (*al-akhira*).[204] A prayer of the Bab was also written in response to questions relating to the meaning of the jihad-oriented tradition of Mufaddal b. ʻUmar. He makes it clear that eschatological expectations spelled out therein could be cancelled through *al-bada*.[205] Though defensive jihad was sanctioned and anticipated in the writings of the Bab, it was hardly realized and is only dimly reflected in the Babi upheavals of the mid-1840s and later.[206] The first thing that Baha'u'llah did in instituting his post-Babi, Baha'i religion in mid-1863, it may be recalled here, was to abolish militaristic jihad and declare all humanity purified and equal in the sight of God.[207]

Sometimes, challenging post-Islamic legalistic and ritualistic dimensions of the new religion of the Bab are found (often in parallel versions) in the two Bayans. They occasionally involve a very focused exclusivism linked to a possibly immanent messianic fulfillment. As far as challenging legalistic directives go, an example might be the injunction to level the non-Babi sacred places (domes, sanctuaries, etc.) on earth (*biqa' al-ard*) then allot whatever remains to the Babi wahid ("Unity," eighteen or nineteen major believers).[208] This directive would have been virtually impossible to fulfill and remains a problematic religious directive. At times, the Bab seems to have desired to all but destroy the existing order before the fullness of the realization of his religion could be actualized. At other times, the Bab called for a more positive transition to eschatological order and regeneration. Even the Baha'i leader 'Abdu'l-Baha (d. 1921) reckoned such above-mentioned harsh directives of the Bab to be the opposite of the Baha'i position of actualizing and promoting the unity and well-being of humankind.[209] Some directives may never have been intended to be rigidly, outwardly realized. Details of these harsh or demanding directives of the Bab can be found in the many summaries of the contents of the Bayans (e.g., by Browne and others).

---

204 See INBMC 91:98. Key references of the Bab to this issue of bada' can be found in several early and some later writings and letters. See, for example, the S. Aʻmal (6007C:450), the later P. Bayan (IV.3, 113–14), and P. Dala'il, 51.

205 INBA Ms 6003C:173 ff. cf. Sachedina, 1981:165–66.

206 The first thing that Baha'u'llah did in instituting his post-Babi, Baha'i religion was to abolish jihad and declare all humanity purified, hence a new unity or new creation (Lambden, 2005).

207 Lambden 2005 cf. MacEoin, 1982.

208 Ar. Bayan IV:12.

209 Makatib II:266.

Certain of the elevated claims of the Bab are dwelt upon in his Bayans; including his frequent claim to be the cosmogonic *nuqta* as a "Primordial Point" at the base of the Arabic/Persian letter B. The apophatic unknowability of ultimate Godhead is frequently underlined as reflected in a new *basmala*.[210] It is often maintained that twelver Shiʿi messianic expectations and apocalyptic scenarios have found literal and/or symbolic fulfillment in the person and religion of the Bab. The messianic *man yuzhiru-hu Allah* (Him whom God shall make manifest) is frequently mentioned. Cryptic reference, as will be demonstrated, is several times made to the possible times of his advent or (more accurately) advents. Many of his numerous ethical and legal directives revolve around generating a receptivity to faith in the coming messiah figure. Both Bayans have been fully translated into French by Nicolas (d. Paris 1939) in the early twentieth century.[211]

THE PERSIAN DALA'IL-I SABʿA (SEVEN PROOFS)

Dating to 1848–49, this seventy-or-so-page P. Dala'il and its shorter (around ten to fifteen-page) Arabic counterpart (al-Dala'il al-sabʿa) are important expressions of religious testimonia (istidlaliyya). The P. Dala'il was written from Maku in c. 1848 for an unidentified, possibly non-Babi, Shaykhi disciple of Sayyid Kazim Rashti. The addressee is sometimes thought to have been the Babi martyr Mulla Muhammad 'Ali, Hujjat Zanjani (d. 1851).[212] It opens with a testimony to God's uniqueness, eternality, and unknowability. The essential identity, endless continuity, and successive appearance of prophets,

210 P. Bayan III.11, 89–92.

211 Cf. the earlier 1865 Gobineau and Hamadani trans.

212 See MacEoin, Sources, 87; Saiedi, Gate, 35. The at one-time Shaykhi identity of the recipient seems to be presupposed. Shaykhi-rooted proof-texts are here and there spelled out, such as the prediction relating to "after a while" (baʿda hin), after 68 (abjad hin) understood as 1269 AH (= 1852–53, the messianic year 9) found in Q. 38:88 and the Kh-Tutunjiyya of Imam 'Ali (see Kh-Tutunjiyya, 1978:168; P. Dala'il, 46; MacEoin, Messiah 366 f.). In this light, the Bab concludes the P. Dala'il most appropriately by supplicating as follows: "I seek the forgiveness of God, thy Lord, at every moment, before the moment and after the moment (kull hin va qabl-i hin va baʿda hin)" (72). This is echoed a year or more later at the end of the fifth Persian section in K. Pan. VII. where we find the words: "in every moment and before [that] moment and after [that] moment (dar har hin va qabl-i hin va baʿda-i hin)" (251). See also the excerpt from the Chahar Shaʿn (Four Modes) ascribed to the Bab and cited MacEoin, *Rituals*, 13, fn.58, 75.

dhikrs, or manifestations of the *mashiyyat-i awwaliyya* (Primal Will of God) is outlined. With the termination of a 13,000-year cycle, this Primal Will has, the Bab asserts, become known through his own nafs ("Logos-Self") which is the *nuqta-yi bayan* (Point of the Bayan), the focal center of divine revelation and guidance.

THE ARABIC AL-DALA'IL AL-SAB'A (SEVEN PROOFS)

This much shorter (ten to fifteen pages), wholly Arabic version of the P. Seven Proofs with a similar dating (c. 1848), again sets down seven Q. rooted testimonia (*dala'il*) often founded upon the revelation of inimitable *ayat* (verses). It commences with the *basmala* with a double superlative, "In the Name of God, the most Unique, the Peerless" (*al-afrad al-afrad*). There follows a further eighteen similar *basmala* verses, then twenty short invocations commencing "in God is God" (*bi-Allah Allah al-fard al-afrad*). Again, largely based on the f-r-d (= "to be unique") Arabic root, this pattern continues by including several prayers, invocations and claims to (subordinate) Divinity with occasional (f-r-d rooted) neologisms (e.g., *firdan*, *firda'*), as well as deep points of theological and chronological insight. The continuity of revelation is again underlined through multiple future theophanies of *man yuzhiru-hu Allah*.[213] The followers' rejection of successive Abrahamic religions is detailed relative to the reception of their successive holy books. This sometimes involves an unusual prophetological chronology involving the appearance of a pre-Mosaic David (pre-tenth century BCE), which may well reflect a cyclic prophetological gnosis unique to factions of the ahl-i haqq (the often Imam 'Ali centered "People of Truth") such as the Dawudiyyun (Davidites).[214]

Several further major works of the Bab are dated to the last few months of his life. They include (parts of) the K. Asma' (Book of Names) and the K. Panj Sha'n (Book of the Five Grades). The possibly final, major work of the Bab, is the Haykal al-Din (Temple of Religion), with two commentaries on portions thereof. The following few paragraphs must serve to introduce these late or final writings of the Bab.

213 Ar. Dala'il, y (= 10).
214 Ar. Dala'il, l (= 12); cf. Jani (ed. Browne), Nuqtat al-kaf, 37; Lambden 1980s/2002.

KITAB AL-ASMA'/KULL SHAY' (THE BOOK OF THE DIVINE NAMES, THE "ALL THINGS")

Toward the beginning of one of the sections in his K. Asma', the Bab states that God created the pleroma of "All-Things" (*kull shay'*) through His Power as something determined or regulated (*taqdir^{an}*), adding that He fashioned "All-Things" (*kull shay'*) through the divine Will (*al-mashiyyat*) as something formulated (*taswir^{an}*).[215] Theological comprehensiveness or "oneness" expressed through 19 (*wahid* ='one, unique') x 19 (*wahid*) amounting to 361, remains an especially influential numerological paradigm within the later writings of the Bab, especially his P. Bayan and K. Asma'. For the Bab, the key Qur'anic phrase *kull shay'* ("all things, everything"), has all manner of deep theological, cosmological, prophetological, numerological, literary, symbolic, and chronological significances.

This massively important, very lengthy (perhaps 3,000 + page), multi-faceted late work of the Bab (c. 1848–49) is rooted in literary form after this *kull shay'* (abjad numerical value 19x19 = 361) pleroma ("fullness, everything") paradigm, again having nineteen wahids ("unities") each with nineteen sections or gates (babs). It is also further subdivided into four subsections which usually extend for several pages.[216] The K. Asma' has been little studied though it has had some unfortunate negative appraisals by a few orientalists and academics who had never seen the whole, complete reorganized text.[217] Today there are no critical or even semi-critical editions of this complex scriptural work. There exist numerous (more than twenty-seven) scattered though perhaps all partial manuscripts of the K. Asma'.[218] Nonetheless it is a very important testimony to the late Arabic style of the Bab's revelations. It should be regarded as among the most theologically weighty writings of the Bab. Among the reasons for this is that the Badi' (new) Babi-Baha'i calendar of nineteen months each with nineteen days (+ four or five intercalary days) is apparently based upon or rooted in one of the sections of the K. Asma'.[219]

215 K. Asma' I. 2, INBMC 29:4 f. The phrase *kull shay'* ("all-things" occurs quite frequently, around 121 times within forty-eight (out of 114) surahs in the Q., e.g., Q. 7:145. For details see Lambden website, "Kitab al-asma' I – The Book of Names."

216 Cf. the P. and Ar. Bayans.

217 See E. G. Browne, Materials, 206–7 and D. M. MacEoin, Sources 91.

218 There are mss. in Russia (St. Petersburg) ("three in Cambridge, seven in London, four in Paris," as MacEoin, noted in 1992 Sources.

219 The exact mss. for this calendral data in the K. Asma' is unclear. Cf. P. Bayan V.III, 152 f.; Zarandi/Shoghi Effendi, DB II in various Baha'i World vols., e.g., vol. 5, 361–65.

Like several other late works of the Bab, the K. asma' is rich in messianic urgency and predictions of the theophany of *man yuzhiru-hu Allah* (Him whom God shall make manifest). It has invocatory depth and expresses the intricacies of the secrets of the many theologically weighty Names of God (*asma' Allah*), sometimes relating them to high-ranking Babi believers. Recited in the original Arabic, numerous verses or phrases within the Kitab al-asma' again have a *Dhikr*-like or invocatory, rhythmic intensity.

KITAB-I PANJ SHAʿN (THE BOOK EXPRESSIVE OF FIVE MODES OF REVELATION)

This Arabic and Persian work was begun on 1 Baha 7 (= 5 Jumadi I 1266/19 March 1850), the commencement of the year of *al-abad* (the All-Eternal), the year seven on the new Badiʿ calendar of the Bab. Almost 450 pages long (in the incomplete printed edition), it was written over the next seventeen days. Each of its twelve sections is in five sub-divisions in line with (a version of) the five modes of revelation (here the fifth mode is the Persian). One of the main features of the K. Panj is its use of streams of invocations, often repeated according to important number patterns such as 19, 38 (= 19+19) and even 95 (5 x 19).[220]

K. Panj I.1 opens with a neo-*basmala* verse, boldly utilizing a superlative form of the Name of God Allah (God; A+Allah = "Most Supreme God"). This is most probably an exaltation of the expected messianic *man yuzhiru-hu Allah*, to whom this opening section is very likely dedicated. Its subsequent fifty-nine sections (in twelve divisions) are sometimes further dedicated to notable followers of the Bab to whom portions of this book were separately communicated. Not all of the identities of the twelve possible recipients are known. Suggestions as to their identity are mostly only tentative. Somc of these followers after whom sections are named were very erudite individuals, as is reflected in the complexity of the K. Panj. This includes the erudite aforementioned Sayyid Yahya Darabi, Vahid. The complex XIIth section may be devoted to him. It is among the most difficult of the writings of the Bab. Opening with a neo-*basmala* utilizing the superlative of the root indicating knowledge or "gnosis" ('-l-m, 'ilm), it continues with very detailed aspects

220 See, e.g., K. Panj, XI.1, 328 ff.; XI.1, 367 ff.

of *'ilm al-hurūf* (the science of the letters) and the construction of talismans in the light of chronological eras. The Bab also treats alchemical issues quite frequently in the K. Panj, especially in its Xth division.[221]

The sixth pentad or division of the K. Panj is believed by some to have been dedicated to Mirza Husayn 'Ali Nuri Baha'u'llah (d. Acre, Palestine, 1892) known through the non-Qur'anic Name of God Baha' ("Glory-Beauty," *abjad* = 9).[222] Azali Babis assert, however, that it is dedicated to Fatima Baraghani (d. 1852) known as Tahira, also allegedly known through the Name of God Baha', on account of her beauty (which is one of the key meanings of baha'). Whatever the case, this section commences with a neo-*basmala*, which reads, *bismi'llah al-abha al-abha* (In the Name of God, the All-Glorious, the most Beautiful) and continues with many different words and phrases containing the use of this Arabic root (b-h-a/w, cf. baha', etc.). Some are neologisms deriving from this triliteral root. Devotional passages follow which are very closely related to the Shi'i Ramadan dawn prayer which, as already noted, opens with a use of the divine attribute baha'. In the K. Panj, God, for example, is addressed as *buhyan al-baha'iyin* (loosely, the Glory dominated One among the glorious ones).[223] In fact, whole sections and parts of the K. Panj are structured according to the Ramadan dawn prayer, the Du'a al-Baha' (as it is sometimes referred to) which was mentioned on p. 179.

In the P. Bayan and K. Panj we find interesting occurrences of the (possibly New Testament rooted) call, *subhan Allah haqq*[an] *haqq*[an] ("Truly, truly" or "Verily, verily, Glorified be God"). This in a tradition related to the Christian naqus, the clapperboard instrument used in the Christian call to prayer, loosely a "bell." In P. Bayan II. 17 we find four successive repetitions of the first part of the Islamic *shahada* (*la ilaha illa Allah*, "There is no God, but God"), each one followed by two, three, four then

---

221 K. Panj X.1, 327 ff. Profitable source critical reference in connection with hadith texts and other materials, should be made to the Manakib Al Abi Talib of Ibn Shahrashūb al-Māzandarānī (d. 588/1192). Therein we find (as elsewhere) the *al-nuqta* (diacritical Point) tradition voiced by 'Ali, and an influential alchemical exchange of this same Imam which is reflected in parts of the KPS (Manaqib II:63; KPS X.1, 336 ff.).

222 In certain writings of the Bab, the word baha' is associated with the Babi messiah man yuzhiru-hu Allah, All the Baha' (glory-beauty) of the Bayan is "Him whom God shall make manifest" (Per. Bay. 3:14; cf. K.Panj S:88). He occasionally used the genitive phrase baha'-Allah, though often not, it seems, exactly as what might be considered a personal name, like the title assumed by Mirza Husayn 'Ali Nuri.

223 Refer, K. Panj VI.1, 172.See also I/I:3 f.; VII/1:316; VII/2:224, etc.

five repitions of *haqq*^{an} ("Verily").[224] Such also seems to be reflected in K. Panj sha'n I. 5 where we at one point find the obligation to recite, "Verily, verily there is no God except God (*la ilaha illa Allah haqq*^{an} *haqq* ^{an})" nineteen times.[225] Many other points of interest, aside from the foregoing, seem related to materials existing in the Manaqib of Ibn Shahrashub (see bib.).[226]

Finally, the following passage from the K.Panj should most likely be taken to indicate the future advent of an infinite number of future theophanies of the messianic figure man yuzhiru-hu Allah (He whom God will make manifest) nine times named below:

> And after the Bayan it is [the theophany of] man yuzhiru-hu Allah (He whom God will make manifest) [1]. And after *man yuzhiru-hu Allah* [1] is *man yuzhiru-hu Allah* [2]. And after *man yuzhiru-hu Allah* [2] is *man yuzhiru-hu Allah* [3]. And after *man yuzhiru-hu Allah* [3] is *man yuzhiru-hu Allah* [4]. And after *man yuzhiru-hu Allah* [4] is *man yuzhiru-hu Allah* [5]. And after *man yuzhiru-hu Allah* [5] is *man yuzhiru-hu Allah* [6]. And after *man yuzhiru-hu Allah* [6] is *man yuzhiru-hu Allah* [7]. And after *man yuzhiru-hu Allah* [7] is *man yuzhiru-hu Allah* [8]. And after *man yuzhiru-hu Allah* [8] is *man yuzhiru-hu Allah* [9].[227]

THE (LAWH-I) HAYKAL AL-DIN ("TEMPLE OF RELIGION") (1266/EARLY–MID-1850)

This medium-length, around sixty-page, very-late (1266 / May/June 1850), quasi-legalistic scriptural Tablet must have been the final main work of the Bab. It is an Arabic compendium of Babi law very closely related to the Arabic Bayan and extending to eight wahids ("unities") mostly with nineteen gates or divisions.[228] Within it are many further examples of novel, messianically charged legalistic enactments of the Bab. They again often aim to "prepare the way" for the advent of *man yuzhiru-hu Allah* or contain regulations

224 See also P. Bayan II.17.
225 K. Panj I.5, 36. cf. three occurrences in V.4, 162 and IX.2., 303. Cf. 28, 36, 204.
226 Examples include statements of Imam 'Ali about the alchemical work (al-san'a) in Manaqib II:63) and those within K. Panj sha'n IX.3 (310 ff.) and X.1 (esp. 336 ff.).
227 K. Panj IX. 4, 314–15, cf. 397.
228 MacEoin, *Sources*, 90–91.

designed to express deep faith and gratitude toward this expected one. Only a few examples can be referenced here:[229]

- To read nothing other than the Bab's verses (III:5).
- To cease work when man yuzhiru-hu Allah appears, not working save at that which he permits (VII:5).
- To present nineteen precious stones to the first believers ("first wahid") in *man yuzhiru-hu Allah* (VIII:5b).

THE LATE MESSIANISM OF THE BAB

The Bab not only claimed to fulfill Islamic messianic predictions himself, but frequently dwelt upon the characteristics of another or, more accurately multiple, great future messiah figure(s) before whom he frequently humbled himself. Future messianism lies at the core of the religion of the Bab. Unlike the Islamic *khatamiyya* (prophetological "sealedness," Q. 33:40), the Bab predicted a future succession of endless theophanies of the aforementioned messianic figure. For the Bab, religion will ever be renewed by God through an ongoing series of successive advents of the *mazhar-i ilahi* (Manifestations of God). In his two Bayans and other later writings, messianism is very central. This coming figure is frequently referred to by means of the phrase *man yuzhiru-hu Allah* (Him whom God shall make manifest).[230] An unusual, messianically loaded designation, it is repeatedly used by the Bab in his later writings. It is found, for example, more than 250 times in the around 350-page P. Bayan, over 280 times in the over 400-page K. Panj, as well as frequently in the very late Haykal al-Din and elsewhere.

The messianic phrase *man yuzhiru-hu Allah* is most likely rooted in terminology found in early Shiʿi messianic expectations. The messianism of the Bab is often expressed in very clear terms, though the precise identity of the coming one and the next "time of the end" remains mysterious. There are diverse, sometimes complex predictions of the time of the forthcoming

229 For some useful details about the Haykal al-din see MacEoin, Sources, 90–91.
230 Especially those traditions featuring z-h-r / yuzhir (He shall manifest) related predictions. Key examples of such phrases can be found in very early messianic traditions registered within the Kitab of Sulaym ibn Qays al-Hilali (d. c. 705 CE). They are also intimated in certain writings of the Great Shaykh, Muhyi al-Din Ibn al-ʿArabi (so Goldziher, 1921).

theophanic advent. It might be in the year nine (1269/1852–53)[231] or nineteen (1279/1862–63), in *ghiyath* (*abjad* = 1511) or *mustaghath* (*abjad* =2001).[232] The immanence of the future messianic advent(s) thus varies greatly. At times these calendral figures express multiple rather than single future messianic advents. Certain messianic statements of the Bab may well be of symbolic rather than strictly chronological import. The Bab also made it clear that the time of the subsequent theophany was known only to God.[233] It may therefore be a very long time away or something especially immanent. Immediately or shortly after his execution, during the early 1850s and 1860s, more than twenty followers of the Bab claimed a high messianic-theophanic status, or to be the expected messianic *man yuzhiru-hu Allah*. Most are now forgotten save Mirza Husayn 'Ali Nuri, Baha'u'llah, the founder of the Baha'i religion.

THE WASIYYAT-NAMA (WILL AND TESTAMENT) ATTRIBUTED TO THE BAB[234]

On the orders the new grand vizier (of Nasir al-Din Shah), Mirza Taqi Khan, Amir Kabir (d. 1852), the Bab was executed as a dangerous religious heretic in the public square in Tabriz on 9 July 1850. Some time prior to this he had likely communicated a five-page Arabic *wasiyyat-nama* (Will and Testament) to the Name of God *al-Azal* (Eternity), indicative of Baha'u'llah's half-brother Mirza Yahya Nuri (d. Famagusta, 1912). This Arabic document accorded Mirza Yahya a key position pending the future theophany of "Him whom God shall make manifest."[235] Toward the beginning of this wasiyyat-nama, the Bab made cryptic reference to himself or (for Baha'is) to Baha'-Allah as one *hayy fi ufuq al-abha* (living in the Abha Horizon).[236] The word *abha* (all-glorious) here is taken by Baha'u'llah

231 In certain of his writings the Bab had alluded to the importance of the year commonly understood by Baha'is to be the year 1269 AH (= 15 October 1852–4 October 1853) indicating the period of Baha'-Allah's call to mazhariyya (being a Manifestation of God) or (loosely) his assumption of Prophethood.

232 See P. Bayan, II. 17, 65 ff., etc.

233 P. Bayan III.15, 100.

234 There are at least two *wasiyyat-nama* (Will and Testament) attributed to the Bab (see Afnan, 2000:196–97).

235 INBMC 64:95–102; Haifa ms; cf. Nicholas, 1905 [Ar-Béyan], 52 f.

236 Refer INBMC 64:96; BWC. Unpublished ms. [unpaginated] 2. cf. GWB CXIII:207. According to at least one of his "seals" of the Edirne period, Baha'-Allah states, "God

and his followers to be an allusion to this one time Babi then founder of the Baha'i religion. For many, he made the religion of the Bab global and massively promoted the sacredness of his writings over more than forty-year period (1844–92).

CONCLUDING SUMMARY NOTE

As a young twenty-five-year-old Persian, the Bab had a wide religious outreach, as is clear within his numerous writings. These he believed to be revelations from a transcendent God. In his world-embracing consciousness, he addressed all humanity and provided them with a new sacred scripture in the language of Islam (Arabic) and in that of his homeland (Persian), which is similar to the Bible being in Hebrew (a Semitic language) and Greek (an Indo-European language). Within twenty-five years of his execution in 1850 at the age of just thirty-one, awareness of his tragic story began to be known in Europe and elsewhere. A desire to investigate his writings developed. From the mid-1860s, orientalist and academic papers began to be written in Europe and tentative translations of a few of his writings surfaced.

A portion of a ms. of the aforementioned K. al-asma' (Book of Names, c. 1849) of the Bab, for example, was obtained within about fifteen years of its writing by Nokolai Khanykov (d. Paris, 1878), a one-time general Russian consul in Tabriz (during 1853–57). In 1864, the German-born theologian, philosopher, and polymathic linguist Johannes Albrecht Bernhard Dorn or (Russ.) Boris Andreevich (d. St. Petersburg, 1881) wrote a Russian article in which he published a typeset, voweled portion of its Arabic text, adding some annotations (see bib.).[237] The following year, in 1865, the notorious Comte de Gobineau (d. Turin, 1882) with much help from his Persian Jewish assistant Lalazar [Eleazar] Hamadani,

---

testifies by virtue of His own Self that I, verily, am one that is alive in the Abha (most beautiful) Horizon and at every instant cries out from that Horizon, 'I, verily, am God, no God is there except me'" (The Baha'i World vol. V, p. 4 + Taherzadeh, RB 1, photograph opposite 78x). Elsewhere, in numerous alwah, Baha'-Allah associates himself with the Bab's phrase *ana hayy fi ufuq al-abha*. An example is found in his c. 1867 L. Sarraj (Ma'ida VII), 69, 89, 94 and the untitled Tablet of Baha'-Allah in Behmardi ed. La'ali 3:15. cf. Mazandarani, KZH II:8.

237 Dorn published the roughly ten-page wahid (Unity) XII bab (section) 1 on the ma'rifa or gnosis of the Name of God 'al-Maskin', meaning (loosely), "the Peaceful/Tranquil/the Dwelling."

managed to translate the Arabic Bayan of the Bab into French (see bib.)[238] Scholars and others within Russia, France, Britain, Italy, and elsewhere, speedily came to engage with the writings of the Bab. Sadly, for most of the twentieth century, the subject of the writings of the Bab, was largely ignored, sidelined or neglected.

In his writings, the Bab had predicted that Christians who converted to his religion would be viewed by him as a qurrat al-'ayn, the solace or "apple of his eye(s)."[239] Another now internationally revered female, Qurrat al-'Ayn, Fatima Baraghani, Tahira (the Pure One) (d. Tehran, 1852) gave her life for his religion after eloquently expounding his writings in both prose and poetry. She was well-remembered by the British Persianist and early admirer of the Bab and his writings, Edward Granville Browne (d. Cambridge, 1926). Browne became fascinated by the Bab in late July 1886 and zealously sought out his followers and his writings, spending a "Year Amongst the Persians" (1887–88). Subsequently, he wrote the following eloquent panegyric of the female Babi martyr Tahira, Qurrat al-'Ayn (executed 1852):

> The appearance of such a woman as Kurratu'l-'Ayn is in any country and any age a rare phenomenon, but in such a country as Persia it is a prodigy—nay, almost a miracle. Alike in virtue of her marvellous beauty, her rare intellectual gifts, her fervid eloquence, her fearless devotion, and her glorious martyrdom, she stands forth incomparable and immortal amidst her countrywomen. Had the Babi religion no other claim to greatness, this were sufficient—that it produced a heroine like Kurratu'l-'Ayn.[240]

It was the case, then, that the writings or revelations of the Bab inspired many pure-hearted Persians and others to acts of great faith and heroism, even martyrdom for the sake of his visionary restructuring of religion and society. His writings generated and continue to generate religious renewal, awe, and astonishment. They cannot and should not be bypassed or forgotten.

---

238 In the *Les Religiones...* of Gobinesu we find a sixty-page French translation of the Arabic Bayan (refer 2nd ed. 1866, 461–543). It was somewhat mistitled, the (Per.!) "Ketab-e-Hukkam" (sic. "The Book of Precepts") for al-Bayan al-'Arabi ("The Arabic Bayan").
239 See words of Bab to Sayyid Yahya Darabi, Wahid, cited Baha'u'llah, L. Sarraj, (Ma'ida VII), 65. Cf. Shoghi Effendi, Dispensation, 9.
240 Browne, Note Q. Trav. Narr., 309.

BIBLIOGRAPHY

General and Miscellaneous Abbreviations

- Basmala = The Qur'anic Bismillah al-rahman al-rahim (In the Name of God, the Merciful, the Compassionate). There are also numerous variants in the writings of the Bab.
- BPT = Baha'i Publishing Trust (various countries and locations).
- BPT (Iran) = Majmū'ah-yi milli-yi matbu'at-i amri (= MMMA).
- BWC = The Bahá'í World Centre (Haifa, Israel).
- Dawn-Breakers = Tarikh-i Nabil-i Zarandi is the first volume of the recreated history of Nabil-i Zarandi by Shoghi Effendi Rabbani entitled "The Dawn-Breakers Nabil's Narrative" (1st ed. 1932). Rep. BPT., Wilmette: Illinois, 1996, etc.
- EGB Coll., = E. G. Browne (1862–1926) collection of mss. largely at the University of Cambridge (UK).
- EI^1–EI^3. The three successive editions of the Leiden: Brill, Encyclopaedia of Islam 1st ed. M. Th. Houtsma, et al. ed. E. J. Brill & Luzac & Co., 1913–38. Rep. E. J. Brill: New York, 1987. 2nd ed. H. A. R. Gibb/P. J. Bearman et al. ed. (EI^2, 1960–2009). 3rd ed. (= EI^3) ed. M. Gaborieau/ Kate Fleet et al. 2007 (now ongoing and online).
- EIr. = *Encyclopædia Iranica*, ed. Ehsan Yarshater, et al. vol. I–, London, 1982–. Online edition, New York, 1996– (ongoing).
- INBMC [or INBAMC] = "Iran National Baha'i [Archives] Manuscript Collection," 100 (+ index vols.), Tehran mid-1970s. This often indicates volumes of bound photocopies of Arabic and Persian manuscripts mostly of the writings of the Bab and Baha'u'llah as well as some letters (alwah, "Tablets") of Abd al-Baha' and select other Islamic [Shi'i-Shaykhi] and Babi-Baha'i secondary sources. The following are among the INBMC vols. which contain writings of the Bab: INBMC 1, 14, 29, 40, 43, 50, 53, 58, 60, 64, 67, 69, 80, 82, 86, 91, and 98.
- K. = Kitab (book, Letter, Communication...).
- Kh. = Khutba (= Literary Oration, Discourse).
- L. = Lawh pl. alwah (scriptural "Tablet").
- MMMA = Majmū'ah-yi milli-yi matbu'at-i amri (Iranian BPT.).
- Ms (pl. mss) Manuscript(s).
- Q. = Qur'an.
- QA. = The Qayyūm al-asma' of the Bab. See T. Sūrat Yūsuf, p. 222.

- R. = Risala (see p. 220).
- S. = Ṣahifa (see p. 220).
- Sh. = Sharh (Commentary).
- Trans. = Translated by...
- T. = Tafsir (Commentary).
- TBA = Tehran Baha'i Archives

Select Writings of Sayyid 'Ali Muhammad Shirazi, the Bab (1819–50)

Primary Sources, Select Arabic (Ar.) and Persian (Per.) writings of the Bab in manuscript (ms., pl. mss.) and published with select abbreviations and occasional indications of probable dating.

Bayan (Revelatory Exposition)

- P. Bayan = Bayan-i farsi, np. nd. c.1847–48. [1] Tehran, printed Azali ed. 1946]; [2] IMBMC 24:1ff ms. dated 1954.
- Ar- Bayan = al-Bayan al-'arabi (c. 1847–48). [1] in 'Abd-al-Razzaq Hasani, al-Babiyūn wa'l-Baha'iyūn, Sidon, 1957, 81–107 ed. [2] INBMC 43:1–68. French trans. in Gobineau, Religions, Appendix: "Ketab-è Hukkam", 409–82.
- Bayan 'Illat tahrim al-maharim (Clarification of Matters Forbidden or Permissible), TBA Ms.6006C, 85–89.

Dala'il sab'a (The Seven Proofs)

- P. Dala'il = Dala'il-i sab'a. IBA (ii) (? = Nicolas ms.106), 104b ff. + n.p. n.d. (Azali edition [Tehran,196?]) 1–72.
- Ar. Dala'il = Dala'il-i sab'ah. np.nd. [Azali ed. Tehran, 196?] (alif-nūn); (Haifa) IBA (?) = Nicolas ms. 106), 102a–104b.

Khutba = Kh- (pl. khutub) "Literary Discourse"/"Oration"

- Kh-Dhikriyya, ms. 5; Afnan, 2000:473–74.
- Kh. Huruf = Khutba on 'ilm al-hurūf INBA 91; INBA 6004C:209–13.
- Kh. Jaliliyya = Khutba prefacing some mss. of the T. Sūrat al-'aṣr. INBMC 40:1–5.
- Kh. Jidda = Khutba at Jeddah. INBAMC 91:61–81. Incomplete text cited in Afnan, 2000, 86–87. Trans. Lambden 2012 (see p. 230).
- Kh. Qahriyya = Khutba-yi qahriyya. INBMC 64:127–50. Afnan, 2000:359–64.

- Khutba fi al-Safina ("The Sermon on the Ship"), a Khutba of the Bab on the sufferings of the Imam Husayn' [1] INBMC 91:73–81; (2). Tehran, INBA 5006C, 317–20.

Kitab = K. (pl. kutub) "Book," "Letter," etc

- K. A'mal = Kitab a'mal al-sana (Book of the [Devotional] Acts of the Year) in INBA ms. 5006C and 1261/1846.
- K. Asma' = Kitab al-asma' ("The Book of Names"), c.1849. INBMC 29: [2] Uncat. ms. Marzieh Gail Coll. Bosch Baha'i Library (USA) [3] Princeton University ms. (3rd series), vol. 30.
- K. Haykal = Haykal al-din. (The Temple of Religion") n.p. n.d. [Tehran, Azali ed. 196?].
- K. Fihrist = Kitab al-fihrist ("The Book of the Index") INBA. Ms 6007C:339–48.
- K. Panj = Kitab-i panj sha'n. ("The Book of the Five Modes"), n.p. n.d. [Tehran Azali ed. 196X?].
- K. Rūh = Kitab al-rūh [incomplete] ("The Book of the Spirit"), Haifa ms. unpublished [Afnan family mss.] [2] INBA 4011C, 61–100.
- K. 'Ulama' = Kitab al-'ulama' ("Letter to the Learned Ones") INBMC 67:206–16; Afnan 2000:107–11.

Lawh (pl. Alwah), Scriptural Tablets or Letters

- Tablet of the Bab to Muhammad before 'Ali' in the Browne coll. ms. F23 (9), 142–44.
- Tablet of the Bab to an unidentified individual (possibly to Baha'u'llah) in the Browne coll. ms. F23 (9), 144–49.
- Lett. Kirmani = Epistle of the Bab to Hajji Mirza Muhammad Karim Khan Kirmani (d. 1288/1871 CE) cited in Kirman's Risala al-Shihab al-thaqib fi rajm al-nawaṣib ("The Piercing Thunderbolt for the Stoning of the Enemies"), Kirman: Matba'at al-Sa'ada, 1353/1975, 25–27. For a typed text and full trans. Lambden Hurqalya website.
- Letter to the 'Ulama' of Tabriz, text in Afnan, 2000:332–37.
- Qismati = Qismati az alwah-i khatt-i nuqta-yi ūla wa Sayyid Husayn Katib (n.p.) [Iran] n.d.

Masa'il Writings, Replies to Questions, Sometimes Composed in the Form of Prayers

- Q. Bada', "Reply to a question about the bada of God" in INBMC 67:172–73.

- Q. Elixir, "Reply to a question about the alchemical Elixir" in INBMC 67:203–04. Trans. Lambden, "The Bab on the alchemical Elixir," https://hurqalya.ucmerced.edu/node/3001
- Q. Mahfuz = Su'al 'an al-lawh al-mahfuz. (Q. 85:22), TBA. ms. 6006C:79–80.
- Q. Zavarih = Reply to the three questions of Mirza Muhammad Sa'id Zavarih on Basit al-haqiqa and other matters. INBMC 69:419–37.

Risala = R. (pl. Rasa'il) = Treatise

- R. Dhahabiyya = Risala Dhahabiyya (The Golden Treatise). cf. Afnan, 2000:449. INBMC 86:70–98.
- R. Furū al-'adliyya, INBA 5010C, 166–75.
- R. Jasad = Risala fi'l-jasad al-nabi (= Sharh kayfiyyat al-mi'raj), INBMC 69:416–18. Trans. Lambden, Hurqalya website.
- [Risala-yi] Khasa'il-i sab'a (= Khasa'il) or (Ar.) al-Sha'a'ir al-sab'a, text cited in a letter of Mulla 'Abd al-Karim Qazvini (d. 1268/1851–52) to the greatest uncle of the Bab, the Khal-i A'zam, Hajji Mirza Sayyid 'Ali, in facsimile in Afnan 'Ahd-i a'la, 99 and typed and summarized by Afnan in ibid., 100.
- Risala fi'l-nahw wa'l-sarf ("Treatise on Grammar and Morphology/Syntax," c. 1845). [1] INBMC 4011C:167–71; [2] INBMC 67:121–25. See p. 231, McCants, 2012.
- R. Nubuwwa = Risala fi'l-nubuwwa al-khassa. INBMC 14:321–92 and see Eschraqi, 2004.
- R. Sulūk = Risala fi'l-sulūk. TBA., ms. 6006C:73–74. See Lawson trans.
- Majmū'ah = A Compendium of fourteen rasa'il (treatises) or variously titled works of the Bab. From the one-time personal library of a certain Baqir Naraqi now held in the Majlis Library Tehran ms. no. 12448.

Ṣahifa = S. (pl. Ṣuhuf) Scroll, Page, Document...

- Ṣahifa a'mal al-sana (Trestise on the religious acts of the Year), manuscript in the Majlis Library Tehran No. 12448 (unpaginated), item one.
- S. Haramayn = Ṣahifa bayn al-haramayn. ("Epistle [written] Between the two shrines [Mecca and Medina]"). A Treatise written for Mirza Muhammad Muhit and Sayyid 'Ali Kirmani, in E. G. Browne, Or. ms. F 7(9):1–125; TBA. ms. 6007C, 348–413 and ms. in the Majlis Library Tehran no. 12448 (unpaginated), item two.

- Ṣahifa [Risala] furū' al-'Adliyya (The Treatise regarding the Branches of Justice), np. nd.
- Ṣahifa Radawiyya. Browne coll. Or F28. no. 6.

Sharh (Commentary) = Sh.

- Sh. Du'a Ghayba (Commentary on the Devotion for the [Period of the] Occultation) or S. Ja'fariyya = Ṣahifa-yi Ja'fariyya. [1] INBMC 60:57–154. [2] INBMC 98:48–108.
- Sh. Hadith Abū Lubayd Makhzumi (Interpretation of the Tradition of Abu Lubayd Makhzumi).
- Sh-Kh-Tutunjiyya (Commentary on an extract from the Sermon of the Gulf) of Imam 'Ali/Sayyid Kazim Rashti.

Surahs (Scriptural Divisions)

- Sūrat al-Ridwan. Ar. text in Afnan, 2000:198–99.

Tafsir (pl. Tafasir) = T. Commentaries on Qur'an texts and Twelver Imami sacred Traditions (hadith/akhbar)

- T. Akhi = Tafsir hadith 'allamani akhi rasūl-Allah ("Commentary upon the Hadith, 'My brother, the Messenger of God'"), INBMC 14:410–17.
- T. 'Ama' = Tafsir, hadith al-'ama' ("Commentary upon the tradition of the 'Theophanic Cloud'"). TBA. ms 6007C:1–16.
- T. 'Aṣr = Tafsir sūra wa'l-'asr (Q. 110), ("Commentary upon the Sūrah of the Afternoon [Era]") [1] INBMC 69:21–119 [2] INBMC 14:105–208.
- T. Baqara = Tafsir sūrat al-baqara (Q. 2) ("Commentary upon the Sūrah of Cow"), INBMC 69:(1 ff.) 157–294 + (Pt. II) 377–410.
- T. Basmala = Tafsir (Hurūf) al-basmala (Commentary upon the [Letters of the] Basmala), TBA ms. 6014C:299–370 [2] Tehran, INBA 6012C:300–93; INBMC 53:1–45.
- T. Ha' (1) = Tafsir al-Ha' (1) (Commentary upon the Letter "H" I), INBMC 14:221–283; INBMC 67:4–52.
- T. Ha' (2) = Tafsir al-Ha' (2) (Commentary upon the Letter "H" II) INBMC 14:284–320; INBMC 67:53–85.
- T. Hamd = Tafsir Sūrat al-hamd (Q.1) ("Commentary upon the Sūra of Praise [Fathiha]"), [1] INBMC 69:120–53; [2] INBA 5014C:84–129; [3] INBA 6010C:5–41.

- T. Kawthar = Tafsir Sūrat al-kawthar ("Commentary upon the Sura of the Abundance"), EGB Coll. ms. Or. F10 [7]; [2] INBMC 53:181–383 [3] INBMC 53:1–45 [4] INBMC 60:1–56; [5] INBMC 64:33–80.
- T. Laylat = Tafsir Laylat al-qadr, (Q. 97) ("Commentary upon the Sura of the Night of Destiny"), INBMC 69:14–21.
- T. Kumayl = Tafsir Hadith Kumayl ibn Ziyad al-Nakha'i (Commentary upon the Hadith of Kumayl), INBMC 53:63–68.
- T. Man 'Arafa = Tafsir hadith man 'arafa nafsahu... ("Commentary upon Hadith of 'Whoso knoweth himself Knoweth his Lord'"), INBMC 14:468–77; [2] INBMC 40:46–53.
- T. Du'a al-Ṣabah ascribed to Imam 'Ali [1] INBMC 14:400–09; [2] 40:55–62.
- T. waw wa'l-saffat ("Commentary on the [letter] 'w' of wa'l-saffat" ("Those arrayed in rows" = Q. 37:1a).
- T. Sūrat Yūsuf [Q. 12] = Qayyūm al-asma' (= QA). [1] QA-1261 = An early Haifa ms. dated 28 Jumadi I 1261/1845 deriving from Muhammad Mahdi ibn Karbala'i Shah Karam. [2] INBMC 3, an early Mulla Husayn associated ms. [3] QA-F11 (9) = CUL. EGB. Coll. ms. F 11 (9), dated 1891.
- QA-Lambden trans. Hurqalya website. Translations of select sūras and pericopae of the Qayyūm al-asma'.
- T. Wajh = Tafsir Nahnu wajh Allah. TBA 6006C: f. 69–70; INBMC 53:568.

Tasbih Fatima

- T. Fatima in Majmū'ah – Majlis Library Tehran (no. 12448) (2), 180–92.

Tilismat (Talismans), Talismanic Haykals (Pentadic Temples) and Dhari'a (Circles)

- 'Kayfiyyat da'irat al-A- [=1] Y- [=10] Q- [=100] Gh- [=1,000] ("On the construction of the da'ira [talismanic] circle 'A-Y-Q-Gh'" in EGB Coll. F .21, 63–65.
- K. da'ira al-thalitha ("Epistle of the Third Circle"), Cambridge University: Browne Coll. ms F. 25 Item iii.

Wasiyya = Wasiyyat-namah

- Wasiyya 1 = Wasiyyat-namah I in Afnan, 2000:196 and 197.
- Wasiyya 2 = Wasiyyat-namah II. An alleged "Will and Testament" of the Bab. [1] BWC: Haifa ms. (unpaginated) [2] INBA 64:95–102.

Ziyarat-Nama (Visitation Tablets)

- Ziyarat-Nama for Shaykh Ahmad al-Ahsa'i in CUL., Browne Coll. Or. ms. F. 20 ff. 85b–87b.
- Al-Ziyarat al-jami'a al-saghira (Lesser Comprehensive Visitation Supplication) in Tehran: Majlis Library ms. no. 12448 unpaginated ms. [141–45].
- al-Ziyarat al-jami'a al-kabira (Greater Comprehensive Visitation Supplication) in Tehran: Majlis Library ms. no. 12448 unpaginated [145–70]. Also, Cambridge, Browne Coll. F. 22 (item 1) and INBMC 50:1–72.

General Translations of Writings of the Bab

Habib Taherzadeh (and others) trans.

- SWB tr. = Selections from the Writings of the Bab. Haifa: Bahá'í World Centre, 133 BE/1976. 2nd. ed. 1978.
- SWB txt. = Muntakhabat Ayat az athar-i Haḍrat-i Nuqta-yi ūla. MMMA, 134 BE/Wilmette. Illinois: BPT. 1978.

Mirza Husayn 'Ali Nūri (1817–92), entitled Baha'- Allah

- Kitab-i badi' (c.1867). Kouchekadeh ms. (personal copy); Kitab-i badi', Prague: Zero Palm Press, 148 BE/1992.
- Lawh-i hurūfat al-muqatta'ah, Ishraq Khavari ed. and comp. Ma'ida-yi asmani, IV, (129 Badi'/1969–70), 49–86.
- Lawh-i 'Ali Muhammad Sarraj in Ishraq Khavari ed. and comp. Ma'ida-yi asmani, VII (129 Badi'/1969–70), 4–118 and INBMC 73:198–231.

'Abdu'l-Baha' 'Abbas (1844–1921)

- Trav.Narr = 1891. ed. and trans. E. G. Browne, *A Traveller's Narrative Written to Illustrate the Episode of the Bab* (by 'Abbas Effendi). 2 vols. Cambridge: CUP. + reprint 2 vols. in one. Amsterdam: Philo Press, 1975.

Shoghi Effendi Rabbani (c. 1896–1957), Writings and Compilations of Writings

- Zarandi ed. and trans. DB/Dawn-Breakers (see p. 217).
- Dispensation = *The Dispensation of Bahá'u'lláh*. London: BPT, 1947 + many reprints.

Secondary and Other Sources: With Select Abbreviations

Afnan, Abu'l-Qasim

- *'Ahd-i a'la zindigani-yi hadrat-i Bab*. Oxford: Oneworld, 2000.

al-Ahsa'i, Ibn Abi Jumhur (d. late fifteenth century)

- *'Awali al-la'ali al-'aziziyya fi'l-ahadith al-diniyya*. 4 vols. Qumm: Matba'at Sayyid al-Shuhada', 1403–5/1983–85.

al-Ahsa'i, Shaykh Ahmad b. Zayn al-Din (d. Mutayrif near Medina, 1241/1826)

- JK = *Jawami' al-kalim*. 2 vols. Tabriz: Muhammad Taqi Nakhjavani, 1273–76/ vol. 1 / i, ii, and iii. 1273/1856 and vol. 2 /I and ii, 1276/1859.
- Sh-Ziyara = *Sharh al-ziyara al-jami'a al-kabira*. Tehran [1267/1850–51]; 4th ed., 4 vols. Kirman, 1355–56/1976–77.

'Ali ibn Abi Talib (d.40/661), first twelver Imam

- Kh-Ttnj = al-Khutba al-Tutunjiyya [Tatanjiyya] ('The Sermon of the Gulf') in Rajab al-Bursi, Mashariq anwar... (see p. 233) 166–70), cf. the partial text throughout Sayyid Kazim Rashti's 1270/1853 commentary and the Lambden intro. and trans. on personal website (see p. 228).
- K. Jafr = *Kitab al-jafr al-jami' wa al-nūr al-lawami'*. Beirut: Dar al-Maktaba al-Tarbiyya. 1987.
- Nahj al-Balagha, (comp.) al-Sharif al-Raḍi, Muhammad ibn al-Husayn, 4 vols. in 1 Beirut: Mu'assat al-A'lami li'l-Matbū'at, 1424/2003.

Amanat, Abbas

- *Resurrection and Renewal: The Making of the Babi Movement in Iran, 1844–1850*. Ithaca and London: Cornell University Press, 1989.
- *Apocalyptic Islam and Iranian Shi'ism*. London: I.B. Tauris, 2009.
- "Persian Nuqtawis and the Shaping of the Doctrine of 'Universal Conciliation' (ṣulh-i kull) in Mughal India." In Orkhan Mir-Kasimov, ed., *Unity in Diversity, Mysticism, Messianism and the Construction of Religious Authority in Islam*. Leiden: Brill, 2014, 367–91.

Anastase, Le Piere

- *al-Dawūdat aw al-Dawūdiyyūn* (*Le Sect des Davidiens*). al-Mashriq: 1903, VI/3, 60–67.

al-'Askari, Hasan (eleventh Shi'ite Imam, d. 260/873–74)

- *al-Tafsīr al-mansūb ilá al-Imām Abī Muḥammad al-Ḥasan ibn 'Alī al-'Askarī*. Qum: Madrasah al-Imām al-Mahdī, 1988.

al-'Ayyashi, Abu l-Naẓr Muhammad b. Mas'ūd (fl. ninth to tenth century)

- *Tafsir al-Qur'an*. ed. Hashim al-Rasul al-Mahallati. 2 vols. Beirut: Mu'assat al-A'la. 1380–1/ 1411/1991.

al-Bahrani, Sayyid Hashim ibn Sulayman (d. c.1110 /1697)

- *Al-Mahajjat fi ma nazal fi'l-Qa'im al-Hujjat*.
- *The Qaem in the Qur'an*. (Shiabooks, Book 1), trans. Sayyid Mohen al-Hosaini al-Milani, 2006, 132 verses of the Holy Qur'an.

Balyuzi, Hasan M. (1908–80)

- 1973. *The Bab: The Herald of the Day of Days*. Oxford, UK: George Ronald.

Bausani, Alessandro

- *Persia Religiosa: Da Zaratustra a Baha'u'llah* (Italian), Milan: Il Saggiatore, 1959.
- *Religion in Iran: From Zoroaster to Baha'u'llah* (trans. J. M. Marchesi), New York: Bibliotheca Persica Press, 2000.

Behmardi, Vahid, ed.

- *La'ali al-hikma* vol. III. (ed. Vahid Behmardi). Rio de Janeiro: Editora Baha'i-Brasil, 198?.
- + William McCants (abridged trans.) "A Stylistic Analysis of the Báb's Writings Abridged Annotated Translation of Vahid Behmardi's 'Muqaddamih-yi dar bárih-yi sabk va siyáq-i áthár-i mubárakih-yi haḍrat-i rabb a'lá'." In OJBS: *Online Journal of Baha'i Studies*, 121/1, 2007.

Brown, Vahid

- "Autobibliography in the Writings of the Báb." In *Lights of 'Irfan* (Wilmette, IL: Irfan Colloquia), vol. 6, 2005:47–68.

Browne, Edward, Granville (1862–1926)

- Personal "Diary" page for 30 July 1886. Reproduced in Momen ed. 1987. Figure 4 (opposite p. 19).

- "The Babis of Persia II: Their Literature and Doctrines." *JRAS*, 21, 1889:881–1009.
- "Writings of the Bab and Ṣubh-i-Ezel." In *A Traveller's Narrative Written to Illustrate the Episode of the Bab*, 2 vols., Cambridge, 1891, I:335–47.
- "A Catalogue and Description of 27 Babi Manuscripts." *JRAS*, 24, 1892a:433–99, 637–710.
- "Some Remarks on the Bábí Texts Edited by Baron Victor Rosen in vols. I and VI of the *Collections Scientifiques de l'Institut des Langues Orientales de Saint-Pétersbourg*." *JRAS*, 24, 1892b:259–335.
- E. G. Browne, ed. and trans., *The Tarikh-i-Jadid, or New History of Mirza 'Ali Mohammed, the Bab*, Cambridge, 1893. Repr. as *The New History...* Amsterdam: Philo Press, 1975.
- "Bab, Babis." In *Hastings Encyclopaedia of Religion and Ethics, vol. II.* Edinburgh: T. & T. Clark, 1909, 299–308.
- N-Kaf = Nuqtat al-kaf (ed.), Browne, Kitab-i Nuqtatu'l-Káf. Compiled by Hajji Mirza Jani of Kashan. London and Leiden: 1910.
- Materials = *Materials for the Study of the Bábí Religion.* Cambridge: CUP, 1918 [Rep.1961] esp. "Further Notes on Babi Literature," in Materials 198–208.

al-Būni, 'Abu al-'Abbas Ahmad ibn 'Ali ibn Yūsuf al-Qurayshi (622/1225)
- *Kitab shams al ma'arif wa lata'if al awwarif* (*The Book of Sun of Gnosis and the Subtleties of the mystics*). Cairo, 1904

al-Bursi, Rajab. al-Hafiz (d. c. 814/1411)
- Mashariq = *Mashariq anwar al-yaqin fi asrar Amir al-Mu'minin.* Beirut: Dar al-Andalus, 1978.

Cole, Juan R.
- 'Chahriq ii' in EIr. vol. IV, Fasc. 6, 644–45.

Dorn, Johannes Albrecht Bernhard / Boris Andreevich (1805–81)
- Die Sammlung von Morgenländischen Handschriften: welche dir Kaiserliche Offentliche Bibliothek zu St. Petersburg in Jahre 1864 Von Hern. v. Chanykov... St. Petersburg: Buchdruckerei der Kaiserlichen Akademie der Wissenschaften erwoben hat von B. Dorn, 1865.

Eschraghi, Armin

- *Frühe Shaikhi und Babi-Thelogie: Die Beweise für Muhammads besonderes Prophetentum (ar- Risala fi ithbat an-nubūwa al-khaṣṣa)*. Leiden: E. J. Brill, 2004.
- "Undermining the Foundations of Orthodoxy: Some Notes on the Bab's Sharia (Sacred Law)" in Lawson ed. 2012, 223–47.

Gobineau, Joseph Arthur Comte de Gobineau (1816–82)

- *Les Religiones et les Philosophies dans l'Asie Centrale.* 2nd ed. Paris: Librarie Académique, Didier et Libraires-Éditeurs qual des Grands-Augustins, 1866.

Goldziher, Ignaz Goldziher (1850–1921)

- "Verhältnis des Bab zu früheren Ṣūfi-Lehren" in *Der Islam*, Zeitschrift für Geschichte und Kulter des Islamischen Oriens 11 (1921), 252–54. Eng. trans. B. Walker and S. N. Lambden in BSB 6:2–3 (Feb. 1992), 65–68.

al-Hasani, 'Abd al-Razzaq

- *Al-Babiyun wa'l-Baha'iyun fi haḍirihim wa madihim: Dirasah daqiqah fi'l-kashfiyya wa'l-shaykhiyya wa fi kayfiyya ẓuhūr al-Babiyya fa-'l-Baha'iyya Sidon.* Lebanon: Matba'at 'al-'Irfan, 1957.

Ibn al-'Arabi, Muhyi al-Din (c. 638 /1240)

- *al-Futūhat al-Makkiyya*, 4 vols. Beirut: Dar Ṣadir n.d. [= Cairo ed.1911, rep. 1968].
- Fusus = *Fuṣūṣ al-Hikam.* Ed. A. 'Afifi. [Cairo] Beirut: Dar al-Kutub al-'Arab, 1946.
- Kitab Insha' al-Dawa'ir. 'Alam al-Fikr. n.d.
- Rasa'il = *Rasa'il Ibn al-'Arabi.* ed. Afifi. Rep. Beirut: Dar Ihya al-turuth al-'arabi. nd.

Ibn Shahrashub al-Mazandarani, Muhammad ibn 'Ali (d. 588/1192)

- *Manāqib Al Abi Talib*, 5 vols. ed. Yusuf Biqa'i. Beirut: Dar al-Murtada, Dar al-Adwa', 1427/1385 Sh. / 1991 + 2007.

Ja'far al-Sadiq [sixthImam]; 'Abd al-Razzaq Gilani (trans.)

- Misbah al-shari'ah wa-miftah 'al-haqiqa - Matn va sharh ba tarjama (text, trans. and comm.) - (al-mansub 'ila 'al-'Imam 'al-Sadiq)... [recension of] Shahid al-Thani. trans. 'Abd al-Razzaq al-Gilani (1676) ed. Bahman Khulū'i.

al-Jili, 'Abd al-Karim ibn Ibrahim (d. c. 832/1428)

- Insan Kamil = *al-Insan al-kamil fi ma'rifat al-awakhir wa'l-awa'il.* 2 vols. in 1. Cairo: Muṣtafa al-Babi al-Halabi, 1375/1956.
- *al-Kahf wa'l-raqim fi sharh bismillah al-rahman al-rahim.* Beirut: Dar al-Kutub al-`Ilmiyya, 1425/2004.

al-Kashani, Hajji Mirza Jani (d. 1852)

- *Kitab-i Nuqtat al-Kaf*, compiled by Hajji Mirza Jani of Kashan between the years A.D. 1850 and 1852, edited from the unique Paris ms. Suppl. Persan 1071. ed. E. G. Browne and Muhammad Qazvini. Leiden: Brill, 1910.

al-Kashani, Mulla Muhsin Fayḍ (d. 1091/1680)

- *Tafsir al-safi fi tafsir kalam Allah al-wafi.* Beirut: Mu'assasat al-A'lami, 1399–1402/1979–82.

Kirmani, Hajji Mirza Muhammad Karim Khan (d. 1288/1871)

- Izhaq al-batil dar radd al-Babiyya ("The Crushing of Falsehood in refutation of Babism"). Completed 12 Rajab 1261/17 July 1845.

Kulayni [Kulini], Abū Ja'far Muhammad (d. 329/941)

- al-Kafi = *Kafi al-Uṣul min al-Kafi* (vols. 1–2). ed. A. A. Ghafari. Beirut: Dar al-Aḍwa, 1405/1985.
- *al-Furū' min al-Kafi* (vols. 3–7). ed. A. A. Ghafari. Beirut: Dar al-Aḍwa, 1405/1961.

Lambden, Stephen N.

- Ph.D. 1980s/2002 = Lambden Ph.D. = "Some Aspects of Isra'iliyyat and the Emergence of the Babi-Baha' Interpretation of the Bible." Unpublished, 1980s/ 2002 Ph.D. thesis, University of Newcastle upon Tyne, UK.
- Hurqalya Publications [= H*] – Personal website hosted at the University of California, Merced. See especially "Haykal – The Writings of the Bab": https://hurqalya.ucmerced.edu/scholarship/haykal-writings-b%C4%81b
- "The Bab on the alchemical Elixir." https://hurqalya.ucmerced.edu/node/3001. 1985.

- "Towards a Complete Translation of Qayyūm al-asma' of the Bab (I–CXI)." Lamben Hurqalya website, https://hurqalya.ucmerced.edu/node/103/ ,1980–2020 (ongoing).
- "An Episode in the Childhood of the Báb." In Peter Smith (ed.), *Studies in Bábí and Bahá'í History, Vol. 3*, Los Angeles: Kalimat Press, 1986, 1–31.
- "The Sinaitic Mysteries: Notes on Moses/Sinai Motifs in Babi and Baha'i Scripture." In Moojan Momen (ed.), *Studies in the Bábí & Bahá'í Religions, Vol. 5* [= Studies in Honour of the Late Hasan M. Balyuzi]. Los Angeles: Kalimat Press, 1988, 64–183.
- "The Background and Centrality of Apophatic Theology in Babi and Baha'i Scripture." In Jack McLean (ed.), *Revisioning the Sacred: New Perspectives on a Baha'i Theology*, Los Angeles: Kalimat Press, 1997, 37–78.
- "Eschatology: Babi-Baha'i." *EIr* VIII, 1998:581–82.
- "The Messianic Roots of Babi-Baha'i Globalism," in *Baha'i and Globalisation*." In (eds.) Margit Warburg, Annika Hvithamar, and Morten Warmind (Aarhus Universitetsforlag, 2005), 17–34.
- The Du'a al-Simat ("Prayer of the Signs") with some notes on the Commentary of Sayyid Kazim Rashti and Babi-Baha'i Intertextualities. Paper presented at the Middle East Studies Association, 2006 (Boston, MA).
- "Kitab-e iqan." (with Sholeh A. Quinn) in *EIr*, 2010 (online) and 2018 (in print).
- Review of MacEoin, "The Messiah of Shiraz: Studies in Early and Middle Babism" (Iran Studies; Leiden: Brill Academic Pub, 2009) in *Religion* (Lancaster, UK) 41/3 (2011b), 514–18.
- "The Sūrah Titles of the Qayyūm al-asma' of Sayyid 'Ali Muhammad Shirazi (1819–50 CE): Gateways to the Earliest Thought of the Bab." Hurqalya website: https://hurqalya.ucmerced.edu/node/401.
- "The Khaṣa'il-i sab'a (The Treatise of the Seven Directives) of Sayyid 'Ali Muhammad Shirazi, the Bab (d. 1850)." The Third International Conference on Modern Religions and Religious Movements and the Bábí-Bahá'í Faiths, 21-23 March 2011a. Hebrew University, Jerusalem.
- "The Tafsir Sūrat Yūsuf–Qayyūm al-asma' of the Bab as the Kitab al-Husayniyya." Unpublished Iranian Studies paper, 2012a.
- "The Khutba al-Jidda (The Literary Sermon at Jeddah) of the Bab." In Lawson and Ghaemmaghani (eds.) "A Most Noble Pattern," 2012b, 146–59.

- "Khatamiyya (Q. 33:40b) and the Liqa' Allah (the Divine Theophany)." Hurqalya website, 2018a: https://hurqalya.ucmerced.edu/node/3141/
- "Joseph as Husayn and the Qayyūm (Deity Self-Subsisting): A Provisional translation of the 5th Sūrah of the Qayyūm al-asma." In BSR (forthcoming), 2019a.
- "The Babi-Baha'i transcendence of khatam al-nabiyyin (Qur'an 33:40) as the 'finality of prophethood'." Hurqalya website: 2019b. PDF here: https://hurqalya.ucmerced.edu/biblical-and-islamic-studies.
- "From Cosmic Firmament to Celestial Interworld: Some notes on the Biblical Hebrew, Aramaic-Syriac or Mandaic roots and Shi'i-Shaykhi developments of the realm commonly designated هورقليا Hūrqalya." (Forthcoming.)

Lawson, B. Todd

- The Qur'an Commentary of the Bab. Ph.D. dissertation. McGill Univ, 1987.
- "Interpretation as Revelation: The Qur'an Commentary of Sayyid 'Ali Muhammad Shirazi, the Bab (1819–50)." In A. Rippin, ed., *Approaches to the History of the Interpretation of the Qur'an*, 1988.
- "Interpretation as Revelation: The Qur'an Commentary of Sayyid 'Ali Muhammad Shirazi, the Bab (1819–50)." *Approaches to the History of the Interpretation of the Qur'an*. Ed. Andrew Rippin. Oxford: Clarendon, 1988. 223–53.
- "The Term 'Remembrance' (dhikr) and 'Gate' (bab) in the Bab's Commentary on the Sura of Joseph." Studies in Honor of the Late Hasan M. Balyuzi. Ed. Moojan Momen. *Studies in the Babi and Baha'i Religions*, vol. 5. Los Angeles: Kalimat Press, 1988. 1–64.
- "The Dawning Places of the Lights of Certainty in the Divine Secrets Connected with the Commander of the Faithful by Rajab Bursi." In Lewisohn (ed.) *The Legacy of Mediaeval Persian Sufism*. London: Khaniqahi Nimatullahi Publications, 1992, 261–76.
- "Akhbari Shi'i Approaches to Tafsir." In Hawting and Shareef (eds.) *Approaches to the Qur'an*. London and New York: Routledge, 1993, 173–210.
- "The Dangers of Reading: Inlibration, Comrnunion, and Transference in the Qur'an Commentary of the Bab." Scripture and Revelation: Papers presented at the First Irfan Colloquium, Newcastle-upon Tyne, England, December 1993, and the Second Irfan Colloquium, Wilmette, USA,

March 1994. Ed. Moojan Momen. *Baha'i Studies Series*, vol. 3. Oxford: George Ronald, 1997, 111–255.
- "The Bab's Epistle on the Spiritual Journey towards God." In *Lights of 'Irfan*: vol. 3. Wilmette, IL: 'Irfan Colloquia, 2002, 49–57.
- *Gnostic Apocalypse and Islam: Qur'an, exegesis, messianism, and the literary origins of the Babi Religion.* London and New York: Routledge, 2011.
- Lawson and Ghaemmaghani (eds.) "A Most Noble Pattern, Collected Essays on the Writings of the Bab, 'Ali Muhammad Shirazi." Oxford: George Ronald, 2012.
- "Coincidentia Oppositorum in the Qayyum al-Asrna: The Terms 'Point' (nuqta), 'Pole' (qutb), 'Center' (markaz), and the Khutbat al-Tatanjiya," https://www.h-net.org/~bahai/bhpapers/vol5/tatanj/tatanj.htm
- *Tafsir as Mystical Experience: Intimacy and Ecstasy in Quran Commentary: Tafsīr sūrat al-baqara of Sayyid ʿAlī Muḥammad Shīrāzī, The Báb (1819–1850).* Leiden, Boston: Brill, 2019.
- Personal website, http://toddlawson.ca/publications/

McCants, William, F.
- Risala fi'l-nahw wa'l-sarf ("Treatise on Grammar and Syntax"). In Lawson (ed.), 2012, 52–87.

MacEoin, Denis
- "The Babi Concept of Holy War." In *Religion*, vol. 12, 1982:2, 93–129.
- "Nineteenth-century Babi talismans." *Studia Iranica*, 14/1, 1985:77–98.
- 'Ahsa'i, Shaykh Ahmad al-. *EIr.* I:674–79.
- 'Bayan (2), December 15, 1988 in *EIr*, Vol. III, Fasc. 8, 878–82.
- [Sources =] *The Sources for Early Babi Doctrine and History, A Survey.* Leiden: E. J. Brill, 1992.
- *Rituals in Babism and Baha'ism (Pembroke Persian Papers 2).* London: British Academic Press, 1994.
- *The Messiah of Shiraz, Studies in Early and Middle Babism.* Leiden: Brill, 2009.

Majlisi, Muhammad Baqir (d. 1111/1699)
- Bihar 2nd ed. = Bihar al-anwar², 110 vols. Beirut: Dar al-Ihya al-Turath al-'Arabi, 1376–94/1956–74 and 1403/1983.

Mazandarani, Mirza Assad-Allah, Fadil-i

- KZH = [Tarikh-i] Zuhur al-haqq. 9 (largely) mss. vols.
- Tarikh zuhur al-haqq. vol. III. n.p., n.d. [Tehran. 1940s?], rep. Hoffheim: Mu'assasat-i Matbu'at-i Baha'i-i Alman, 2008.

Mohammad Hosseini, Nosratollah

- *Hadrat-i Bab*. Dundas, Ontario: Institute for Baha'i Studies, 1995.

Momen, Moojan.

- "The Trial of Mulla 'Ali Bastami: A Combined Sunni-Shi'i fatwa against the Bab." *Iran*, 20, 1982:113–43.
- (ed.) *Selections from the Writings of E. G. Browne on the Bábí and Bahá'í Religions*. [= SWEGB] Oxford: George Ronald, 1987.
- "Darabi, Sayyid Yahya." In *EIr*. VII:10–11.

Momen, Moojan and Stephen N. Lambden

- "Some Sources for Early Babi Doctrine and History: A Survey by Denis MacEoin." *Review in Iranian Studies*, vol. 28, no. 3/4 (Summer–Autumn, 1995), 263–65.

National Spiritual Assembly of the Baha'is of the United States and Canada.

- *The Bahá'í World*, vol. V (1932–34). New York: Baha'i Publishing Committee, 1936.

Nicholas, A. L. M. (1864–1939)

- S-Preuves = *Le Livre des Sept Preuves de la mission du Bab*. Paris: Maisonneuvre, 1902.
- *Seyyed Ali Mohammed dit Le Bâb*. Paris: Dujarric & Co., 1905.
- Ar-Béyan = *Le Béyan Arabe, Le Livre Sacré Bábyse*. Paris: Ernest Leroux, 1905.
- P-Béyan = *Le Béyan Persan*, trans. A. L. M. Nicolas, 4 vols. Paris: Librarie Paul Geuthner, 1911–14.

Nicholson, R. A. (ed.)

- *A Descriptive Catalogue of the Oriental MSS. Belonging to the late E. G. Browne*. Cambridge: CUP, 1932.

Nomanul Haq, Syed

· *Names, Natures, and Things: The Alchemist Jaabir ibn Hayyaan and his Kitaab al-Ahjaar (Book of Stones).* Dordrecht, London, Boston: Kluwer Academic Publishers, 1993.

al-Nu'mani, Abi 'Abdallah Muḥammad ibn Ibrahim ibn Ja'far (d. 360/970)

· *Kitab al-Ghayba*, Beirut: Mu'assasat al-A'la li'l-Matbu'at, 1403/1983.

Quinn, Sholeh A.

· "Muhammad Shah Qajar in Four Early Writings of the Bab," in Lawson ed. 2012:160–175.

al-Qumi, 'Abbas (d. 1319/1901)

· Mafatih al-Jinnan. Dar Ihya al-Turath al-'Arabi, 1422/2001

Rabbani, Ahang

· *The Genesis of the Bábi-Bahá'í Faiths in Shíráz and Fárs. Mírzá Habíbu'lláh Afnán.* (trans. and annotated by Ahang Rabbani). Leiden: Brill, 2008.

Rajab al-Bursi, al-Hafiz, Radi al-Din Rajab ibn Muhammad (d. Tūs, c. 814/1411)

· *Mashariq anwar al-yaqin fi asrar Amir al-Mu'minin.* Beirut: Dar al-Andalus, 1978.

al-Rashti, Sayyid Kazim al-Husayni (d. Karbala, 1259/1843)

· Sh-Ism = Risala fi sharh wa tafsir ism Allah al-a'zam. School of Oriental and African Studies Library. Ms. Ar. 92308 fol. 271a–74a.
· Sh-Qasida = Sharh al-qasida al-lamiyya. Tabriz. 1270/1853.
· Sh-Ttnj[2] = *Sharh al-khutba al-tutunjiyya*, 3 vols. 2nd ed. Hajji Mirza 'Abd al-Rasul al-Ihqaqi, Kuwait: Jami'a al-Imam al-Muhammad Ṣadiq 1421/2001.
· Sh-Du'a al-simat = *Sharh du'a' al-simat wa... Sharh hadith al-qadr.* Beirut: Mu'assat Fikr al-Awhad / Syria [Damascus]: al-Sayyida Zaynab, 1423/2002.

Sachedina, A. A.

· *Islamic Messianism: The Idea of Mahdi in Twelver Shi'ism.* Albany: SUNY Press, 1981.

Saiedi, Nader

- *Gate of the Heart: Understanding the Writings of the Bab*. Canada: Wilfred Laurier Univ. Press, 2008.

Taherzadeh, Adib

- *The Revelation of Bahá'u'lláh, vol. 4, Mazra'ih & Bahjí*, 1877–92. Oxford: George Ronald, 1987.

Volkov, Denis V.

- "Khanykov, Nikolai." In *EIr*. XVI/4, 2018:419–24.

Wilson, Samuel Graham

- "The Bayan of the Bab." *Princeton Theological Review*, Vol. XIII, 1915: 633–54.

Zarandi, Muhammad (Nabil) (d. 1892)

- Tarikh [= DB] ed. and trans. (Part I) Shoghi Effendi as "The Dawn-Breakers: Nabil's Narrative of the Early Days of the Baha'i Revelation." Wilmette: Baha'i Pub. Trust, 1st ed. 1932? Many later editions, 1974.

5

Interpretation as Revelation

The Qur'án Commentary of the Báb, Sayyid 'Alí Muḥammad Shírází (1819–50)

TODD LAWSON

Abstract: This chapter attempts to describe and place in context two of the earliest writings of the Báb. Both writings are commentaries on the Qur'án. The earliest of these, a commentary on the Chapter of the Cow, was written before the Báb made his claim to be the promised one; the second is the famous Qayyúm al-Asmá or Commentary on the Chapter of Joseph. Apart from pointing out the dramatic differences in style and content between these two commentaries, this chapter offers some observations on the nature of these contents, the history of the ideas put forth, and their relationship to Shí'í Islam and the thought of Shaykh Ahmad al-Ahsá'í and Sayyid Kázim Rashtí.

The writings of the Báb are many. On his own estimate, they exceed 500,000 verses.[1] In the past, these writings have been examined by scholars mainly for what they have to tell us about the history of the Bábí movement. The purpose of this discussion is to draw attention to the literature itself in order to begin an evaluation of what must surely be one of the most important questions to be raised not only by students of the Bábí and Bahá'í religions, but also by those interested in the history of nineteenth-century Iran, upon which the dramatic events associated with the name of the Báb made such a vivid mark. That question – How did the Báb read the Holy Book of Islam? – will automatically be of interest to those engaged in studying the history of the interpretation of the Qur'án. It should be mentioned that *tafsír* represents only one of several types of exposition to which the Báb applied himself. That it should be regarded as among the most important types is clear from the mere fact that it comprises a large percentage of his extant work and that it was by means of a *tafsír* that he first made his claims known.

It was the *Tafsír súrat Yúsuf*, also known as the *Qayyúm al-asmá*, which the Báb's earliest followers used to propagate his cause. It has been referred to by Bahá'u'lláh (1817–92) as "the first, the greatest, and mightiest of all books,", and by Shoghi Effendi (1897–1957) as being "universally regarded, during almost the entire ministry of the Báb, as the Qur'án of the people of the *Bayán*."[2] In addition to this work, are three other major *tafsír*s extant, and a series of shorter commentaries.[3]

---

1 The Báb, *Bayán-i fársí* (= *Le Béyan Persan*, trans. A.-L.-M. Nicolas (Paris, 1011–14), iii. 113. See also the discussion of the amount of the Báb's work that has survived in Denis MacEoin, *The Sources for Early Bábí Doctrine and History: A Survey* (Leiden, 1992, hereafter *Sources*), 11–41.

2 *Bahá'u'lláh*, the title assumed by Mirzá Ḥusayn 'Alí Núrí, was the founder of the Bahá'í faith. This comment is found in his *Kitáb-i Íqán* (Cairo, n.d.), 180 = *Kitáb-i-Íqán: The Book of Certitude*, translated by Shoghi Effendi (Wilmette, 1970), 231. The second statement is from Shoghi Effendi, great-grandson of Bahá'u'lláh and eventual Guardian of the Bahá'í faith (*walí amru'lláh*), *God Passes By* (Wilmette, 1970), 23.

3 All works of the Báb referred to in this chapter are, unless otherwise noted, still in manuscript. The following are the titles of his works which contain the word *tafsír* or *sharḥ* (the first four being in chronological order): (1) *Tafsír súrat al-baqara* (covers the first *juz'* of the Qur'án); (2) *Tafsír súrat Yúsuf* (Q. 12); (3) *Tafsír súrat al-kawthar* (Q. 108); (4) *Tafsír súrat wa'l-aṣr* (Q. 103); (5) *Tafsír súrat al-ḥamd* (Q. 1, distinct from (1) above, which also includes commentary on Q. 1, the *súrat al-fátiḥa*); (6) *Tafsír súrat al-tawḥíd* (Q. 112); (7) *Tafsír súrat al-qadr* (Q. 97); (8) *Tafsír basmala* (on the Quranic phrase "*Bismilláhir raḥmánir raḥím*/In the name of God, the Merciful, the Compassionate";

It appears that all of these belong to the earliest period of the Báb's career and are, therefore, important in themselves as a source for his earliest thought.[4]

As will be seen, some of this material represents a distinct type of scriptural interpretation; this is particularly apparent in the *Tafsír súrat Yúsuf*, excerpts from which will appear later in this chapter. That there are problems connected with the proper categorization of some of these writings is something Browne suggested long ago. In speaking of the above-mentioned *tafsír* he said: "A *Commentary* in the strict sense of the word it is not, but rather a mystical and often unintelligible rhapsody."[5]

In the following pages an attempt will be made to show some aspects of this work and one other of the Báb's *tafásír* to try to indicate, in however limited a form, some elements of the logic of structure and content of this important composition while calling attention to the clear transformation of style and thought between it and the earlier *Tafsír súrat al-baqara*. Before proceeding directly to the texts, a brief outline of the life of the Báb will help put the following discussion in perspective.

LIFE OF THE BÁB

The Báb was born in Shíráz on 20 October 1819 (1 Muḥarram 1235) into a family of fairly prosperous merchants. His father died when he was about six years old, and the responsibility for his upbringing devolved upon his uncle. His formal education consisted of five or six years at a local *maktab* under the direction of one Shaykh 'Ábid, who happened to be an adherent of the then somewhat popular Shaykhí school. It appears that the Báb, whose name was 'Alí Muḥammad, was not particularly fond of school, although according to some reports, this antipathy was not the result of any intellectual incapacity. On the contrary, the few reports which exist tend to

(9) *Tafsír-i há'* (commentary on the significance of the Arabic letter *há'*, the 26th of the alphabet; (10) *Tafsír áyat al-kursí* (Q. 2:255); (11) *Tafsír áyat al-núr* (Q. 24:35); (12) *Tafsír ḥadíth Kumayl*; (13) *Tafsír ḥadíth járíya;* (14) *Tafsír naḥnu wajhu'lláh*. Not all of these works concern Quranic material.

4 E. G. Browne, "Báb, Bábís," *Encyclopaedia of Religion and Ethics* (New York, 1909), ii. 305a.

5 E. G. Browne, "Some Remarks on the Bábí Texts Edited by Baron Victor Rosen in vols. I and VI of the *Collections Scientifiques de l'Institut des Langues Orientales de Saint-Pétersbourg*," *JRAS*, 24 (1892), 261.

show the Báb at this early stage as the owner of a precociously inquisitive and outspoken nature.[6]

At age ten the Báb left the *maktab* and five years later moved with his uncle to Búshihr to pursue the family business there. After about four years of working in partnership with his uncle, the Báb became independent. There is disagreement about what the Báb's attitude to trade was, but so far no compelling evidence has been brought to light to support the statement that this basic attitude was negative.[7] It was while the Báb was in Búshihr that he began to write various religious works. Although it is not known exactly what these were, they probably included essays on various theological topics and eulogies of the Imáms. Some of these were apparently written at the request of certain of his fellow merchants. There is also an indication that even before voicing any particular claim to spiritual authority, the Báb had aroused a certain amount of attention, and even ill will, by the production of these earliest works.[8]

In 1840, the Báb closed his business and left Búshihr for the region of the 'Atabát (lit. "thresholds," it refers to the shrine cities of Iraq: Najaf, Karbalá', Káẓimayn, and Sámarra), where he remained for nearly a year.[9] It was during this time that he attended lectures by Sayyid Káẓim Rashtí, the undisputed successor of Shaykh Aḥmad al-Aḥsá'í, founder of the Shaykhí school. It seems that the Báb's family did not approve of his preoccupation with things religious and that his marriage, in 1842, was arranged in the hope of inducing him to concentrate his attention more on the practicalities of existence. Prior to his marriage, while he was still in Karbalá', it is said that the Báb became acquainted with and attracted a certain amount of

6 H. M. Balyuzi, *The Báb, The Herald of the Day of Days* (Oxford, 1973), 34–39. Other treatments of the Báb's life are: Abbas Amanat, *Resurrection and Renewal: The Making of the Babi Movement in Iran, 1844–1850* (Los Angeles, 2005), 109–52; Denis MacEoin, *The Messiah of Shiraz: Studies in Early and Middle Bábism* (Leiden, 2009), 155–63. An important discussion of the problems associated with the biography of the Báb is Stephen N. Lambden, "An Episode in the Childhood of Sayyid 'Alí Muḥammad, the Báb," in Peter Smith, ed., *In Iran: Studies in Bábí and Bahá'í History*, iii (Los Angeles, 1986), 1–31.

7 The Báb's statement, cited by MacEoin, *Messiah*, 156, that a dog belonging to a Jew is to be preferred to the people of the bazaar because of the latter's lack of religious devotion, must be seen as an indictment of the people themselves and not their occupation.

8 See Balyuzi, 40; *Messiah*, 157–58.

9 Opinion is divided on just how long the Báb stayed in Karbalá', where Sayyid Káẓim Rashtí, second leader of the Shaykhí school (see p. 240), held his classes. The discussion appears rooted in polemic; sources favorable to the Báb prefer a shorter length of time.

respect and admiration from a number of Shaykhís, some of whom later became his followers.[10] Even his arch-critic, Muḥammad Karím Khán Kirmání says in his polemical *Izháq al-báṭil* that, although he himself never met the Báb, it was true that he had been held in respect in Karbalá' and that he did in fact meet and serve Sayyid Káẓim during his sojourn there, however long it had been.[11]

The picture that emerges, then, is of a pious young man, who, despite a lack of formal training in the higher religious sciences was nevertheless motivated to produce religious works, the nature of which was sufficiently impressive to win the respect of his readers. Indeed, it was undoubtedly the very fact of this lack of training, together with his status as a merchant, which called attention to his undeniable spiritual and literary gifts. Thus a variation on the Islamic theme of the "unlettered prophet" begins to take shape. In this connection it is also interesting, and perhaps instructive with reference to the way in which Muḥammad's so-called illiteracy may be understood, to observe that the Báb was manifestly not illiterate; in fact, many of his writings were produced before witnesses. That these works were written by one untutored, or at best self-taught, and perhaps even more convincingly, that they were written with astonishing speed and fluency, combined to present an evidentiary miracle comparable, in every way, to the Qur'án itself.[12]

In 1844, shortly after the death of Sayyid Káẓim, the Báb put forth his claim, in writing, to be in direct contact with the Hidden Imám and so a locus of tremendous spiritual authority. Mullá Ḥusayn and seventeen other young Shaykhís, including the famous poetess Ṭáhira, gave their allegiance to him, and the Bábí religion was born. Some months later, the Báb departed on his pilgrimage, returning to Shíráz in March 1845. As a result of the activities of his followers, he was now arrested for the first time and shortly released. In 1846, the Báb took up residence in Iṣfahán where he remained from September of that year until March 1847, shortly after his powerful protector, Iṣfahán's governor-general, Manúchihr Khán, died on 21 February. At this time he was arrested by government troops and escorted to the western frontier of Iran where he was to spend the rest of his life in secluded imprisonment.

---

10 See Peter Smith and Moojan Momen, "The Bábí Movement: A Resource Mobilization Perspective," in P. Smith, ed., *In Iran*, 60 and references.

11 Cited in *Messiah*, 160.

12 See, e.g., A.-L.-M. Nicolas, *Seyyed 'Alí Mohammed dit le Báb* (Paris, 1905), 234.

During this last stage of his career, the Báb continued to experience and record revelations. It was at this time that his Persian *Bayán* was written, together with many prayers, *ajwiba*, and other correspondence to his by now numerous following throughout Iran. According to Nabíl, the Báb, during the nine months he was held in the castle at Máku, produced no less than nine complete commentaries on the Qur'án.[13]

As is well known, the Báb's literary activity came to an end on 9 July 1850, when he was publicly executed in Tabríz.[14]

THE SHAYKHÍ SCHOOL

In a "Foreword" to his account of the first hundred years of the Bábí–Bahá'í religion, Shoghi Effendi asserts the significance of the Shaykhíya in Bábí and Bahá'í history:

> I shall seek to represent and correlate, in however cursory a manner, those momentous happenings which have insensibly, relentlessly, and under the very eyes of successive generations, perverse, indifferent or hostile, transformed a heterodox and seemingly negligible offshoot of the Shaykhí school of the Ithná-'Asharíyyih sect of Shiʿah Islám into a world religion.[15]

The "seemingly negligible offshoot" here mentioned is, of course, the Bábí religion. It has already been mentioned that the Báb's teacher, Shaykh 'Ábid, was a follower of the Shaykhí school. It is also known that several of the Báb's merchant relatives were attracted to the teachings of this movement.[16] As was mentioned previously, the Báb himself attended the lectures of Sayyid Káẓim Rashtí and in at least two of his works directly refers to him as "my teacher" (*mu'allimí*).[17] It is therefore important that at least some brief state-

13 Mullá Muḥammad Zarándí (*Nabíl*), *The Dawn-Breakers: Nabíl's Narrative of the Early Days of the Bahá'í Revelation*, translated and edited by Shoghi Effendi (Wilmette, 1932, hereafter, *Nabíl*), 31. The nine commentaries appear to have been lost.

14 There is some disagreement about the exact date; see Moojan Momen, ed., *The Bábí and Bahá'í Religions, 1844–1944: Some Contemporary Western Accounts* (Oxford, 1981), 77–82.

15 Shoghi Effendi, *God Passes By*, xii.

16 *Nabíl*, 30.

17 The two works are *Risálat al-sulúk* and *Tafsír súrat al-baqara*. They are, as it happens, possibly the two earliest of the Báb's works remaining to us.

ment on the history and teachings of the Shaykhí school be offered here so that a better understanding may be gained of the context in which the Báb wrote his Qur'án commentaries.

The founder of the Shaykhíya, or the *Kashfíya* as its adherents preferred to be designated, was Shaykh Aḥmad ibn Zayn al-Dín ibn Ibráhím ibn Ṣaqr ibn Ibráhím ibn Dághir al-Aḥsá'í. He was born in 1753 in an oasis region in Baḥrayn (namely al-Aḥsá') apparently of pure Arab lineage, where his family had been followers of the Shí'í version of orthodoxy for five generations. From his early childhood, it was clear that Shaykh Aḥmad was strongly predisposed to the study of religious texts and traditions. By the age of five he could read the Qur'án, and during the remainder of his primary education he studied Arabic grammar and became exposed to the mystical and philosophical expressions of Ibn 'Arabí (d. 638/1240) and the less well-known Ibn Abí Jumhúr (d. after 906/1501), author of the *Kitáb al-mujlí*. In 1772, Shaykh Aḥmad left his home to pursue advanced religious studies in the area of the 'Atabát in Iraq. He received his first *ijáza* ("permission to teach") from the renowned scholar Sayyid Muḥammad Mahdí *Baḥr al-'Ulúm* (d. 1797), and eventually six others from various recognized teachers.[18]

Shaykh Aḥmad returned to Baḥrayn for a few years, where he married and pursued his scholarship. Then, as a result of the Wahhábí attack on his native al-Aḥsá, he fled to Baṣra in 1797 and remained in the religious centers there and other localities of Iraq and Iran until shortly before the end of his life. He died on pilgrimage to Mecca in 1826 and was buried in the sacred Baqí' cemetery of Medina. The work of Shaykh Aḥmad was continued by his favorite student, the aforementioned teacher of the Báb, Sayyid Káẓim Rashtí (1798–1843/4). After the death of Sayyid Káẓim, his students divided into several groups, one centered around the personality of Muḥammad Karím Khán Kirmání, another around Sayyid 'Alí Muḥammad, the Báb.

18 The literature on the Shaykhí movement has grown in recent years. Works consulted for this article are: Vahid Rafati, "The Development of Shaykhí Thought in Shí'í Islam," unpublished Ph.D. thesis (UCLA, 1979); Said Amir Arjomand, *The Shadow of God and the Hidden Imam: Religion, Political Order, and Societal Change in Shi'ite Iran from the Beginning to 1890* (Chicago, 1984), see index, "Shaykhism"; Mangol Bayat, *Mysticism and Dissent: Socioreligious Thought in Qajar Iran* (Syracuse, 1982), 37–58; Henry Corbin, *En Islam iranien* (Paris, 1971–72), iv. 205–300. An important recent summary of Shaykh Aḥmad's life and work is Idris Samawi Hamid, "Shaykh Aḥmad al-Aḥsā'ī," in *Philosophy in Qajar Iran*, edited by Reza Pourjavady, Leiden & Boston: Brill, 2019, 66–124.

SHAYKHÍ TEACHINGS

The distinguishing features of this school, as is the case with most Muslim religious sects, are related to the manner in which spiritual authority was to be defined. At this time, the Shí'í world was experiencing an active controversy carried on by the followers of two groups called the *Uṣúlíya* and the *Akhbáríya*. These terms refer to the way each group tended to support its statements on Islamic law and theology. The debate was based on the question of whether *ijtihád* "exerting independent individual effort to form an opinion," rather than wholesale acceptance of the guidance contained in the preserved statements (*akhbár*) of Muḥammad and the Imáms, was the best way to resolve the questions of religion, which would of course include questions of law. Finally, the *Uṣúlíya*, those in favor of *ijtihád*, won the day and for the last 250 years this basic attitude and method has held sway in most of the Shí'í world.

Shaykh Aḥmad grew up in one of the last bastions of the *Akhbárí* approach, and his synthesis may be seen as a radicalization of this method. By means of propounding a doctrine of the Perfect Shí'a/Shí'í (*al-shí'at al-kummal/al-shí'í al-kámil*), an obvious adaption of the Ṣufí idea of the Perfect Man (*al-insán al-kámil*), Shaykh Aḥmad was able, at least in theory, to circumvent the restrictions imposed by either of the two aforementioned methods and arrive at a much less fettered and independent position vis-à-vis the reinterpretation of the raw material of the Islamic religion – the Qur'án, the *sunna*, and the teachings of the Imáms which were preserved in the *akhbár*. In short, this doctrine held that the Perfect Shí'a was always present on earth as a direct link to the Hidden Imám, Muḥammad ibn al-Ḥasan, the twelfth Imám of the Shí'a who disappeared from public ken at the age of six after succeeding his late father as Imám, and whose occultation had now lasted nearly 1,000 years. While neither Shaykh Aḥmad nor Sayyid Káẓim ever publicly claimed the rank of Perfect Shí'í, it seems fairly certain that their followers considered them as such.

Shí'ism has traditionally based itself on five main principles: divine unity (*tawḥíd*), prophethood (*nubúwa*), return (*ma'ád*), the imámate (*imáma*), and divine justice (*'adl*). Shaykh Aḥmad reduced these to three by combining "justice" with "unity" and placing the "return" in the category of "prophethood." To these three, Unity, Prophethood, and the Imámate, was added the idea of the Perfect Shí'a, sometimes referred to by the Shaykhíya as the Fourth Support (*al-rukn al-rábiʿ*) of religion, an allusion, in parallel, to the four pillars of God's throne (*ʿarsh, kursí*).[19] Other distinguishing characteristics of the beliefs held by the Shaykhís pertained to eschatology, in which a corporeal resurrection was denied in favor of a somewhat complex recourse to a separate reality in which resurrection of one's spiritual or subtle (*laṭíf*) body underwent a process designated by the familiar terminology *maʿád, qiyáma*, and so forth. Surely the emphasis here is on the denial of the scientifically untenable bodily resurrection which so many Muslim thinkers prior to Shaykh Aḥmad also found impossible to believe.[20] Shaykh Aḥmad's contribution here is in the form of a sufficiently detailed and appealing possible alternative – even the most hard-bitten sceptic could never completely deny the totally spiritual process which Shaykh Aḥmad propounded. These three features, the doctrine of the Perfect Shíʿa, the extreme veneration of the Holy Family, and the denial of bodily resurrection are perhaps the most important with regard to the relationship of Bábism to Shaykhism.

The doctrine of the Perfect Shíʿa was inseparable from the Shaykhí apophatic theology which implied a virtual deification[21] of this Holy Family, the Fourteen Pure Ones (*chahárdah maʿṣúm*) of orthodoxy: Muḥammad, Fáṭima, ʿAlí, al-Ḥasan, al-Ḥusayn, and the remaining Imáms of Twelver Shíʿism. God here is eternally unknowable (rather than remote), and makes His will known through various stages. Eternally crucial to this process is the twofold institution of prophethood/imamate, so that whenever any positive

---

19 Concern with the doctrine of the Fourth Support is, therefore, one of the most convincing evidences that the Báb was writing his first *tafsír* in a Shakyhí milieu. Early in his commentary on *súrat al-baqara* he says that the Fourth Support is, in fact, the main body of the Shíʿa. That the Báb understood the Fourth Support in this way is also evidence that at this time he did not harbor any claims to the special spiritual authority implied by other uses of this term, or he did not want to be perceived as doing so. Cf. the way in which the Shaykhís were eventually to discuss the idea of the Fourth Support (viz., as *ecclesia spiritualis*) in Corbin, *En Islam iranien*, iv. 274–86, esp. 285. Also, see D. MacEoin, "Early Shaykhí Reactions to the Báb and his Claims," in M. Momen, ed., *Studies in Bábí and Baha'i History*, I (Los Angeles, 1982), 1–42.

20 See Oliver Leaman, *An Introduction to Medieval Islamic Philosophy* (Cambridge, 1985), 17.

21 This statement must be tempered by reference to the innumerable assertions of the servitude of Muḥammad and the Imáms to the essence of God. It would be misleading in the extreme to suggest incarnationism. See a characteristic statement on this question by the Báb himself in his *Risálah-yi iʿtiqádát* in *Majmúʿah-yi áthár-yi ḥaḍrat-i Aʿlá*, Iran National Bahá'í Archives (hereafter INBA) lxix (1976), 411–16.

statement about divinity is made, its proper and immediate reference is to this institution and the bearers of its authority. The Prophet and Imáms are a different order of creation as mediators between the otherwise unknowable God and humanity. The Perfect Shí'a acts as mediator between the Imáms, represented by the twelfth, the now hidden Muḥammad ibn al-Ḥasan, and general humanity. Therefore when the Báb claimed to have received the *Tafsír súrat Yúsuf* from the Hidden Imám (see p. 263), even though he did not explicitly claim for himself the title of Perfect Shí'í, those Shaykhís who were his first readers were already convinced of the necessity for such a link as a *báb* ("gate"), even if they were not agreed as to who was best qualified to act as such, or, less important, what the exact name for such a link should be.

Before leaving the subject, it is important to point out that up until the period of time in which the Báb wrote, the Shaykhíya were probably not yet seen as a separate sect of Twelver Shí'ism. According to Rafati:

> Although the terms "Shaykhí," "'Posht-i Sarí," and "Kashfíya" refer to a certain group of people, and were intended to distinguish them from the rest of the Shí'a, the group solidarity and identity of the Shaykhís was in fact not so distinct as to sharply separate them from the rest of the Shí'í community of Iran as an independent sect or even branch of Twelver Shí'a. The Shaykhís considered themselves true Shí'a who thought and behaved in accordance with the teaching of the Shí'í *imáms*; they did not consider themselves innovators.
>
> It is difficult to believe that during Shaykh Aḥmad's lifetime he was considered the founder of a new school of thought within the Shí'í framework. However, as time went on and the nature of his ideology received greater intellectual attention, a group of fundamentalist *'ulamá'* perceived a radical distinction between his views and the established doctrines of the Shí'a and increasingly differentiated themselves from the Shaykhís. The Shaykhí school, then, gained more group solidarity as it developed historically, reacting as a group against the main body of the Shí'a when it encountered social and intellectual opposition.[22]

22 Rafati, 48–49. For a helpful summary of the points which came to be regarded as representing the most important differences between the Shaykhís and the Shí'a, see Moojan Momen, *An Introduction to Shí'í Islám: The History and Doctrines of Twelver Shí'ism* (Oxford and New Haven, 1985), 226–28. On the importance of the doctrine of the Perfect Shí'í, see Browne, "Báb, Bábís," in *ERE*, ii. 300a–b. See now, Amir-Moezzi "An Absence" (in Bib.).

TAFSÍR WORKS

Among the Báb's writings there are numerous works of *tafsír*.[23] Some of these are commentaries on such important traditions (*akhbár*) as the *Ḥadíth al-járíya* or the *Ḥadíth Kumayl*. Most of the others are commentaries on either a complete *súra* of the Qur'án or one of its more notable verses, such as the Light Verse (Q. 24:35) or the Throne Verse (Q. 2:255). These commentaries present a broad range of ideas and exegetical techniques – to such a degree that any attempt to discuss all of them here would ultimately be meaningless. This is so in spite of the fact that they all seem to come from the same general period, usually referred to as early Bábism.[24] Despite the astonishingly varied nature of the style and content of these commentaries, or more accurately because of it, they are of course extremely valuable for a study of the development of the Báb's teaching. Collectively they represent a unique corpus of Islamic scriptural commentary.

Of the numerous titles in this genre, however, four stand out as major works. In chronological order they are the commentaries on *al-baqara* (*súras* 1 and 2), *Yúsuf* (*súra* 12), *al-kawthar* (*súra* 108), and *wa'l-'aṣr* (*súra* 103). In the following discussion attention will be focused exclusively on the first two of these commentaries.[25]

Tafsír súrat al-baqara

The Báb was just under twenty-five when he completed the first volume of this work in Muḥarram 1259.[26] The work was therefore completed a

23 See n. 3.

24 Browne, "Báb, Bábís," *ERE*, ii. 305a.

25 The other two works deserve some brief mention at this time, inasmuch as they both exhibit one of the more distinctive exegetical procedures of the Báb, and one which is not applied by him to the two *súras* under detailed discussion here. Both *súras* 108 and 103, which are among the shortest chapters in the Qur'án, are explained by the Báb not verse by verse, or even word by word, but rather letter by letter. In this way, the Quranic material is "exploded" by the commentator in an attempt to mine it for as much meaning as possible. For a study of this method, which is not new with the Báb, see Todd Lawson, "The Dangers of Reading: Inlibration, Communion and Transference in the Qur'án Commentary of the Báb," in M. Momen, ed., *Scripture and Revelation: Papers presented at the First Irfan Colloquium Newcastle-upon-Tyne, England, December 1993 and the Second Irfan Colloquium Wilmette, USA, March 1994* (Oxford, 1997), 171–215.

26 Numerous manuscripts of this work, which represents a commentary on the complete first *juz'* of the Qur'án, exist. Five copies have been consulted for this discussion: Cambridge, Browne F. 8; INBA 6014 C; the privately published limited transcription,

month or so before he made his momentous claim to Mullá Ḥusayn, the young Shaykhí "seminarian," on the evening of 22 May 1844 (4–5 Jumádá al-Awwal, 1260). In corroboration of this dating, Mullá Ḥusayn is reported to have noticed this *tafsír* resting on a shelf in the Báb's house during the course of that very evening.[27] This earliest sustained religious work by the Báb includes a brief commentary on the *Súrat al-fátiḥa* (Q. 1), which is prefaced, in some manuscripts, by an introduction noteworthy for the reference it makes to the date on which the composition was begun. Here the Báb says that the night before he began the work, he had a dream in which the entire city of Karbalá' (*[al-]arḍ al-muqaddasa*) rose bit by bit into the air and came to rest before his house in Shíráz, whereupon he was informed of the approaching death of Sayyid Káẓim Rashtí, the Shaykhí leader to whom he refers here as his revered teacher (*al-'álim al-khalíl mu'allimí*).[28]

The way in which the *Súrat al-fátiḥa* is treated is in some ways characteristic of the rest of the commentary. For the Báb, meaning may be derived from the book chiefly by way of relating its contents to the Holy Family (Muḥammad, Fáṭima, and the twelve Imáms). To this end, each of the seven verses of the opening *súra* is designated as an "authoritative scripture" (*kitáb*) of one of these sacred figures. Beginning with Muḥammad, these include (in this order) 'Alí, Fáṭima, al-Ḥasan, al-Ḥusayn, Ja'far (al-Ṣádiq), and finally Músá ibn Ja'far. As will be seen, the number seven plays an

---

in xerox, found in *Majmú'ah-yi áthár-yi ḥaḍrat-i A'lá*, Iran National Bahá'í Archives (INBA), lxix (1976), 157–410; two uncatalogued MSS. in the Princeton University "Bábí Collection". Many thanks to Mr. James Weinberger, former curator of the Near Eastern Collection, Princeton University, for access to these last two items. All references in this chapter are to INBA, which has been paginated in the xerox copy.

A word should also be said about the notorious vol. ii of the Báb's *Tafsír súrat al-baqara*. According to Nicolas (n. 12), this was among those works by the Báb which were stolen from him during his pilgrimage (see 45–46). However, MacEoin, "Critical," 36, lists a MS. of the Bibliothèque Nationale which he says may be this missing volume. An examination of BN Or. 5805 indeed discloses that it is a commentary on the 2nd *juz'* of the Qur'án. At this time, however, it is not possible to ascribe its authorship to the Báb with complete confidence. The MS. in the British Library (BL Or. 7845) is a similar case. Finally, a few pages of a commentary on the second *juz'* are found in *Majmú'ah* (mentioned in n. 21), 377–410. There seems to be some important stylistic differences between this material and the preceding *tafsír*, one example being a much more frequent use of the first person.

27 See the *Táríkh-i jadíd* as quoted by E. G. Browne, "Catalogue and Description of 27 Bábí Manuscripts," *JRAS*, 24 (1892), 496.

28 INBA 6.

important part throughout this work.[29] In this instance, the seven names represent the different names by which each of the fourteen Pure Ones are known. That is, each of the names Muḥammad, ʻAlí, al-Ḥasan, and al-Ḥusayn may be applied to more than one figure of this group. The names Fáṭima, Jaʻfar, and Músá, however, may be used in reference to a single figure. The name Muḥammad is applicable not only to the prophet himself but also to Muḥammad al-Báqir, the fifth Imám (d. 113/731–32), Muḥammad al-Jawád, the ninth Imám (d. 220/835), and Muḥammad ibn al-Ḥasan al-ʻAskarí, the twelfth Imám, also known as al-Mahdí (disappeared 260/873–74). The name ʻAlí may properly designate not only the first Imám (d. 40/661), but also his grandson the fourth Imám, ʻAlí ibn al-Ḥusayn (d. 94/712–13), the eighth Imám, ʻAlí al-Riḍá (d. 202/817–18), and ʻAlí al-Hádí, tenth Imám (d. 254/868). The name al-Ḥasan may be applied to both the second Imám (d. 50/670) and the eleventh (d. 260/873–74). The result is that although there are fourteen different personalities involved, it may be said that there are in reality only seven different names. That the Báb has chosen to associate each verse with one of these seven names has, as will be seen, implications for the way in which he understood one of the more common names for this *súra*, namely, *al-sabʻ al-matháni* (cf. Q. 15:187), the meaning of which is in any case disputed by the classical exegetes.[30] Later in the commentary, the Báb states that one of the results

29 The question, often raised, of Ismáʻílí ("Sevener") influence on the Báb is probably best answered by emphasizing the importance of Shaykhí influence on his writings (see Rafati, 167). The better question to ask would be about the Ismáʻílí influence on the writings of Shaykh Aḥmad and the later elaboration of his thought, especially by Sayyid Káẓim Rashtí. Following Amanat, the Shaykhí movement may best be understood as a synthesis of "three major trends of thought in post-Safavid Shíʻism: the theosophic school of Isfahan (*ḥikmat-i iláhí*), which itself benefited from the theoretical Sufism of Ibn ʻArabí and the ʻOriental' theosophy (*ḥikmat-i ishráq*) of Suhravardí, and the *Akhbárí* 'traditonalist' school of Bahrain which traced its chain of transmitters to the early narrators of *ḥadíth* mostly by way of 'intuitive' perception and the Gnosticism which was diffused in the Shíʻí milieu and was strongly influenced by crypto-Ismáʻílí ideas as well as other heterodoxies of southern and southwestern Iran" (Amanat, 48). It would appear that Browne's advice and hope, written more than a hundred years ago, that "a full and critical study of the Shaykhí doctrines would...form an indispensable preliminary to such a philosophical history of the Bábís as must someday be written" (Browne, Báb, Bábís', *ERE*, ii. 300b), remains to be completely acted upon.

30 See p. 255. Also, see Maḥmoud Ayoub, "The Prayer of Islam: A Presentation of *súrat al-fátiḥa* in Muslim Exegesis," *Journal of the American Academy of Religion, Thematic Issue*, 47 (1979), 635–47, esp. 638.

of the process of creation is that seven becomes fourteen.[31] Thus this opening chapter, which is also known as the "Mother of the Book" (*umm al-kitáb*) because in it is contained the essence of the entire Qur'án, may be likened to the divine will which, in Shaykhí thought, is represented by the pleroma or "fullness" of the Holy Family who manifest this will through the process of the self-manifestation of divine glory, *tajallí*, and may be understood as containing, in potential, all creation.[32]

One of the main concerns of the *Tafsír súrat al-baqara* is in fact the propounding of this particular metaphysical principle. This, together with the method adopted for such – constant reference to the Holy Family as the principle of this process – is the most distinctive and distinguishing feature of the work and may be designated by the rather awkward term "imamization." It is unlikely that this represents, at the time and place it was written, a polemic in the context of an immediate Sunní–Shí'í debate.[33] Rather, it would seem that this method of interpretation is linked to at least two factors. The first is that it reflects the intense veneration in which the Imáms were held by the Shaykhís,[34] and, of course, the Shaykhí

31 INBA 112–13, *ad* Q. 2:29: "It is He who created for you all that is in the earth, then He lifted Himself to heaven and levelled them seven heavens; and He has knowledge of everything." The Báb's comment here is: "Seven, when it undergoes (*karrarat*) the processes of origination and creation, becomes Fourteen." Fourteen, in this context, functions as a symbol of totality.

32 For the idea of *tajallí*, much used by the Shaykhís, but which as a technical term in Muslim discussions of ontology and metaphysics has a much longer history, see Rafati, 69–101. For one of the major antecedents for Shaykhi usage, see Toshihiko Izutsu, *Sufism and Taoism: A Comparative Study of Key Philosophical Concepts* (Berkeley, 1984), 152–58.

33 Such "imamization" is reflected in the most important *tafsír* works of Akhbárí Shí'ism. See e.g., Muḥsin Fayḍ al-Káshání (d.1092/1680), *Tafsír al-ṣáfí*, 5 vols. (Beirut, 1979) and Sayyid Háshim al-Baḥrání (d. 1107/1695), *Tafsír al-burhán* (Tehran, 1334 Sh.). On these authors and Akhbárí hermeneutic see the pioneering work of Corbin, *En Islam iranien*, i. chs. 4 and 5 and more recently Todd Lawson, 'Akhbárí Shí'í Approaches to *Tafsír*', in Colin Turner, ed., *The Koran: Critical Concepts in Islamic Studies* iv (New York, 2004), 163–97.

34 This veneration is one of the main reasons the Shaykhíya ran foul of the more orthodox and rationalistic interpretations of Shí'ism, which did in fact denounce the group as extremist (*ghulát*) on several occasions. In his *Tafsír súrat al-baqara* it is clear that the Báb was sensitive to such charges. Very early on in the work he cites the following tradition from al-Báqir, the fifth Imám: "O concourse of the Shí'a... Be the true Shí'a and take a middle position (*al-numraqat al-wuṣṭá*) so that even the one who is excessive in their belief and practice (*al-ghálí* = 'extremist'), might return to you and the one who does not do enough (*al-tálí*) might catch up to you." See INBA 20.

influence on the author of this work. But perhaps more importantly, especially for understanding the eventual development of the Báb's teaching, it allows the Báb to assert his complete independence from all others, including Shaykh Aḥmad and Sayyid Káẓim (who are not mentioned in the main body of the *tafsír*),[35] apart from the Holy Family and, of course, the Qur'án itself.

A ready example of the Báb's allegorical method is found at Q. 2:26: "God is not ashamed to strike a similitude even of a gnat, or aught above it."[36] Here the "gnat" is explained as being 'Alí himself, while "whatever is above it," *má fawqahá*, is none other than Muḥammad. This interpretation is not new with the Báb; it is found in at least three other well-known Shí'í commentaries where it is ascribed to the sixth Imám, Ja'far al-Ṣádiq. Unlike his practice in similar instances in the commentary, the Báb cites no authority here. The adoption of this interpretation must therefore be seen as an example of the abundantly attested and universally approved process of selection from the overall tradition (rather than "creation") as a means of offering an original interpretation, which is so characteristic of Muslim religious scholarship.[37] That the Báb was creative in the modern sense as well will be seen in what follows when we turn to the *Tafsír súrat Yúsuf.*

A more extended allegory is found at Q. 2:49–51 in the Báb's reading of the story of Moses in the wilderness with his troublesome retinue:

> (49) And when We delivered you from the folk of Pharaoh who were visiting you with evil chastisement, slaughtering your sons, and sparing your women; and in that was a grievous trial from your Lord. (50) And when We divided for you the sea and delivered you, and drowned Pharaoh's folk while you were beholding. (51) and when We appointed with Moses forty nights then you took to yourselves the Calf after him and you were evildoers.

---

35 They are, however, referred to in the *Tafsír súrat Yúsuf,* as e.g., the "two gates" (*bábayn*). It is just this kind of terminological association, which, of course, represents a doctrinal or philosophical affinity, that was so instrumental in the Báb's winning to his cause a number of Shaykhís.

36 All translations of the Qur'án are from A. J. Arberry, *The Koran Interpreted* (Oxford, 1964). In some cases a translation has been slightly adapted.

37 Al-Baḥrání, *al-Burhán*, i. 70; 'Abd 'Alí al-Ḥuwayzí, *Tafsír núr al-thaqalayn* (Qom [1382–5/1962–5]) i. 37–38; al-Ṭabrisí, *Majma' al-bayán fí tafsír al-Qur'án* (Beirut, 1380/1961), i. 38.

The Báb says verse 49 is being addressed (*mukháṭabat*[an] *li-*) to Fáṭima, her husband and her father.[38] "Pharaoh" stands for 'Umar,[39] while "his folk" stands for "wherever *kufr*, *shirk* or *sharr* exist, because these are the various places where he appears (*maẓáhir nafsihi*)." In this place the specific reference is to Yazíd (d. 683), the Umayyad caliph responsible for the killing of Ḥusayn, the third Imám, in 680. Thus, the Quranic "slaughtering of your sons" is a direct reference to "the sons of the Messenger and their lord, Abú 'Abd Alláh al-Ḥusayn."

At this point, the Báb embarks upon a rather lengthy discussion to justify why God would allow such a heinous deed as the murder of one of the Holy Family to take place. During the course of this discussion, the Báb compares the killing of Ḥusayn with the sin of Adam. The main point seems to be that this apparent victory of evil over goodness, the murder of an Imám, was not due to any weakness in Ḥusayn. On the contrary, the Imám, because of the strength of his perfect (*mu'tadil:* harmonious) body, would have been able to destroy the whole world had such been the divine purpose.

At verse 50 the "sea" is the "sea of divine power." Those being addressed are the "People of Infallibility" (*ahl al-'iṣma*), another name for the Holy Family. "The meaning of the second 'Pharaoh'," says the Báb, "is the one who rejected the signs of 'Alí, upon him be peace, which exists in all things." "Moses," at verse 51, "according to its primary meaning (*fa'l-murád bi'l-ḥaqíqat al-awwalíya*) is 'Muḥammad'." "Forty" is understood as referring to 'Alí and the ten proofs (*ḥujaj*) from his progeny. The Báb explains as follows: 'Alí stands for thirty since he lived for thirty years after the death of Muḥammad. "Forty" is arrived at when reference is made to the ten remaining Imáms. That is, those who were allowed to fulfill their missions. The mission of the last or twelfth Imám is at this time still incomplete; therefore the number "ten" would pertain to the length of time spent in the wilderness precisely because the long-awaited arrival of the last Imám will signal the end of this spiritual banishment.[40] "Nights" alludes to the concealment of the glory of the Imáms by the darkness of disbelief (*kufr*).

---

38 Two of the MSS. add "and her grandfather/ancestor" (*jadd*), although this word is not quite so clear in INBA 179.

39 The actual name in the text is *Abú'l-shurúr*, "Father of iniquities," a traditional Shí'í way of referring to, according to the Shí'a, one of the arch-villains of history. See Goldziher, *Richtungen*, 288, 298.

40 Cf. Q. 7:142 where God extends the desert sojourn of Moses and the Children of Israel from 30 to 40 nights.

One of the Quranic evidences of this disbelief was the choosing of the "calf" which was actually Abú Bakr (*al-awwal*) as a legatee (*waṣí*). Therefore the "evildoers" are those who gave their allegiance (*bay'a*) to him.

This section is concluded with a reference to the *Qá'im*, whose return will cause all that has been alluded to in the foregoing to appear.[41] This is an example of the idea that each divine dispensation (*ẓuhúr*) sets in motion a replay of the major events of a primal sacred history. Later, in some of his other writings, the Báb refers to his very first followers, the eighteen "Letters of the Living," as the reappearance of the Holy Family, the Fourteen Pure Ones, and the four *abwáb* ("gates"); those leaders of the early Shí'í community who are believed to have been in touch with the Hidden Imám, Muḥammad ibn al-Ḥasan, during the so-called Lesser Occultation (873–939).[42]

In the course of this interpretation, the Báb alludes to the metaphysics from which it ultimately springs. Repeated reference is made, for example, to the process of divine self-manifestation – *tajallí-*. Once again, the commentary on *Súrat al-fátiḥa* provides a characteristic example. The third verse of the opening *súra* is characterized by the Báb as the "Book (*kitáb*) of Fáṭima." He continues by saying that:

> God has put in it all that is hers and all that pertains to her. This verse is the Garden of Grace. God has provided its shade for whoever believes in her and loves her after he has properly recognized her – according to what she manifested to that recognizer (*li'l-'árif*) by means of his own capacity for understanding. At that time this garden will open to him.[43]

The operative phrase here is: *kamá tajallat li'l-'árif lahu bihi.*[44] An interesting parallel to this usage is found in the *Fuṣúṣ al-ḥikam* of the great mystic Ibn 'Arabí. Here the author discusses *tajallí*, or the way in which God makes himself known to humanity, with these words: *fa-waṣafa nafsahu laná biná*, "He has described Himself to us by means of us," or, less concisely: "He has described Himself to us by means of our own ability and willingness to

41 INBA 179–84.

42 *Messiah*, 337.

43 INBA 7–8. The Quranic verse thus explained is *al-raḥmán al-raḥím*, "the Merciful, the Compassionate."

44 My thanks to Dr. Muhammad Afnan for suggesting the above translation (personal communication, summer 1984).

perceive His description."[45] It is not intended to go into great detail here on the relation of the Báb's thought to that of Ibn 'Arabí, nor is it intended to go into great detail about the Báb's thought per se. Attention is drawn to this subject only by way of indicating the kinds of ideas which find expression during the task the Báb has set for himself (and which is the subject of this discussion), namely, the interpretation of the Qur'án. Suffice it to say that both the Báb and Ibn 'Arabí appear to rely for the ultimate justification of such a view on Q. 41:53: "We shall show them Our signs in the horizons and in themselves, till it is clear to them that this is the truth." The frequency with which this formulation (*lahu bihi*) is encountered in the *Tafsír súrat al-baqara* throws into sharp relief the curious fact that there seems to be no mention of it at all, at least in these terms, in the *Tafsír súrat Yúsuf*.

The metaphysics is related also to ethical concerns in one interesting passage of the *Tafsír súrat al-baqara, ad* Q. 2:3: "[Those] who believe in the Unseen, and perform the prayer, and expend of that We have provided them." Here the Báb chooses to comment on the significance of "faith"' (*imán*) represented in the above translation by the word "believe." In his introductory remarks to this lengthy section he says the following:

> If man knew how God created His creation, no one would ever blame another. This means that God has created mankind (*khalq*) according to the creatures' already existing propensities for acceptance or rejection [of the truth]. The cause of rejection is the same as the cause of acceptance, namely choice (*ikhtiyár*). God has given to each what he deserves according to his already existing propensity (*bi-má huwa 'alayhi*). This divine knowledge is the knowledge of potentialities.[46]

The object of the discussion is an extended treatment of the problems surrounding the perennial puzzle posed by the idea of an individual's free will and God's role in determining a person's fate. Once again, statements of the Báb appear to have much in common with the views of Ibn 'Arabí, in particular his notoriously difficult idea of *al-'ayán al-thábita*.[47] It is probable that the similarity here with Ibn 'Arabí is due more to traces of

45 Ibn al-'Arabí, *Fuṣúṣ al-ḥikam*, ed. 'Affífí (Cairo, 1946), i. 53.
46 INBA 22: *wa law 'alima al-nás kayf khalaqa Alláh al-khalq lam yalum aḥad^{un} aḥad^{an}*.
47 See, e.g., Izutsu, 159, where the author defines *al-'ayán al-thábita* as the "eidetic realities" of possible things. A possible thing becomes actualized in the phenomenal world, each according to the requirements of its own personal archetype.

Ibn 'Arabí's thought existing in the teaching of the Shaykhís (which, as has been said, is acknowledged to be the single most important influence on the way the Báb expressed his ideas) than to any direct borrowing by the Báb from Ibn 'Arabí directly. Indeed, in one of his later *tafásír*, the Báb makes it clear that he does not agree with Ibn 'Arabí at all on at least one point.[48]

Continuing with the Báb's commentary on this same verse, we are soon in the presence of another major pattern in the work. The importance of the number seven has already been mentioned and briefly illustrated; a few more brief examples are added here for further elaboration.

In his discussion of *imán*, the Báb speaks of seven different levels or grades (*marátib*). The first is applied to the people of the garden, or paradise, of the Divine Will (*ahl jannat al-mashíya*). The remaining six grades are respectively applicable to the people of the heaven of Divine Purpose (*al-iráda*), the sea of the Divine Decree (*baḥr al-qadr*), Eden (*'adn*), Divine Permission (*al-idhn*), Eternity (*khuld*), and finally Refuge, or Repose (*ma'wá*). Other examples of this seven-fold structure of spirituality may be found in the *tafsír* at Q. 2:1, where eight gardens, or paradises, and seven hells are described. Here, each hell is but the shadow of the heaven above it. The reason that there are only seven is because the highest heaven casts no shadow. In fact, it is completely isolated from the rest of the structure. The highest heaven represents the Absolute of the apophatic theological model.[49] At Q. 2:2 we are introduced to seven classes of people;[50] at Q. 2:5 we read of seven different grades of lordship (*rubúbíya*).[51] A final example is at Q. 2:22, where seven heavens and seven earths are enumerated.[52]

Another example of the Báb's exegesis may be taken, once again, from Q. 2:3, which is divided into two parts for the purposes of the commentary: "[Those] who believe in the Unseen, and perform the prayer." *Al-Ghayb* ("The Unseen") is interpreted the following way. The Báb says that it represents Muḥammad because he is truly known only by himself and only God knows his true nature (*kunh*). The specific place [of this hidden true nature]

48 *Tafsír súrat wa'l-'aṣr*, MS. Cambridge, Browne F. 9 (6), fol. 71ʳ. On the idea of the pre-existing capacity of believers, see now the important study by F. Kazemi, "Mysteries of Alast" in *BSR* 15(2009): 39–66.

49 In the Báb's words: *lá ḍidd lahá [al-jannat al-úlá] wa lá ẓill, bal fi'l-ḥaqíqa khalwa min al-jinán wa'l-jinán khalwa minhá; wa hiya jannat al-tawḥíd.* INBA 9.

50 INBA 14.

51 INBA 38–40.

52 INBA 81–82.

(*wa maḥall tafṣíl hádhá'l-ghayb*)[53] is none other than the currently concealed (*fí'l-ghayba*) *Qá'im*, Muḥammad ibn al-Ḥasan. The Báb then quotes a tradition from the sixth Imám, Ja'far al-Ṣádiq, wherein several stages of the Quranic *al-ghayb* are enumerated.[54] It has already been explained how for the Báb, who at the time of writing this particular commentary was making use of the terminology and thought of the Shaykhís,[55] the number seven represents the totality of the Holy Family. While it may be of some interest to try and determine other influences apart from the Shaykhí school, to insist on such would be to miss this most important point. One of the more pertinent lessons to be learned here, it would seem, is how the number seven can have importance for both the *Ithná 'Asharíya* (Twelvers) and the so-called *Sab'iya* (Seveners), or the Ismá'ílíya.[56]

To conclude this somewhat random sampling from the earliest of the Báb's Qur'án commentaries, which is also his first major written work, attention will be paid to his reading of the word *ṣalát* (prayer, divine service) in this same verse Q. 2:3. First, its performance symbolizes obedience to Muḥammad, his legatees and his progeny, which in turn represents, in the aggregate, absolute *waláya*. From the beginning to the end of its performance, *ṣalát* is the "form of divine aloneness" (*ṣúrat al-tafríd*), the temple of divine unity (*haykal al-tawḥíd*), and the "outward representation of love or allegiance" (*shabaḥ al-waláya*). However, none but Muḥammad and his Family performs it properly, because *ṣalát* is the foremost station of distinction between the lover and the Beloved (God). The Holy Family is the collective bearer of this love and as such is the object of the famous *ḥadíth qudsí*, "I was a hidden treasure and desired to be known, therefore I created mankind [*khalq* here refers specifically to the Holy Family, according to the Báb's interpretation] in order to be known." Thus it is through the Imám that "lordship" (*rubúbíya*) appeared and "servitude" (*marbúbíya*) was perfected. The perfect performance of *ṣalát* by the Imáms is therefore

53 INBA 23 has *tafḍíl*, an obvious scribal error.

54 INBA 23–24.

55 See, e.g., the description of Shaykh Aḥmad's ontology and his "absolute distinction between Possible Being and Necessary Being," which is illustrated by a seven-stage hierarchy, in Rafati, 103–4.

56 See, e.g., one of the four Twelver Shí'í canonical books of *ḥadíth*, al-Kulayni (d. 328–939 or 329/940), *al-Uṣúl min al-káfí* (Tehran, n.d.) i. 249, no. 27 where one of its chapters is headed: The chapter of "There is nothing in heaven or earth but that it is [made or exists] according to the number seven"/ *báb fí annahu lá yakún shay' fí'l-samá' wa'l-arḍ illá bi-'l-sab'a.*

an ability or quality directly from God (*waṣf Alláh*) which they have been endowed with by means of their own innate capacities (*lahum bihim*). While in the case of others who perform *ṣalát*, this ability comes from the Imáms. This is a perfect example of the Shaykhí teachings referred to earlier.[57]

The Báb then states that the Imáms are in fact the seven *mathání*. This becomes clear when the worshipper recites the *Fátiḥa*, in each verse of which God has described one of the Holy Family by means of the tongue of the servant who, in the course of two prostrations, will have uttered the seven verses of the *Fátiḥa* twice, which is, of course, an affirmation of the sanctity of the Fourteen Pure Ones. If the prayer is performed in this spirit, then the worshipper has succeeded in performing it as properly as he can. The prayer has then become a meeting with the Beloved and the Face of the Worshipped One; a true means of spiritual elevation, *mi'ráj*, for the believer.[58]

Having briefly examined this very early work of the Báb, which, it must be remembered, was written before his declaration in which he claimed special spiritual authority (and is therefore concerned more with Shí'í tradition than with any new system), we will now turn to a *tafsír* of a very different order.

Tafsír súrat Yúsuf

Within no more than a few months of writing the commentary discussed above, the Báb began his commentary on the Quranic story of Joseph (Q. 12). This *tafsír* is utterly different in all of its aspects from the *Tafsír súrat al-baqara*. Unlike the previous commentary, this work contains no direct references to doctrinal discussions on such important Shaykhí topics as the Fourth Support, and no architectonic metaphysical representations.[59] Although allegory and typological exegesis are still among the chief methods

---

57 See pp. 242–4 in this chapter.

58 INBA 26. The use of the word *mi'ráj* here brings an association with another distinctive aspect of Shaykhí theology. While the mainstream of both "orthodoxies," Sunní and Shí'í, interpret the account of Muḥammad's ascent, Mi'raj, through the seven heavens as an actual journey, the Shaykhí school taught that the story should be taken rather more figuratively. Therefore the journey was indeed accomplished, but in the spiritual realm of *húrqalyá* and not in the world of mundane experience. See Rafati, 115. On the Shaykhí understanding of worship, see Corbin, *En Islam iranien*, i. 194.

59 There are, on occasion lists of "spiritual types" such as are found in the *Tafsír súrat al-baqara*. See, e.g., Haifa MS., *Tafsír súrat Yúsuf*, 226, where nine types are detailed. Oblique reference to the "Fourth Support" may also be found, e.g., ibid., 107.

of the actual interpretation, they are of a somewhat different character. Indeed, direct interpretation of the verse represents only a comparatively small portion of the material. In one way, the work is much more structured, taking as its model the Qur'án in its use of *súra* divisions, and in another way much less logical, in that it is often difficult to see just how the text is tied to the Quranic material itself. It is also a very long work and one in which a variety of concerns, images, terminology, laws, exhortations, and prayers are presented, frequently with only the vaguest indication of such genre shifts. Interestingly, there seems to be no verbatim citation of *ḥadíth*. What is offered in the next few pages is merely a very brief description of the work. The intention is to give some idea of the kinds of problems which the *tafsír* presents to the student of the history of Qur'án commentary, to point out the dramatic difference between the two works which are the subject of this chapter, and to offer some very general conclusions.

The *Tafsír súrat Yúsuf*, also known as the *Qayyúm al-asmá*[60] and the *Aḥsan al-qaṣaṣ*, which is of course the name which the Qur'án gives to the Sura of Joseph (Q. 12:3), was described in some detail by Rosen in 1877, and discussed by Browne in 1889 and again in 1892.[61] Since then it has received a certain amount of attention from scholars concerned chiefly with the social history of the Bábí movement.[62] Several manuscripts of the work exist, two of which have been consulted for the purposes of this study.[63] The older of the two, and therefore perhaps the most reliable, was transcribed in 1261/1845 and differs from the later manuscript in many details. The work itself is quite long, the manuscript of 1261 running to 234 pages, with each 9.5 x 17.5 cm.[64] page bearing 25 lines of closely written text. This manuscript is housed in Haifa at the Bahá'í World Centre Archives and Library.

60 "Colui che s'erge sugli Attributi," as translated by Alessandro Bausani, *Persia Religiosa, da Zarathustra a Bahá'ú'lláh* (Milan, 1959), 460. I translate this as "He who is beyond the divine attributes."

61 In the study cited in n. 5. For the 1889 discussion see Browne, *JRAS*, 21 (1889), 904–6.

62 Moojan Momen, "The Trial of Mullá 'Alí Bastami: A Combined Sunni-Shí'í Fatwa against the Báb," *Iran* 20 (1982), 113–43. This important article contains the translation of several excerpts from the *Tafsír*. See also Amanat, *Resurrection*, 201–7 and *Messiah*, q.v. index, *Qayyúm al-asmá'*. See now the numerous translations and commentaries on this *tafsír* at Stephen N. Lambden's invaluable website, https://hurqalya.ucmerced.edu/.

63 For a fairly complete list of MSS. see MacEoin, *Survey*, 195–96. The two used by me here are xerox copies of the Cambridge, Browne F. 11 (9), dated 1891, and the Haifa MS., date 1261, which according to MacEoin, *Survey*, 14, was discovered relatively recently. All further references are to pages of a xerox of the Haifa MS, hereafter cited as *QA*.

64 Dimensions of the area covered by the text, not the actual size of the page.

The text is modelled after the Qur'án, with use of disconnected introductory letters, *súra* divisions, and verse divisions. In fact, the older Haifa manuscript, in imitation of the *sajda al-tiláwa* tradition for the Qur'án, carries the instruction *sajda wájiba* "prostration necessary" at various places on the margin of the text where the word *sajada* or some derivative occurs, to indicate that a prostration should be performed while reading the particular verse. In addition, the Haifa manuscript supplies at the head of 111 *súra*s (each chapter of the commentary is called a *súra* by the Báb) the number of verses, which in this manuscript is invariably forty-two and the Cambridge manuscript, where the verses number forty, indicates the place of revelation for each *súra*, which is invariably Shíráz.[65] The number of verses (42) is thought to represent the *abjad* value of the word *balá*, which according to the Qur'án, was the word used to convey humanity's assent to the primordial divine covenant (Q. 7:172).[66]

Immediately following this comparatively technical information comes the standard Islamic *basmala*: "In the name of God, the Merciful, the Compassionate." This occurs, without exception, at the beginning of each chapter and is followed by the verse from the Qur'án which is to be the subject of the commentary in a particular *súra*. However, the first *súra* of the *Tafsír* does not contain such a citation, and is anyway of a slightly different order from the rest, being something of an introduction.

Continuing this imitation of the form of the Qur'án, the Báb has placed between the *áya* to be commented upon and the main text of each *súra* (except four),[67] a series of disconnected letters, in imitation of the *ḥurúf muqaṭṭaʿát* in the Qur'án, some of which are indeed Quranic. Thus chapter 3, *Súrat al-Imán*, bears the two disconnected letters *Ṭá' Há'*. While the vast majority of these sets of letters must remain at this stage somewhat mysterious, it is interesting to note that at the head of *súra*s 108 and 109, the

65 Thus a typical chapter heading in the Cambridge MS. would appear as follows: *Súrat al-imán, wa hiya Shíráziya wa hiya arbaʿún áya.*

66 Dr. Muḥammad Afnán, personal communication. Concerning the Cambridge MS., Browne notes in "Some Remarks," *JRAS*, 24 (1892), 262, that the *abjad* value of the Quranic *lí*, "to me" or "before me," is 40. The prepositional phrase is, of course, from the Qur'án (Q. 12:4) where Joseph relates his dream to his father: "Daddy, I saw eleven stars, and the sun and the moon: I saw them bowing down before me (*lí*)." In either case, the number of verses in each *súra* is taken to be symbolic of either acceptance, or the assertion, of spiritual authority.

67 *Súra*s 1, 2, 52, and 95 in *QA*. Incidentally, there are many blank spaces in the headings of the *súra*s of the Cambridge MS. It appears that the scribe intended to insert rubrications in these blanks which would carry such information as the number of verses and so on.

following combinations occur: *'Ayn-Lám-Yá'* and *Mím-Ḥá'-Mím-Dál,* giving the proper names 'Alí and Muḥammad. The titles of these two *súra*s are, respectively, *al-Dhikr* ("the Remembrance") and *al-'Abd* ("the Servant"), both of which represent titles which are assumed by the Báb in the course of his commentary. It is likely, therefore, that these two names pertain first of all to the Báb himself (Sayyid 'Alí Muḥammad) and indirectly to the first Imám and the Prophet Muḥammad. Needless to say, the ambiguity was likely not an accident.[68]

Following the disconnected letters there are usually one or perhaps two verses (terminations of which are marked in *QA* by the typical Quranic verse-marker, an independent *há' marbúṭa*, and in the Cambridge MS. by means of a space), which offer some variation on the frequent Quranic introductory formula: This is the Book! *dhálika al-kitáb...* (Q. 2:2) or [This is a] Book sent down to you! *kitáb^{un} unzila ilayka...* (Q. 7:2), which has been shown to be one of the common elements shared by those *súra*s which carry disconnected letters.[69] A few examples will serve as illustrations.

Súra 1, *al-Mulk* ("Dominion"), begins after the title material described above. As mentioned, this is the only chapter of the *Tafsír* not written under a verse from the *Súrat Yúsuf,* nor does it have introductory disconnected letters:

> (1) *al-ḥamdu li-lláh alladhí nazzala'l-kitáb 'alá 'abdihi b-'l-ḥaqq li-yakuna li-'l-'álamín siráj^{an} wahháj^{an}.*[70]

Súra 2, *al-'Ulamá* ("The Learned"):

> (1) *Alif Lám Mím, dhálika al-kitáb min 'indi Alláh al-ḥaqq fi shán al-dhikr qad kána bi'l-ḥaqq ḥawl al- nár manzúl^{an}*; (2) *wa inna naḥnu qad ja'alná'l-áyát fí dhálika'l-kitáb mubín^{an}* [sic].[71]

Súra 3, *al-Imán* ("Faith"):

68 *QA* 223 and 225 respectively. It is suggested that these disconnected letters actually function as the Báb's authorial signature for the work as whole. See Todd Lawson, *The Quran, Epic and Apocalypse* (London 2017), 165–67.

69 Alford Welch, "al-Ḳur'án," *EI*² v. 414a.

70 *QA* 3.

71 *QA* 5.

> (1) *Ṭá' Ḥá'*; (2) *Alláh qad anzala 'l-Qur'án 'alá 'abdihi li-ya'lama 'l-nás anna Alláh qad kána 'alá kulli shay' qadír^an^.*[72]

Súra 37, *al-Ta'bír* ("Interpretation"):

> (1) *Fá' 'Ayn Sín Nún;* (2) *al-ḥamdu li-lláh alladhí anzala 'alá 'abdihi al-kitáb li-yakúna 'alá 'l-'álamín bi'l-kalimat al-'alí shahíd^an^.*[73]

The slightly variant *Súra* 59, *al-Af'ida* ("the Perceptive Hearts"), as one example, has the following, which is, however, still concerned with the way God communicates to mankind:

> (1) *Káf Há' 'Ayn Ṣád*; (2) *Alláh qad akhbara'l-'ibád bi'l-ism al-akbar: an lá iláh illá huwa al-ḥayy al-qayyúm.*[74]

Finally, the example of *Súra* 111, *al-Mu'minín* ("the Believers") is offered by way of emphasizing the more or less standard pattern that obtains throughout the work:

> (1) *Alif Lám Mím*; (2) *inná naḥnu qad ja'alná baynakum wa bayna al-qurá' 'l-mubáraka min ba'd al-báb hádhá unás^un^ ṭáhirín yad'úna 'l-nás ilá dín Alláh al-akbar wa lá yakháfúna min dún Alláh al-ḥaqq 'an shay' ulá'ika hum qad kánú aṣḥáb al-riḍwán fí umm al-kitáb maktúb^an^*; (3) *wa inná naḥnu qad ja'alná hádhá 'l-kitáb áyát li-ulí al-albáb alladhína yusabbiḥúna al-layl wa 'l-nahár wa lá yafturúna* [cf. Q. 21:20] *min amr Alláh al-ḥaqq min laday al-báb 'alá dharra min ba'ḍ al-shay' qiṭmír^an^.*[75]

This then gives some idea of the Báb's conscious desire to make his *Tafsír* structurally resemble or imitate the Qur'án. It is not known whether one of the reasons *súra* 12 was chosen was because the number of its verses closely approximates the total number of Quranic suras,[76] although the

72 *QA* 6.
73 *QA* 67.
74 *QA* 116.
75 *QA* 231.
76 *Súra* 21, *al-Anbiyá* ("The Prophets") has 112 verses, while *Súras* 17, *al-Isrá'* ("The Night Journey") and 12 both have 111. No *súra* has 114 verses, the number which corresponds exactly to the total number of *súras* in the Qur'án.

effect of this coincidence was undoubtedly not lost upon the readers of the commentary. The Quranic story of Joseph is a favorite among Muslims because it contains within the confines of a single sustained narrative the major subjects of importance to Islam including its link with past religions.[77] The *Súrat Yúsuf* had also been the subject of earlier discrete commentaries and elaborations. Thus, the renowned Abú Ḥámid al-Ghazzálí (d. 505/1111) composed a somewhat mystical *tafsír* on this *súra*.[78]

The influential mystic Ibn al-ʻArabí also took up the Quranic Joseph in his *Fuṣús al-ḥikam* as a basis for his discussion of the spiritual imagination.[79] It would seem also that the choice of the *Súrat Yúsuf* as the subject of this commentary of the Báb's is connected with a long tradition which reveres the story of Joseph as representing the spiritual mystery of *taqíya*, pious concealment of the truth, which is so important in Shíʻí religiosity in general,[80] and Shaykhí religious thinking in particular. According to *Nabíl*, Mullá Ḥusayn, the young Shaykhí who was the first to accept the Báb's claim, had once asked the Shaykhí leader, Sayyid Káẓim Rashtí, to write a commentary of the *Súrat Yúsuf*. His teacher responded that such a task was beyond his abilities, but that "the great One, who comes after me will, unasked, reveal it for you. That commentary will constitute one of the weightiest testimonies of His truth, and one of the clearest evidences of the loftiness of his position."[81] Rashtí's response here would appear to be conditioned by numerous *ḥadíth/akhbár* which state that the *Qá'im* will resemble Joseph in several respects.[82] Throughout the Báb's commentary it seems clear that he is seeing himself as Joseph, in that the Quranic story is read as a prefigurement, however allegorical, of the Báb's own mission.

77 According to al-Thaʻlabí (d. 437/1036), *Qiṣaṣ al-anbiyá'*, the story of Joseph is the most beautiful (*aḥsan*) "because of the lesson concealed in it, on account of Yúsuf's generosity and its wealth of matter, in which prophets, angels, devils, jinn, men, animals, birds, rulers and subjects play a part." See B. Heller, "Yúsuf ibn Yaʻqúb," *EI²*, *ad loc*. See now, Firestone (in Bib.).

78 Abú Ḥámid al-Ghazzálí, *Tafsír súrat Yúsuf* (Tehran, 1895). This composition has virtually nothing in common with the Báb's, except, of course, the Quranic citations from the *Súrat Yúsuf*.

79 Ibn al-ʻArabí, *Fuṣús*, i. 99–106.

80 As when Jacob warns Joseph not to tell his dream to his brothers (Q. 12:5). The concealment (*ghayba*) of the Imám is considered a kind of *taqíya*. See R. Strothmann, "*Ṭaḳíya*," *EI¹*, *ad loc*.

81 *Nabíl*, 59.

82 Muḥammad ibn ʻAlí al-Qummí ibn Bábúya, *Ikmál al-dín wa itmám al-niʻma fí ithbát al-rajʻa* (Najaf, 1360/1970), 18.

After the disconnected letters and the above-mentioned introductory verses that claim divine revelation, the next section of a given *súra* begins. It is this section which is most difficult to characterize in general terms because of the variety of content and even method which may appear in it. Largely speaking, the last section of a *súra* is where the Báb turns his attention directly to the verse of the *Súrat Yúsuf* under which a particular *súra* of the *Tafsír* is composed. The method of exegesis, then, is usually a simple paraphrase of said verse in which the Báb makes various substitutions with words which give a meaning much more specific to his own situation and claims. In the course of his exegesis, there is never recourse to the usual markers of an interpretative statement which are frequent in the classical tradition and, as we saw, frequent in the Báb's earlier *Tafsír súrat al-baqara*. Thus, such words as *ay* or *ya'ní* (that is) or *al-murád* (the meaning or intention [of the Qur'án here is]), or even *aqúlu* (I say [about this verse the following]). Rather, the exegetical equivalences are offered by the Báb as much closer to the Quranic material than would be the case if the above words, along with the semantic distance to be traveled their use implies, were used.[83] Before giving examples of this kind of commentary, it may be of interest to discuss in some detail the first *súra* of the Báb's *Tafsír súrat Yúsuf*, the previously excerpted *Súrat al-Mulk*.

This *súra*, which is in fact the part of the work that was written in the presence of Mullá Ḥusayn on the night of 22 May 1844/4–5 Jumádá al-Awwal 1260, forms a kind of introduction to the whole, and is unusual in that it has neither disconnected letters nor does it cite a verse of the *Súrat Yúsuf* to be commented upon. Evidence that it is indeed part of a commentary on the Qur'án does not occur until well into the text, where the following statement is found as verse 10 of the *Súrat al-Mulk*.

> God has ordained that this book (*dhálika al-kitáb*) in explanation of the most beautiful story (*tafsír aḥsan al-qaṣaṣ*) be brought out [from

83 This method may be a reflex of the idea contained in the famous Shí'í *ḥadíth* which quotes the fifth Imám al-Báqir as: "It is we who are the meanings (*ma'ání*). We are the Hand of God, His vicinity, His tongue, His command, His decision, His knowledge, His truth. We are the Face of God which is turned toward the terrestrial world in your midst. He who recognizes us has certitude for an *imám*. He who rejects us has Hell as an *imám*." This is cited in Corbin, *En Islam iranien*, i. 194 (my translation of Corbin's French). The interesting statement "we are the meanings," among other things, takes for granted the absolute spiritual authority implied in the act of paraphrasing the Qur'án.

> its occultation] with Muḥammad bin al-Ḥasan bin 'Alí bin Muḥammad bin 'Alí bin Músá bin Ja'far bin Muḥammad bin 'Alí bin al-Ḥusayn bin 'Alí bin Abí Ṭálib to His servant [the Báb] that it/he might be a convincing Proof of God (*ḥujjat Alláh*) from the Remembrance unto all the worlds.[84]

The title of this *súra*, *al-Mulk* ("dominion, ownership, kingship, rule") is related to the fact that the entire chapter, rather than dealing with subjects directly connected to an understanding of the twelfth chapter of the Qur'án, is a sustained and impassioned challenge first to Muḥammad Sháh, the reigning monarch of Iran at the time, and then to his prime minister, Ḥájí Mírzá Aqásí, to submit to the command of the Remembrance (*dhikr*, that is the Báb). In the course of this *súra* we encounter several elements which are, however, characteristic of the whole book. The first of these is the proclamation of the Báb's spiritual rank, either as Gate (*báb*) or Remembrance (*dhikr*), to name only two of the several different designations which are used throughout the text in this way.[85] Then there are the fluent paraphrases of the Qur'án, the call to absolute obedience, the summons to the world beyond Iran, the invocation of laws (*aḥkám*), the language, and the imagery which is striking in the extreme. An example of this last is the Báb's juxtaposition of opposites. In the *Súrat al-Mulk*, one reads, for example: *inna al-nár fí nuqṭati'l-má' li-lláh al-ḥaqq sájid*[an] *'alá 'l-arḍ* ("the fire in the atom of water is itself prostrate before God the Truth upon the earth").[86] This may be a simple case of an echo of basic alchemical imagery, particularly in this instance. In later *súra*s, however, this combining of opposites takes on original characteristics which seem to somehow designate the source of the Báb's inspiration.[87]

84 *QA* 3; cf. the translation of this verse by Browne, *JRAS*, 21 (1889), 908.

85 Some others are Word (*kalima*), Ariser (*qá'im*) of the year one thousand, the blessed tree in Sinai, and the Resurrection (*qiyáma*). For a discussion of these and other emblems of spiritual authority, see M. Afnan and W. S. Hatcher, "Western Islamic Scholarship and Bahá'í Origins," *Religion*, 15 (1985), 29–51.

86 *QA* 3 verse 19. In this same *súra* the following statement occurs: *wa inna qad sayyarná 'l-jibál 'alá 'l-arḍ* (cf. Q. 18:47) *wa l-nujúm 'alá 'l-'arsh ḥawl al-nár fí quṭb al-má' min ladá' l-dhikr bi-lláh al-ḥaqq* ("We have set the mountains in motion upon the earth, and the stars upon the Throne around the fire in the atom of water in the presence of the Remembrance through God the Truth"). *QA* 4, verse 42.

87 Another more dramatic example of this "figure" is: "We have apportioned mountains on the earth, and placed the earth upon the water, and the musky air [we have caused to come forth] from under the hot coldness (*al-ḥarr al-bard*), *QA* 137. Numerous other examples could be cited. The coincidence of opposites is a frequent figure in this work. The Báb's use of it here is undoubtedly influenced by such important and obscure

To resume the general description of this *tafsír*, the third section of a given *súra* may consist of a running exegetical paraphrase of extended sections of the Qur'án. For example, chapters 52 and 53, *Súrat al-Faḍl* ("Excellence") and the *Súrat al-Ṣabr* ("Patience"),[88] present a detailed rewriting of the first fifty or so verses of the second *súra* of the Qur'án, *Súrat al-Baqara*. Here the exegesis is of a completely different order than that found in the earlier major work by the Báb studied earlier.

At Q. 2:2–5, we have:

> *Qur'án*
> That is the Book, wherein is no doubt, a guidance to the godfearing who believe in the Unseen, and perform the prayer, and expend of that We have provided them; who believe in what has been sent down to thee and what has been sent down before thee, and have faith in the Hereafter; those who are upon guidance from their Lord, those are the ones who prosper.

> *The Báb*
> By thy Lord! Thou [the Hidden Imám, and by implication the Báb himself] art the Book wherein there is no doubt, and thou art praiseworthy in the estimation of God. Those who believe in the Remembrance of God, in his Unseeness (*ghayba*), and rule among mankind with truth by means of his verses, we will, in very truth,[89] bestow upon them, as a blessing from Our side, a great reward. Those are upon a guidance with the Remembrance of God, and those are the ones who hastened first, in truth, in the Book of God.[90]

Another more extended example of this running paraphrase may be found in *súras* 80 to 95 inclusive,[91] which treats most of the Quranic material from

---

traditions as the *Khuṭbat al-taṭanjíya*. See, Todd Lawson, *Gnostic Apocalypse in Islam: Qur'an, Exegesis, Messianism, and the Literary Origins of the Babi Religion* (London and New York, 2012), 75–92.

88 *QA* 100–5.

89 "In very truth" translates a frequent "refrain" throughout this work, *'alá al-ḥaqq bi'l-ḥaqq* (or some variation of this). In the Qur'án, *al-Ḥaqq* is one of the many divine names and attributes. The translation here does not carry the all-important reference to divinity: God is *al-Ḥaqq*, "The Truth/Reality" par excellence.

90 *QA* 100.

91 *QA* 160–95.

Q. 10:57 up to the first few verses of Q. 17. A more or less random example is the Báb's rewriting of Q. 10:87.

> *Qur'án*
> And We revealed unto Moses and his brother, "Take you, for your people, in Egypt certain houses; make your houses a direction for men to pray to; and perform the prayer; and do thou give good tidings to the believers."
>
> *The Báb*
> And We revealed to Moses and his brother, "Take you [or, set aside] in the Egypt of the hearts, for the people of the earth, houses consecrated to the exclusive divine unity (*aḥadíya*) of the Most Great Remembrance of God, the Living. And He is God, the Knowing, the Judge." And verily God made them [houses] a direction for men to pray to, and to perform all the prayers in, so give good tidings to the sincere servants of God.[92]

As mentioned previously, the fourth section of a given *súra* usually returns to the verse of the Qur'án under which it is written. The method, again, is a paraphrase of which the last two of the following three examples are characteristic. The second chapter, *Súrat al-'Ulamá'*, is written under Qur'án 12:1: *Alif Lám Rá'* – Those are the signs of the Manifest Book. The *súra* thus ends with a commentary on these three disconnected letters. The Báb says that God created the letter *alif* to represent that servant of His [the Báb himself?] who is strong in the divine cause (*amr*). The letter *lám* signifies the ascendancy of His/his[?] rule (*ḥikmuhu*) over the rule of the Book [the Qur'án?]. The letter *ra"* was made by God for the spreading (*inbisáṭ*) of His cause according to the way it has been ordained in the Mother Book.

Súra 71, *al-Qalam* ("the Pen"), is written under Qur'án 12:70: "Then, when he had equipped them with their equipment, he put his drinking-cup into the saddlebag of his brother. Then a herald proclaimed, 'Ho, cameleers, you are robbers!'" The Báb's paraphrase of this verse is as follows:

> Verily, We command the angels to place the drinking-cup of the Remembrance in the saddlebags of the believers, by the leave of

92 *QA* 161.

> God, the Exalted, and God is Knower of all things. O herald (*al-mu'adhdhin*), cry out! O cameleers, you are robbers. Indeed the cup of the Remembrance is concealed from you in the highest station, in very truth. And God is the Preserver of all things. And God is powerful over all things.[93]

The metaphors in this paraphrase-commentary (drinking-cup = Remembrance; saddlebag = believers) are similar to the previously cited "Egypt of the hearts." In this instance, however, they refer to a subject raised in the *Tafsír súrat al-baqara,* namely: one's innate, and in a sense predetermined, capacity for accepting or rejecting the Imám as the manifestation of divinity, in this case represented by the Báb. The believers are therefore privileged to be so because they hold within themselves the "signs" of the Remembrance, here represented by "drinking-cup." Likewise, the "robbers" are prevented from accepting the truth because these signs have been withheld from them due to their own pre-creational natures.[94]

The *Súrat al-Ḥajj* ("'the Pilgrimage"), number 103, is written under Qur'án 12:102: "This is of the tidings of the Unseen that We reveal to thee; thou wast not with them when they agreed upon their plan, devising." The Báb's paraphrase is as follows:

> This commentary (*dhálika al-tafsír*) is of the tidings of the Cloud of Unknowing (*al-'amá'*), written upon the leaf of the heart by the permission of God, the Exalted, in the vicinity of the sacred fire. Verily, God has revealed to you the tidings of the Unseen that you were the Most Great Truth, when their word conflicted, lying. God is, in very truth, Witness over you.[95]

It is important to point out, before offering a few concluding remarks, that one of the strongest evidences that the Báb here is claiming divine revelation is the first two words of this verse: *dhálika al-tafsír* perfectly echoes, participates in and appropriates the considerable authority of the Quranic *dhálika al-kitáb* "This is the Book," as the Qur'án continues, "wherein is

93 *QA* 145.
94 On this idea see Kazemi, "Mysteries," *passim.*
95 *QA* 214. *Al-'amá'* is a frequent term in this work. For an in-depth treatment of the history of its usage and its spiritual significance, see Stephen N. Lambden, "An Early Poem of Bahá'u'lláh: The Sprinkling of the Cloud of Unknowing (*Rashḥ-i 'Amá'*)," *Bahá'í Studies Bulletin,* 3, no. 2 (1984), 4–114, esp. 42 to end.

no doubt, a guidance to the godfearing" (Q. 2:2). By "mimicking" the Quranic verse here the Báb's message is unmistakable. He wants the reader to understand that this *Tafsír* is much more than a mere commentary. It is in fact a new revealed scripture about which there can be no doubt – a guidance to the god-fearing.

CONCLUSIONS

> In order to account for the triggering of the interpretative process, we must assume at the outset that the production and reception of discourse... obey a very general rule of pertinence, according to which if a discourse exists there must be a reason for it. So that when at first glance a given discourse does not obey this rule, the receiver's spontaneous reaction is to determine whether the discourse might not reveal its pertinence through some particular manipulation. "Interpretation"...is what we call this manipulation.[96]

The examples of the textual concerns of the *Tafsír súrat Yúsuf* which have been provided here, along with the general description of the work, are sufficient to make possible a few very general observations. While it is clear that the work is most unusual vis-à-vis the greater Islamic exegetical tradition, or for that matter any other genre of Arabic literature, it would appear that by categorizing the work as *tafsír* the author wished it to be read and judged in this context. This, of course, raises the question of what in fact distinguishes *tafsír* from other types of literature. It should not be assumed that since the Báb was not a typical religious scholar that he was therefore unaware of the standard works of *tafsír*,[97] or that he thought this work of his should be received as a continuation of that tradition. Rather, the contrary

96 Tzvetan Todorov, *Symbolism and Interpretation*, trans. Catherine Porter (Ithaca, 1982), 28.

97 E.g., one of the few mentions of any but an Imám in the *Tafsír súrat al-baqara* is a reference to the "author of *al-Ṣáfí*," i.e., Muḥsin Fayḍ Káshání, author of the *Tafsír al-ṣáfí*. The reference itself is not flattering (see *Majmú'a*, 402). Káshání is criticized for his purely superficial (*qishr maḥḍ*) interpretation of Q. 2:143 (INBA ends its commentary at v. 141). In addition, the Báb says that he has not referred to the *tafsír* of the *'ulamá'* because "such is not worthy of the purpose of this book." It must be noted that these words come in the course of the commentary on the second *juz'* of the Qur'án, the authorship of which is open to debate.

would seem to be the case, particularly in view of the earlier *Tafsír súrat al-baqara*, which, however different from the main sources of orthodox Shíʿí Qur'án commentary it may be, exhibits many of the usual approaches and methods found in those works. In composing the later commentary, the *Tafsír súrat Yúsuf*, the Báb was attempting a break with or abandonment of a tradition which he saw as moribund, particularly so in the context of the advent of a new order for which he himself claimed to be the herald. In addition, as was noted earlier, there was a certain amount of eschatological expectation focused on the awaited appearance of one who would produce a commentary on the twelfth *súra* of the Qur'án.

Browne's statements that the work is inappropriately titled notwithstanding, it is abundantly clear that not only does it offer interpretative statements on the *Súra* of Joseph, but comments on a large portion of the rest of the Qur'án in the process, through paraphrase and other innovative methods. Unusual, there is no doubt. To say that it is not interpretive, or that it does not make clear what the Qur'án meant, at least to the Báb and his immediate readership, is either not to have read it, or to have imposed upon it too rigid a notion about what constitutes *tafsír*, which is after all fundamentally only "explanation." Given the method of allegorical and typological exegesis which is fluently and ceaselessly expressed in the constant use of such rhetorical devices as metaphor and simile, in addition to the "heresy of paraphrase" and the exploitation of ambiguity—all of which have been cast in an unabashed imitation of the Qur'án[98]—the work is clearly one of interpretation. This composition is the result of a reordering of the basic elements of the scripture of Islam which have been fully internalized by the author and finally transformed by him through the twin but opposite processes of imitation and inspiration to become finally an original "act" of literature. Taken as a whole, this remarkable work of the 25-year-old merchant from Shíráz, representing as it does a text within a text which strives to interpret itself, offers a concrete and literary example of a singularly heroic attempt to transform what became known much later, and in a culture quite alien to his own, as the hermeneutic circle, into a hermeneutic spiral.[99]

98 The Báb repeatedly asserts that the work is in fact the *same* Qur'án that was revealed to Muḥammad; see, e.g., Habib Taherzadeh, et al., (trans.), *Selections from the Writings of the Báb* (Haifa, 1978), 67.

99 Cf. Mohammed Arkoun, "Lecture de la Fátiḥa," in his *Lectures du Coran* (Paris, 1982), 41–67, esp. 49. Here the author, who appears to be speaking from a Sunní standpoint, makes a reference to Ricoeur's definition of the "cercle herméneutique" in setting forth what he considers to be eight principles, either explicit or implicit, of classical exegesis. I stress the

By comparing these two works, which were written at about the same time, we see how differently the act of interpretation, springing yet from the same mind, is capable of expressing itself. And with the second work, not only do we have a new example for the history of *tafsír*, but because the work itself is a call to action, we also have the rather startling example of *tafsír* directly affecting history—in a sense, becoming history.[100]

BIBLIOGRAPHY

Unpublished Manuscript Sources of the Writings of the Báb

Tafsír súrat al-baqara

INBA = Tehran Baha'i Archives 6014C, xerox from the library of H. M. Balyuzi, pagination added.
Cambridge University, Browne F. 8.
INBA 69 = *Majmú'ah-yi áthár-yi ḥaḍrat-i A'lá*, Iran National Bahá'í Archives, lxix (1976), 157–410.
Two uncatalogued MSS. in the Princeton University "Bábí Collection".
All references to the Báb's *Tafsír súrat al-baqara* in this chapter are to INBA.

Tafsír súrat al-baqara, 2nd juz' (partial)

Bibliothèque nationale de France Or. 5805.
British Library Or. 7845.
Majmú'ah-yi áthár-yi ḥaḍrat-i A'lá, Iran National Bahá'í Archives (INBA), lxix (1976), 377–410.

Sunní nature of the schema because in it he presents his seventh principle in the following terms: "The disappearance of the prophet has enclosed all believers in a hermeneutic circle: each confronted, henceforth, a text which re-presents the Word; each must 'believe in order to understand and understand in order to believe'." (My translation of Arkoun's French.) By comparison, it would appear that the same thing occurred within Twelver Shí'í Islam, or at least was perceived later to have occurred, with the disappearance of the twelfth Imám.

100 I am grateful to Prof. H. Landolt, McGill University, for his very kind interest, encouragement, and assistance with this study.

Risálat al-sulúk

Tehran Bahá'í Archives MS. 6006. C., 73–74.

Risálah-yi i'tiqádát

Majmú'ah-yi áthár-yi ḥaḍrat-i A'lá, INBA lxix (1976), 411–16.

Tafsír súrat wa'l-'aṣr

Cambridge University, Browne F. 9 (6).

Tafsír súrat Yúsuf

QA = Haifa uncatalogued MS., dated 28 Jumádá al-Awwal 1261[= 3 June 1845] (pagination added).
Cambridge University, Browne F. 11 (9), dated 1891.

Published Writings of the Báb, Bahá'u'lláh and Shoghi Effendi

The Báb, *Bayán-i fársí* (= *Le Béyan Persan*, 4 vols., translated by Alphonse Louis Marie Nicolas (Paris: Paul Geuthner, 1911–14.
The Báb, *Selections from the Writings of the Báb*, translated by Habib Taherzadeh et al. Bahá'í World Centre: Haifa, 1978.
Bahá'u'lláh, *Kitáb-i Íqán* (Cairo: n.d.= *Kitáb-i-Íqán: The Book of Certitude*. Translated by Shoghi Effendi, Wilmette, Il.: Bahá'í Publishing Trust, 1970.
Shoghi Effendi, *God Passes By*. Wilmette, Il.: Bahá'í Publishing Trust, 1970.

Secondary Sources

Unpublished

Afnan, Muhammad, Conversations and other private communications between 1986 and 2016.
Hamid, Idris Samawi. "The Metaphysics and Cosmology of Process According to Shaykh 'Aḥmad al- Aḥsā'ī: Critical Edition, Translation and Analysis of 'Observations in Wisdom'." Unpublished Ph.D. thesis (State University of New York at Buffalo, 1998).

Landolt, Hermann A., Conversations and other private communications between 1982 and 1987.

Rafati, Vahid. "The Development of Shaykhí Thought in Shí'í Islam." Unpublished Ph.D. thesis (University of California at Los Angeles, 1979).

Published

Afnan, Muhammad and William S. Hatcher. "Western Islamic Scholarship and Bahā'ī Origins." *Religion* 15, no. 1 (1985): 29–51.

Amanat, Abbas. *Resurrection and Renewal: The Making of the Babi Movement in Iran, 1844–1850*. Ithaca, N.Y.: Cornell University Press, 1989.

Amir-Moezzi, Mohammad Ali. "An Absence Filled with Presences: Shaykhiyya Hermeneutics of the Occultation (Aspects of Twelver Shiite Imamology VII)." In *The Twelver Shia in Modern Times: Religious Culture and Political History*, edited by Rainer Brunner and Werner Ende, 38–57. Social, Economic and Political Studies of the Middle East and Asia 72. Leiden: Brill, 2001.

Arberry, Arthur John, trans. *The Koran Interpreted*. London: Oxford University Press, 1972.

Arjomand, Said Amir. *The Shadow of God and the Hidden Imam: Religion, Political Order, and Societal Change in Shi'ite Iran from the Beginning to 1890*. Chicago: University of Chicago Press, 1984.

Arkoun, Mohammed. "Lecture de la Fátiḥa," in his *Lectures Du Coran*. Paris: G.-P. Maisonneuve et Larose, 1982, 41–67.

Ayoub, Mahmoud. "The Prayer of Islam: A Presentation of Sūrat al-Fātiha in Muslim Exegesis." In *Studies in Qur'an and Tafsir*, 635–47. Chico, CA: American Academy of Religion, 1979.

Baḥrānī, Hāshim ibn Sulaymān, al-. *Kitāb Al-Burhān Fī Tafsīr al-Qur'ān*, 4 vols. Tehran: Chāp'khānah-i Āfatāb, 1956/1375.

Balyuzi, Hasan M. *The Bāb: The Herald of the Day of Days*. Oxford: G. Ronald, 1973.

Bausani, Alessandro. *Persia Religiosa: Da Zaratustra a Bahā'u'llāh*. Milan: Il Saggiatore, 1959.

Bausani, Alessandro. *Religion in Iran: From Zoroaster to Baha'u'llah*. Translated by J. M. Marchesi. New York: Bibliotheca Persica Press, 2000.

Bayat, Mangol. *Mysticism and Dissent: Socioreligious Thought in Qajar Iran*. Syracuse, N.Y.: Syracuse University Press, 1982.

Browne, Edward Granville. "The Bábís of Persia. II. Their Literature and Doctrines." *Journal of the Royal Asiatic Society of Great Britain and Ireland*, New Series, 21, no. 4 (October 1889): 881–1009.

Browne, Edward Granville. "Some Remarks on the Bábí Texts Edited by Baron Victor Rosen in Vols. I and VI of the *Collections Scientifiques de l'Institut Des Langues Orientales de Saint-Pétersbourg*." *Journal of the Royal Asiatic Society of Great Britain and Ireland*, New Series, 24, no. 2 (April 1892): 259–335.

Browne, Edward Granville. "Catalogue and Description of 27 Bábí Manuscripts." *Journal of the Royal Asiatic Society of Great Britain and Ireland*, New Series, 24, no. 3 (July 1892): 433–99.

Browne, Edward Granville. "Báb, Bábís," in James Hastings, editor, *Encyclopaedia of Religion and Ethics* (New York, 1909), ii. 305a.

Corbin, Henry. *En Islam iranien: Aspects spirituels et philosophiques*. 4 vols. Paris: Gallimard, 1971.

Firestone, R. "Yūsuf b. Ya'ḳūb." In *Encyclopaedia of Islam*, edited by P. Bearman, T. Bianquis, C. E. Bosworth, E. van Donzel, and W. P. Heinrichs, 11:352. Brill, n.d.

Ghazzālī, Abū Hāmid al-. *Tafsīr Sūrat Yūsuf*. Tehran: n.p., 1895.

Goldziher, *Richtungen*, 288, 298. Goldziher, Ignaz. *Die Richtungen Der Islamischen Koranauslegung: An Der Universität Upsala Gehaltene Olaus-Petri-Vorlesungen*. Boston: Adamant Media Corp., 2003. See also now: Goldziher, Ignaz. *Schools of Koranic Commentators*. Edited and translated by Wolfgang H. Behn. Wiesbaden: Harrassowitz in Kommission, 2006.

Hamid, Idris Samawi. "Shaykh Aḥmad Al-Aḥsā'ī." In *Philosophy in Qajar Iran*, edited by Reza Pourjavady, 1st ed., 127:66–124. Handbook of Oriental Studies, Section One: The Near and Middle East. Leiden & Boston: Brill, 2019.

Heller, Bernát. "Yūsuf b. Ya'ḳūb." In *Shorter Encyclopaedia of Islam*, edited by H. A. R. Gibb and J. H. Kramers, 646–48. Leiden: E. J. Brill, 1974.

Huwayzi, 'Abd 'Alī, al-. *Kitāb tafsīr nūr al-thaqalayn*. Edited by H. al-Mahallati. 5 vols. Qumm: Matba'at al-'Ilmiyya, 1382–85/1962–65.

Ibn al-'Arabī, Muhyi al-Dīn. *Fuṣūṣ al-ḥikam*. Edited by Abū al-'Alā Affifi. 2 vols. Beirut: Dār al-kitāb al-'Arabī, 1966.

Ibn Bābawayh, Muhammad ibn 'Alī. *Kitāb ikmāl al-dīn wa itmām al-ni'ma fī ithbāt al-raj'a*. Najaf: Matba'at al-Haydarīya, 1389/1970.

Izutsu, Toshihiko. *Sufism and Taoism: A Comparative Study of Key Philosophical Concepts*. Berkeley: University of California Press, 1983.

Kāshānī, Mullā Muḥammad Muḥsin *Fayḍ*, al-. *Tafsīr al-ṣāfī*. Edited by Ḥusayn A'lamī. 5 vols. Beirut: Mu'assasat al-A'lamī lil-Maṭbū'āt, 1399.

Kazemi, Farshid. "Mysteries of Alast: The Realm of Subtle Entities ('Alam-i Dharr) and the Primordial Covenant in the Babi-Baha'i Writings." *Bahá'í Studies Review* 15 (2009): 39–66.

Kulaynī al-Rāzī, Abū Ja'far Muḥammad b. Ya'qūb, al-. *al-Usûl min al-kâfî*. 2 vols. Tehran: Dār al-Kutub al-Islāmiyya, 1374 [1954].

Lambden, Stephen N. "An Early Poem of Mirza Husayn 'Ali Bahá'u'lláh: The Sprinkling of the Cloud of Unknowing (*Rashḥ-i 'Ama'*)." *Bahá'í Studies Bulletin* 3, no. 2 (1984): 4–114.

Lambden, Stephen N. "An Episode in the Childhood of the Báb." In *In Iran*, edited by Peter Smith, 3:1–31. Studies in Bâbî and Bahâ'î History. Los Angeles: Kalimáta Press, 1986.

Lambden, Stephen N. https://hurqalya.ucmerced.edu/.

Lawson, Todd. "Akhbārī Shī'ī Approaches to Tafsīr." In *The Koran: Critical Concepts in Islamic Studies*, edited by Colin Turner, Reprint., 163–97. IV: Translation and Exegesis. New York and London: Routledge Curzon, 2006 (first published 1993).

Lawson, Todd. "The Dangers of Reading: Inlibration, Communion and Transference in the Qur'an Commentary of the Báb." In Moojan Momen, editor, *Scripture and Revelation: Papers Presented at the First Irfan Colloquium Newcastle-upon-Tyne, England, December 1993 and the Second Irfan Colloquium Wilmette, USA, March 1994*, 171–215. Oxford: George Ronald, 1997.

Lawson, Todd. *Gnostic Apocalypse in Islam: Qur'an, Exegesis, Messianism, and the Literary Origins of the Babi Religion*. London and New York: Routledge, 2012.

Lawson, Todd. *The Quran, Epic and Apocalypse*. London: Oneworld Academic, 2017.

Lawson, Todd. *Tafsir as Mystical Experience: Intimacy and Ecstasy in Quran Commentary: Tafsīr sūrat al-baqara of Sayyid 'Alī Muḥammad Shīrāzī, The Báb (1819–1850)*. Vol. 14. Texts and Studies on the Qur'ān 14. Leiden: Brill, 2018.

Leaman, Oliver. *An Introduction to Medieval Islamic Philosophy*. Cambridge: Cambridge University Press, 1985.

MacEoin, Denis. "Early Shaykhí Reactions to the Báb and his Claims," in Moojan Momen, editor, *Studies in Bábí and Baha'i History*, 1, Los Angeles: Kalimát Press, 1982.

MacEoin, Denis. *The Sources for Early Bábí Doctrine and History: A Survey.* Leiden: E. J. Brill, 1992.

MacEoin, Denis. *The Messiah of Shiraz: Studies in Early and Middle Bábism.* Leiden: Brill, 2009.

Momen, Moojan. *The Bábí and Bahá'í Religions, 1844–1944: Some Contemporary Western Accounts.* Oxford: George Ronald, 1981.

Momen, Moojan. "The Trial of Mullā 'Alī Basṭāmī: A Combined Sunnī-Shī'ī Fatwā against the Bāb." *Iran* 20 (January 1982): 113–43.

Momen, Moojan. *An Introduction to Shí'í Islám: The History and Doctrines of Twelver Shí'ism.* Oxford and New Haven: George Ronald and Yale University Press, 1985.

Nicolas, Alphonse Louis Marie. *Seyyèd Ali Mohammed dit Le Bâb.* Paris: Dujarric, 1905.

Smith, Peter and Moojan Momen, "The Bábí Movement: A Resource Mobilization Perspective," in *In Iran: Studies in Bábí and Bahá'í History*, edited by Peter Smith, 3:33–93. Los Angeles: Kalimát Press, 1986.

Strothmann, Rudolph. In *Shorter Encyclopaedia of Islam*, edited by H. A. R. Gibb and J. H. Kramers, 561–62. Leiden: E. J. Brill, 1974.

Ṭabrisī, Abū 'Alī, al-. *Majma' al-bayān fī tafsīr al-Qur'ān.* Vol. 1. Beirut: Dār al-Fikr wa Dār al-Kitāb al-Lubnānī, 1377/1957.

Todorov, Tzvetan. *Symbolism and Interpretation.* Translated by Catherine Porter. Ithaca, N.Y.: Cornell University Press, 1982.

Welch, A. T., Paret, R. and Pearson, J. D. "al-Ḳur'ān," in: *Encyclopaedia of Islam, Second Edition.* Edited by: P. Bearman, Th. Bianquis, C. E. Bosworth, E. van Donzel, W. P. Heinrichs. Consulted online on 22 August 2019, http://dx.doi.org.myaccess.library.utoronto.ca/10.1163/1573-3912_islam_COM_0543.

Zarandi, Mullá Muḥammad Zarándí.(*Nabíl*), *The Dawn-Breakers: Nabíl's Narrative of the Early Days of the Bahá'í Revelation.* Translated and edited by Shoghi Effendi, Wilmette, Il.: Bahá'í Publishing Trust, 1974.

6

The Social Basis of the Bābī Upheavals in Iran (1848–53)

A Preliminary Analysis[1]

MOOJAN MOMEN

Abstract: This chapter attempts to understand the social basis for the Bābī upheavals that affected Iran in 1848–52. It examines the available accounts of these upheavals and creates tables of the social background and geographical origin of the participants in these events. The evidence presented seems to indicate that in the cities and towns of Iran those who became followers of the Bāb were drawn from all social classes, with a slight preponderance from the ʿ*ulamā*, who also provided the leadership of the movement. The spread of the Bābī movement across the villages of Iran was more patchy. Where a religious or secular leader became a Bābī much of the village would also become Bābīs, but this only occurred in a small proportion of the villages of Iran. There do not appear to have been conversions from the religious minorities nor from the nomadic tribes. There is some evidence that some

1 This chapter is a revised version of a paper that was presented at the Third Baha'i Studies Seminar at the University of Lancaster, England, in April 1979 and published in the *International Journal of Middle East Studies* 15 (1983), 157–83. I am grateful to Peter Smith for his suggestions about the paper and to Iraj Saniee for assistance with statistical analysis.

geographical regions of Iran responded more than other regions. Patterns of conversion and the networks that formed the basis for these conversions are also described and discussed.

INTRODUCTION

In the middle of the nineteenth century, Iran was shaken by a series of serious upheavals caused by the Bābī movement.[2] Although of short duration, these upheavals engulfed the entire country and had far-reaching effects in that they formed the first of a chain of events that led on the one hand, to the Constitutional Movement in Iran, and on the other, to the establishment of the now world-wide Bahāʾī Faith.

Sayyid ʿAlī Muḥammad Shīrāzī (1819–50) took the title, the Bāb, in 1844 and advanced a religious claim. Initially this claim appeared to be only that he was in communication with the Hidden Imām (the Imām Mahdī),[3] and the claim was directed principally at the adherents of the Shaykhī school who had just suffered the loss of their leader, Sayyid Kāẓim Rashtī, and were in search of another leader. After a few years, however, it became

2 On the history of the Bābī movement, see: J. A. de Gobineau, *Les Religions et Philosophies dans l'Asie Centrale*, 1st ed. (Paris, 1865), 10th ed. (Paris, 1957), 131–319 and Appendix; E. G. Browne, *A Traveller's Narrative, written to illustrate the Episode of the Bāb* (Cambridge, 1891); idem, *The Tārīkh-i-Jadīd; or, New History of Mīrzā ʿAlī Muḥammad the Bāb* (Cambridge, 1893); A.-L.-M. Nicolas, *Seyyèd Ali Mohammed dit le Bâb* (Paris, 1905); Nabīl, *Nabīl's Narrative: The Dawn-Breakers*, trans. and ed. Shoghi Effendi (Wilmette, IL, 1962); H. M. Balyuzi, *The Bāb* (Oxford, 1973); M. Momen, *The Bābī and Bahāʾī Religions (1844–1944): Some Contemporary Western Accounts* (Oxford, 1981). And since the first publication of this article: Peter Smith, *The Babi and Baha'i Religions: From Messianic Shiʿism to a World Religion* (Cambridge: Cambridge University Press, 1987), 1–56. I also include here Abbas Amanat, *Resurrection and Renewal: The Making of the Babi Movement in Iran, 1844–1850* (Ithaca: Cornell University Press, 1989), despite the unwarranted and in places outright false statements made about me in the preface to the new edition of this book (Los Angeles, 2005). I will leave it to readers to judge for themselves, on the basis of the evidence of the present chapter, the truth of assertions such as that I have "questioned the relevance of socio-political dynamics in the birth and development of the Babi movement"; or that I have written "from a pre-modernist, divine-interventionist perspective in which human agency does not seem to have a place"; or that I have a "regrettable disregard for conventions of scholarly citation" – these being but some of a number of egregious and unjustifiable statements that he makes.

3 Regarding the Bāb's claims, see M. Momen, "The Trial of Mullā ʿAlī Bastāmī: A combined Sunnī-Shīʿī *fatwā* against the Bāb," *Iran*, 20 (1982), 140–42.

clear that the Bāb's claim involved more than this. Almost simultaneously, in the summer of 1848, at his own trial in Tabrīz before the crown prince, Nāṣiru'd-Din Mīrzā (who would become shah less than two months later), and at a conference of his followers at Badasht in Khurāsān, the claim was put forward that the Bāb was in fact the Imām Mahdī returned and that he was the bearer of a new revelation from God which abrogated the Islamic dispensation, the Qur'ān and the *Sharīʿah.*

Such a claim was a direct challenge to the Islamic hierarchy and was immediately followed by the raising of the Black Standard in Khurāsān (see pp. 281–2), an action that was seen as a challenge to the state. Shortly afterwards, there occurred the first of the major Bābī upheavals at Shaykh Ṭabarsī in Māzandarān (October 1848–May 1849). This was followed by the first Nayrīz upheaval (May–June 1850) and the prolonged Zanjān upheaval (May 1850–January 1851). The Bāb himself was put to death in Tabrīz on 9 July 1850. One and a half years after the termination of the Zanjān upheaval, there occurred on 15 August 1852 an attempted assassination of Nāṣiru'd-Dīn Shāh by a group of Bābīs. This led in the next few months to the arrest and execution of a large number of Bābīs in Tehran and elsewhere. A year later there was a second Nayrīz upheaval (October–December 1853).

Following this bloody repression, the Bābī movement went underground only to re-emerge two decades later as the Bahāʾī movement. The social and economic teachings of the Bāb undoubtedly had widespread appeal and influenced the Reformist and Constitutionalist movements that were to emerge a few decades later to an extent that is at present insufficiently appreciated, as the American scholar Nikki Keddie has pointed out.[4]

The manner in which the Bāb was able within a very short space of time to amass a considerable number of followers has led some scholars to look for underlying social and economic factors as an explanation. And, certainly, there was plenty of cause for social unrest in Iran during the period 1800–50.

Probably the first to examine the Bābī movement from an economic and social viewpoint was the Russian scholar Mikhail Ivanov.[5] Writing from a Marxist viewpoint, he has examined the situation in Iran at this time. Ivanov's description of the social and economic crisis in Iran is well supported by

4 N. Keddie, "Religion and Irreligion in early Iranian Nationalism," *Comparative Studies in Society and History*, 4 (1962), 274–75.

5 M. S. Ivanov, *Babidski Vostanii i Irane (1848–1852)* (Moscow, 1939); idem, "Babism" and "Babi Uprisings" in *Great Soviet Encyclopedia, vol.* 2 (New York, 1973), 521. See also V. Minorsky, review of *Ivanov's Babidski Vostanii, Bulletin of the School of Oriental and African Studies*, 11/4 (1946), 878–80.

evidence from other sources. With regard to the balance of trade, Ivanov cites some interesting evidence. The principle trade route for Iran from 1830 to 1880 was the Istanbul–Erzerum–Tabrīz route which carried most of the import and export trade. Ivanov's figures, taken from Russian sources on the overall trading balance for Tabrīz for the period 1833–47, compare well with figures compiled by the British consul in Tabrīz (see Table 1). These figures are for total foreign trade centred in Tabrīz, including Russian trade, and demonstrate a large deficit to Iran.

TABLE 1. Balance of the Trade with Europe and Russia at Tabrīz

	Total exports	Total imports	Annual deficit
Russian observer[a] annual average 1833–47	£260,306	£726,886	£466,580
British Consul[b] (Abbott) March 1844–March 1845	£369,057	£703,204	£334,147
British Consul[c] (Stevens) 1848	£343,738	£830,773	£487,035

a. Calculated from Ivanov, quoted in Minorski, review of Ivanov, *Bābīdski Vostani i Iran* (see note 4), 879.

b. *Parliamentary Papers*, vol. 53 (for 1849), 357.

c. *Parliamentary Papers*. vol. 55 (for 1851), 864.

The situation was also bad for Iran at Būshihr where there was an annual trade deficit of approximately £74,000 on average over the period 1817–23.[6] The small trading surplus which there may have been in trade with Central Asia could not have made much difference to these figures. The size of this deficit in the balance of payments can be better appreciated when one remembers that the total revenue of the state at this time, in both cash and kind, was of the order of £1,250,000.[7]

6 Calculated from C. Issawi, *The Economic History of Iran (1800–1914)* (Chicago, 1971), 90–91.

7 Calculated from India Office estimates made in 1836, quoted in Issawi, *Economic History*, 361. In considering the balance of trade, it is impossible, of course, to assess the amount of smuggling that occurred. Most authorities seem agreed that, overall, its effect on the balance of trade was in Iran's favour. However, this must be set against the large amount of money spent by Iranian pilgrims in Iraq, as well as the pious benefactions made to the Holy Shrines there.

Such massive and continuing deficits resulted in a considerable drain of gold and silver from the country. The economic consequences of this may for a number of years have been cushioned by the immense booty brought back from India by Nadir Shah. However, the continuing drain of gold and silver on account of these factors was beginning to be felt by the 1840s. Progressive debasement of the coinage and other factors led to an inflation rate of between 70 and 150 per cent in the period from 1843–61, with some important commodities such as wheat and barley tripling in price.[8]

Apart from the purely economic consequences of the trade with Europe, there was also the social disruption caused by the import of European manufactured goods leading to the decline and even death of many traditional local industries. Especially hard hit were Iranian merchants who, hampered by a corrupt and extortionate administration, were no match for European mercantile firms that were favoured by trade agreements and protected by strong consular powers.

In addition to these social and economic factors, the two military defeats by Russia in 1804–13 and 1826–28, as well as Iran's humiliation at the hands of the English over Herat in 1838, were the first time that the vast superiority of the West and Iran's degradation from the glories of Safavid rule and Nadir Shah's conquests were clearly demonstrated to intelligent Iranians; a fact of which they were henceforth constantly reminded by the haughty demeanour and manifest power of European diplomatic and consular personnel. Moreover, the farcical proceedings of Ḥāj Mirzā Aqasi, Muḥammad Shāh's prime minister, the pervasive corruptness of the administration, the sorry state of the Army and the obscurantism and greed of most of the clerical class (the *ʿulamā*), could only serve to increase the general dissatisfaction and restlessness of the people.

Thus, Ivanov sees the Bābī movement as "a popular mass movement, born out of definite social conditions and directed against the ruling class."[9] Ivanov stresses the merchant-class background of the Bāb and the influence this had on his teaching: such matters as the high standing given to trade as a profession; the legalization of interest; the inviolability of commercial correspondence. Ivanov then asserts that a new phase of the movement began with the emergence of Mullā Muḥammad ʿAlī Bārfurūshī (Quddūs), who was of a peasant family and promoted such ideas as the abolition of all

8 Issawi, *Economic History*, 342.

9 Ivanov quoted in Minorsky's review, 878.

taxes and private property.[10] He describes the Bābī upheavals as risings of "peasants, artisans, urban poor, and small trades-people" against feudalism and "enslavement of the country by foreign capital."[11] He contends that it was the particular circumstances in Iran that led to the leadership of the movement by the lower clergy and small-trade bourgeoisie.[12]

Keddie has pointed out the similarity between the Bābī uprisings in Iran and the Taiping revolt in China. She has noted the similarities in the leadership of the movement, the nature of the revolts, the influence of Christianity and the West, the social content of the teachings of the two movements (including some elements of community of property, strict regulation of personal morality, and an enhanced position for women), and the nationalistic tendency (with the revival of the solar calendar and a Zoroastrian theory of elements).[13] Keddie has also referred to the social and economic impact of the West and the probable hastening effect this had on such movements as Babism.[14]

The British scholar Peter Avery has looked to "an element in the movement's origins of the protest of the south against the north, a protest articulated by merchants who were prospering from trade through Shiraz and its port of Bushire, and through the cities of Yazd and Kerman with their port Bandar Abbas, with both the Indian subcontinent and Mesopotamia"[15] in order to explain the impetus acquired by the movement.

Finally, the Iranian scholar Farhad Kazemi has reviewed the economic, social, and political dislocation in Iran in the first half of the nineteenth century and has pointed out that many of the factors laid down by Max Weber as precipitating the emergence of a charismatic leader were fulfilled in Iran at this time.[16]

Although they have referred to the economic and social factors leading to the emergence of Babism, Ivanov, Keddie, and Kazemi have all been careful to stress the cultural, historical, and religious continuity of Bābī teaching. They have noted the importance of the Shīʿī doctrine of the Mahdī as well as the linking role of the Shaykhī movement in this continuity. Thus,

10 Ibid., 879–80
11 Ivanov, "Babi Uprisings," 521.
12 Ibid.
13 Keddie, "Religion and Irreligion," 268–70.
14 Ibid., 270.
15 P. Avery, *Modern Iran* (London, 1965), 53.
16 F. Kazemi, "Some Preliminary Observations on the Early Development of Babism," *Muslim World*, 63 (1973), 119–122.

as Kazemi has noted, unlike Weber's charismatic leader, the Bāb did not stress the break with the past.[17] Indeed much of the Bāb's writings revolve around emphasising and explaining this continuity. However, we shall not explore that theme in this chapter.[18]

In the present work, I shall attempt to make a more detailed analysis than any made hitherto of the social background of those persons who followed the Bāb, and in particular those who participated in the Bābī upheavals. I shall also consider the question of the contribution of social and economic factors to the spread of the Bābī movement.

THE SHAYKH ṬABARSĪ UPHEAVAL: 1848–49

Of the four major Bābī upheavals in the period from 1848 to 1853, unquestionably the most important was that at Shaykh Ṭabarsī, and this for the following reasons:

1. The Bāb himself instructed Mullā Ḥusayn to initiate this episode by raising the Black Standard in Khurāsān and journeying westward. The Bāb moreover issued a general call to his disciples to rally to the Black Standard.
2. This episode involved the two leading disciples of the Bāb, Mullā Muḥammad ʿAlī Bārfurūshī (Quddus), and Mullā Ḥusayn Bushrūʾī, and a total of nine of the eighteen "Letters of the Living," the first and leading disciples of the Bāb. The Zanjān and Nayrīz upheavals involved none of the "Letters of the Living," and were each led by one of the Bāb's prominent disciples. Two of the "Letters of the Living," the famous Ṭāhirih (Qurratu'l-ʿAyn) and Sayyid Ḥusayn Yazdī, the Bāb's secretary, died in the Tehran executions of 1852.
3. This episode evoked a widespread response from the Bābīs with groups setting out from all over the country to join Mullā Ḥusayn. Many succeeded in doing so while others failed on account of the efforts of the royal troops. Among the latter were Sayyid Yaḥyā

17 Ibid., 122.
18 However, see the following book published since the first publication of this article: Todd Lawson, *Gnostic Apocalypse and Islam: Qur'an, Exegesis, Messianism and the Literary Origins of the Babi Religion* (London: Routledge, 2012).

> Dārābī who was later to lead the Nayrīz upheaval, Mīrzā Ḥusayn ʿAlī Nūrī (Bahā'u'llāh), and several persons who later perished in the 1852 holocaust in Tehran. There was no similar widespread support for the other two upheavals.

Thus, the participants at Shaykh Ṭabarsī may be considered as a representative cross-section of the most active and enthusiastic followers of the Bāb. For this reason, and also because of the fact that the details of those participating have been more carefully recorded, more attention will be focused here on this episode.

In July 1848, Mullā Ḥusayn Bushrūʾī, on the Bāb's instructions, raised a Black Standard in Mashhad and set off westward. The implications of such an act for the religious hierarchy and for the government were, no doubt, obvious to all. First, there was the well-known tradition ascribed to Muḥammad: "Should you see Black Standards coming from Khurāsān, then go to them, for there you will find the Mahdī, the Vicegerent of God."[19] Second, it was from just such an action, the raising of a Black Standard in Khurāsān, that the ʿAbbasids had succeeded in overthrowing the Umayyad dynasty.

Mullā Ḥusayn was not, however, challenged by the government during his march from Khurāsān—probably because it coincided with the confusion arising from the death of Muḥammad Shāh. Just outside Bārfurūsh, however, there was a clash between the Bābīs and the populace which resulted in Mullā Ḥusayn taking up positions around the Shrine of Shaykh Ṭabarsī and building defensive fortifications. The ensuing conflict lasted from mid-October 1848 to early May 1849.

Estimates of the total number of Bābīs at Shaykh Ṭabarsī differ widely. The higher estimates, such as 1,500 in the official court history, the *Nāsikhu't-Tawārikh*,[20] may be the result of exaggeration by the Shāh's troops in order to allay their discomfiture over their failure to defeat a poorly armed, untrained group of civilians for such a lengthy period. The Bābī and Bahāʾī histories seem to agree that Mullā Ḥusayn arrived at Shaykh Ṭabarsī with 313 men (although this figure is undoubtedly influenced by fact that this was the number of companions of the Prophet

---

19 See, for example, Ahmad ibn Hanbal, *Musnad* vol. 5 (Cairo, 1313/1896), Hadith of Thawbān, 677. See also *Nabīl's Narrative*, 351.

20 Lisānu'l-Mulk, *Nāsikhu't-Tawārīkh*, quoted in Browne, *Traveller's Narrative*, vol. 2, 179.

Muhammad at the Battle of Badr and there was a Shīʿī prophecy that the same number would accompany the Imām Mahdī on his return).[21] However, a considerable number of Bābīs joined after this, including some from the surrounding villages.[22] I will discuss the probable total number of participants below.

In the second volume of his *Tārikh-i Shuhadā-yi Amr*, the Iranian Bahāʾī historian Muḥammad ʿAlī Malik-Khusravī has gathered whatever names and biographical details are available on the Bābī participants at Shaykh Ṭabarsī. His most important sources include three manuscript accounts by survivors of the episode,[23] two histories based on accounts given by other survivors,[24] the *Nuqṭatu'l-Kāf*, the *Tārikh-i Jadīd*, and a number of other sources.[25]

Total Number of Bābīs at Shaykh Ṭabarsī

The information provided by Malik-Khusravī may be supplemented from another source. One of the most important sources, the *Tārikh-i-Mīmiyyih* by Mahjūr, gives an analysis by towns of origin of the 313 persons who accompanied Mullā Ḥusayn as he entered Māzandarān from Mashhad. Such a list is not, of course, complete since this represents a very early stage in this episode, but it serves as a check on Malik Khusravī's list. I have compared the two lists in Table 3.[26]

21 See, for example, ʿAbdu'l-Bahā in Browne, *Traveller's Narrative*, vol. 2, 37; and *Nabīl's Narrative*, 354.

22 Other estimates of the total number of Bābīs include those of Farrant, British Charge d'Affaires: about 500; Dolgoruki, Russian Minister: 1,500; Ferrier, French Agent: 1,200; Mackenzie, British Consul, Rasht: 400–500. For details see M. Momen, *The Bábí and Bahá'í Religions*, 91–99.

23 Luṭf-ʿAlī Mīrzā Shīrāzī, Mīr Abū-Ṭālib Shahmīrzādī, and Ḥājī Nāṣir Qazvīnī.

24 *Nabīl's Narrative*, based on the accounts of five survivors; and the *Tārīkh-i-Mimiyyih* by Sayyid Muḥammad Ḥusayn Mahjūr Zavāriʾī, based on the accounts of three survivors.

25 M A. Malik-Khusravī Nūrī, *Tārīkh-i-Shuhadā-yi Amr*, 3 vols. (Tehran, 130 BE/1973). For list of sources relating to Shaykh Ṭabarsī see vol. 1, 16–18.

26 I have compared Mahjūr's list in three sources: Fāḍil Māzandarānī, *Ẓuhūru'l-Ḥaqq*, vol. 3 (n.p., n.d.), 124 n.; manuscript (F28, Browne Collection, Cambridge University Library), 18; manuscript used by Malik-Khusravī (photocopy of manuscript in private hands), 18. There are no discrepancies in the numbers cited save that the third-named source gives the number of Zanjānīs as 13 rather than the 12 given in the other two sources. All three sources occasionally misspell names, e.g., Siyāmī for *Miyāmī*, Rūmī for Urūmī, etc.

TABLE 2. Occupations of Bābī participants at Shaykh Ṭabarsī

	Major *'ulamā*[a]	Minor *'ulamā*[b]	Nobility, land owners and high government officials	Wholesale merchants (*tujjār*)	Skilled retail merchants (guilded)[d]	Urban workers (guilded)[e]	Unskilled urban workers[f]	Peasantry[g]	Unclassified[h]			TOTAL
									a	b	c	
Khurāsān, including Qā'in and Simnān	6	62	1	1	3	5	4	1	12	43	6	144
Māzandarān and Gīlān	4	28	7	0	0	7	1	5	9	19	10	90
Ādharbāyjān	0	6	0	0	0	0	0	0	2	2	0	10
Qazvīn and Khamsih (Zanjān)	0	6	0	3	1	2	0	0	14	0	0	26
Tehran and Qum	4	1	1	0	0	0	1	0	1	1	0	9
Kashān and Maḥallāt	0	4	0	0	0	0	0	0	0	0	0	4
Iṣfahān	0	8	2	1	4	19	0	0	12	7	0	53
Fārs	0	5	1	0	0	0	0	0	6	0	0	12
Yazd and Kirmān	0	2	0	0	0	4	0	0	4	0	0	10
'Iraq	0	0	0	0	1	0	0	0	1	1	1	4
Origin unknown	0	0	0	0	0	2	0	0	0	0	1	3
TOTAL	14	122	12	5	9	39	6	6	61	73	18	365

a. Includes three *mujtahids*; three *Imām-Jum'ihs*, one Mutavallī-Bāshī of Qum; two described as having a circle of *ṭullāb;* one on account of his being called a *muḥaqqiq-i-'ahd;* one on account of his being said to have had *riyāsat-i dīnī* in his area; two on account of being young sons of the above. Finally, there is one major Sufi *murshid* (of Tehran) who is not strictly speaking of the *'ulamā* but is put here as being a "religious leader".

b. Includes all mullās (*akhūnds*) and religious students (*ṭullāb, talāmīdh*), also two *pīshnamāzes*, two *mutavallīs*, and one *mu'azzin*. Of course, many of the minor *'ulamā* engaged in other occupations. The only ones noted by Malik-Khusravī were: one *hakkāk* (engraver) of Māzandarān, one *gandum-pāk-kun* (wheatsifter) of Isfahan, and one *aṭṭār* (druggist) of Khursān. These three have been included in this category.

c. Includes one *mustawfī*, one Afsharid prince, and also seven Māzandarānīs who were members of an important landowning family.

d. Includes one described as *dastmāl-gīrih-zan* (marriage broker?), two *sarrafs* (money-changers/brokers), and one who is described as being an agent for a wholesale merchant.

e. Includes one man described as *payvand* (grafter?).

f. Includes all retainers and personal servants.

g. includes one man, Āqā Bayk-i Lur, who was presumably a tribesman.

h. No information as to occupation available. These have been subdivided thus: [a] urban; belonging to large and medium-sized towns—see p. 293; [b] rural; belonging to small towns and villages—see p. 293; [c] unknown origin. Some twenty-six persons in the unclassified category had either "Mīrzā" or "Shaykh" in front of their names, indicating that they had at least received an education.

TABLE 3. Town Origins of Participants: Comparison of the Lists of Mahjūr and Malik-Khusravī

	Mahjūr	Malik-Khusravī		Mahjūr	Malik-Khusravī
Iṣfahānī	40	40	**Qazvīnī**	10	16
Ardistānī	7	11	**Hamadānī**	6	0
Shīrāzī	8	11	**Tabrīzī**	5	1
Kirmāni	3	4	**Zanjānī**	12/13[d]	10
Mashhadī	22	5 (20)[a]	**Kirmānshāhī**	3	0
Bushrū'ī	24	22	**Bārfurūshī**	4	16
Turbatī	5	8[b]	**Bihnamirī**	40	18
Hirātī	14	8[c]	**Shāhrūdī**	3	0
Turshīzī	10	6	**Amulī**	2	4
Kākhakī	4	0	**Shaykh Ṭabarsī**	2	4
Miyāmi	19	31	**Khū'ī**	3	4
Qā'inī	4	2	**Kanī**	2	3
Tihrānī	9	2	**Yazdī**	3	6
Kāshānī	6	0	**Shahmīrzādī**	9	6
Qumī	12	4	**Urūmī**	3	1
Sangsarī	10	26	**Indian**	4	0
Karbalā'ī	5	1			

a. Five persons are specifically designated as being Mashhadīs by Malik-Khusravī, Another fifteen are designated Khurāsānī which I have considered as meaning being from Mashhad (although I recognise that this is not always the case). In Table 5 these have been entered in the fourth column.

b. From villages in the area of Turbat-i-Ḥaydarī: Mihnih, Dūghābād, Fayḍābād, and 'Abdu'llāhābād

c. These are included in the Khurāsān figures in Table 5.

d. See note 26.

The principal discrepancies which appear between the two lists in Table 3 can be explained as follows:

1. Mahjūr's list was compiled at a very early stage of the proceedings and many, especially Māzandarānīs, joined after this.
2. Malik-Khusravī's sources seem to display an ethnocentric bias in that non-Persian participants are not named. Thus, of five persons from Karbalā, fourteen from Hirāt, and four Indians in Mahjūr's list, only one Karbalā'ī and eight Hirātīs are named in Malik-Khusravī's sources.
3. Similarly, certain towns such as Kashān, Shāhrūd, Hamadān, and Kirmānshāh are not represented in Malik-Khusravī's sources. This may be because of the absence of any survivors from that town who would have recorded the names of their fellow townsmen.

We may make a speculative attempt at completing Malik-Khusravī's list by adding each positive difference between his and Mahjūr's list (see Table 4).

Thus, the number of Bābī participants at Shaykh Ṭabarsī was probably between 540 and 600 (allowing for some others who may have joined after Mahjūr's listing and who were not named in one of Malik-Khusravī's sources). Therefore Malik-Khusravī's list probably represents approximately 65 per cent of the Bābī participants at Shaykh Ṭabarsī.

Rural/Urban Origin of Bābī Participants at Shaykh Ṭabarsī

Taking Malik-Khusravī and Mahjūr as a basis, we may now assess the number of people at Shaykh Tabarsi from rural and urban backgrounds; see Table 5a.

The grouping together of small towns and villages in Table 5a is not, however, totally satisfactory and so in Table 5b I have repeated totals for other categories, but separated the category of small towns and villages into its component parts as explained in the notes below Table 5b.

It is worth noting the large contribution made to these totals by five small towns and villages: Bushrūyih in Khurāsān (24 persons); Bihnamīr[27] in Māzandarān (40 or more persons); Miyāmay, near Shāhrūd (31 persons);

27 Browne gives this name wrongly as Bahmīz, owing to a simple transposition of a dot. See *Tārīkh-i-Jadīd*, 67 and note, 364; and *Nuqṭatu'l-Kāf*, 191.

TABLE 4. An Estimate of Total Numbers at Shaykh Ṭabarsī

	Malik-Khusravī	Positive difference between the two lists	Final total
Khurāsān	144	2 Mashhadīs 2 Bushrū'īs 6 Hirātīs 4 Turshīzīs 4 Kakhakīs 2 Qā'inīs 3 Shahmīrzādīs	167
Māzandarān and Gīlān	90	102[a]	192
Adharbāyjān	10	4	14
Qazvīn and Khamsih	26	3 Zanjānīs	29
Tehran and Qum	9	7 Tihrānīs 8 Qumīs	24
Kāshān and Maḥallat	4	6 Kāshānīs	10
Iṣfahān	53		53
Fārs	12		12
Yazd and Kirmān	10		10
Kirmānshāh and Hamadān	0	3 Kirmānshāh 6 Hamadān	9
'Irāq	4	4 Karbalā'īs	8
India	0	4 Indians	4
TOTALS	362		532

a. Since Mahjūr's list applies only to Mullā Ḥusayn's companions prior to their entry into Māzandarān, a different method has been used to obtain this figure. It is clear that a large number of Māzandarāni villagers joined the Bābīs. The only figure I have found for these villagers is the reference to 120 Māzandarānīs under the Bihnamīrī chief, Aqa Rasūl (Browne, *New History*, 67). Therefore, I have subtracted the 18 Bihnamīrīs already listed in Malik-Khusravī from 120 to arrive at this number.

TABLE 5a. Rural/Urban Origin of Bābī Participants at Shaykh Ṭabarsī

	Large towns (>22,000)	Medium-sized towns (7–22,000)	Small towns and villages (<7,000)	Unknown	Outside Iran
Khurāsān	7	13	118	15	14[a]
Māzandarān and Gilān	0	24	155	13	0
Adharbāyjān	8	6	2	0	0
Qazvīn and Khamsih	13	13	3	0	0
Tehran and Qum	9	12	3	0	0
Kāshān and Maḥallāt	0	6	4	0	0
Iṣfahān	41	0	12	0	0
Fārs	11	0	1	0	0
Yazd and Kirmān	10	0	0	0	0
Kirmānshāh and Hamadān	9	0	0	0	0
ʿIrāq	0	0	0	0	8
India	0	0	0	0	4
Origin Unknown	0	0	0	3	0
TOTALS	108	74	298	31	26

a. The Khurāsānis in the fifth column are from Hirāt.

Source: This table was compiled on the basis of the list of towns given by Thomson in *Parliamentary Papers*, vol. 69 (for 1867–68), 507–15; reprinted in Issawi, *Economic History*, 28. Also in French in *Bull. Soc. Geog., 5e ser.*, vol. 18 (1869), 15–40. This does not imply, however, that I agree with all the details of this list. (In Thomson's table there are 12 large towns with populations of greater than 22,000 and 23 medium-sized towns with populations 7,000–22,000.)

and Shahmīrzād (9 persons) and Sangsar[28] (26 persons), both near Simnān. Thus a total of 129 or more persons are from these five locations. The totals for Bihnamīr and Bushrūyih are probably underestimated.

TABLE 5b. Rural/Urban Origin of Bābī Participants at Shaykh Ṭabarsī

Large towns (>22,000)	108
Medium-sized towns (7–22,000)	74
Small towns (2–7,000)	28[a]
Villages	269
Tribesmen	1[b]
TOTAL	480
Origins Unknown and Outside Iran	57
FINAL TOTAL	537

a. Consisting of Ardistān (11), ʿAliyābād (5), Qāʾin (4), Maḥallāt (4), Ṭabas (1), Nayrīz (1), Bajistān (1), Najafābād (1).

b. Āqā Bayk Lūr

Concerning the 365 participants listed by Malik-Khusravī, the following additional information is available:

1. There were 54 survivors, a large number of whom (22) were, as may be expected, Māzandarānīs, who had local contacts and knew the terrain. This total of 54 however includes a number of persons who betrayed their comrades and thus managed to escape with their lives.
2. Malik-Khusravī only names some 13 persons as being Shaykhīs who had become Bābīs, which may indicate that although in the early years Shaykhīs were the majority of the Bāb's followers (all 18 "Letters of the Living" were Shaykhīs), by this time the Bāb's appeal had widened considerably and former Shaykhīs were no longer numerically important, although of course the importance of such figures as Mullā Ḥusayn Bushrūʾī and Mullā Muḥammad

28 Browne gives these two names wrongly as Shāh-Mīrzā and Dasak-sar. See *Tarikh-i-Jadid*, 104, and note 1 (which indicates how the mistake was made).

ʿAlī Bārfurūshī (Quddūs), both former Shaykhīs, can hardly be overlooked. Also, there may be a tendency to underestimate the number of Shaykhīs since they were not a clearly defined sect at this time and there were probably many who were inclined to Shaykhī views but were not formally identified as such. Indeed, those mentioned as Shaykhīs by Malik-Khusravī tend to be only those who had travelled to Karbalā to study under Sayyid Kāẓim Rashtī. Thus, the Bushrū'īs who were present had become Bābīs through Mullā Ḥusyan Bushrū'ī and had probably previously been Shaykhīs.

3. There were 34 Sayyids among the 365 listed by Malik-Khusravī – probably a higher proportion than in the general population in Iran.

THE NAYRĪZ UPHEAVALS OF 1850 AND 1853

It is much more difficult to obtain information about the Bābī participants in the Nayrīz and Zanjān upheavals since these have not been studied in such detail as Malik-Khusravī's study of Shaykh Ṭabarsī. Concerning Nayrīz, we know that it was a small town in Iran, which Lovett in 1872 estimated to have a population of 3,500.[29] It consisted of three quarters (*mahallihs*)[30] and was famous principally for the growing of fruit.

The man who brought the Bābī movement to Nayrīz was Sayyid Yaḥyā Dārābī who was given the title Vaḥīd by the Bāb. Vaḥīd was the son of one of the most famous of the contemporary *ʿulamā*, Sayyid Jaʿfar Dārābī, known as Kashfī. Vaḥīd received the usual theological training, but he was not an adherent of the Shaykhī school.

Vaḥīd had gone to Tehran in 1849 hoping to join the Bābīs at Shaykh Ṭabarsī, but was informed that the way was blocked by the besieging army. He remained for a time in Tehran at the house of Mīrzā Ḥusayn ʿAlī Bahā'u'llāh, and then in late 1849 set out for Yazd where he had a house. His presence in Yazd provoked an upheaval which at one time had the deputy governor of that town besieged in his own citadel. Eventually, Vaḥīd's position in Yazd became untenable and he set out from Yazd towards the province of Fārs. He travelled slowly, stopping at several villages to preach

29 B. Lovett, "Surveys on the road from Shiraz to Baum," *Journal Royal Geographical Society*, 42 (1872), 203.
30 Ibid.

to the populace of Babism. He eventually reached Nayrīz where he had previously married the daughter of Ḥājī Shaykh ʿAbdu'l-ʿAlī the *Imām-Jumʿih* of the Chinār-Sūkhtih quarter and a *qaḍī.*

Shortly after Vaḥīd's arrival at Nayrīz there was conflict between him and the governor, Zaynu'l-ʿĀbidīn Khān. Vaḥīd retired to a fort just outside Nayrīz together with a number of companions: the Nayrīz upheaval had begun.

As at Shaykh Ṭabarsī, the government troops, finding themselves unable to deal with the Bābīs, resorted to trickery in order to bring about the surrender of the Bābīs, and then ordered a general massacre.

This first Nayrīz upheaval was followed three years later by a second episode, every bit as bloody as the first, although this time the main fighting occurred in the hills outside Nayrīz where the Bābīs took up positions and defended themselves against the troops. At the end of this conflict there was another general massacre and some 200 heads of Bābīs, as well as several hundred Bābī women and children and about 80 Bābī male prisoners were sent to Shīrāz.

As I have stated previously, the sources for the two Nayrīz upheavals are not very detailed. I have obtained most information from *Nabīl's Narrative*, Nicolas' *Seyyèd Ali Mohammed*, and Muhammad Shafīʿ-Rawḥānī's *Lamʿātu'l-Anwār.*[31] To this I have added information drawn from a manuscript, *Vaqayiʿ-i Ḥayratangīz-i Nayrīz-i Mishkbīz*, by Shaykh Muḥammad Ḥusayn. The first two works are both based principally on a manuscript history by Mirzā Shafiʿ[32] and mostly list names of those killed ("martyrs") whereas the third work concentrates on the survivors of these two episodes. Unfortunately, however, none of these works give much biographical detail and hence the listing is very incomplete.

Occupations of Bābī Participants in the Two Nayrīz Upheavals

Table 6 gives the occupations of the participants in the two Nayrīz upheavals. No attempt has been made to separate the two episodes because most of those participating in the second had also taken part in the first.

31 Tehran (130 BE/1973).

32 I am assuming that the history of Nayrīz listed as an anonymous work by Nicolas (*Seyyèd Ali Mohammed*, 51) is by Mīrzā Shafīʿ Rawḥānī on account of the great similarity between Nabīl's and Nicolas' version of events in the first Nayrīz upheaval.

Origins of Participants at the Two Nayrīz Upheavals

Vaḥīd himself, although described as Dārābī, was in fact born and brought up in Yazd. Of the 337 persons listed in Table 6, 7 are from Yazd, 7 from Istahbānāt, 1 from Bavānāt, and the remaining 322 persons were Nayrīzīs. (See also comments in the next section.)

TABLE 6. Occupations of Bābī Participants at Nayrīz

Occupation classification	Number of participants
Major *'ulamā*	6[a]
Minor *'ulamā*	60[b]
Nobility, landowners, and high government officials	11[c]
Wholesale merchants (*tujjār*)	0
Retail merchants (guilded)	6
Skilled urban workers (guilded)	19
Unskilled urban workers	3
Peasantry	5[d]
Unclassified (urban)	0
Unclassified (rural)	227[e]
Unclassified (origin unknown)	0
TOTAL	337

a. Consists of Vaḥīd himself, 2 *Imām-Jum'ihs*, 1 *Shaykhu'l-Islām* of Bavānāt, and 2 young sons of one of the *Imām-Jum'ihs*.

b. One of the Mullās listed here is also said to have been a gilder (*mudhahhib*).

c. Includes 2 relatives of the governor and 2 *kadkhudās*.

d. These were 5 agriculturalists who lived in Nayrīz and worked the orchards there. To call them peasants is probably not wholly accurate.

e. Includes 1 *darvish*. Most of these would have been fruit-growers.

Total Numbers of Bābī Participants at the Two Nayrīz Upheavals

As before, there are many estimates of the total number of Bābī participants in these upheavals. For the first upheaval, the *Nāsikhu't-Tawārīkh* states that initially 300 Bābīs occupied the fort and that later their numbers grew to 2,000.[33] Ḥasan Fasā'ī, in the *Fārs-Nāmih Nāsirī,* states that initially there were 500 Bābīs and that their numbers swelled to more than 3,000.[34] According to Nicolas' Bābī source, the number was 700–800.[35] There are fewer figures for the second upheaval. Nicolas states that at the end of this episode 603 women and 80 male prisoners were taken captive to Shīrāz.[36] *Nabīl's Narrative* gives the numbers as 600 women prisoners, 180 male prisoners and 180 male "martyrs"; a total of 960.[37]

We may arrive at an estimate of the numbers of Bābīs involved in the Nayrīz upheavals by a different means. We know that on Vaḥīd's arrival at Nayrīz almost the whole of one of the town's quarters, the Chinār-Sūkhtih quarter,[38] together with some people of the other quarters, flocked to hear him speak and became his followers; Nabīl gives the numbers as 1,000 persons of the Chinār-Sūkhtih quarter and 500 from other parts of Nayrīz.[39] Now, it cannot be assumed that all of those who flocked to Vaḥīd in the heat of the moment after his address in the mosque continued to follow him once it became clear that an armed conflict was inevitable and that their lives would be at stake. Nevertheless, this gives us an estimate for the population of the Chinār-Sūkhtih quarter that compares well with Lovett's statement that the town's population was 3,500 spread over three quarters.[40] By the time of the second episode, the town had become sharply polarised, with all the Bābīs living in the Chinār-Sūkhtih quarter.

---

33 Lisānu'l-Mulk, *Nāsikhu't-Tawārīkh*, quoted in Browne, *Traveller's Narrative*, vol. 2, 183.

34 H. Busse (trans.), *History of Persia under Qajar Rule* (New York, 1972), 291–92.

35 Nicolas, *Seyyèd Ali Mohammed*, 398.

36 Ibid., 422.

37 *Nabīl's Narrative*, 644

38 This quarter is named variously as "Chinār-Sūkhtih" by Nabīl, "Chinār-Shāhī" by Mīrzā Shafī' Rawḥānī, and "Mahallih-yi Bālā" by Lovett.

39 *Nabīl's Narrative*, 478–79.

40 See note 27.

From these different statements, I would be inclined to put the Bābī population of Nayrīz participating in the two upheavals at about 1,000. The number of persons that Vaḥīd brought with him to Nayrīz was insignificant beside this. There are stated to have been 72 persons,[41] of whom 20 were from Istahbānāt[42] and many of the rest from Yazd. At least 5 *'ulamā* from Istahbānāt participated in the second episode.[43]

We may safely assume, moreover, that from a sociological point of view, the followers of Vaḥīd consisted of a representative cross-section of a quarter in a small rural town.

THE ZANJĀN UPHEAVAL: 1850–51

The Bābī leader in the Zanjān episode was another man of extraordinary capacities, Mulla Muḥammad 'Alī Zanjānī. Before the rise of Babism, he had been given the title Ḥujjatu'l-Islām (the Proof of Islam), and he was later named by the Bāb, Ḥujjat. Ḥujjat's father was one of the leading *'ulamā* of Zanjān, and Ḥujjat had acquired the usual theological education with the *'ulamā* of Karbalā and Najaf before returning to Zanjān, on his father's death, in order to take up his father's position. But there was already the element of friction between Ḥujjat and the *mujtahids* of Zanjān because in 'Irāq Ḥujjat had espoused the doctrines of the anti-*mujtahid* Akhbārī school. The *'ulamā* of Zanjān complained to Muḥammad Shāh, who brought Ḥujjat to Tehran to be examined. Ḥujjat acquitted himself well before an assembly of *'ulamā* and returned to Zanjān with the king's favour. Then came the advent of Babism and Ḥujjat's enthusiastic avowal of it. This added fuel to the complaints of the *'ulamā* of Zanjān, and eventually, after a comparatively minor incident, violence broke out and the town was divided into two halves, the eastern half being in the hands of the Bābīs.

This episode lasted longer than the others, some eight months in all. Zanjān was a much larger and more important town than Nayriz, and the number of Bābī participants was greater. This time the siege ended not so much by treachery, as by the gradual attrition of the Bābīs.

Unfortunately, our sources for Zanjan are even poorer than for Nayrīz

41 *Nabīl's Narrative*, 483–84.
42 Ibid., 481.
43 Nicolas, *Seyyèd Ali Mohammed*, 415

and Shaykh Ṭabarsī. I have used *Nabīl's Narrative* and Nicolas' *Seyyèd Ali Mohammed* (both of these use the manuscript history of Ḥusayn Zanjānī, and the latter has in addition a history by Āqā Naqd-ʿAlī). I have also used Āqā ʿAbdu'l-Aḥad Zanjānī's memoirs translated by Browne. These sources yielded only sixty-eight names and very little biographical information.

Occupations of Bābī Participants at Zanjān

Table 7 gives the occupations of the Bābī participants at Zanjān.

TABLE 7. Occupations of Babi Participants at Zanjān

Occupation classification	**Number of participants**
Major ʿ*ulamā*	5[a]
Minor ʿ*ulamā*	5
Nobility, landowners, and high government officials	7[b]
Wholesale merchants (*tujjār*)	0
Retail merchants (guilded)	3
Skilled urban workers (guilded)	9
Unskilled urban workers	3
Peasantry	0
Unclassified (urban)	35
Unclassified (rural)	0
Unclassified (origin unknown)	0
TOTAL	67

a. Consists solely of Hujjat and his family.

b. Includes one physician (*ṭabīb*) and one surgeon (*jarrāḥ*), both of whom also owned property.

Origins of Bābī Participants at Zanjān

Of the sixty-eight names, all were from Zanjān barring two. One of these was from Shīrāz and one from Baku.

Total Numbers of Bābī Participants at Zanjān

As before, the Muslim Iranian sources have exaggerated the number of Bābīs present, presumably once again to make light of the inability of the shah's troops to take the town. The *Nāsikhu't-Tawārīkh* gives the grossly inflated figure of 15,000 Bābīs,[44] which is several thousand greater than the probable total population of Zanjān at this time. Nabīl estimates a total of 1,800 "martyrs"[45] with 500 women prisoners at the end of the siege,[46] and 100 women and children taken prisoner earlier in the siege;[47] a total of 2,400 which does not take into account a number of desertions from the Bābī side that were reported to have occurred. Shaykh ʿAlī Bakhsh gives the figure of 3,000 including deserters[48] and Āqā ʿAbdu'l-Aḥad states that there were 3,000, of whom about 1,000 deserted when Ḥujjat explained to them their probable fate.[49] Āqā ʿAbdu'l-Aḥad also states that there were sixty barricades with nineteen men at each barricade.[50] This would require 1,140 men, and if we assume an equal number of women were involved, a total of 2,280.

All in all, it would appear that if we take a total of 2,250 Bābī participants, excluding deserters, we would not be far wrong. In the Bābī accounts there is only slight support for the contention that there was widespread involvement of Bābīs from villages surrounding Zanjān as Ivanov has stated.[51]

From the point of view of the social background of the Bābī participants, in all probability this consisted of a representative cross-section of the population of a medium-sized Iranian town. An interesting social comment on the Bābīs of Zanjān is to be found in the history of Mīrzā Ḥusayn Zanjānī, a survivor of the episode:

44 Lisānu'l-Mulk, *Nāsikhu't-Tawārīkh*, quoted in Browne, *Traveller's Narrative*, vol. 2, 180.

45 *Nabīl's Narrative*, 580.

46 Ibid., 573.

47 Ibid., 569.

48 E. G. Browne, "Personal Reminiscences of the Bābī Insurrection at Zanjān in 1850," *Journal Royal Asiatic Society*, 19 (1897), 768.

49 Ibid., 809. *Nabīl's Narrative*, 568, also reports some desertions.

50 Browne, "Personal Reminiscences," 809.

51 Ivanov, "Babi Uprisings," 521. *Nabīl's Narrative* (550), however, describes Zaynab, the Bābī heroine of the episode, as a village maiden. Also, Joseph Ferrier, the French Agent in Tehran, in his report states that there were 6,000 Bābīs in Zanjān and triple that number in the surrounding villages. However, Ferrier's sources of information were not, in general, very good. See Momen, *Bābī and Bahā'ī Religions*, 114–126.

> And as for the Bābīs, whichever of them were of the poorer classes of the town, or the traders or the sayyids or the religious students (*ṭullāb*) or others resisted the enemy with complete constancy, and began to build fortifications. Some who were of the rich, and wealth had become a veil for them, went over to the side of the Muslims, and these were those whose place had always been at the head of the assembly or in front of the pulpit (*minbar*).[52]

THE TEHRAN EPISODES OF 1850 AND 1852

There were two major episodes in Tehran. The first, in 1850, is known as the "Seven Martyrs of Tehran" whereas the second in 1852, following an attempt on the life of the shah, was a much more serious affair involving the arrest and execution of a large number of Bābīs.

The Seven Martyrs of Tehran, 1850

In Tehran in 1850, a number of Bābīs were arrested and seven put to death. These seven are named by Nabīl as follows:[53]

1. Ḥājī Mirza Sayyid ʿAlī Shirazī, merchant (*tājir*).
2. Mīrzā Qurbān-ʿAlī Bārfurūshī, a Sufi *murshid* of the Niʿmatu'llāhī order.
3. Ḥājī Mullā Ismāʿīl Qumī, an *akhūnd*.
4. Sayyid Ḥusayn Turshīzī, a *mujtahid*.
5. Ḥājī Muḥammad Taqī Kirmānī, merchant (*tājir*).
6. Sayyid Murtaḍā Zanjānī, merchant (*tājir*).
7. Muḥammad Ḥusayn Marāghiʾī, government official.[54]

About these seven men, Browne has written, echoing the words of the authors of the *Tārīkh-i Jadīd* and the *Nuqṭatu'l-Kāf*:

52 Manuscript in private hands, 13.

53 *Nabīl's Narrative*, 446–58.

54 I have assumed that the Mīrzā Muḥammad Ḥusayn Tabrīzī mentioned in *Tārīkh-i-Jadīd* (252, 255–56, and alternate reading in note on 256) is identical to Muḥammad Ḥusayn Marāghiʿī, mentioned in *Nabīl's Narrative*, 458.

> They were men representing all the more important classes in Persia—divines, dervishes, merchants, shopkeepers, and government officials; they were men who had enjoyed the respect and consideration of all; they died fearlessly, willingly, almost eagerly, declining to purchase life by that mere lip-denial, which, under the name of *ketmān* or *taḳiya*, *is* recognised by the Shiʿites as a perfectly justified subterfuge in case of peril; they were not driven to despair of mercy as were those who died at Shaykh Ṭabarsī and Zanjān; and they sealed their faith with their blood in the public square of the Persian capital wherein is the abode of the foreign ambassadors accredited to the Shāh.[55]

Even in the geographical spread of their home towns, these seven men represented all Iran, with one of them each being from Fārs, Māzandarān, Khurāsān, Ādharbāyjān, Kirmān, Khamsih, and Qum. It would have been difficult to have picked seven men who were more representative of all that was most respected in mid-nineteenth century Iran.

The Tehran Executions of 1852

Following the disturbances of 1850, there was a period of one and a half years in which the Bābī movement appears to have become quiescent. A group of the Bābīs of Tehran, however, plotted to assassinate Nāṣiru'd-Dīn Shāh, whom they held to be responsible for the death of their leader and their comrades.

The assassination attempt failed and there ensued a large number of arrests and executions. We have been given, however, two somewhat contradictory pictures of the executions. The official government newspaper at the time, *Rūznāmih-yi Vaqāyiʿ-yi Ittifāqiyyih*, states that some thirty or forty men were arrested and most of these executed individually, some by the official executioner and some by various groups of government officials and other bodies. On the other hand, the French diplomat and writer, Arthur Comte de Gobineau, who joined the French legation in Tehran only two years after this episode, speaks of large numbers of Bābīs, including women and children marching, en masse, to their death at the hands of the official executioners.[56] There is some

55 Browne, *Traveller's Narrative*, vol. 2, 216.
56 Gobineau, *Religions*, 267.

support for Gobineau's version in a newspaper account of 400 Bābīs having been put to death.[57]

If, however, the second view is correct, it is surprising that no names or even descriptions of these other martyrdoms have been given in any Bābī, Bahā'ī or Muslim source. For this analysis, therefore, I have been compelled to rely on the thirty-five names listed in the government newspaper[58] to which I have only added the famous Bābī heroine, Ṭāhirih Qurratu'l-'Ayn. Biographical details of these individuals were obtained from various sources; in particular, the third volume of Malik-Khusravī's *Tārīkh-i Shuhadā-yi Amr.*

Occupations of the Bābīs Executed in Tehran in 1852

Table 8 (overleaf) gives the occupations and geographical distribution of the Bābīs executed in Tehran in 1852.

CONCLUSIONS

From the information accumulated, it is possible to discern the principal features of each episode. The Zanjān and Nayrīz episodes were localised urban upheavals centred on one charismatic personality who had been converted to Babism and succeeded in attracting a large proportion of the populace of the town to the new movement and thereby exciting the opposition of the *'ulamā*. There is little evidence from the various accounts of the upheavals or from the names analysed in this chapter for supposing any major degree of support among the peasantry, or any large-scale movement of Bābīs from other parts of Iran, to support their co-religionists in these two towns.

The upheaval at Shaykh Ṭabarsī was altogether of a different character. Here, with the raising of the Black Standard in Khurāsān, there was a definite challenge to the existing order. The most enthusiastic of the Bābīs from all parts of Iran came to enlist under Mullā Ḥusayn's banner.

57 *Daily News* (London) and *Morning Post* (London), 1 November 1852. This report was based on accounts published in Istanbul newspapers which in turn were based on news arriving from Tabriz. See Momen, *Bābī and Bahā'ī Religions*, 12, 134.
58 Issue no. 82, 10 Dhu'l-Qa'dih 1268 (27 August 1852), quoted in Malik-Khusravi, *Tārīkh*, vol. 3, 56–65.

TABLE 8. Occupations and Geographical Origins of the Bābīs Executed in Tehran in 1852

	Major *ʿulamā*	Minor *ʿulamā*	Nobility, landowners, and high government officials	Wholesale merchants (*tujjār*)	Retail merchants (guilded)	Skilled urban workers (guilded)	Unskilled urban workers	Peasantry	Unclassified (urban)	Unclassified (rural)	Unclassified (origin unknown)	TOTAL
Khurāsān	2	0	0	0	0	0	0	0	1	0	3	6
Māzandarān and Gīlān	0	2	2	0	0	0	0	0	0	3	0	7[a]
Ādharbayjān	0	1	0	0	0	1	1	0	0	0	0	3
Qazvīn and Khamsih	0	2	0	0	0	0	0	0	0	0	2	4
Tehran and Qum	0	1	1	0	0	0	0	0	0	0	0	2
Kāshān and Maḥallāt	0	0	0	1	1	0	0	0	0	0	0	2
Iṣfāhān	0	0	0	1	0	0	0	0	0	3	0	4
Fārs	0	1	1	0	1	0	0	0	1	1	0	5[b]
Yazd and Kirmān	0	2	0	0	0	0	0	0	0	0	0	2
Unknown	0	0	0	0	0	0	0	0	0	0	1	1
	2	9	4	2	2	1	1	0	2	7	6	36

a. Those listed for Māzandarān are persons arrested in Tākur after Mīrzā Yaḥyā's abortive attempt to instigate an uprising there to coincide with the attempted assassination of the Shāh. These were brought to Tehran and executed there.

b. Two of those from Fārs were arrested after the first Nayrīz upheaval and had been held in prison in Tehran since that time.

The attempted assassination of the Shāh may be described in contemporary terms as an act of urban terrorism planned by a small group and carried out by about twelve Bābīs in Tehran. Apart from an abortive attempt by Mīrzā Yaḥyā to incite an uprising in Tākur, Māzandarān, to coincide with the attempted assassination, there are no accounts of attacks in other parts of Iran in this period.

A Comparative Analysis

The listings presented here are not of course a representative cross-section of the Bābīs. They are almost certainly weighted in favour of the influential classes, the *ʿulamā* and merchants, and against the poorer classes.

Because the Shaykh Ṭabarsī upheaval involved the participation of Bābīs from all over Iran—persons whom we may consider as the most enthusiastic of the new community even if not representative of the whole community—and because our figures for it are more complete than for the other upheavals, it would be worthwhile to examine these figures more closely. In trying to compare these figures with those for Iran as a whole at that time, we are of course greatly hindered by the lack of information about mid-nineteenth-century Iran.

Figures for the total population of Iran at this time vary widely from Thomson's estimate of 4,400,000 (in 1867)[59] to Blau's 10,000,000 (in 1850).[60] But various writers throughout the last half of the nineteenth century were more agreed on the relative proportions of urban, rural, and nomadic peoples (see Table 9a).

The most striking difference to be noted from Table 9a is the lack of nomads among the Bābīs. If, for the time being, the nomads are excluded and the figures analysed further, Table 9b is obtained.

From Table 9b, it is clear that, if one ignores Schindler (on account of the problem outlined in note c of Table 9b), the distribution of the Bābīs at Shaykh Ṭabarsī according to whether they came from a large town, medium-sized town, small town, or village is very similar to that of the general population of Iran as estimated by Thomson (excluding the nomadic element), with perhaps a slight preponderance of those who came from medium-sized towns. In general, then, it may be said that there was no significant bias towards either urban or rural backgrounds among the Bābīs at Shaykh Ṭabarsī.

59 Thomson, *Parliamentary Papers*, vol. 69 for 1867–68, 507–15.

60 E. O. Blau, *Commerciale Zustande Persiens* (Berlin, 1858), 1.

TABLE 9a. Population of Iran Compared with the Bābīs at Shaykh Ṭabarsī

Source	Total population	Towns	Villages	Nomads
Blau, 1857[a]	10,000,000	30%	40%	30%
Thomson, 1867[b]	4,000,000	22.7%	38.6%	38.6%
Mounsey, 1870[c]	5,000,000	20%	50%	30%
Schindler, 1884[d]	7,654,000	25.6%	49.4%	24.9%
Mean		24.5%	44.5%	30.8%
Bābīs at Shaykh Ṭabarsī		43.8%	56%	0.2%

(The totals do not all add up to exactly 100% because of the rounding up and down of percentages, which has been done to avoid giving the impression that these are precise figures rather than estimates.)

a. Blau (see note 60), 1.

b. Thomson (see Source note to Table 5a).

c. A. H. Mounsey, *A Journey through the Caucasus and the interior of Persia* (London, 1872), 96–97.

d. A. H. Schindler, quoted in Mr Dickson's report. *Parliamentary Papers,* vol. 76 (for 1884–85), 7.

TABLE 9b. Population of Iran Compared with Bābīs at Shaykh Ṭabarsī (excluding nomadic tribesmen)

	Thomson, 1867[a]	Schindler, 1885[b]	Shaykh Ṭabarsī
Large towns (>22,000)	20.7%	12.9%	22.5%
Medium-sized towns (7–22,000)	10.7%	2.5%[c]	15.4%
Small towns (2–7,000)	5.5%	18.7%	5.8%
Villages	62.9%	65.9%	56%

(The totals do not all add up to exactly 100% because of the rounding up and down of percentages, which has been done to avoid giving the impression that these are precise figures rather than estimates.)

a. Calculated from Thomson (see Source note to Table 5a).

b. Calculated from Schindler (see Source note to Table 9a).

c. This is almost certainly an underestimate since Schindler does not give in his table a number of medium-sized towns such as Bārfurūsh, Sārī, Qūchān, Turshīz, etc., which would have increased this figure at the expense of small towns.

We are, unfortunately, insufficiently informed of the social structure in Iran to be able to perform a similar analysis with the data of Table 2 with respect to occupations. But in view of the fact that 37.3 per cent of the 365 persons listed by Malik-Khusravī were *ʿulamā*, one must suspect a strong bias towards this group. It has been said that the *ʿulamā* who were converted to Babism were principally the minor *ʿulamā*. However, in this group of 136 *ʿulamā* there were three *mujtahids*, and that cannot be far from the normal proportion of *mujtahids* to other clerics and *tullāb*. It would be true to say, however, that the leadership among the Bābīs was vested in the minor *ʿulamā* group to a large extent, although even here, Ḥujjat and Vaḥīd were major religious leaders.

The Role of Women

Most accounts of Babism are agreed that one of its major social thrusts was towards an amelioration of the social position of women. The Bāb himself does not seem to have written a great deal on this theme, apart from forbidding temporary marriage, restricting the number of wives that a man may have to two, and allowing men and women to mix socially to a limited extent.[61] However, the proceedings of the famous Bābī heroine, Ṭāhirih (Qurratu'l-ʿAyn) and in particular her symbolic act in discarding the veil at the conference of Badasht, as well as the evident approval of her actions by the Bāb, would indicate that this was a basic feature of the Bābī movement.

There were no women among the Bābīs at Shaykh Tabarsi and this is not surprising in view of the circumstances of the siege. At Zanjān and Nayrīz, however, the women played an important role. During the Zanjān episode, the British consul, Keith Abbott, visited the scene of the operations and reported to Sir Justin Sheil, the British minister: "They [the Bābīs] fight in the most obstinate and spirited manner, the women even, of whom several have been killed, engaging in the strife."[62]

It was during the Zanjān upheaval that a latter-day Joan of Arc arose in the person of Zaynab, a young Bābī girl who donned the apparel of the men and participated in the fighting with such courage and success that she

---

61 Persian Bayān (F12 and F13, Browne Collection, Cambridge University Library; references given as *vāḥid:bāb*), 6:7, 8:15, 8:10, respectively.

62 Abbott to Sheil, 30 August 1850, enclosed in Sheil to Palmerston, 5 September 1850, FO 60 153, in Momen, *Bābī and Bahāʾī Religions*, 11.

soon became the terror of the royal troops and was put in command of one section of the Bābī defences.[63]

At Nayrīz also, the women played an important part, Nabīl records: "The uproar caused by their [the Bābīs] womenfolk, their amazing audacity and self-confidence, utterly demoralized their opponents and paralysed their efforts."[64] It would seem that in the second Nayrīz upheaval, the Bābī women outnumbered the men, whose ranks had been thinned by the first episode.

Other Social Groups

It is worth recording here the absence from the Bābī lists of any persons from the main religious minorities: Christians, Jews, and Zoroastrians.[65]

We have already noted the almost complete absence of any of the nomadic tribesmen who formed a large part of the country's population. Indeed, there does not seem to have been any effort made by the Bābīs themselves to reach this part of the population. There is also what some may regard as a surprising sparsity of Sufi *darvishes* in the Bābī lists—only two at Shaykh Ṭabarsī and one of the "Seven Martyrs of Ṭehran."[66] In this context, it is interesting to note that according to the Bābī historian Sayyid Muhammad Ḥusayn Mahjūr Zavāri'ī, when Lutf-ʿAlī Mīrzā joined Mullā Ḥusayn Bushrū'ī's party dressed in the garb of a *darvīsh*, he was instructed by Mullā Ḥusayn to change his clothing.[67]

---

63 *Nabīl's Narrative*, 549–52.

64 Ibid., 487.

65 Baha'i sources mention a single Zoroastrian in Kāshān and a few Jews in Hamadan who became a Bābīs (see M. Momen, *The Baha'i Communities of Iran, 1851–1921: Volume 2: The South of Iran*, Oxford, forthcoming; see chapters on Kashan and Hamadan). But the reference in one source to twenty-five or thirty families having become Bābīs in Shīrāz is due to an error, see M. Momen, "Early Relations between Christian Missionaries and the Bābī and Bahā'ī Communities," in *Studies in Bábí and Bahá'í History*, vol. 1 (ed. M. Momen, Los Angeles: Kalimat Press, 1982), 49–82; see 79 n. 8.

66 At Nayriz, there was a man who is just named as "Darvīsh" (Shafī-Rawḥānī, *Lamaʿātu'l-Anwār*, 293). Similarly, Nicolas records the name of a man called Mashhadi Darvish (*Seyyèd Ali Mohammed*, 414).

67 Manuscript F28, Browne Collection, Cambridge University Library, 12.

The Social Basis of Babism

If we now turn our attention to the various statements made by Ivanov, Kazemi, and others, as noted previously, we can examine these statements in the light of the facts that have been presented.

Taking into consideration the fact that the classes indicated by Ivanov as constituting the bulk of the Bābī movement (peasants, artisans, urban poor, and small tradesmen) must also have represented the vast majority of the population of Iran at this time, one can find little evidence to support Ivanov's ideas. Although one would agree with Ivanov that leadership of the movement was vested in the minor *ʿulamā*, one is forced to point out that quite apart from the leadership, a good part of the following was of the same category. Although the Bāb himself was a member of a mercantile family, there is little evidence that merchants whether wholesale (*tujjār*) or retail played a prominent role. All in all, Bausani seems to be nearer the mark when he writes: "The Bab's followers were drawn not only from the lower classes and the growing middle class of traders, but even from the aristocracy."[68]

Much of Ivanov's thesis is based on an obscure and difficult passage in the *Nuqṭatu'l-Kāf*[69] in which, according to Ivanov's interpretation, Mullā Muḥammad ʿAlī Quddūs Bārfurūshī addresses the Bābīs gathered at the Conference of Badasht, saying that the "old order had died away and the believers were freed of the old duties,"[70] that property was usurpation, and whoever was willing to renounce it was relieved of the obligation to pay taxes.[71] On a closer examination of the text, however, it would seem that there are no grounds for even asserting that this passage represents a speech made by Mullā Muḥammad ʿAlī (rather than one of the lengthy and obscure digressions which the author of the *Nuqṭatu'l-Kāf* frequently makes). Although it cannot be denied that Mullā Muḥammad ʿAlī was of peasant origin, his theological training at Mashhad and Karbalā would have tended to make him identify with the *ʿulamā* rather than the peasants, and certainly whatever is extant of his writings confirms this view of him as one of the *ʿulamā* concerned with theological issues rather than a peasant

68 A. Bausani, *The Persians* (London, 1971), 166.
69 145–53. See also Browne's comment on this passage, *Tārīkh-i-Jadīd*, 356–57.
70 Minorsky's review, 880.
71 Ibid.

revolutionary concerned with social ones.[72] Even in the case of Ṭāhirih, who is usually thought of as a champion of women's advancement, there is little evidence of such preoccupations in her writings.[73] She would first and foremost appear to have been a zealous advocate of the Bāb's religious claims and only secondarily a social reformer.

Ivanov refers to the effect that the West may have had as a catalyst in promoting Babism. He refers to the Bābī upheavals as a popular rising against feudalism and enslavement to foreign capital.[74] The main groups feeling the effects of the West in Iran at this time were the craftsmen and artisans who were being deprived of their livelihood by the influx of Western manufactured goods; the wholesale merchants who were increasingly unable to compete with the Western merchants (who were backed by powerful consular authorities); and, to a lesser extent at this stage, the peasant classes who were being forced into greater poverty by the increasing demand by landlords for payment in cash rather than in goods.[75]

Although it is true that there was a group of craftsmen and artisans at Shaykh Ṭabarsī and, in particular, a group of eighteen who came from Iṣfahān, the latter represented less than half of the total number coming from Iṣfahān (forty-two) and even then, nine of them were builders (*bannā*) whose livelihood could hardly have been affected by Western competition. If the resentment of craftsmen and artisans was an important factor in the Bābī upheavals, one would have expected a much larger number of such persons from the important manufacturing towns of Iṣfahān, Kāshān, Yazd, Hamadān, and Shīrāz. Moreover, one may have expected Bābī disturbances in these towns.[76] We have already noted that

72 Manuscript F43, Browne Collection, Cambridge University Library; mss. Or. 5110 and Or. 6256, Oriental Manuscripts, British Library. F43 and Or. 5110 are the same work, which appears to be a series of discourses or possibly letters. Or. 6256 is an incomplete copy of the same work.

73 See letters by her in Browne, *Tārīkh-i-Jadīd*, 434–41, and in Fāḍil Māzandarānī, *Ẓuhūru'l-Ḥaqq*, vol. 3, 484–532; also her poetry in E. G. Browne, *Materials for the Study of the Bābī Religion* (Cambridge, 1918), 343–51.

74 Ivanov, "Babi Uprisings," 521.

75 See N. Keddie, *Historical Obstacles to Agrarian Change* (Claremont, 1950), 4–7. Also quoted in Issawi, *Economic History*, 54–57.

76 Indeed, there were disturbances in these towns completely unconnected with the Bābī movement. There were disturbances in Isfahān connected with Ahmad Mirza Safavi (see H. Algar, *Religion and State in Iran* [Berkeley: 1969], 126–28); in Yazd, connected with Muḥammad ʿAbdu'llāh who only became a Bābī in the last few months of his life, having led an urban uprising that went on for several years; in Mashhad, the Sālār was in revolt against the Qājārs and was in receipt of

there was no large-scale participation by the merchant class who, in any case, as Kazemi has pointed out,[77] had little to gain and much to lose by joining the Bābīs. Although it is true that a number of peasants and villagers joined the Bābīs at Shaykh Ṭabarsī, this seems to have been more at the instigation of a local religious leader who had been converted to Babism rather than out of a desire for social reform. This was certainly the case at Bushrūyih, Sangsar, and Shahmīrzād, while the case of Bihnamīr is even more remarkable in that the forty or more persons from the village who joined the Bābīs at Shaykh Ṭabarsī did so under the leadership of the local landowner, Āqā Rasūl Bihnamīrī, and therefore could hardly be regarded as peasants "rising against feudalism"[78] as Ivanov would have them.

It should be noted, by way of a parenthesis at this point, that although the Bābīs were frequently accused by government and religious sources (and the Europeans in Iran who usually reflected these sources)[79] of being communists and preaching anarchy, immorality, and the community of property and even of wives, these accusations should not be taken too seriously as there is in Iran almost a tradition of accusing any heterodox movement of holding these views. The Ismāʿīlīs and the Mazdakites were similarly accused.[80] As Gobineau has pointed out:

> It is a type of accusation made respectable by its antiquity, and one may perhaps regard it as the mark of the oldest religious hatred in the world... It was used against the Ophites [a Christian Gnostic sect], the Carmatians [Qarmaṭīs], the disciples of Mani, and others; the Muslims have used it against the Nuṣayrīs and, as we see, against the Bābīs. Thus, generalised this argument loses its value, and after one reads the laws of His Sublime Highness [the Bāb], it becomes evident that we must consider it simply as an insult.[81]

---

considerable assistance from the townspeople; on the death of Muḥammad Shāh, there were disturbances in a number of urban centres including Shīrāz, Kirmānshāh, Tabrīz, and even in Tehran.

77 Kazemi, "Preliminary Observations," 130–31.

78 Ivanov, "Babi Uprisings," 521.

79 See dispatches of Sheil and Dolgoruki and other European sources, quoted in Momen, *Bābī and Bahāʾī Religions*, 4–8, 44–45.

80 Bausani, *The Persians*, 98.

81 Gobineau, *Religions*, 313.

With regard to the accusation of community of property among the Bābīs, there would seem to be some justification for this. Thus, in Āqā ʿAbdu'l-Aḥad's account of the Zanjān upheaval there is the following:

> After this His Holiness the Martyr [Mullā Muḥammad ʿAlī Zanjānī Ḥujjat] commanded his followers that they should all be as one family and one household, and that all things, from eatables to clothing, whatever there was, should be divided for use; and his followers did even as he commanded so that they even opened their houses to one another, and passed in and out in unity and concord.[82]

Similarly, the Bābīs in Shaykh Tabarsi are reported to have pooled their money in order to pay for food which was then prepared and served to all.[83] But these actions were taken under extreme circumstances at a time when hostilities had become inevitable and cannot therefore be taken as representing normal policy. With respect to this moreover, Curzon has commented:

> Nor does there seem to be any greater justice in the charges of socialism, communism, and immorality, that have been so freely levelled at the youthful persuasion. Certainly, no such idea as communism in the European sense, i.e., a forcible redistribution of property, or as socialism in the nineteenth century sense, i.e., the defeat of capital by labour, ever entered the brain of the Bāb or his disciples. The only communism known to and recommended by him was that of the New Testament and the early Christian Church, viz., the sharing of goods in common by members of the faith, and the exercise of alms-giving, and an ample charity. The charge of immorality seems to have arisen partly from the malignant inventions of opponents, partly from the much greater freedom claimed for women by the Bāb, which in the Oriental mind is scarcely dissociable from profligacy of conduct.[84]

Gobineau has written of the Bāb having come into contact with Jews and Christians in his youth,[85] while Keddie states that "the Bāb was probably

82 Browne, "Personal Reminiscences," 793.

83 Malik-Khusravī, *Tārīkh*, vol. 1, 171–76.

84 G. N. Curzon, *Persia and the Persian Question* (2 vols., London. 1892); see vol. 1, 501–2.

85 Gobineau, *Religions*, 134.

influenced by Christian ideas."[86] It would seem to me that there was very little opportunity for the Bāb to come into any significant contact with the West. Although the redoubtable Christian missionary, Henry Martyn, had visited Shīrāz in 1811, there were no resident Europeans there from that time until the 1860s. It is true that the Bāb was for a number of years in Būshihr, where there was a British Resident of the East India Company. But at this time the staff at the Residency was very small and there is no evidence that the Bāb had direct dealings with them. Similarly, it is doubtful whether any of the other disciples of the Bāb had any contact with Europeans in this period when there had not as yet developed the widespread presence of European consuls, missionaries and merchants that characterised Iran towards the end of the nineteenth century.[87] Nor with the lack of printing facilities in Iran, was there yet any opportunity for the diffusion of European ideas by this means. Although it is tempting to look to the widespread revolutionary ferment in Europe, which came to a climax in 1848, for parallels with the Bābī movement, the vast mass of Iranians at this time were totally unaware of what was happening in Europe and completely unaffected by the revolutionary propaganda.

We can find little in our analysis to support Avery's contention of there being an element of the protest of the south against the north in the Bābī upheavals. By far, the largest groups in the Shaykh Ṭabarsī episode were from Khurāsān and Māzandarān as may be expected from the fact that Mullā Ḥusayn began his march from Khurāsān and ended it in Māzandarān. Moreover, of the other two upheavals, Nayrīz was in the south, but the larger and more prolonged Zanjān upheaval was in the north.

86 Keddie, "Religion and Irreligion," 268–69.

87 The American Protestant missionaries who arrived in 1834 confined their work to the Nestorian Christian villages around Lake Urmiyyih. They therefore had almost no impact on the Muslim majority until 1872 when the Tehran mission was set up and work among Muslims begun. The Iranian historian Firaydūn Ādamiyyat wrote in the early editions of his book *Amīr Kabīr va Īrān* (see for example the 2nd edition, Tehran, 1323/1944, 243–44) that the Bābī movement was concocted during a meeting between the British agent and traveller Arthur Conolly and Mullā Ḥusayn Bushrū'ī. Adamiyyat gives as his source for this assertion Conolly's book, *Journey to the North of India Overland from England through Russia, Persia and Affghaunistaun* (2 vols., London, 1834). However, one can read both volumes of this book from cover to cover without finding a single mention of Mullā Ḥusayn or Babism or anything that might reasonably be said to be an allusion to this episode. After being challenged by the Iranian historian Mojtaba Monovi, Adamiyyat removed this passage from later editions of his book.

What then can be said about the social basis of Babism from our analysis? We know that the Bābī doctrine was spread through Iran principally by the eighteen "Letters of the Living" who were all minor *ʿulamā*, having been students of Sayyid Kāẓim Rashtī, the Shaykhī leader. The "Letters of the Living" and other emissaries of the Bāb moved from town to town and village to village, in each place converting a few persons. Those converted to Babism were drawn from all social classes with a preponderance from the *ʿulamā*, who also provided the leadership of the movement. The manner of preaching varied from one emissary to another. Some would teach the new religion cautiously and secretively, whereas others, particularly after about the year 1847, taught the new religion openly and even from the *minbar* (pulpit).

In most places, only a handful of persons would be converted to the new religion, but occasionally there would occur the conversion of a large number of people in one town and this was usually due to the conversion of an important local figure, often one of the leading *ʿulamā*, who would bring in those who followed him in religious matters. This is what happened in Zanjān where Mullā Muḥammad ʿAlī's conversion led to about one-quarter of the town becoming Bābīs; and also in Nayrīz where the conversion of Ḥājī Shaykh ʿAbdu'l-ʿAlī, a judge (*qāḍī*) and Friday prayer leader (*Imām-Jumʿih*) of the Chinār-Sūkhtih quarter, as well as the fame and influence of Vaḥīd, his son-in-law, led to the conversion of about one-third of the town. These were the two largest towns in which such a course of events occurred, and as we know, a violent upheaval ensued in each case. In some other smaller places, a similar phenomenon occurred. In Sangsar and Shahmīrzād, the conversion of the prominent local religious leader, Āqā Sayyid Aḥmad, caused the conversion of a large number of persons. In Bihnamīr, by contrast, it was as a result of the conversion of a local landowner, Āqā Rasūl, that a large number of persons was converted.

Although it seems probable that there was at this time great social and economic dislocation in Iran, and this undoubtedly induced a spirit of turmoil which would facilitate the spread of any new message, the message brought by the emissaries of the Bāb seems to have been primarily a religious one rather than a social one. The conversions that occurred would appear to have been more on the basis of a conviction in the Bāb's divine inspiration and an acceptance of his claim of fulfilling prophecy rather than out of enthusiasm for a programme of social reform or by way of social protest. The majority of Bābīs inclined to this religious element, and this includes the most important leaders of the Bābīs and, of course, the Bāb himself. Even the armed conflicts which occurred at Shaykh Ṭabarsī, Nayrīz, and Zanjān would seem to be considered by the Bābīs who participated in them either as the necessary fulfilment of prophecies associated with the advent of the Hidden Imām Mahdī or as measures of self-defence against the attacks of their enemies, but only to a very minor extent as a means of bringing about political or social reform.

There were a few persons, however, who joined the Bābī movement as a means of overturning the existing state of affairs and introducing a new social order. The author of the *Nuqṭatu'l-Kāf* may have been one such person with his reference to the renunciation of property and abolition of taxes as well as his abusive references to the Qājārs. Another such person was the Yazdī *Lūṭī-garī* (gang) leader, Muḥammad ʿAbdu'llāh who had been in revolt against the government for a number of years before adopting Babism. It would seem that this minority revolutionary-reformist strain in Babism continued into the second half of the nineteenth century as the Azalī branch. Mīrzā Yaḥyā Azal had himself been of a revolutionary turn of mind. He was closely involved in the plot to assassinate Nāṣiru'd-Dīn Shāh in 1852, and just before this plot was implemented, he had left for his native Tākur in Māzandarān to organise a simultaneous Bābī uprising in that region. The Azalīs were later to produce such notable reformists and constitutionalist figures as Shaykh Aḥmad Rūḥī, Mīrzā Āqā Khān Kirmānī, and Mīrzā Yaḥyā Dawlatābādī. There was a tendency in the Azalī branch to become further and further removed from religious matters and such figures as Shaykh Aḥmad Rūḥī and Mīrzā Āqā Khān Kirmānī were openly atheistic in their later writings.[88]

The majority of Bābīs, who as we have noted were mainly concerned with religious matters, went on in later years to become followers of Mīrzā Ḥusayn ʿAlī Bahā'u'llāh, who was himself much opposed to violence and armed conflict as a means of advancing the new religion. One of his first acts when later assuming leadership of the movement was to forbid religious warfare (*jihād*). The fact that the Bābīs who became Bahā'īs were quite content to lay aside their weapons and no further uprising occurred despite the growth of the movement, is a further indication that the majority of the Bābīs were not motivated by considerations of revolt or social reform. The Bahā'īs became increasingly removed from political activity and more concerned with religious issues.

88 M. Bayat, *Mysticism and Dissent: Socioreligious Thought in Qajar Iran* (Syracuse, 1982).

7

The Babi–State Conflicts of 1848–50[1]

SIYAMAK ZABIHI-MOGHADDAM

Abstract: Mid-nineteenth-century Iran was the scene of four clashes between the Babis and the Qajar state, in which several thousand Babis and government troops and irregulars died. Drawing on eyewitness accounts and other primary sources, this chapter challenges the common depiction of these events as Babi uprisings aimed at subverting the ruling dynasty. As the Babi religion spread, the clerical establishment's opposition to the movement and tensions between the Babis and hostile elements in the surrounding Muslim community grew. In a context of political instability, the central government moved to suppress the Babis, whom it blamed for the disturbance of public order. During the early years of the movement, unlike later, the community responded to attacks with defensive warfare. This chapter investigates the circumstances of the conflicts that occurred between 1848 and 1850 and offers an analysis of the objectives of the Babi participants as reflected in the sources.

1 Part of this chapter was first published in Siyamak Zabihi-Moghaddam, "The Babi-State Conflict at Shaykh Tabarsi," *Iranian Studies*, vol. 35, nos. 1–3 (2002), 87–112.

Between 1848 and 1853, Iran was the scene of four major clashes between the Babis and the Qajar state. These clashes unfolded in Mazandaran (1848–49), Zanjan (1850–51), and Nayriz (1850, 1853). They resulted in the deaths of at least 2,700 Babis and many more government troops and irregulars. They shaped in significant ways and for years to come the authorities' views of the Babi movement and later the Baha'i community. The outbreak of hostilities in Nayriz and Zanjan in 1850 in the wake of the Mazandaran episode was responsible for the authorities' decision to execute the Bab. His death and the killing of a large number of his followers, including many leading figures, dealt a severe blow to the Babi movement and contributed to its almost entire collapse by the mid-1850s.[2]

This chapter investigates the circumstances of the first three Babi–state conflicts and offers an analysis of the objectives of the Babi participants. The Babis' clashes with government forces are often described as "uprisings" or "insurrections" and are perceived as a series of unsuccessful attempts by the Babis to subvert the ruling dynasty. This view is reflected in the contemporary sources—most importantly official Qajar chronicles and Western diplomatic reports—and has since been adopted by many scholars. It does not, however, rest on a careful examination and analysis of the available evidence. To understand these conflicts and to find meaningful interpretations of the Babis' objectives, it is necessary to establish what happened and examine how the Babi participants themselves understood their circumstances and their own actions.

Multiple accounts of these conflicts produced by different parties are available, making it possible to reconstruct the course of the events and assess the objectives of the Babis fairly reliably. The Babi, Baha'i, and Azali primary sources are particularly relevant in this regard. They are the most detailed of the existing sources, include several eyewitness accounts, and, crucially, reflect the Babi participants' perceptions of their situation and intentions.

Based on a careful study of the primary sources, the following observations may be made concerning the Babis' objectives. In the case of the Mazandaran episode, a group of Babis traveling through the province was attacked and found themselves trapped. They determined to fight a

2 For the Babi movement in general, see Abbas Amanat, *Resurrection and Renewal: The Making of the Babi Movement in Iran, 1844–1850* (Ithaca; London: Cornell University Press, 1989).

defensive war as a testimony to the truth of their cause. In Nayriz, when a prominent Babi with many supporters among the townspeople disregarded the governor's order not to enter the town, the latter gathered an army and attacked the Babis, triggering the conflict. The Babis were willing to fight the governor's forces, but they had had no plans to oust him or seize control of the town. In Zanjan, it was the governor's failed attempt to arrest the leader of the large local Babi community that sparked the hostilities. The governor ordered the town to be divided into opposing camps and launched a war against the Babis. The Zanjani Babis responded with strictly defensive warfare and had no intention of seizing power. In none of these conflicts, which were confined to small localities, did the Babi participants aspire to set up an alternative, Babi rule to replace the established government.

Among the Babi–state clashes, the Mazandaran episode at the shrine of Shaykh Tabarsi marked a turning point in the history of the Babi movement. It was the first time that the state, hitherto content with incarcerating the Bab in a remote corner of the country, began to actively suppress the Babis. The death of Muhammad Shah and the accession to power of Nasir al-Din Shah and his premier Mirza Taqi Khan Amir Kabir were crucial for this change of policy. In addition, being the first of the Babi–state clashes, the struggle of Tabarsi influenced the developments that led to the later battles. Following the Shaykh Tabarsi episode, the state acted more swiftly and forcefully against the Babis when hostilities erupted in Nayriz and Zanjan.

In the long history of government sanctioned violence toward the Babi and Baha'i communities, which continues to this day, it is only in this early period that the members of the community responded by fighting back. By the mid-1860s Baha'u'llah had publicly claimed to be the *man yuẓhiruhu'llāh* ("He whom God shall make manifest")—the messianic figure foretold by the Bab. The large majority of the Iranian Babis accepted his claim. Even before then, Baha'u'llah had become the de facto leader of the Babi community and had bent his energies to transforming their outlook and behavior. From the mid-1850s on, Baha'u'llah repeatedly condemned the use of violence and advocated that the only legitimate way to promote the religion of God was through persuasion by arguments and adherence to an ethical code of conduct. Later, as the founder of a new religion, Baha'u'llah emphasized, in addition to strict nonviolence, obedience to temporal authorities and shunning of political strife.

BABI CLASHES WITH THE STATE: NEITHER SOCIAL PROTEST NOR OFFENSIVE HOLY WAR

Some scholars have argued that the Babi movement was essentially a social protest "directed against the ruling class."[3] They have linked its emergence to economic strains generated under the impact of the West. Available evidence, however, does not substantiate this view. A study of the social background of the Babis involved in the clashes with the state does not indicate any large representation of peasants or urban craftsmen and artisans—the groups that would have been most affected by economic strains.[4] We have information about the social and occupational background of about half the Babi participants in the Shaykh Tabarsi conflict and know that a significant number of them belonged to the 'ulama' class.[5] We know less about those that were involved in the first Nayriz conflict and even less about the participants in the Zanjan battle. In all probability, the Babis in the latter locality represented a cross-section of the town's inhabitants and in the former a cross-section of one of the town's quarters.[6] Given the available information about the Babi participants, it is difficult to argue that these upheavals were rooted in socio-economic factors. In general, the picture that emerges from the accounts of these conflicts penned by the Babi eyewitnesses themselves or later Baha'i and Azali chroniclers reveals the deep religious concerns of the Babi actors.

Some scholars have emphasized the religious, as opposed to socio-economic, grounds for the Babi upheavals, but have nevertheless interpreted them as Babi rebellions against the Qajar state. Browne writes that the Babis aimed to replace Qajar rule with a Babi theocracy in the

3 V. Minorsky, "M. S. Ivanov: *The Babi Risings in Iran in 1848–1852*, Trudi of the Oriental Institute of the Academy of Sciences of the USSR, vol. 30, Moscow 1939," *Bulletin of the School of Oriental and African Studies*, vol. 11 (1946), 878. See also Kurt Greussing, "The Babi Movement in Iran 1844–52: From Merchant Protest to Peasant Revolution," in János M. Bak, Gerhard Benecke, eds., *Religion and Rural Revolt* (Manchester: Manchester University Press, 1984), 256–69.

4 See Moojan Momen, "The Social Basis of the Bābī Upheavals in Iran (1848–53): A Preliminary Analysis," *International Journal of Middle East Studies*, vol. 15, no. 2 (1983), 157–83. This article is reprinted in the present volume. Momen has discussed Ivanov's study, but many of the points he raises apply equally to Greussing's article.

5 In addition to the article by Momen, see Amanat on the structure of the Babi community in Chapter 3 of the present volume.

6 Momen, "Social Basis of the Bābī Upheavals," 169–70.

immediate future and to establish a reign of the saints.[7] Algar sees the Babi movement as a heresy of Shiʿi origin that sought to overthrow orthodoxy by force. He maintains that the Babi rebellion began in the summer of 1848, when Mulla Husayn-i-Bushru'i, the Bab's most renowned disciple, marched toward Mazandaran at the head of a band of Babis.[8] MacEoin has proposed the view that "[b]etween 1847 and 1850, following the Bāb's announcement that he himself was the Qā'im, his followers took up arms to begin the last crusade or share in the messianic woes in the hope of hastening the final restitution of things."[9] Like Browne, MacEoin states that the Babis intended to establish a "Bābī theocracy" and "the immediate rule of the saints on earth."[10] He links the clashes between the Babis and the state to a Babi concept of an "offensive" jihad, but maintains that at Shaykh Tabarsi and in Nayriz and Zanjan, the Babis proclaimed a "defensive" jihad against the Qajar state and its forces.[11] He also suggests that the Babis attempted unsuccessfully to transform these local upheavals into "a more widely-based revolutionary struggle against the forces of unbelief," and he gives a number of factors for their failure.[12] In sum, he argues that the Babis, because of their views concerning the coming of the Qa'im, who, according to prevailing Shiʿi beliefs, was expected to usher in the final battle between the forces of good and evil, and because of the

7 Edward G. Browne, *Materials for the Study of the Bábí Religion* (Cambridge: Cambridge University Press, 1918), xv; idem, ed. and trans., *The Táríkh-i-Jadíd or New History of Mírzá 'Alí Muḥammad the Báb* (Cambridge: Cambridge University Press, 1893), xvi. This idea was proposed as early as 1850s. Lady Sheil maintained that the "real doctrine" of the religion of the Bab was the "reign of the Saints" (Lady Mary L. Sheil, *Glimpses of Life and Manners in Persia: With Notes on Russia, Koords, Toorkomans, Nestorians, Khiva, and Persia* [London: John Murray, 1856], 179). The notion may well have originated with her husband, Justin Sheil, the British Minister in Tehran. In his dispatch of 12 February 1850, Justin Sheil wrote: "The votaries of this sect consider that their own supremacy has been decreed, and that to the Saints it is lawful to acquire by whatever means the wealth and goods of the Ungodly" (quoted in Moojan Momen, *The Bábí and Bahá'í Religions, 1844–1944: Some Contemporary Western Accounts* [Oxford: George Ronald, 1981], 5).

8 Hamid Algar, *Religion and State in Iran, 1785–1906: The Role of the Ulama in the Qajar Period* (Berkeley; Los Angeles: University of California Press, 1969), 144.

9 Denis MacEoin, "From Babism to Baha'ism: Problems of Militancy, Quietism, and Conflation in the Construction of a Religion," *Religion*, vol. 13, no. 3 (1983), 222.

10 Denis MacEoin, "Bahā'ī Fundamentalism and the Academic Study of the Bābī Movement," *Religion*, vol. 16, no. 1 (1986), 70; idem, "From Babism to Baha'ism," 222.

11 Denis MacEoin, "Babism," *Encyclopædia Iranica*; idem, "The Babi Concept of Holy War," *Religion*, vol. 12, no. 2 (1982), 121.

12 "Babi Concept of Holy War," 121. Cf. idem, "Babism," 316; idem, "Bahā'ī Fundamentalism," 70. MacEoin's discussion of the circumstances of the Babi upheavals is tendentious. In the following sections, a few examples are discussed.

Bab's statements on jihad, actively sought to provoke confrontations with the Qajar state and the 'ulama'—the main representatives of the forces of evil in their eyes.

Since the publication of MacEoin's articles, Saiedi has carried out a more thorough and comprehensive study of jihad in the writings of the Bab.[13] Moreover, he has examined this theme in the context of the Bab's entire religious system. He argues persuasively that "although the Báb did not formally and explicitly abrogate holy war, He effectively eliminated it within His Dispensation."[14] Saiedi's discussion is not confined to jihad but includes all the severe laws regarding non-believers found in the Persian Bayān, the most important of the Bab's later writings, the composition of which began in late 1847. He rests his argument on three significant and related observations. He notes that the Bab's later statements clearly show that only a Babi king had authority to enforce the severe laws of the Bayān, including jihad. He then shows that those laws could only be enforced after the cause of the Bab had been "exalted," which, as envisaged by the Bab, would happen at the advent of Him Whom God Shall Make Manifest, the bearer of a new divine revelation whose coming is promised in the writings of the Bab.[15] Finally, Saiedi notes that the Bab also attached certain stipulations to his severe laws, making their implementation conditional on logically impossible conditions.[16]

It is also relevant to note that the many references to the theme of jihad in the early writings of the Bab as, for example, the injunction in the Qayyūm al-Asmā' regarding the believers purchasing arms in expectation of a struggle, were intended to establish the Bab's religious authority in the eyes of his primarily Shi'i audience and were, therefore, in conformity with common Shi'i beliefs concerning the Qa'im. The Bab deliberately modeled the concept of jihad in the Qayyūm al-Asmā' and in other works

13 Nader Saiedi, *Gate of the Heart: Understanding the Writings of the Báb* (Waterloo, Ont.: Wilfrid Laurier University Press, 2008), chapter 14.

14 Ibid., 368.

15 It is relevant here to note that the Bab also clearly stated that all his laws would be subject to the approval of Him Whom God Shall Make Manifest. Baha'u'llah, whom the large majority of the Babis accepted as the promised one of the religion of the Bab, abrogated jihad altogether when he declared to be Him Whom God Shall Make Manifest.

16 *Gate of the Heart*, 362–67. For jihad in the Bab's writings, see also Saiedi (Chapter 2) and Eschraghi (Chapter 8) in this volume.

written before the Persian Bayān on the Shiʿi concept of jihad.[17] In a later work, the Dalā'il-i-Sab'ih, the Bab clarifies that, in the Qayyūm al-Asmā', he enjoined the observance of the laws of the Qur'an, so that his audience "might regard His Faith as similar to their own, perchance they would not turn away from the Truth..."[18]

The argument that the Babis intended to establish a "Bābī theocracy" through a "holy war" is primarily based on references to Babi kings in the Bab's "later" writings, most importantly the Persian Bayān.[19] As noted, however, these same writings, in effect, precluded the possibility of waging an offensive jihad on several accounts, including the fact that a Babi king had to be in power before offensive jihad could be waged. There are no provisions in the Bayān for rank-and-file Babis, without a Babi king, to declare offensive jihad. Neither are there provisions for the Babis to wage a jihad in order to put a Babi king into power.

Not only did the Bab effectively preclude the possibility of an offensive jihad in his later writings, he also never issued a call to wage jihad to overthrow the Qajar regime, even after Muhammad Shah's "rebuff of the Báb's summons to become his follower and the commencement of sustained persecution of the Babis."[20]

After examining the issue of jihad in the Bab's writings, we can now turn to the question of the objectives of the Babis who were involved in the upheavals of 1848–50. To address this question, all the available primary sources, most importantly the Babi-Baha'i accounts, will be utilized. Before embarking on an analysis of the events and circumstances around the Babi–state conflicts, however, it is useful to review the primary sources.

---

17 MacEoin notes that the concept of jihad in the Qayyūm al-Asmā' and other works written before the Persian Bayān resembles the Shiʿi concept of jihad, but he does not mention the Bab's explanation that it was so by design ("Babi Concept of Holy War," 107).

18 The Bab, *Dalā'il-i-Sab'ih* (n.p., n.d.), 29; idem, *Selections from the Writings of the Báb* (Haifa: Bahá'í World Centre, 1978), 119.

19 See MacEoin, "Bahā'ī Fundamentalism," 70.

20 Peter Smith and William P. Collins, "Babi and Baha'i Millennialism," in Catherine Wessinger, ed., *The Oxford Handbook of Millennialism* (Oxford; New York: Oxford University Press, 2011), 480. MacEoin is well aware of this fact and attempts to explain it by suggesting that offensive jihad was not declared "probably because it was regarded as wrong to declare a holy war unless there was a reasonable chance of success—a condition clearly lacking in the case of the Bābīs" ("Babi Concept of Holy War," 121). The Bab's later writings make it clear, however, that offensive holy war could not be declared, whatever the conditions.

REVIEW OF THE PRIMARY SOURCES OF THE BABI UPHEAVALS

The struggle of Shaykh Tabarsi is the best-documented of all the Babi–state clashes. The most important sources are the Babi and Baha'i accounts by three survivors of the event, Lutf-'Ali Mirzay-i-Shirazi, Mir Abu-Talib-i-Shahmirzadi, and Haji Nasir-i-Qazvini. These accounts were written independently of each other. Less important, but still valuable, is the history by Mahjur-i-Zavari'i, an early Babi chronicle of the event. A document of singular importance about this event is the edict of Nasir al-Din Shah to the governor of Mazandaran.[21]

The major sources for the first Nayriz conflict are the late Baha'i eyewitness account by Mulla Muhammad-Shafi'-i-Nayrizi, who was only a small

21 Of the three eyewitness accounts of the Tabarsi struggle, Lutf-'Ali Mirzay-i-Shirazi's chronicle is the earliest and most extensive (Untitled history, n.d., Browne Manuscripts, Or. F. 28, item 3, Cambridge University Library, Cambridge). The author was executed in 1852. His chronicle was therefore written within three years and three months of the conclusion of the Mazandaran episode. Mir Abu-Talib-i-Shahmirzadi's narrative was written much later, but before 1888 (Untitled history, n.d., uncatalogued photocopy of autograph manuscript, Afnan Library, Sandy, Bedfordshire). Haji Nasir-i-Qazvini's eyewitness account is much shorter than the other two ("Tārīkh-i-janāb-i-Ḥājī Naṣīr-i-Shahīd," in 'Abd al-'Ali 'Ala'i, ed., *Tārīkh-i-Samandar va Mulḥaqqāt* [Tehran: Mu'assasiy-i-Millīy-i-Maṭbū'āt-i-Amrī, 131 B.E./1974–5], 499–520). He wrote his narrative not long before he died in prison in 1300/1882–83. Sayyid Muhammad-Husayn-i-Zavari'i Mahjur seems to have written his account titled "Vaqāyi' al-Mīmīyyih" in 1278/1861–62 (n.d., Browne Manuscripts, Or. F. 28, item 1, Cambridge University Library, Cambridge). Nasir al-Din Shah's edict to the governor of Mazandaran is published in facsimile in *The Bahá'í World*, vol. 5 (New York: Bahá'í Publishing Committee, 1936), 58. Ruhu'llah Mehrabkhani gives an English translation of this edict in *Mullá Ḥusayn: Disciple at Dawn* (Los Angeles: Kalimát Press, 1987), 249–51.

In addition to the above accounts, there is a Baha'i narrative by Aqa Sayyid Muhammad-Rida Shahmirzadi, the youngest brother of the above-mentioned Mir Abu-Talib-i-Shahmirzadi (Untitled history, n.d., uncatalogued photocopy of autograph manuscript, Afnan Library, Sandy, Bedfordshire). It contains some information about the Mazandaran episode. His account seems to have been written in the 1890s. There is also a brief Muslim account by a certain Shaykh al-'Ajam. It was probably written in 1860. It was published by Bernhard Dorn (also Boris Andreevich Dorn) under the title "Min Kalām-i-Shaykh al-'Ajam-i-Māzandarānī" (in "Nachträge zu dem Verzeichniss der von der Kaiserlichen öffentlichen Bibliothek erworbenen Chanykov'schen Handschriften und den da mitgetheilten Nachrichten über die Baby und deren Koran, von B. Dorn," *Bulletin de l'Académie Impériale des Sciences de St.-Pétersbourg*, vol. 9 [1866], 205–11). Habib Borjian has provided an English translation of this account ("A Mazandarani Account of the Babi Incident at Shaikh Tabarsi," *Iranian Studies*, vol. 39, no. 3 [2006], 381–99).

child when the conflict took place, and the much earlier, albeit brief, narrative by Sayyid Ibrahim-i-Nayrizi, an exceptionally unbiased description of the events by a well-informed Muslim.[22]

With regard to the Zanjan battle, the late narrative by Mirza Husayn-i-Zanjani, a Baha'i who obtained his information from Baha'i and Muslim eyewitnesses to the event, and the later account by Aqa 'Abd al-Ahad-i-Zanjani, an Azali Babi who was a small child residing in the Muslim side of the town during the episode, are highly significant.[23]

---

22 Mulla Muhammad-Shafi'-i-Nayrizi may have written his history in or around 1880. He used information obtained from survivors who were older than him. A photocopy of a manuscript of Mulla Muhammad-Shafi''s history exists in the Afnan Library (Untitled history, n.d., uncatalogued photocopy of manuscript, Afnan Library, Sandy, Bedfordshire). The manuscript was transcribed by two Baha'is probably in the early 1930s. This is the text cited in this article. Fadil-i-Mazandarani and Nicolas had access to a different version of Mulla Muhammad-Shafi''s account.

Sayyid Ibrahim-i-Nayrizi's account contains much valuable information and is also more accurate than the later sources available (see "Sanadī dar bāriy-i-Sayyid Yaḥyā," in Iraj Afshar, ed., *Chihil Sāl Tārīkh-i-Īrān dar Dawriy-i-Pādishāhīy-i-Nāṣir al-Dīn Shāh* [Tehran: Asāṭīr, 1989], vol. 2, 635–40). The account was written on an inner wall of the mosque in the Bazar quarter of Nayriz. It consists of two parts written on separate occasions. The first part contains the narrative of the first Nayriz episode. The second part is much shorter and deals with the assassination of the governor of Nayriz, which triggered the Babi upheaval of 1853. His account is dated 1270 (beginning in October 1853); however, the date was obviously added to the text after it was written. Internal evidence indicates that the account was actually not written before early 1271 (c. November 1854). Referring to Mihr-'Ali Khan-i-Nuri, one of the two commanders of the army that fought against the Nayrizi Babis in 1850, the author gives his title as Shuja' al-Mulk. It was in early 1271 that Mihr-'Ali Khan received this title (see the announcement in the official national newspaper, *Rūznāmiy-i-vaqāyi'-i-ittifāqīyyih*, Thursday, 17 Safar 1271/9 November 1854, 1–2).

In addition to these two sources, Haj Mirza Hasan-i-Fasa'i's history of the province of Fars in the Qajar period published in 1313/1895–96 under the title *Fārsnāmiy-i-Nāṣirī* includes an account of the two Nayriz conflicts (Mansur Rastigar Fasa'i, ed. [Tehran: Amīr Kabīr, 1367 Sh./1988–89], 2 vols.). The author was a learned *ṣūfī*. His account of the first Nayriz conflict is in many respects similar to the account given in the official Qajar history the *Nāsikh al-Tavārīkh*, but contains additional details.

23 Mirza Husayn-i-Zanjani completed his narrative in or around 1880 (Untitled history, n.d., Ms. orient. Oct. 1216, Staatsbibliothek, Berlin). He identifies two of his informants: the Baha'i women Karbala'i Havva and Kulthum Khanum (History, f. 21b). His narrative remains unpublished.

Aqa 'Abd al-Ahad-i-Zanjani's father was the *kad-khudā* (mayor) of one of the quarters of the town. Aqa 'Abd al-Ahad's family seems to have been among the supporters of Hujjat, the leader of the Zanjani Babis. None of them, however, participated in the battle on the Babis' side. Aqa 'Abd al-Ahad wrote his account in response to a request from Browne. His autograph manuscript is dated Ramadan 1309 (Untitled history, Ramadan 1309 [April 1892], Browne Manuscripts, Or. F. 25, item 6, Cambridge University

The general histories of the Babi and Baha'i religions also provide information about these conflicts. Of these histories the most important is the narrative by the Baha'i chronicler Nabil-i-Zarandi. Although Nabil himself was not a participant in any of the conflicts, he was an early convert who knew many of the Babi survivors and had obtained information from them about these events. He also had access to eyewitness accounts that are unavailable or may no longer exist. The volume published under the title *Kitáb-i-Nuqṭatu'l-Káf* is also relevant. It contains the earliest general history of the Babi religion.[24]

In addition to the aforementioned narrative by Sayyid Ibrahim-i-Nayrizi, the most important Muslim accounts of these clashes are in the two main official histories of the period, *Nāsikh al-Tavārīkh* by Mirza Muhammad-Taqi

---

Library, Cambridge). Browne translated the text into English and published it with additional notes in 1897 (Edward G. Browne, trans., "Personal Reminiscences of the Bābī Insurrection at Zanjān in 1850, written in Persian by Āqā 'Abdu'l-Aḥad-i-Zanjānī," *Journal of the Royal Asiatic Society*, vol. 29, no. 4 [1897], 761–827). His translation is occasionally inaccurate.

The accounts by Mirza Husayn and Aqa 'Abd al-Ahad provide valuable information about the Babi participants' perception of the episode but are not very useful as regards the chronology of the events. Although not free from internal discrepancies and errors, the *Nāsikh al-Tavārīkh* is the best source for the chronology of the Zanjan episode.

24 Yar-Muhammad-i-Zarandi Nabil became a Babi in 1849. He began writing his narrative in August 1888 and completed it in November 1890. Shoghi Effendi translated and edited the part of Nabil-i-Zarandi's chronicle that deals with the history of the Babi religion (Nabil-i-Zarandi, *The Dawn-Breakers: Nabíl's Narrative of the Early Days of the Bahá'í Revelation*, Shoghi Effendi, trans. and ed. [Wilmette, Ill.: Bahá'í Publishing Committee, 1932]). Nabil's narrative is far more comprehensive and detailed than the *Nuqṭatu'l-Káf.* A critical edition of the *Nuqṭatu'l-Káf* was published by Browne (Edward G. Browne, ed., *Kitáb-i-Nuqṭatu'l-Káf: Being the Earliest History of the Bábís compiled by Ḥájjí Mírzá Jání of Káshán between the years A.D. 1850 and 1852* [Leyden; London: E. J. Brill; Luzac & Co., 1910]). Internal evidence indicates that the historical part of the text was completed by January 1852. For a detailed discussion of the *Nuqṭatu'l-Káf,* see William McCants and Kavian Milani, "The History and Provenance of an Early Manuscript of the *Nuqtat al-kaf* Dated 1268 (1851–52)," *Iranian Studies*, vol. 37, no. 3 (2004), 431–49; Milani, "Noqṭat al-Kāf," *Encyclopædia Iranica.*

Another source that may be mentioned here is Mirza Husayn-i-Hamadani's account. It is the second earliest general history of the Babi movement. Browne published a parallel edited translation of two versions of this history in 1893 (*Táríkh-i-Jadíd*). One of these versions, the manuscript F. 55 (9) in Browne's collection at the Cambridge University Library, is the "Tārīkh-i-Badī'-i-Bayānī," a revised version of Mirza Husayn-i-Hamadani's work prepared by the Baha'i scholar Aqa Muhammad-i-Qa'ini. Mirza Husayn-i-Hamadani wrote his history in the 1870s. With regard to the Babi–state conflicts, it does not add much new information to what is already available in the *Nuqṭatu'l-Káf.*

Lisan al-Mulk Sipihr and *Rawḍat al-Ṣafāy-i-Nāṣirī* by Rida-Quli Khan-i-Hidayat. Contemporary diplomatic reports and accounts by Western travelers and missionaries also contain important information about these events.[25]

AN OUTLINE OF THE CONFLICT AT SHAYKH TABARSI, SEPTEMBER 1848–MAY 1849

The conflict at Shaykh Tabarsi in Mazandaran lasted eight months and left an estimated 1,500 dead, almost a third of whom were Babis. Half of the eighteen Letters of the Living, the core of the leadership of the Babi movement, lost their lives in this episode. Near the end of the conflict, between 10,000 to 12,000 troops and irregulars were engaged in fighting a few hundred Babis. Decades later the memory of the battle at Shaykh Tabarsi was still fresh in the minds of the inhabitants of Mazandaran.

The prelude to the conflict was a march from Khurasan to Mazandaran by a group of Babis led by Mulla Husayn-i-Bushru'i, the first of the Letters of the Living (July–September 1848). From there, the Babis intended to continue their march to Azarbaijan to meet the Bab and possibly rescue him from his confinement. Initially, the band numbered about 200, some of whom were armed. On 12 Shavval 1264/11 September 1848 (only a few days after the death of Muhammad Shah on 4 September), the party reached Barfurush, the chief commercial town in Mazandaran.[26] Upon their arrival, the Babis were met by a mob of 3,000 to 4,000 townspeople and

25 Muhammad-Taqi Lisan al-Mulk Sipihr's *Nāsikh al-Tavārīkh: Tārīkh-i-Qājārīyyih* (Jamshid Kiyanfar, ed. [Tehran: Asāṭīr, 1377 Sh./1998–99]) and Rida-Quli Khan-i-Hidayat's *Rawḍat al-Ṣafāy-i-Nāṣirī* (vol. 10 [Qum: Markazī, Khayyām, Pīrūz, (1340) Sh./1961–62]) record the history down to the year 1274/1857–58. A wide collection of Western reports and accounts is published in Momen, *Bábí and Bahá'í Religions*. A number of reports by the Russian Minister in Tehran and one by the Russian consul in Astarabad are available in Prince Dolgorukov, "Excerpts from Dispatches written during 1848–1852 by Prince Dolgorukov, Russian Minister to Persia," *World Order*, vol. 1, no. 1 (1966), 17–24.

26 Lutf-'Ali Mirzay-i-Shirazi, History, 24. For Barfurush, see Xavier de Planhol, "Bābol i. The Town," *Encyclopædia Iranica*. In this study, whenever possible, the observation-based lunar calendar current in Iran, instead of the regulated, fixed Islamic calendar, has been used to determine the corresponding dates in the Gregorian calendar.

villagers who refused to let them enter the town. Mulla Husayn instructed the Babis to turn back, but meanwhile the mob shot and killed two of them. Thus, he and a few others counter-attacked and drove back the mob, which succeeded in attacking a couple more times. In the meantime, Babis who arrived later took lodging in the caravansary of the town. They were exhausted from the long trip, during which several had fallen ill and one had died. In the following days, hundreds of people from nearby villages joined the mob and several times attacked the Babis. The attacks stopped with the arrival of 'Abbas-Quli Khan-i-Larijani, a prominent Mazandarani chief (*sarkardih*), and the Babis made an agreement with him that they would leave the area.

When the Babis left Barfurush, a crowd of townspeople followed them, and Khusraw-i-Qadi-Kala'i, a brigand, joined the Babis with his armed men, ostensibly to protect them. Khusraw, whose intent was actually to loot the Babis, led them around the countryside while his men and other local people began secretly killing them off. When the Babis discovered this, they killed Khusraw, drove off his men, and took refuge in the nearby shrine of Shaykh Tabarsi (22 Shavval 1264/21 September 1848).[27] The shrine consisted of a building housing the Shaykh's tomb[28] and a grassy enclosure surrounded by a wall two meters high. Browne, who visited Shaykh Tabarsi years later, wrote that it was "a place of little natural strength."[29] The site was not chosen for strategic reasons. As the Babis expected to be attacked, they built four small towers around the shrine, from which they kept watch over the area. Over the next two to three months, Quddus, who was the last of the Letters of the Living, and others joined the Babis at Shaykh Tabarsi, and their number rose to about 500.

When Nasir al-Din Shah heard that the Babis were entrenched at Shaykh Tabarsi, he gave orders to the chiefs of Mazandaran to wipe them out.[30] A number of local chiefs soon arrived with a militia nearly 4,000 strong. On 25 Muharram 1265/22 December 1848, the Babis made a sortie in daylight, surprised and routed their enemies, and killed seventy or more, including

27 Lutf-'Ali Mirzay-i-Shirazi, History, 52–53.

28 It is commonly believed that his name was Shaykh Ahmad-ibn-i-'Aliyy-ibn-i-Abi-Talib-i-Tabarsi. He lived in the twelfth century.

29 Edward G. Browne, *A Year Amongst the Persians: Impressions as to the Life, Character, and Thought of the People of Persia, Received during Twelve Months' Residence in that Country in the Years 1887–8* (London: Adam and Charles Black, 1893), 565.

30 Sipihr, *Nāsikh al-Tavārīkh*, vol. 3, 1019; Hidayat, *Rawḍat al-Ṣafā*, vol. 10, 433.

the commander of the army. They also captured a huge amount of ammunition, provisions, and about a hundred horses.[31] This was of great importance to the Babis, as their own equipment was completely inadequate. On their arrival at Shaykh Tabarsi, the Babis may have had many swords and daggers, but only seven muskets and perhaps five horses.[32]

After this defeat, the shah gave emphatic orders to his uncle, Prince Mahdi-Quli Mirza, the newly appointed governor of Mazandaran, to eradicate the Babis. He also issued an edict, dated 3 Safar 1265/29 December 1848, which referred to the Babi movement as a "fresh heresy" (*bid'at*), the extermination of which was required by the religion and Shi'i doctrine. A note in the shah's own handwriting read: "It is true...you must exert yourself to the utmost in this affair. This is not a trifling amusement. The fate of our religion and of Shi'i doctrine hangs in the balance."[33] The edict reveals a significant measure of religious motivation on the part of the young shah for the suppression of the Babis.

Sometime during the first half of January 1849, the prince-governor arrived at a village near Shaykh Tabarsi. He did not launch an attack immediately, as he was waiting for reinforcements. The Babis had started digging a ditch around the shrine on 1 Safar 1265/27 December 1848 and were building a fort. They also began storing provisions in preparation for a siege. When the Babis discovered that the prince was waiting for 'Abbas-Quli Khan-i-Larijani and his forces, they decided to strike first. On the night of 29 Safar 1265 (the night of 23–24 January 1849), some 200 Babis sortied from their fortifications and routed the government forces.[34]

Four days later, 'Abbas-Quli Khan arrived with his forces, whose number

---

31 Sipihr (*Nāsikh al-Tavārīkh*, vol. 3, 1021) and Hidayat (*Rawḍat al-Ṣafā*, vol. 10, 434) write that in this attack the Babis massacred the people of the village of Afra, where the militia of the Mazandarani chiefs had entrenched themselves. The Babi and Baha'i sources do not refer to any such massacre. Browne is mistaken in stating that according to the author of the *Nuqṭatu'l-Káf*, the Babis, on this occasion, killed "the soldiers and villagers alike" (*Táríkh-i-Jadíd*, 362). The *Nuqṭatu'l-Káf* (161–62) only refers to the demolition of the village and the appropriation of provisions. The text indicates that this was in retaliation for the villagers permitting the militia to use their village. Had the Babis killed the inhabitants, it would not make sense to refer only to the destruction of their village and appropriation of their property as the punishment inflicted on them.

32 Lutf-'Ali Mirzay-i-Shirazi, History, 43–44, 75.

33 *Bahá'í World*, vol. 5, 58; Mehrabkhani, *Mullá Ḥusayn*, 250–51.

34 Lutf-'Ali Mirzay-i-Shirazi, History, 91.

gradually rose to about 6,000.[35] On the night of 9 Rabiʿ I 1265 (the night of 2–3 February 1849), over 200 Babis attacked ʿAbbas-Quli Khan's troops. In the clash, some 400 of the troops, including many chiefs, lost their lives. The high casualties among the troops were partly owing to their shooting and slashing at each other in the dark in the confusion following the Babis' attack. This time the Babis suffered many casualties. More than forty of them, including Mulla Husayn-i-Bushru'i, were killed during the battle or died later of their injuries. On the following day, the troops attacked the fort, apparently in order to collect the wounded and some of their dead and bury other bodies where they had fallen. When they retreated, the Babis went out to the battlefield to fetch their own dead. They found that the Babi corpses had been decapitated, burned, or both. On seeing this, the Babis exhumed and decapitated the bodies of the soldiers and mounted their heads on poles near the fort.[36]

Soon the prince-governor returned with a new army, ʿAbbas-Quli Khan joined forces with him, and the number of troops and irregulars gradually reached 10,000 to 12,000.[37] The fort was now completely surrounded, and supplies were cut off. In late February or early March, the troops stormed the fort but were repelled. At about this time, a detachment of soldiers with two cannons, two mortars, and two howitzers arrived at Shaykh Tabarsi, and a heavy bombardment of the fort began in the second half of March.

By early April the Babis had used up all their supplies of rice and grain and had already slaughtered and consumed the thirty or so horses that were left and were living on grass. Since ʿAbbas-Quli Khan and the Mazandarani chiefs had failed to capture the fort in spite of their superior forces, the government in Tehran dispatched Sulayman Khan-i-Afshar (about 9 April).[38] Under Sulayman Khan's command, tunnels were dug to the fort, and mines

35 Ibid., 99; Barthélémy Semino, *Zhinirāl Semino dar Khidmat-i Īrān-i ʿAṣr-i Qājār va Jang-i Hirāt: 1236–1266 hijrīy-i qamarī/Le Général Semino en Iran Qâjâr et la Guerre de Hérat: 1820–1850*, Mansoureh Ettehadieh (Nezam Mafi), S. Mir-Mohammad Sadegh, eds. (Tehran: Nashr-i-Tārīkh-i-Īrān, 1997), 192 (Semino's letter of 16 June 1849).

36 Lutf-ʿAli Mirzay-i-Shirazi, History, 112; Abu-Talib-i-Shahmirzadi, History, 16; Nasir-i-Qazvini, "Tārīkh," 510–11; Mahjur, "Vaqāyiʿ al-Mīmīyyih," 64–65; Browne, *Nuqṭatu'l-Káf*, 177; Sipihr, *Nāsikh al-Tavārīkh*, vol. 3, 1027; Hidayat, *Rawḍat al-Ṣafā*, vol. 10, 439–40.

37 Lutf-ʿAli Mirzay-i-Shirazi, History, 119; Nasir-i-Qazvini, "Tārīkh," 515; Ferrier to de LaHitte, 21 February 1850, quoted in Momen, *Bábí and Bahá'í Religions*, 95.

38 Amir Kabir suspected ʿAbbas-Quli Khan of having become a Babi. See Semino's letter of 16 June 1849 in *Zhinirāl Semino*, 192.

were placed under two of its towers. When preparations were completed, the mines were ignited, and the fort was stormed from four directions. This second general assault also failed. Shortly afterwards, thirty or more Babis deserted the fort, but the leader of the group and perhaps a few others were shot dead by the troops, and the rest were captured and killed later. By this time the troops had discovered that the Babis left the fort at night to collect grass, so they continued firing on the area around the fort throughout the night. From then on, for the last nineteen days of the siege, the Babis were reduced to eating the putrefied meat, skin, and bones of their dead horses, and even the leather of their saddles.

The siege was brought to an end when the prince-governor resorted to treachery. The Babis were promised safety if they left the fort. Copies of the Qur'an were sealed and sent to confirm the pledge. On the afternoon of 15 Jumada II 1265/9 May 1849, the surviving Babis, some 220 in number, evacuated the fort. Once outside, they were disarmed and with few exceptions massacred (10 May 1849).[39]

THE OBJECTIVES OF THE BABIS AT SHAYKH TABARSI

In his narrative, Nabil-i-Zarandi writes that Mulla Husayn unfurled the "Black Standard" on the Bab's instruction as the group of Babis embarked on their march to Mazandaran.[40] In the Shi'i prophetic traditions, there are references to black standards proceeding from Khurasan, which signify the advent of the Qa'im. Nabil quotes a tradition that refers to the black standard and adds that this standard "was carried aloft all the way from the city of Mas͟hhad to the shrine of S͟hayk͟h Ṭabarsí," where it was flown until the fall of the fort.[41] Commenting on Nabil's statements, various scholars have drawn attention to the significance of the raising of black standards.[42] They have argued that apart from its messianic overtones, fulfilling literally the prophecies about the appearance of the Qa'im in Khurasan, raising black standards also had political implications. It was exactly by such an act that the 'Abbasids began their rebellion against the Umayyads, which ended

39 Abu-Talib-i-Shahmirzadi, History, 21, 32–33, 36. See also Browne, *Nuqṭatu'l-Káf*, 192; Nabil, *Dawn-Breakers*, 399–400; Sipihr, *Nāsikh al-Tavārīkh*, vol. 3, 1035–36.

40 *Dawn-Breakers*, 324–25.

41 Ibid., 351.

42 See Momen, "Social Basis of the Bābī Upheavals," 161; MacEoin, "Babi Concept of Holy War," 115.

with the overthrow of the latter. However, the main issue is what such an act meant to the Babis, and how it was interpreted by the authorities and the public. In this respect, it is noteworthy that there is no evidence that contemporaries attached any political significance to such an act. The Qajar chronicles are silent on this issue, and there is no mention of the government being alarmed by it or taking any notice of it at all. An explanation for this, that is, how a banner could be flown without attracting suspicion, can be found in the custom of *chāvush-khānī* (recitation by a *chāvush*), which was common at the time.[43]

The *chāvush* was a guide who took people on pilgrimage to Mecca, the 'Atabat (i.e., the Shi'i shrine cities of Iraq), or Mashhad. In order to encourage people to join him, he would chant poems praising the Prophet or the Imams and would hoist a special banner to announce the imminent pilgrimage.[44] Lutf-'Ali Mirza's account indicates that the Babis in Mulla Husayn's party were apprehensive about being attacked and attempted to conceal their identity by claiming to be pilgrims on their way to Karbala'.[45] Considering the practice of *chāvush-khānī*, the Babis would have been able to fly a black banner without necessarily arousing suspicion. However, there is evidence suggesting that Nabil's portrayal of this event is not entirely correct.

None of the earlier accounts mentions any such episode. In fact, Lutf-'Ali Mirza's account contains evidence that makes it seem rather doubtful. Lutf-'Ali Mirza had joined Mulla Husayn's band shortly before their entry into Mazandaran. He comments in passing on Mulla Husayn's black garment, saying that this was the meaning of the black standard from Khurasan reported in the tradition.[46] This suggests that the travelers were not flying black standards at all at that time. There is corroboratory evidence in the account by Mir Abu-Talib-i-Shahmirzadi, who joined the Babis after they entered the shrine of Shaykh Tabarsi. He refers several times in his narrative to the prophecies about the black standards having been fulfilled. However, he implies that the Babis "understood Mulla Husayn to be the Standards from Khurasan."[47] The *Nuqṭatu'l-Káf*, too,

43 I am grateful to Saleh Molavinegad for drawing my attention to the practice of *chāvush-khānī*.

44 Ghulam-Husayn Yusufi, "Čāvoš," *Encyclopædia Iranica*.

45 History, 2–3, 8–9.

46 Ibid., 19.

47 History, 25; cf. 7–8. Nabil may have had access to a different version of Mir Abu-Talib's account. In his rendering of the passage in question, Mulla Husayn is "the bearer" of the "Black Standard" (*Dawn-Breakers*, 407).

contains references to the various standards in the prophecies. It is stated that the "Khurasani Standard" refers to "janāb-i-Sayyid al-Shuhadā—peace be upon him—who set out from Khurasan [Mulla Husayn-i-Bushru'i]."[48] Considering this evidence, it seems likely that the Babis did not carry black standards on the way to Mazandaran. Even if they did, they apparently did not attach any eschatological significance to them. Rather, they viewed the act of Mulla Husayn and his party, who set out on a march from Khurasan, as the fulfillment of the prophecies concerning the black standards.

Elsewhere in his narrative, Nabil gives the number of the Babis at Shaykh Tabarsi as 313.[49] Like the black standard, the figure 313 has eschatological significance. According to some traditions, the companions of the Qa'im number 313, which is the numerical value of the word *jaysh* (army), that is, the *jaysh* of the Qa'im.[50] It is not unlikely that an emphasis on the literal fulfillment of such prophecies led to the circulation among the Babis of stories about the carrying of the black standard and the number of participants at Shaykh Tabarsi being exactly 313, which subsequently found their way into Nabil's narrative.

Evidence as to why Mulla Husayn and some 200 Babis were heading for Mazandaran is scanty. Mulla Husayn had shortly before been forced to leave Mashhad. The region was unstable due to Salar's rebellion; a clash had occurred between the Babis and the local people in Mashhad,[51] and such clashes would have worsened the situation. Mulla Husayn reportedly once remarked that his sole purpose in leaving Mashhad had been to "exalt the word of God and attain martyrdom."[52] It seems, however, that he had another, more concrete aim as well. One of the objectives of the conference of Badasht (June–July 1848) was to deliberate on how the Bab could be rescued from prison.[53] Avarih, the author of a late Baha'i history, states that it was decided there that the Babis should go to the fortress in Azarbaijan (i.e., Chahriq), where the Bab was imprisoned, and once there ask Muhammad Shah to release the Bab, or liberate him by force if

---

48 Browne, 153.

49 *Dawn-Breakers*, 354.

50 See Mohammad Ali Amir-Moezzi, "Eschatology iii. In Imami Shi'ism," *Encyclopædia Iranica*.

51 This clash is discussed on p. 331 of this chapter.

52 Lutf-'Ali Mirzay-i-Shirazi, History, 18; cf. 88.

53 Shoghi Effendi, *God Passes By*, rev. ed. (Wilmette, Ill.: Bahá'í Publishing Trust, 1974), 31.

necessary, avoiding conflict with the state as far as possible.[54] It was probably because of the bastinado inflicted on the Bab in Tabriz (April 1848) that the Babis determined to rescue their leader.[55] According to Shaykh Kazim-i-Samandar, Mulla Husayn's party intended to proceed to Azarbaijan to meet the Bab.[56] Hidayat, one of the two main Qajar court chroniclers of this period, also states that Mulla Husayn's original intention was to go to Chahriq to liberate the Bab.[57]

The existing sources do not clarify the Bab's attitude toward his followers' plan to rescue him. His rescue, if carried out by force, would amount to interfering in the affairs of the state. Apparently, the Babis regarded such an act as legitimate, as it was in response to persecution. It is difficult to conjecture the course of action that the Babi band would have taken had it succeeded in rescuing the Bab. Nowhere in the available Babi or Baha'i accounts is there any clear indication of their future plans. The only clue given is that they intended to go to the Shiʿi shrine cities of Iraq.[58] If this is taken at face value, it would suggest that the Babis in Mulla Husayn's party intended to leave the country. However, considering the fate of Mulla 'Ali Bastami, the Bab's emissary to the 'Atabat,[59] it is hard to imagine that they would have fared any better there, in the heartland of the Shiʿi world, than in Iran.

It is important to have a sense of the context in which the Babis' march to Mazandaran took place. Three months earlier, the Bab had been brought to Tabriz, the provincial capital, and interrogated in the presence of the crown prince and the clergy (about 23 April 1848).[60] On this occasion the Bab had

54 'Abd al-Husayn Avarih, *Al-Kavākib al-Durrīyyih fī Ma'āthir al-Bahā'īyyih*, vol. 1 (Cairo: al-Sa'āda, 1923), 129. Avarih erroneously writes Maku instead of Chahriq.

55 See Hidayat, *Rawḍat al-Ṣafā*, vol. 10, 428.

56 Shaykh Kazim-i-Samandar-i-Qazvini, "Tārīkh-i-janāb-i-Samandar," in 'Abd al-'Ali 'Ala'i, ed., *Tārīkh-i-Samandar va Mulḥaqqāt* (Tehran: Mu'assasiy-i-Millīy-i-Maṭbū'āt-i-Amrī, 131 B.E./1974–75), 168. Samandar makes this statement in his short biography of one of the survivors of the Mazandaran conflict, whom he had met.

57 *Rawḍat al-Ṣafā*, vol. 10, 422, 428–29. Cf. Edward G. Browne, ed. and trans., *A Traveller's Narrative Written to Illustrate the Episode of the Báb* (Cambridge: Cambridge University Press, 1891), vol. 2, 189.

58 Lutf-'Ali Mirzay-i-Shirazi, History, 88. Cf. Browne, *Nuqṭatu'l-Káf*, 166; Nabil, *Dawn-Breakers*, 324; Sipihr, *Nāsikh al-Tavārīkh*, vol. 3, 1014; Hidayat, *Rawḍat al-Ṣafā*, vol. 10, 431.

59 See Moojan Momen, "The Trial of Mullā 'Alī Basṭāmī: A Combined Sunnī-Shī'ī Fatwā against the Bāb," *Iran*, vol. 20 (1982), 113–43.

60 According to Nabil, the trial of the Bab took place toward the end of July 1848 (*Dawn-Breakers*, 301). There is, however, evidence that the trial occurred in the second

publicly declared himself to be the Qa'im (the Hidden Imam or the Mahdi), a claim that posed a serious challenge to the clergy and one for which he was bastinadoed. There had been sporadic cases of persecution of the Babis prior to April 1848, but after the Bab's trial in Tabriz, such incidents seem to have occurred more frequently, as the clergy, infuriated by the open challenge of the Bab and encouraged by the punishment imposed on him, stepped up its attempts to incite the authorities and the populace to persecute the Babis. An early account by Dr. Austin H. Wright, an American missionary stationed near Chahriq, where the Bab was held in confinement, indicates that when the Bab was brought to Tabriz for trial, the government also issued an order that the Babis "wherever found should be fined and punished."[61] Two episodes preceding the march of Mulla Husayn's band to Mazandaran, one in Mashhad and the other in Niyala after the Babi conclave in Badasht, should be viewed in the light of these increased tensions involving the Babis. Both episodes occurred in the summer of 1848.

In the Mashhad episode, after a fight between a young Babi and a servant of one of the local religious leaders, the Babi involved was beaten and dragged through the streets by a string through his nose. About seventy Babis, armed with swords, attempted to rescue him, and in the clashes that occurred, a few of the townspeople and Babis were injured.[62] It was this episode that led to Mulla Husayn's expulsion from Mashhad, after which he set out on his march to Mazandaran. At the Badasht conclave, Qurrat al-'Ayn Tahirih, the only woman among the Letters of the Living, had appeared unveiled in a gathering of Babis, signaling the abrogation of Islamic law and the commencement of the *qīyāmat* (resurrection). Later, on hearing the news that the Babis had discarded the *sharī'a*, and rumors of immoral acts being committed, the inhabitants of the village of Niyala in Mazandaran attacked the Babis who had arrived there from Badasht, killing and injuring some and plundering their belongings.[63]

---

half of April 1848. See letters from Aqa Sayyid Husayn-i-Katib and Khal-i-Asghar in Abu'l-Qásim Afnán, *'Ahd-i-A'lā: Zindigānīy-i-Ḥaḍrat-i-Bāb/The Bábí Dispensation: The Life of the Báb* (Oxford: Oneworld, 2000), 337–39. See also Siyamak Zabihi-Moghaddam, "Mu'arrifīy-i-Kitāb. *'Ahd-i-A'lā: Zindigānīy-i-Ḥaḍrat-i-Bāb*," *Payām-i-Bahā'ī*, no. 253 (December 2000), 40.

61 *The Literary World*, vol. 8, no. 228 (14 June 1851), 470. Wright's letter is dated 10 February 1851.

62 Mahjur, "Vaqāyi' al-Mīmīyyih," 6–8; Abu-Talib-i-Shahmirzadi, History, 23, 46–47; Samandar, "Tārīkh-i-janāb-i-Samandar," 168. See also Nabil, *Dawn-Breakers*, 288–89.

63 Nabil, *Dawn-Breakers*, 298–300; Munirih Khanum, *Munírih Khánum: Memoirs and Letters*, Sammireh Anwar Smith, trans. (Los Angeles: Kalimát Press, 1986), 15–16.

The atmosphere of hostility toward the Babis is corroborated by Lutf-'Ali Mirza's account. He writes that when the band of Babis headed by Mulla Husayn entered Mazandaran, they encountered the party of Prince Khanlar Mirza, the new governor of the province (second half of August). When the prince discovered that they were Babis, he angrily said to several of them: "You are all Babis and *mufsid-i fi'l-arḍ* ('the corrupt on the earth')[64] and killing you is obligatory," and that Muhammad Shah had ordered that wherever they were found they should be killed.[65] Other sources do not refer to Muhammad Shah giving orders to kill the Babis. Still, the incident reflects the tension that surrounded the Babis at the time. Previously, on Lutf-'Ali Mirza's advice, Mulla Husayn had instructed the Babis to stand guard at night.[66]

When the Babi band, near Barfurush, received news of the death of Muhammad Shah, they headed toward the town. The Babis must have been aware that trouble might break out there due to the presence of Sa'id al-'Ulama', an influential cleric who was extremely hostile toward the Babis. It appears, however, that they had no alternative. Shortly before this, they had been forced to leave the village of Arim because of complaints from some of the local people who had objected to the Babis occupying their pasture-land; others had complained that foodstuffs had become scarce because the Babis paid so well that everybody went to them to sell their rice and other stuffs. The people had threatened to attack the Babis at night if they did not leave.[67] Muhammad Shah's death complicated this situation radically. The Babis could no longer move from place to place, as they risked attacks by robbers exploiting the temporary anarchy or by local people or authorities who might take them for a band of plunderers.[68] A letter, written from the provincial capital Sari shortly after Muhammad Shah's death, reads: "...Saree [Sari]...is the only town not in a disturbed state in all Mazandaran, and the roads are infested by robbers in every direction."[69] Barfurush was the major

64 An Islamic concept based on Qur'an 5:32 and other verses.
65 History, 14.
66 Ibid., 4, 6.
67 Ibid., 20–21.
68 See Nasir-i-Qazvini, "Tārīkh," 504.
69 Anonymous, 12 September 1848, "Translation: Extract of a letter from a person sent to M. [Mazandaran] by Colonel F. [Farrant]," "Enclosed Farrant's No. 85 of 1848," The National Archives of the UK, Foreign Office Records, FO 60/138. Lieutenant-Colonel Francis Farrant was the British Chargé d'Affaires in Tehran. Cf. Lutf-'Ali Mirzay-i-Shirazi, History, 25–26; Robert Grant Watson, *A History of Persia from the Beginning of the Nineteenth Century to the Year 1858* (London: Smith, Elder and Co., 1866), 360.

town most easily accessible from Arim. Here, the Babis would be able to find provisions sufficient for their numbers until the situation stabilized.

Describing the Babis' entry into Barfurush, neither of the two main official histories of the period, *Nāsikh al-Tavārīkh* and *Rawḍat al-ṣafā*, states that the Babis were attacked. Lutf-'Ali Mirza's eyewitness account clearly states that they were, as do other Babi and later Baha'i sources, and Shaykh al-'Ajam's account seems to confirm this. The latter writes that news had reached Barfurush that 500 Babis had rebelled and were intent on making a surprise attack. The people of Barfurush armed themselves and waited for the Babis in order to kill them. When the Babis arrived, a clash occurred, during which Mulla Husayn killed seven or eight people.[70] Though there may have been more casualties among the townspeople in this first clash, they were relatively few, suggesting that the Babis had not intended to attack the inhabitants. In contrast, when Mulla Husayn and his fellow Babis made sorties against the besieging troops at Shaykh Tabarsi, they proved capable of imposing significant casualties on their enemies.

After leaving Barfurush, the Babis reluctantly agreed that Khusraw-i-Qadi-Kala'i and his armed men should escort them. The Babis were followed by a vengeful mob from Barfurush, and they were strangers to the inhospitable surroundings of Mazandaran, with its narrow paths, thick forests, and impassable marshland. When the Babis discovered that their escort had killed some of them and intended to kill the rest of the party and steal their goods, they killed Khusraw in the middle of the night and attacked and dispersed his men. Leaving behind all their belongings, the Babis pursued the escort and attacked a village which they thought was Qadi-Kala. On returning from this attack, the Babis discovered that none of their possessions were left and thus they made their way, with the help of a local guide whom they had taken prisoner, to the nearby shrine of Shaykh Tabarsi.

The Babis decided to stay at Shaykh Tabarsi because they could not move on. The Babi survivors' accounts show that the party's leader, Mulla Husayn, was aware that they had reached the end of their journey. On entering the shrine, he addressed his companions, saying that this was the place all of them would be killed.[71] Lutf-'Ali Mirza describes the agony of the Babis when they heard that there was no escape from "martyrdom." After Muhammad Shah's death, it was no longer possible for them to proceed with their initial plan of rescuing the Bab. Apart from the general lawlessness in the region and

70 "Min Kalām-i-Shaykh al-'Ajam," 206–7; Borjian, "A Mazandarani Account," 391.
71 Lutf-'Ali Mirzay-i-Shirazi, History, 54.

the risk of being attacked by robbers, the Babis' enemies wanted to avenge the blood of those killed in Barfurush, as well as that of Khusraw and his men. The Babis would make an easy target for their enemies if they attempted to travel the narrow byways of Mazandaran. Their dialect as well as their dress would reveal that they were strangers.[72] Haji Nasir-i-Qazvini's account indicates that the Babis expected the townspeople to attack.[73] It seems that word had also been sent to nearby villages that the Babis were infidels whom it was lawful to kill and plunder.[74] For a time after the Babis entered the shrine of Shaykh Tabarsi, the people from Qadi-Kala and other villages robbed all the strangers in the area and even killed a few.[75] In short, the Babis were trapped, so they began erecting some rudimentary defenses around the shrine. The fact that the first major attack on the Babis did not come for three months was only due to the absence of the chiefs and notables of Mazandaran, who had been obliged to go to Tehran for the coronation of the shah.[76] In the meantime the inhabitants of Qadi-Kala attacked the Babis at the shrine.[77]

Under these circumstances, the motifs of jihad (i.e., defensive holy war) and martyrdom fully emerged. The Babis, like the general Shiʿi population of Iran, were well acquainted with these motifs. To them, the advent of the Qa'im marked the culmination of Shiʿi history. As the struggle began, it appeared to the Babis that the episode of Karbala' was being re-enacted. For them, the Qajars were the new Umayyads, and their clerical enemies were the eschatological figures who would wage war against the Qa'im. The first major attack on the Babis at Shaykh Tabarsi occurred in Muharram, the very month in which the Imam Husayn was martyred. Mulla Husayn referred specifically to this in his interview with the prince's emissary and drew a parallel to the Umayyads and the Imam Husayn.[78]

Certain factors indicate that the Babis were not intent on insurrection. Their limited arms and equipment, consisting initially of swords and daggers, eighteen muskets, and a few horses, as well as the children and elderly among the party, made them unfit for a struggle against a trained army.[79] If the actions of the Babis at Shaykh Tabarsi were part of a Babi plan aimed

72 See ibid., 61; Mahjur, "Vaqāyiʿ al-Mīmīyyih," 37.
73 "Tārīkh," 504.
74 Lutf-ʿAli Mirzay-i-Shirazi, History, 36.
75 Abu-Talib-i-Shahmirzadi, History, 3.
76 Sipihr, *Nāsikh al-Tavārīkh*, vol. 3, 1017; Hidayat, *Rawḍat al-Ṣafā*, vol. 10, 433.
77 Browne, *Nuqṭatu'l-Káf*, 160. Cf. Nabil, *Dawn-Breakers*, 345.
78 Lutf-ʿAli Mirzay-i-Shirazi, History, 87; Mahjur, "Vaqāyiʿ al-Mīmīyyih," 42.
79 See Lutf-ʿAli Mirzay-i-Shirazi, History, 43–44, 80.

at overthrowing the state, it seems reasonable that Babis elsewhere would have sought to take advantage of the instability created by the death of the shah. It was then that uprisings and disorder broke out in many parts of the country, and Salar, the leader of the revolt in Khurasan, used the opportunity to consolidate his position. For another one and a half years, his rebellion engaged a substantial part of the country's military resources. Without support from outside, the fall of the fort of Shaykh Tabarsi was obviously only a matter of time. In siege warfare, it is always factors outside the fortress that decide the success or failure of the defenders.[80] Therefore, preparing for defensive warfare at Shaykh Tabarsi would not serve any end in itself if other Babis did not conduct insurrectionary activities in other parts of the country. It would seem that they were in a position to do so, if that was what they intended. For example, Mulla Muhammad-'Aliy-i-Zanjani Hujjat, who led the Babis of his town during the most severe of the Babi–state clashes less than two years later, escaped from the capital while the Mazandaran episode was unfolding. He had a large following in Zanjan and had been in contact with them during his confinement in Tehran. As the first major attack on Shaykh Tabarsi came in the second half of December, three and a half months after the death of the shah, and the conflict lasted until May, it seems that the Zanjani Babis would have had sufficient time to organize a revolt there, had they been instructed to do so. Another Babi leader, Aqa Sayyid Yahyay-i-Darabi Vahid, who less than two years later would be involved in the first Nayriz conflict, had many supporters in this town, as well as in Yazd. He, too, would seem to have been in a position to stage a rebellion. Neither Hujjat nor Vahid, however, nor any of the other Babis, attempted to organize a revolt. In spite of his imprisonment, the Bab was in communication with his followers, and while at one point he may have instructed them to join the Babis at Shaykh Tabarsi, he never issued an order for a Babi offensive jihad.

The early Babi and later Baha'i narratives of the Shaykh Tabarsi episode do not indicate that the participants aspired to establish a Babi theocracy. The claim of the court historian Sipihr that Mulla Husayn promised his fellow Babis kingship and rulership of various lands and provinces[81] stands in sharp contrast to the statements in these accounts that Mulla Husayn, soon

80 "In war history, there is no known case of a defender, once encircled in a fortress, being able to compel the attacker to call off a siege alone and with his own resources. Defense of a fortress is always a battle to gain time" (Gert Bode, "Siege," in Trevor N. Dupuy, editor-in-chief, *International Military and Defense Encyclopedia* [Washington D. C.; New York: Brassey's (US), Inc., 1993], vol. 5, 2417).

81 *Nāsikh al-Tavārīkh*, vol. 3, 1019.

after the Babis entered Mazandaran and encountered the party of Prince Khanlar Mirza, warned his companions that all of them would be killed. He told them that whoever wanted to leave had to do it then and that "it will not be possible to leave later. They will close the roads and spill our blood. Soon the enemies will attack from all sides."[82]

The eyewitness accounts show that the Babis did not view themselves as insurrectionists and that in response to the authorities, they denied such an objective. Several sources refer to an exchange of messages between the Babis and Prince Mahdi-Quli Mirza. According to Lutf-'Ali Mirza, the prince-governor sent a strongly worded message to Mulla Husayn, accusing the Babis of stirring up mischief. The message also said that the Babis were no match for the royal troops and that they should leave the province. Lutf-'Ali Mirza then gives a summary of Mulla Husayn's exchange with the prince's emissary saying that the emissary remarked that the Babis should produce a miracle to prove the truth of their cause, and that the prince would join forces with them if they did so and attempt to overthrow Nasir al-Din Shah.[83] Mulla Husayn answered that the greatest miracle, the revelation of verses, had already been performed, but that they had denied it. He asked why they would not, instead, gather their 'ulama' to engage in logical arguments with the Babis. If the 'ulama' defeated the Babis in argument, they could kill them; otherwise, the 'ulama' should accept the cause of truth.[84] The interview was interrupted when Mulla Husayn went to get Quddus's response to the prince's message. On returning, Mulla Husayn angrily related to the emissary what the Babis had suffered, saying that it was their enemies, and not the Babis, who had caused mischief. To the prince's remark about the superiority of the royal troops, Mulla Husayn answered that truth always prevailed over falsehood, and that if the whole world united to assail him, he would wage war against it, until he either was martyred or defeated his adversaries.[85]

In response to the prince's remark that if the Babis produced a miracle, he would join forces with them in order to overthrow the shah, Mulla

82 Lutf-'Ali Mirzay-i-Shirazi, History, 18–19. Cf. Browne, *Nuqṭatu'l-Káf*, 155–56; Nabil, *Dawn-Breakers*, 326.

83 History, 83–84. This indicates that the prince-governor believed the Babis were intent on insurrection.

84 Ibid., 84–85. The request of the Babis at Shaykh Tabarsi for a meeting with the 'ulama' is also reported in Mir Abu-Talib-i-Shahmirzadi's eyewitness account (History, 12). See also Browne, *Nuqṭatu'l-Káf*, 163.

85 Lutf-'Ali Mirzay-i-Shirazi, History, 85–88.

Husayn said that he did not seek the sovereignty of the ephemeral world, and reproached the prince and the enemies for ascribing such objectives to the Babis, whom they did not even know. He also remarked that he had left Mashhad "with the aim of spreading the truth," in whatever way might prove possible, "whether by overcoming falsehood or by means of the sword or by suffering martyrdom..." He refused to leave the province, saying, "I shall make manifest the cause of God by means of the sword," and adding that he had been deceived in Barfurush by the "sardar-i-Larijani," that is, 'Abbas-Quli Khan-i-Larijani, and that he would not be deceived again and would not disperse his few companions until they had overcome all their enemies or had all been killed. Mulla Husayn hinted at the prince's dishonesty and occasionally called the shah a puppy. He concluded the interview by writing a short answer to the prince.[86] Obviously, the Babis were not begging for mercy. Mulla Husayn's reference to 'Abbas-Quli Khan and his hints at the prince's dishonesty indicate that he believed that the prince could not be relied on, and that the prince's only intention was to get the Babis out of the fort so that they could be killed more easily. Mulla Husayn's remarks, as related by Lutf-'Ali Mirza, also clearly show the Babis' determination to disseminate their cause and to defend themselves. Mulla Husayn's boldness also suggests that if the Babis at Shaykh Tabarsi really aimed to overthrow the shah, they would not have hesitated to say so.[87]

86 Ibid., 88–89.

87 In his article "Babi Concept of Holy War" (115–17), MacEoin provides an analysis of the objectives of the Babis at Shaykh Tabarsi. Citing Lutf-'Ali Mirza's history, he comments that Mulla Husayn refused to leave Mazandaran as "requested" by the prince (116). To call the prince's demand that the Babis should leave Mazandaran a "request" is misleading. The prince had received emphatic instructions from Nasir al-Din Shah in person to eradicate the Babis, and shortly afterwards the shah had issued a royal decree ordering him to "cleanse the realm of this filthy and reprobate sect, so that not a trace of them remains" (*Bahá'í World*, vol. 5, 58; Mehrabkhani, *Mullá Ḥusayn*, 251). The Babis had heard about the prince's mission and knew that Mazandarani troops had been ordered to assist him. Some of the local people who had initially expressed their support for the Babis had now reneged. The prince's message was phrased in harsh language and accused the Babis of stirring up mischief (Lutf-'Ali Mirzay-i-Shirazi, History, 82–83). This cannot be called a "request."

MacEoin refers to Mulla Husayn's statement about not departing from Mazandaran "until the cause of God is manifested" ("Babi Concept of Holy War," 116), but leaves out his remark that he had once been deceived by 'Abbas-Quli Khan in Barfurush, and that he would not be deceived again (Lutf-'Ali Mirzay-i-Shirazi, History, 89). All this makes it clear that Mulla Husayn believed that the prince's "request" was a trick, and that if the Babis agreed and left the fort, they would all be killed.

Mulla Husayn and his companions knew that they were fighting a war they could not win. They hoped that the manner of their fighting would be a testimony to the truth and power of the Babi cause.

THE CALM BETWEEN STORMS: MAY 1849–MAY 1850

The conflict at Shaykh Tabarsi set the stage for future clashes between government forces and the Babis, and provided the script for how those clashes were to play out. It revealed to the Babis, the 'ulama', and the local authorities the attitude of the central government toward the Babis and how it could be expected to act in similar situations. After the struggle of Tabarsi, it was clear to the Babis that they had little chance of reaching an understanding with the state. At the same time, Amir Kabir's actions had strengthened the hand of the 'ulama' against the Babis, even though this had not been his objective. Moreover, the Amir's policy had signaled to the local authorities that the central government did not tolerate any compromise with the Babis; to secure their hold on office, they would have to take a hard stance against the Babis.

Suppressing the Babi movement had become a high priority for Amir Kabir soon after he had assumed office. His actions against the Babis were shaped by circumstances rather than religious bigotry. The country was already in a state of turmoil when Muhammad Shah died. Gross mismanagement in the later years of Aqasi's premiership had caused much discontent. The state treasury was almost empty, bringing the government to the verge of bankruptcy. Following the shah's death, disorder broke out in various parts of the country, and the rebellion in Khurasan gained support. To stabilize the position of the new government and to proceed with his reform plans, Amir Kabir needed to restore order in the country. The spread of the Babi movement, he estimated, could not but cause disorder.

Amir Kabir blamed the Babis for upholding religious doctrines that were anathema to the 'ulama', who considered themselves the chief custodians of religious orthodoxy. It was clear to him that the Babis' beliefs and their activities in propagating their faith could not but provoke opposition from the 'ulama' and the masses subservient to them. The 'ulama' could not be expected to concede to the Babis the right to exist within Iranian society, as that would weaken their power over the population. In view of the above, the Amir was not willing to take a neutral stance toward the Babis.

Amir Kabir was also alarmed by the spread of the Babi religion among state officials and civil servants as well as within the ranks of the military. On 7 March 1849, at the height of the Shaykh Tabarsi upheaval, Prince Dolgorukov, the Russian Minister in Tehran, made the following observation:

> However, no matter how serious this question may be [that is, the success of Salar's rebellion in Khurasan], it has not preoccupied society to the same extent ever since the sectaries of the Bab have apparently had the tendency to grow in all parts of the Kingdom. The Amir confessed to me that their number can be already put at 100,000; that they have already appeared in southern provinces; that they are found in large numbers in Tihran itself; and that, finally, their presence in Adhirbayjan is beginning to worry him very much.[88]

The following year, Lieutenant-Colonel Justin Sheil, the British Minister in Tehran, wrote: "It is conjectured that in Teheran this religion has acquired votaries in every class, not even excluding the artillery and regular Infantry. Their numbers in this city, it is supposed, may amount to about two thousand persons."[89] The Amir probably feared that the continued spread of the Babi religion, in addition to leading to disturbances around the country, would create tensions within the ranks of the government and the military and thus affect the functioning of the state and impede and, in the worst case, jeopardize his reform program. Such considerations, coupled with his tendency to use excessive force, seem to have determined his harsh policy toward the Babis.

For several months after the conclusion of the Shaykh Tabarsi episode, there was no incidence of any serious confrontation between the authorities and the Babis. This changed, however, when Aqa Sayyid Yahyay-i-Darabi Vahid, the most influential among the Bab's supporters, entered Yazd to propagate the Babi religion. His activities ultimately led to the first Nayriz conflict.

Vahid arrived in Yazd in around January 1850.[90] Prior to his conversion to the religion of the Bab, he had been a prominent cleric associated with the court of Muhammad Shah. Vahid was born in Yazd, one of his two wives

88 "Excerpts from Dispatches," 19.

89 Report to Palmerston, 12 February 1850, quoted in Momen, *Bábí and Bahá'í Religions*, 6.

90 Yazd is located in central Iran. In 1867, it had an estimated population of 40,000. See Hooshang Amirahmadi, *The Political Economy of Iran under the Qajars: Society, Politics, Economics, and Foreign Relations, 1796–1926* (London; New York: I.B. Tauris, 2012), 19, Table 3.2.

and their children, as well as two of his brothers, resided there, and he also enjoyed some support among the townspeople. Vahid's activities soon aroused the opposition of the 'ulama', and Aqa Khan-i-Irvani, the deputy-governor of Yazd, attempted to arrest him. He may have feared the consequences for his own position if he failed to act against the Babi leader. The Babis were determined to defend their leader against the authorities' action, and clashes occurred between the two sides. In the meantime, a certain Muhammad-i-'Abd Allah, a ruffian leader, intervened in the fighting on Vahid's side.

Muhammad-i-'Abd Allah had previously come into conflict with the authorities. Following the death of Muhammad Shah, he had received payments from the wealthy to use his influence to stop the ruffians in Yazd from pillaging the population. Later, the central government had acted to put an end to the menace caused by Muhammad-i-'Abd Allah.[91] In late 1849, another governor had been appointed, and the deputy-governor, Aqa Khan-i-Irvani, had executed one of the ruffians shortly after his arrival in Yazd. This had prompted Muhammad-i-'Abd Allah to rebel against Aqa Khan, but he had been defeated and forced to seek hiding (about late November–early December 1849).[92]

When clashes occurred between the local government and the Babis following the arrival of Vahid, Muhammad-i-'Abd Allah emerged from hiding and came to Vahid's rescue, probably in the hope of regaining his lost influence in the town as well as taking revenge on Aqa Khan. He might have thought that the Babis were willing to join forces with him. Against the background of the Shaykh Tabarsi conflict and the deteriorating situation of the Babis in the country, malcontents like Muhammad-i-'Abd Allah were likely to consider the Babis as potential allies against local authorities.

Muhammad-i-'Abd Allah forced the deputy-governor to take refuge in the town's citadel and laid siege to it. The 'ulama' of Yazd, however, fearing the Babis' influence, rallied the support of the townspeople for Aqa Khan, and Muhammad-i-'Abd Allah and his gang were attacked and dispersed.[93] All in all, seven or more Babis and some thirty government soldiers and ruffians might have been killed during the Yazd episode.[94] Vahid left Yazd

91 Sipihr, *Nāsikh al-Tavārīkh*, vol. 3, 959, 1002–3.

92 Ibid., 1076–77.

93 See Sheil to Palmerston, 12 February 1850, quoted in Momen, *Bábí and Bahá'í Religions*, 107.

94 See Browne, *Nuqṭatu'l-Káf*, 224. See also A.-L.-M. Nicolas, *Tārīkh-i-Sayyid 'Alī-Muḥammad Ma'rūf bih Bāb*, 'A. M. F. ['Ali-Muhammad Farahvashi], trans. (n.p., 1322 Sh./1943–44), 421. Cf. Fadil-i-Mazandarani, *Ẓuhūr al-Ḥaqq*, vol. 3, 480.

at this time. After his departure, the deputy-governor persecuted Vahid's supporters and executed two or more of the Babis in Yazd.[95]

There is no indication that Vahid sought an alliance with Muhammad-i-'Abd Allah; he certainly did not fight on his side. The central government, however, took a different view of the events in Yazd. Shortly after the disturbances there, over a dozen Babis were arrested in Tehran (19 February 1850). They were given the choice of denying their faith or facing death. By 21 February, seven of them, all people of some prominence, had already been executed in public on Amir Kabir's order.[96] They had been accused of conspiring to assassinate the shah, the premier, and the Imam-Jum'ih of Tehran. The general public, however, did not believe the authorities' claims.[97] The charges were in all probability fabricated. Following the disturbances in Yazd, Amir Kabir may well have intended to teach the Babis a lesson by executing some of the members of the movement in Tehran.

Leaving Yazd, Vahid traveled south to the province of Fars, spreading the Babi message as he passed through towns and villages. His activities would often lead to some conversions, but would also provoke the opposition of some of the 'ulama' and other figures. In Bavanat, a local clerical leader, the Shaykh al-Islam, together with many others became Babis, and some of them joined Vahid on his journey. Vahid then approached Nayriz intending to enter the town, and reached within a short distance of it,[98] but changed his route when the governor ordered him to stay away and went to Istahbanat. He then visited Fasa, where his presence excited opposition. From there he went to Runiz and then back to Istahbanat. Vahid's father was born in Istahbanat and many of his relatives lived there. From Istahbanat, Vahid headed to Nayriz, once again, accompanied by some twenty people, and this time he entered the town while the governor was temporarily away. The first battle of Nayriz began shortly thereafter.[99]

95 Browne, *Nuqṭatu'l-Káf*, 224; Ibrahim-i-Nayrizi, "Sanadī," 635; Nabil, *Dawn-Breakers*, 474–75; Asadu'llah Fadil-i-Mazandarani, "Kitāb-i-Ẓuhūr al-Ḥaqq," vol. 2, n.d. [c. 1932], uncatalogued photocopy of manuscript, Afnan Library, Sandy, Bedfordshire, 406–7.

96 Ferrier to de LaHitte, 21 February 1850, quoted in Momen, *Bábí and Bahá'í Religions*, 104. Cf. Nabil, *Dawn-Breakers*, 443–58.

97 Sheil to Palmerston, 22 February 1850, quoted in Momen, *Bábí and Bahá'í Religions*, 102.

98 Vahid arrived at the shrine of Khajih Ahmad-i-Ansari about seven km west of Nayriz (Ibrahim-i-Nayrizi, "Sanadī," 636).

99 For Vahid's journey in Fars, see Ibrahim-i-Nayrizi, "Sanadī," 636; Muhammad-Shafi'-i-Nayrizi, History, 1–3.

THE NAYRIZ CONFLICT OF MAY–JUNE 1850

The first Nayriz conflict lasted about a month and resulted in the deaths of close to 1,000 people.[100] The atrocities committed against the community during this struggle and the harsh treatment meted out to the surviving Babis drove some of them to seek vengeance, and sowed the seeds of the second conflict in that town.

Nayriz is located almost 220 km east of the provincial capital Shiraz. In 1850, it may have had a population of about 3,000.[101] By the time the conflict began, one-quarter of the inhabitants may have converted to the Babi faith. Nayriz was Vahid's second home town. His Nayrizi wife and their son lived there, and Vahid had many admirers in the town. When the news of Vahid's arrival in Runiz, some seventy km west of Nayriz, reached the people in the latter town, many left to greet him there. On hearing this, the governor of Nayriz, Haji Zayn al-'Abidin Khan-i-Nayrizi, sent word that those who had given their allegiance to Vahid should expect to be killed and have their wives captured, but Vahid's devotees ignored his warning.[102] After the disturbances in Yazd, Amir Kabir surely would have wanted to capture Vahid. The governor feared the reaction of the court in the capital if he allowed Vahid to enter the town.[103] Vahid arrived in Nayriz on 5 Rajab 1266/18 May 1850[104] and immediately went to the local mosque near his residence in the Chinar-Sukhtih quarter, where he had many supporters. A crowd of several hundred, many of whom were armed with swords and muskets, had assembled there to meet him.[105] According to the account

100 The figure for the total casualties of the two sides appears in Ibrahim-i-Nayrizi, "Sanadī," 639–40.

101 Early in the 1870s, Beresford Lovett reported the population of Nayriz to be about 3,500 ("Surveys on the Road from Shiraz to Bam," *Journal of the Royal Geographical Society of London*, vol. 42 [1872], 203).

102 Muhammad-Shafi'-i-Nayrizi, History, 3; Nabil, *Dawn-Breakers*, 476–77; Fadil-i-Mazandarani, "Ẓuhūr al-Ḥaqq," vol. 2, 408.

103 See Ibrahim-i-Nayrizi, "Sanadī," 636; Browne, *Nuqṭatu'l-Káf*, 225; Fadil-i-Mazandarani, "Ẓuhūr al-Ḥaqq," vol. 2, 410.

104 Fadil-i-Mazandarani, "Ẓuhūr al-Ḥaqq," vol. 2, 409. Nabil (*Dawn-Breakers*, 478) and Muhammad-Shafi' Ruhani Nayrizi (*Lama'āt al-Anvār*, vol. 1 [Tehran: Mu'assasiy-i-Millīy-i-Maṭbū'āt-i-Amrī, 130 B.E./1973–74], 57) note that Vahid entered Nayriz on 15 Rajab/28 May.

105 According to Ibrahim-i-Nayrizi, close to 900 people were present ("Sanadī," 636). Cf. Muhammad-Shafi'-i-Nayrizi, History, 4. Relying on information provided by Mulla Muhammad-Shafi', Nabil puts the number of the assembled crowd at 1,500 (*Dawn-Breakers*, 478–79). See also Fadil-i-Mazandarani, "Ẓuhūr al-Ḥaqq," vol. 2, 409.

by Mulla Muhammad-Shafi'-i-Nayrizi, Vahid informed the crowd that he had come to proclaim the word of God and warned of dire consequences if he stayed. He said that troops would be sent against them and that they would be killed, their wives made captive, and their property plundered. The assembled crowd, however, entreated him to stay and expressed their readiness to sacrifice their lives and their all.[106]

Haji Zayn al-'Abidin Khan had retreated to the village of Qatru (Qatruyih), located some forty km east of Nayriz.[107] This region was famous in Fars for the tribal horsemen and musketeers who, on demand, volunteered to serve in the irregular forces of local governors. The governor was intent on returning to Nayriz and gathered a 1,500-man strong army.[108] When news reached Vahid that the governor had gathered an army and was about to enter Nayriz, he instructed some of his followers to take possession of an old fort outside the town—the fort of Khajih near the Chinar-Sukhtih quarter.[109] On his return to Nayriz, Haji Zayn al-'Abidin Khan made his fortified residence in the Bazar quarter his stronghold. For a few days, various dignitaries and religious figures from Nayriz and Istahbanat attempted to mediate between the governor and Vahid to prevent bloodshed.[110] The governor then ordered his musketeers to shoot at the Chinar-Sukhtih quarter, which resulted in the injury of one of the Babis. This incident prompted many of the residents to evacuate the quarter to avoid getting embroiled in hostilities.[111] At daybreak on the following day Vahid and some of his supporters rode out to the fort of Khajih (c. 15 Rajab/28 May). This move enabled them to better defend themselves. It also helped to keep the Babi women and children in the Chinar-Sukhtih quarter out of harm's way. The Babis at the fort were initially about seventy in number.[112]

Haji Zayn al-'Abidin Khan did not consider the Babis a serious threat.

106 History, 3–4.

107 Ibrahim-i-Nayrizi, "Sanadī," 636; Muhammad-Shafi'-i-Nayrizi, History, 3; Nabil, *Dawn-Breakers*, 477. Cf. Hidayat, *Rawḍat al-Ṣafā*, vol. 10, 457.

108 Ibrahim-i-Nayrizi, "Sanadī," 636. Cf. Muhammad-Shafi'-i-Nayrizi, History, 5.

109 Muhammad-Shafi'-i-Nayrizi, History, 5.

110 Ibrahim-i-Nayrizi, "Sanadī," 636.

111 Sayyid Ibrahim-i-Nayrizi's account ("Sanadī," 636) indicates that many left the Chinar-Sukhtih quarter after this incident, but according to Mulla Muhammad-Shafi' (History, 5–6), only a few went to the governor. Cf. Nabil, *Dawn-Breakers*, 482.

112 Muhammad-Shafi'-i-Nayrizi, History, 6; Nabil, *Dawn-Breakers*, 482; Fadil-i-Mazandarani, "Ẓuhūr al-Ḥaqq," vol. 2, 411. Sayyid Ibrahim ("Sanadī," 636) and Sipihr (*Nāsikh al-Tavārīkh*, vol. 3, 1107) put the number of the Babis at the fort at this time at 180 to 200 and 300, respectively.

He sent 500 of his men to deal with Vahid and his companions, but they were attacked and repelled by the Babis. He then sent additional forces, but they were again defeated by the Babis. Shortly afterwards, Haji Zayn al-'Abidin Khan himself arrived, accompanied by his brother, who was a former governor of Nayriz, and other relatives, and his army set up camp near the fort. The Babis made sorties on two consecutive nights. The second time, the governor's forces were completely routed, his brother was killed, and two or three of the latter's sons were taken captive.[113] Following this defeat, the governor retreated to the village of Qatru.

At this time, on Vahid's order, the defense of the fort was organized, and some Babis were assigned specific tasks. A water-cistern was also constructed in the fort. More Babis joined their co-religionists at the fort, swelling their numbers to several hundred.[114] The Babis' victory over Haji Zayn al-'Abidin Khan's forces broadened the support for Vahid among the townspeople.[115] It also struck fear into the hearts of the Babis' opponents, some of whom fled Nayriz.[116]

When the news of the clashes in Nayriz reached Firuz Mirza Nusrat al-Dawlih, the newly appointed governor of Fars, who was on his way to the provincial capital Shiraz, he prompted the Vazir of Fars to dispatch troops

113 The account of these early skirmishes is primarily based on Ibrahim-i-Nayrizi, "Sanadī," 636–38. Some of these skirmishes are not reported in the other sources. See Muhammad-Shafi'-i-Nayrizi, History, 6–7; Nabil, *Dawn-Breakers*, 482–83; Fadil-i-Mazandarani, "Ẓuhūr al-Ḥaqq," vol. 2, 411; Sipihr, *Nāsikh al-Tavārīkh*, vol. 3, 1107–8; Hasan-i-Fasa'i, *Fārsnāmiy-i-Nāṣirī*, vol. 1, 793. Cf. Hidayat, *Rawḍat al-Ṣafā*, vol. 10, 457.

114 Nicolas writes that the number of the Babi defenders at the fort reached 700 to 800 (*Tārīkh-i-Sayyid 'Alī-Muḥammad*, 429). These figures are based on a manuscript of the episode by Mulla Muhammad-Shafi' that Nicolas had in his possession. According to the copy of Mulla Muhammad-Shafi''s account consulted for this chapter, Vahid had some 500 dedicated supporters, but he permitted only about seventy of them to enter the fort, and a few managed to get permission to enter the fort through intermediaries (History, 8–9). Fadil-i-Mazandarani notes that reportedly 400 Babis were eventually ready for combat in the fort and in the town ("Ẓuhūr al-Ḥaqq," vol. 2, 414). Ruhani writes that the number of the Babis at the fort at one point reached 600, and finally 1,000 (*Lama'āt al-Anvār*, vol. 1, 63, 72, 74). Sipihr puts the number of the Babi fighters at this time at over 2,000 (*Nāsikh al-Tavārīkh*, vol. 3, 1108).

It appears that the Babis in the Chinar-Sukhtih quarter also prepared some defenses (see Muhammad-Shafi'-i-Nayrizi, History, 5, 8; Fadil-i-Mazandarani, "Ẓuhūr al-Ḥaqq," vol. 2, 414). These must have been very rudimentary, since, in Nayriz, unlike Zanjan, there did not occur a street-to-street and house-to-house battle at the end of the conflict.

115 Sipihr, *Nāsikh al-Tavārīkh*, vol. 3, 1108. Cf. Ibrahim-i-Nayrizi, "Sanadī," 638.

116 Vahid had appointed an executioner, and on his instruction, twelve of the Babis' enemies were executed. See Ibrahim-i-Nayrizi, "Sanadī," 638. Cf. Muhammad-Shafi'-i-Nayrizi, History, 9, 11; Fadil-i-Mazandarani, "Ẓuhūr al-Ḥaqq," vol. 2, 415.

and two cannons to Nayriz.[117] Leaving Shiraz in early June, these troops joined forces with the army gathered by Haji Zayn al-'Abidin Khan, and their number rose to some 5,000.[118] They proceeded toward Nayriz, where they camped near the fort of Khajih. After a few days, the Babis in the fort made a sortie at night and were joined by fellow Babis from the town, who attacked the army's camp from another direction. During this battle, the cries of the Babi women in Nayriz, cheering the Babi fighters on, could be heard from every side and contributed to demoralizing the troops. The engagement lasted about eight hours, and the casualties were high on both sides, with the Babis suffering sixty or so dead and many injured. Soon afterwards, the Babis made a second night attack on the troops and killed many soldiers.[119] On hearing the news of these setbacks, Firuz Mirza gave orders for fresh troops to proceed to Nayriz. On 19 and 20 June additional forces and two cannons were dispatched.[120] Before these forces reached their destination, however, the conflict ended with the Babis' defeat, as discussed below.

Two consecutive defeats convinced the army commanders that they could not win the battle without substantive casualties. They decided, therefore, to lure the Babis out of the fort by a trick. They suspended fighting for a few days, feigned devotion to Vahid, and expressed their desire to end hostilities. Similar to the conflict in Mazandaran, they sealed a copy of the Qur'an and sent it to the fort, swearing that they desired no more bloodshed and wished to investigate the religious claims of the Babis. They invited Vahid to come to the camp of the army together with a few of his

117 Report of Mirza Mahmud, the British agent in Shiraz, for 24 May to 5 June 1850, quoted in Momen, *Bábí and Bahá'í Religions*, 110; Sipihr, *Nāsikh al-Tavārīkh*, vol. 3, 1108; Hasan-i-Fasa'i, *Fārsnāmiy-i-Nāṣirī*, vol. 1, 793.

118 Sipihr, *Nāsikh al-Tavārīkh*, vol. 3, 1108–9; Hidayat, *Rawḍat al-Ṣafā*, vol. 10, 457; Fadil-i-Mazandarani, "Ẓuhūr al-Ḥaqq," vol. 2, 416.

119 Muhammad-Shafi'-i-Nayrizi, History, 12; Nabil, *Dawn-Breakers*, 487; Fadil-i-Mazandarani, "Ẓuhūr al-Ḥaqq," vol. 2, 417; Ibrahim-i-Nayrizi, "Sanadī," 638; Hasan-i-Fasa'i, *Fārsnāmiy-i-Nāṣirī*, vol. 1, 794; Sipihr, *Nāsikh al-Tavārīkh*, vol. 3, 1109; Mirza Mahmud's report for 4 to 20 June 1850, quoted in Momen, *Bábí and Bahá'í Religions*, 110. Hasan-i-Fasa'i writes that 150 Babis and 300 soldiers were reportedly killed in the first engagement. Sipihr, however, claims that, at the most, four soldiers were killed and five injured. In the second engagement, according to Hasan-i-Fasa'i, the Babis lost almost 50 men and the troops close to 100. There is no mention of this second clash in Mulla Muhammad-Shafi'-i-Nayrizi's account or in Nabil's narrative, which derives its information mainly from the former source.

120 Mirza Mahmud's report for 4 to 20 June 1850, quoted in Momen, *Bábí and Bahá'í Religions*, 110. Cf. Sipihr, *Nāsikh al-Tavārīkh*, vol. 3, 1110.

companions to establish the truth of the Babi religion and promised to submit to him if he did so.[121]

Vahid left the fort on 17 June 1850 accompanied by a few of his companions.[122] He had agreed with the Babi defenders that they should suspend fighting and wait to receive word from him. Contrary to their pledge, the army commanders put Vahid under arrest shortly after his arrival in their camp. He was soon forced to write a message to his companions, instructing them to evacuate the fort. One of the Babis who had accompanied Vahid to the camp was to deliver the message. It is related that Vahid secretly wrote a second message, warning the Babi defenders not to be tricked by the army commanders, and entrusted it to the same companion to deliver it to the Babis at the fort. This companion, however, chose to betray Vahid, informed Haji Zayn al-'Abidin Khan of the second message, and was instructed to deliver only the first.[123]

Though perplexed by the message they received, the Babis at the fort could not bring themselves to disregard their leader's order. They left the fort at night, some carrying their arms with them. Many of these were intercepted and killed by the soldiers and the governor's men, while others managed to hide. After the fort of Khajih was captured and the Babi defenders were neutralized, Vahid was killed, and his body was subjected to indignities (late June).[124] The Chinar-Sukhtih quarter, where most of the Babis lived, was plundered and occupied for three to four weeks by the troops, including the newly arrived forces from Shiraz. Even part of the Bazar quarter was plundered. The soldiers also searched for and managed to seize some of the Babi men. The women were also captured. The fort of Khajih was burnt down.[125]

---

121 Muhammad-Shafi'-i-Nayrizi, History, 13–14; Browne, *Nuqṭatu'l-Káf*, 226–27. Cf. Nabil, *Dawn-Breakers*, 488–89.

122 For this date, see Mirza Mahmud's report for 23 June to 3 July 1850, quoted in Momen, *Bábí and Bahá'í Religions*, 110–11.

123 See Muhammad-Shafi'-i-Nayrizi, History, 14–16; Nabil, *Dawn-Breakers*, 490–91; Fadil-i-Mazandarani, "Ẓuhūr al-Ḥaqq," vol. 2, 419–20; Browne, *Nuqṭatu'l-Káf*, 227–28.

124 Muhammad-Shafi'-i-Nayrizi, History, 16–18; Nabil, *Dawn-Breakers*, 491–94, 499; Fadil-i-Mazandarani, "Ẓuhūr al-Ḥaqq," vol. 2, 428; Ibrahim-i-Nayrizi, "Sanadī," 639. Nabil writes that Vahid was killed on 18 Sha'ban 1266/29 June 1850 (*Dawn-Breakers*, 499). Mirza Mahmud's report for 23 June to 3 July 1850 indicates that this date cannot be completely wrong (Momen, *Bábí and Bahá'í Religions*, 110–11).

125 See Mirza Mahmud's reports for 23 June to 3 July and 1 to 16 July 1850, quoted in Momen, *Bábí and Bahá'í Religions*, 110–11; Ibrahim-i-Nayrizi, "Sanadī," 639; Muhammad-Shafi'-i-Nayrizi, History, 20; Browne, *Nuqṭatu'l-Káf*, 229. See also Nabil, *Dawn-Breakers*, 494–95; Fadil-i-Mazandarani, "Ẓuhūr al-Ḥaqq," vol. 2, 421–22.

Some thirty-six Babi men and about fifty Babi women were taken to Shiraz. They were accompanied by soldiers carrying on bayonets the severed heads of the slain Babis.[126] Of the Babi captives in Shiraz, many were executed on Firuz Mirza's order, while others perished in prison. Haji Zayn al-'Abidin Khan had kept some of the wealthier Babis in his own custody in Nayriz. He extorted heavy sums from them and confiscated their property. Some of the surviving Babis were made to "suffer an anguishing death," while others were subjected to all manner of torture for a long time.[127] The cruelties inflicted on these Babis contributed to triggering the second Nayriz conflict (1853). Two of the survivors were also among the small group of Babis that plotted to assassinate Nasir al-Din Shah in August 1852.

AN ANALYSIS OF THE OBJECTIVES OF VAHID AND THE BABIS IN NAYRIZ

Compared with the accounts of the episode at Shaykh Tabarsi, the available sources on the first Nayriz conflict are fewer and less accurate. The most detailed source about this conflict is the narrative by Mulla Muhammad-Shafi'-i-Nayrizi, an eyewitness to the first and second Nayriz conflicts. He was merely six years old in 1850, however, and must have heavily relied on other eyewitnesses and informants for his narrative. Moreover, he wrote his account many years later. As a result, some important details are missing, and it is not fully accurate. Among the early accounts, those by the two official historians of this period and Western diplomatic reports are short and also contain relatively many inaccuracies. The exception is the narrative by Sayyid Ibrahim-i-Nayrizi, which appears to be accurate, but it is also very brief. All this makes an analysis of the objectives of the Babis in Nayriz a more difficult task compared with the Mazandaran episode.

According to Mulla Muhammad-Shafi', Vahid's objective in coming to Nayriz was to deliver the divine message.[128] His account suggests that not so many of Vahid's supporters had become Babis previously and that Vahid wished to convert them to the Babi religion. As stated earlier, on the very

126 Mirza Mahmud's report for 1 to 16 July 1850, quoted in Momen, *Bábí and Bahá'í Religions*, 111; Fadil-i-Mazandarani, "Ẓuhūr al-Ḥaqq," vol. 2, 425. Cf. Sipihr, *Nāsikh al-Tavārīkh*, vol. 3, 1110.

127 Muhammad-Shafi'-i-Nayrizi, History, 20–21; Nabil, *Dawn-Breakers*, 495–99; Fadil-i-Mazandarani, "Ẓuhūr al-Ḥaqq," vol. 2, 423.

128 History, 4. Cf. Nabil, *Dawn-Breakers*, 479.

day of Vahid's arrival, several hundred people assembled in a mosque to meet him. Mulla Muhammad-Shafi''s account suggests that the majority of those who came to hear Vahid speak in the mosque during the ten days or so that he was in Nayriz before the conflict began accepted the Babi faith.[129] There is no mention in the available sources of Vahid having visited Nayriz previously, following his conversion in 1846, though it is known that he traveled in Iran to spread the Bab's message.[130] The available sources only relate that Vahid, immediately after his conversion, sent some of the Bab's writings to his father-in-law, who wielded religious authority and was the head of the religious students in the Chinar-Sukhtih quarter of Nayriz.[131] It thus seems that the conversion of the large majority of Vahid's supporters occurred during his visit in May 1850.[132]

When Vahid decided to enter Nayriz in defiance of the governor's order, he anticipated that the governor was likely to take action against him. For this reason, he immediately warned his followers about the prospect of a clash if he stayed. He knew that if a conflict broke out, his supporters would not have any realistic chance of winning it. As reported by Mulla Muhammad-Shafi', Vahid had no misgivings about this. For him, however, the meaning and significance of the conflict did not revolve and depend on victory. This is also indicated by the manner of Vahid's warfare. Retreating to a fort outside Nayriz only allowed Vahid to delay defeat. As was the case with the siege at Shaykh Tabarsi, it was only a matter of time before the Babi forces would be vanquished.

The fact that Vahid left the fort of Khajih when he was invited by the army commanders to prove the validity of the Babi cause to them also indicates that, for him, the issue was not victory. He must have known that he was putting himself in danger by going to the army camp. The claim by the court historian Sipihr that Vahid left the fort because he realized that the

129 History, 4–5. Nicolas goes so far as to state that all the inhabitants of the Chinar-Sukhtih quarter became Babis at this time (*Tārīkh-i-Sayyid ʿAlī-Muḥammad*, 424).

130 In one of his treatises, Vahid refers to the date of his visit to Shiraz, where he met the Bab and converted to the Babi cause. This was in Jumada I 1262/April–May 1846 (see Fadil-i-Mazandarani, *Ẓuhūr al-Ḥaqq*, vol. 3, 471).

131 Fadil-i-Mazandarani, *Ẓuhūr al-Ḥaqq*, vol. 3, 465.

132 Even those of Vahid's supporters who may have already identified themselves, at least to some extent, with the Babi cause at the time of Vahid's arrival would not have understood the full implications of the Bab's claims, as these became clear only gradually. Thus, Vahid's intention of coming to Nayriz was probably twofold: to win new converts to the Babi cause, and to acquaint those who already considered themselves Babis more fully with the religion they had embraced.

Babis' resistance was futile is baseless.[133] The fact that the Babis in Nayriz had no chance of winning a war against the government was apparent to Vahid from the beginning. Moreover, Vahid's companions were ready to continue to fight, had it not been for the treachery of the Babi messenger who persuaded them to evacuate the fort. Vahid was aware of the treacherous intentions of the army commanders, but felt obligated to comply with their request and leave the fort in order to "complete the proof" and out of reverence for the Qur'an.[134]

The question remains why Vahid was willing to engage in a battle against the governor, knowing that it could only end in his defeat. There is a story about Vahid that is relevant to this question. Probably in the first half of 1848, Vahid's travels had brought him to Tehran. It is reported that, on one occasion when Tahirih was present, Vahid was engaged in quoting Qur'anic verses and Islamic traditions in vindication of the religion of the Bab, when, suddenly, he was interrupted by Tahirih, who declared that now was not the time for quoting traditions; it was the time for "action" and "sacrifice."[135] Tahirih herself attempted in late 1848 to join the Babis at Shaykh Tabarsi but failed. Her sentiments, as reflected in this story, echoed those of many of her co-religionists about the way they were to respond to the challenges posed by the Bab's continued imprisonment and the public's growing hostility toward the movement. The above anecdote, with its reference to sacrifice, provides some clues as to why Vahid did not shy away from a battle with Haji Zayn al-'Abidin Khan.

Vahid could have pursued his activities proclaiming the Babi cause elsewhere rather than in Nayriz. Either way it could be expected that at one point he would be arrested and killed. As discussed earlier, shortly after the episode in Yazd, several well-known Babis had been executed in the capital on Amir Kabir's orders. Vahid was the most prominent Babi in the country. If he continued his activities spreading the Babi religion, he would before long suffer a similar fate. Thus, insofar as his own life was concerned, Vahid's decision to go to Nayriz would not change anything. Its significance was because of the consequences it could have for his many supporters. Despite the risks involved, Vahid chose to go to Nayriz to proclaim the Babi cause. As

---

133 *Nāsikh al-Tavārīkh*, vol. 3, 1110. Sipihr also states that Vahid was losing the support of his companions. Sayyid Ibrahim-i-Nayrizi's description of what happened, however, is more consistent with the account given in the Babi and Baha'i sources ("Sanadī," 638–39).

134 Browne, *Nuqṭatu'l-Káf*, 227; Nabil, *Dawn-Breakers*, 489.

135 'Abdu'l-Baha, *Memorials of the Faithful*, Marzieh Gail, trans., 2nd printing (Wilmette: Bahá'í Publishing Trust, 1975), 200.

noted earlier, however, he did not intend to stay, and it was only because of the insistence of his devotees, who ardently pleaded with him not to leave, that he changed his mind and remained in Nayriz.

A sense of mutual devotion and obligation existed between Vahid and his admirers in Nayriz. For Vahid, that obligation entailed a responsibility to acquaint them with the Bab's message. To his admirers, the prospect of getting killed in a battle by the side of Vahid appeared more honorable than seeing him leave the town, expecting that he would fall at the hands of his enemies in another place, probably under more humiliating circumstances. The majority of them joined Vahid fully cognizant of the dire consequences that their actions could have. Once his supporters had made their choice, Vahid no longer feared a confrontation with the governor. If it happened, it could serve to proclaim the cause of the Bab and vindicate its truth.

The Babi-Baha'i sources focus on the predominantly religious aspects of the conflict for the Babi participants. Initially, however, another factor seems to have been at play. According to the official histories of the period, Nayriz was in a state of uprising against its governor when Vahid entered the town.[136] The governor had been forced to leave Nayriz and was busy raising an army in the neighboring region of Qatru. The official Qajar chronicles, however, provide no information as to the nature and scale of the rebellion in Nayriz. They do not comment on the grievances of the townspeople, the social classes and groups involved, or their numerical strength. There is also no mention in the official accounts of a Babi involvement in this rebellion. They merely state that those who had rebelled to get rid of the governor joined Vahid.[137] Haj Mirza Hasan-i-Fasa'i gives a similar account of this rebellion in his *Fārsnāmiy-i-Nāṣirī*. The "mischief-makers," he notes, numbered close to 500, and they all joined Vahid after he entered Nayriz.[138] Although Mulla Muhammad-Shafi' does not refer to any rebellion by the townspeople, he, as well as Sayyid Ibrahim-i-Nayrizi, indicate that many of the townspeople who went to the mosque of the Chinar-Sukhtih quarter to meet Vahid were armed.

The scant information that can be gleaned from the available sources suggests that the governor had antagonized many of the townspeople. It is

136 Sipihr, *Nāsikh al-Tavārīkh*, vol. 3, 1106; Hidayat, *Rawḍat al-Ṣafā*, vol. 10, 457. See also Ibrahim-i-Nayrizi, "Sanadī," 636.

137 Sipihr, *Nāsikh al-Tavārīkh*, vol. 3, 1106–7; Hidayat, *Rawḍat al-Ṣafā*, vol. 10, 457.

138 Vol. 1, 792.

reported, for example, that a nephew of the governor by the name Mirza Muhammad-Ja'far was among those who joined Vahid. He became a Babi after Vahid's arrival. The governor had previously killed Mirza Muhammad-Ja'far's father. He had also imprisoned Mirza Muhammad-Ja'far and several of his brothers and ordered that they be starved to death. A sympathizer, however, had supplied the prisoners with food and water.[139] It is likely that many of those who had rebelled against the governor converted to the Babi religion in the brief interval between Vahid's arrival and the beginning of hostilities in Nayriz. Many of them may have already been among Vahid's devotees or may have held him in high regard because of his credentials as a prominent *'ālim*. Their grievances against the governor may explain why they were willing to risk a confrontation with him.

To the Babis, hundreds of whom were new converts, the coming struggle had a profound meaning. In their view, they would be fighting for the cause of the Qa'im. They considered Vahid as a representative of the Qa'im. At one point after the conflict began, a dozen of the Babis' enemies were executed in Nayriz on Vahid's instructions. These executions served to emphasize Vahid's authority as the Qa'im's representative to pass judgment on those who had fought against his "helpers."

Conflict always involves more than one party, however. Haji Zayn al-'Abidin Khan's decision to open fire on the homes of Vahid's supporters was the immediate cause of the outbreak of hostilities. When the governor had earlier banned Vahid from entering Nayriz, it was partly out of fear for the reaction of the shah's court.[140] But he must also have anticipated that Vahid's arrival would complicate the situation. Haji Zayn al-'Abidin Khan may have considered Vahid a potential foe because of his Babi beliefs. Moreover, if many of those who had rebelled against him were also admirers of Vahid, Haji Zayn al-'Abidin Khan would have had added reason to keep Vahid at a distance. His actions suggest, however, that he did not consider the Babis a match for his forces. Underestimating their resolve and commitment, he did not take the necessary precautions, and hence his men were defeated by the Babis four times before troops arrived from Shiraz.

Although the arrival of Vahid and the conversion of many of the inhabitants of Nayriz to the Babi religion added a new dimension to the tensions

139 Ruhani, *Lama'āt al-Anvār*, vol. 1, 258–60; Muhammad-'Ali Faydi, *Nayrīz-i-Mushkbīz* (Tehran: Mu'assasiy-i-Millīy-i-Maṭbū'āt-i-Amrī, 130 B.E./1973–74), 83–85.

140 See Ibrahim-i-Nayrizi, "Sanadī," 636; Browne, *Nuqṭatu'l-Káf*, 225; Fadil-i-Mazandarani, "Ẓuhūr al-Ḥaqq," vol. 2, 410.

between the townspeople and Haji Zayn al-'Abidin Khan, it strengthened the latter's hand in one significant way. What might have been previously perceived by the authorities in Shiraz and Tehran as a local dispute between the governor and a segment of the townspeople acquired a completely new character and significance following the arrival of Vahid. It had now turned into a conflict between the Qajar state and the Babis. The authorities in Tehran, once informed of the developments in Nayriz, could be expected to demand swift and decisive action against the Babis. Haji Zayn al-'Abidin Khan could also be sure to receive assistance from the government in Shiraz. Similarly, he could count on the backing of the 'ulama', which would be important for mobilizing local forces of volunteers as well as exerting pressure on the provincial government to act against the Babis. It is reported that when the conflict began, Haji Zayn al-'Abidin Khan, besides asking for military assistance from the provincial government, sent letters to the 'ulama' and dignitaries of Shiraz.[141]

The Babi-Baha'i sources of the Nayriz conflict do not comment on the attitude of the local 'ulama' toward the fighting. This may well be because the 'ulama' of Nayriz and nearby towns were completely overshadowed by the stature and prominence of Vahid. Another noteworthy feature of the conflict was the attempt by some local dignitaries and religious figures to mediate between the Babis and the governor. The account by Sayyid Ibrahim-i-Nayrizi indicates that various dignitaries and *sādāt* (descendants of the Prophet Muhammad) of Nayriz and some of the 'ulama' of Istahbanat tried to prevent the conflict.[142] Their attitude and position indicate the ties that connected the new and old Babis with the Muslim population of the area. The conflict largely severed these ties and contributed to the emergence of a distinct Babi community in Nayriz. The second Nayriz conflict that occurred three years later only deepened the breach between the Babis and the wider Muslim community.

Lasting only a month, the fighting in Nayriz did not present a major challenge to the authorities in Tehran. In terms of the casualties of the troops, this conflict did not compare with either the Mazandaran struggle, which had ended the previous year, or the Zanjan episode, which began about the same time but continued for seven and a half months.

141 Muhammad-Shafi'-i-Nayrizi, History, 11.
142 "Sanadī," 636.

HUJJAT AND THE 'ULAMA' OF ZANJAN

Mulla Muhammad-'Aliy-i-Zanjani entitled Hujjat, the leader of the Babis in Zanjan, was a popular clerical figure in the town before his conversion to the Babi religion in 1846. As an *akhbārī 'ālim*, he had become involved in serious disputes with other leading Zanjani 'ulama', who were *uṣūlīs*.[143] Hujjat believed that the authority of the *uṣūlī mujtahids* was a self-arrogation that did not rest on the text of the Qur'an and the traditions of the Imams. This fact and Hujjat's habit of denouncing the 'ulama' were the major causes of the disputes. Besides this, Hujjat's views on certain legal matters were considered heretical by the other 'ulama'. He also exhibited a harsh attitude toward some current abuses that were generally tolerated by the other 'ulama' in a tacit understanding with the local authorities. His popularity and influence among the townspeople also aroused the jealousy of the other prominent 'ulama' and added fuel to their opposition to Hujjat.[144]

These frictions and disputes prompted the 'ulama' of Zanjan to lodge a complaint against Hujjat at the court of Muhammad Shah, as a result of which he was summoned to Tehran. Baha'i accounts maintain that at about the time the Bab passed through Zanjan on his way to the prison-fortress of Maku in Azarbaijan (April 1847), the shah, for a second time, ordered the transfer of Hujjat to the capital.[145] An important contemporary document, a petition against Hujjat endorsed by eighteen 'ulama' and lay individuals and dated Jumada I 1263/April–May 1847, seems to corroborate this dating.[146] Interestingly, while this petition denounces Hujjat for his allegedly corrupt and heretical views and practices, it does not refer to him as a Babi. As attested by the Babi-Baha'i accounts, Hujjat had embraced the

143 For an overview of the differences between the *akhbārī* and *uṣūlī* schools of Shi'i Islam, see Moojan Momen, *An Introduction to Shi'i Islam: The History and Doctrines of Twelver Shi'ism* (Oxford: George Ronald, 1985), 222–25.

144 For a discussion of Hujjat's early disputes with the established 'ulama' of Zanjan, see John Walbridge, "The Babi Uprising in Zanjan: Causes and Issues," *Iranian Studies*, vol. 29, nos. 3–4 (1996), 342–44.

145 Nabil, *Dawn-Breakers*, 533–37; Husayn-i-Zanjani, History, ff. 4b–5a. Cf. 'Abd al-Ahad-i-Zanjani, History, ff. 4b–5a; Browne, "Personal Reminiscences," 777–78. The pieces of information provided in the Babi, Baha'i, and Azali sources and the Qajar chronicles about the events involving Hujjat and the Babis in Zanjan prior to and during the conflict of 1850 do not always correspond with each other. Due to constraint of space, only some of the discrepancies in the existing sources are discussed in this chapter.

146 This petition was published in the daily newspaper *Iṭṭilā'āt*, 20 Azar 1354/11 December 1975, 10–11. Walbridge discusses its contents in "Babi Uprising in Zanjan," 343–44, 348. Internal evidence indicates that it was prepared outside Zanjan.

Bab's message about a year earlier. By this time, many of Hujjat's supporters had likely followed their leader into the Babi religion. The absence of any reference to the religion of the Bab in the text of the aforementioned petition, however, implies that they did not openly profess and propagate their new faith.

After arriving in Tehran, Hujjat was barred from returning to Zanjan. He was still in the city when Muhammad Shah died (September 1848), and after the outbreak of the Mazandaran conflict, he heard that Amir Kabir intended to put him to death.[147] This prompted Hujjat to escape from the capital and make his way to Zanjan (early 1849). At about the same time, Amir Aslan Khan Majd al-Dawlih, the maternal uncle of Nasir al-Din Shah, was appointed governor of Zanjan and was instructed by Amir Kabir to arrest and send Hujjat to the capital. The Zanjan conflict broke out a year later.

THE ZANJAN EPISODE OF MAY 1850–JANUARY 1851

In May 1850 the town of Zanjan witnessed the beginning of what became the bloodiest of the Babi–state conflicts of mid-nineteenth-century Iran. An estimated 20,000 troops and irregulars, armed with eighteen or more pieces of artillery, fought against the Babis.[148] Zanjan may have had a population of around 12,000 at the time.[149] The Babis, including the women and chil-

---

147 Nabil, *Dawn-Breakers*, 539, 555.

148 Momen, *Bábí and Bahá'í Religions*, 114; Sipihr, *Nāsikh al-Tavārīkh*, vol. 3, 1062–68. The text of the account of the Zanjan episode in this edition of the *Nāsikh al-Tavārīkh* contains at least two significant typographical errors and omissions as compared with the text edited by Jahangir Qa'im-Maqami: Muhammad-Taqi Lisan al-Mulk Sipihr, *Nāsikh al-Tavārīkh: Dawriy-i-Kāmil-i-Tārīkh-i-Qājārīyyih* (Tehran: Amīr Kabīr, 1337 Sh./1958–59).

149 Different estimates (in brackets below) have been offered for the population of Zanjan in various years of the nineteenth century. See, for example, M. Tancoigne, *A Narrative of a Journey into Persia, and Residence at Teheran: Containing a Descriptive Itinerary from Constantinople to the Persian Capital* (London: William Wright, 1820), 83 (10,000); Horatio Southgate, *Narrative of a Tour through Armenia, Kurdistan, Persia, and Mesopotamia: With Observations on the Condition of Mohammedanism and Christianity in Those Countries* (New York: D. Appleton & Co., 1840), vol. 2, 44 (8,000); Alexander Mackay, *Elements of Modern Geography*, 12th ed. (Edinburgh; London: William Blackwood and Sons, 1872), 164 (15,000); Samuel Graham Wilson, *Persian Life and Customs: With Scenes and Incidents of Residence and Travel in the Land of the Lion and the Sun*, 3rd ed. (Chicago: Student Missionary Campaign Library, 1895), 145 (20,000).

dren, may have initially numbered 4,000 or more, thus constituting about one-third of the inhabitants. The majority of the Babis participated in the conflict, and about 1,800 lost their lives. The casualties of the government troops and the local militia were probably much higher, with one Western observer reporting that an estimated 4,500 soldiers had been killed during the siege.[150]

Two months before the conflict began, Salar's rebellion in Khurasan had finally been crushed. His revolt had engaged the military resources of the country for three years. In terms of loss of life and financial costs as well as duration, it proved to be the most significant single rebellion during the entire Qajar reign.

The existing accounts of the Zanjan episode disagree about important details, including the dating and order of the events prior to the outbreak of open warfare on 17 May. Unlike the Mazandaran and Nayriz episodes, there is no early eyewitness account that may help assess the credibility of conflicting statements. The course of the fighting presented is primarily reconstructed on the basis of the *Nāsikh al-Tavārīkh* and Western diplomatic dispatches. There are, however, some discrepancies between these sources, as well as within the *Nāsikh al-Tavārīkh.*

The episode that eventually led to the conflagration in Zanjan was a fight between a Babi boy and a Muslim man. Nicolas cites an account of this incident by the Babi boy. The Babi boy was walking home with his teacher, who was also a Babi, when a Muslim neighbor of the boy's family blocked their way, brandishing a knife while drunk. The Babi boy stabbed and injured the man. He later managed to escape, but his teacher was arrested.[151] Sometime after this incident, Hujjat sent a petition to Amir Aslan Khan Majd al-Dawlih, the governor, asking him to release the young Babi, but his petition was ignored. He then renewed his request and offered to pay a fine; when this was again rejected, Hujjat's messenger forced the release of the prisoner. The governor had until this time failed to carry out Amir Kabir's instruction

150 Ferrier to de LaHitte, 24 February 1851, quoted in Momen, *Bábí and Bahá'í Religions*, 124.

151 Nicolas, *Tārīkh-i-Sayyid 'Alī-Muḥammad*, 362–63. The Babi boy in question was Naqd-'Ali, a brother to Aqa 'Abd al-Ahad-i-Zanjani, the author of the Azali eyewitness account of the Zanjan episode. The latter has also given the account of this incident (History, ff. 5b–6a). However, it differs in some details from Naqd-'Ali's account. Naqd-'Ali is referred to as a Babi in the available sources. No one from his family, however, participated in the Zanjan conflict on the Babis' side. They stayed in the Muslim side of the town during the conflict.

about arresting Hujjat for fear of the reaction of his supporters and because they always escorted their leader. Urged by the 'ulama' and presented with a plan, however, he now resolved to arrest Hujjat.[152]

On Friday 4 Rajab 1266/17 May 1850, a party of ruffians and others approached the mosque of Hujjat, but was repelled by the Babi guards. In the clashes that occurred, Sipihr notes, some forty people were injured, including one of the governor's men. Two people were also killed, including a son of a local clergy. After being dispersed by the Babi guards, some of the ruffians encountered an unarmed Babi, attacked and severely injured him, and took him to the governorate, where he was killed. His naked body was thrown out into the public square of the town as a warning to those who entertained any sympathies for Hujjat. The governor also ordered that a crier go through the town and instruct the Muslim populace to go to the western side of the town, warning that the Babi side of the town would soon be destroyed by government troops. Assisted by the 'ulama', who were inciting the populace against the Babis, the governor also began recruiting reinforcements from the neighboring villages. The 'ulama' had succeeded in launching a holy war against the Babis.[153]

On the following day, the Babis secured the fort of 'Ali-Mardan Khan inside the town.[154] This move also provided the Babis with a shelter for the women and children and a secure site for storing provisions and some weapons. They were preparing for a long struggle. The next day (Sunday 6 Rajab/19 May), Sipihr maintains, a group of Babis made an unsuccessful attempt to capture the governor at his residence.[155]

On 25 May, within hours after the news of the disturbances in Zanjan

---

152 Husayn-i-Zanjani, History, ff. 6a–7a; Nabil, *Dawn-Breakers*, 540–41; 'Abd al-Ahad-i-Zanjani, History, ff. 6a–7a; Browne, "Personal Reminiscences," 781–82.

153 Husayn-i-Zanjani, History, ff. 6b–8a; Nabil, *Dawn-Breakers*, 541–44; Sipihr, *Nāsikh al-Tavārīkh*, vol. 3, 1061. Diverging from Mirza Husayn-i-Zanjani's narrative, Dhabih's account, interpolated into a version of Mirza Husayn-i-Hamadani's history, maintains that the attempt to arrest Hujjat was carried out after the crier went through the town causing the townspeople to separate into opposing camps (Browne, *Táríkh-i-Jadíd*, 143–44). Had this been the case, it would have robbed the governor's plan to arrest Hujjat of the element of surprise. See also 'Abd al-Ahad-i-Zanjani, History, ff. 9a–11a; Browne, "Personal Reminiscences," 787–92.

154 Sipihr, *Nāsikh al-Tavārīkh*, vol. 3, 1061; Nabil, *Dawn-Breakers*, 544–45. The account by Mirza Husayn-i-Zanjani puts this event at a later date (History, f. 11b). See also Browne, *Táríkh-i-Jadíd*, 145–46.

155 *Nāsikh al-Tavārīkh*, vol. 3, 1061–62. Cf. Nabil, *Dawn-Breakers*, 545.

had reached Tehran, a battalion of infantry, 400 cavalry, and three pieces of artillery were dispatched.[156] Amir Kabir's swift response indicated the seriousness with which he viewed the events in Zanjan. These and other troops arrived in Zanjan in early Sha'ban (around mid-June). Earlier, on 20 Rajab/2 June, cavalry troops had arrived from the nearby town of Sultaniyyih.

Zanjan was surrounded by a wall built of unbaked clay that was seven to eight meters high. The Babis controlled the eastern half of the town and commanded over four of its six gates.[157] They had raised some thirty barricades and had posted over 1,000 fighting men and boys to defend them and to keep watch on the enemy.[158] The Babis had also constructed two guns. They collected and fired back at the army cannon-balls shot at them.[159]

Sipihr's account in the *Nāsikh al-Tavārīkh* suggests that the first major assault on the Babis' positions came on 20 Sha'ban/1 July. Tunnels were dug to one of the barricades of the Babis. Once exploded, Majd al-Dawlih and the army commanders attacked and captured the barricade. This was followed by a lull of several days.[160] On 9 July, the Bab was executed by a firing squad in Tabriz at the order of Amir Kabir. He had been a prisoner of the state for several years, and contact with his followers had been severely restricted. His execution, Amir Kabir thought, would crush the spirits of his followers and deal a severe blow to the movement. The troops in Zanjan may have hoped that the news of the Bab's execution would cause the Babis to desert Hujjat, but they continued their resistance.

Among the Babi fighters was a peasant girl by the name Zaynab. Early during the conflict, when the Babis were erecting barricades, she had persuaded Hujjat to give her permission to participate in the struggle. Cutting her hair and dressing like a man, she had joined the defenders of one of the barricades. She fought the assailing troops for five months before she was

156 Sheil to Palmerston, 25 May 1850, quoted in Momen, *Bábí and Bahá'í Religions*, 115. Cf. Sipihr, *Nāsikh al-Tavārīkh*, vol. 3, 1062.

157 Anitchkov to Prince Vorontsov, 29 July 1850, quoted in Momen, *Bábí and Bahá'í Religions*, 117.

158 Nabil, *Dawn-Breakers*, 549. According to Mirza Husayn-i-Zanjani, about 1,800 Babis defended thirty-one barricades (History, ff. 9b–10a). Sipihr states that the Babis had erected forty-eight barricades (*Nāsikh al-Tavārīkh*, vol. 3, 1064). Aqa 'Abd al-Ahad-i-Zanjani mentions sixty barricades (History, f. 19a); Browne, "Personal Reminiscences," 809.

159 Stevens to Palmerston, 31 July 1850; Abbott to Sheil, 30 August 1850; quoted in Momen, *Bábí and Bahá'í Religions*, 117–18. See also 'Abd al-Ahad-i-Zanjani, History, f. 20a; Browne, "Personal Reminiscences," 811.

160 Sipihr, *Nāsikh al-Tavārīkh*, vol. 3, 1062.

killed. Her courage and fearlessness prompted Hujjat to name her Rustam-'Ali. She was not the only female who, disguised as a man, had joined the Babi combatants.[161]

The troops' slow advancement compelled the authorities in Tehran to dispatch additional forces to Zanjan.[162] On 15 Ramadan/26 July, a regiment that had newly arrived in Zanjan, together with other regular forces as well as irregular militias, launched a fresh attack and succeeded in capturing another Babi barricade, but not before suffering some fifty casualties.[163]

Amir Kabir was determined to put an end to the Babi resistance quickly. He sent a message that if Hujjat's men were not defeated, captured, and sent to the capital within a few days, the army commanders would be severely punished. On 25 Ramadan/5 August, government forces, together with volunteer fighters from among the townspeople, made another attempt to break through the Babi lines, but without any definite result. Many were killed on both sides during this engagement.[164]

At about this time, the bazaar of Zanjan was set on fire. The bazaar stretched from the eastern part of the town to its western boundary. After the commencement of fighting, the bazaar had been divided into two parts separated by an artificial wall. The state chronicles maintain that the Babis were responsible for this fire. This is likely since the fire engaged the townspeople and gave the Babis an opportunity to reconstruct and strengthen their barricades. Moreover, the Babis had earlier moved all the provisions in their shops to the fort. There was no activity in the section of the bazaar that stretched through the eastern, Babi part of Zanjan, while some shops still stayed open in the western, Muslim side of the town. Thus, the Babis may have gained the most out of this fire. According to Mirza Husayn-i-Zanjani, however, 320 Babi shops were also set alight. His narrative suggests that Muslims and Babis both had a share in starting the fire. Whoever was responsible, the fire brought about a lull of a couple of weeks in the fighting.[165]

161 Husayn-i-Zanjani, History, ff. 17b–18a; Nabil, *Dawn-Breakers*, 549–52, 559; 'Abd al-Ahad-i-Zanjani, History, ff. 15b–16b; Browne, "Personal Reminiscences," 802–3. Rustam is a mythological hero in Persian literature. Sipihr refers to the activities of a fifteen- or sixteen-year-old Babi girl who assisted the Babi fighters (*Nāsikh al-Tavārīkh*, vol. 3, 1066). She may have been a different person than Rustam-'Ali.

162 Sipihr, *Nāsikh al-Tavārīkh*, vol. 3, 1062.

163 Ibid., 1062–63.

164 Ibid., 1063.

165 Husayn-i-Zanjani, History, f. 9a; 'Abd al-Ahad-i-Zanjani, History, f. 11b; Browne, "Personal Reminiscences," 792–93; Sipihr, *Nāsikh al-Tavārīkh*, vol. 3, 1060, 1063. Cf. Hidayat, *Rawḍat al-Ṣafā*, vol. 10, 449.

Close to ninety days since the inception of hostilities had passed when Amir Kabir dispatched Muhammad Khan-i-Mirpanj, the former Military Commander of Tabriz, with 3,000 troops and six cannons and two mortars. He arrived in Zanjan on 8 Shavval/17 August.[166] Muhammad Khan served as the commanding officer of the government forces for the remaining period of the siege. On the very night of his arrival, a heavy bombardment of the Babis' positions began.[167]

The Babi women and even children supported the struggle. According to the Baha'i chronicler Nabil,

> Men and women laboured with unabating fervour to strengthen the defences of the fort and reconstruct whatever the enemy had demolished. What leisure they could obtain was consecrated to prayer. Every thought, every desire, was subordinated to the paramount necessity of guarding their stronghold against the onslaughts of the assailant. The part the women played in these operations was no less arduous than that accomplished by their men companions. Every woman, irrespective of rank and age, joined with energy in the common task. They sewed the garments, baked the bread, ministered to the sick and wounded, repaired the barricades, cleared away from the courts and terraces the balls and missiles fired upon them by the enemy, and, last but not least, cheered the faint in heart and animated the faith of the wavering. Even the children joined in giving whatever assistance was in their power to the common cause, and seemed to be fired by an enthusiasm no less remarkable than that which their fathers and mothers displayed.[168]

By late August, Muhammad Khan had managed to drive the Babis from their hold on the northern wall and confine them to the southeastern corner of the town. He was able to fire at the Babi positions from the

166 Sipihr, *Nāsikh al-Tavārīkh*, vol. 3, 1063–64; Hidayat, *Rawḍat al-Ṣafā*, vol. 10, 450; Muhammad-Sadiq Diya'i, "Sanadī rāji' bih Shūrish-i-Bābīyān-i-Zanjān," *Yaghmā*, vol. 20, no. 3 (1346 Sh./1967–68), 164. Cf. Dolgorukov to Seniavin, 31 July 1850 (Julian)/12 August 1850 (Gregorian), quoted in Mikhail Sergeevich Ivanov, *Babidskie vosstaniya v Irane (1848–1852)* (Moscow: Trudy Instituta Vostokvedeniya XXX, 1939), 154. See also Momen, *Bábí and Bahá'í Religions*, 118. The date of this dispatch given in the latter source is one day off. Muhammad Khan-i-Mirpanj was later granted the title Amir-i-Tuman.

167 Nabil, *Dawn-Breakers*, 557–58. Cf. Husayn-i-Zanjani, History, ff. 12a–12b.

168 *Dawn-Breakers*, 563.

bastions he had newly captured and from within the town. The Babis now controlled only one-quarter of the town. To many observers, their defeat seemed near. The British Consul Keith Abbott, however, was of a different opinion. Writing from the army camp before Zanjan, he made the following observation:

> The resistance of the Bâbees appears to have been most determined and conducted with much skill. These people have erected Barricades and have loop-holed all the houses in their quarter, so that though their numbers are now greatly reduced by desertion and casualties and they are said not to have more than 300 fighting men left, their position is so strong that it must no doubt be a matter of considerable difficulty to dislodge them.[169]

Muhammad Khan attempted at one point to trick the Babis into believing that Nasir al-Din Shah had decided to abandon the Zanjan campaign and that government forces wished to end the fighting. Hostilities were suspended, and a copy of the Qur'an was sealed and sent to Hujjat with an invitation for him to send a delegation of the Babis to meet Muhammad Khan. Although Hujjat believed that the commander only intended to trick the Babis, he decided to respond to his invitation out of respect for the Qur'an. Some elder Babis together with nine small boys were chosen to represent Hujjat, but after arriving in the army camp, Muhammad Khan ordered their arrest.[170]

A renewed effort was made to persuade the Babis to lay down arms after the arrival of 'Aziz Khan-i-Mukri in late August. 'Aziz Khan was the commander of the armed forces directly responsible to Amir Kabir. He was on his way to Yerevan to meet the Grand Duke of Russia. The Amir had instructed him to take command of the operations in Zanjan on his way to Yerevan, in the hope that 'Aziz Khan would be able to bring the matter to a speedy end. Initially, 'Aziz Khan ordered the release of some Babi prisoners.[171] However, as it did not persuade the Babis to lay down arms, he launched an attack, but soon had to give up. All the captive Babis, however, were killed at his

169 Letter to Sheil, 30 August 1850, quoted in Momen, *Bábí and Bahá'í Religions*, 118.
170 Husayn-i-Zanjani, History, ff. 18a–19a; Nabil, *Dawn-Breakers*, 563–66. Mirza Husayn-i-Zanjani also writes that Muhammad Khan had some of these Babis killed in a painful manner.
171 Sipihr, *Nāsikh al-Tavārīkh*, vol. 3, 1064.

order.[172] 'Aziz Khan stayed in Zanjan very briefly and left without having achieved anything.

Toward the end of August, six pieces of heavy cannons and fresh supplies of ammunition were dispatched from Tehran.[173] At about this time, Amir Kabir sacked three of the army commanders as a punishment for their failure to subjugate the Babis.[174] The 'ulama' of Zanjan had accused one of these of having become a Babi, and the Amir seems to have become suspicious of him. Their sack also served as a warning to the remaining army commanders that the Amir meant business. Amir Kabir's attitude and methods are also evident in a letter he wrote to Mirza Ibrahim Khan Muzaffar al-Dawlih, the brigadier of the regiment of the district of Khamsih. In it, the Amir threatened that the brigadier, as well as the governor and Muhammad Khan would all be held culpable for any negligence evinced in the case of the "accursed" Mulla Muhammad-'Ali (i.e., Hujjat) and demanded that he be seized, whether dead or alive.[175]

As the bombardment of the fort continued, the Babis' casualties mounted, but they did not cease fighting, causing Amir Kabir to become increasingly frustrated. In late November, the British Consul in Tabriz, Richard W. Stevens, reported that "a large reinforcement" was on the way to Zanjan and noted that Amir Kabir "has authorized, if necessary, the destruction of the town and a general massacre."[176] In early December a major breakthrough came with the capture of the fort of 'Ali-Mardan Khan by the Garrus regiment.[177] This regiment had earlier won important victories for the central government during the campaign against Salar. The troops also took captive about a hundred of the Babi women and children, who "were brought to the camp, and made over to the soldiers."[178]

172 Report of a secretary of the Russian Embassy, enclosed Dolgorukov to Seniavin, 23 September 1850 (Julian)/5 October 1850 (Gregorian), quoted in Ivanov, *Babidskie vosstaniya v Irane*, 154–56; Momen, *Bábí and Bahá'í Religions*, 119–20.

173 Abbott to Sheil, 30 August 1850, quoted in Momen, *Bábí and Bahá'í Religions*, 118.

174 Cf. Sipihr, *Nāsikh al-Tavārīkh*, vol. 3, 1065.

175 Cyrus Ghani, *Yāddāshthāy-i-Duktur Qāsim-i-Ghanī*, vol. 6 (Tehran: Zuvvār, 1367 Sh./1988–89), 357. In this source, the name of the recipient is erroneously given as Zafar al-Dawlih.

176 Report to Palmerston, 29 November 1850, quoted in Momen, *Bábí and Bahá'í Religions*, 121.

177 Nabil maintains that the troops found an opportunity to force their passage into the fort when Hujjat was hit in the arm by a bullet, prompting the Babi defenders to rush to him (*Dawn-Breakers*, 569–70). It seems, however, that Hujjat was wounded sometime after the fall of the fort.

178 Stevens to Sheil, 9 December 1850, quoted in Momen, *Bábí and Bahá'í Religions*, 121.

After the capture of the fort, only the house of Hujjat and some adjacent buildings remained in the hands of the Babis, but they were still putting up a fierce resistance.[179] It appears from the Baha'i and Azali sources that at this time, Hujjat permitted his men to attack the troops to drive them back from the nearby houses. Until then the Babis had fought in a strictly defensive manner. Sword in hand, Hujjat himself joined his fellow Babis, but during one such attack he was shot in the arm and died of his injury within a week or so (c. 29 December 1850).[180] The buildings adjacent to Hujjat's house were one after another razed to the ground by artillery fire and explosions. By 6 January 1851, the remaining Babis had laid down their arms. The army commanders had vowed to spare the lives of the Babi survivors and had sealed a copy of the Qur'an to confirm their pledge.

Of the injured Babis, almost none survived the cold of the winter and the hardships that they were exposed to. The Babi fighters who had surrendered or had been held captive—seventy-six in number—were for the most part bayoneted to death; some were blown from the mouth of a cannon, and a few were pardoned and released.[181] Some of the Babi men, together with a few who were captured after the conclusion of the fighting, were sent to Tehran. Four of these were executed in the capital on 28 Rabi' II 1267/2 March 1851.[182] The Babi women and children were taken to the stable in the house of Mirza Abu al-Qasim-i-Zanjani, one of the leading clerics of the town. There they were forced to recant their faith before being entrusted to the care of their Muslim relatives. They were also stripped of the last valuables that they had managed to retain. Some of the Babi children died there. Those of Hujjat's family who had survived the conflict were sent to Shiraz.

179 Anitchkov to the Viceroy of the Caucasus, 11 December 1850 (Julian)/23 December 1850 (Gregorian), quoted in Momen, *Bábí and Bahá'í Religions*, 121.

180 'Abd al-Ahad-i-Zanjani, History, f. 20a; Browne, "Personal Reminiscences," 811–12; Husayn-i-Zanjani, History, f. 20a; Sipihr, *Nāsikh al-Tavārīkh*, vol. 3, 1068–69; Ferrier to de LaHitte, 24 January 1851, quoted in Momen, *Bábí and Bahá'í Religions*, 122–33; Browne, *Táríkh-i-Jadíd*, 161. Nabil writes that Hujjat died on 5 Rabi I 1267/9 January 1851, after having endured the pain caused by his wound for nineteen days (*Dawn-Breakers*, 573). This date cannot be correct. The news of Hujjat's death had reached the Sayyid-i-Mujtahid by the night preceding 3 Rabi I 1267/7 January 1851. See Diya'i, "Sanadī," 164.

181 Sipihr, *Nāsikh al-Tavārīkh*, vol. 3, 1068–69; Sheil to Palmerston, 6 January 1851; Stevens to Palmerston, 25 January 1851; quoted in Momen, *Bábí and Bahá'í Religions*, 123. Sipihr openly states that the governor's promise to spare the lives of the Babi defenders was a trick.

182 *Rūznāmiy-i-vaqāyi'-i-ittifāqīyyih*, Friday, 3 Jumada I 1267/7 March 1851, 1.

The Zanjan episode led to the almost complete disappearance of the Babi community there. The survivors were too afraid to identify themselves as Babis. Many were absorbed into the Muslim population of the town. When the British Iranologist Edward Browne visited Zanjan in November 1887, the town had not yet recovered from the ravages of the conflict.

AN ANALYSIS OF THE OBJECTIVES OF HUJJAT AND THE ZANJANI BABIS

Zanjan is located halfway between Tehran and Tabriz. The latter city, the provincial capital of Azarbaijan and the seat of the crown prince, was the largest urban center in the country. There were large concentrations of troops in both Tabriz and Tehran. In his report written a month after the news of the clashes in Zanjan had reached Tehran, Sheil commented on Zanjan's position: "It is not a little strange that Zenjan, within the reach of all the military resources of Tehran and Azarbaijan, should make an attempt at revolt."[183] There was no chance that a rebellion in Zanjan could succeed. This would have been apparent to the Babis and the authorities alike.

Long before the fighting began, the Babis of Zanjan had become a cause of concern to the authorities in the capital. Already in March 1849, while the Shaykh Tabarsi conflict was underway, Dolgorukov commented on rumors about the Babis' numbers in Zanjan and noted that by their very presence, "they threaten to disrupt the public order."[184] A year later, about two months before the first clashes occurred, he wrote that in Zanjan "[the Babis'] number reaches 2,000 people, and the ideas spread by them among the people incite common discontent."[185] Exaggerated and fabricated reports about the Babis' numbers and activities were also reaching the capital. The official histories of the period put the number of the Babis in the Zanjan district at 10,000 to 15,000.[186] The court historian Sipihr also accuses the Babis of sharing in common their wives and property and claims that many had joined Hujjat in the hope of laying hands on the women and property

183 Report to Palmerston, 25 June 1850, quoted in Momen, *Bábí and Bahá'í Religions*, 115.

184 Report to Nesselrode, 7 March 1849, quoted in ibid., 114.

185 Report to Nesselrode, 14 March 1850, quoted in ibid.

186 Hidayat claims that Hujjat had gathered around himself 10,000 to 15,000 men from the town and the district (*Rawḍat al-Ṣafā*, vol. 10, 448), while Sipihr provides the figure of about 15,000 (*Nāsikh al-Tavārīkh*, vol. 3, 1059).

of Muslims.[187] It is likely that these reports originated with the 'ulama' of Zanjan and perhaps even the governor. Although their exaggerated nature might have been apparent to Amir Kabir, such reports must have alarmed the Tehran authorities.

Shortly before the conflict broke out, Salar's rebellion in Khurasan had been decisively and finally crushed, freeing a significant portion of the country's military resources. Thus, the timing of the conflict did not work to the advantage of the Babis. Hujjat had returned to Zanjan in early 1849, while the conflict at Shaykh Tabarsi was still in progress.[188] Some Zanjani Babis had earlier gone to Mazandaran to join the defenders of the fort at Shaykh Tabarsi. Others were preparing arms in secret in anticipation of a conflict in Zanjan.[189] If Hujjat's intention had been rebellion with a view to seizing control of the town, he would have had a much better chance while Salar's rebellion and the Shaykh Tabarsi conflict were still underway. On his return, however, he did not attempt to stage an insurrection.

Majd al-Dawlih, "a cruel man, tactless and given to rages," had received specific instructions from the Amir to arrest and send Hujjat to Tehran.[190] For a long time, however, he did not make any move against Hujjat. When he finally did attempt to arrest Hujjat, he must have been sure that his position in a coming struggle with the Babis was secure. When that attempt failed, the governor instructed the Muslim population of the town to leave the Babis' quarters and began gathering a militia army from the environs of Zanjan. He could also count on military assistance from outside. While it is not known whether he had already received assurances from Amir Kabir about this, it is known that the Amir sent reinforcements as soon as he received news of the events in Zanjan. The manner of his response was so notable that it prompted the British Minister in Tehran to describe it as "an instance unexampled in Persia of military celerity."[191]

Majd al-Dawlih's attempt to arrest Hujjat was a response to the forced release by Hujjat's messenger of a fellow believer. Hujjat's supporters must have considered that their action was likely to provoke a response from the governor, but they may not have predicted the nature of that response. It would have been clear to them, however, that a confrontation with the

187 *Nāsikh al-Tavārīkh*, vol. 3, 1059.
188 Ibid.
189 Husayn-i-Zanjani, History, f. 6a.
190 Walbridge, "Babi Uprising in Zanjan," 352.
191 Sheil to Palmerston, 25 May 1850, quoted in Momen, *Bábí and Bahá'í Religions*, 115.

local government would lead to the involvement of the central government, which could not but end in their defeat. A conflict involving the Babis would have been quite different from popular risings against local governors, which were not uncommon during the Qajar era. In Zanjan itself, three years earlier, an attack by a mob had forced the town's cruel and unpopular governor to flee. After investigating the issue, the central authorities had decided not to take action against the populace but to appoint a new governor.[192] For a popular rebellion to succeed, however, the backing of the 'ulama' or at least their neutrality would have been essential; this, however, was an impossibility in the case of the Babis. Moreover, following the clash at Shaykh Tabarsi and the disturbances in Yazd, Amir Kabir's position had only hardened against the Babis. Thus, the Babis in Zanjan could be certain that a conflict with the local authority would lead to the involvement of the central government and would be pursued until the Babis were fully crushed. Hence, Hujjat and his supporters had nothing to win from initiating a clash with the local government. They were, however, willing to take a risk in order not to let an innocent Babi languish in the governor's prison.

Amir Kabir was seriously concerned about the large number of the Babis in Zanjan. He seems to have thought that, by eliminating Hujjat, he could defuse a potentially dangerous situation. He had no interest in starting a costly conflict, however. Whatever his initial hopes and calculations may have been, once hostilities broke out, his goal became to annihilate the Babis. As mentioned earlier, toward the end of the conflict, Stevens, the British consul in Tabriz, reported: "The Ameer-i-Nizam [Amir Kabir] has authorised, if necessary, the destruction of the town and a general massacre."[193]

While neither the Babis nor the Amir had any interest in a bloody war in Zanjan, the same did not apply to another party to the conflict: the local 'ulama'. They were irreconcilably opposed to the Babi religion and had a history of conflict with Hujjat as well. The 'ulama' would not settle for anything short of the total suppression of the Zanjani Babis. Had Hujjat agreed to let himself get arrested, and had his supporters consented to this, it would have gone a long way to satisfy the 'ulama', but they would have not tolerated the presence of a Babi community in the town, even without

192 Sipihr, *Nāsikh al-Tavārīkh*, vol. 2, 913–14; *Iṭṭilā'āt*, 20 Azar 1354/11 December 1975, 10; Walbridge, "Babi Uprising in Zanjan," 348 n. 32.

193 Report to Palmerston, 29 November 1850, quoted in Momen, *Bábí and Bahá'í Religions*, 121.

Hujjat as its head. The 'ulama' must have anticipated that Hujjat's supporters would not ignominiously deliver him into their hands and that many of them would rather choose to fight and die for their common cause. They were, however, ready to seize an opportunity to obliterate Babi dissent in Zanjan regardless of the costs.

According to Mirza Husayn-i-Zanjani, when the governor decided to arrest Hujjat in May 1850, it was in response to the clergy's insistence.[194] The most senior of them, the Sayyid-i-Mujtahid, was present in the governorate on the day the attempt to arrest Hujjat was made, and he took part in the killing of the Babi captive who was brought there.[195] The Sayyid-i-Mujtahid issued a fatwa for jihad against the Babis and later went so far as to describe it as binding even on women, noting that Muslim women did not need to obtain permission from their husbands to join in the jihad against the Babis.[196] The governor would not have taken action against Hujjat without assurances from the 'ulama' that they would declare a holy war against the Babis.

For their part, the Babis blamed the 'ulama' for initiating the conflict. This is the purport of a letter from Hujjat to one of the 'ulama' of Zanjan, written after the town was divided into opposing camps. In this letter, Hujjat accuses the 'ulama' of deceiving the governor, implying that they had prompted the governor to assail the Babis for their own gain.[197] He further maintains that the clerics' war against the Babis was not sanctioned in any religion or by any of God's commands, asserts that no harm will come to them from the Babis, asks the unnamed *'ālim* to tell the governor to scatter the forces that he had gathered, and adds that the Babis were willing to continue to be loyal citizens. He also accuses the 'ulama' of having betrayed the shah by disturbing the peace of his land.

It is possible that Hujjat wrote similar letters to other 'ulama' of Zanjan. His appeal was ignored, however. Approaching the 'ulama' in this vein was one of the ways through which Hujjat attempted to stop further bloodshed in the town. He also appealed, two months into the conflict, to the Turkish

194 History, f. 6b. See also Hujjat's letter in Fadil-i-Mazandarani, *Ẓuhūr al-Ḥaqq*, vol. 3, between 182 and 183. Cf. 'Abd al-Ahad-i-Zanjani, History, f. 7a; Browne, "Personal Reminiscences," 783.

195 Husayn-i-Zanjani, History, f. 7b.

196 See passages from a work that the Sayyid-i-Mujtahid was composing while the conflict was underway, quoted in Diya'i, "Sanadī," 164.

197 See facsimile of Hujjat's autograph letter published in Fadil-i-Mazandarani, *Ẓuhūr al-Ḥaqq*, vol. 3, between 182 and 183.

and British ministers in Tehran and the British acting consul in Tabriz to mediate in the fighting.[198] Amir Kabir, however, was determined to pursue the fighting to its very end. Commenting on Hujjat's letters to foreign diplomats in Tehran, Dolgorukov observed that "my English colleague is of the opinion that it would be very difficult to force the Persian government to consent to foreign intervention in favor of the above-mentioned sectaries."[199]

Once it became clear that a conflict was imminent, some of the Babis abandoned Hujjat and moved to the Muslim part of the town. A few even joined government forces and fought against the other Babis.[200] The majority, however, chose to stand by Hujjat's side and fight. Their determination was owing to a new sense of religious zeal, which strengthened the bonds of loyalty and solidarity that predated Hujjat's conversion. They saw Hujjat as the representative of the Qa'im, his "proof" among the people.[201] Fighting alongside Hujjat was equivalent to fighting for the cause of the Qa'im. Thus, to the Zanjani Babis, the struggle had a profound religious significance. They joined the battle and continued to fight even though they knew that they would ultimately be defeated.

For some time after the town was divided into two camps, Hujjat spoke to his followers about what they could expect. Mirza Husayn-i-Zanjani reports that Hujjat cautioned the Babis not to think that they were the disciples of the Qa'im and would therefore become triumphant over the peoples of the world through the power of their swords; observed that they would rather become victorious through sacrificing their lives and property; warned that as had happened at Shaykh Tabarsi, they would all be killed; and advised that those who did not have the strength to bear this should go to the Muslim side. What was going to happen, he further explained, was part of the turmoil of the Latter Days—the eschatological calamities that were to follow the advent of the Qa'im.[202] Similarly, Aqa 'Abd al-Ahad's account indicates that from the beginning of the conflict until the end, time and again Hujjat made it clear to his companions that

198 Sheil to Palmerston, 22 July 1850; Dolgorukov to Seniavin, 26 September 1850; quoted in Momen, *Bábí and Bahá'í Religions*, 116–17. See also Browne, *Nuqṭatu'l-Káf*, 233–34.

199 Report to Seniavin, 26 September 1850, quoted in Momen, *Bábí and Bahá'í Religions*, 117.

200 Sipihr, *Nāsikh al-Tavārīkh*, vol. 3, 1066–67.

201 The term *ḥujjat* literally means "proof."

202 History, f. 8b.

they were free to leave and save their lives. He did not wish them to stay out of a sense of shame or compulsion.[203]

The Baha'i and Azali sources of the Zanjan battle indicate that the Babis carried out strictly defensive warfare. Hujjat's companions refrained from making sorties against the troops and irregulars that were encamped outside the city walls or had entrenched themselves in the town, even though this would have been to their advantage. Initially, the Babis had control over half of Zanjan. Hujjat's companions were surely capable of making surprise attacks on their enemies at night. There is, however, no report of such attacks, not even in the Muslim sources. According to Mirza Husayn-i-Zanjani, some of Hujjat's companions had specifically sought his permission to carry out sorties against the troops, but Hujjat had declined.[204] His objective of pursuing a strictly defensive strategy was to demonstrate clearly to the authorities and those fighting against the Babis that his companions were not intent on revolt and seizure of the town.[205]

Only toward the end of the fighting, after the fall of the fort of 'Ali-Mardan Khan, Hujjat ordered attacks on the advancing forces of the enemy. Mirza Husayn-i-Zanjani and Aqa 'Abd al-Ahad-i-Zanjani refer to these attacks by the terms *jihād* and *qitāl* (fighting) and contrast them with the Babis' earlier strategy, which they describe as *difā'* (defense). Their accounts indicate that Hujjat ordered a jihad only when the Babis' defeat was imminent.[206] As was noted earlier, the troops captured a large number of Babi women and children when they seized control of the fort. The troops were taking captive additional Babi women and young girls as they captured or demolished the remaining Babi houses one after another. The fall of the fort had thus rendered Babi women and children defenseless. According to Aqa 'Abd al-Ahad-i-Zanjani, some of the Babi females were sold to the people of Zanjan and elsewhere or were carried away to other towns and villages. He also writes that girls twelve years of age were bought and sold

203 History, f. 18b. Cf. Browne, "Personal Reminiscences," 808. Browne's translation of the relevant passage is inaccurate. See also Husayn-i-Zanjani, History, f. 19a.

204 History, f. 11b. This was before the arrival of Muhammad Khan-i-Mirpanj in August.

205 Ibid.

206 Mirza Husayn-i-Zanjani, History, ff. 9a, 20a; 'Abd al-Ahad-i-Zanjani, History, ff. 19b–20a; Browne, "Personal Reminiscences," 810–12 (Browne has translated the term jihad as "battle for the faith"). Aqa 'Abd al-Ahad-i-Zanjani may have had access to Mirza Husayn-i-Zanjani's account, and his description of the Babis' initial fighting as *difā'* and the later attacks as jihad may be based on the latter's account. He does not refer to Mirza Husayn-i-Zanjani's work, however.

for one *qirān*.[207] It was under such circumstances and with the purpose of delaying, to the extent possible, the advancement of the troops that Hujjat permitted his companions to launch attacks. Although Mirza Husayn and Aqa 'Abd al-Ahad both use the term jihad, it is clear that the Babis' warfare was nothing but defensive.

Not only did the Babis refrain from making sorties against the troops, they, under Hujjat's instructions, showed strong discipline in their fighting. This is attested to in the account by Prince 'Ali-Quli Mirza.[208] Citing Mirza Abu al-Qasim-i-Zanjani, one of the leading clerics in the town and a major adversary of the Babis, 'Ali-Quli Mirza writes that a few Babis had run into this cleric in a street at night and had the opportunity to kill him but had refrained from it, saying that they had not been instructed to do so. According to Mirza Abu al-Qasim-i-Zanjani, the Babis could have killed many of the 'ulama' in Zanjan, but they did not.[209]

The Babis' manner of warfare did not change the perception of the observers, all of whom had from the outset labeled their actions as a revolt against the state.[210] The central government was only interested in a swift restoration of peace and order by subduing the Babis. The Amir had neither a desire to ascertain the circumstances that had precipitated the conflagration in Zanjan, nor was he interested in exploring measures that might lead to a truce between the parties, a scenario which was in any case impossible given the hard-line attitude of the 'ulama'. The Zanjani 'ulama' were not seeking to make peace with Hujjat and his Babi supporters. Their position spelled out for the government what may have appeared to it as the most practical solution to the conflict: the complete defeat of the Babis.

207 History, f. 18b; Browne, "Personal Reminiscences," 808.

208 Prince 'Ali-Quli Mirza I'tidad al-Saltanih wrote his account "Mutanabbi'īn" in 1295/1878. The portion of this work that deals with the Babis was edited by 'Abd al-Husayn Nava'i and published in 1333 Sh./1954–55 under the title *Fitniy-i-Bāb* (3rd ed., Tehran: Bābak, 1362 Sh./1983–84). It contains some first-hand information about the Zanjan episode and the events following the 1852 attempt on the life of the shah. The other parts of this work that pertain to the Babi–state clashes, however, mirror the account in the *Nāsikh al-Tavārīkh* and provide no new information.

209 Nava'i, *Fitniy-i-Bāb*, 72–73. It should be stated, however, that according to Mirza Husayn-i-Zanjani, two Babis had committed brutalities and had therefore been expelled by Hujjat from among the Babis. They had then joined the enemy and later acted as guides to an army commander, who had penetrated the Babi positions to assassinate Hujjat (History, ff. 14b–15a).

210 See, for example, Sheil's report to Palmerston dated 25 June 1850, quoted at the beginning of this section.

On the whole, the available evidence, including, not least, the defensive character of the Babis' warfare, indicates that their intention had not been to rebel against the state authority. This is also supported by the Babis' understanding of the episode, as reflected, for example, in Hujjat's letter to one of the 'ulama' of Zanjan. Once the conflict had begun, however, it assumed a profound religious significance for the Babis, and they resolved to defend themselves with all their force against their enemies. As John Walbridge puts it, the Babis' final "war aim" was to emulate the Imam Husayn and his small band of the faithful. They "had no choice but to fight for their honor before God. There was no other option, neither hope of victory nor of honorable surrender."[211] Unable to change the outcome of the battle, which was sealed from the outset and was evident to all parties, the Babis determined to turn the battle into a proclamation of their tenacious faith in the advent of the Qa'im.

CONCLUSION

In the eyes of contemporaries, the Babi–state clashes were triggered by Babi attempts at revolt. A close study of these conflicts, however, does not substantiate this view. The Bab's claims to Mahdihood and prophethood and the Babis' active propagation of the new religion posed a threat to the position of the 'ulama' and weakened their influence and sway in society. As the Babi religion spread and the claims of the Bab became better known, the clerical establishment's opposition to the Babi movement grew fiercer and the incidence of attacks on the Babis increased, often provoking a response. These developments in turn alarmed the authorities, who blamed the Babis for disturbing the public order.

When the death of Muhammad Shah threw the country into chaos, the Babis that were passing through Mazandaran were seen as insurrectionists, and the young Nasir al-Din Shah and Amir Kabir ordered their extirpation. In their opposition to the followers of the new religion, the former was mainly motivated by religious bigotry and the latter by political considerations. A year after the conclusion of the Mazandaran struggle, conflicts broke out in Nayriz and Zanjan. The Babis' warfare was defensive in all these episodes. By fighting bravely against a far superior force and facing a heroic death, the followers of the Bab saw an opportunity to vindicate their faith.

211 "Babi Uprising in Zanjan," 353.

BIBLIOGRAPHY

'Abd al-Ahad-i-Zanjani, Aqa, Untitled history (Ramadan 1309 [April 1892]), Browne Manuscripts, Or. F. 25, item 6, Cambridge University Library, Cambridge.

'Abdu'l-Bahá, *Memorials of the Faithful*, Marzieh Gail, trans., 2nd printing (Wilmette: Bahá'í Publishing Trust, 1975).

Abu-Talib-i-Shahmirzadi, Mir, Untitled history, n.d., uncatalogued photocopy of autograph manuscript, Afnan Library, Sandy, Bedfordshire.

Afnán, Abu'l-Qásim, *'Ahd-i-A'lā: Zindigānīy-i-Ḥaḍrat-i-Bāb/The Bábí Dispensation: The Life of the Báb* (Oxford: Oneworld, 2000).

Afshar, Iraj, ed., *Chihil Sāl Tārīkh-i-Īrān dar Dawriy-i-Pādishāhīy-i-Nāṣir al-Dīn Shāh* (Tehran: Asāṭīr, 1989), vol. 2.

'Ala'i, 'Abd al-'Ali, ed., *Tārīkh-i-Samandar va Mulḥaqqāt* (Tehran: Mu'assasiy-i-Millīy-i-Maṭbū'āt-i-Amrī, 131 B.E./1974–75).

Algar, Hamid, *Religion and State in Iran, 1785–1906: The Role of the Ulama in the Qajar Period* (Berkeley; Los Angeles: University of California Press, 1969).

Amanat, Abbas, *Resurrection and Renewal: The Making of the Babi Movement in Iran, 1844–1850* (Ithaca; London: Cornell University Press, 1989).

Amirahmadi, Hooshang, *The Political Economy of Iran under the Qajars: Society, Politics, Economics, and Foreign Relations, 1796–1926* (London; New York: I.B. Tauris, 2012).

Amir-Moezzi, Mohammad Ali, "Eschatology iii. In Imami Shi'ism," *Encyclopædia Iranica.*

Anonymous, 12 September 1848, "Translation: Extract of a letter from a person sent to M. [Mazandaran] by Colonel F. [Farrant]," "Enclosed Farrant's No. 85 of 1848," Foreign Office Records, FO 60/138, The National Archives of the UK, Kew, Surrey.

Avarih, 'Abd al-Husayn, *Al-Kavākib al-Durrīyyih fī Ma'āthir al-Bahā'īyyih*, vol. 1 (Cairo: al-Sa'āda, 1923).

Bab, The, *Dalā'il-i-Sab'ih* (n.p., n.d.).

—, *Selections from the Writings of the Báb* (Haifa: Bahá'í World Centre, 1978).

Bahá'í World, The, vol. 5 (New York: Bahá'í Publishing Committee, 1936).

Bode, Gert, "Siege," in Trevor N. Dupuy, editor-in-chief, *International Military and Defense Encyclopedia* (Washington D. C.; New York: Brassey's [US], Inc., 1993), vol. 5, 2417–22.

Borjian, Habib, "A Mazandarani Account of the Babi Incident at Shaikh Tabarsi," *Iranian Studies*, vol. 39, no. 3 (2006), 381–99.

Browne, Edward G., ed., *Kitáb-i-Nuqṭatu'l-Káf: Being the Earliest History of the Bábís compiled by Ḥájjí Mírzá Jání of Káshán between the years A.D. 1850 and 1852* (Leyden; London: E. J. Brill; Luzac & Co., 1910).

—, *Materials for the Study of the Bábí Religion* (Cambridge: Cambridge University Press, 1918).

—, trans., "Personal Reminiscences of the Bābī Insurrection at Zanjān in 1850, written in Persian by Āqā 'Abdu'l-Aḥad-i-Zanjānī," *Journal of the Royal Asiatic Society*, vol. 29, no. 4 (1897), 761–827.

—, ed. and trans., *The Táríkh-i-Jadíd or New History of Mírzá 'Alí Muḥammad the Báb* (Cambridge: Cambridge University Press, 1893).

—, ed. and trans., *A Traveller's Narrative Written to Illustrate the Episode of the Báb* (Cambridge: Cambridge University Press, 1891), vol. 2.

—, *A Year Amongst the Persians: Impressions as to the Life, Character, & Thought of the People of Persia, Received during Twelve Months' Residence in that Country in the Years 1887–8* (London: Adam and Charles Black, 1893).

Diya'i, Muhammad-Sadiq, "Sanadī rāji' bih Shūrish-i-Bābīyān-i-Zanjān," *Yaghmā*, vol. 20, no. 3 (1346 Sh./1967–68), 162–64.

Dolgorukov, Prince, "Excerpts from Dispatches written during 1848–1852 by Prince Dolgorukov, Russian Minister to Persia," *World Order*, vol. 1, no. 1 (1966), 17–24.

Dorn, Bernhard, "Nachträge zu dem Verzeichniss der von der Kaiserlichen öffentlichen Bibliothek erworbenen Chanykov'schen Handschriften und den da mitgetheilten Nachrichten über die Baby und deren Koran, von B. Dorn," *Bulletin de l'Académie Impériale des Sciences de St.-Pétersbourg*, vol. 9 (1866), 202–31.

Fadil-i-Mazandarani, Asadu'llah, "Kitāb-i-Ẓuhūr al-Ḥaqq," vol. 2, n.d. [c. 1932], uncatalogued photocopy of manuscript, Afnan Library, Sandy, Bedfordshire.

—, *Kitāb-i-Ẓuhūr al-Ḥaqq*, vol. 3 ([Tehran: Āzurdigān], c. 1944).

Faydi, Muhammad-'Ali, *Nayrīz-i-Mushkbīz* (Tehran: Mu'assasiy-i-Millīy-i-Maṭbū'āt-i-Amrī, 130 B.E./1973–74).

Ghani, Cyrus, *Yāddāshthāy-i-Duktur Qāsim-i-Ghanī*, vol. 6 (Tehran: Zuvvār, 1367 Sh./1988–89).

Greussing, Kurt, "The Babi Movement in Iran 1844–52: From Merchant Protest to Peasant Revolution," in János M. Bak, Gerhard Benecke, eds.,

Religion and Rural Revolt (Manchester: Manchester University Press, 1984), 256–69.

Hasan-i-Fasa'i, Haj Mirza, *Fārsnāmiy-i-Nāṣirī*, Mansur Rastigar Fasa'i, ed. (Tehran: Amīr Kabīr, 1367 Sh./1988–89), 2 vols.

Hidayat, Rida-Quli Khan, *Rawḍat al-Ṣafāy-i-Nāṣirī*, vol. 10 (Qum: Markazī, Khayyām, Pīrūz, [1340] Sh./1961–62).

Husayn-i-Zanjani, Mirza, Untitled history, n.d., Ms. orient. Oct. 1216, Staatsbibliothek, Berlin.

Ibrahim-i-Nayrizi, Sayyid, "Sanadī dar bāriy-i-Sayyid Yaḥyā," in Iraj Afshar, ed., *Chihil Sāl Tārīkh-i-Īrān dar Dawriy-i-Pādishāhīy-i-Nāṣir al-Dīn Shāh* (Tehran: Asāṭīr, 1989), vol. 2, 635–40.

Ivanov, Mikhail Sergeevich, *Babidskie vosstaniya v Irane (1848–1852)* (Moscow: Trudy Instituta Vostokvedeniya XXX, 1939).

Khan Bahadur, Agha Mirza Muhammad, "Some New Notes on Babiism," *Journal of the Royal Asiatic Society*, vol. 59, no. 3 (July 1927), 443–70.

Literary World, The, vol. 8, no. 228 (14 June 1851).

Lovett, Beresford, "Surveys on the Road from Shiraz to Bam," *Journal of the Royal Geographical Society of London*, vol. 42 (1872), 202–12.

Lutf-'Ali Mirzay-i-Shirazi, Untitled history, n.d., Browne Manuscripts, Or. F. 28, item 3, Cambridge University Library, Cambridge.

MacEoin, Denis, "The Babi Concept of Holy War," *Religion*, vol. 12, no. 2 (1982), 93–129.

—, "Babism," *Encyclopædia Iranica*.

—, "Bahā'ī Fundamentalism and the Academic Study of the Bābī Movement," *Religion*, vol. 16, no. 1 (1986), 57–84.

—, "From Babism to Baha'ism: Problems of Militancy, Quietism, and Conflation in the Construction of a Religion," *Religion*, vol. 13, no. 3 (1983), 219–55.

Mackay, Alexander, *Elements of Modern Geography*, 12th ed. (Edinburgh; London: William Blackwood and Sons, 1872).

Mahjur-i-Zavari'i, Sayyid Muhammad-Husayn, "Vaqāyi' al-Mīmīyyih," Browne Manuscripts, Or. F. 28, item 1, Cambridge University Library, Cambridge.

McCants, William, and Kavian Milani, "The History and Provenance of an Early Manuscript of the *Nuqtat al-kaf* Dated 1268 (1851–52)," *Iranian Studies*, vol. 37, no. 3 (2004), 431–49.

Mehrabkhani, Ruhu'llah, *Mullá Ḥusayn: Disciple at Dawn* (Los Angeles: Kalimát Press, 1987).

Milani, Kavian S., "Noqṭat al-Kāf," *Encyclopædia Iranica.*

Minorsky, V., "M. S. Ivanov: *The Babi Risings in Iran in 1848–1852*, Trudi of the Oriental Institute of the Academy of Sciences of the USSR, vol. 30, Moscow 1939," *Bulletin of the School of Oriental and African Studies*, vol. 11 (1946), 878–80.

Momen, Moojan, *The Bábí and Bahá'í Religions, 1844–1944: Some Contemporary Western Accounts* (Oxford: George Ronald, 1981).

—, *An Introduction to Shi'i Islam: The History and Doctrines of Twelver Shi'ism* (Oxford: George Ronald, 1985).

—, "The Social Basis of the Bābī Upheavals in Iran (1848–53): A Preliminary Analysis," *International Journal of Middle East Studies*, vol. 15, no. 2 (1983), 157–83.

—, "The Trial of Mullā 'Alī Basṭāmī: A Combined Sunnī-Shī'ī Fatwā against the Bāb," *Iran*, vol. 20 (1982), 113–43.

Muhammad-Rida Shahmirzadi, Aqa Sayyid, Untitled history, n.d., uncatalogued photocopy of autograph manuscript, Afnan Library, Sandy, Bedfordshire.

Muhammad-Shafi'-i-Nayrizi, Mulla, Untitled history, n.d., uncatalogued photocopy of manuscript, Afnan Library, Sandy, Bedfordshire.

Munirih Khanum, *Munírih Khánum: Memoirs and Letters*, Sammireh Anwar Smith, trans. (Los Angeles: Kalimát Press, 1986).

Nabil-i-Zarandi, *The Dawn-Breakers: Nabíl's Narrative of the Early Days of the Bahá'í Revelation*, Shoghi Effendi, trans. and ed. (Wilmette, Ill.: Bahá'í Publishing Committee, 1932).

Nasir-i-Qazvini, Haji, "Tārīkh-i-janāb-i-Ḥājī Naṣīr-i-Shahīd," in 'Abd al-'Ali 'Ala'i, ed., *Tārīkh-i-Samandar va Mulḥaqqāt* (Tehran: Mu'assasiy-i-Millīy-i-Maṭbū'āt-i-Amrī, 131 B.E./1974–75), 499–20.

Nava'i, 'Abd al-Husayn, ed., *Fitniy-i-Bāb*, 3rd ed. (Tehran: Bābak, 1362 Sh./1983–84).

Nicolas, A.-L.-M., *Tārīkh-i-Sayyid 'Alī-Muḥammad Ma'rūf bih Bāb*, 'A. M. F. ['Ali-Muhammad Farahvashi], trans. (n.p., 1322 Sh./1943–44) [Persian translation of A.-L.-M. Nicolas, *Seyyèd Ali Mohammed dit le Bâb* (Paris: Dujarric, 1905)].

Planhol, Xavier de, "Bābol i. The Town," *Encyclopædia Iranica.*

Ruhani Nayrizi, Muhammad-Shafi', *Lama'āt al-Anvār*, vol. 1 (Tehran: Mu'assasiy-i-Millīy-i-Maṭbū'āt-i-Amrī, 130 B.E./1973–74).

Saiedi, Nader, *Gate of the Heart: Understanding the Writings of the Báb* (Waterloo, Ont.: Wilfrid Laurier University Press, 2008).

Samandar-i-Qazvini, Shaykh Kazim, "Tārīkh-i-janāb-i-Samandar," in 'Abd al-'Ali 'Ala'i, ed., *Tārīkh-i-Samandar va Mulḥaqqāt* (Tehran: Mu'assasiy-i-Millīy-i-Maṭbū'āt-i-Amrī, 131 B.E./1974–75), 12–370.

Semino, Barthélémy, *Zhinirāl Semino dar Khidmat-i Īrān-i 'Aṣr-i Qājār va Jang-i Hirāt: 1236–1266 hijrīy-i qamarī/Le Général Semino en Iran Qâjâr et la Guerre de Hérat: 1820–1850*, Mansoureh Ettehadieh (Nezam Mafi), S. Mir-Mohammad Sadegh, eds. (Tehran: Nashr-i-Tārīkh-i-Īrān, 1997).

Shaykh al-'Ajam, "Min Kalām-i-Shaykh al-'Ajam-i-Māzandarānī," in Bernhard Dorn, "Nachträge zu dem Verzeichniss der von der Kaiserlichen öffentlichen Bibliothek erworbenen Chanykov'schen Handschriften und den da mitgetheilten Nachrichten über die Baby und deren Koran, von B. Dorn," *Bulletin de l'Académie Impériale des Sciences de St.-Pétersbourg*, vol. 9 (1866), 205–11.

Sheil, Lady Mary L., *Glimpses of Life and Manners in Persia: With Notes on Russia, Koords, Toorkomans, Nestorians, Khiva, and Persia* (London: John Murray, 1856).

Shoghi Effendi, *God Passes By*, rev. ed. (Wilmette, Ill.: Bahá'í Publishing Trust, 1974).

Sipihr, Muhammad-Taqi Lisan al-Mulk, *Nāsikh al-Tavārīkh: Dawriy-i-Kāmil-i-Tārīkh-i-Qājārīyyih*, Jahangir Qa'im-Maqami, ed. (Tehran: Amīr Kabīr, 1337 Sh./1958–59).

—, *Nāsikh al-Tavārīkh: Tārīkh-i-Qājārīyyih*, Jamshid Kiyanfar, ed. (Tehran: Asāṭīr, 1377 Sh./1998–99), 3 vols.

Smith, Peter and William P. Collins, "Babi and Baha'i Millennialism," in Catherine Wessinger, ed., *The Oxford Handbook of Millennialism* (Oxford; New York: Oxford University Press, 2011), 474–91.

Southgate, Horatio, *Narrative of a Tour through Armenia, Kurdistan, Persia, and Mesopotamia: With Observations on the Condition of Mohammedanism and Christianity in Those Countries* (New York: D. Appleton & Co., 1840), vol. 2.

Tancoigne, M., *A Narrative of a Journey into Persia, and Residence at Teheran: Containing a Descriptive Itinerary from Constantinople to the Persian Capital* (London: William Wright, 1820).

Walbridge, John, "The Babi Uprising in Zanjan: Causes and Issues," *Iranian Studies*, vol. 29, nos. 3–4 (1996), 339–62.

Watson, Robert Grant, *A History of Persia from the Beginning of the Nineteenth Century to the Year 1858* (London: Smith, Elder and Co., 1866).

Wilson, Samuel Graham, *Persian Life and Customs: With Scenes and Incidents of Residence and Travel in the Land of the Lion and the Sun*, 3rd ed. (Chicago: Student Missionary Campaign Library, 1895).

Yusufi, Ghulam-Husayn, "Čāvoš," *Encyclopædia Iranica.*

Zabihi-Moghaddam, Siyamak, "The Babi-State Conflict at Shaykh Tabarsi," *Iranian Studies*, vol. 35, nos. 1–3 (2002), 87–112.

—, "Mu'arrifīy-i-Kitāb. *'Ahd-i-A'lā: Zindigānīy-i-Ḥaḍrat-i-Bāb*," *Payām-i-Bahā'ī*, no. 253 (December 2000), 37–42.

8

From Babi Movement to the Baha'i Faith

Some Observations About the Evolution of a New Religion

ARMIN ESCHRAGHI

Abstract: The Baha'i faith is an independent religion founded in an Islamic environment. Its tenets nevertheless are based upon a new understanding of God, man, and religion, one which differs fundamentally from traditional Islamic ideas. Its founder, Baha'u'llah, gradually initiated his followers into his new teachings. In this process of introducing new values and ideals, the earlier Babi movement played a key role in preparing the ground for promoting innovative ideas. In this chapter we will examine this gradual process with regard to topics such as tradition vs. innovation, messianism, violence in the name of God, and the idea of "divine law."

The Babi movement, which was founded by Sayyid Ali-Muhammad Shirazi (1819–50) known as the "Bab" (lit. gate), is no doubt among the most important movements in the history of modern Iran. Several features distinguish its teachings from the ideas of the many political activists and social reformers that appeared in the nineteenth and twentieth centuries. These reformers generally went to great lengths to present their ideas as being in accordance with existing tradition, either because they were in fact traditionalists themselves, or because they feared that their ideas would be deemed "heretical" by certain powerful factions of the Shiite clergy. As a result they made every effort to present their ideas, no matter how innovative and modernist in nature, as being in total accordance with established Islamic tradition and by this means legitimize advancing them.[1] Many attempts were made to achieve what seems to be impossible, namely to present modern, innovative ideas while remaining entirely within the bounds of established norms.

The Bab, on the other hand, did not consider tradition as sacrosanct. Rather he declared that, throughout history, it was blind loyalty to outlived patterns and age-old beliefs that caused backwardness and decline in human society and kept men from recognizing the truth. To put it in other words: while many tried to find answers to the problems and challenges of their time in their assumption of a glorious past – in this case: the Golden Age of early Islam, the "true spirit" of "pristine Muhammadanism" (*Islam-i nab-i Muhammadi*) – the Bab focused the attention of his followers upon the future. In this spirit, in 1847 he carried out a revolutionary step by formally declaring the end of the Islamic Dispensation and abolishing its Sacred Law (*shari'ah*).

Such an act was not, in itself, unique. In fact, over the centuries there had been others who, driven by their apocalyptic views, declared Sacred Law as obsolete, since they believed that the world was soon coming to

1 Yusuf Khan Mustashar'ud-Dawlih (d. 1895), a well-known reformist during the reign of Nasir-ud-Dan Shah (d. 1896), in his essay "Yik Kalimih" [One Word] tried to prove that Western codified law was entirely in line with the Qur'an and *hadith* literature. See the Persian-English edition by Seyed-Ghorab and McGlinn, *One Word – Yak Kaleme*, Leiden 2010. See also Iradj Eschraghi, *Tajaddud-kh^{w}ahi va islah-gara'i dar Iran*, 2nd ed., Forugh: Köln, 2018, 91–100. Another activist, Malkam Khan (d. 1908), a Christian himself, stated: "In Islam, every Mujtahid can turn to the traditions (*ahadith va sunan*), that boundless ocean, and by force of interpretation, install new laws. Therefore, rather than stating that our laws stem from France or England we should say that they derive from Islam." Quoted from Eschraghi, *Tajaddud-kh^{w}ahi*, 110.

an end, or would enter into a "new cycle." Also, some Sufis and "esoteric" Shiite groups voiced antinomian ideas, such as the law being but an outward shell which should be cast away once man attained true knowledge. The Bab did not share such views, and he was the only prophetic figure to go a step further: not merely abolishing the Law but actually replacing it with a new one. Through this act he unequivocally expressed his intent to initiate fundamental change and break away from tradition.

The Babi faith is neither an Islamic sect, nor is it a mere political or social movement. It has all the features of an independent religion. With the Bab as its prophetic figure and his numerous writings constituting its holy scripture, the new faith contains distinct teachings concerning theology, *Menschenbild*, prophetology, ethics, as well as ritual practices (prayer, pilgrimage, fasting...).[2] As we shall see, the Bab's replacement of the Islamic Law with his own Sacred Law was, more than anything else, a symbolic act. Had he not done so, the independence of his faith would not have been recognized and most probably, it would have been deemed a mere reform movement within Shiʿism or a short-lived social or political upheaval, to be confined to a mere footnote in history. But the Bab's principal intent seems to have been, by means of a pointed defection from tradition, to prepare the people of Iran to engage in a challenging and painful process not just of reform, but of fundamental renewal.

SOME GENERAL OBSERVATIONS ON THE BAB'S SACRED LAW

During the six years of his ministry, the Bab penned a large number of Persian and Arabic treatises. During the first years of his mission, he set forth his innovative and sometimes revolutionary teachings while at the same time remaining within the Shiite framework which shaped his prospective addressee's intellectual horizon. Since his audience was comprised of Muslims, he made frequent recourse to the tenets, terminology and doctrine of that religious tradition, and his writings therefore conform to the conventional genres of classical Islamic scholarship, namely exegesis

2 For more on this see A. Eschraghi, "Undermining the Foundations of Orthodoxy: Some Notes on the Bab's Sharia (Sacred Law)," in: Todd Lawson and Omid Ghaemmaghami, *A Most Noble Pattern. Collected Essays on the Writings of the Bab, Ali Muhammad Shirazi (1819–50)*, George Ronald: Oxford, 2012, 175–95.

(*tafsir*) of the Qur'an, discussions of prophetic traditions (*hadith*), theology (*kalam*) and philosophy (*falsafah, hikmah*), prayers and, to a very modest extent, jurisprudence (*fiqh*).

The literary output of the Bab is vast and its particular theological, philosophical, and exegetical topics deserve detailed study. However, there appear to be three pivotal themes that are found throughout all of his writings, albeit expressed in different ways: 1) the expectation of a messianic figure; 2) epistemology, i.e., how to obtain knowledge of God and His representatives on earth; and 3) the question of authority (*wilayah*), namely the God-given legitimacy of religious and political leaders.

For his immediate audience these three themes were closely intertwined and the revolutionary implications of his treatment of them were much more obvious to them than to a modern Western reader: according to tradition the quest for knowledge met its goal in acknowledging the "Imam" of any given time, as this Imam was the sole legitimate worldly and spiritual leader, destined to reveal himself when the time was ripe, to overthrow or kill all worldly kings and rulers, who had wrongfully usurped his power, and eventually to establish a rule of justice in accordance with the Law of God. Only when read against the background of certain key doctrines of Shiʿism and of contemporary religious and political discourse, can the revolutionary impact of the Bab's message be appreciated.

Although this might not be obvious at first sight, in fact many of the Bab's new laws and ordinances are actually related to discussions about "authority." He clearly challenged the legitimacy of clerical leadership and denied the religious Learned many of their traditional privileges. The authority of Shiite clerics was based upon the concept of "vicegerency" (*niyabah*). The Imam, according to their belief, was the sole ruler, and no secular government was legitimate. But since the Imam had gone into occultation (*ghaybah*) and the time of his return was unknown, some of the more politically ambitious and powerful clerics claimed that every secular ruler must be subordinate to the religious Learned and bow to their judgment (see p. 381).

When in 1844, the Bab claimed to be a representative of the Hidden Imam, this may have been considered as a rather moderate statement, particularly in comparison with the much higher theophanic claims (*mazhariyyah*) that he put forward from 1847 onwards. Nevertheless, his earliest claim already posed a severe challenge to clerical authority, as during the presence of a mouthpiece of the Imam himself, the need of other representatives stood in question. Moreover, from the earliest days of his ministry the

Bab repeatedly challenged the Learned to face him and demonstrate their ability to interpret the Qur'an, and write treatises and verses against him (*mubahalah*).

Although the Bab called himself a representative of the promised Mahdi, and some time later, to be the Imam himself, he nevertheless declined to fulfill many of the expectations held by the votaries of traditional Shiʿism. Most importantly, he did not show any inclination to establish "God's rule on earth," i.e., to invite the people to overthrow the rule of the shah (king) and to inaugurate a theocratic government. He called on secular rulers to observe justice and trustworthiness toward their peoples and not to manifest selfish pride and tyranny. But unlike the clerics who considered every worldly ruler per se as a usurper of the Imam's legitimate power, the Bab never challenged or denied the shah's right to rule.

While he recognized the legitimacy of worldly rule, which could – if somewhat anachronistically – be termed as a condoning of secular government, the Bab fundamentally challenged the structure of clerical authority. During the Qajar (1779–1926) dynasty the religious Learned had obtained unprecedented power by claiming to be the Hidden Imam's representatives, while the shah's authority depended to a considerable extent upon their approval and goodwill,[3] a fact that weakened the position of his government. Now, the Bab struck at the very foundations of Shiite clerical authority by presenting his own competing claim to be the representative of the Hidden Imam. A number of his new rules and laws can be understood as serving the overall goal of limiting the worldly power and influence of religious authorities: e.g., prohibitions of congregational obligatory prayer, of preaching from pulpits, of issuing death verdicts, and of declaring others to be infidels. The kissing of hands as a gesture of humility toward religious authorities as well as the confession of sins to any human being with the expectation of thereby achieving redemption were likewise prohibited. He denounced what he called the excessive study of classical Arabic with its peculiarities of grammar – a prerogative of the religious Learned – to be futile, and forbade trade which employed the holy dust gathered from the Shrines of

3 The second Qajar king Fath-Ali Shah (1797–1834) spent much of his reign looking for ways to secure religious legitimization for his rule. For a while he sympathized with Akhbarism and Shaykhism, before ultimately adopting Usulism. It was Shaykh Ja'far Naraqi who issued a decree permitting him to rule. His grandson and successor, Muhammad Shah (1834–48), was more inclined toward Sufism than any of the three clerical schools, as his prime minister and mentor Hajji Mirza Aqasi was a member of a particular Sufi order.

the Imams. These few examples are representative of many ordinances in the Bab's Holy Law that target the social and financial power of the clerics. For it was not merely the conservative and traditionalist agenda of the clerics but also their openly political ambitions and their determination to challenge the authority of the state, which had become a major obstacle in the way of any meaningful change and reform.[4]

MESSIANISM IN THE BAB'S WRITINGS

According to his own testimony, the Bab's most important work was the *Persian Bayan* (lit. exposition, explanation), his most elaborate book of laws, written in 1847 while in solitary confinement in Maku, a remote fortress in the Sunni region of Azarbaijan. This book contains ordinances related to a new calendar and rituals such as prayer, fasting, pilgrimage, burial rites, etc. A considerable number of these ordinances appear to be of a symbolic nature, expressive of fundamental principles, rather than intended to be implemented by the faithful. These would include his command to produce various talismanic devices, to transcribe the writings of the Bab in particular ways and to build shrines with a quite extraordinary architecture. Other laws were directly related to issues of contemporary society, such as the introduction of printing-houses and the installment of a postal system, so all people had access to news and information, as well as personal matters such as marriage and divorce, the education of children, and the station of women.

Even a superficial glance at the *Persian Bayan* will find that virtually every law and statement is related to "Him whom God shall manifest," a messianic figure who, according to the Bab, will appear in the future and replace the law of the *Bayan* with a new one. The British orientalist Edward G. Browne, who made extensive studies of Babism and of the *Persian Bayan* in particular wrote:

> We cannot fail but to be struck by the fact that when the Bab was a prisoner and an exile at Maku, probably well aware of what his ultimate fate would be, he showed far more anxiety about the reception which should be accorded to 'Him whom God shall manifest'

4 For a more detailed discussion including references see A. Eschraghi, "Undermining."

> than about himself... Almost every ordinance in the Beyan is similarly designed to be a perpetual reminder of 'Him whom God shall manifest'.[5]

The Bab claimed to be the promised one of Shiite Islam. Yet he did not announce himself as the final messenger from God. Rather he drew the attention of his followers to another, subsequent messianic figure. However, as we shall presently see, Babi expectation of a promised savior differs fundamentally from "classical" or traditional messianism.

One popular understanding of "religion" at the time of the Bab was that it represented a code of fixed and unchallengeable laws which covered all major and minor aspects of human life and were to be observed in minute detail, as both true happiness in this world and salvation in the afterlife, depended upon such observance. Messianic expectation played a key role as it taught believers that in the face of tests and tribulations they should diligently adhere to, and never deviate in the slightest from, the straight path set forth by religious tradition. They should endure all manner of sufferings until salvation came, through divine intervention, in the appearance of a savior. On the day of judgment, they were assured, the stricter one's adherence to the divine ordinances (as explained and defined by the religious Learned), the larger would be his reward and the greater his assurance of admittance into Paradise. Such a mindset, obviously, encouraged traditionalism and conservatism and tended to be skeptical of or outright hostile to innovation and change.

The messianism of the Bab on the other hand was of a different nature. Throughout his writings he repeatedly pointed out that it had always been blind obedience and attachment to tradition which had led to stagnation and hindered men from recognizing the appearance of the Prophets of God. Contrary to traditional Shiite messianism, which invited the faithful believers to perseverance in observing tradition and inaction in addressing new challenges,[6] the Bab created what has been called in the Christian

5 Quoted in: M. Momen (ed.) *Selections from the Writings of E. G. Browne on the Babi and Baha'i Religions*, George Ronald: Oxford, 1987, 232. See also *Bayan- Farsi*, n.p. n.d., Vahid 4, Bab 4 (from here on quoted as *Bayan* x:y).

6 This point of criticism was made by Ruhollah Khomeini (d. 1989) in his early 1970s lectures on "Islamic Governance." He stated that since it was unclear when the Mahdi would come, rather than to passively await his appearance, the believers needed to actively promote the application of divine law and the establishment of an Islamic State. Cf. *Hukumat-i Islami*, Intisharat-i Amir: Tehran, 1981, 22.

context "messianic unrest." His exposition of divine Law reiterated two fundamental points: 1) The believers should not trust that the promised one would appear in the distant future, rather he could appear at any time; and 2) the believers should be prepared to abandon their previous convictions and whatever they habitually considered to be sacred, for such flexibility could well be a prerequisite for the recognition of a new messenger of God.

In this vein he constantly admonished his followers to be vigilant lest they hear of the promised one's revelation but fail to recognize it. This "constant reminder," to reiterate the words of E. G. Browne, found its expression in a number of ordinances, from which but a few examples shall suffice. In every meeting they should keep one empty chair for him.[7] If a hundred thousand men were to go on pilgrimage and, amid circumambulation would hear his call, they should immediately halt and hasten toward him.[8] No one should cause grief for another soul,[9] and no teacher should beat a child,[10] lest they unknowingly hurt the promised one.

The Bab repeatedly warned his followers to never consider their present understanding and convictions as sacred and unchallengeable and not to regard these as the divine standard, adequate for judging the truth of the promised one. Surely it was uncritical adherence to traditions of the past which had prevented the people of previous ages from accepting the prophets who appeared to them. It is perhaps in this vein that he instructed his followers not to attribute miracles to him and to adhere closely to the only unchallengeable proof of his truth, i.e., the divine verses revealed by him. All believers in God, according to the Bab, had the capacity to understand the Book of God[11] and were free to come to their own understanding of its contents, while no one could claim to truly understand its meaning or be entitled to impose his ideas upon others. The only authoritative interpreter of the Bab's words was to be the promised one himself.[12] The Bab went even so far as to state that should anyone lay claim to being the promised one, no one should oppose him, for one could not be sure that his claim was not true.[13] What is even more striking is that the Bab did not even consider his own verses to be unchallengeable. Rather, just as he affirmed that the Qur'an had

7 *Bayan* 9:1.
8 *Bayan* 8:2.
9 *Bayan* 7:18.
10 *Bayan* 6:11.
11 *Bayan* 6:8.
12 *Bayan* 2:2.
13 *Bayan* 6:8.

been replaced with his *Bayan*, when the promised one appeared, the Bab's writings would also be abolished (*mahv*) and no longer serve as the divine touchstone for distinguishing truth from falsehood.[14] "He whom God shall manifest" had the right to reveal himself whenever he liked, in whatever manner he wished, and no one had the right to question him or argue with him, not even on the basis of the Bab's writings. In fact, his followers were prohibited to even ask questions of the promised one.[15]

According to the Bab the future was not pre-ordained or carved in stone. Rather, everything (including divine law) was in a permanent mode of change and evolution. This worldview differs fundamentally from the traditional Islamic eschatology, which considers divine revelation to be sealed, and recounts in great detail the numerous "signs of the Hour" and the many things that will occur at the time of the Mahdi's appearance.

THE LATER DEVELOPMENT OF THE BABI MOVEMENT

The Babi movement spread quickly through all strata of Iranian society, and a considerable number of people were attracted to it.[16] The followers of the Bab did not belong to one particular class or ethnic group, nor were they confined to a specific region of the country. They were clerics, court members, ministers, peasants, traders, workers, etc. The reasons why the Babi movement spread so fast, and what needs of the Iranian people its teachings addressed, remain to be investigated. Within a couple of years thousands had joined its ranks, and proven their allegiance through the sacrifice of their lives.

It lies in the nature of such a mass movement that many Babis were not thoroughly acquainted with the teachings of the Bab. Their Prophet was in prison, out of reach for the vast majority of his followers, and only communicated with them through letters. Making copies of these writings and disseminating them was difficult and potentially dangerous. Moreover, the Bab's writings employed the terminology of Shiite esotericism, as well as the Bab's own peculiar style and neologisms, which made them difficult to

14 *Bayan* 2:6.
15 *Bayan* 3:1. This law was later abrogated by Baha'u'llah, *The Most Holy Book*, Baha'i World Centre: Haifa, 1992, para. 126 (from here on quoted as KA x:y).
16 On this topic see Peter Smith and Moojan Momen, *The Babi Movement: A Resource Mobilization Perspective*, in Peter Smith (ed.), *In Iran: Studies in Babi and Baha'i History vol. 3*, Los Angeles: Kalimat Press, 1986, 33–93; and Chapter 6 in this volume.

grasp for most readers, and sometimes incomprehensible. It can therefore be fairly assumed that many Babis were not aware of the Bab's actual teachings on every subject he addressed, and not surprisingly, some of their ideas and actions did not mirror his intentions.

When local clerics instigated attacks on the Babis by the populace as well as government forces in three different regions of Iran, a number of the followers of the Bab entrenched themselves in local fortresses, and in one case withdrew to a certain quarter of a town, took up arms and fought back. Such action only seems to have escalated the conflict so that after a few months of fighting, the majority of them were dead.[17] Moreover, the death verdict which a number of clerics had publicly issued two years earlier against the Bab and which the government had ignored thus far, was now carried out. Apparently, the way things were presented to the prime minister Amir Kabir (d. 1851) made him believe that the Babis, much like other seditious and rebellious groups active at the time, posed a threat to the government and in particular to its ambition of strengthening the state's central authority over the entirety of the country.[18] He thus gave the order for the execution of the Bab; in July 1850 he was, in a public show of force, put to death in a square in Tabriz by a large firing squad.

The prominent Iranian historian F. Adamiyat (1920–2008) comes to an interesting conclusion:

> Siyyid Ali-Muhammad [the Bab] did not seek war and rebellion. He was in fact a kind man and hatred was not in his nature... Rather, it was the Mullahs that considered him a threat... Even the letter of the Prime Minister of the time (Mirza Aqasi) clearly shows that the government did not heed the clerics' attempts to initiate a crackdown on the Bab. Another important point to note is that the Bab, when first confronted with the Mullahs' hostility, turned to the government.[19]

17 It has often been claimed that the Babis instigated attacks with the ultimate aim of overthrowing the shah and establishing a theocracy. While a certain element of militancy on their behalf cannot be denied, this was more likely rooted in their Shiite apocalypticism and in the environment and culture in which they lived than derived from the teachings of the Bab. For more, see Chapter 7 in this volume.

18 On this see p. 387 of this chapter.

19 *Amir Kabir va Iran*, 444, here quoted from Homa Nategh, *Iran dar rah-yabi-yi farhangi 1834–1848*, London 1988, 69. Cf. also the Bab's letter to Muhammad Shah written in Maku in 1847/8, quoted in A. Afnan, *Ahd-i A'la*, Oneworld: Oxford, 2000, 299–304. Relevant excerpts can be found in *Selections from the Writings of the Bab*, Baha'i World Centre: Haifa, 1976, 1:6.

And another historian, Homa Nategh (1935–2016) adds:

> It seems that Amir Kabir did not gain any advantage from persecuting and killing the Babis. In fact, he remained alone. Being fond of innovation, progress and development, he should have tried to win the support of reformers in challenging the authoritarian reign of Nasir-ud-Din Shah as well as the religious tyranny [of the clerics]. As we have seen, the Babis at the very least in the beginning of their efforts to spread their beliefs [lit. ideals], turned to men of state. One could even say, they were with the latter, not against them.[20]

In 1852 a number of Babis decided to assassinate the shah in revenge for the execution of the Bab and the killing and imprisonment of so many of his followers.[21] Their attempt upon the shah's life failed, and led to an unprecedented wave of persecution across the whole country. Among those killed were all the known leading figures of the movement. A number of Babis found refuge in the neighboring country of Iraq which was under Ottoman Rule. For about ten years the community remained virtually without leadership. Mirza Yahya Nuri (1831–1912), "Subh-i-Azal" who considered himself the Bab's "vicegerent" (*wasi*) or representative, lived in hiding and avoided all contact with his fellow believers. As a consequence, a number of other Babis put forth leadership claims; nonetheless, none of them were able to gain enough support to unite and lead the community.

BAHA'U'LLAH AFTER THE BAB'S MARTYRDOM

Mirza Husayn-Ali Nuri "Baha" or "Baha'u'llah" (1817–92) was among the many followers of the Bab, who were imprisoned after the failed assassination attempt. He spent several months in a dungeon in Tehran, but eventually the government became convinced that he had not had a part in the plot and his life was spared.[22] He was released on condition that he

20 *Rah-yabi-yi farhangi*, ibid.

21 On the background and circumstances of this attempt see Moojan Momen, "Millennialism and Violence: The Attempted Assassination of Nasir al-Din Shah of Iran by the Babis in 1852," in: *Nova Religio: The Journal of Alternative and Emergent Religions*, vol. 12, no. 1 (August 2008), 57–82.

22 M. Khormuji, *Haqayiq-ul-Akhbar*, Tehran 1984, 116; Sipihr Lisan-ul-Mulk, *Nasikh-ut-Tavarikh*, ed. J. Kiyanfar, Tehran, 1998, vol. iii, 1189.

leave Iran and go into exile. Baha'u'llah had, from the outset, opposed all violence including armed resistance.[23] According to his own testimony it was during his incarceration in a Tehran prison, that he resolved to erase all traces of militancy among the Babis:

> Day and night, while confined in that dungeon, We meditated upon the deeds, the condition, and the conduct of the Babis, wondering what could have led a people so high-minded, so noble, and of such intelligence, to perpetrate such an audacious and outrageous act against the person of His Majesty. This Wronged One, thereupon, decided to arise, after His release from prison, and undertake, with the utmost vigor, the task of regenerating this people.[24]

In 1853, having been released from prison, Baha'u'llah reached Baghdad. During the subsequent decade he managed to transform the mindset of the remaining Babis, convincing them to abandon the militant elements which were part of their Islamic heritage, such as the doctrines of "Holy War" (*jihad*) and "retaliation in kind" (*qisas*). He later referred to this occurrence in these words:

> Strife and conflict befit the beasts of the wild. It was through the grace of God and with the aid of seemly words and praiseworthy deeds that the unsheathed swords of the Babi community were returned to their scabbards. Indeed, through the power of good words, the righteous have always succeeded in winning command over the meads of the hearts of men.[25]

In 1863 the Ottoman government complied with a request of the Persian Court and banished Baha'u'llah farther away from the border between the two kingdoms, first to Istanbul, then in the same year to Edirne and finally,

23 See for example MacEoin, "The Babi Concept of Holy War," in *Religion* 12:2 (1982), 93–129; idem, "From Babism to Baha'ism: Problems of Militancy, Quietism, and Conflation in the Construction of a Religion," in *Religion* 13:3 (1983), 219–55. For a critical discussion of this view see N. Saiedi, *Gate of the Heart. Understanding the Writings of the Bab*, Wilfrid Laurier University Press: n.p. 2008, 339 passim.

24 Baha'u'llah, *Epistle to the Son of the Wolf*, Baha'i Publishing Trust: Wilmette 1988[3], para 33 (from now on quoted as ESW xy).

25 *Lawh-i Dunya*, in *Tablets of Baha'u'llah revealed after the Kitab-i-Aqdas*, Baha'i World Centre: Haifa 1978, 7:7 (from now on quoted as *Tablets* x:y).

in 1868, to 'Akka. Before leaving Baghdad, Baha'u'llah revealed his claim to be Him whom God shall make manifest, the messianic figure promised by the Bab, to a few trusted individuals. During his stay in Edirne (1863–68) he sent numerous letters and epistles (*alvah*, "Tablets") to the Babis in Iran in which he gradually disclosed his station. Toward the end of the Edirne period and during the first years in 'Akka he went even further, sending a number of letters to the rulers of Iran, the Ottoman Empire, France, Britain, Russia, and even the Pope, thus symbolically addressing the peoples of the world through their leaders and making known to them his claims and his teachings. Baha'u'llah passed away in 1892 just outside the city of 'Akka.

BABI MESSIANISM AND THE QUESTION OF LEADERSHIP

The vast majority of Babis in Iran and Iraq eventually accepted Baha'u'llah's claim. Only a mere handful followed his much younger half-brother Mirza Yahya Nuri "Azal" or "Subh-i-Azal" (1831–1912) whom they considered to be a "vicegerent" of the Bab. The members of this group are usually referred to as "Azalis" or "Bayanis." They did not succeed in establishing an autonomous religious identity or an organized community of their own. The only known authentic Azali writings stem from the late nineteenth and early twentieth centuries and are mere anti-Baha'i polemics. In other words, as is often the case with those engaged in religious schisms and counter-claims, the Azalis never moved beyond opposition to the Baha'is and thus failed to articulate and promote any teachings of their own.[26] There is ample anecdotal evidence from remaining Azali families in Isfahan and other towns, that their leaders observed "dissimulation" (*taqiyyah*)[27] and enjoined it upon their followers.

26 The notion that the Azalis were underdogs who preserved true Babism but were outmaneuvered by their more ambitious and strategically-minded co-religionists is to a considerable extent grounded in the work of E. G. Browne. That such a notion, which does not hold up in the light of sources, has become relatively popular in academic circles is principally attributable to the virtual absence of any critical study of Azali literature. It is remarkable that a scholar like E. G. Browne with such intimate knowledge of Babi and Baha'i history, who cited and published a number of important documents, never said much about Azal's writings, apart from general praise, and did not prepare any of his works for publication. Fortunately, Azal's writings are nowadays available online. The Baha'i writer Farham Sabet in a recent study of the transition from Babism to the Bahai faith employs Azali sources to an unprecedented extent and offers many fresh insights: *Mumashat-i Hadrat-i Baha'u'llah dar izhar-i amr* (unpublished manuscript).

27 *Taqiyyah* (lit. fear, prudence) means, that believers should conceal or, according to

In the late 1880s, one particularly important figure, Hadi Dawlat-Abadi is said to have cursed the Bab from the pulpit of a mosque during Friday prayer in order to save his life – and to keep up his good relationship with the powerful local cleric, Mullah Muhammad-Taqi Najafi. It seems that strict adherence to "dissimulation" led the remaining Azalis to eventually merge with the Muslims in their environment and to more or less disappear as a distinct group. Beyond the occasional unverifiable rumors, for many decades there has been no trace of activities or proof for the actual existence of an Azali or any other Babi community.[28]

The main theological problem for the followers of the Bab was that a considerable portion of Bayanic laws appeared to presume the existence of a society where the population and its rulers would be Babis. Other laws seemed to be utterly impractical due to the impossible conditions to which they were subject.[29] Yet other laws were most likely symbolic in nature. Those who, like the Azalis, believed that the Bab's many statements about the revelation of "Him whom God shall make manifest" referred to a distant future, i.e., at least one or two thousand years, faced a dilemma. In the event that the laws of the *Bayan* could not be implemented for centuries to come

---

some, even deny outright their belief, when threatened or in danger.

28 Moreover, for much of the twentieth century and at least the past four or five decades not a single individual has gained prominence as an "Azali", "Babi", or "Bayani." Alleged "Bayani" activities on the internet, since carried out in complete anonymity, do not allow one to come to any conclusions about the number and the identity of whoever is behind them.

Going further back in history, a number of prominent activists and literati of the late nineteenth/early twentieth century, such as Malik-ul-Mutakallimin, Siyyid Jamal-ud-Din Wa'iz, Yahya Dawlat-Abadi and, in particular, Azal's two sons-in-law, Mirza Aqa Khan-i Kirmani and Shaykh Ahmad-i Ruhi, are often denominated "Babi" or "Azali" in works of Iranian history. But their views on the Bab and his teachings are entirely unclear. If they considered themselves "Babis," what did it mean to them? What were their motives and intentions? Moreover, what has not yet been properly explained is the intellectual relationship between these individuals and Azal. Are they to be considered his students or disciples? Did any of the political ideas they promoted and for which they gained historical prominence, stem from Azal or were they inspired by his writings? There is no evidence in their literary output (nor in that of Azal for that matter) that this was the case. The family of Yahya Nuri itself is no longer active and he was apparently buried according to Muslim rites, in Cyprus. Cf. M. Momen, "The Cyprus Exiles," in *Baha'i Studies Bulletin*, 5:3–6:1 (1991), 84–113.

It would seem therefore that what has kept the issue of "Azali-Babism" alive is none other than the frequent reference to it in works of Muslim anti-Baha'i polemicists.

29 The most glaring example of this is daily prayer which is obligatory but nowhere described in any detail. But what is more, the direction of prayer is supposed to be toward "Him whom God shall make manifest."

without the conversion of the masses, and their governance by Babi monarchs, what was their relationship to the Babi law to be? A number of Babis abandoned religious law altogether and considered it unnecessary. Others decided to continue obeying Islamic Law for practical reasons, presumably hoping that another solution would become manifest in the future. The vast majority of Babis accepted Baha'u'llah's claim to be "Him whom God shall make manifest" and his approach to the *Bayan*.

SOME GENERAL OBSERVATIONS ON BAHA'U'LLAH'S SACRED LAW

Azal claimed to be the Bab's vicegerent, and the custodian and preserver of his law. Baha'u'llah, on the other hand, claimed to be the recipient of a new revelation from God and thus asserted his authority to change, to abolish and to replace the Bab's laws and ordinances. During the first few years of his mission the Bab had insisted that his followers adhere to Islamic Law, and it was only from 1847 onwards that he declared it abolished and replaced by the law of the *Bayan*. In like manner, Baha'u'llah initially instructed his followers to observe the Bab's *Bayan*,[30] but in 1873, about halfway through his ministry, he revealed the *Most Holy Book*, which reformed, amended, and effectively replaced Babi law.

The Bab's replacement of the Islamic *shari'ah* with a new law was, no doubt, a revolutionary step. Yet, as his writings demonstrate, this revolution was expressed employing the terminology and referencing the traditional framework of Islamic theological and legal discourse. Notwithstanding the fact that the Bab himself had made it abundantly clear throughout the *Bayan* that his commands are symbols for spiritual or ethical principles, the *Bayan* to a considerable extent appears to be a book of laws.

Baha'u'llah's *Most Holy Book* on the other hand, while it is sometimes called a "book of laws," is in fact, much like the Qur'an and other Holy Books, a composite work with many facets and not to be confused with a systematic and detailed legal code. The *Most Holy Book*, which in its length resembles an epistle, treats a wide variety of topics and contains

30 See for example the celebrated Arabic prayer commonly referred to as "Tablet to Ahmad," written a few years before Baha'u'llah's own *Most Holy Book* (c. 1873) and addressed to the Babis in Iran. In it he extols the Bab in high terms and calls the *Bayan* the "Mother Book."

key theological, mystical and ethical concepts, and historical references. Most of the ordinances and commandments found in this book refer to the spiritual discipline of the individual believer, e.g., prayer, meditation, fasting, and pilgrimage. Others refer to the social life of the believer, including inheritance, marriage, divorce, burial, as well as theft and murder. Yet others are exhortations that enjoin trustworthiness, justice, forbearance, truthfulness, and cleanliness. When most laws are described, focus is not laid on practical details but rather on underlying ethical or spiritual principles.

According to his own testimony, Baha'u'llah withheld his pen for many years from responding to his followers' frequent inquiries with regard to legal questions.[31] He stated that after the revelation of the *Bayan*, there was no essential need for revealing further laws. However, out of compassion for mankind, he decided to lessen their burden and alter the laws of the Bab.[32] It seems that Baha'u'llah considered spiritual knowledge and virtue, not legal provisions, as the true foundation of divine religion. Laws, according to him, were derived from knowledge and hence whoever was deprived of knowledge would not be able to obey the laws.[33]

The idea that the Prophet Muhammad revealed a complete code of law, pertaining to all general and specific issues, encompassing even the most intimate aspects of life, is prominent in classical Islam.[34] Traditionalist clerics teach that all matters, be they related to politics, science, economy, medicine, nutrition or to any other aspect of collective or individual human life, are treated in the divine scriptures. It is for the religious Learned to study them and discover the answers to all current and future problems in order that they may guide mankind in a direction that will be pleasing to God.

Baha'u'llah on the other hand deliberately left many issues to be decided by future generations of his followers. One example is the issue of clothing and of the growing of a beard, both of which were accorded much importance in traditional Islam. Baha'u'llah did not rule on the veiling of women,

---

31 KA 98.

32 KA 142.

33 Cf. *Lawh-i Nasir*, in: *Majmu'iy-i Alvah-i Mubarakih*, Cairo n.d., 179. The original wording is this:

احکام فرع عرفان بوده و خواهد بود. و نفوسی که از
اصل محتجب مانده اند چگونه به فرع ان تشبث نمایند.

34 Cf. Ruhollah Khomeini, *Kashf-i Asrar*, Qom, n.d. [1941], 107.

nor did he involve himself in contemporary discussions about whether wearing "Western" garb was lawful (*halal*) or prohibited (*haram*). Rather he left these issues to the judgment of the individual:

> The choice of clothing and the cut of the beard and its dressing are left to the discretion of men. But beware, O people, lest ye make yourselves the playthings of the ignorant.[35]

Another example is his strong emphasis on the principle of moral integrity and in particular of chastity. Baha'u'llah condemned adultery, fornication (*zina*), and sodomy (*liwat*). Yet he did not engage in detailed legalistic expositions, listing all the diverse practices of human beings, passing judgment upon the legality of each one. He left these questions, if and whenever they related to the public sphere, to be handled by democratically elected institutions ("Houses of Justice").[36] In his writings the most important issues are those pertaining to morality, and they are not to be promoted through ever more detailed discussions of legal questions or by establishing mechanisms where believers control and sanction each other's behavior. When it comes to such matters as pertain to their private lives, individuals are for the most part responsible only to God. Religious life, according to Baha'u'llah, is thus not to be centered around legal questions, and therefore he did not seek to establish a code of laws that would cover every possible situation that could occur. He aimed at fostering virtue, knowledge, and reason.

In other words: Baha'u'llah's faith is based upon virtues and ideals, while the manner of their implementation and realization in practical life is left to the responsibility of the individual believer. Characterizing his faith as "legalistic" or applying the standards of traditional religious jurisprudence to it, would be mistaken, whether by friends or enemies.[37] Baha'u'llah quite openly declared that his mission was not to promote laws, but rather to give rise to human perfections and to uplift their souls, so that the true

35 *Bisharat*, in: Tablets 3:12.

36 KA 19, 49, 107.

37 A common topic in traditional Islamist anti-Baha'i polemics is the alleged incompleteness and therefore "futility" of Baha'u'llah's "*shari'a*," since it is silent on so many topics which classical Islamic jurists consider to be of great importance. Such criticism is based upon a number of premises and a particular mindset, which are then projected onto Baha'u'llah's message, but are in fact incompatible with it and therefore inadequate for passing any judgment on Baha'u'llah's teachings.

station of man and of human reason could become universally manifest.[38] He wrote, in this vein:

> Think not that We have revealed unto you a mere code of laws. Nay, rather, We have unsealed the choice Wine with the fingers of might and power. To this beareth witness that which the Pen of Revelation hath revealed. Meditate upon this, O men of insight![39]

> The purpose of the one true God, exalted be His glory, hath been to bring forth the Mystic Gems out of the mine of man...[40]

SOME FURTHER OBSERVATIONS ON THE BAHA'I FAITH'S EVOLUTION FROM THE BABI MOVEMENT

When immediately prior to leaving Baghdad in 1863 (see p. 389) Baha'u'llah disclosed to a few Babis his claim to be the promised one of the *Bayan*, he accompanied this disclosure with the declaration of three important principles:

> First, that in this Revelation the law of the sword hath been annulled. Second, that ere the expiration of one thousand years whosoever advanceth a prophetic claim is false. By "year" a full year is intended, and no exegesis or interpretation is permitted in this matter. And third, that at that very hour God, exalted be His Glory, shed the full splendor of all His names upon all creation.[41]

A number of key concepts are enshrined in this passage, three of which will be briefly discussed: messianism and the coming of a new revelation, ritual impurity, and religious legitimization of violence.[42]

---

38 *Ayat-i Ilahi*, Baha'i-Verlag: Hofheim, 148 BE, 189. The original text is as follows:
اين ظهور از براي اجراي حدودات ظاهره نيامده ... بلكه لأجل ظهورات كماليه در انفس انسانيه و ارتفاع ارواحهم الي المقامات الباقية و ما يصدّقه عقولهم ظاهر و مشرق شده تا آنكه كلّ فوق ملک و ملكوت مشي نمايند

39 KA 5.

40 ESW 16.

41 *Days of Remembrance. Selections from the Writings of Baha'u'llah for Baha'i Holy Days*, Baha'i World Centre: Haifa 2016, 9:1.

42 For a discussion of the passage see also N. Saiedi, *Logos and Civilization. Spirit, History, and Order in the Writings of Baha'u'llah*, University of Maryland, 2000, 242 passim.

Messianism

Muslims believe the Prophet Muhammad to be the final messenger of God prior to the Day of Judgment. Yet, they also believe in a future savior ("Mahdi") who will be sent by God. Shiite Muslims in particular believe that one of Muhammad's offspring, the so-called Twelfth Imam has gone into hiding over a thousand years ago, and they long for his miraculous return. The Bab claimed to be that long-awaited messianic figure, but also strongly emphasized the coming of yet another Manifestation of God, "Him whom God shall make manifest," whose appearance was near. (The Bab taught that there would be an ongoing series of prophetic cycles and God would send further "Manifestations" in the future.) Baha'u'llah then claimed to be that messianic figure foretold by the Bab and affirmed that the next Manifestation of God would appear in no less than a thousand years.

Islam, Babism, and the Baha'i faith therefore represent three different approaches to messianism and expectation, each having far-reaching implications for the worldview of their followers.

In Islam (much as in Christianity and Judaism) the time of the messianic figure's advent is indeterminate. The expectations surrounding it have often been associated with violence and militancy: the messianic figure shall punish and kill all the enemies of God and render his own followers triumphant over all others. The Messiah/Mahdi will redeem the righteous believers and set straight whatever men are incapable of putting in order. Furthermore, he will judge men according to their allegiance to tradition, deviation from which being considered a sin. As pointed out previously, one practical implication of such a mindset of "passive messianism" is skepticism toward any change and reform initiated by man alone. It is considered safer to wait for the Messiah/Mahdi to restore the correct order of things, than to take unguided action and risk making them worse.

The messianic expectancy fostered by the Bab, on the contrary, was transformed into an instrument to guard the believers against backwardness and stagnation and to encourage them to constantly question their own convictions and traditions, lest they become sanctified and unchallengeable and eventually turn into an obstacle for recognizing the next Manifestation. In other words: the kind of messianism taught by the Bab promoted constant reconsideration of ideas and convictions. Contrary to classical messianism, "Him whom God shall make manifest" would not confirm beliefs and traditions of old, cherished by the believers, but rather he would initiate a new start, a whole "new creation" and dispense with former convictions if needed.

This is exemplified by comparing the use of a certain term in traditional Islamic discourse and in the Bab's writings. For Muslim theologians "*bid'ah*" (innovation, something new and unprecedented) designates a deviation from "sunnah" (established tradition) and carries very negative connotations. It can best be compared to the Western term "heresy."[43] The Bab, on the other side, did not shy away from "*bid'ah*" and, from his earliest writings onwards, used the term countless times referring to himself, his message, his revealed verses, etc. No doubt he was fully aware of the controversial connotations of this term.

In Baha'u'llah's writings, things take yet another turn as messianic expectancy is virtually abolished. While it is true that in very rare instances he made reference to future "Manifestations of God," he refrained from sharing any details, prophecies, signs or the like regarding the circumstances of their appearance. There is no attempt to raise messianic expectations, rather they are discouraged. In most of his writings he claimed that all the hopes and expectations of the past are fulfilled in his revelation and that the period of waiting was now over.

With his proclamation that for at least a thousand years there would appear no recipients of divine revelation, he virtually abolished the traditional concept of "messianism." The believers were told with unprecedented clarity that they should no longer wait for a savior but should rather take on responsibility, open-mindedly investigate all matters for themselves and work for the betterment of the world. The time of prophethood (*nubuvvah*) and messengership (*risalah*) had ended,[44] and the age of reason and wisdom (*'aql*) had dawned.[45]

Ritual Impurity (najasah)

In a number of religious traditions, including Zoroastrianism, Judaism and, in particular, Shiite Islam, the concept of ritual purity is pivotal and has led to considering outsiders or non-believers as ritually impure. Such

43 In a statement (*hadith*) attributed to Muhammad in various slightly differing versions he says "every innovation [in religion] means misguidance, and all misguidance leads to hellfire."

44 ESW 168; cf. *Ishraqat*, n.p., n.d., 293.

45 KA 189, *Lawh-i Salman*, in *Majmu'iy-i Alvah-i mubarakih*, 125.

impurity is not connected to matters of hygiene; it is considered a spiritual concept. Whoever comes in contact with impure matter, needs to observe specific rituals to restore his purity. Shiite clerics have been particularly obsessed with the minute practical details of this concept and produced a vast literature on the topic over the course of centuries and to the present.

The Bab addressed this topic in the *Bayan* and employed the established Islamic terminology when treating it, but he offered an entirely new approach. In one passage, he listed things that "purify" others (*mutahhirat*), and at first glance it might seem a mirror-image of Shiite legal discourse. However, he also lists "the believers" and "the book of God" as purifiers.[46] Obviously such a notion renders the whole idea of impurity obsolete. Concern with the question of purity and the many details surrounding it only makes sense, after all, when the believers are afraid of losing purity and having to restore it. But according to the Bab, if a believer comes into contact with something impure, he renders it pure, not vice versa. In other words: impurity is no longer the stronger, dominating principle; purity is. Severe restrictions on associating with non-believers, as the Shiite clerics imposed them, made no sense in the Bab's worldview.

Although the Bab might have abolished the practical consequences of the concept of "ritual impurity," he presented this idea within the framework and mindset of classical Shiite jurisprudence. It was Baha'u'llah who went a step further and universalized this teaching in clear and unambiguous terms, referencing the passage cited from his aforementioned Baghdad declaration.

> God hath, likewise, as a bounty from His presence, abolished the concept of "uncleanness," whereby divers things and peoples have been held to be impure. He, of a certainty, is the Ever-Forgiving, the Most Generous. Verily, all created things were immersed in the sea of purification when, on that first day of Ridvan, We shed upon the whole of creation the splendors of Our most excellent Names and Our most exalted Attributes. This, verily, is a token of My loving providence, which hath encompassed all the worlds. Consort ye then with the followers of all religions, and proclaim ye the Cause of your Lord, the Most Compassionate; this is the very crown of deeds, if ye be of them who understand.[47]

46 *Bayan* 15:14; cf. 5:7; 6:2.
47 KA 75.

Holy War and Religious Legitimization of Violence

One of the most important principles laid down by Baha'u'llah is the abolishment of "Holy War", i.e., violence in the name of God. As we have already seen, Shiite traditions portray the promised Imam not as a spiritual or moral teacher, but as a military leader who will rise with the sword to take revenge on his foes and shed their blood, before then redeeming his faithful servants.[48] In other words: Shiite messianism is marked by strong, violent, and apocalyptic elements.

The Bab, being well-aware of such expectations, in his earliest writings addressed this mindset and proclaimed that the "Day of Permission" (*yawm-ul-idhn* [the Imam's permission to wage war]) had arrived.[49] Shortly afterwards however, when a number of Babis, as ordered by the Bab, gathered in Karbala – an Iraqi town with particular relevance to Shiite messianism – presumably awaiting the start of the final apocalyptic battle, the Bab refrained from joining them and asked them to disperse. In letters of the time he explains that he reacted thus to the hostility of the clerics and out of fear that any blood would be shed.[50] The Bab's unwillingness to go along with traditional expectations cost him the support of many followers who must have hoped to be among the Mahdi's companions in the final battle.

The Bab received criticism from both ends, some voicing their opposition to his, as they deemed, "illegitimate" call to *jihad* in the first place. Others argued that as a representative of the Imam, by abstaining from fighting against the infidels, he had failed his duty.[51]

But it seems more probable that the Bab's initial declaration of *jihad* was

---

48 Such traditions are abundant and can be found in all major and minor classical collections of *Hadith*. See for example Shaykh Ahmad al-Ahsa'i, *Kitab ar-Raj'ah*, Ad-Dar al-'Alamiyyah: Beirut 1993, 100 ("His business will be to kill and he will accept no one's repentance.") or 116 ("God sent Muhammad as a token of his bounty, but the Qa'im will be a token of His wrath.")

49 The two early works in particular, *Qayyum al-Asma'* and *Kitab ar-Ruh*, contain a number of such passages. See A. Eschraghi, *Frühe Shaikh- und Babi-Theologie. Die Darlegung der Beweise für Muhammads besonderes Prophetentum (Ar-Risala fi Ithbat an-Nubuwa al-Khassa)*, Brill: Leiden, 2004, 166–69 for references and further discussion of the topic.

50 Cf. the letter to Mulla Abdu'l-Khaliq-i Yazdi, printed in: A. Afnan, *Ahd-i A'la*, 184.

51 An example of a Muslim polemic on this topic is found in Abu Talib Shirazi, *Asrar-ul-'Aqayid*, Dar-ul-Kutub-il-Islamiyyah: Tehran, n.d. [2nd revised edition], vol ii, 84–104. The author states that the Bab's claim to be the Mahdi could not be true since he did not take up the sword. The addressee of the Bab's *Risalah Dhahabiyyah* must have voiced similar objections, as can be discerned from the text.

a symbolic way of announcing the advent of a new Day, couched in terms that were suited to his addressee's intellectual mindset. His call to *jihad* was also part of a way of voicing his claim as the Imam's representative and thus establishing his authority over the clerics. Among the first to have realized this was Muhammad Karim Khan Kirmani (d. 1810–73), leader of a particular school of Shiite Islam, and an adversary of the Bab. Within a year of the Bab's first secret declaration, Kirmani started writing polemics against him. Pointing out that according to established Shiite belief only the Hidden Imam had the right to declare Holy War, Kirmani concluded that the Bab, by calling for *jihad*, had "usurped the station of the Holy Prophet's offspring and taken up their place."[52]

The Bab's announcement of *jihad* was at a time when his identity was still kept a secret and he only had a handful of followers. But when there were thousands of Babis across the country willing to fight, he even forbade the killing of anyone. In the *Persian Bayan* he emphasized that God had prohibited the slaying of any soul, more than anything else, and in the most strict manner. If so much as the mere thought of it crossed anyone's mind, it would immediately render him an unbeliever and subject him to punishment from God. Furthermore, death verdicts were not permitted "against anyone, at any time, under any circumstances and under any condition."[53]

Despite these clear injunctions a number of Babis, as we have seen, between 1848–52 took up arms against government forces in three cities or regions of the country (Zanjan, Nayriz and Shaykh Tabarsi in Mazandaran). As is clear from the relevant sources, they were driven by different motivations. Some merely acted in self-defense against attacks instigated by local clerics. Others were convinced that the end of times had arrived and they were to fight alongside the promised one. But there is no evidence that the Babis followed a plan to overthrow the government or intended to establish control over the state or even a specific region of the country.[54] Rather than pursuing a systematic effort and initiating steps of their own, they merely reacted, were thus drawn into fighting, and entrenched themselves with no clear strategy whatsoever.

The question remains, what the teachings of the Bab were on war and

52 *Tir-i Shihab*, typed manuscript online www.alabrar.info. For a detailed discussion see also A. Eschraghi, *Irtibat-i Karim Khan Kirmani ba adyan-i Babi va Baha'i*, in Safiniy-i-ʿIrfan, vol. ix, 46–74.

53 *Bayan* 4:5.

54 Cf. Siyamak Zabihi-Moghaddam, "The Babi-State Conflict at Shaykh Tabarsi," in *Iranian Studies*, 2002, 35:1–3, 87–112.

non-violence. There are, for instance, passages in the *Bayan* that seem to speak of a Babi king or ruler who should establish control over Iran and cleanse it of all non-Babis. But a literal reading of such statements would lead to irreconcilable contradictions. In the very same chapter the Bab goes on to state that this provision referred exclusively to those Babi kings who held power, and should never be put into practice in places where it meant harm or would cause the slightest grief to anyone.[55] The path to guidance, he stated, was one of love and compassion, not of force and coercion.[56] God in his infinite mercy had decreed, that to no one was given the right to cause grief to another soul.[57] The carrying of arms was prohibited, unless the shah gave permission, the reason being that no man should commit what would instill fear in the hearts of others.[58] Under such conditions, it becomes clear that "Holy War" against non-believers with the goal to convert or conquer was impractical.

Moreover, the prerequisite for *jihad*, according to the Bab, was the existence of a Babi king having been instated. Before that, there could be no legal way to start *jihad* to establish a Babi state. It had to be the other way around: first establish a rule, and then the king could issue the command to fight; which then would be practically devoid of meaning. Could it be that the (few and scattered references) related to *jihad* in the *Bayan* were, like the earlier ones, merely symbolic in nature?

Again, a look at the historical circumstances might shed some light on this question. As has been discussed, according to classical Shiite jurisprudence, only the twelfth Imam is the legitimate spiritual and worldly ruler and during the time of his occultation any king is a usurper. Over time a number of Shiite clerics developed the doctrine of "vicegerency" (*niyabah*) and reached different conclusions. Some held that there should be no cooperation with any worldly government whatsoever, others believed that the kings should obey the clerics in order to make sure that their rule was in accordance with divine law. And another rather small number of Mullahs claimed that it should be the Learned themselves who would rule.[59] Despite their differences all three groups held in common that there was no such thing as a legitimate secular authority separate from religion. The

55 *Bayan* 5:5.
56 *Bayan* 2:16.
57 *Bayan* 7:18.
58 *Bayan* 7:6.
59 Cf. Muhsin Kadivar, *Nazariyihay-i dawlat dar fiqh-i Shi'ih*, Nashr-i Nay: Tehran 1378⁴, idem, *Hukumat-i Wala'i*, Nashr-i Nay: Tehran 1377.

Bab, in turn, made it clear not least throughout his numerous letters to the Iranian monarch Muhammad Shah (d. 1848) that he, speaking as the Imam's representative or the Imam himself, had no desire for kingship or for the authority to issue verdicts, like the clerics.[60] Quite significantly, he tells the shah to accept his message and cast away all worldly power, but if he were to reject the Bab's claim he should cling to his kingship and let the Bab be in peace.[61] He neither tells the shah to succumb to his authority and become a mere servant and carry out his orders, nor does he call for his overthrow should he refuse to accept his call.

In order to be able to better appreciate the significance of the Bab's teachings on the authority of the king and the clerics, it is particularly illuminating to consider the example of a near-contemporary and particularly fateful religious verdict (*fatva*) issued by a prominent cleric, Siyyid Muhammad-i Isfahani "Mujahid" (d. 1826). He decreed that it was in fact a religious obligation to conquer Russia and thus was able to effectively pressure the country into the so-called second Russo-Persian War (1826–28), against the will of the shah and the crown-prince Abbas Mirza and even the Russians who showed no interest in yet another armed conflict. According to Qajar court chronicles, the reins of authority slipped out of the monarch's hands into those of a "bunch of unworthy and incapable men." The "mob and rabble preferred the verdict of the Mullahs over the king's command," and "unconditionally heeded the Mujtahid's [senior cleric] call to jihad." "All over the country, the situation became such that whenever the honorable monarch spoke against the Mullahs' verdict, the people of Iran would rise in opposition to the king of Islam."[62]

The second Russo-Persian War ended with a historic defeat for Iran, sealed with the so-called "Turkmenchay Treaty." It meant a permanent loss of significant territories and posed heavy burdens on the Iranian people in terms of reparation payment. According to the court chronicle, Siyyid-i Mujahid was, as a consequence of the martyrdom of a number of illustrious inhabitants of Tabriz, "severely maltreated by the vulgar people of Tabriz"

60 Cf. Letter of the Bab to Muhammad Shah, printed in A. Afnan, *Ahd-i A'la*, 103. The original text:

«ما اراد ملک الدنیا ولا الآخرة و لا حکم الفتوی مثل العلماء...»

61 Cf. Letters of the Bab to Muhammad Shah from Maku (quoted in A. Afnan, *Ahd-i A'la*, 299–304, Selections,1:6) and from Chahriq (ibid., 354).

62 Rida-Quli Khan Hidayat, *Rawdat-us-Safay-i Nasiri*, ed. Kiyanfar, Tehran 1385[2], vol. xiv, 7835 passim.

and therefore decided to leave the battleground and died shortly after on the way back.[63] Sometime later, another prominent cleric, Mullah Muhammad-Taqi Baraghani (d. 1847) would make the crown prince responsible for the disaster, as his intentions had not been pure.[64]

With this immediate historical background in mind, it becomes clear that this is yet another prescription of the Bab's that carries a symbolic meaning. The Bab's statement that authority to call for war rested exclusively with the shah, with no mention of the clerics, can be seen as addressing the events and the aftermath of the war with Russia, which had occurred a mere two decades earlier. The consequences of a senior cleric's meddling with politics were still widely felt.

Whatever the case, the Bab's statements on *jihad* are ambiguous and can, no doubt, be interpreted in different ways. Baha'u'llah, however, much like on other topics such as ritual purity, did not leave any room for ambiguity or misunderstanding when it came to religious legitimization of violence. From as early as 1852, the beginning of his prophetic career, up until his passing in 1892, in countless letters and writings, addressed to his followers but also to individual clerics and kings, he reiterated his stance that there was no religious legitimacy whatsoever for violence against non-believers. There was no law or permission to wage Holy War, no matter who would call for it.

CONCLUSION

In the second half of the twentieth century, Iranian writers, generally associated with the political Left, have presented Babism as a revolutionary movement, which "mirrored the desires of those classes developing toward bourgeoisie and the democratic wishes and demands of workers and peasants." Baha'u'llah was portrayed as having led the movement away from its initial goal by quenching the fire of its revolutionary zeal.[65] However it would be more accurate to say that while the Babi movement was aimed at destroying the structure of the spiritual and political authority of Shiite

63 Ibid., 7846, 7848. Cf. also M. Bamdad, *Sharh-i Hal-i Rijal-i Iran*, Tehran 1371[4], vol. iii, 285; Sipihr Lisan-ul-Mulk, *Nasikh-ut-Tavarikh*, vol. i, 363–404.

64 M. Tunukabuni, *Qisas-ul-Ulama*, Ed. B. Karbasi, Tehran 1383, 30.

65 Ihsan Tabari, *Barkhi barrasiha darbariy-i jahanbinihay-i ijtima'i dar Iran*, Berlin 1387[4], 620.

clerics, it was Baha'u'llah who turned it into a constructive force aimed at building up a new society.

While it is true that Baha'u'llah's writings, from a literary point of view, closely mirror (at times) Islamic, or more precisely, mystic terminology, in fact his teachings mark a fundamental break with Islam in terms of worldview, the image of man, the very idea of religion itself and its role in this world. It is a faith on its own, separate from Islam. Babism, on the other hand, can be portrayed as an intermediate stage between Islam and a wholly new religion.

Based on this premise, the Bab's role was to challenge age-old convictions and diminish the hold of clerical power over people's minds. In other words, his mission was to tear down the power structure of society, while Baha'u'llah, subsequently, was to proclaim a new thought system, based upon ideas and values that were suited to the current needs of society.[66]

The gradual process of introducing new teachings can be observed in reference to fundamental issues such as man's role in and responsibility for the betterment of society (see p. 398 on messianism and apocalypticism), and in regulations governing the association of believers with those outside their own faith. Contrary to classical Islam and scriptural Babism, Baha'u'llah permitted such association not only to be unrestricted but deemed it desirable and praiseworthy.[67]

This process was also reflected in some of the minor, and at times obscure, regulations of the *Bayan*: According to popular belief at the time of the Bab, ordinary Muslims were obliged "to submit in utter deference

66 Some passages in the writings of Shoghi Effendi, great-grandson of Baha'u'llah and head of the Baha'i faith from 1921–57, seem to support this premise and the line of reasoning presented above: "The severe laws and injunctions revealed by the Bab can be properly appreciated and understood only when interpreted in the light of his own statements regarding the nature, purpose and character of his own Dispensation. As these statements clearly reveal, the Babi Dispensation was essentially in the nature of a religious and indeed social revolution, and its duration had therefore to be short, but full of tragic events, of sweeping and drastic reforms. Those drastic measures enforced by the Bab and his followers were taken with the view of undermining the very foundations of Shiite orthodoxy, and thus paving the way for the coming of Baha'u'llah. To assert the independence of the new Dispensation, and to prepare also the ground for the approaching Revelation of Baha'u'llah, the Bab had therefore to reveal very severe laws, even though most of them were never enforced. But the mere fact that he revealed them was in itself a proof of the independent character of his Dispensation and was sufficient to create such widespread agitation, and excite such opposition on the part of the clergy that led them to cause his eventual martyrdom." (Quoted from KA, n. 109).

67 KA 144; *Bisharat* 5, 25, 29.

and servility whatever was peerless and valuable amongst their possessions to the Mullahs."[68] The Bab then declared in the *Bayan* that in the early days of Islam, whenever a country was conquered, whatever was peerless among the spoils of war, belonged to Muhammad. Now it likewise belonged to "the Manifestation of God" (i.e., the Bab or "Him whom God shall make manifest").[69] This is yet another example wherein the Bab symbolically shifted attention away from the clerics toward himself and denied them their claimed privilege as representatives of the Imam. Baha'u'llah then proceeded, in the *Most Holy Book*, to abolish the provision altogether.[70]

The Bab had identified and addressed the main obstacles to progress. But it was Baha'u'llah who pivoted to the needs of a future society. His teachings were summarized and articulated, in the 1870s and 80s, in his several letters to kings and rulers,[71] in the *Most Holy Book*, in a number of subsequent letters often described as "appendices" (*mutammimat*) to that book,[72] and finally in 1891 in his last major work, which may be considered his spiritual testimony, an Epistle outwardly addressed to a cleric in Isfahan, but actually to the Shah of Iran, and in the final analysis, to the people of the world.

In these works, the core teachings of Baha'u'llah were detailed, many of which stand in obvious contrast with the established norms of his time. Among them universal peace, unrestricted association with and mutual friendship between the members of all faiths, and in fact all peoples of the world, equality of men and women, emphasis on education for children whether boys or girls, praise of freedom, establishment of consultative assemblies, praise of a free press, condonement and encouragement of scientific progress, emphasis on the high value and constructive role of music and the arts, praise of reason and, not least, the coming of age (*'asr-i bulugh*) of humanity.[73]

---

68 See the autobiography of the cleric and political activist Ibrahim Zanjani: *Khatirat-i Shaykh Ibrahim-i Zanjani*, ed. M. Salih, Tehran 1380, 59, cf. 5.

69 *Bayan* 5:6.

70 KA 114.

71 These are collected in *The Summons of the Lord of Hosts*, Baha'i World Centre: Haifa 2002.

72 These are contained in *Tablets*.

73 Cf. in particular *Tablets*, chapters 3–8, 11, and the *Most Holy Book*.

BIBLIOGRAPHY

Afnan, Abul-Qasim. *Ahd-i A'la*. Oneworld: Oxford, 2000.

Bab. *Bayan-i Farsi*, n.p., n.d. [Tehran 1950s?].

_____ *Selections from the Writings of the Bab*. Baha'i World Centre: Haifa, 1976.

Baha'u'llah. *Ayat-i Ilahi*. Baha'i-Verlag: Hofheim, 148 BE.

_____ *Days of Remembrance. Selections from the Writings of Baha'u'llah for Baha'i Holy Days*. Baha'i World Centre: Haifa, 2016.

_____ *Epistle to the Son of the Wolf*. Baha'i Publishing Trust: Wilmette, 1988[3].

_____ *Majmu'iy-i Alvah-i Mubarakih*. Cairo n.d.

_____ *The Most Holy Book*. Baha'i World Centre: Haifa, 1992.

_____ *The Summons of the Lord of Hosts*. Baha'i World Centre: Haifa, 2002.

_____ *Tablets of Baha'u'llah revealed after the Kitab-i-Aqdas*. Baha'i World Centre: Haifa, 1978.

Bamdad, Mihdi. *Sharh-i Hal-i Rijal-i Iran*. Tehran, 1371.

Eschraghi, Armin. *Frühe Shaikhi- und Babi-Theologie. Die Darlegung der Beweise für Muhammads besonderes Prophetentum (Ar-Risala fi Ithbat an-Nubuwa al-Khassa)*. Brill: Leiden, 2004.

_____ "Undermining the Foundations of Orthodoxy: Some Notes on the Bab's Sharia (Sacred Law)." In: Todd Lawson and Omid Ghaemmaghami, *A Most Noble Pattern. Collected Essays on the Writings of the Bab, Ali Muhammad Shirazi (1819–50)*, George Ronald: Oxford, 2012, 175–95.

Eschraghi, Iradj. *Tajaddud-khwahi va islah-gara'i dar Iran*. 2nd edition. Forugh: Cologne, 2018.

Hidayat, Rida-Quli Khan. *Rawdat-us-Safay-i Nasiri*. Ed. Kiyanfar. Tehran, 1385[2].

Kadivar, Muhsin. *Hukumat-i Wala'i*. Nashr-i Nay: Tehran, 1377.

_____ *Nazariyihay-i dawlat dar fiqh-i Shi'ih*. Nashr-i Nay: Tehran, 1378.

Khomeini, Ruhollah. *Hukumat-i Islami*. Intisharat-i Amir: Tehran, 1981.

_____ *Kashf-i Asrar*. Qom, n.d. [1941?].

Khormuji, M. *Haqayiq-ul-Akhbar*. Tehran, 1984.

MacEoin, Denis. "The Babi Concept of Holy War." In: *Religion*, 12:2 (1982), 93–129.

_____ "From Babism to Baha'ism. Problems of Militancy, Quietism, and Conflation in the Construction of a Religion." In: *Religion*, 13:3 (1983), 219–55.

Momen, Moojan. "The Cyprus Exiles." In *Baha'i Studies Bulletin*, 5:3–6:1 (1991), 84–113.

_____ "Millennialism and Violence: The Attempted Assassination of Nasir al-Din Shah of Iran by the Babis in 1852." In: *Nova Religio: The Journal of Alternative and Emergent Religions*, vol. 12, no. 1 (August 2008), 57–82.

_____ *Selections from the Writings of E. G. Browne on the Babi and Baha'i Religions*. Oxford: George Ronald, 1987.

Nategh, Homa. *Iran dar rah-yabi-yi farhangi 1834–1848*. London, 1988.

Saiedi, Nader. *Gate of the Heart: Understanding the Writings of the Bab*. Wilfried Laurier University Press: n.p., 2008.

_____ *Logos and Civilization: Spirit, History, and Order in the Writings of Baha'u'llah*. University of Maryland: 2000.

Sipihr Lisan-ul-Mulk. *Nasikh-ut-Tavarikh*. ed. J. Kiyanfar. Tehran, 1998.

Smith, Peter and Momen, Moojan. "The Babi Movement: A Resource Mobilization Perspective." In Peter Smith (ed.), *In Iran: Studies in Babi and Baha'i History vol. 3*, Los Angeles, Kalimat Press, 1986, 33–93.

Tabari, Ihsan. *Barkhi barrasiha darbariy-i jahanbinihay-i ijtima'i dar Iran*. Berlin 1387.

Tunukabuni, Muhammad-Ali. *Qisas-ul-Ulama*. ed. B. Karbasi. Tehran, 1383.

Zanjani, Ibrahim. *Khatirat-i Shaykh Ibrahim-i Zanjani*. ed. M. Salih. Tehran, 1380.

9

“The hand of God is not chained up”

Notes on Two Salient Themes in the Prose Writings of Ṭáhirih Qurratu’l-‘Ayn

OMID GHAEMMAGHAMI[1]

Abstract: A proper assessment of the philosophical and intellectual talents of the Bábí martyr Ṭáhirih Qurratu’l-‘Ayn (d. 1852) requires a careful study of her prose writings. This chapter offers remarks on two central themes encountered in these works. The first is the continuation of divine revelation, the appearance of the promised Qá’im of Shí‘í Islam in the person of the Báb, and intimations of the identity, mission, and station of “Him whom God shall make manifest”; the second is the urgent need for love and friendship among the Bábí faithful in their interactions with one another, and for forbearance and wisdom in delivering the message of the Báb to others.

1 The author wishes to thank Dr. Mina Yazdani and Ms. Vida Rastegar-Ghaemmaghami for their comments on an earlier draft.

INTRODUCTION

The figure of Ṭáhirih Qurratu'l-'Ayn is one of the most striking features of the religion founded by 'Alí-Muḥammad-i-Shírází, known as the Báb (d. 1850). Executed at the age of thirty-five for her deeds as much as her words, Ṭáhirih was an eloquent speaker, a gifted poet, and a prolific scholar.[2] Whereas much of her poetry has been published, translated, and studied, the painstaking, difficult, and prodigious work of methodically identifying, cataloguing, collating, authenticating, and analyzing the many extant letters, treatises, prayers, and homilies written by or attributed to Ṭáhirih remains a desideratum.[3] In this short chapter, I will

2 Studies on and references to Ṭáhirih include Abbas Amanat, *Resurrection and Renewal: The Making of the Babi Movement in Iran, 1844–1850* (Los Angeles: Kalimát Press, 2005 [paperback edition]), 295–331; Nuṣratu'lláh Muḥammad-Ḥusayní, *Ḥaḍrat-i-Ṭáhirih* (Madrid: Intishárát-i-Niḥal, 2012 [2nd edition]); Muḥammad Afnán, *Majmú'iy-i-Maqálát*, [vol. 1] (Dundas, Ontario: 'Andalíb, 2013), 228–86; the articles compiled in the anthology edited by Sabir Afaqi, *Táhirih in History: Perspectives on Qurratu'l-'Ayn from East and West* (Los Angeles: Kalimát Press, 2004); Farzaneh Milani, *Veils and Words: The Emerging Voices of Iranian Women Writers* (London: I.B. Tauris, 1992), 77–99; Farzaneh Milani, *Sword Not Words: Iranian Women Writers and Freedom of Movement* (Syracuse: Syracuse University Press, 2011), 105–27; Negar Mottahedeh, *Representing the Unpresentable: Historical Images of National Reform from the Qajars to the Islamic Republic of Iran* (New York: Syracuse University Press, 2008); Todd Lawson, "The Authority of the Feminine and Fatima's Place in an Early Work of the Bab," in *The Most Learned of the Shi'a*, edited by Linda S. Walbridge (Oxford: Oxford University Press, 2001), 94–96; Abbas Amanat, *Iran: A Modern History* (New Haven: Yale University Press, 2017), 241–45; Abbas Amanat, *Apocalyptic Islam and Iranian Shi'ism* (London: I.B. Tauris, 2009), 120; 'Alí al-Wardí, *Hákadhá Qatalú Qurrata'l-'Ayn* (Köln: Al-Kamel Verlag, 1991); the collection of poems compiled and translated by Amin Banani, et al., *Táhirih: A Portrait in Poetry (Selected Poems of Qurratu'l-'Ayn)* (Los Angeles: Kalimát Press, 2005); Majmú'ah Mina'l-Mu'allifín, *Buká'u'ṭ-Ṭáhirah* (Damascus: Dáru'l-Madá, 2008); Sayfí Ibráhím Sayfí, *Qurratu'l-'Ayn (Aṭ-Ṭáhirah) va'l-Bábíyyah* (New Delhi: Mir'át Publications, 2001). Extensive bibliographies of primary and secondary sources on Ṭáhirih and the Bábí movement in eastern and western languages produced up to the early 1990s are available in Anjuman-i-Adab va Hunar (editor), *Khúshihhá'í az Kharman-i-Adab va Hunar 3: Dawriy-i-Ṭáhirih.* (Darmstadt: Reyhani, 1992), 135–42; and idem, *Khúshihhá'í az Kharman-i-Adab va Hunar 4: Dawriy-i-Qalam-i-A'lá* (Darmstadt: Reyhani, 1993), 206–22. Harvard University recently digitized a number of writings attributed to Ṭáhirih as part of its Women's Worlds in Qajar Iran project. This collection is publicly available at www.qajarwomen.org/fa/items/1030A1.html.

3 On Ṭáhirih's poetry, see now Banani, et al., *Táhirih: A Portrait in Poetry* and the three collections published in the original language and translated into English by Hatcher and Hemmat entitled *The Poetry of Ṭáhirih* (Oxford: George Ronald, 2002); *Adam's Wish: Unknown Poetry of Ṭáhirih* (Wilmette: Bahá'í Publishing Trust, 2008); and *The*

briefly examine two salient and recurring themes encountered in Ṭáhirih's prose writings: the continuation of divine revelation and the paramount need for love and friendship.

PROGRESSIVE REVELATION

The most critical theme in Ṭáhirih's letters and treatises is the renewal of revelation and the appearance of the promised one. Abbas Amanat draws attention to the prevalence of "the theme of progressive revelations" in works that have survived from the first two years of her career as a Bábí.[4] Ṭáhirih states in her writings that Messengers and Prophets—whom she calls, among other things, "Translators of the Divine Will and the Tongues of His Decree" (*tarájimiy-i-ma<u>sh</u>íyyat va alsiniy-i-irádiy-i-ú*)—have appeared to guide humanity throughout history.[5] She stresses that "all" of the "Manifestations of the Kingdom of God's Cause" (*maẓáhir-i-amr*) who appeared in the past have promised the advent of the revelation of the Báb and celebrated its virtues. The Day of Resurrection foretold in the Books and Scriptures of the past is, according to Ṭáhirih, the appearance of the Báb, whom she identifies as the awaited messianic Qá'im of Twelver <u>Sh</u>í'í Islam.[6] In her writings, Ṭáhirih extols the Báb as "the speaking Tongue of God and His true Guardian," "the blessed crimson Tree," "the Revelation of light from the horizon of Bahá," "the Remembrance of God, the Exalted, the Most High," "the Mystery of Mysteries," "the Fountain of Destiny," "the decisive Decree," "the greatest Proof of God," "the Gate of endless effusions," "the most great Master," "the most radiant Light," "the Ruler of creation," "the supreme Luminary," "a shining Lamp," "the awaited Soul," "the Seal of gates," "the Point of the beginning and the end," "the Most Great Name," "He who stands on the Tuṭunjayn," "the Gate of Him Who is the Invisible of Invisibles," "the Guide of those who are lost in bewilderment," "the Treasure of the poor and destitute," "the Fortress of them who

---

Quickening: Unknown Poetry of Ṭáhirih (Wilmette: Bahá'í Publishing Trust, 2011). On her prose writings in particular, see Denis MacEoin, *The Sources for Early Bābī Doctrine and History* (Leiden: Brill, 1992), 107–16; Amanat, *Resurrection and Renewal*, 301 n. 41.

4 Amanat, *Resurrection and Renewal*, 301.

5 Fáḍil-i-Mázindarání, *Kitáb-i-Ẓuhúru'l-Ḥaqq*, vol. 3 (Hofheim: Bahá'í-Verlag, 2008), 379.

6 Fáḍil-i-Mázindarání, *Kitáb-i-Ẓuhúru'l-Ḥaqq*, vol. 3, 287–88.

seek refuge," and "the Most Noble Pattern."[7] These and other epithets and titles deployed in Ṭáhirih's writings to praise and speak of the Báb reveal her understanding of his station, in addition to her impressive command of the Quran, hadith, the writings of the Báb, and the works of Shaykh Aḥmadu'l-Aḥsá'í (d. 1826), the founder of what came to be known as the Shaykhí movement, and Shaykh Aḥmad's successor, Siyyid Káẓim-i-Rashtí (d. 1843), under whom Ṭáhirih studied for several years.

The theme of progressive revelation is emphasized in one of Ṭáhirih's earliest surviving works, dated one year after the Báb's declaration, in which she expatiates upon the exigency of a new divine Messenger. Echoing one of the key arguments of the Báb, presented throughout his writings, Ṭáhirih avers that just as Muḥammad's greatest proof was the Quran, the Báb's greatest proofs are his verses, singling out "the blessed commentary"[8]—a reference to the Qayyúmu'l-Asmá', the Báb's commentary on the Súrih of Joseph, known throughout the ministry of the Báb as the Quran of the Bábís—from which Ṭáhirih cites often in her writings, and which she is said to have translated into Persian.[9] Addressing the Báb's Shaykhí opponents in the same work, she asks rhetorically if those who rejected the Messenger of God (Muḥammad) said anything different than what those who now oppose the Báb are saying, namely, that "He [Muḥammad] brought a new exposition [*bayán* or *bayyán*] that does not conform with our grammatical rules and conventions?"[10]

7 See Muḥammad Afnán, *Majmú'iy-i-Maqálát*, [vol. 1], 274; Fáḍil-i-Mázindarání, *Kitáb-i-Ẓuhúru'l-Ḥaqq*, vol. 3, 266, 267; Muḥammad-Ḥusayní, *Ḥaḍrat-i-Ṭáhirih*, 505. Each of these epithets and descriptions is rooted in the Quran, hadiths (esp. Shí'í hadiths), the writings of the Báb, and the writings of Shaykh Aḥmad and Siyyid Káẓim. On the locution "the Most Noble Pattern" (*Ar-rasmu'l-akram*), which also appears in the writings of the Báb (see the collections of the Iranian National Bahá'í Archives (INBA), 14:62, available at www.afnanlibrary.org/docs/persian-arabic-mss/inba/), see Lawson, "Introduction," in Todd Lawson and Omid Ghaemmaghami (eds.), *A Most Noble Pattern* (Oxford: George Ronald, 2012), ix–x.

8 Fáḍil-i-Mázindarání, *Kitáb-i-Ẓuhúru'l-Ḥaqq*, vol. 3, 380.

9 For examples of passages from the Qayyúmu'l-Asmá' cited by Ṭáhirih, see Fáḍil-i-Mázindarání, *Kitáb-i-Ẓuhúru'l-Ḥaqq*, vol. 3, 378, 383. Ṭáhirih is also said to have translated into Persian the Ṣaḥífiy-i-Makhzúnih, another early work of the Báb, to which the Báb refers in the Qayyúmu'l-Asmá'. See Nuṣratu'lláh Muḥammad-Ḥusayní, *Ḥaḍrat-i-Báb* (Dundas, Ontario: Institute for Bahá'í Studies in Persian, 1995), 754.

10 Fáḍil-i-Mázindarání, *Kitáb-i-Ẓuhúru'l-Ḥaqq*, vol. 3, 382. Cf. In the chapter of his Kitábu'l-Asmá' on the name of God *al-Abyan*, the Báb deploys the neologism *bayyán* (which can mean both "Exposition" and "Expounder") and expresses a preference for calling his main doctrinal work *bayyán* (with a *tashdíd* on the letter *yá'*), though he also permits referring to it as *bayán* (meaning "Exposition"), inasmuch as *bayyán* can refer

Extolling the Báb as "the greatest proof of God" and the Manifestation of "the Self of God, the Most High" in a treatise addressed to one of the Shí'í ulama, Ṭáhirih maintains that God has the power of raising any of His servants to be His Proof (*ḥujjah*),[11] Gate (*báb*), Prophet (*nabí*), or Messenger (*rasúl*). Invoking the Quranic locution "no change can you find in God's mode of dealing" (Quran 33:62, 35:43, 48:23), she stresses that God's greatest Sunnah (meaning mode of dealing, method, precedent, and practice) has been to raise, in each and every age, a new Manifestation, implying that not only has He raised a new Messenger in the Báb, but that He will continue to send Divine Emissaries in the future. She then makes an intriguing statement: for those who have eyes to see, there are no differences between a Prophet, a Messenger, or a Gate.[12] This statement demonstrates that Ṭáhirih, and likely others from among the Báb's earliest disciples, perceived, soon after the Báb's declaration, that by adopting the title of "Báb," Siyyid 'Alí Muḥammad-i-Shírází was only ostensibly introducing himself as a gate of the Hidden Imám. Rather, by adopting the title of "Báb," he was in fact proclaiming himself, from the beginning of his ministry, to be the Gate of God, the Gate of the figure referred to explicitly in the Báb's later writings as "Him whom God shall make manifest," and a new Messenger on par with Moses, Jesus, and Muḥammad.

The theme of a new Divine Revelation is present in a novel interpretation given by Ṭáhirih to Quran 5:64, "'The hand of God,' say the Jews, 'is chained up.' Chained up be their own hands; and for that which they have said, they were accursed. Nay, outstretched are both His hands!"[13] Ṭáhirih alludes or refers to this verse in several of her works.[14] The prevailing interpretation of "the hand of God is chained up" in exegetical sources, shaped, it seems, at least partly by anti-Semitic stereotypes and tropes, is that of miserliness. Reading the verse literally, most commentators suggest that it either reprimands the Jewish people for complaining that God has withheld His provision from them, or admonishes them for mocking the dire financial

at once to both the book and to God, its Author.

11 This is an ambivalent term that refers varyingly to Messengers, Prophets, Imáms, the four emissaries of the twelfth Imam from the period of the Minor Occultation, or the ulama in Shí'í (including Shaykhí) sources.

12 Muḥammad-Ḥusayní, *Ḥadrat-i-Ṭáhirih*, 537.

13 Translated by Shoghi Effendi in Bahá'u'lláh, *The Kitáb-i-Íqán: The Book of Certitude* (Wilmette: Bahá'í Publishing Trust, 1931/1983), 136, adapted from J. M. Rodwell's translation.

14 See, e.g., Fáḍil-i-Mázindarání, *Kitáb-i-Ẓuhúru'l-Ḥaqq*, vol. 3, 379, 384, 388.

situation in which the early Muslim community in Medina found itself. Ṭáhirih affirms that "the hand of God is not chained up" (*dast-i-parvardigár bastih níst*) but reads (viz., understands) the verse in a different manner. She appears to allude to a rare hadith attributed in Shí'í sources to the eighth Imám, 'Alí ar-Riḍá (d. 818), where the verse "'The hand of God,' say the Jews, 'is chained up'" is interpreted by ar-Riḍá not as an expression of miserliness but rather to say that "They [the Jewish people] meant that God has brought His *amr* to an end and will not bring forth a new thing again... He will not add anything to (his *amr*)."[15] Scholars have noted the difficulty in translating the term *amr* (lit., command, order, cause, affair, among other things) in the Quran and hadith sources owing to its multifarious uses. It is clear that *amr* in these sources often has eschatological and apocalyptic connotations; "divine Cause"[16] and "divine command"[17] have been suggested as the best approximate translation in English. In other words, according to ar-Riḍá, Quran 5:64 reproaches the Jewish people at the time of Muḥammad who opposed him on the basis that the *amr* of God brought by Moses to them was the *only* divine Cause, and that God would never raise a new prophet with a new divine Cause again. Ṭáhirih universalizes this reading of the verse and applies it to all religious communities—and in particular the Muslim community of her own time—who contend that their Messenger is the final Messenger or allege that God is incapable of sending a new Emissary and adding to His *amr*. Ṭáhirih proclaims more than once in her writings that "Day after Day, the cycle of the universe is progressively advancing upward. There can be no suspension to the effusions of His all-encompassing grace."[18] It is important to note that the word deployed by Ṭáhirih in this passage, *taraqqí*, translated as "progressively advancing upward," connotes social and educational progress, and is related to notions of refinement, development, and prosperity.

Ṭáhirih, furthermore, affirms in her writings that divine revelation will not cease with the Báb, echoing the most salient theme in the Báb's writings.

15 Cited in Ash-Shaykhu'ṣ-Ṣadúq, *'Uyún Akhbári'r-Riḍá* (Tehran: Nashr-i-Jahán, 1378 AH/1958–59), vol. 1, 182, 189.

16 Todd Lawson, *Gnostic Apocalypse and Islam* (London: Routledge, 2012), index, s.v. "divine cause (*al-amr*)"; Amanat, *Resurrection and Renewal*, 252 (here Amanat translates *amru'lláh* in one of the Tablets of the Báb as "Divine cause").

17 Amanat, *Iran: A Modern History*, 246; Abbas Amanat, *Resurrection and Renewal*, 149.

18 Fáḍil-i-Mázindaráni, *Kitáb-i-Ẓuhúru'l-Ḥaqq*, vol. 3, 387. A similar statement is made in idem, 388. The translation here is cited from Amanat, *Resurrection and Renewal*, 302–3, slightly amended.

The Báb has referred indirectly or directly throughout his writings to the imminent appearance of a figure whom he began in 1847 to refer to as "Him whom God shall make manifest." Rather than appoint a successor or foretell the appearance of another prophet, the Báb commanded his followers to await the advent of "Him whom God shall make manifest," to whom he also alluded as, among other ciphers, "the Son of 'Alí" (that is, "Ḥusayn") and "238" (the numerical equivalent of the name "Ḥusayn-'Alí").[19] From sources available to the Bahá'í chronicler Muḥammad-i-Zarandí, surnamed Nabíl-i-A'ẓam (d. 1892), it appears that Ṭáhirih had intuited that this figure was none other than her co-religionist, the Bábí disciple Mírzá Ḥusayn-'Alíy-i-Núrí, known at the time as Jináb-i-Bahá', who later assumed the title Bahá'u'lláh (d. 1892).[20] The eldest son of Bahá'u'lláh, Mírzá 'Abbás-i-Núrí, known as 'Abdu'l-Bahá (d. 1921), who met Ṭáhirih as a child, has noted that in her speeches, Ṭáhirih expatiated upon the principle of progressive revelation, declared boldly the appearance of the promised one, and anticipated the declaration of Bahá'u'lláh as the promised one of the Bayán:

> The purport of her discourse, which was supported by a range of arguments, as well as by the Qur'án and the traditions of the Prophet, was that in every age an illustrious and distinguished Individual must be the focal Centre of the circle of guidance, the Pole Star of the firmament of the most excellent Law of God, and a perspicuous Leader; that all may defer to Him; and that in this day that illustrious and distinguished Individual is the Báb, Who has manifested Himself. Although her speech was eloquent, yet when she perceived that Bahá'u'lláh was to raise another call and shine forth with another radiance, she became even more enkindled and reached a state that can hardly be described. She forsook all patience and composure and well-nigh rent asunder the veil of concealment. Night and day she would at turns speak forth and cry out, laugh aloud, and weep bitterly.[21]

---

19 Nader Saiedi, *Gate of the Heart* ([Waterloo]: Wilfred Laurier University Press, 2008), 344–51.

20 [Nabíl-i-Zarandí], *The Dawn-Breakers: Nabíl's Narrative of the Early Days of the Bahá'í Revelation*, trans. and ed. Shoghi Effendi (Wilmette: Bahá'í Publishing Trust, 1932/1999), 285, 286 and 293.

21 'Abdu'l-Bahá, "Ṭáhirih and the Conference of Badasht," from *Twelve Table Talks Given by 'Abdu'l-Bahá in 'Akká*, trans. the Bahá'í World Centre, available at www.bahai.org/r/608439669. For the original Persian text, see 'Abdu'l-Bahá, *Muntakhabátí az Makátíb-i-Ḥaḍrat-i-'Abdu'l-Bahá*, vol. 4 (Hofheim: Bahá'í-Verlag, 2000), 20.

The frequent allusions to Jináb-i-Bahá' in Ṭáhirih's poetry were noted by Shoghi Effendi (d. 1957), 'Abdu'l-Bahá's successor as head of the Bahá'í community: "It was from her pen that odes had flowed attesting, in unmistakable language, not only her faith in the Revelation of the Báb, but also her recognition of the exalted and as yet undisclosed mission of Bahá'u'lláh."[22] Familiarity with her poetry, and likely historical accounts of Ṭáhirih's veneration of Jináb-i-Bahá', led the renowned German Islamicist Annemarie Schimmel (d. 2003) to note that Ṭáhirih "hailed (Jináb-i-Bahá') as the awaited leader of the [Bábí] community."[23] Her association with Jináb-i-Bahá' is further suggested by Abbas Amanat as one of the motivations for her murder in the aftermath of the failed assassination attempt on Náṣiri'd-Dín S͟háh in 1852.[24]

The prose writings of Ṭáhirih contain references as well as what appear to be enigmatic allusions to Jináb-i-Bahá'. In her prose writings, Ṭáhirih appears to refer indirectly to Jináb-i-Bahá' as the letter *záy* and "the Countenance of Glory" (*ṭal'atu'l-bahá'*).[25] Some of the many references to "Ḥusayn" in her writings give the impression of being allusions to Jináb-i-Bahá'. If this hypothesis is correct, these references suggest that Ṭáhirih understood that Jináb-i-Bahá' was the return of Imám Ḥusayn, a claim that Jináb-i-Bahá' appears to have begun making to select individuals as early as 1851.[26] In a prayer Ṭáhirih beseeches God to "Shield from every misfortune Him Whom Thou hast supported with victory, He Whose return [Ḥusayn]—the Mystery of Muḥammad—hath been promised, and grant that the day of attaining His presence (*yawm-i-liqá'-i-ú*) may be made manifest." Seemingly alluding in the same prayer to Jináb-i-Bahá' as "the Point of

---

22 Shoghi Effendi, *God Passes By* (Wilmette: Bahá'í Publishing Trust, 1944/1999), 74. Bahá'u'lláh has written about Ṭáhirih's veneration of him and cited verses from her poetry. See 'Abdu'l-Ḥamíd Is͟hráq-K͟hávarí, compiler, *Má'idiy-i-Ásmání*, vol. 7 ([Tehran]: Mu'assisiy-i-Millíy-i-Maṭbú'át-i-Amrí, 129 B.E.), 98–99. See also John S. Hatcher and Amrollah Hemmat, *The Poetry of Ṭáhirih* (Oxford: George Ronald, 2002), 83–99; Baharieh Rouhani Ma'ani, *Leaves of the Twin Divine Trees* (Oxford: George Ronald, 2008), 373–74.

23 Annemarie Schimmel, "Qurrat al-ʿAyn Ṭāhirah," *Encyclopedia of Religion*, 2nd ed. (Detroit: Thomson Gale, 2005), vol. 11, 7575.

24 Abbas Amanat, *Pivot of the Universe: Nasir al-Din Shah Qajar and the Iranian Monarchy, 1831–1896* (Berkeley: University of California Press, 1997), 215.

25 Muḥammad-Ḥusayní, *Ḥaḍrat-i-Ṭáhirih*, 556. The numerical equivalence of the letter *záy* according to abjad reckoning is seven, which is the number of letters in Ḥusayn-'Alí, Bahá'u'lláh's given name.

26 [Nabíl-i-Zarandí], *The Dawn-Breakers* (trans. and ed., Shoghi Effendi), 32–33, 593–94.

Bahá'" (*nuqṭatu'l-bahá'* and *nuqṭiy-i-bahá'*) and to the Báb and Bahá'u'lláh as "the Twin Points" (*nuqṭatayn*), she supplicates God to "Protect all who circumambulate the Twin Points and keep them steadfast in Thy most great Cause (*amr-i-a'ẓam*), so that they may behold the Point illuminating their inmost realities."[27]

In a separate prayer, Ṭáhirih writes:

> Lo, I bow down in adoration before the Face of Ḥusayn, for verily, He hath returned. I humble myself, moreover, before the Most Great Countenance [the Báb] Who hath believed in Him [Ḥusayn = Jináb-i-Bahá'] and affirmed that He [Ḥusayn = Jináb-i-Bahá'] is the Point Whose advent God promised through His utterance, and recorded through His verse, "We decreed heretofore in the Scriptures that My righteous Servants shall inherit the earth after the appearance of the Remembrance."[28] Verily, it hath been revealed in the Bayán that He [Ḥusayn = Jináb-i-Bahá'] is, of a truth, Him Whom God shall make manifest. O my Lord! Can He Who shall be made manifest [Ḥusayn = Jináb-i-Bahá'] be anyone other He Who hath appeared [the Báb]? No, and to this Thy most august and all-compelling Glory beareth me witness, for verily, He hath appeared with proofs, Scriptures, and the splendors of divine decree![29]

This passage suggests that Ṭáhirih perceived that: 1. Imám Ḥusayn, whose return after the rise of the Qá'im is expected in Shí'í hadiths, had returned in

27 Muḥammad-Ḥusayní, *Ḥaḍrat-i-Ṭáhirih*, 540. See the interpretative comments on this prayer by 'Abdu'l-Ḥusayn Ávárih in his *Al-Kavákibu'd-Durríyyah fí Ma'áthiri'l-Bahá'íyyah* (Cairo: Maṭba'atu's-Sa'ádah, 1923), vol. 1, 275, 278–81. A. Q. [Abu'l-Qásim] Faizi has also commented on this passage, having translated it from an unidentified source manuscript, in his *Explanation of the Symbol of the Greatest Name* (New Delhi: Baha'i Publishing Trust, n.d.), 9–10: "Tahirih, in one of her epistles, says, 'O my God! O my God! The veil must be removed from the face of the Remnant of the Lord. O my God! Protect Husayn the mystery of Muhammad and advance the day of reunion with him... Make the point of Baha, O my God, to circulate... O my God! Protect all who circumambulate the twin points and keep them steadfast in Thy most Great Cause, so that they might behold the point sending forth light upon them.'"

28 Quran 21:105.

29 Muḥammad Afnán, *Majmú'iy-i-Maqálát*, [vol. 1], 272. The same passage with some modification is recorded in Muḥammad-Ḥusayní, *Ḥaḍrat-i-Ṭáhirih*, 562. See also idem, 585–86 n. 24. Muḥammad-Ḥusayní, *Ḥaḍrat-i-Ṭáhirih*, 479, comments that Ṭáhirih alludes in another prayer to Bahá'u'lláh by use of the third person pronoun (both singular and plural) *íshán*. This pronoun is often used when talking about an absent person or people.

the person of Bahá'u'lláh; 2. the Báb had confessed his belief in Bahá'u'lláh; 3. Bahá'u'lláh is him whom God shall make manifest, the promised one of the Bayán; 4. Bahá'u'lláh and the Báb are intrinsically one. Ṭáhirih's interpretation of Quran 21:105 in this passage is highly original. In some Shí'í Quran commentaries, the locution "My righteous servants" is defined as the Qá'im—the messianic twelfth Imám of Shí'í Islam—and his companions, but Ṭáhirih appears to suggest that "My righteous Servants" is Him whom God shall make manifest, who is the return of Imám Ḥusayn, and who has appeared after "the Remembrance" (*adh-dhikr*), a key epithet of the Báb. Ṭáhirih thus implies that so great is the station of Him whom God shall make manifest that he is alluded to in the Quran with the plural form of the word "Servants," not unlike how the Bible and the Quran, in certain verses, describe God in plural terms.

LOVE, FRIENDSHIP, AND FORBEARANCE

A second salient theme in Ṭáhirih's prose works, in particular in her letters to fellow Bábís, is love, friendship, and compassion. Ṭáhirih echoes the words of the Báb, who refers to God's Messengers as Trees of love (*ashjár-i-maḥabbat*).[30] In the Persian Bayán, his most important and seminal work, the Báb affirms that "no act of worship is nearer unto His acceptance than bringing joy to the hearts of the believers, and none more remote than inflicting sorrow upon them."[31] Elsewhere in the same work, he states, "He [God] hath cherished and will ever cherish the desire that all men may attain His gardens of Paradise with utmost love, that no one should sadden another, not even for a moment, and that all should dwell within His cradle of protection and security..."[32] And in the Kitábu'l-Asmá', speak-

30 The Báb, from the sixth Báb of sixth Váḥid of the Persian Bayán, available in the collections of the Iranian National Bahá'í Archives (INBA), vol. 96, at www.afnanlibrary.org/docs/persian-arabic-mss/inba/, fol. 139.

31 This is a translation, authorized by the Bahá'í World Centre, of a passage from the Persian Bayán, cited in 'Alí-Akbar Furútan, *The Story of My Heart: Memoirs of 'Alí-Akbar Furútan*, trans. Mahnaz Aflatooni Javid (Oxford: George Ronald, 1984), 199. For a discussion of this and related passages in the writings of the Báb, see Saiedi, *Gate of the Heart*, 322–23, 325, 306, 314; Amanat, *Resurrection and Renewal*, 114, 243, 374 n. 12.

32 The Báb, *Selections from the Writings of the Báb*, compiled by the Research Department of the Universal House of Justice, trans., Habib Taherzadeh with the assistance of a Committee at the Bahá'í World Centre (Haifa: Bahá'í World Centre, 1976), 86.

ing in the voice of God, the Báb states, "We have created you from one tree and have caused you to be as the leaves and fruit of the same tree, that haply ye may become a source of comfort to one another. Regard ye not others save as ye regard your own selves, that no feeling of aversion may prevail amongst you so as to shut you out from Him Whom God shall make manifest on the Day of Resurrection. It behooveth you all to be one indivisible people..."[33] In a letter written with the intention of buoying the spirit of her co-religionists and strengthening the faith of weak believers, Ṭáhirih invokes the same sentiments in declaring that the only path that God has created to attain His Presence and win His good-pleasure is the path of love and friendship:

> God hath made love and friendship the only path to attaining the Court of His glory and grace. No other path hath He ordained save the path of intimate association and friendship. O my God! I yearned for Thine obedience and found it not save in loving Thy lovers. Know ye that God hath made love His religion. The Throne of the Most High circleth around this love, so *become as true brethren*[34] *in the one and indivisible religion of God, free from distinction, for verily God desireth that your hearts should become mirrors unto your brethren in the Faith, so that ye find yourselves reflected in them, and they in you. This is the true Path of God, the Almighty,* and verily, He is God, the All-Possessing, the All-Praised![35]

She reiterates the same exhortation in a separate letter:

> Hearken to my call and return not to your former states. Dwell not in the homes of the sowers of dissension after having become united

33 The Báb, *Selections from the Writings of the Báb*, 129.

34 Cf. Quran 3:103; 9:11.

35 Fáḍil-i-Mázindarání, *Kitáb-i-Ẓuhúru'l-Ḥaqq*, vol. 3, 275. A typo exists in the original text on this page: *ṣiráṭu'l-'azíz* has been written as *aṣ-ṣiráṭu'l-'azíz*. The passage in italics here and in the next selection is quoted nearly verbatim from the Qayyúmu'l-Asmá'. The translation of this passage is published in the Báb, *Selections from the Writings of the Báb*, 56. For a summary in Persian of a portion of the passage by Ṭáhirih, see Muḥammad-Ḥusayní, *Ḥaḍrat-i-Ṭáhirih*, 483–84. According to 'Abdu'l-Bahá, when Ṭáhirih embraced the religion of the Báb, she forsook her two grown sons, who chose to turn away and repudiate the new faith, and never sought to see them again. She would instead assert that all the friends of God are her children. See 'Abdu'l-Bahá, *Makátíb-i-'Abdu'l-Bahá*, vol. 3 (Egypt: Faraju'lláh Zakíyyu'l-Kurdí, 1922), 421–22.

> in harmony. *Become as true brethren in the one and indivisible religion of God, free from distinction, for verily God desireth that your hearts should become mirrors unto your brethren in the Faith, so that ye find yourselves reflected in them, and they in you. This is the true Path of God, the Almighty,* and verily, He is God, the Exalted, the Great![36]

Intimately connected to the theme of love and compassion are Ṭáhirih's frequent exhortations to her fellow Bábís to be forbearing and to eschew conflict and contention (*mujádilih*) when presenting the message of the Báb to others. In the Bayán, the Báb asserts that the "path to guidance is one of love and compassion, not of force and coercion. This hath been God's method in the past, and shall continue to be in the future!"[37] Ṭáhirih similarly urges her fellow believers to penetrate the hearts of their interlocutors with wisdom and forbearance, and not through confrontation and argumentation.[38] In the same vein, she interprets verses in the Quran that mention *jihád* (the duty to struggle, strive, or engage in warfare against the enemies of Islam), *qatl* (to kill; to cause carnage), and *qitál* (to fight, combat, and engage in battle), and likewise words derived from the *j – h – d* and *q – t – l* trilateral roots, e.g., *mujáhidih,* in spiritual terms, divesting these words of any notion of outward violence or militancy.[39] To cite just one example, the command *faqtulú anfusakum* in Quran 2:54 (commonly translated as "slay each other" or "kill those who have been guilty of a crime"), understood by some Quran commentators, jurists, and increasingly by groups that advocate violence, as providing divine licence to kill, Ṭáhirih interprets spiritually as meaning "kill your egos, entreat repentance from your Creator, and present yourselves before your Lord for reckoning and take your share. Truly this

36 Fáḍil-i-Mázindaráni, *Kitáb-i-Ẓuhúru'l-Ḥaqq*, vol. 3, 284. The phrase *'alá khaṭṭi's-savá'* in this and in the previous passage, translated as "free from distinction" in *Selections from the Writings of the Báb*, warrants a comment. The word *savá'* denotes equality and is etymologically derived from the same root as the words commonly used in Arabic and Persian for equality: *musává* and *tasávi*. The phrase *'alá khaṭṭi's-savá'* means literally "on the line of equality" or "on the stroke of equality." It is a stronger and clearer turn of phrase than the more common Arabic idiom *'ala's-savá'*, which means "in like manner," and from which are derived such expressions as *hum 'alá ḥaddin savá'*, meaning "they are the same; they are equal."

37 The Báb, *Selections from the Writings of the Báb*, 77.

38 Fáḍil-i-Mázindaráni, *Kitáb-i-Ẓuhúru'l-Ḥaqq*, vol. 3, 384.

39 On the juxtaposition of *mujáhadih* and *mujádilih* in Ṭáhirih's writings, translated by Amanat as "spiritual endeavor" and "rational argumentation," see Amanat, *Resurrection and Renewal*, 302.

mortal life passes away like the passing of a cloud[40] (*fa-inna'l-'umr yamurr marra's-saḥáb*)..."[41]

BIBLIOGRAPHY

'Abdu'l-Bahá [Mírzá 'Abbás-i-Núrí]. *Makátíb-i-'Abdu'l-Bahá*, vol. 3. Egypt: Faraju'lláh Zakíyyu'l-Kurdí, 1922.

———. *Muntakhabátí az Makátíb-i-Ḥaḍrat-i-'Abdu'l-Bahá*, vol. 4. Hofheim: Bahá'í-Verlag, 2000.

Afaqi, Sabir, editor. *Táhirih in History: Perspectives on Qurratu'l-'Ayn from East and West*. Los Angeles: Kalimát Press, 2004.

Afnán, Muḥammad. *Majmú'iy-i-Maqálát* [vol. 1]. Dundas, Ontario: 'Andalíb, 2013.

Amanat, Abbas. *Apocalyptic Islam and Iranian Shi'ism*. London: I.B. Tauris, 2009.

———. *Iran: A Modern History*. New Haven: Yale University Press, 2017.

———. *Pivot of the Universe: Nasir al-Din Shah Qajar and the Iranian Monarchy, 1831–1896*. Berkeley: University of California Press, 1997.

———. *Resurrection and Renewal: The Making of the Babi Movement in Iran, 1844–1850*. Los Angeles: Kalimát Press, 2005 [paperback edition].

Anjuman-i-Adab va Hunar, editor. *Khúshihhá'í az Kharman-i-Adab va Hunar 3: Dawriy-i-Ṭáhirih*. Darmstadt: Reyhani, 1992.

———. *Khúshihhá'í az Kharman-i-Adab va Hunar 4: Dawriy-i-Qalam-i-A'lá*. Darmstadt: Reyhani, 1993.

Ávárih, 'Abdu'l-Ḥusayn. *Al-Kavákibu'd-Durríyyah fí Ma'áthiri'l-Bahá'íyyah*, vol. 1. Cairo: Maṭba'atu's-Sa'ádah, 1923.

The Báb [Siyyid 'Alí-Muḥammad-i-Shírází]. *Selections from the Writings of the Báb*, compiled by the Research Department of the Universal House of Justice and translated by Habib Taherzadeh with the assistance of a Committee at the Bahá'í World Centre. Haifa: Bahá'í World Centre, 1976.

---

40 Cf. Quran 27:88.

41 Fáḍil-i-Mázindarání, *Kitáb-i-Ẓuhúru'l-Ḥaqq*, vol. 3, 272. Such passages may be juxtaposed with frequent depictions of Ṭáhirih as "militant." For example, in the span of twenty-seven pages, Hamid Dabashi employs the qualifier "militant" nine times to refer to Ṭáhirih and her companions. Hamid Dabashi, *Shi'ism: A Religion of Protest* (Cambridge: The Belknap Press of Harvard University Press, 2011), 170–97. On misrepresentations of Ṭáhirih in anti-Bahá'í polemical sources and Western sources, see Mina Yazdani, "Layers of Veils Covering the Woman Who Unveiled," forthcoming.

Bahá'u'lláh [Mírzá Ḥusayn-'Alíy-i-Núrí]. *The Kitáb-i-Íqán: The Book of Certitude*, translated by Shoghi Effendi. Wilmette: Bahá'í Publishing Trust, 1931/1983.

Banani, Amin, editor and translator, with Jascha Kessler and Anthony A. Lee. *Táhirih: A Portrait in Poetry (Selected Poems of Qurratu'l-'Ayn)*. Los Angeles: Kalimát Press, 2005.

Dabashi, Hamid. *Shi'ism: A Religion of Protest*. Cambridge: The Belknap Press of Harvard University Press, 2011.

Fayzi, A. Q. [Abu'l-Qásim]. *Explanation of the Symbol of the Greatest Name*. New Delhi: Baha'i Publishing Trust, n.d.

Furútan, 'Alí-Akbar. *The Story of My Heart: Memoirs of 'Alí-Akbar Furútan*, translated by Mahnaz Aflatooni Javid. Oxford: George Ronald, 1984.

Hatcher, John and Amrollah Hemmat. *Adam's Wish: Unknown Poetry of Ṭáhirih*. Wilmette: Bahá'í Publishing Trust, 2008.

———. *The Poetry of Ṭáhirih*. Oxford: George Ronald, 2002.

———. *The Quickening: Unknown Poetry of Ṭáhirih*. Wilmette: Bahá'í Publishing Trust, 2011.

Ishráq-Khávarí, 'Abdu'l-Ḥamíd, compiler. *Má'idiy-i-Ásmání*, vol. 7. [Tehran]: Mu'assisiy-i-Millíy-i-Maṭbú'át-i-Amrí, 129 B.E.

Lawson, Todd. "The Authority of the Feminine and Fatima's Place in an Early Work of the Bab." In *The Most Learned of the Shi'a*, edited by Linda S. Walbridge, 94–127. Oxford: Oxford University Press, 2001.

———. *Gnostic Apocalypse and Islam*. London: Routledge, 2012.

———. "Introduction," in *A Most Noble Pattern*, edited by Todd Lawson and Omid Ghaemmaghami, ix–xv. Oxford: George Ronald, 2012.

Ma'ani, Baharieh Rouhani. *Leaves of the Twin Divine Trees*. Oxford: George Ronald, 2008.

MacEoin, Denis. *The Sources for Early Bābī Doctrine and History*. Leiden: Brill, 1992.

Majmú'ah Mina'l-Mu'allifín. *Buká'u'ṭ-Ṭáhirah*. Damascus: Dáru'l-Madá, 2008.

Mázindaráni, [Asadu'lláh] Fáḍil-i-. *Kitáb-i-Ẓuhúru'l-Ḥaqq*, vol. 3. Hofheim: Bahá'í-Verlag, 2008.

Milani, Farzaneh. *Sword Not Words: Iranian Women Writers and Freedom of Movement*. Syracuse: Syracuse University Press, 2011.

———. *Veils and Words: The Emerging Voices of Iranian Women Writers*. London: I.B. Tauris, 1992.

Mottahedeh, Negar. *Representing the Unpresentable: Historical Images of*

National Reform from the Qajars to the Islamic Republic of Iran. New York: Syracuse University Press, 2008.
Muḥammad-Ḥusayní, Nuṣratu'lláh. *Ḥaḍrat-i-Báb.* Dundas, Ontario: Institute for Bahá'í Studies in Persian, 1995.
———. *Ḥaḍrat-i-Ṭáhirih.* Madrid: Intis̲h̲árát-i-Niḥal, 2012 [2nd edition].
[Nabíl-i-Zarandí]. *The Dawn-Breakers: Nabíl's Narrative of the Early Days of the Bahá'í Revelation,* translated and edited by Shoghi Effendi. Wilmette: Bahá'í Publishing Trust, 1932/1999.
Ṣadúq, As̲h̲-S̲h̲ayk̲h̲u'ṣ-. *'Uyún Ak̲h̲bári'r-Riḍá.* Tehran: Nas̲h̲r-i-Jahán, 1378 AH/1958–59.
Saiedi, Nader. *Gate of the Heart.* [Waterloo]: Wilfred Laurier University Press, 2008.
Sayfí, Sayfí Ibráhím. *Qurratu'l-'Ayn (Aṭ-Ṭáhirah) va'l-Bábíyyah.* New Delhi: Mir'át Publications, 2001.
Schimmel, Annemarie. "Qurrat al-ʿAyn Ṭāhirah." In *Encyclopedia of Religion,* 2nd edition, edited by Lindsay Jones, vol. 11, 7574–75. Detroit: Thomson Gale, 2005.
Shoghi Effendi. *God Passes By.* Wilmette: Bahá'í Publishing Trust, 1944/1999.
Wardí, 'Alí al-. *Hákad̲h̲á Qatalú Qurrata'l-'Ayn.* Köln: Al-Kamel Verlag, 1991.
Yazdani, Mina. "Layers of Veils Covering the Woman Who Unveiled." Forthcoming.

10

Babi-Baha'i Books and Believers in E. G. Browne's *A Year Amongst the Persians*

SHOLEH A. QUINN

Abstract: This chapter explores aspects of the Orientalist E. G. Browne's account of his stay in Iran in 1887–88. While there, he traveled to various parts of the country, spending time in the major cities of Tehran, Isfahan, Shiraz, Yazd, and Kirman. Browne was particularly interested in meeting Babi-Baha'i believers, having become knowledgeable about the new religion while still in England. He was particularly keen to obtain Babi and Baha'i books, and learn first-hand about the religious beliefs of the people he met. This chapter explores the books that Browne encountered while in Iran, the beliefs that people articulated to him in the discussions he recorded, and possible correlations between the two, using Browne's published travel account and the personal diaries upon which he based his book.

INTRODUCTION

The celebrated Orientalist Edward Granville Browne (1862–1926) is well known in Babi-Baha'i studies as one of the earliest pioneers in the scholarly study of the Babi and Baha'i religions. His many articles and books focusing largely on Babi history, and his translations of historical works and scripture helped establish a field of study relatively soon after the passing of Muhammad 'Ali Shirazi "the Bab" (1819–50), founder of the Babi religion. Baha'is today best remember Browne for just a few paragraphs of his extensive writing, where he powerfully memorialized his meeting with Mirza Husayn 'Ali Nuri, "Baha'u'llah" (1817–92), founder of the Baha'i religion, in a "pen portrait" that has been reproduced dozens of times.[1]

The impact of Browne's distinguished career as a professor at the University of Cambridge and specialist in Persian literature resonates to this day, when it is difficult to open a scholarly book treating any aspect of Iranian history or literature without finding reference to his scholarship. His documenting of the Iranian Constitutional Revolution, his magisterial four-volume history of Persian literature, his efforts in publishing dozens of editions and translations of Persian texts, all contribute to making him one of the foremost scholars of his time in his fields of specialty.

Several books and articles have already been written focusing on Browne's relationship with the Babi and Baha'i religions. In 1970, Hasan Balyuzi—both a descendant of the family of the Bab, who are known as the "Afnan," and one of the "Hands of the Cause of God" (*ayadi-yi amr Allah*), a title originally designated by Baha'u'llah for leading Baha'is—published his *Edward Granville Browne and the Baha'i Faith*.[2] In writing his book, Balyuzi drew on original documents, such as Browne's correspondence with 'Abdu'l-Baha, son of Baha'u'llah and leader of the Baha'i community after his father's passing, and family archives, including his own father's correspondence with Browne. Some seventeen years after the publication of Balyuzi's book, Moojan Momen published his *Selections from the Writings of E. G. Browne on the Babi and Baha'i Religions* in 1987.[3] This volume not only

Author's Note: I am grateful to Stephen N. Lambden, Moojan Momen, Ma Vang, and especially John Gurney for providing me with helpful comments on this chapter. I take full responsibility, of course, for all errors.

1 Browne, *A Traveller's Narrative*, xxxix–xli.

2 Balyuzi, *Edward Granville Browne*. See *EIr*, 'Afnān,' and *EIr*, 'Ayādī-e amr Allāh.'

3 *Selections from the Writings of E. G. Browne*. Hereafter cited as *SWE*.

brings together most of Browne's articles on the Babi and Baha'i religions, but also includes helpful additions such as a list of the Browne archives at Cambridge and annotations to Browne's writings. More recently, a number of articles on Browne have been published by Christopher Buck and Youli Ioannesyan on aspects of Browne's relationship with Baha'u'llah.[4]

In spite of the important contributions noted here, Browne's own writings have not been sufficiently explored for the wealth of information they provide on the Babis and Baha'is. One of Browne's books, his *A Year Amongst the Persians*, is particularly useful for the insights it provides regarding the Iranian Babi-Baha'i communities of the late nineteenth century. *A Year Amongst the Persians* has been hailed as a "classic" in Victorian-era travel writing.[5] Published in 1893, Browne wrote the book based on the diaries that he kept while living in and traveling through Iran from 1887–88. Moojan Momen has pointed to the importance of *A Year Amongst the Persians* for Babi-Baha'i studies, stating that one of Browne's most important contributions to the field was his "description of the early Baha'i community in Iran, which is the only detailed description that we have from someone who was not a Baha'i."[6] Despite the critical acclaim the book has received, it remains a curious fact that, perhaps because of Browne's own fame and considerable personal charisma, scholarship on the book has focused on the person of the observer rather than on the people and practices that he observed.

Browne's fluency in Persian and his complete immersion in Persian life allowed him to communicate effectively with the people he met during his travels. This, along with his outstanding writing ability, helped him bring the characters he met to life while placing them within the context of their everyday lives. None of this means, of course, that Browne was an uninterested party. Indeed, Edward Said's groundbreaking study, *Orientalism*, cautions that outsiders do not always understand everything they see and hear, that they bring their own assumptions and attitudes to the table, and that their writings need to be used in a critical fashion.[7]

The origins of Browne's interests in the Babi religion are well known, as he explains how he first encountered it when he read Joseph Arthur

4 See, for example, Buck and Ioannesyan, "Baha'u'llah's Bishārāt," 3–28, and Buck and Ioannesyan, "Scholar Meets Prophet," 21–38.

5 Browne, *A Year Amongst the Persians*. Hereafter cited as *YAP*.

6 *SWE*, 12.

7 See Said, *Orientalism*. Geoffrey Nash has placed Browne's writings in the context of Orientalism. See Nash, *From Empire to Orient*.

Gobineau's (1816–82) *Religions et philosophies dans l'Asie Centrale* in 1865.[8] Browne describes his discovery of this book in his diary entry for July 30, 1886, stating that he "read Gobineau's Religions et Philosophies dans L'Asie Centrale – which pleased & interested me so much that I took it out. In there was much interesting information about the Bábís in it."[9] By the next day, Browne had already finished reading the Babi section of this book.[10] A year later, in 1887, Browne had completed both his medical studies and a course of study in Oriental languages. On 30 May of that year, the news came that he had been elected a Fellow of Pembroke College, Cambridge. This allowed him to undertake a journey to Persia, with the blessing of his father—Sir Benjamin Chapman Browne, Lord Mayor of Newcastle upon Tyne (for two consecutive years, 1885–87) and an important shipping engineer—in order to improve his Persian language skills and learn as much as he could about Persia and the Persians before assuming his position at Cambridge. Browne left for Iran in September 1887, arriving in the northern Iranian city of Tabriz on 1 November. Traveling through Iran on horseback, his main stopping points were Tehran (23 November 1887– 7 February 1888), Isfahan (20 February–6 March), Shiraz (21 March–13 April), Yazd (5-24 May), and Kerman (4 June–19 August).

The source material that has survived related to the Babi and Baha'i religions reveals very little about the followers of the Bab and Baha'u'llah in nineteenth-century Iran, especially in terms of their everyday lives, the nature of their religious interactions and activities, and the access they themselves had to Babi and Baha'i scripture and other texts. This chapter seeks to fill this gap by examining two related questions: what were the believers in Iran reading, and how did they articulate their beliefs to Browne? We will demonstrate that the believers whom Browne met in the four Iranian cities of Isfahan, Shiraz, Yazd, and Kirman, were not all reading the same texts and, furthermore, they articulated a variety of understandings of the new religions to Browne.[11]

---

8 *SWE*, 3. See also Gobineau, *Religions et philosophies*.

9 *SWE*, 18. Figure 4 on this page reproduces the page from Browne's diary describing his discovery of Gobineau's book.

10 In addition to writing about Iran, Gobineau "may be considered as a harbinger of genetic racism." See *EIR*, "Gobineau, Joseph Arthur de". For more on how Gobineau's racist writings influenced Browne in his own writing, see Nash, *From Empire to Orient*, 142–43.

11 While these were not the only places that Browne visited, they were the places where he spent the most time with believers.

Part of the reason why *A Year Amongst the Persians* lends itself so well to addressing these issues is that, in terms of books and reading, Browne himself was an avid bibliophile and he asked the people he met specifically about their books.[12] Later he would say this about Babi-Baha'i bibliophilia: "For liberal as the Babis are in all else, they hoard their books as a miser does his gold; and if a Babi were to commit a theft, it would be some rare and much-prized manuscript which would vanquish his honesty."[13] In addition to his interest in obtaining books, Browne was also interested in talking to people. Indeed, he participated in many detailed and extensive discussions with individuals of all religious backgrounds, so the text contains a great deal of information about Babi/Baha'i religious self-understanding, and how that self-understanding was transmitted to non-believers in 1887–88.

TERMINOLOGY AND IDENTIFICATIONS

Browne employed a specific terminology in his writing about the Babi and Baha'i religion, especially in early works such as his *Year Amongst the Persians*. In particular, he uses the term "Babi" as a generic umbrella term that included the two factions of believers associated with the original Babi movement: Baha'is and Azalis. Occasionally he uses the term "Behaist" to refer to a follower of Baha'u'llah, and from time to time he writes "Azali" to refer to a follower of Mirza Yahya "Subh-i Azal." I have chosen, here, to use the more general term "believer" to refer to the religionists of all three—whether Babi, Baha'i, or Azali—that Browne encountered.[14]

ISFAHAN

Browne did not encounter any believers who explicitly identified themselves to him as Babis or Baha'is until he reached Isfahan. There, he asked

12 In using the word "books," I am referring to the mostly hand-copied manuscripts that Browne obtained rather than published volumes.

13 *YAP*, 595.

14 In his *SWE*, editor Moojan Momen used the original diary that Browne kept of his travels and very helpfully identifies most of the people in Browne's *YAP*, since Browne disguised the names of some of the Baha'is he met in order to protect them. Balyuzi's *Edward Granville Browne* also provides helpful background information on some of the individuals whom Browne met.

a Persian employed at the English Church Mission House in New Julfa, where he was staying, to put him in touch with some Babis, or at least to get him some of their books.[15] About a week later, he still had not made any contact until he encountered a couple of trinket sellers, or *dallals,* whom he met on the porch of the Church Mission House. These *dallal*s were selling "the usual collection of carpets, brasswork, trinkets, and old coins," and they proceeded to show him their goods. Browne was not interested in the souvenirs, and just as he was trying to dismiss them by offering ridiculously low amounts for their wares, one of them whispered to him, "You are afraid we shall cheat you. I am not a Musulmán that I should desire to cheat you. I AM A BÁBÍ."[16] Browne expressed great surprise upon hearing this, and replied to the *dallal*: "You are a Bábí!...Why, I have been looking for Bábís ever since I set foot in Persia. What need to talk about these wares, about which I care but little? Get me your books if you can; that is what I want—your books, your books!"[17]

The next day, the Babi *dallal,* whom Browne later identifies as Javad Aqa (or Mirza Javad), a relative of the great Baha'i calligrapher Mishkin Qalam, returned and brought Browne two books, "a manuscript copy of the *Íḳán* ('Assurance')," and a copy of Abdu'l Baha's commentary on the tradition, "I was a Hidden Treasure, and I desired to be known; therefore I created creation that I might be known," both of which Browne purchased.[18] He also showed Browne samples of Mishkin Qalam's

---

15 *YAP*, 222.

16 *YAP*, 223.

17 *YAP*, 224; *SWE*, 23. In his Diary, Browne states, "After that, the Persian dallâls came, with some curiosities and I had a long talk with them. One of them coming close to me told me that he was a Babi and therefore I could trust him. [English in Sanskrit text. I am grateful to Fariba Hedayati for deciphering the English/Sanskrit text in this passage.] I was very pleased at this discovery and asked him to obtain for me some of their books which he promised to do and also he said he would take me on Saturday to the house of their chief where I could discuss the religion - he also said he had been beaten for attending the service at the church here." (English in Persian script). Browne, Diary 2, 264. A third version of this appears in one of Browne's early articles on the Babis: "The Babis of Persia": "'I am not a Musulmán that I should desire to cheat you; I am a Bábí.' My astonishment at this frank avowal was only equalled by my delight, and I replied to him, 'If you are indeed a Bábí, you may, perhaps, be able to assist me in obtaining some books which will tell me about your beliefs.' Seeing that I was really anxious to learn about them, he not only promised to do this, but also offered to take me to his house on the following Saturday, where I should meet the chief Bábí in Isfahán." Browne, "The Bábís of Persia", 488; *SWE*, 148.

18 *YAP*, 226; *SWE*, 23. The first title refers to Baha'u'llah's *Kitab-i Iqan.*

calligraphy, but Browne was not allowed to purchase them, as he was told that "the sale of these works of art was limited entirely to the Bábí community."[19]

Browne met only a few believers while in Isfahan. The most important individual was Haji Mirza Haydar 'Ali Isfahani (d. 1920).[20] Haji Mirza Haydar 'Ali impressed Browne a great deal, but although they had a chance to converse, Browne did not provide details about their discussion.[21] Browne did have an extensive conversation with Javad Aqa, the *dallal.* Earlier, Browne had expressed to Javad Aqa a desire to visit the resting place of Haji Mirza Hasan, the "King of Martyrs" (*Sultan al-shuhada*) and Haji Mirza Husayn, the "Beloved of Martyrs" (*Mahbub al-shuhada*), who were killed for their faith some eight years earlier, in 1879.[22] Arrangements were thus made for the visit and on the designated day, Javad Aqa took him to the general area and a poor Babi grave digger pointed out the specific burial site. As they were leaving, Browne was moved by the kindness of the grave digger, and tried to express this to Javad Aqa. In reply, Javad Aqa told Browne that the Babis were closer and more sympathetic to Christians than Muslims. He pointed out the similarities between the Baha'i religion and Christianity, especially between the Bab and Christ, noting their wisdom even during their childhood, their pure and blameless lives, and their execution by a "fanatical priesthood" and a paranoid government. He also noted similarities in Christian and Babi belief: monogamy, personal cleanliness, and freedom for women. Javad Aqa then proceeded to accuse Muslims, especially mullas, of being superstitious in their expectations of the return of the Mahdi and for not being able to recognize the Bab.[23] Browne appears to have concluded

---

19 *YAP*, 225–26; *SWE*, 24–25.

20 *YAP*, 229; *SWE*, 29.

21 Browne writes in his diary that, "We had innumerable tea & kalyáns, & much talk, so that I did not leave till 4:15..." Diary 2, 267.

22 *YAP*, 227–28.

23 *YAP*, 231–38. "Mirza Javad told me that in their shariat there was no ghusl [ablutions], no legal impurity,: no man was considered unclean because he belonged to another sect: nothing was unlawful but wine: tea was much commended: the prohibition formerly uttered against kalyáns was withdrawn: circumcision & polygamy & the veil were abolished: the fast was changed to 19 days preceding the Naw Rúz: the salutation was 'Alláhu Abhá.' As a matter of fact their women want the veil & their sons are circumcised owing to the exigencies of circumstances – but this is only provisional." Browne, Diary 2, 268–69. It is interesting to note that in his diary, Browne does not state that Javad Aqa made these explicit statements about or comparisons with Christianity. For a discussion of the childhood of the Bab and of Christ, see Lambden, "An Episode in the Childhood of the Bab," 1–32.

that believers in Iran at this time had a tendency to elevate Christianity at the expense of Islam, at least when speaking with him. He acknowledged this practice in more general terms when he wrote, shortly after his return to England: "That they [the Babis] adapt their conversation to those with whom they are speaking there is no doubt."[24]

SHIRAZ

When Browne left Isfahan, he next headed to Shiraz, which was in many ways the place he was looking forward to visiting the most. Indeed, he expressed his joy upon seeing Shiraz for the first time: "Words cannot describe the rapture which overcame me as, after many a weary march, I gazed at length on the reality of that whereof I had so long dreamed..."[25] He described the same moment in his diary in a lengthier passage:

> [I] rode on full of expectancy till after a sudden turn to the right, I suddenly came in view of Shíráz, lying green & beautiful almost at my feet. I shall never as long as I live forget the thrill of ecstasy which I experienced as at last the long-expected sight burst upon me. Yes, after so many weary miles march, there at last was beautiful Shíráz, the goal of my long pilgrimage – I almost wept for joy – No illusion – no disappointment here-: more beautiful than I had dreamed of or hoped for – smiling fair amidst its lovely gardens of cypresses and plane trees – its green domes standing up in the fresh air – was Shíráz, the darling city of Háfiz & Sa'dí.[26]

Browne carried with him a letter of introduction to the Baha'is of Shiraz from Haji Mirza Haydar 'Ali, and was scheduled to meet with the designated individual mentioned in the letter, but before he could do so, he ran into a certain Mirza 'Ali Aqa, with whom he had been well acquainted in England.[27] Mirza 'Ali Aqa was later known as 'Ali Muhammad Khan, Muvaqqar al-Dawlah, and became "Governor of the Gulf Ports and Minister

24 Browne, "The Bábís of Persia," 882; *SWE*, 188.
25 *YAP*, 284.
26 Browne, Diary 2, 302–3.
27 *YAP*, 327; *SWE*, 38.

for Public Works."[28] He was a member of the Afnan family and father of the aforementioned Hasan Balyuzi. Browne would go on to spend a great deal of time with Mirza 'Ali Aqa during his stay in Shiraz.

Books in Shiraz

Browne later noted the context and the extent to which he heard believers read their books in Shiraz:

> I saw a great deal of the Bábís; and, sometimes in their houses, sometimes in the beautiful gardens which surround the city, and which alone render it worthy of all the praises bestowed upon it by Háfiz and a host of other poets, I used to sit with them for hours, hearing their books read, listening to their anecdotes or arguments, and discussing their doctrines.[29]

Mirza 'Ali Aqa showed Browne two Baha'i books in his home. Browne describes these as "a small work called *Madaniyyat* ('Civilisation'), lithographed in Bombay, one of the few secular writings of the Bábís. Another was the *Kitáb-i-Aḳdas* ('Most Holy Book') which contains the codified prescriptions of the sect in a brief compass."[30] Mirza 'Ali Aqa told him to study the latter carefully. Browne later obtained a copy of this book for himself.[31]

But Browne was not satisfied with just these two books, and explicitly asked the Babis in Shiraz "about the books which they prized most highly." In response, they said that the Bab had composed about 100 treatises of different lengths, but they were all called *Bayan* (exposition).[32] *Bayan* is a term the Bab himself sometimes used for the totality of his writings, and the believers in Shiraz appear to have used the term in the same way.[33] They also told him that Baha'u'llah had written an equivalent number of books and letters. Browne of course was interested in obtaining as many of these volumes as possible and asked if they were all in Shiraz. They told him that the books were "scattered about the country in the hands of the believers,"

28 *SWE*, 38.
29 Browne, "The Bábís of Persia," 495; *SWE*, 155.
30 *YAP*, 328. The first of these two volumes has been translated into English as *The Secret of Divine Civilization*. Its full title in Persian is *Risala-yi Madaniyya*.
31 *YAP*, 328; *SWE*, 39.
32 *YAP*, 343.
33 Personal communication, Stephen N. Lambden, 27 June 2015.

and in Shiraz itself, "the total number of separate works is altogether about a dozen."[34]

Browne then asked which of all of these works were the few that were of "greater value," so that he could focus his efforts on obtaining those, and he was given a list of five titles: (1) the *Kitab-i Aqdas* (which he had already seen), (2) the [*Kitab-i*] *Iqan* (which he already owned), (3) the *Suwar-i 'Ilmiyya*, (4) Prayers and exhortations, and (5) "a history of the early events of this 'manifestation,' written by one who desired to keep his name secret."[35] Items 3 and 4 are not individual titles, but rather categories of texts that the Bab himself gave to the totalities of his revelations. Indeed, *Suwar-i ilmiyya* (surahs to do with *'ilm*, or science/knowledge) and prayers are two categories listed in the Bab's *Kitab-i panj sha'an*.[36] Of these books and categories of books, Browne was particularly interested in obtaining the *Kitab-i Aqdas* and the history, and eventually he received copies of both of these. He was also very interested in the poetry of Qurrat al-'Ayn, but they told him that while some of her poetry still existed, they did not have any in Shiraz.[37]

Reading in Shiraz

While in Shiraz, Browne also had the opportunity to see some believers engaged in reading books. For example, one day he attended a gathering in a garden with Mirza 'Ali Aqa and three other guests, whom he described as "all men past middle age, grave and venerable in appearance."[38] Two of these were Afnans whom he had met before. The third had a white turban, and had brought with him two books. Momen identifies him as Haji Mirza 'Abd al-Hamid, who first became a Babi when he heard the Bab's speech in the Vakil mosque.[39] Mirza 'Ali suggested that Haji Mirza 'Abd al-Hamid should read from his books, and they chose to read the

34 *YAP*, 343.

35 *YAP*, 343–44. Browne, Diary 2, 314. This final item most likely refers to *A Traveler's Narrative*, written by 'Abd al-Baha. Browne later received a copy of this volume when he went to Palestine and visited Baha'u'llah. He went on to edit and translate the manuscript and included in his introduction his famous pen portrait describing his encounter with Baha'u'llah. Browne did not learn until after he published *A Traveller's Narrative* that 'Abdu'l Baha was the author. See Browne, *A Traveller's Narrative*.

36 For a discussion of this, see Stephen N. Lambden, Chapter 4, in this volume.

37 *YAP*, 343–45.

38 *YAP*, 348.

39 *YAP*, 348; *SWE*, 62.

"Epistle to Napoleon III."[40] Browne naturally asked to look at the volume, and noted that it also contained the *Kitab-i Aqdas* in its entirety, and other epistles addressed to the Queen of England, the Emperor of Russia, the Shah of Persia, the Pope of Rome, and a Turkish minister who had oppressed the Babis (Tablet to Fuad Pasha). This book also contained a couple of letters addressed to believers, one of whom was the Babi missionary that Browne had met in Isfahan. Browne states that these epistles were known collectively as *Surah-i Haykal*.[41] The second book that Haji Mirza 'Abd al-Hamid had was a larger volume, known as "The Perspicuous Book" (*Kitab-i Mubin*).[42]

Later during his stay in Shiraz, Browne went to the home of one of the Afnans to meet one of the most learned Babis in Shiraz (Fazil-i Zarqani) and there he was shown several more books he had not seen before: (1) an epistle to a Christian, (2) an epistle addressed to one of Mirza 'Ali Aqa's uncles containing consolations for his father's death and his own bankruptcy, and (3) a specimen of *Khatt-i tanzili* ("revelation writing").[43] All the texts that Browne encountered while in Shiraz are listed at the end of this chapter.

Overall, the believers that Browne met in Shiraz were mostly Afnans from the mercantile class. They were primarily engaged in reading the works of Baha'u'llah as opposed to the writings of the Bab, and they had far more books in their possession than the believers Browne had met in Isfahan.

To what extent did the believers express familiarity with the contents of these scriptural tablets when they spoke to Browne about their faith? Browne attended many gatherings in Shiraz and provides much detail about who was present and the topics they discussed. Space only allows mention of one or two representative discussions. The first was an extensive conversation between three people who were part of a larger group of guests in attendance: (1) Browne, (2) a young *sayyid* by the name of Aqa Sayyid Muhammad 'Ali, who was a student of theology and later taught logic and philosophy in Shiraz (Browne never learned his name), and (3) Haji Mirza

40 *YAP*, 348.

41 *YAP*, 349. See also n. 1, where Browne states that he published abstracts of these letters in the *Journal of the Royal Asiatic Society* in October 1889 and that the *Surah-i Haykal* was published by Baron Rosen.

42 *YAP*, 348–49; *SWE*, 62–63. Browne states in his diary that it was a "large M.S. containing many súras of different lengths, but without particulars of the place or occasion of their revelation." Browne, Diary 2, 325. This book was later published in Bombay, India (1890) as *Athar-i Qalam-i A'la* vol. 1 *al-Kitab al-Mubin*.

43 *YAP*, 359.

Hasan Khartumi.[44] The full guest list, along with their names as identified by Momen, is as follows:

1. Mirza 'Ali Aqa.
2. Haji Mirza Hasan—Haji Mirza Husayn of Shiraz, known as Khartumi, who was a leading Baha'i of Shiraz.
3. Mirza Muhammad—Mirza Muhammad Baqir Dihqan, the son of Haji Abu al-Hasan Bazzaz. He was the head of post office in Shiraz, and one of the mainstays in Shiraz community.
4. A young *sayyid*—Aqa Sayyid Muhammad Ali, a student of theology at the time, later taught logic and philosophy in Shiraz—Browne never learned his name.
5. Aqa Sayyid Husayn Afnan—a merchant and Mirza 'Ali Aqa's maternal uncle, son of Haji Mirza Abu al-Qasim, and Shoghi Effendi's grandfather.
6. 1–2 other people.[45]

Browne tells us that he attended this gathering of believers wanting to learn specific things about their religion, but notes that his teachers did not readily disclose these to him: "Disregarding those details of persons, past events, and literary history about which I was so desirous to learn, they proceeded to set forth the fundamental assumptions on which their faith is based in a manner which subsequent experience rendered familiar to me."[46]

The many topics of discussion included (1) the purpose of life—which they told him was to know God, (2) how to recognize a new prophet, (3) when a revelation is abrogated, (4) the station of Zoroaster, and (5) the concept of *jihad*, or holy war in Islam. Regarding this last point, Browne states that the Prophet Muhammad's actions were defended by the young *sayyid*. Finally, they also discussed (6) the return of Christ being like a thief in the night, and (7) the notion of progressive revelation.[47]

As the conversation continued, another topic was introduced, one that would come up repeatedly during Browne's time in Iran: that of the station of Baha'u'llah. Beginning with his time in Shiraz, Browne repeatedly expressed shock and surprise when he heard certain people state that they

44 *YAP*, 329–30; *SWE*, 41.
45 *YAP*, 329–30; *SWE*, 41.
46 *YAP*, 330–31.
47 *YAP*, 330–43.

believed Baha'u'llah was God. In this gathering, Haji Mirza Hasan Khartumi compared Christ to Baha'u'llah, and asked Browne, "Did He [Christ] not declare that one should come to comfort His followers, and perfect what He had begun? Did He not signify that after the Son should come the Father?" Browne's response was one of shock: "Do you mean, I demanded in astonishment, that you regard Behá as the Father? What do you intend by this expression? You cannot surely mean that you consider Behá to be God Himself?"[48] This led to further discussion in which Haji Mirza Hasan provided an analogy for the concept of the father as being one in an assembly "who is wiser than all the rest," and in this way, he said, "So may Behá be called 'the Father' of Christ and of all preceding prophets."[49]

There is a scriptural basis for this assertion in the writings of Baha'u'llah that Browne encountered. As previously noted, one of the scriptural tablets (*alvah*) that the Shiraz believers had in their possession and presumably had read was Baha'u'llah's Tablet to the Pope. About halfway through that text we find a statement which scripturally contextualizes Haji Mirza Hasan's comment: "This is the day whereon the Rock crieth out and shouteth, and celebrateth the praise of its Lord, the All-Possessing, the Most High, saying: 'Lo! The Father is come, and that which ye were promised in the Kingdom is fulfilled!'"[50]

This issue of the station of the Manifestation and the potential station of human beings came up in another gathering in Shiraz on 6 April 1888,

48 *YAP*, 340; *SWE*, 50–51.

49 *SWE*, 51. Browne states in his diary that "I found it very difficult to get satisfactory answers out of them, as they shifted their ground continually. For instance, they began arguing with me on the basis of their religion being the perfecting of the law of Christ, & likened the ahkám to his commands – e.g. 'prefer rather that ye should be killed than that you should kill.' They said Behá was Christ come back 'as a thief in the night' according to his promise – nay – even 'the Father' himself. I asked them what they meant by this: whether they meant that Behá was God. They asked me what I understood by Christ's divinity, & then said – 'As if in the present company, there were one present much more learned than all the rest, he might be said spiritually speaking, to be the Father of the rest, so might Behá be said to be the Father of Christ.' I then asked them, if their religion were the perfecting of Christ's law, what they thought of Islám, which would then appear an interpolation. This they would not admit, but avoided discussing the question, saying it would take up too much time. The seyyid & I then differed as to the right any 'prophet' had to use force to propagate his religion. He talked about *lutf* [kindness] and *qahr* [wrath], but I declined to admit the latter was an attribute of God." Browne, Diary 2, 313–14.

50 Baha'u'llah, *Asar-i qalam-i a'la* vol. 1, 36; trans., *The Summons of the Lord of Hosts*, 59. Here, "the Rock" is most probably an allusion to the papacy, since Peter was considered, in the Catholic view, "the Rock" upon which the Church was established.

this time at the home of one of the Afnans.[51] There, Browne had a discussion with the main guest, Mulla 'Abd Allah, also known as Fazil-i Zarqani, or "Kamil," whom Momen identifies as a scholar in the fields of logic and philosophy.[52] Some four days prior to this gathering, on 2 April 1888, Browne had received a copy of the *Kitab-i Aqdas* [*al-Kitab al-aqdas*], read through the entire text, in part with Mirza 'Ali Aqa—even making plans for them to translate it together into English—and already had a number of technical questions about its contents.[53] He was particularly interested in understanding a verse that seemed to condemn Sufis who claim inward or hidden knowledge: "And there are amongst them such as lay claim to the inner and the inmost (mystery). Say, 'O liar! By God, what thou hast is but husks which we have abandoned to you as bones are abandoned to the dogs.'"[54] Browne said to Fazil-i Zarqani:

> Surely...not only is the doctrine of the Ṣúfís in many ways near akin to your own, but it is also purer and more spiritual by far than the theology of the *mullás*. Do you condemn Manṣúr-i-Ḥalláj for saying 'I am the Truth' (*Anâ'l-Ḥaḳḳ*), when Behá makes use of the same expression? Do you regard Jalálu'd-Dín Rúmí as a liar when you continually make use of the *Maṣnaví* to illustrate your ideas?[55]

Fazil-i Zarqani's answer was negative, as he explained that those verses were directed toward those who "pretended inward illumination." He added that since there were long intervals between manifestations, "there must be in the world silent manifestations of the Spirit intrinsically not less perfect than the speaking manifestations whom we call prophets. The only difference is that a 'claim' (*iddi'a*) is advanced in the one case and not in the other."[56] Interestingly, Fazil-i Zarqani's remarks combine the Shi'i notion of the silent and the speaking Imam with, as Momen notes, Sufi notions of the perfect

51 Browne, Diary 2, 328.

52 *YAP*, 354; *SWE*, 68.

53 Browne received a copy of the *Kitab-i Aqdas* from Mirza 'Ali Agha on Monday 2 April 1888. See Browne, Diary 2, 319. Even before this, though, the two friends had discussed translating the text into English. See Browne, Diary 2, 308–9.

54 *YAP*, 355; Baha'u'llah, *Kitab-i Aqdas*, 31; trans., 36.

55 *YAP*, 355. Al-Hallaj was the Sufi mystic who was executed in 922 and who famously stated, "I am the truth/I am God."

56 *YAP*, 357. The discussion in Browne, Diary 2, 328–29 is much more technical and extensive. The discussion continues in Browne, Diary 3, 338.

man who is always alive in the world.[57] The fact that Fazil-i Zarqani gave Browne this answer suggests that impact of Shi'i/Sufi influences on Baha'i thought at this time, at least on this particular individual.

YAZD

Browne's next stop was Yazd. In stark contrast with the relatively large number of books he saw in Shiraz, in Yazd he saw only two volumes: (1) the *Lawh-i Shaykh Baqir*, and (2) the *Alvaḥh-i Salatin* (Tablets to the Kings). He also saw a small amount of poetry, perhaps because the most important Baha'i whom he met in Yazd was the celebrated poet from Lahijan, Aqa 'Ali Ashraf, better known as 'Andalib, who showed him these two books.[58] 'Andalib had been driven out of his native Lahijan and imprisoned in Rasht due to his having become a Baha'i. After spending some time in Qazvin, he had made his way to Yazd, where he met Browne.[59] 'Andalib read to Browne some of his own poems, and also copied down for him some of Qurrat al-'Ayn's poems.[60] Browne also saw some Babi poems by a certain Jinab-i Maryam, whom he identifies as Mulla Husayn's sister.[61]

Despite the relatively fewer number of books that the believers in Yazd whom Browne met had in their possession, they still held many gatherings with Browne, as in Shiraz. In such meetings, he had wide ranging discussions with the believers, often raising with them the same sorts of questions he posed to the believers in Shiraz. Two familiar issues arose in Yazd: the station of Baha'u'llah and the relationship of Christ to Muhammad. The second meeting Browne attended took place in a garden owned by the merchant Haji Sayyid Mirza, whom Momen identifies as the son of Haji Mirza Sayyid Hasan, the Afnan-i Kabir (d. 1892).[62] Also attending this gathering

57 *SWE*, 71. On the silent (*samit*) and speaking (*natiq*) Imam, see Matti Moosa, *Extremist Shiites*, 314.

58 For these Tablets, reference can only be found in Browne, Diary 3, 370. See also Browne, Diary 3, 338, for another reference to the *Lawh-i Baqir*, which was addressed to Muhammad Baqir, whom Baha'u'llah referred to as "the wolf" (*zib*).

59 For more information on 'Andalib before his meeting with Browne, see Balyuzi, *Eminent Bahá'ís*, 60–74.

60 *YAP*, 436–37.

61 *YAP*, 443. This reference would be to Mulla Husayn Bushru'i, the first individual to believe in the Bab and the first of the *Huruf al-hayy* ("Letters of the Living"). See *EIr*, "Bošrū'ī, Mollā Moḥammad-Ḥosayn."

62 *YAP*, 398; *SWE*, 85.

was the poet 'Andalib (b. 1853), whom Browne ended up chatting with alone for quite a while. 'Andalib began the conversation by expressing his opinion that Jews had failed to recognize Jesus, and suggested that perhaps Christians had done the same with Baha'u'llah: "May not you Christians have done the same...with regard to Him whose advent you expect, the promised 'Comforter'?"[63] He gave the example of the Carmelite monks who were awaiting the return of Christ in a monastery not too far from Acre. 'Andalib then asked Browne to "consider the parable of the Lord of the vineyard," summarizing the story in which, after Christ was killed, the "Lord of the vineyard" would "come and destroy the husbandmen, and will give the vineyard unto others."[64] This caused Browne to ask in astonishment, "Do you then regard Behá as the Lord of the vineyard, that is to say, as God himself?"[65] Browne had already heard an affirmative answer to this question in Shiraz, and there, as in Yazd, he uses the word "astonishment" in describing his response to what he heard. In reply, 'Andalib asked him, "What say your own books?... Who is He who shall come after the Son?" Browne answered this with yet another question, "Well, but what then say you of Muhammad."[66] And thus ensued another discussion, similar to Browne's conversation with the *dallal* in Isfahan, about the relative stations of Christ, Muhammad, and Baha'u'llah. In this instance, 'Andalib affirmed Browne's comment that Christ's station was higher than that of Muhammad.[67]

63 *YAP*, 433–34.
64 *YAP*, 433–34.
65 *YAP*, 434.
66 *YAP*, 434.
67 *YAP*, 433–35; *SWE*, 90–91. In his diary covering these discussions, Browne does not convey any sense of "astonishment:" "The discusser of yesterday ['Andalib] was there, and later on when Haji Seyyid Mírzá had left, he began to talk to me about the zuhúr- 'How was it,' he said, 'that the Jews, though expecting the promised Messiah, failed to recognize Christ?' I said, 'because they looked only at the outward meaning of the words, & had conceived a certain idea of their expected Messiah which was fake, & hence not realized,' 'Well,' he said, 'might it not be the same with the Christians? Might they too not have misunderstood the prophecies of Christ's coming again? Might he not have COME, & they failed to understand or realize it, like the Carmelite monks who are waiting within a little distance of Acre, while the promised son of God has come within a few miles of them?' He then quoted many texts on the coming of Christ, especially dwelling on the parable of the vineyard: that after the son came, & was killed, the owner of the vineyard himself was to come. I asked about the relation of Mohammadanism to these: for, I said, if it were true that these prophecies referred to this zuhúr, they could not be also taken as referring to Muhammad. He said that Muhammad was a messenger, as it were, coming to announce the approach of the owner of the vineyard. I said that in that case he was less than the son, who was killed, & this he agreed to." Browne, Diary 3, 366–67.

Two days later, Haji Sayyid Mirza invited Browne to spend the day with him and his friends in one of his gardens situated outside the town, on the road to Taft. A number of guests attended the gathering, but Browne again mostly spoke with 'Andalib. 'Andalib once more put forth the notion of "progressive revelation," and explained how he regarded the prophets as successive manifestations of divine will. Browne asked about the superiority or greater perfection of one manifestation over another, and in reply, 'Andalib stated that "from the standpoint of the Absolute it [the superiority of one Manifestation of God over another] is incorrect," but that "from our human point of view...we are entitled to speak thus."[68] He used the analogy of the sun being hotter in the summer than in the winter, or warmer one day than another, to explain the differences in station of the Manifestation of God.[69]

Later, as he did in Shiraz, Browne asked Haji Sayyid Mirza about the difference between Sufis like al-Hallaj (d. 1111), the mystic who experienced *fana*, or annihilation in God, thereby claiming "*ana al-haqq*" or "I am the Truth," and Baha'u'llah's similar claim of "I am God."[70] In Shiraz, Fazil-i Zarqani had stated that the difference between the divinity statements of al-Hallaj and Baha'u'llah was that Baha'u'llah made a claim, but there would always be a perfect man in the world. Haji Sayyid Mirza's response was to draw an analogy of the sun shining into a mirror. He said that the difference was between the sun reflected in a mirror, which would be al-Hallaj, and the sun itself, which would be Baha'u'llah.[71] Haji Sayyid Mirza's statement is inclusive yet hierarchical: he asserts the supremacy of Baha'u'llah over Sufis like al-Hallaj, no matter how elevated al-Hallaj's claim, yet he does not dismiss al-Hallaj's theophanic assertion. In Yazd, then, Browne engaged in discussions very similar to those he had in Shiraz. He posed similar questions to those he raised in other towns, and received a variety of answers, many of which corroborated earlier responses, despite the fact that the believers he spoke with did not have very many books in their possession.

68 *YAP*, 436–37.
69 *YAP*, 436–37.
70 *YAP*, 438.
71 *YAP*, 438. See Browne, Diary 3, 371, for a slightly more extensive and technical description of this discussion.

KIRMAN

Browne spent more time in Kirman than any other place in the country, and met a wide range of people of all backgrounds, as he himself observed: "In no town which I visited in Persia did I make so many friends and acquaintances of every grade of society, and every shade of piety and impiety, as at Kirman."[72] During his stay in Kirman, Browne lodged in a garden house outside the Nasiri gate. He also spent much time with people he referred to as "dervishes and qalandars," but who were in reality largely Baha'i converts. What Browne experienced in Kirman bears some similarity to the account of another individual who also visited the town and wrote about his impressions: Haji Mirza Haydar 'Ali Isfahani. Isfahani, who had visited many Iranian cities to teach the Baha'i religion, describes the socio-religious landscape that he saw in Kirman in a rather negative light. He states that the people who became believers later reverted back to their original religious identity. He ascribes this to the deep-rooted indeterminate religious identities of the people belonging to different groups such as Shaykhis, Sufis, and dervishes mixing freely.[73]

In Kirman, Browne attended many gatherings where believers shared their religious understandings with him. On some of these occasions, he saw and obtained Babi/Baha'i books, and in others, he attended gatherings where people were reading such books. A summary of the books that Browne saw in Kirman can be found at the end of this chapter. It is important to note that these gatherings were not formal meetings where theological matters were debated. Rather, Browne describes them as uninhibited, freewheeling discussions in which he, a 26-year-old young adult, was trying to understand the beliefs of his new friends. One of the main themes in many of his conversations was again the question of divinity in relation to human beings. For example, early on while in Kirman, Browne attended a meeting at the home of Mirza 'Ali Riza Khan, who was Ali Riza Khan Mahallati, later I'tizad al-Vuzara, a Baha'i.[74] Two guests at that gathering were individuals with whom he would spend a great deal of time in subsequent weeks: a Baha'i named Usta 'Askar Nukhud-biriz, son of 'Ali Zhu'l Fiqar, who as his name indicates, was a pea parcher by profession.[75] He also met a certain Shaykh

72 *YAP*, 475.
73 See Isfahani, *Bihjatu'ul-sdur*, 247.
74 *SWE*, 110.
75 *YAP*, 500; *SWE*, 110.

"Ibrahim," who was really Shaykh Sulayman Sultanabadi, a Baha'i living in the home of Mirza Rahim Khan Burujirdi, the Farrash Bashi.[76] Also present was Mirza Muhammad Khan, a Ni'matullahi dervish.[77] This gathering (and subsequent gatherings) in Kirman was more religiously diverse than in other cities—it notably included a Ni'matullahi dervish—yet the believers seemed to speak openly in front of him, unlike their more circumspect co-religionists in other cities. After lunch, Browne spoke with Usta 'Askar, the pea parcher. During this conversation, Usta 'Askar started talking to him in what Browne characterized as "a very wild strain," one with which he subsequently said "became only too familiar."[78] The kinds of comments that Browne labeled as "wild"—not just at this meeting but also later gatherings—all had to do with the notion that divinity could be found in ordinary people. For example, Browne explains how Usta 'Askar said to him, "If you would see Adam, I am Adam; if Noah, I am Noah; if Abraham, I am Abraham," and so forth. When Browne asked him, "Why do you not say at once 'I am God'," Usta 'Askar's answer was "yes, there is naught but He."[79]

This idea was expressed again at a later date when Browne was a guest at home of Usta 'Askar himself. Others present at this gathering were Aqa Fathullah, whom Browne describes as a young Azali minstrel and poet, who was singing verses in praise of the Bab; Shaykh Sulayman; 'Abdullah, a servant of the Farrash-bashi and a friend of Shaykh Sulayman; a post official whom Browne says he will call Haydar Allah; and Usta 'Askar's brother. According to Browne, the talk again became very "wild," as the guests were "declaring themselves to be one with the Divine Essence, and calling upon me by such titles as '*Jenáb-i-Ṣáḥib*' and '*Ḥaẓrat-i-Firangí*' to acknowledge that there was 'no one but the Lord Jesus' present."[80]

On 24 June 1888, three days after this get-together, Browne hosted a gathering at his own residence in Kirman. The people who attended were Usta 'Askar the pea parcher, Shaykh Sulayman, a certain Aqa Muhammad Hasan of Yazd, whose real identity was Aqa Muhammad 'Ali Yazdi, Fathullah

76 See *SWE*, 108.
77 *YAP*, 500; *SWE*, 111.
78 *YAP*, 501–2.
79 *YAP*, 501–2.
80 *YAP*, 520–29; *SWE*, 114–20. Browne does not seem to have considered the possibility that his friends in Kirman may have deliberately spoken to him in an exaggerated manner simply because they knew that their words would shock him. While Browne was narrating his account in his role as "observer," those whom he was writing about could very well have been attempting to subvert the "orientalist" gaze by needling Browne in this way.

the Azali minstrel, and 'Abdullah.[81] On this day, Browne took opium for the first time, and gradually became addicted to the drug. Browne explains the circumstances under which this happened, describing how he was suffering from ophthalmia, a painful eye condition, that was not getting any better. After insisting that he try an ultimately ineffective remedy of egg whites and hollyhock leaves, Usta 'Askar then suggested that Browne smoke a pipe of opium to help relieve the pain, which he did.[82] At that gathering, they also talked about religion. The conversation began with the topic of progressive revelation, but then the Azali minstrel sang an ode of Qurrat al-'Ayn, and eventually Browne was told to "go to Acre and see God." Browne again expressed his horror at what he called "anthropomorphism." The Azali minstrel made things worse by telling him "You are to-day the Manifestation of Jesus, you are the Incarnation of the Holy Spirit, nay, did you but realize it, you are God!" Shaykh Sulayman agreed with the minstrel, and told Browne that Baha'u'llah had said to him, "Verily I am a man like unto you," which he understood to mean that whatever station Baha'u'llah attained, everyone else could also attain.[83]

When the Azali minstrel asked Browne why he was so offended, he said that he objected to the believers kissing the Aqdas on one hand and then violating all of its laws on the other (Shaykh Suleyman had become extremely drunk on this and indeed most occasions). The shari'ah-minded Browne was reminded, in relation to Shaykh Sulayman, that "old habits will force themselves to the surface at times..."[84] Earlier, Browne had learned about Shaykh Sulayman's horrific experiences during his imprisonment, when he was nearly killed for his faith, and of his visit to Acre to see Baha'u'llah, who he said told him to stop preaching "the doctrine" because he had "already suffered enough in God's way."[85]

Shaykh Sulayman's statements about the Quranic "meeting with God" (*liqa' Allah*) reflect what the Bab and Baha'u'llah have said in their own writings about this notion, which they interpreted as meeting the Manifestation of God in person. For example, in the scriptural tablet Effulgences (*Tajalliyat*), Baha'u'llah says that "Attainment unto the Divine Presence (*liqa' Allah*) can

81 I am grateful to John Gurney for identifying Aqa Muhammad 'Ali Yazdi, an important believer from Rafsanjan.

82 *YAP*, 533–34.

83 *YAP*, 534–38.

84 *YAP*, 538–41; *SWE*, 121–22. For the notion of "shari'ah-mindedness," see Hodgson, *The Venture of Islam*, 238.

85 *YAP*, 523–24.

be realized solely by attaining His [Baha'u'llah's] presence."[86] This passage certainly aligns with Shaykh Sulayman's encouraging Browne to "Go to Acre and see God."[87]

Browne had several opportunities to be present when people were reading sacred texts aloud, and it is interesting to note that Kirman was the only place that he visited where he witnessed people reading the writings of the Bab. At the first such gathering that he attended, the following individuals were present: 'Abd al-Husayn, the opium-kneader, Haydarullah Beg, Nasrullah Beg of the post office, a dervish named Habibullah, Usta 'Askar the pea parcher, the prince-telegraphist's secretary, and Shaykh Suleyman. The last to walk in was a dervish boy, who brought a qalyan and said "Allahuabha," leading Browne to conclude that "All those present, indeed, were Babis."[88]

After lunch, Browne continued:

> as we sat sipping our tea and taking an occasional whiff of opium, quantities of Bábí poems by Ḳurratu'l-'Ayn, Suleymán Khán, Nabíl,

---

86 (Clarification added). Baha'u'llah, *Majmu'ah-i az alvah-i Jamal-i Aqdas-i Abha*, 27; trans., *Tablets of Baha'u'llah*, 50.

87 The notion of the incarnation of Divinity in the human temple is clearly rejected in the writings of Baha'u'llah. He states: "To every discerning and illumined heart it is evident that God, the unknowable Essence, the divine Being, is immensely exalted beyond every human attribute, such as corporeal existence, ascent and descent, egress and regress... He is and hath ever been veiled in the ancient eternity of His Essence, and will remain in His Reality everlastingly hidden from the sight of men... No tie of direct intercourse can possibly bind Him to His creatures. He standeth exalted beyond and above all separation and union, all proximity and remoteness." Baha'u'llah, *Kitab-i Iqan*, 98. Shoghi Effendi (1897–1957), the Guardian of the Baha'i faith and the leader of the Baha'i community 1921–57, clarified this issue as follows: "The divinity attributed to so great a Being [Baha'u'llah] and the complete incarnation of the names and attributes of God in so exalted a Person should, under no circumstances, be misconceived or misinterpreted. The human temple that has been made the vehicle of so overpowering a Revelation must, if we be faithful to the tenets of our Faith, ever remain entirely distinguished from that 'innermost Spirit of Spirits' and 'eternal Essence of Essences'—that invisible yet rational God Who, however much we extol the divinity of His Manifestations on earth, can in no wise incarnate His infinite, His unknowable, His incorruptible and all-embracing Reality in the concrete and limited frame of a mortal being." Shoghi Effendi, *The World Order of Baha'u'llah*, 112–13. For an extensive and detailed study on the notion of the "Meeting with God" in Babi and Baha'i texts, see Lambden, "Transcendance Bābī-Bahā'ī de *khatam al-nabiyyīn*," 1–57. An updated and English version of this paper is available online as "The Bābī-Bahā'ī Transcendence of khātam al-nabiyyīn."https://hurqalya.ucmerced.edu/sites/hurqalya.ucmerced.edu/files/page/documents/lambden-_seal_2018-f30.pdf. See also Fananapazir, "A Tablet of Mīrzā Husayn 'Alī Bahā'u'llāh to Jamāl-i Burūjirdī," 4–13.

88 *YAP*, 573–74.

> Rawḥá (a woman of Ábádé), and others, were produced and handed round or recited, together with the Báb's Seven Proofs (*Dalá'il-i-Sab'a*), Behá's *Lawḥ-i Naṣír*, and other tracts and epistles.[89]

Browne was able to obtain of a selection of these items for his collection.

On 20 July 1888, that same day, Browne had been invited to meet a mystery guest who turned out to be a female Mulla, whom he describes as the "Manifestation of Ḳurrat al-ayn."[90] Browne was shocked to see a woman in the room, and equally shocked that they called her "Mullá."[91] Eventually eight to nine other people joined them, including Shaykh Sulayman and his friend 'Abdullah. This time, Browne was shown the *Kalimat-i Maknuna* or "Hidden Words of Fatima."[92]

One of the books that Browne was most eager to obtain was the *Bayan* of the Bab. He tried to acquire a copy in Kirman, but it was not until the end of his stay there that arrangements were made for him to obtain a manuscript copy of this important text, consisting of an exposition of the Bab's developed teachings. He had to stop in a village near Bahramabad (Rafsanjan) after leaving Kirman and there he was able, with considerable effort, to have the manuscript placed in his possession.[93]

In Kirman, Browne experienced something of the electric and ecstatic atmosphere of people who certainly had access to texts—more so, in fact, than in Isfahan or Yazd—but who at the same time expressed excitement over their belief that God was resident in Acre, and they were spiritually and in some cases literally intoxicated with the idea that they could partake of that divinity. There is some scriptural evidence for this attitude. In Baha'u'llah's Lawh-i Ashraf, dating to the Edirne period, we find the following statement: "Say: The first and foremost testimony establishing His truth is His own Self (*nafs*). Next to this testimony is His revelation (*zuhur*). For whoso faileth to recognize either the one or the other He hath established the words (*ayat*) He hath revealed as proof of His reality and truth."[94] In encouraging Browne to go to

89 *YAP*, 574.
90 *YAP*, 568.
91 *YAP*, 568.
92 *YAP*, 568.
93 *YAP*, 593–96.
94 Baha'u'llah, *Muntakhabati az asar-i-hazrat-i Baha' Allah*, 105; trans. as *Gleanings from the Writings of Bahá'u'lláh*, 52. I am grateful to Roger Prentice for bringing this passage to my attention.

Acre, the believers in Kirman seem to have taken this statement to heart. While less shari'ah-minded, perhaps, than their counterparts in Shiraz, Isfahan, or Yazd, their ecstatic enthusiasm made an unforgettable impression on Browne.

CONCLUSION

A Year Amongst the Persians provides a unique window into the nascent Baha'i communities in Iran, providing knowledge about the books they possessed, and their beliefs. Of the cities that Browne visited, the believers of Shiraz had the largest number of books in their possession, and Yazd had the fewest. In terms of beliefs, the diverse communities that Browne visited reflected different understandings of the new religion of Baha'u'llah. Among the main topics that they explored was the relationship between the Babi-Baha'i religion and Christianity, the station of Baha'u'llah, and the possible divinity of human beings. Everywhere that Browne went, he found believers who were not only willing, but eager to share their understandings of the new faith with him. Throughout it all, Browne remained open to their comments and kept talking to them, however surprised and shocked he may have been at what he heard.[95]

THE TEXTS BROWNE ENCOUNTERED IN IRAN

Books in Isfahan

1. A manuscript of the Iqan ("Assurance").
2. Abdu'l Baha's commentary on the tradition "I was a Hidden Treasure."

95 Towards the end of his stay in Kirman, Browne met the prince-telegraphist, and describes their conversation in his diary: "The Prince talked more openly – & said he was in doubt about Ezel & Behá; what did I think about the Nuḳta-i-Beyán - I said I could not deny him, & he agreed." Browne, Diary 3, 460.

Books in Shiraz

Books Browne hears mentioned

1. *Suwar-i Ilmiyya.*
2. Prayers and exhortations (hears about).
3. The [*Kitāb-i*] *Īqān* (Baha'u'llah) (already owns).

Writings Browne asks about but does not obtain

1. The poetry of Qurrat al-'Ayn.

Books Browne sees

1. Madaniyat ('Abdu'l Baha's *Secret of Divine Civilization*).
2. *Surah-i Haykal* (Baha'u'llah).
3. Epistle to Napoleon III, Queen of England, Emperor of Russia, Shah of Persia, Pope of Rome, and a Turkish minister who had oppressed the Babis [Tablet to Fu'ad Pasha] (Baha'u'llah).
4. A couple of letters addressed to believers, one of which was written to the Babi missionary that Browne had met in Isfahan.
5. "The Perspicuous Book" (*Kitab-i Mubin*).
6. An epistle to a Christian.
7. An epistle containing consolations addressed to one of Mirza 'Ali's uncles for his father's death, and his own bankruptcy.
8. A specimen of "revelation writing" (*khatt-i tanzili*).

Books in Kirman

Books that Browne sees

1. A book of poetry by Nabil.
2. A lithograph copy of the *Kitab-i Iqan.*
3. *Kalimat-i Maknuna* (*Hidden Words*).

Books that Browne is lent

1. A copy of a poem in praise of Baha'u'llah, by Na'im.

Books that Browne heard read out loud

1. Karim Khan's refutations of Babi doctrine.
2. Poems by Kurratu'l-'Ayn, Suleyman Khan, Nabil, Rawha (a woman of Abade), and others.
3. The Bab's Seven Proofs (*Dala'il-i-sab'a*).

4. Baha'u'llah's Lawḥ-i Nasir.
5. Other tracts and epistles.[96]

Browne obtained copies of a selection of the following items:

1. Poems by Qurrat al-'Ayn (Tahirah), Sulayman Khan, Nabil, Rawha (a woman of Abade), and others.
2. The Bab's Seven Proofs (*Dala'il-i-sab'a*).
3. Baha'u'llah's Lawh-i Nasir.
4. Other tracts and epistles.

BIBLIOGRAPHY

Baha'u'llah. *Athar-i Qalam-i A'la* vol. 1 *al-Kitab al-Mubin*. (Bombay, 1890); trans. as *The Summons of the Lord of Hosts*. (Haifa: Bahá'í World Centre, 2002).

___ *Kitab-i Aqdas*. (Haifa: Bahá'í World Centre, 1995); trans. (Wilmette, Ill.: Baha'i Publishing Trust, 1993).

___ *Kitab-i Iqan*. (Wilmette: Baha'i Publishing Trust, 1931).

___ *Majmu'a-i az alvah-i Jamal-i Aqdas-i Abha kih ba'd az Kitab-i Aqdas nazil shudah*. (Hofheim/Germany: Bahá'í-Verlag, 1980); trans. as *Tablets of Baha'u'llah Revealed after the Kitab-i-Aqdas*. (Wilmette: Baha'i Publishing Trust, 1988).

___ *Muntakhabati az asar-i-hazrat-i Baha' Allah*. (Hofheim-Langenhain: Bahá'í-Verlag, 1984); trans. as *Gleanings from the Writings of Baha'u'llah*. (Wilmette: Baha'i Publishing Trust, 1990).

Balyuzi, H. M. *Edward Granville Browne and the Bahá'í Faith*. (Oxford: George Ronald, 1970).

___ *Eminent Baha'is in the Time of Baha'u'llah*. (Oxford: George Ronald, 1985).

Browne, E. G. "The Babis of Persia," *Journal of the Royal Asiatic Society* 21 (1889): 485–526.

___ Diary 2, Pembroke College MS LC.II.74; Diary 3, Pembroke College, Cambridge, MS LC.II.75.

___ *A Year Amongst the Persians: Impressions as to the Life, Character, and Thought of the People of Persia*. (London: Adam and Charles Black, 1893).

Browne, E. G. (ed. and trans.) ['Abdu'l Baha] *A Traveller's Narrative Written*

96 *YAP*, 525.

to Illustrate the Episode of the Bab. (Cambridge: Cambridge University Press, 1891).

Buck, C. and Ioannesyan, Y. "Baha'u'llah's Bishārāt (Glad-Tidings): A Proclamation to Scholars and Statesmen." *Baha'i Studies Review* 16 (2010): 3–28.

___ "Scholar Meets Prophet: Edward Granville Browne and Baha'u'llah (Acre, 1890)." *Baha'i Studies Review* 20 (2014): 21–38.

Encyclopædia Iranica (*EIR*). S.v., "Afnān," by M. Momen; s.v., "Ayādī-e amr Allāh," by D. MacEoin; s.v., "Bošrū'ī, Mollā Moḥammad-Ḥosayn," by Denis M. MacEoin; s.v., "Gobineau, Joseph Arthur de," by J. Calmard.

Fananapazir, K. "A Tablet of Mīrzā Husayn 'Alī Bahā'u'llāh to Jamāl-i Burūjirdī," *Baha'i Studies Bulletin* 5 (1991), 4–13.

Gobineau, J. *Religions et philosophies dans l'Asie Centrale.* (Paris: Didier, 1865).

Hodgson, M. G. S. *The Venture of Islam: Conscience and History in a World Civilization*, vol. 1, *The Classical Age*. (Chicago: University of Chicago Press, 1974).

Isfahani, Haji Mirza Haydar 'Ali. *Bihjatu'ul-sdur.* (Hofheim, Germany: Bahá'í-Verlag, 2002).

Lambden, S. N. "An Episode in the Childhood of the Bab," in *In Iran: Studies in Babi and Baha'i History*, ed. Peter Smith, 1–32. (Los Angeles: Kalimat Press, 1986).

___ "Transcendance Bābī-Bahā'ī de *khatam al-nabiyyīn* (Coran, 33:40), comme 'fin de la prophétie,"' trans. Louis Henuzet, in *Exclusivisme ou pluralism: Un défi pour la conciliation des doctrines religieuses, traduction de travaux bahá'ís par Louis Henuzet.* (Brussels: Maison d'éditiones Bahá'íes, 2018), 1–57. Expanded Eng. version: "The Bābī-Bahā'ī Transcendence of khātam al-nabiyyīn (Qur'ān 33: 40) as the 'Finality of Prophethood'." https://hurqalya.ucmerced.edu/sites/hurqalya.ucmerced.edu/files/page/documents/lambden-_seal_2018-f30.pdf.

Momen, M. (ed.) *Selections from the Writings of E. G. Browne on the Babi and Baha'i Religions.* (Oxford: George Ronald, 1987).

Moosa, M. *Extremist Shiites: the Ghulat Sects.* (Syracuse: Syracuse University Press, 1988).

Nash, G. *From Empire to Orient: Travellers to the Middle East 1830–1926.* (London: I.B. Tauris, 2005).

Said, E. *Orientalism.* (New York: Vintage, 1994).

Shoghi Effendi. *The World Order of Baha'u'llah.* (Wilmette, Ill: Bahá'í Publishing Trust, 2nd rev. ed., 1974).

Index